Mausi : madame

Mela : pèlerinage

Mitahi : pain sucré frit et croustillant

Namaste : se dit pour saluer quelqu'un, en joignant les mains devant la poitrine

Narial pani : lait de coco

Okra : hibiscus cultivé pour ses fruits

Paan : chique de bétel

Paan-sopari : *idem*

Paise : centime de la roupie

Panipuri : petit beignet rempli de jus de tamarin

Peda : bonbon

Pora : omelette parsie

Purdha : voile porté par les musulmanes

Puri : galette frite

Salwar khamez : tenue féminine composée d'une tunique arrivant au genou et d'un pantalon bouffant

Samosa : beignet de viande et de légumes

Shenai : instrument de musique ressemblant au hautbois

Shrikhand : yaourt sucré

Shukria : merci

Taxiwalla : chauffeur de taxi

Tilla : point rouge que les Indiennes portent au milieu du front

OHIO REVISED CODE

ANNOTATED

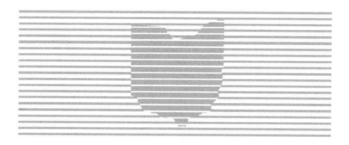

Title 29
Crimes
Procedure
Appendix—Law Prior to July 1, 1996

THOMSON
— ★ — ™
WEST

Mat# 40401338

DEDICATION

To the Bench and Bar
whose members preserve and protect
the rule of law in American society

STATE OF OHIO
OFFICE OF THE SECRETARY OF STATE

Pursuant to the authority vested in me, I, J. Kenneth Blackwell, Secretary of State, do hereby state that I have provided copies of the enrolled acts of the Ohio General Assembly, as filed in my office, to this publisher for publication of the Ohio Revised Code.

Given under my hand and the seal of the office of the Secretary of State, in the city of Columbus, this 30th day of August, 2006.

J. Kenneth Blackwell
Secretary of State

PREFACE

Baldwin's™ *Ohio Revised Code Annotated* has been published and maintained since 1921. Through the years, Banks–Baldwin™ met the changing needs of Code users by continuously improving both editorial content and the level of service provided to subscribers. Now published by West in casebound format, *Baldwin's ORC* sets the standard for quality editorial information and user-friendliness. With every content feature known to have value in an annotated Code, and all information presented for maximum user convenience, it is the first state code designed for practice in the 21st century. (Please consult the User's Guide in Volume 1 for additional information.)

This appendix to Title 29 contains statutes effective prior to July 1, 1996—the date on which the Omnibus Criminal Sentencing Act, 1995 S 2, took effect—and is current through 1995 S 144, File 49 of the 121st GA (1995-1996).

Editorial features include:

LEGISLATIVE HISTORY

A complete legislative history, in reverse chronological order, follows each section of law.

HISTORICAL AND STATUTORY NOTES

Editorial notes are inserted where necessary to supplement and clarify legislative history or interpretation; they typically call attention to matters such as endorsements or opinions from the Legislative Service Commission, legislative discrepancies, and analogous subject matter.

"Pre–1953 H 1 Amendments" are noted in reverse chronological order for selected sections that existed prior to creation of the Revised Code by 1953 House Bill 1.

WESTLAW ELECTRONIC RESEARCH GUIDES

Westlaw electronic research guides have been inserted to facilitate efficient access to West's computer assisted legal research system for the latest laws and cases. See page XIII.

ANCILLARY RESEARCH AIDS

Other research aids in this set include a User's Guide (in Volume 1); a list of abbreviations; tables of titles and tables of contents; and analyses of chapters and sections.

PREFACE

ACKNOWLEDGMENT

We express our gratitude and appreciation to members of the Bench and Bar, Ohio's law librarians and law schools, the members and staff of the Ohio Secretary of State's Office, the Legislative Service Commission, and others whose timely suggestions have contributed materially to the successful planning and development of *Baldwin's Ohio Revised Code Annotated*.

WEST

Cleveland, Ohio
October, 2006

RELATED PRODUCTS FROM WEST

Baldwin's Ohio Practice, Business Organizations
Jason C. Blackford

Baldwin's Ohio Practice, Civil Practice
James M. Klein, Stanton G. Darling II & Dennis G. Terez

Baldwin's Ohio Practice, Criminal Law 2d
Lewis R. Katz, Paul C. Giannelli,
Beverly J. Blair, Judith P. Lipton

Baldwin's Ohio Practice, Ohio Criminal Justice
Lewis R. Katz, Paul C. Giannelli & Case Western Reserve University

Baldwin's Ohio Practice, Ohio Statutory Charges
Dennis G. Terez

Baldwin's Ohio Practice, Domestic Relations Law 4th
Beatrice K. Sowald & Stanley Morganstern

Baldwin's Ohio Practice, Evidence 2d
Paul C. Giannelli & Barbara Rook Snyder

Baldwin's Ohio Practice, Rules of Evidence Handbook
Paul C. Giannelli & Barbara Rook Snyder

Baldwin's Ohio Practice, Merrick–Rippner Probate Law 6th
Angela G. Carlin

Baldwin's Ohio Practice, Local Government Law—Township
Rebecca C. Princehorn

Baldwin's Ohio Practice, Local Government—Municipal
John E. Gotherman, Harold W. Babbit, & James F. Lang

Baldwin's Ohio Practice, Local Government—County
William T. Conard II

Ohio Appellate Practice
Judge Mark P. Painter and Douglas R. Dennis

Ohio Arrest, Search and Seizure
Lewis R. Katz

Ohio Consumer Law
Legal Aid Society of Cleveland,
Harold L. Williams, Ed.

RELATED PRODUCTS

Ohio Domestic Violence Law

Judge Ronald B. Adrine & Alexandria M. Ruden

Ohio Driving Under the Influence Law

Judge Mark P. Painter

Ohio Employment Practices Law

Bradd N. Siegel & John M. Stephen

Ohio Felony Sentencing Law

Judge Burt W. Griffin & Lewis R. Katz

Ohio Juvenile Law

Paul C. Giannelli &
Patricia McCloud Yeomans

Ohio Landlord Tenant Law

Frederic White

Ohio Personal Injury Practice

Ohio Planning and Zoning Law

Stuart Meck & Kenneth Pearlman

Ohio School Law Handbook

Susan C. Hastings, Richard D. Manoloff,
Timothy J. Sheeran & Gregory W. Stype

Trial Handbook for Ohio Lawyers

Richard M. Markus

Baldwin's Ohio School Law Journal

Mary A. Lentz, Ed.

Code News

David S. Collins, Ed.

Domestic Relations Journal of Ohio

Stanley Morganstern, Ed.

Finley's Ohio Municipal Service

Price D. Finley, Ed.

Probate Law Journal of Ohio

Robert M. Brucken, Ed.

Workers' Compensation Journal of Ohio

Jerald D. Harris, Ed.

Baldwin's Ohio School Law

Susan C. Hastings, Richard D. Manoloff,
Timothy J. Sheeran & Gregory W. Stype

RELATED PRODUCTS

NEED RESEARCH HELP?

You can get quality research results with free help—call the West Reference Attorneys when you have questions concerning Westlaw or West Publications at 1–800–733–2889.

INTERNET ACCESS

Contact the West Editorial Department directly with your questions and suggestions by e-mail at west.editor@thomson.com.

Visit West's home page at west.thomson.com.

WESTLAW ELECTRONIC RESEARCH GUIDE

Westlaw—Expanding the Reach of Your Library

Westlaw is West's online legal research service. With Westlaw, you experience the same quality and integrity that you have come to expect from West books, plus quick, easy access to West's vast collection of statutes, case law materials, public records, and other legal resources, in addition to current news articles and business information. For the most current and comprehensive legal research, combine the strengths of West books and Westlaw.

When you research with westlaw.com you get the convenience of the Internet combined with comprehensive and accurate Westlaw content, including exclusive editorial enhancements, plus features found only in westlaw.com such as ResultsPlus™ or StatutesPlus.™

Accessing Databases Using the Westlaw Directory

The Westlaw Directory lists all databases on Westlaw and contains links to detailed information relating to the content of each database. Click Directory on the westlaw.com toolbar. There are several ways to access a database even when you don't know the database identifier. Browse a directory view. Scan the directory. Type all or part of a database name in the Search these Databases box. The Find a Database Wizard can help you select relevant databases for your search. You can access up to ten databases at one time for user defined multibase searching.

Retrieving a Specific Document

To retrieve a specific document by citation or title on westlaw.com click **Find&Print** on the toolbar to display the Find a Document page. If you are unsure of the correct citation format, type the publication abbreviation, e.g., **xx st** (where xx is a state's two-letter postal abbreviation), in the Enter Citation box and click **Go** to display a fill-in-the blank template. To retrieve a specific case when you know one or more parties' names, click **Find a Case by Party Name**.

KeyCite®

KeyCite, the citation research service on Westlaw, makes it easy to trace the history of your case, statute, administrative decision or regulation to determine if there are recent updates, and to find other documents that cite your document. KeyCite will also find pending legislation relating to federal or state statutes. Access the powerful features of KeyCite from the westlaw.com toolbar, the **Links** tab, or KeyCite flags in a document display. KeyCite's red and yellow warning flags tell you at a glance whether your document has negative history. Depth-of-treatment stars help you focus on the most important citing references. KeyCite Alert allows you to monitor the status of your case, statute or rule, and automatically sends you updates at the frequency you specify.

WESTLAW GUIDE

ResultsPlus™

ResultsPlus is a Westlaw technology that automatically suggests additional information related to your search. The suggested materials are accessible by a set of links that appear to the right of your westlaw.com search results:

- Go directly to relevant ALR® articles and Am Jur® annotations.
- Find on-point resources by key number.
- See information from related treatises and law reviews.

StatutesPlus™

When you access a statutes database in westlaw.com you are brought to a powerful Search Center which collects, on one toolbar, the tools that are most useful for fast, efficient retrieval of statutes documents:

- Have a few key terms? Click **Index**.
- Know the common name? Click **Popular Name Table**.
- Familiar with the subject matter? Click **Table of Contents**.
- Have a citation or section number? Click **Find by Citation**.
- Or, simply search with Natural Language or **Terms and Connectors**.

When you access a statutes section, click on the **Links** tab for all relevant links for the current document that will also include a KeyCite section with a description of the KeyCite status flag. Depending on your document, links may also include administrative, bill text, and other sources that were previously only available by accessing and searching other databases.

Additional Information

Westlaw is available on the Web at www.westlaw.com.

For search assistance, call the West Reference Attorneys at 1–800–REF–ATTY (1–800–733–2889).

For technical assistance, call West Customer Technical Support at 1–800–WESTLAW (1–800–937–8529).

TABLE OF TITLES
BALDWIN'S
OHIO REVISED CODE ANNOTATED

*

ABBREVIATIONS

A	Amended
A B A J	American Bar Association Journal
Abs	Ohio Law Abstract
Admin L Rev	Administrative Law Review, American Bar Association
Akron L Rev	Akron Law Review
AFSCME	American Federation of State, County and Municipal Employees
Alb L J Sci & Tech	Albany Law Journal of Science and Technology
ALR	American Law Reports Annotated
ALR2d	American Law Reports Annotated, Second Series
ALR3d	American Law Reports Annotated, Third Series
ALR4th	American Law Reports Annotated, Fourth Series
ALR5th	American Law Reports Annotated, Fifth Series
ALR Fed	American Law Reports Annotated, Federal
Am	Amended, Amendment
Am Crim L Rev	American Criminal Law Review
Am Dec	American Decisions
Am Jur	American Jurisprudence
Am Jur 2d	American Jurisprudence, Second Series
Am L Rec	American Law Record
Am L Reg	American Law Register
Am Rep	American Reports
App	Appellate Court
App	Ohio Appellate Reports
App(2d)	Ohio Appellate Reports, Second Series
App(3d)	Ohio Appellate Reports, Third Series
App R	Rules of Appellate Procedure
Ariz L Rev	Arizona Law Review
Art	Article
Assn	Association
A–TF	Amended and Transferred From
A–TT	Amended and Transferred To
Auth	Authority
B	Weekly Law Bulletin
Babbit's Ohio Mun Serv	Babbit's Ohio Municipal Service
Baldwin's Ohio Sch L J	Baldwin's Ohio School Law Journal
Baldwin's Ohio Sch Serv	Baldwin's Ohio School Service
Bd	Board
Bldg	Building
B.R.	Bankruptcy Reporter
Brook L Rev	Brooklyn L Rev
BTA	Ohio Board of Tax Appeals
B U L Rev	Boston University Law Review
Bull	Weekly Law Bulletin
Bus Law	Business Lawyer
Cap U L Rev	Capital University Law Review
Case W Res L Rev	Case Western Reserve University Law Review

ABBREVIATIONS

CC	Ohio Circuit Court Reports
CCA	United States Circuit Court of Appeals
CC(NS)	Ohio Circuit Court Reports, New Series
CCR	Rules of Court of Claims of Ohio
CD	Ohio Circuit Decisions
CFR	Code of Federal Regulations
CF Stds	Court Facility Standards
Ch	Chapter
Cin B Ass'n Rep	Cincinnati Bar Association Report
Cir	Circuit Court
Cities & Villages	Cities and Villages, Ohio Municipal League
CIV DISC	Civil Discovery
Civ R	Rules of Civil Procedure
CJC	Code of Judicial Conduct
C.J.S.	Corpus Juris Secundum
Clev B J	Cleveland Bar Journal
Clev L Rec	Cleveland Law Record
Clev L Reg	Cleveland Law Register
Clev L Rep	Cleveland Law Reporter
Clev–Marshall L Rev	Cleveland–Marshall Law Review
Clev St L Rev	Cleveland State Law Review
CMR	Court–Martial Reports
Colum Hum Rts L Rev	Columbia Human Rights Law Review
Colum J Gender & L	Columbia Journal of Gender and Law
Colum J L & Soc Probs	Columbia Journal of Law and Social Problems
Columbus B Briefs	Columbus Bar Briefs
Co	Company
COC	Ohio Court of Claims
Comm	Commission
Commr	Commissioner
Com.Pl.	Common Pleas Court
Conf	Conflicting
Const	Constitution
Cornell L Rev	Cornell Law Review
Corp	Corporation
CP	Common Pleas Court
CPR	Code of Professional Responsibility
CRC	Ohio Civil Rights Commission
Crim L J Ohio	Criminal Law Journal of Ohio
Crim R	Rules of Criminal Procedure
CSCR	Cincinnati Superior Court Reports
CSS	Court Security Standards
Ct	Court
D	Ohio Decisions
Dayton	Dayton Reports
Dayton B Briefs	Dayton Bar Briefs
dba	doing business as
DC	District Court
Dept	Department

ABBREVIATIONS

Dick L Rev	Dickinson Law Review
Dist	District
Div	Division
Dom Rel	Domestic Relations Court
Domestic Rel L J Ohio	Domestic Relations Journal of Ohio
DPID Reg	Death Penalty Indigent Defense Regulations
DR	Disciplinary Rules, Code of Professional Responsibility
D Repr	Ohio Decisions, Reprint
Duq L Rev	Duquesne Law Review
E	Enacted
EBR	Environmental Board of Review (pre 1997)
EBR	Environmental Review Appeals Commission (1997 and after)
EC	Ethical Considerations, Code of Professional Responsibility
Ed	Education
eff.	Effective
Elections Op	Ohio Elections Commission Opinions
Envtl L J Ohio	Environmental Law Journal of Ohio
Envtl Monthly	Environmental Monthly
ERAC	Environmental Review Appeals Commission
Ethics Op	Ohio Ethics Commission Opinions
Evid R	Ohio Rules of Evidence
ex rel	on the relation of
Fam L Quar	Family Law Quarterly, American Bar Association
F	Form
F.	Federal Reporter
F.2d	Federal Reporter, Second Series
F.3d	Federal Reporter, Third Series
F. Cas	Federal Cases
Fed	Federal
Fed Appx	Federal Appendix
Finley's Ohio Mun Serv	Finley's Ohio Municipal Service
Fla L Rev	University of Florida Law Review
Forum	Forum, American Bar Association
F.R.D.	Federal Rules Decisions
FR Serv	Federal Rules Service
FR Serv(2d)	Federal Rules Service, Second Series
F.Supp	Federal Supplement
F.Supp(2d)	Federal Supplement, Second Series
GC	General Code of Ohio
Geo L J	Georgetown Law Journal
Gotherman's Ohio Mun Serv	Gotherman's Ohio Municipal Service
Gov Bar R	Supreme Court Rules for the Government of the Bar
Gov Jud R	Supreme Court Rules for the Government of the Judiciary
H	House Bill
Harv L Rev	Harvard Law Review
HCR	House Concurrent Resolution
Health L J Ohio	Health Law Journal of Ohio
HJR	House Joint Resolution

ABBREVIATIONS

HR . . . . .House Resolution
HWFB .Hazardous Waste Facility Board
Inc . . . . .Incorporated
Ind L J . . . . .Indiana Law Journal
Indus Rel Rep . . . . .Industrial Relations Report
Iowa L Rev . . . . .Iowa Law Review
IRC . . . . .Internal Revenue Code
J Fam L . . . . .Journal of Family Law (University of Louisville)
J L & Com . . . . .Journal of Law and Commerce
J L & Educ. . . . . .Journal of Law and Education
J L & Health . . . . .Journal of Law and Health
J Min L & Pol'y. . . . . .Journal of Mineral Law and Policy
J Nat Resources & Envtl
  L . . . . .Journal of Natural Resources and Environmental Law
Joint Legis Ethics Comm . . . .Joint Legislative Ethics Commission
Jud Cond . . . . .Code of Judicial Conduct
Juv . . . . .Juvenile Court
Juv R .Rules of Juvenile Procedure
Ky Bench & B . . . . .Kentucky Bench and Bar
Ky L J . . . . .Kentucky Law Journal
Lake Legal Views . . . . .Lake Legal Views, Lake County Bar Association
Law & Fact . . . . .Law & Fact, Cuyahoga County Bar Association
LBA Bull . . . . .Louisville Bar Association News Bulletin
L.Ed. .Lawyers' Edition, United States Supreme Court Reports
L.Ed.2d . . . . .Lawyers' Edition, United States Supreme Court Reports,
                                              Second Series
Legal Reference Serv Q . . . . .Legal Reference Services Quarterly
Louisville Law . . . . .Louisville Lawyer
LRA . . . . .Lawyers Reports Annotated
LRA(NS). . . . . .Lawyers Reports Annotated, New Series
Ltd . . . . .Limited
May Ed R . . . . .Mayor's Court Education and Procedure Rules
Md L Rev . . . . .Maryland Law Review
Mental Disability L Rep . . . . .Mental Disability Law Reporter
Mercer L Rev . . . . .Mercer Law Review
Mfg . . . . .Manufacturing
Misc. .Ohio Miscellaneous Reports
Misc(2d) . . . . .Ohio Miscellaneous Reports, Second Series
M J. . . . . .Military Justice Reporter
Muni . . . . .Municipal Court
Nat'l L J . . . . .National Law Journal
N D L Rev . . . . .North Dakota Law Review
N.D.Ohio . . . . .Northern District Ohio
N.E. . . . . .Northeastern Reporter
N.E.2d. . . . . .Northeastern Reporter, Second Series
NEA. .National Education Association
Neb L Rev . . . . .Nebraska Law Review
N Ky L Rev . . . . .Northern Kentucky Law Review
N Ky St L F . . . . .Northern Kentucky State Law Forum
NP . . . . .Ohio Nisi Prius Reports

ABBREVIATIONS

NP(NS)	Ohio Nisi Prius Reports, New Series
Nw U L Rev	Northwestern University Law Review
O	Ohio Reports
OAC	Baldwin's Ohio Administrative Code
OAG	Opinions of the Ohio Attorney General
OAPSE	Ohio Association of Public School Employees
OBR	Ohio Bar Reports
OCA	Ohio Courts of Appeals Reports
O Const	Ohio Constitution
OCRC	Ohio Civil Rights Commission
OEA	Ohio Education Association
OFD	Ohio Federal Decisions
OFT	Ohio Federation of Teachers
Ohio	Ohio Reports
Ohio App	Ohio Appellate Reports
Ohio App.2d	Ohio Appellate Reports, Second Series
Ohio App.3d	Ohio Appellate Reports, Third Series
Ohio B Ass'n Serv Letter	Ohio Bar Association Service Letter
Ohio C.C.	Ohio Circuit Court Reports
Ohio C.C.N.S.	Ohio Circuit Court Reports, New Series
Ohio C.D.	Ohio Circuit Decisions
Ohio Civ Prac J	Ohio Civil Practice Journal
Ohio Ct.Cl.	Ohio Court of Claims
Ohio Com.Pl.	Ohio Common Pleas Court
Ohio Dec.	Ohio Decisions
Ohio Dec. Reprint	Ohio Decisions, Reprint
Ohio F.Dec.	Ohio Federal Decisions
Ohio L Rep	Ohio Law Reporter
Ohio Law	Ohio Lawyer
Ohio Law Abs.	Ohio Law Abstract
Ohio Misc.	Ohio Miscellaneous Reports
Ohio Misc.2d	Ohio Miscellaneous Reports, Second Series
Ohio N.P.	Ohio Nisi Prius Reports
Ohio N.P.N.S.	Ohio Nisi Prius Reports, New Series
Ohio N U L Rev	Ohio Northern University Law Review
Ohio Sch Boards Ass'n J	Ohio School Boards Association Journal
Ohio St.	Ohio State Reports
Ohio St.2d	Ohio State Reports, Second Series
Ohio St.3d	Ohio State Reports, Third Series
Ohio St B Ass'n Rep	Ohio State Bar Association Report
Ohio St L J	Ohio State Law Journal
Ohio Tax Rev	Ohio Tax Review
Ohio Trial	Ohio Trial, Ohio Academy of Trial Lawyers Education Foundation
OJur 3d	Ohio Jurisprudence, Third Series
OLS	Baldwin's Ohio Legislative Service Annotated
OMR	Baldwin's Ohio Monthly Record
OO	Ohio Opinions
OO(2d)	Ohio Opinions, Second Series
OO(3d)	Ohio Opinions, Third Series

ABBREVIATIONS

Or L Rev	Oregon Law Review
ORC	Baldwin's Ohio Revised Code
OS	Ohio State Reports
OS(2d)	Ohio State Reports, Second Series
OS(3d)	Ohio State Reports, Third Series
OSLJ	Ohio State Law Journal
OS Unrep	Ohio State Unreported
O.Supp.	Ohio Supplement
Otto	Otto's Supreme Court Reports
Pa B A Q	Pennsylvania Bar Association Quarterly
Pa Law	Pennsylvania Lawyer
Pa St B Ass'n Bull	Pennsylvania State Bar Association Bulletin
PBR	Personnel Board of Review
PConf	Possibly or Partially Conflicting
Pepp L Rev	Pepperdine Law Review
Prob	Probate Court
Prob & Trust J	Probate and Trust Journal
Prob L J Ohio	Probate Law Journal of Ohio
Civ Discovery Edition	PRO/GRAM Civil Discovery Edition
Civ Litig Edition	PRO/GRAM Civil Litigation Edition
PUCO	Public Utilities Commission of Ohio
R	Repealed
RBR	Reclamation Board of Review (pre 1997)
RBR	Reclamation Commission (1997 and after)
RC	Ohio Revised Code
R–E	Repealed and Reenacted
RRD	RC 119.032 rule review date(s)
Rep R	Supreme Court Rules for the Reporting of Opinions
RS	Revised Statutes of Ohio
S	Senate Bill
St Mary's L J	St. Mary's Law Journal
SCR	Senate Concurrent Resolution
S.Ct.	United States Supreme Court Reporter
SCt R	Rules of Practice of the Supreme Court of Ohio
S.D.Ohio	Southern District Ohio
SERB	State Employment Relations Board
Shingle	The Shingle, Philadelphia Bar Association
SJR	Senate Joint Resolution
SR	Senate Resolution
Stat	Statutes
State Employment Rel Board Q	State Employment Relations Board Quarterly
Sub	Substitute
Sup R	Rules of Superintendence for Courts of Ohio
TC	Tax Court (United States)
Temp L Q	Temple Law Quarterly
Temp L Rev	Temple Law Review
TF	Transferred From
Title Topics	Title Topics, Ohio Land Title Association
TJS	Trial Court Jury Use and Management Standards

ABBREVIATIONS

Tol B Ass'n News . . . . Toledo Bar Association Newsletter
Traf R . . . . Ohio Traffic Rules
Trial . . . . Trial, Association of Trial Lawyers of America
TT . . . . Transferred To
Twp . . . . Township
UCBR . . . . Unemployment Compensation Board of Review (pre 1997)
UCBR . . . . Unemployment Compensation Review Commission (1997 and after)
UCC . . . . Uniform Commercial Code
U Cin L Rev . . . . University of Cincinnati Law Review
U Colo L Rev . . . . University of Colorado Law Review
UCRC . . . . Unemployment Compensation Review Commission
U Dayton L Rev . . . . University of Dayton Law Review
U Pa L Rev . . . . University of Pennsylvania Law Review
U Pitt L Rev . . . . University of Pittsburgh Law Review
U Rich L Rev . . . . University of Richmond Law Review
U.S. . . . . United States Supreme Court Reports
USC . . . . United States Code
USCA . . . . United States Code Annotated
USLW . . . . United States Law Week
USP.Q. United States Patent Quarterly
USP.Q.2d . . . . United States Patent Quarterly, Second Series
U Tol L Rev . . . . University of Toledo Law Review
v . . . . versus
v . . . . volume, Ohio Laws
VCC R . . . . Rules of Court of Claims of Ohio, Victims of Crime Compensation Section
Vill L Rev . . . . Villanova Law Review
W . . . . Withdrawn
W . . . . Wright's Ohio Supreme Court Reports
Wall. . . . . Wallace's Supreme Court Reports
Wake Forest L Rev . . . . Wake Forest Law Review
Washburn L J . . . . Washburn Law Journal
WL . . . . Westlaw reference number
W.L.B. . . . . Weekly Law Bulletin
WLG . . . . Weekly Law Gazette
WLJ . . . . Western Law Journal
WLM . . . . Western Law Monthly
Workers' Compensation J
 Ohio . . . . Workers' Compensation Journal of Ohio
W Reserve U L Rev . . . . Western Reserve University Law Review
Wright . . . . Wright's Ohio Supreme Court Reports

*

TABLE OF CONTENTS

Title 29—Crimes—Procedure

Appendix—Law Prior to July 1, 1996

CITE THIS BOOK

OHIO REV. CODE ANN. §2901.01 (Baldwin 2006 APPX.)

*

BALDWIN'S OHIO REVISED CODE ANNOTATED

Title XXIX

CRIMES—PROCEDURE APPENDIX

Law effective prior to July 1, 1996

Publisher's Note: 1995 S 2—the Omnibus Criminal Sentencing Act—applies to offenses committed on or after July 1, 1996.

Westlaw Computer Assisted Legal Research

Westlaw supplements your legal research in many ways. Westlaw allows you to

- update your research with the most current information
- expand your library with additional resources
- retrieve current, comprehensive history and citing references to a case with KeyCite

For more information on using Westlaw to supplement your research, see the Westlaw Electronic Research Guide, which follows the Preface.

CHAPTER 2901

GENERAL PROVISIONS

GENERAL PROVISIONS

GENERAL PROVISIONS

2901.01   Definitions

As used in the Revised Code:

(A) "Force" means any violence, compulsion, or constraint physically exerted by any means upon or against a person or thing.

(B) "Deadly force" means any force which carries a substantial risk that it will proximately result in the death of any person.

(C) "Physical harm to persons" means any injury, illness, or other physiological impairment, regardless of its gravity or duration.

(D) "Physical harm to property" means any tangible or intangible damage to property which, in any degree, results in loss to its value or interferes with its use or enjoyment. "Physical harm to property" does not include wear and tear occasioned by normal use.

(E) "Serious physical harm to persons" means any of the following:

(1) Any mental illness or condition of such gravity as would normally require hospitalization or prolonged psychiatric treatment;

(2) Any physical harm which carries a substantial risk of death;

(3) Any physical harm which involves some permanent incapacity, whether partial or total, or which involves some temporary, substantial incapacity;

(4) Any physical harm which involves some permanent disfigurement, or which involves some temporary, serious disfigurement;

(5) Any physical harm which involves acute pain of such duration as to result in substantial suffering, or which involves any degree of prolonged or intractable pain.

(F) "Serious physical harm to property" means any physical harm to property which does either of the following:

(1) Results in substantial loss to the value of the property, or requires a substantial amount of time, effort, or money to repair or replace;

(2) Temporarily prevents the use or enjoyment of the property, or substantially interferes with its use or enjoyment for an extended period of time.

(G) "Risk" means a significant possibility, as contrasted with a remote possibility, that a certain result may occur or that certain circumstances may exist.

(H) "Substantial risk" means a strong possibility, as contrasted with a remote or significant possibility, that a certain result may occur or that certain circumstances may exist.

(I) "Offense of violence" means any of the following:

(1) A violation of sections 2903.01, 2903.02, 2903.03, 2903.04, 2903.11, 2903.12, 2903.13, 2903.21, 2903.22, 2905.01, 2905.02, 2905.11, 2907.02, 2907.03, 2907.12, 2909.02, 2909.03, 2909.04, 2909.05, 2911.01, 2911.02, 2911.11, 2911.12, 2917.01, 2917.02, 2917.03, 2917.31, 2919.25, 2921.03, 2921.34, 2921.35, 2923.12, and 2923.13 of the Revised Code;

(2) A violation of an existing or former municipal ordinance or law of this or any other state or the United States, substantially equivalent to any section listed in division (I)(1) of this section;

(3) An offense, other than a traffic offense, under an existing or former municipal ordinance or law of this or any other state or the United States, committed purposely or knowingly, and involving physical harm to persons or a risk of serious physical harm to persons;

(4) A conspiracy or attempt to commit, or complicity in committing, any offense under division (I)(1), (2), or (3) of this section.

(J)(1) "Property" means any property, real or personal, tangible or intangible, and any interest or license in such property. "Property" includes, but is not limited to, cable television service, computer data, computer software, financial instruments associated with computers, and other documents associated with computers, or copies of the documents, whether in machine or human readable form. "Financial instruments associated with computers" include, but are not limited to, checks, drafts, warrants, money orders, notes of indebtedness, certificates of deposit, letters of credit, bills of credit or debit cards, financial transaction authorization mechanisms, marketable securities, or any computer system representations of any of them.

(2) As used in this division and division (M) of this section, "cable television service," "computer," "computer software," "computer system," "computer network," and "data" have the same meaning as in section 2913.01 of the Revised Code.

(K) "Law enforcement officer" means any of the following:

(1) A sheriff, deputy sheriff, constable, police officer of a township or joint township police district, marshal, deputy marshal, municipal police officer, member of a police force employed by a metropolitan housing authority under division (D) of section 3735.31 of the Revised Code, or state highway patrol trooper;

(2) An officer, agent, or employee of the state or any of its agencies, instrumentalities, or political subdivisions, upon whom, by statute, a duty to conserve the peace or to enforce all or certain laws is imposed and the authority to arrest violators is conferred, within the limits of such statutory duty and authority;

(3) A mayor, in his capacity as chief conservator of the peace within his municipal corporation;

(4) A member of an auxiliary police force organized by county, township, or municipal law enforcement authorities, within the scope of such member's appointment or commission;

(5) A person lawfully called pursuant to section 311.07 of the Revised Code to aid a sheriff in keeping the peace, for the purposes and during the time when such person is called;

(6) A person appointed by a mayor pursuant to section 737.01 of the Revised Code as a special patrolman or officer during riot or emergency, for the purposes and during the time when such person is appointed;

(7) A member of the organized militia of this state or the armed forces of the United States, lawfully called to duty to aid civil authorities in keeping the peace or protect against domestic violence;

(8) A prosecuting attorney, assistant prosecuting attorney, secret service officer, or municipal prosecutor;

(9) An Ohio veterans' home policeman appointed under section 5907.02 of the Revised Code.

(L) "Privilege" means an immunity, license, or right conferred by law, or bestowed by express or implied grant, or arising out of status, position, office, or relationship, or growing out of necessity.

(M) "Contraband" means any property described in the following categories:

(1) Property that in and of itself is unlawful for a person to acquire or possess;

(2) Property that is not in and of itself unlawful for a person to acquire or possess, but that has been determined by a court of this state, in accordance with law, to be contraband because

4

of its use in an unlawful activity or manner, of its nature, or of the circumstances of the person who acquires or possesses it;

(3) Property that is specifically stated to be contraband by a section of the Revised Code or by an ordinance, regulation, or resolution;

(4) Property that is forfeitable pursuant to a section of the Revised Code, or an ordinance, regulation, or resolution, including, but not limited to, forfeitable firearms, dangerous ordnance, and obscene materials;

(5) Any controlled substance, as defined in section 3719.01 of the Revised Code, or any device, paraphernalia, money as defined in section 1301.01 of the Revised Code, or other means of exchange that has been, is being, or is intended to be used in an attempt or conspiracy to violate, or in a violation of, Chapter 2925. or 3719. of the Revised Code;

(6) Any gambling device, paraphernalia, money as defined in section 1301.01 of the Revised Code, or other means of exchange that has been, is being, or is intended to be used in an attempt or conspiracy to violate, or in the violation of, Chapter 2915. of the Revised Code;

(7) Any equipment, machine, device, apparatus, vehicle, vessel, container, liquid, or substance that has been, is being, or is intended to be used in an attempt or conspiracy to violate, or in the violation of, any law of this state relating to alcohol or tobacco;

(8) Any personal property that has been, is being, or is intended to be used in an attempt or conspiracy to commit, or in the commission of, any offense or in the transportation of the fruits of any offense;

(9) Any property that is acquired through the sale or other transfer of contraband or through the proceeds of contraband, other than by a court or a law enforcement agency acting within the scope of its duties;

(10) Any computer, computer system, computer network, or computer software that is used in a conspiracy to commit, an attempt to commit, or in the commission of any offense, if the owner of the computer, computer system, computer network, or computer software is convicted of or pleads guilty to the offense in which it is used.

(N) A person is "not guilty by reason of insanity" relative to a charge of an offense only if he proves, in the manner specified in section 2901.05 of the Revised Code, that at the time of the commission of the offense, he did not know, as a result of a severe mental disease or defect, the wrongfulness of his acts.

(1991 S 144, eff. 8–8–91; 1991 H 77; 1990 S 24; 1988 H 708, § 1)

2901.02   Classification of offenses

As used in the Revised Code:

(A) Offenses include aggravated murder, murder, aggravated felonies of the first, second, and third degree, felonies of the first, second, third, and fourth degree, misdemeanors of the first, second, third, and fourth degree, minor misdemeanors, and offenses not specifically classified.

(B) Aggravated murder when the indictment or the count in the indictment charging aggravated murder contains one or more specifications of aggravating circumstances listed in division (A) of section 2929.04 of Revised Code, and any other offense for which death may be imposed as a penalty, is a capital offense.

(C) Aggravated murder and murder are felonies.

(D) Regardless of the penalty which may be imposed, any offense specifically classified as a felony is a felony, and any offense specifically classified as a misdemeanor is a misdemeanor.

(E) Any offense not specifically classified is a felony if imprisonment for more than one year may be imposed as a penalty.

(F) Any offense not specifically classified is a misdemeanor if imprisonment for not more than one year may be imposed as a penalty.

(G) Any offense not specifically classified is a minor misdemeanor if the only penalty which may be imposed is a fine not exceeding one hundred dollars.

(1984 H 380, eff. 4–3–84; 1982 H 269, § 4; 1982 S 199; 1972 H 511)

2901.03 Common law offenses abrogated; offense defined; contempt or sanction powers of courts or general assembly not affected

(A) No conduct constitutes a criminal offense against the state unless it is defined as an offense in the Revised Code.

(B) An offense is defined when one or more sections of the Revised Code state a positive prohibition or enjoin a specific duty, and provide a penalty for violation of such prohibition or failure to meet such duty.

(C) This section does not affect any power of the general assembly under section 8 of Article II, Ohio Constitution, nor does it affect the power of a court to punish for contempt or to employ any sanction authorized by law to enforce an order, civil judgment, or decree.

(1972 H 511, eff. 1–1–74)

2901.04 Rules of construction

(A) Sections of the Revised Code defining offenses or penalties shall be strictly construed against the state, and liberally construed in favor of the accused.

(B) Rules of criminal procedure and sections of the Revised Code providing for criminal procedure shall be construed so as to effect the fair, impartial, speedy, and sure administration of justice.

(1972 H 511, eff. 1–1–74)

2901.05 Presumption of innocence; proof of offense; of affirmative defense; as to each; reasonable doubt

(A) Every person accused of an offense is presumed innocent until proven guilty beyond a reasonable doubt, and the burden of proof for all elements of the offense is upon the prosecution. The burden of going forward with the evidence of an affirmative defense, and the burden of proof, by a preponderance of the evidence, for an affirmative defense, is upon the accused.

(B) As part of its charge to the jury in a criminal case, the court shall read the definitions of "reasonable doubt" and "proof beyond a reasonable doubt," contained in division (D) of this section.

(C) As used in this section, an "affirmative defense" is either of the following:

(1) A defense expressly designated as affirmative;

(2) A defense involving an excuse or justification peculiarly within the knowledge of the accused, on which he can fairly be required to adduce supporting evidence.

(D) "Reasonable doubt" is present when the jurors, after they have carefully considered and compared all the evidence, cannot say they are firmly convinced of the truth of the charge. It is a doubt based on reason and common sense. Reasonable doubt is not mere possible doubt, because everything relating to human affairs or depending on moral evidence is open to some possible or imaginary doubt. "Proof beyond a reasonable doubt" is proof of such character that an ordinary person would be willing to rely and act upon it in the most important of his own affairs.

(1978 H 1168, eff. 11–1–78; 1972 H 511)

2901.06 Battered woman syndrome

(A) The general assembly hereby declares that it recognizes both of the following, in relation to the "battered woman syndrome:"

(1) That the syndrome currently is a matter of commonly accepted scientific knowledge;

(2) That the subject matter and details of the syndrome are not within the general understanding or experience of a person who is a member of the general populace and are not within the field of common knowledge.

(B) If a person is charged with an offense involving the use of force against another and the person, as a defense to the offense charged, raises the affirmative defense of self-defense, the person may introduce expert testimony of the "battered woman syndrome" and expert testimony that the person suffered from that syndrome as evidence to establish the requisite belief of an imminent danger of death or great bodily harm that is necessary, as an element of the affirmative defense, to justify the person's use of the force in question. The introduction of any expert testimony under this division shall be in accordance with the Ohio Rules of Evidence.

(1990 H 484, eff. 11–5–90)

2901.07   DNA testing of certain prisoners

(A) As used in this section, "DNA analysis" and "DNA specimen" have the same meanings as in section 109.573 of the Revised Code.

(B)(1) A person who is convicted of or pleads guilty to committing an offense listed in division (D) of this section and who is sentenced to a term of imprisonment shall submit to a DNA specimen collection procedure administered by the director of rehabilitation and correction or the chief administrative officer of the detention facility, jail, or workhouse in which the person is serving the term of imprisonment. If the person serves the term of imprisonment in a state correctional institution, the director of rehabilitation and correction shall cause the DNA specimen to be collected from the person during the intake process at the reception facility designated by the director. If the person serves the term of imprisonment in a county, multicounty, municipal, municipal-county, or multicounty-municipal detention facility or a jail or workhouse, the chief administrative officer of the detention facility, jail, or workhouse shall cause the DNA specimen to be collected from the person during the intake process at the detention facility, jail, or workhouse. In accordance with division (C) of this section, the director of rehabilitation and correction or the chief administrative officer of the detention facility, jail, or workhouse in which the person is serving the term of imprisonment shall cause the DNA specimen to be forwarded to the bureau of criminal identification and investigation no later than fifteen days after the date of the collection of the DNA specimen. The DNA specimen shall be collected in accordance with division (C) of this section.

(2) If a person is convicted of or pleads guilty to committing an offense listed in division (D) of this section, is serving a term of imprisonment for that offense, and did not provide a DNA specimen pursuant to division (B)(1) of this section, prior to the person's release from imprisonment, the person shall submit to, and director of rehabilitation and correction or the chief administrative officer of the detention facility, jail, or workhouse in which the person is serving the term of imprisonment shall administer, a DNA specimen collection procedure at the state correctional institution, detention facility, jail, or workhouse in which the person is serving the term of imprisonment. In accordance with division (C) of this section, the director of rehabilitation and correction or the chief administrative officer of the detention facility, jail, or workhouse in which the person is serving the term of imprisonment shall cause the DNA specimen to be forwarded to the bureau of criminal identification and investigation no later than fifteen days after the date of the collection of the DNA specimen. The DNA specimen shall be collected in accordance with division (C) of this section.

(3) If an inmate is released on parole, furlough, or other release, is under the supervision of the adult parole authority, is returned to a state correctional institution for a violation of a condition of his parole, furlough, or other release, was or will be serving a term of imprisonment for committing an offense listed in division (D) of this section, and did not provide a DNA specimen pursuant to division (B)(1) or (2) of this section, the inmate shall submit to, and the director of rehabilitation and correction shall administer, a DNA specimen collection procedure at the state correctional institution in which the person is serving the term of imprisonment. In accordance with division (C) of this section, the director of rehabilitation and correction shall cause the DNA specimen to be forwarded to the bureau of criminal identification and investigation no later than fifteen days after the date of the collection of the

DNA specimen. The DNA specimen shall be collected from the inmate in accordance with division (C) of this section.

(C) A physician, registered nurse, licensed practical nurse, duly licensed clinical laboratory technician, or other qualified medical practitioner shall collect in a medically approved manner the DNA specimen required to be collected pursuant to division (B) of this section. No later than fifteen days after the date of the collection of the DNA specimen, the director of rehabilitation and correction or the chief administrative officer of the county, multicounty, municipal, municipal-county, or multicounty-municipal detention facility, jail, or workhouse in which the person is serving the term of imprisonment shall cause the DNA specimen to be forwarded to the bureau of criminal identification and investigation in accordance with procedures established by the superintendent of the bureau under division (H) of section 109.573 of the Revised Code. The bureau shall provide the specimen vials, mailing tubes, labels, postage, and instructions needed for the collection and forwarding of the DNA specimen to the bureau.

(D) The director of rehabilitation and correction and the chief administrative officer of the county, multicounty, municipal, municipal-county, or multicounty-municipal detention facility or jail or workhouse shall cause a DNA specimen to be collected in accordance with divisions (B) and (C) of this section from a person in its custody who is convicted of or pleads guilty to one of the following offenses:

(1) A violation of section 2903.01, 2903.02, 2905.01, 2905.04, 2907.02, 2907.03, 2907.04, 2907.05, 2907.12, or 2911.11 of the Revised Code;

(2) An attempt to commit a violation of section 2907.02, 2907.03, 2907.04, 2907.05, or 2907.12 of the Revised Code;

(3) A violation that arose out of the same facts and circumstances and same act as did a charge against the person of a violation of section 2907.02, 2907.03, 2907.04, 2907.05, or 2907.12 of the Revised Code that was previously dismissed.

(E) The director of rehabilitation and correction or a chief administrative officer of a detention facility, jail, or workhouse described in division (B) of this section is not required to comply with this section until the superintendent of the bureau of criminal identification and investigation gives agencies in the criminal justice system, as defined in section 181.51 of the Revised Code, in the state official notification that the state DNA laboratory is prepared to accept DNA specimens.

(1995 H 5, eff. 8–30–95)

2901.08   Delinquency adjudications deemed convictions

If a person is alleged to have committed an offense and if the person previously has been adjudicated a delinquent child or juvenile traffic offender for a violation of a law or ordinance, the adjudication as a delinquent child or as a juvenile traffic offender is a conviction for a violation of the law or ordinance for purposes of determining the offense with which the person should be charged and, if the person is convicted of or pleads guilty to an offense, the sentence to be imposed upon the person relative to the conviction or guilty plea.

(1995 H 1, eff. 1–1–96)

2901.09   Taking life of the president, or of a person in line of succession to the presidency—Repealed

(1972 H 511, eff. 1–1–74; 1953 H 1; GC 12406)

2901.10   Taking life of a governor or lieutenant governor—Repealed

(1972 H 511, eff. 1–1–74; 1953 H 1; GC 12407)

JURISDICTION, VENUE, AND LIMITATIONS OF PROSECUTIONS

2901.11   Criminal law jurisdiction

(A) A person is subject to criminal prosecution and punishment in this state if any of the following occur:

(1) He commits an offense under the laws of this state, any element of which takes place in this state;

(2) While in this state, he conspires or attempts to commit, or is guilty of complicity in the commission of an offense in another jurisdiction, which offense is an offense under both the laws of this state and such other jurisdiction;

(3) While out of this state, he conspires or attempts to commit, or is guilty of complicity in the commission of an offense in this state;

(4) While out of this state, he omits to perform a legal duty imposed by the laws of this state, which omission affects a legitimate interest of the state in protecting, governing, or regulating any person, property, thing, transaction, or activity in this state;

(5) While out of this state, he unlawfully takes or retains property and subsequently brings any of such property into this state;

(6) While out of this state, he unlawfully takes or entices another and subsequently brings such other person into this state.

(B) In homicide, the element referred to in division (A)(1) of this section is either the act which causes death, or the physical contact which causes death, or the death itself. If any part of the body of a homicide victim is found in this state, the death is presumed to have occurred within this state.

(C)(1) This state includes the land and water within its boundaries and the air space above that land and water, with respect to which this state has either exclusive or concurrent legislative jurisdiction. Where the boundary between this state and another state or foreign country is disputed, the disputed territory is conclusively presumed to be within this state for purposes of this section.

(2) The courts of common pleas of Adams, Athens, Belmont, Brown, Clermont, Columbiana, Gallia, Hamilton, Jefferson, Lawrence, Meigs, Monroe, Scioto, and Washington counties have jurisdiction beyond the north or northwest shore of the Ohio river extending to the opposite shore line, between the extended boundary lines of any adjacent counties or adjacent state. Each of those courts of common pleas has concurrent jurisdiction on the Ohio river with any adjacent court of common pleas that borders on that river and with any court of Kentucky or of West Virginia that borders on the Ohio river and that has jurisdiction on the Ohio river under the law of Kentucky or the law of West Virginia, whichever is applicable, or under federal law.

(D) When an offense is committed under the laws of this state, and it appears beyond a reasonable doubt that the offense or any element thereof took place either in Ohio or in another jurisdiction or jurisdictions, but it cannot reasonably be determined in which it took place, such offense or element is conclusively presumed to have taken place in this state for purposes of this section.

(1992 S 371, eff. 1–17–93; 1972 H 511)

2901.12 Venue

(A) The trial of a criminal case in this state shall be held in a court having jurisdiction of the subject matter, and in the territory of which the offense or any element of the offense was committed.

(B) When the offense or any element of the offense was committed in an aircraft, motor vehicle, train, watercraft, or other vehicle, in transit, and it cannot reasonably be determined in which jurisdiction the offense was committed, the offender may be tried in any jurisdiction through which the aircraft, motor vehicle, train, watercraft, or other vehicle passed.

(C) When the offense involved the unlawful taking or receiving of property or the unlawful taking or enticing of another, the offender may be tried in any jurisdiction from which or into which the property or victim was taken, received, or enticed.

(D) When the offense is conspiracy, attempt, or complicity cognizable under division (A)(2) of section 2901.11 of the Revised Code, the offender may be tried in any jurisdiction in which the conspiracy, attempt, complicity, or any of its elements occurred.

(E) When the offense is conspiracy or attempt cognizable under division (A)(3) of section 2901.11 of the Revised Code, the offender may be tried in any jurisdiction in which the offense that was the object of the conspiracy or attempt, or any element thereof, was intended to or could have taken place. When the offense is complicity cognizable under division (A)(3) of section 2901.11 of the Revised Code, the offender may be tried in any jurisdiction in which the principal offender may be tried.

(F) When an offense is considered to have been committed in this state while the offender was out of this state, and the jurisdiction in this state in which the offense or any material element of the offense was committed is not reasonably ascertainable, the offender may be tried in any jurisdiction in which the offense or element reasonably could have been committed.

(G) When it appears beyond a reasonable doubt that an offense or any element of an offense was committed in any of two or more jurisdictions, but it cannot reasonably be determined in which jurisdiction the offense or element was committed, the offender may be tried in any such jurisdiction.

(H) When an offender, as part of a course of criminal conduct, commits offenses in different jurisdictions, he may be tried for all of those offenses in any jurisdiction in which one of those offenses or any element of one of those offenses occurred. Without limitation on the evidence that may be used to establish such course of criminal conduct, any of the following is prima-facie evidence of a course of criminal conduct:

(1) The offenses involved the same victim, or victims of the same type or from the same group.

(2) The offenses were committed by the offender in his same employment, or capacity, or relationship to another.

(3) The offenses were committed as part of the same transaction or chain of events, or in furtherance of the same purpose or objective.

(4) The offenses were committed in furtherance of the same conspiracy.

(5) The offenses involved the same or a similar modus operandi.

(6) The offenses were committed along the offender's line of travel in this state, regardless of his point of origin or destination.

(I)(1) When the offense involves a computer, computer system, or computer network, the offender may be tried in any jurisdiction containing any location of the computer, computer system, or computer network of the victim of the offense or any jurisdiction in which the alleged offender commits any activity that is an essential part of the offense.

(2) As used in this section, "computer," "computer system," and "computer network" have the same meaning as in section 2913.01 of the Revised Code.

(J) When the offense involves the death of a person, and it cannot reasonably be determined in which jurisdiction the offense was committed, the offender may be tried in the jurisdiction in which the dead person's body or any part of the dead person's body was found.

(K) Notwithstanding any other requirement for the place of trial, venue may be changed upon motion of the prosecution, the defense, or the court, to any court having jurisdiction of the subject matter outside the county in which trial otherwise would be held, when it appears that a fair and impartial trial cannot be held in the jurisdiction in which trial otherwise would be held, or when it appears that trial should be held in another jurisdiction for the convenience of the parties and in the interests of justice.

(1989 S 64, eff. 10–26–89; 1986 H 49; 1972 H 511)

2901.13 Limitation of criminal prosecutions

(A) Except as otherwise provided in this section, a prosecution shall be barred unless it is commenced within the following periods after an offense is committed:

(1) for a felony other than aggravated murder or murder, six years;

(2) for a misdemeanor other than a minor misdemeanor, two years;

(3) for a minor misdemeanor, six months.

(B) If the period of limitation provided in division (A) of this section has expired, prosecution shall be commenced for an offense of which an element is fraud or breach of a fiduciary duty, within one year after discovery of the offense either by an aggrieved person, or by his legal representative who is not himself a party to the offense.

(C) If the period of limitation provided in division (A) of this section has expired, prosecution shall be commenced for an offense involving misconduct in office by a public servant as defined in section 2921.01 of the Revised Code, at any time while the accused remains a public servant, or within two years thereafter.

(D) An offense is committed when every element of the offense occurs. In the case of an offense of which an element is a continuing course of conduct, the period of limitation does not begin to run until such course of conduct or the accused's accountability for it terminates, whichever occurs first.

(E) A prosecution is commenced on the date an indictment is returned or an information filed, or on the date a lawful arrest without a warrant is made, or on the date a warrant, summons, citation, or other process is issued, whichever occurs first. A prosecution is not commenced by the return of an indictment or the filing of an information unless reasonable diligence is exercised to issue and execute process on the same. A prosecution is not commenced upon issuance of a warrant, summons, citation, or other process, unless reasonable diligence is exercised to execute the same.

(F) The period of limitation shall not run during any time when the corpus delicti remains undiscovered.

(G) The period of limitation shall not run during any time when the accused purposely avoids prosecution. Proof that the accused absented himself from this state or concealed his identity or whereabouts is prima-facie evidence of his purpose to avoid prosecution.

(H) The period of limitation shall not run during any time a prosecution against the accused based on the same conduct is pending in this state, even though the indictment, information, or process which commenced the prosecution is quashed or the proceedings thereon are set aside or reversed on appeal.

(1972 H 511, eff. 1-1-74)

2901.14   Administering medicine when intoxicated—Repealed

(1972 H 511, eff. 1-1-74; 1953 H 1; GC 12410)

2901.15   Prescribing secret medicine—Repealed

(1972 H 511, eff. 1-1-74; 1953 H 1; GC 12411)

2901.16   Attempt to procure abortion—Repealed

(1972 H 511, eff. 1-1-74; 1953 H 1; GC 12412)

2901.17   Testimony in abortion prosecutions—Repealed

(1972 H 511, eff. 1-1-74; 1953 H 1; GC 12412-1)

2901.18   Torturing or punishing another—Repealed

(1972 H 511, eff. 1-1-74; 131 v S 382; 1953 H 1; GC 12428)

2901.19   Maiming or disfiguring another—Repealed

(1972 H 511, eff. 1-1-74; 1953 H 1; GC 12416)

2901.20   Hazing—Repealed

(1972 H 511, eff. 1-1-74; 1953 H 1; GC 12417)

CRIMINAL LIABILITY

2901.21   Requirements for criminal liability

(A) Except as provided in division (B) of this section, a person is not guilty of an offense unless both of the following apply:

(1) His liability is based on conduct which includes either a voluntary act, or an omission to perform an act or duty which he is capable of performing;

(2) He has the requisite degree of culpability for each element as to which a culpable mental state is specified by the section defining the offense.

(B) When the section defining an offense does not specify any degree of culpability, and plainly indicates a purpose to impose strict criminal liability for the conduct described in such section, then culpability is not required for a person to be guilty of the offense. When the section neither specifies culpability nor plainly indicates a purpose to impose strict liability, recklessness is sufficient culpability to commit the offense.

(C) As used in this section:

(1) Possession is a voluntary act if the possessor knowingly procured or received the thing possessed, or was aware of his control thereof for a sufficient time to have ended his possession.

(2) Reflexes, convulsions, body movements during unconsciousness or sleep, and body movements that are not otherwise a product of the actor's volition, are involuntary acts.

(3) "Culpability" means purpose, knowledge, recklessness, or negligence, as defined in section 2901.22 of the Revised Code.

(1972 H 511, eff. 1–1–74)

2901.22   Culpable mental states

(A) A person acts purposely when it is his specific intention to cause a certain result, or, when the gist of the offense is a prohibition against conduct of a certain nature, regardless of what the offender intends to accomplish thereby, it is his specific intention to engage in conduct of that nature.

(B) A person acts knowingly, regardless of his purpose, when he is aware that his conduct will probably cause a certain result or will probably be of a certain nature. A person has knowledge of circumstances when he is aware that such circumstances probably exist.

(C) A person acts recklessly when, with heedless indifference to the consequences, he perversely disregards a known risk that his conduct is likely to cause a certain result or is likely to be of a certain nature. A person is reckless with respect to circumstances when, with heedless indifference to the consequences, he perversely disregards a known risk that such circumstances are likely to exist.

(D) A person acts negligently when, because of a substantial lapse from due care, he fails to perceive or avoid a risk that his conduct may cause a certain result or may be of a certain nature. A person is negligent with respect to circumstances when, because of a substantial lapse from due care, he fails to perceive or avoid a risk that such circumstances may exist.

(E) When the section defining an offense provides that negligence suffices to establish an element thereof, then recklessness, knowledge, or purpose is also sufficient culpability for such element. When recklessness suffices to establish an element of an offense, then knowledge or purpose is also sufficient culpability for such element. When knowledge suffices to establish an element of an offense, then purpose is also sufficient culpability for such element.

(1972 H 511, eff. 1–1–74)

2901.23   Organizational criminal liability

(A) An organization may be convicted of an offense under any of the following circumstances:

(1) The offense is a minor misdemeanor committed by an officer, agent, or employee of the organization acting in its behalf and within the scope of his office or employment, except that if the section defining the offense designates the officers, agents, or employees for whose conduct the organization is accountable or the circumstances under which it is accountable, such provisions shall apply.

(2) A purpose to impose organizational liability plainly appears in the section defining the offense, and the offense is committed by an officer, agent, or employee of the organization

acting in its behalf and within the scope of his office or employment, except that if the section defining the offense designates the officers, agents, or employees for whose conduct the organization is accountable or the circumstances under which it is accountable, such provisions shall apply.

(3) The offense consists of an omission to discharge a specific duty imposed by law on the organization.

(4) If, acting with the kind of culpability otherwise required for the commission of the offense, its commission was authorized, requested, commanded, tolerated, or performed by the board of directors, trustees, partners, or by a high managerial officer, agent, or employee acting in behalf of the organization and within the scope of his office or employment.

(B) When strict liability is imposed for the commission of an offense, a purpose to impose organizational liability shall be presumed, unless the contrary plainly appears.

(C) In a prosecution of an organization for an offense other than one for which strict liability is imposed, it is a defense that the high managerial officer, agent, or employee having supervisory responsibility over the subject matter of the offense exercised due diligence to prevent its commission. This defense is not available if it plainly appears inconsistent with the purpose of the section defining the offense.

(D) As used in this section, "organization" means a corporation for profit or not for profit, partnership, limited partnership, joint venture, unincorporated association, estate, trust, or other commercial or legal entity. "Organization" does not include an entity organized as or by a governmental agency for the execution of a governmental program.

(1972 H 511, eff. 1–1–74)

2901.24   Personal accountability for organizational conduct

(A) An officer, agent, or employee of an organization as defined in section 2901.23 of the Revised Code may be prosecuted for an offense committed by such organization, if he acts with the kind of culpability required for the commission of the offense, and any of the following apply:

(1) In the name of the organization or in its behalf, he engages in conduct constituting the offense, or causes another to engage in such conduct, or tolerates such conduct when it is of a type for which he has direct responsibility;

(2) He has primary responsibility to discharge a duty imposed on the organization by law, and such duty is not discharged.

(B) When a person is convicted of an offense by reason of this section, he is subject to the same penalty as if he had acted in his own behalf.

(1972 H 511, eff. 1–1–74)

2901.241   Assault with a dangerous or deadly weapon—Repealed

(1972 H 511, eff. 1–1–74; 128 v 560)

Historical and Statutory Notes

Ed. Note: See now 2903.11 for provisions analogous to former 2901.241.

2901.25   Assault and battery, and menacing threats—Repealed

(1972 H 511, eff. 1–1–74; 1953 H 1; GC 12423)

Historical and Statutory Notes

Ed. Note: See now 2903.13, 2903.21, and 2903.22 for provisions analogous to former 2901.25.

Pre–1953 H 1 Amendments: RS 6823

2901.251 Throwing stones at persons—Repealed

(1972 H 511, eff. 1–1–74; 131 v H 146)

Historical and Statutory Notes

Ed. Note: See now 2903.11 and 2903.13 for provisions analogous to former 2901.251.

2901.252 Assault of law enforcement officer or fireman, or state or federal militia— Repealed

(1972 H 511, eff. 1–1–74; 132 v H 996)

Historical and Statutory Notes

Ed. Note: See now 2903.11 and 2903.13 for provisions analogous to former 2901.252.

2901.26 Kidnapping—Repealed

(1972 H 511, eff. 1–1–74; 1953 H 1; GC 12424)

Historical and Statutory Notes

Ed. Note: See now 2905.01 and 2905.02 for provisions analogous to former 2901.26.

Pre–1953 H 1 Amendments: 115 v Pt 2, 73; RS 6824

2901.27 Abducting person for purpose of extortion—Repealed

(1972 H 511, eff. 1–1–74; 1953 H 1; GC 12427)

Historical and Statutory Notes

Ed. Note: See now 2905.01 for provisions analogous to former 2901.27.

Pre–1953 H 1 Amendments: 117 v 485, § 1; 115 v Pt 2, 73; 101 v 263; 95 v 648, § 1

2901.28 Abduction resulting in death—Repealed

(1972 H 511, eff. 1–1–74; 1953 H 1; GC 13386)

Historical and Statutory Notes

Ed. Note: See now 2903.01 for provisions analogous to former 2901.28.

Pre–1953 H 1 Amendments: 115 v Pt 2, 90, § 1; 95 v 648, § 2

2901.29 Jurisdiction—Repealed

(1972 H 511, eff. 1–1–74; 1953 H 1; GC 13386–1)

Historical and Statutory Notes

Ed. Note: See now 2901.11 for provisions analogous to former 2901.29.

Pre–1953 H 1 Amendments: 115 v Pt 2, 90, § 2

MISSING CHILDREN

2901.30 Police handling of missing child case

(A) As used in sections 2901.30 to 2901.32 of the Revised Code:

(1) "Information" means information that can be integrated into the computer system and that relates to the physical or mental description of a minor including, but not limited to, height, weight, color of hair and eyes, use of eyeglasses or contact lenses, skin coloring, physical or mental handicaps, special medical conditions or needs, abnormalities, problems, scars and

marks, and distinguishing characteristics, and other information that could assist in identifying a minor including, but not limited to, full name and nickname, date and place of birth, age, names and addresses of parents and other relatives, fingerprints, dental records, photographs, social security number, driver's license number, credit card numbers, bank account numbers, and clothing.

(2) "Minor" means a person under eighteen years of age.

(3) "Missing children" or "missing child" means either of the following:

(a) A minor who has run away from or who otherwise is missing from the home of, or the care, custody, and control of, his parents, parent who is the residential parent and legal custodian, guardian, legal custodian, or other person having responsibility for the care of the minor;

(b) A minor who is missing and about whom there is reason to believe he could be the victim of a violation of section 2905.01, 2905.02, 2905.03, 2905.04, or 2919.23 of the Revised Code.

(B) When a law enforcement agency in this state that has jurisdiction in the matter is informed that a minor is or may be a missing child and that the person providing the information wishes to file a missing child report, the law enforcement agency shall take that report. Upon taking the report, the law enforcement agency shall take prompt action upon it, including, but not limited to, concerted efforts to locate the missing child. No law enforcement agency in this state shall have a rule or policy that prohibits or discourages the filing of or the taking of action upon a missing child report, within a specified period following the discovery or formulation of a belief that a minor is or could be a missing child.

(C) If a missing child report is made to a law enforcement agency in this state that has jurisdiction in the matter, the law enforcement agency shall gather readily available information about the missing child and integrate it into the national crime information center computer within twelve hours following the making of the report. The law enforcement agency shall make reasonable efforts to acquire additional information about the missing child following the transmittal of the initially available information, and promptly integrate any additional information acquired into such computer systems.

Whenever a law enforcement agency integrates information about a missing child into the national crime information center computer, the law enforcement agency promptly shall notify the missing child's parents, parent who is the residential parent and legal custodian, guardian, or legal custodian, or any other person responsible for the care of the missing child, that it has so integrated the information.

The parents, parent who is the residential parent and legal custodian, guardian, legal custodian, or other person responsible for the care of the missing child shall provide available information upon request, and may provide information voluntarily, to the law enforcement agency during the information gathering process. The law enforcement agency also may obtain available information about the missing child from other persons, subject to constitutional and statutory limitations.

(D) Upon the filing of a missing child report, the law enforcement agency involved promptly shall make a reasonable attempt to notify other law enforcement agencies within its county and, if the agency has jurisdiction in a municipal corporation or township that borders another county, to notify the law enforcement agency for the municipal corporation or township in the other county with which it shares the border, that it has taken a missing child report and may be requesting assistance or cooperation in the case, and provide relevant information to the other law enforcement agencies. The agency may notify additional law enforcement agencies, appropriate county children services boards, and appropriate county departments of human services exercising children services functions, about the case, request their assistance or cooperation in the case, and provide them with relevant information.

Upon request from a law enforcement agency, a county children services board or a county department of human services exercising children services functions shall grant the law enforcement agency access to all information concerning a missing child that the board or department possesses that may be relevant to the law enforcement agency in investigating a missing child report concerning that child. The information obtained by the law enforcement agency shall be used only to further the investigation to locate the missing child.

(E) Upon request, law enforcement agencies in this state shall provide assistance to, and cooperate with, other law enforcement agencies in their investigation of missing child cases.

The information in any missing child report made to a law enforcement agency shall be made available, upon request, to law enforcement personnel of this state, other states, and the federal government when the law enforcement personnel indicate that the request is to aid in identifying or locating a missing child or the possible identification of a deceased minor who, upon discovery, cannot be identified.

(F) When a missing child has not been located within thirty days after the date on which the missing child report pertaining to him was filed with a law enforcement agency, that law enforcement agency shall request the missing child's parents, parent who is the residential parent and legal custodian, guardian, or legal custodian, or any other person responsible for the care of the missing child, to provide written consent for the law enforcement agency to contact the missing child's dentist and request the missing child's dental records. Upon receipt of such written consent, the dentist shall release a copy of the missing child's dental records to the law enforcement agency and shall provide and encode the records in such form as requested by the law enforcement agency. The law enforcement agency then shall integrate information in the records into the national crime information center computer in order to compare the records to those of unidentified deceased persons. This division does not prevent a law enforcement agency from seeking consent to obtain copies of a missing child's dental records, or prevent a missing child's parents, parent who is the residential parent and legal custodian, guardian, or legal custodian, or any other person responsible for the care of the missing child, from granting consent for the release of copies of the missing child's dental records to a law enforcement agency, at any time.

(G) A missing child's parents, parent who is the residential parent and legal custodian, guardian, or legal custodian, or any other persons responsible for the care of a missing child, immediately shall notify the law enforcement agency with which they filed the missing child report whenever the child has returned to their home or to their care, custody, and control, has been released if he was the victim of an offense listed in division (A)(3)(b) of this section, or otherwise has been located. Upon such notification or upon otherwise learning that a missing child has returned to the home of, or to the care, custody, and control of his parents, parent who is the residential parent and legal custodian, guardian, legal custodian, or other person responsible for his care, has been released if he was the victim of an offense listed in division (A)(3)(b) of this section, or otherwise has been located, the law enforcement agency involved promptly shall integrate the fact that the minor no longer is a missing child into the national crime information center computer.

(H) Nothing contained in this section shall be construed to impair the confidentiality of services provided to runaway minors by shelters for runaway minors pursuant to sections 5119.64 to 5119.68 of the Revised Code.

(1990 S 3, eff. 4–11–91; 1984 S 321)

2901.31   Cooperation in national information efforts

Law enforcement agencies in this state shall cooperate fully with the United States attorney general in the collection of information that would assist in the identification of unidentified deceased persons and information that would assist in the location of missing persons under the "Federal Missing Children Act of 1982," 96 Stat. 1259, 28 U.S.C.A. 534, as amended.

Law enforcement agencies in this state that are investigating missing children cases shall utilize the records and information compiled by the United States attorney general pursuant to that act when the circumstances of an investigation indicate that the records and information may be of assistance and when the act authorizes it.

(1984 S 321, eff. 4–9–85)

2901.32 Regulation of solicitations for missing child information distribution

(A) No organization shall solicit contributions for the purpose of distributing materials containing information relating to missing children unless it complies with all of the following requirements:

(1) It has been incorporated under Chapter 1702. of the Revised Code or the nonprofit corporation law of another state for a period of two years prior to the time of the solicitation of contributions.

(2) It has been exempt from federal income taxation under subsection 501(a) and described in subsection 501(c)(3), 501(c)(4), 501(c)(8), 501(c)(10), or 501(c)(19) of the Internal Revenue Code of 1954, 68A Stat. 3, 26 U.S.C. 1, as now or hereafter amended, for a period of two years prior to the time of the solicitation of contributions.

(3) It does not use fund-raising counsel, professional solicitors, commercial co-venturers, or other charitable organizations, as these terms are defined in section 1716.01 of the Revised Code, to solicit such contributions.

(B) No organization that solicits contributions for the purpose of distributing materials containing information relating to missing children shall expressly state or imply in any way that it is affiliated with, or is soliciting contributions on behalf of, an organization established to assist in the location of missing children without the express written consent of that organization.

(C) Whoever violates division (A) or (B) of this section is guilty of improper solicitation of contributions for missing children, a misdemeanor of the third degree.

(1990 H 486, eff. 11–7–90; 1984 S 321)

2901.33 Child stealing—Repealed

(1972 H 511, eff. 1–1–74; 1953 H 1; GC 12425)

2901.34 Conspiracy to abduct—Repealed

(1972 H 511, eff. 1–1–74; 1953 H 1; GC 13386–5)

2901.35 Denial of privileges at restaurants, stores, and other places by reason of color or race—Repealed

(1972 H 511, eff. 1–1–74; 1953 H 1; GC 12940, 12941)

2901.36 Bar to prosecution—Repealed

(1972 H 511, eff. 1–1–74; 1953 H 1; GC 12942)

2901.37 Libel—Repealed

(1972 H 511, eff. 1–1–74; 126 v 575; 1953 H 1; GC 13383)

2901.38 Blackmailing—Repealing

(1972 H 511, eff. 1–1–74; 1953 H 1; GC 13384)

2901.39 Threatening letters—Repealed

(1972 H 511, eff. 1–1–74; 1953 H 1; GC 13385)

2901.40 Abandonment of destitute, infirm, or aged parents—Repealed

(1972 H 511, eff. 1–1–74; 126 v 429; 1953 H 1; GC 12429)

2901.41 Bond to support parent—Repealed

(1972 H 511, eff. 1–1–74; 1953 H 1; GC 12430)

2901.42 Parent whom child need not aid—Repealed

(1972 H 511, eff. 1–1–74; 131 v S 119; 1953 H 1; GC 12431)

2901.43   Conspiracy to deprive any person of equal protection of state laws prohibited—Repealed

(1972 H 511, eff. 1–1–74; 131 v S 294)

2901.44   Threat of damage to building or other real or personal property—Repealed

(1972 H 511, eff. 1–1–74; 131 v H 703)

2901.45   Adulterating candy or food—Repealed

(1973 H 716, eff. 1–1–74; 1972 S 538)

CHAPTER 2903

HOMICIDE AND ASSAULT

HOMICIDE

HOMICIDE

2903.01 Aggravated murder; specific intent to cause death

(A) No person shall purposely, and with prior calculation and design, cause the death of another.

(B) No person shall purposely cause the death of another while committing or attempting to commit, or while fleeing immediately after committing or attempting to commit kidnapping, rape, aggravated arson or arson, aggravated robbery or robbery, aggravated burglary or burglary, or escape.

(C) Whoever violates this section is guilty of aggravated murder, and shall be punished as provided in section 2929.02 of the Revised Code.

(D) No person shall be convicted of aggravated murder unless he is specifically found to have intended to cause the death of another. In no case shall a jury in an aggravated murder case be instructed in such a manner that it may believe that a person who commits or attempts

19

to commit any offense listed in division (B) of this section is to be conclusively inferred, because he engaged in a common design with others to commit the offense by force and violence or because the offense and the manner of its commission would be likely to produce death, to have intended to cause the death of any person who is killed during the commission of, attempt to commit, or flight from the commission of or attempt to commit, the offense. If a jury in an aggravated murder case is instructed that a person who commits or attempts to commit any offense listed in division (B) of this section may be inferred, because he engaged in a common design with others to commit the offense by force or violence or because the offense and the manner of its commission would be likely to produce death, to have intended to cause the death of any person who is killed during the commission of, attempt to commit, or flight from the commission of or attempt to commit the offense, the jury also shall be instructed that the inference is nonconclusive, that the inference may be considered in determining intent, that it is to consider all evidence introduced by the prosecution to indicate the person's intent and by the person to indicate his lack of intent in determining whether the person specifically intended to cause the death of the person killed, and that the prosecution must prove the specific intent of the person to have caused the death by proof beyond a reasonable doubt.

(1981 S 1, eff. 10–19–81; 1972 H 511)

2903.02   Murder

(A) No person shall purposely cause the death of another.

(B) Whoever violates this section is guilty of murder, and shall be punished as provided in section 2929.02 of the Revised Code.

(1972 H 511, eff. 1–1–74)

2903.03   Voluntary manslaughter

(A) No person, while under the influence of sudden passion or in a sudden fit of rage, either of which is brought on by serious provocation occasioned by the victim that is reasonably sufficient to incite the person into using deadly force, shall knowingly cause the death of another.

(B) Whoever violates this section is guilty of voluntary manslaughter, an aggravated felony of the first degree.

(1982 H 269, § 4, eff. 7–1–83; 1982 S 199, H 103; 1972 H 511)

2903.04   Involuntary manslaughter

(A) No person shall cause the death of another as a proximate result of the offender's committing or attempting to commit a felony.

(B) No person shall cause the death of another as a proximate result of the offender's committing or attempting to commit a misdemeanor of the first, second, third, or fourth degree or a minor misdemeanor.

(C) Whoever violates this section is guilty of involuntary manslaughter. Violation of division (A) of this section is an aggravated felony of the first degree. Violation of division (B) of this section is an aggravated felony of the third degree.

(D)(1) In addition to any penalty imposed upon the offender under division (C) of this section and section 2929.11 of the Revised Code, if an offender is convicted of or pleads guilty to a violation of division (A) or (B) of this section and if the felony or misdemeanor that the offender committed or attempted to commit, that proximately resulted in the death of the other person, and that is the basis of the offender's violation of division (A) or (B) of this section included, as an element of that felony or misdemeanor offense, the offender's operation or participation in the operation of a motor vehicle, motorcycle, snowmobile, locomotive, watercraft, or aircraft while he was under the influence of alcohol, a drug of abuse, or alcohol and a drug of abuse, both of the following apply:

(a) The offender's driver's or commercial driver's license or permit or nonresident operating privilege shall be permanently revoked pursuant to section 4507.16 of the Revised Code;

(b) The offender is not eligible for shock probation, probation, or shock parole pursuant to section 2947.061, 2951.02, or 2967.31 of the Revised Code if any of the following apply relative to the offender:

(i) He previously has been convicted of or pleaded guilty to a violation of division (A) or (B) of this section in which the felony or misdemeanor that he committed or attempted to commit, that proximately resulted in the death of the other person, and that is the basis of the offender's violation of division (A) or (B) of this section included, as an element of that felony or misdemeanor offense, his operation or participation in the operation of a motor vehicle, motorcycle, snowmobile, locomotive, watercraft, or aircraft while he was under the influence of alcohol, a drug of abuse, or alcohol and a drug of abuse;

(ii) He previously has been convicted of or pleaded guilty to a violation of a municipal ordinance that is substantially similar to division (A) or (B) of this section and the felony or misdemeanor that he committed or attempted to commit, that proximately resulted in the death of the other person, and that is the basis of the offender's violation of the municipal ordinance that is substantially similar to division (A) or (B) of this section included, as an element of that felony or misdemeanor offense, his operation or participation in the operation of a motor vehicle, motorcycle, snowmobile, locomotive, watercraft, or aircraft while he was under the influence of alcohol, a drug of abuse, or alcohol and a drug of abuse;

(iii) He previously has been convicted of or pleaded guilty to a violation of section 1547.11, 2903.06, 2903.07, 2903.08, 4511.19, or 4511.192 of the Revised Code, division (B) or (D) of section 4507.02 of the Revised Code, section 4507.38 or 4507.39 of the Revised Code as those sections existed prior to September 24, 1986, a municipal ordinance that is substantially similar to section 2903.06, 2903.07, 2903.08, 4511.19, or 4511.192 of the Revised Code, or a municipal ordinance that is substantially similar to section 4507.38 or 4507.39 of the Revised Code as those sections existed prior to September 24, 1986;

(iv) He has accumulated twelve points pursuant to section 4507.021 of the Revised Code within one year of the offense;

(v) He was driving under suspension at the time he committed the offense.

(2) In determining, for purposes of division (D)(1) of this section, whether an offender was under the influence of alcohol, a drug of abuse, or alcohol and a drug of abuse at the time of the commission of his violation of division (A) or (B) of this section, the trier of fact may consider as competent evidence the concentration of alcohol in the offender's blood, breath, or urine as shown by a chemical test taken pursuant to section 1547.111 or 4511.191 of the Revised Code. The offender shall be presumed to have been under the influence of alcohol if there was, at the time the bodily substance was withdrawn for the chemical test, a concentration of ten-hundredths of one per cent or more by weight of alcohol in the offender's blood, ten-hundredths of one gram or more by weight of alcohol per two hundred ten liters of his breath, or fourteen-hundredths of one gram or more by weight of alcohol per one hundred milliliters of his urine.

(1994 H 236, eff. 9–29–94; 1993 S 62, § 4, eff. 9–1–93; 1992 S 275; 1982 H 269, § 4, S 199; 1972 H 511)

2903.05 Negligent homicide

(A) No person shall negligently cause the death of another by means of a deadly weapon or dangerous ordnance as defined in section 2923.11 of the Revised Code.

(B) Whoever violates this section is guilty of negligent homicide, a misdemeanor of the first degree.

(1972 H 511, eff. 1–1–74)

2903.06 Aggravated vehicular homicide; effects of conviction for violations on penalties; repeat offenders

(A) No person, while operating or participating in the operation of a motor vehicle, motorcycle, snowmobile, locomotive, watercraft, or aircraft, shall recklessly cause the death of another.

(B) Whoever violates this section is guilty of aggravated vehicular homicide, an aggravated felony of the third degree. If the offender previously has been convicted of or pleaded guilty to an offense under this section, section 2903.07 or 2903.08 of the Revised Code, or section 2903.04 of the Revised Code in a case in which the offender was subject to the sanctions described in division (D) of that section, aggravated vehicular homicide is an aggravated felony of the second degree.

If the jury or judge as trier of fact finds that the offender was under the influence of alcohol, a drug of abuse, or alcohol and a drug of abuse, at the time of the commission of the offense, then the offender's driver's or commercial driver's license or permit or nonresident operating privilege shall be permanently revoked pursuant to section 4507.16 of the Revised Code.

When the trier of fact determines whether the offender was under the influence of alcohol, a drug of abuse, or alcohol and a drug of abuse, the concentration of alcohol in the offender's blood, breath, or urine as shown by a chemical test taken pursuant to section 1547.111 or 4511.191 of the Revised Code may be considered as competent evidence, and the offender shall be presumed to have been under the influence of alcohol if there was at the time the bodily substance was withdrawn for the chemical test a concentration of ten-hundredths of one per cent or more by weight of alcohol in the offender's blood, ten-hundredths of one gram or more by weight of alcohol per two hundred ten liters of his breath, or fourteen-hundredths of one gram or more by weight of alcohol per one hundred milliliters of his urine.

(C) If the offender previously has been convicted of or pleaded guilty to a violation of this section, section 2903.04 of the Revised Code in a case in which the offender was subject to the sanctions described in division (D) of that section, section 1547.11, 2903.07, 2903.08, 4511.19, or 4511.192 of the Revised Code, division (B) or (D) of section 4507.02 of the Revised Code, section 4507.38 or 4507.39 of the Revised Code as those sections existed prior to September 24, 1986, a municipal ordinance that is substantially similar to section 2903.07, 2903.08, 4511.19, or 4511.192 of the Revised Code, a municipal ordinance that is substantially similar to section 4507.38 or 4507.39 of the Revised Code as those sections existed prior to September 24, 1986, or a municipal ordinance that is substantially similar to section 2903.04 of the Revised Code in a case in which the offender would have been subject to the sanctions described in division (D) of that section had he been convicted of a violation of that section, if the offender has accumulated twelve points pursuant to section 4507.021 of the Revised Code within one year of the offense, or if in the commission of the offense the offender was driving under suspension or operating a motor vehicle while under the influence of alcohol, a drug of abuse, or alcohol and a drug of abuse, he shall not be eligible for shock probation, probation, or shock parole pursuant to section 2947.061, 2951.02, or 2967.31 of the Revised Code.

(1993 S 62, § 4, eff. 9–1–93; 1992 S 275; 1990 S 131; 1989 S 49, H 381; 1986 S 262, H 428, S 356, H 265; 1982 S 432; 1973 H 716; 1972 H 511)

2903.07 Vehicular homicide; effects upon penalties of being under influence of alcohol or drug of abuse; repeat offenders

(A) No person, while operating or participating in the operation of a motor vehicle, motorcycle, snowmobile, locomotive, watercraft, or aircraft, shall negligently cause the death of another.

(B) Whoever violates this section is guilty of vehicular homicide, a misdemeanor of the first degree. If the offender previously has been convicted of an offense under this section, section 2903.06 or 2903.08 of the Revised Code, or section 2903.04 of the Revised Code in a case in which the offender was subject to the sanctions described in division (D) of that section, vehicular homicide is a felony of the fourth degree.

If the jury or judge as trier of fact finds that the offender was under the influence of alcohol, a drug of abuse, or alcohol and a drug of abuse, at the time of the commission of the offense, then the offender's driver's or commercial driver's license or permit or nonresident operating privileges shall be permanently revoked pursuant to section 4507.16 of the Revised Code.

When the trier of fact determines whether the offender was under the influence of alcohol, a drug of abuse, or alcohol and a drug of abuse, the concentration of alcohol in the offender's blood, breath, or urine as shown by a chemical test taken pursuant to section 1547.111 or 4511.191 of the Revised Code may be considered as competent evidence and the offender shall be presumed to have been under the influence of alcohol if there was at the time the bodily substance was withdrawn for the chemical test a concentration of ten-hundredths of one per cent or more by weight of alcohol in the offender's blood, ten-hundredths of one gram or more by weight of alcohol per two hundred ten liters of his breath, or fourteen-hundredths of one gram or more by weight of alcohol per one hundred milliliters of his urine.

(C) If the offender previously has been convicted of or pleaded guilty to a violation of this section, section 2903.04 of the Revised Code in a case in which the offender was subject to the sanctions described in division (D) of that section, section 1547.11, 2903.06, 2903.08, 4511.19, or 4511.192 of the Revised Code, division (B) or (D) of section 4507.02 of the Revised Code, section 4507.38 or 4507.39 of the Revised Code as those sections existed prior to September 24, 1986, a municipal ordinance that is substantially similar to this section, section 2903.08, 4511.19, or 4511.192 of the Revised Code, a municipal ordinance that is substantially similar to section 4507.38 or 4507.39 of the Revised Code as those sections existed prior to September 24, 1986, or a municipal ordinance that is substantially similar to section 2903.04 of the Revised Code in a case in which the offender would have been subject to the sanctions described in division (D) of that section had he been convicted of a violation of that section, if the offender has accumulated twelve points pursuant to section 4507.021 of the Revised Code within one year of the offense, or if in the commission of the offense the offender was driving under suspension or operating a motor vehicle while under the influence of alcohol, a drug of abuse, or alcohol and a drug of abuse, he shall not be eligible for shock probation, probation, or shock parole pursuant to section 2947.061, 2951.02, or 2967.31 of the Revised Code.

(1993 S 62, § 4, eff. 9–1–93; 1992 S 275; 1990 S 131; 1989 H 381; 1986 S 262, H 428, S 356, H 265; 1982 S 432; 1973 H 716; 1972 H 511)

2903.08 Aggravated vehicular assault

(A) No person, while operating or participating in the operation of a motor vehicle, motorcycle, snowmobile, locomotive, watercraft, or aircraft, shall recklessly cause serious physical harm to another person.

(B) Whoever violates this section is guilty of aggravated vehicular assault, a felony of the fourth degree. If the offender previously has been convicted of an offense under this section, section 2903.06 or 2903.07 of the Revised Code, or section 2903.04 of the Revised Code in a case in which the offender was subject to the sanctions described in division (D) of that section, aggravated vehicular assault is a felony of the third degree.

If the jury or judge as trier of fact finds that the offender was under the influence of alcohol, a drug of abuse, or alcohol and a drug of abuse, at the time of the commission of the offense, then the offender's driver's or commercial driver's license or permit or nonresident operating privileges shall be permanently revoked pursuant to section 4507.16 of the Revised Code.

When the trier of fact determines whether the offender was under the influence of alcohol, a drug of abuse, or alcohol and a drug of abuse, the concentration of alcohol in the offender's blood, breath, or urine as shown by a chemical test taken pursuant to section 1547.111 or 4511.191 of the Revised Code may be considered as competent evidence and the offender shall be presumed to have been under the influence of alcohol if there was at the time the bodily substance was withdrawn for the chemical test a concentration of ten-hundredths of one per cent or more by weight of alcohol in the offender's blood, ten-hundredths of one gram or more by weight of alcohol per two hundred ten liters of his breath, or fourteen-hundredths of one gram or more by weight of alcohol per one hundred milliliters of his urine.

(C) If the offender previously has been convicted of or pleaded guilty to a violation of this section, section 2903.04 of the Revised Code in a case in which the offender was subject to the sanctions described in division (D) of that section, section 1547.11, 2903.06, 2903.07, 4511.19, or 4511.192 of the Revised Code, division (B) or (D) of section 4507.02 of the Revised Code, section 4507.38 or 4507.39 of the Revised Code as those sections existed prior to September 24, 1986, a municipal ordinance that is substantially similar to this section, section 2903.07, 4511.19, or 4511.192 of the Revised Code, a municipal ordinance that is substantially similar to section 4507.38 or 4507.39 of the Revised Code as those sections existed prior to September 24, 1986, or a municipal ordinance that is substantially similar to section 2903.04 of the Revised Code in a case in which the offender would have been subject to the sanctions described in division (D) of that section had he been convicted of a violation of that section, if the offender has accumulated twelve points pursuant to section 4507.021 of the Revised Code within one year of the offense, or if in the commission of the offense the offender was driving under suspension or operating a motor vehicle while under the influence of alcohol, a drug of abuse, or alcohol and a drug of abuse, he is not eligible for shock probation, probation, or shock parole pursuant to section 2947.061, 2951.02, or 2967.31 of the Revised Code.

(1994 H 236, eff. 9–29–94; 1993 S 62, § 4, eff. 9–1–93; 1992 S 275; 1990 S 131)

2903.09 Trustee for dependent child or pregnant wife of person convicted of abandonment, torture or neglect—Repealed

(1972 H 511, eff. 1–1–74; 1969 H 1; 132 v S 65; 1953 H 1; GC 12970–1, 12970–2)

ASSAULT

2903.10 Definitions

As used in sections 2903.13 and 2903.16 of the Revised Code:

(A) "Functionally impaired person" means any person who has a physical or mental impairment that prevents him from providing for his own care or protection or whose infirmities caused by aging prevent him from providing for his own care or protection.

(B) "Caretaker" means a person who assumes the duty to provide for the care and protection of a funtionally [sic] impaired person on a voluntary basis, by contract, through receipt of payment for care and protection, as a result of a family relationship, or by order of a court of competent jurisdiction. "Caretaker" does not include a person who owns, operates, or administers, or who is an agent or employee of, a care facility, as defined in section 2903.33 of the Revised Code.

(1988 H 642, eff. 3–17–89)

2903.11 Felonious assault

(A) No person shall knowingly:

(1) Cause serious physical harm to another;

(2) Cause or attempt to cause physical harm to another by means of a deadly weapon or dangerous ordnance, as defined in section 2923.11 of the Revised Code.

(B) Whoever violates this section is guilty of felonious assault, an aggravated felony of the second degree. If the victim of the offense is a peace officer, as defined in section 2935.01 of the Revised Code, felonious assault is an aggravated felony of the first degree.

(1983 S 210, eff. 7–1–83; 1982 H 269, S 199; 1972 H 511)

2903.12 Aggravated assault

(A) No person, while under the influence of sudden passion or in a sudden fit of rage, either of which is brought on by serious provocation occasioned by the victim that is reasonably sufficient to incite the person into using deadly force, shall knowingly:

(1) Cause serious physical harm to another;

(2) Cause or attempt to cause physical harm to another by means of a deadly weapon or dangerous ordnance, as defined in section 2923.11 of the Revised Code.

(B) Whoever violates this section is guilty of aggravated assault, a felony of the fourth degree. If the victim of the offense is a peace officer, as defined in section 2935.01 of the Revised Code, aggravated assault is a felony of the third degree.

(1984 H 37, eff. 6–22–84; 1983 S 210; 1982 H 269, S 199, H 103; 1972 H 511)

2903.13 Assault

(A) No person shall knowingly cause or attempt to cause physical harm to another.

(B) No person shall recklessly cause serious physical harm to another.

(C) Whoever violates this section is guilty of assault, a misdemeanor of the first degree.

(1) If the offense is committed by a caretaker against a functionally impaired person under his care, assault is a felony of the fourth degree. If the offense is committed by a caretaker against a functionally impaired person under his care, if the offender previously has been convicted of or pleaded guilty to a violation of this section or section 2903.11 or 2903.16 of the Revised Code, and if in relation to the previous conviction the offender was a caretaker and the victim was a functionally impaired person under the offender's care, assault is a felony of the third degree.

(2) If the offense is committed in any of the following circumstances, assault is a felony of the fourth degree, and the sentence of imprisonment imposed upon the offender shall be served consecutively to any other sentence of imprisonment imposed upon the offender:

(a) The offense occurs in or on the grounds of a state correctional institution or an institution of the department of youth services, the victim of the offense is an employee of the department of rehabilitation and correction, the department of youth services, or a probation department or is on the premises of the particular institution for business purposes or as a visitor, and the offense is committed by a person incarcerated in the state correctional institution, a person institutionalized in the department of youth services institution pursuant to a commitment to the department of youth services, or a probationer, furloughee, or parolee;

(b) The offense occurs in or on the grounds of a local correctional facility, the victim of the offense is an employee of the local correctional facility or a probation department or is on the premises of the facility for business purposes or as a visitor, and the offense is committed by a person who is under custody in the facility subsequent to his arrest for any crime or delinquent act, subsequent to his being charged with or convicted of any crime, or subsequent to his being alleged to be or adjudicated a delinquent child.

(c) The offense occurs off the grounds of a state correctional institution and off the grounds of an institution of the department of youth services, the victim of the offense is an employee of the department of rehabilitation and correction, the department of youth services, or a probation department, the offense occurs during the employee's official work hours and while he is engaged in official work responsibilities, and the offense is committed by a person incarcerated in a state correctional institution or institutionalized in the department of youth services who temporarily is outside of the institution for any purpose or by a probationer, parolee, or furloughee.

(d) The offense occurs off the grounds of a local correctional facility, the victim of the offense is an employee of the local correctional facility or a probation department, the offense occurs during the employee's official work hours and while he is engaged in official work responsibilities, and the offense is committed by a person who is under custody in the facility subsequent to his arrest for any crime or delinquent act, subsequent to his being charged with or convicted of any crime, or subsequent to his being alleged to be or adjudicated a delinquent child and who temporarily is outside of the facility for any purpose or by a probationer, parolee, or furloughee.

(3) If the victim of the offense is a peace officer, a fire fighter, or a person performing emergency medical service, while in the performance of their official duties, assault is a felony of the fourth degree.

(4) As used in this section:

(a) "Peace officer" has the same meaning as in section 2935.01 of the Revised Code.

(b) "Fire fighter" has the same meaning as in section 3937.41 of the Revised Code.

(c) "Emergency medical service" has the same meaning as in section 4765.01 of the Revised Code.

(d) "Local correctional facility" means any county, multicounty, municipal, municipal-county, or multicounty-municipal jail or workhouse, any minimum security misdemeanant jail established under section 341.23 or 753.21 of the Revised Code, or any other county, multicounty, municipal, municipal-county, or multicounty-municipal facility used for the custody of persons arrested for any crime or delinquent act, persons charged with or convicted of any crime, or persons alleged to be or adjudicated a delinquent child.

(e) "Employee of a local correctional facility" means any person who is an employee of the political subdivision or of one or more of the affiliated political subdivisions that operates the local correctional facility and who operates or assists in the operation of the facility.

(1994 H 571, eff. 10–6–94; 1994 S 116, eff. 9–29–94; 1992 H 561, eff. 4–9–93; 1988 H 642; 1972 H 511)

Historical and Statutory Notes

Ed. Note: A special endorsement by the Legislative Service Commission states, "Comparison of these amendments [1994 H 571, eff. 10–6–94 and 1994 S 116, eff. 9–29–94] in pursuance of section 1.52 of the Revised Code discloses that they are not irreconcilable, so that they are required by that section to be harmonized to give effect to each amendment." In recognition of this rule of construction, changes made by 1994 H 571, eff. 10–6–94, and 1994 S 116, eff. 9–29–94, have been incorporated in the above amendment. See *Baldwin's Ohio Legislative Service*, 1994 Laws of Ohio, pages 5–1152 and 5–690, for original versions of these Acts.

2903.14   Negligent assault

(A) No person shall negligently, by means of a deadly weapon or dangerous ordnance as defined in section 2923.11 of the Revised Code, cause physical harm to another.

(B) Whoever violates this section is guilty of negligent assault, a misdemeanor of the third degree.

(1972 H 511, eff. 1–1–74)

2903.15   Presumption;   defenses—Repealed

(1972 H 511, eff. 1–1–74; 1973 S 62; 1970 H 84)

2903.16   Failing to provide for functionally impaired person

(A) No caretaker shall knowingly fail to provide a functionally impaired person under his care with any treatment, care, goods, or service that is necessary to maintain the health or safety of the functionally impaired person when this failure results in physical harm or serious physical harm to the functionally impaired person.

(B) No caretaker shall recklessly fail to provide a functionally impaired person under his care with any treatment, care, goods, or service that is necessary to maintain the health or safety of the functionally impaired person when this failure results in serious physical harm to the functionally impaired person.

(C)(1) Whoever violates division (A) of this section is guilty of knowingly failing to provide for a functionally impaired person, a misdemeanor of the first degree. If the offender previously has been convicted of or pleaded guilty to a violation of this section, or a violation of section 2903.11 or 2903.13 of the Revised Code, and if the victim of the previous offense was a functionally impaired person under the offender's care, a violation of division (A) of this section is a felony of the fourth degree.

(2) Whoever violates division (B) of this section is guilty of recklessly failing to provide for a functionally impaired person, a misdemeanor of the second degree. If the offender previously has been convicted of or pleaded guilty to a violation of this section, or a violation of section 2903.11 or 2903.13 of the Revised Code, and if the victim of the previous offense was a functionally impaired person under the offender's care, a violation of division (B) of this section is a felony of the fourth degree.

(1988 H 642, eff. 3–17–89)

MENACING;   STALKING

2903.21   Aggravated menacing

(A) No person shall knowingly cause another to believe that the offender will cause serious physical harm to the person or property of such other person or member of his immediate family.

(B) Whoever violates this section is guilty of aggravated menacing, a misdemeanor of the first degree.

(1972 H 511, eff. 1–1–74)

2903.211   Menacing by stalking

(A) No person by engaging in a pattern of conduct shall knowingly cause another to believe that the offender will cause physical harm to the other person or cause mental distress to the other person.

(B) Whoever violates this section is guilty of menacing by stalking, a misdemeanor of the first degree. If the offender previously has been convicted of or pleaded guilty to a violation of this section involving the same person who is the victim of the current offense, menacing by stalking is a felony of the fourth degree.

(C) As used in this section:

(1) "Pattern of conduct" means two or more actions or incidents closely related in time, whether or not there has been a prior conviction based on any of those actions or incidents.

(2) "Mental distress" means any mental illness or condition that involves some temporary substantial incapacity or mental illness or condition that would normally require psychiatric treatment.

(1992 H 536, eff. 11–5–92)

2903.212   Bail

(A) Except when the complaint involves a person who is a family or household member as defined in section 2919.25 of the Revised Code, if a person is charged with a violation of section 2903.21, 2903.211, 2903.22, or 2911.211 of the Revised Code or a violation of a municipal ordinance that is substantially similar to one of those sections and if the person, at the time of the alleged violation, was subject to the terms of any order issued pursuant to section 2903.213, 2933.08, or 2945.04 of the Revised Code or previously had been convicted of or pleaded guilty to a violation of section 2903.21, 2903.211, 2903.22, or 2911.211 of the Revised Code that involves the same complainant or a violation of a municipal ordinance that is substantially similar to one of those sections and that involves the same complainant, the court shall consider all of the following, in addition to any other circumstances considered by the court and notwithstanding any provisions to the contrary contained in Criminal Rule 46, before setting the amount and conditions of the bail for the person:

(1) Whether the person has a history of violence toward the complainant or a history of other violent acts;

(2) The mental health of the person;

(3) Whether the person has a history of violating the orders of any court or governmental entity;

(4) Whether the person is potentially a threat to any other person;

(5) Whether setting bail at a high level will interfere with any treatment or counseling that the person is undergoing.

(B) Any court that has jurisdiction over violations of section 2903.21, 2903.211, 2903.22, or 2911.211 of the Revised Code or violations of a municipal ordinance that is substantially similar to one of those sections may set a schedule for bail to be used in cases involving those violations. The schedule shall require that a judge consider all of the factors listed in division (A) of this section and may require judges to set bail at a certain level or impose other reasonable conditions related to a release on bail or on recognizance if the history of the alleged offender or the circumstances of the alleged offense meet certain criteria in the schedule.

(1992 H 536, eff. 11–5–92)

2903.213   Anti–stalking protection order as pretrial condition of release

(A) Except when the complaint involves a person who is a family or household member as defined in section 2919.25 of the Revised Code, upon the filing of a complaint that alleges a violation of section 2903.21, 2903.211, 2903.22, or 2911.211 of the Revised Code, the complainant may file a motion that requests the issuance of an anti-stalking protection order as a pretrial condition of release of the alleged offender, in addition to any bail set under Criminal

Rule 46. The motion shall be filed with the clerk of the court that has jurisdiction of the case at any time after the filing of the complaint. If the complaint involves a person who is a family or household member, the complainant may file a motion for a temporary protection order pursuant to section 2919.26 of the Revised Code.

(B) A motion for an anti-stalking protection order shall be prepared on a form that is provided by the clerk of the court, which form shall be substantially as follows:

"Motion for Anti-stalking Protection Order

_____Court

Name and address of court

State of Ohio

v. No. _____

_____

Name of Defendant

(Name of person), the complainant in the above-captioned case, moves the court to issue an anti-stalking protection order containing terms designed to ensure the safety and protection of the complainant in relation to the named defendant, pursuant to its authority to issue such an order under section 2903.213 of the Revised Code.

A complaint, a copy of which has been attached to this motion, has been filed in this court charging the named defendant with a violation of section 2903.21, 2903.211, 2903.22, or 2911.211 of the Revised Code.

I understand that I must appear before the court, at a time set by the court not later than the next day that the court is in session after the filing of this motion, for a hearing on the motion, and that any anti-stalking protection order granted pursuant to this motion is a pretrial condition of release and is effective only until the disposition of the criminal proceeding arising out of the attached complaint.

_____

Signature of complainant

_____

Address of complainant"

(C) As soon as possible after the filing of a motion that requests the issuance of an anti-stalking protection order, but not later than the next day that the court is in session after the filing of the motion, the court shall conduct a hearing to determine whether to issue the order. The complainant shall appear before the court and provide the court with the information that it requests concerning the basis of the motion. If the court finds that the safety and protection of the complainant may be impaired by the continued presence of the alleged offender, the court may issue an anti-stalking protection order, as a pretrial condition of release, that contains terms designed to ensure the safety and protection of the complainant, including a requirement that the alleged offender refrain from entering the residence, school, business, or place of employment of the complainant.

(D)(1) Except when the complaint involves a person who is a family or household member as defined in section 2919.25 of the Revised Code, upon the filing of a complaint that alleges a violation of section 2903.21, 2903.211, 2903.22, or 2911.211 of the Revised Code, the court, upon its own motion, may issue an anti-stalking protection order as a pretrial condition of release of the alleged offender if it finds that the safety and protection of the complainant may be impaired by the continued presence of the alleged offender.

(2) If the court issues an anti-stalking protection order under this section as an ex parte order, it shall conduct, as soon as possible after the issuance of the order but not later than the next day the court is in session after its issuance, a hearing to determine whether the order should remain in effect, be modified, or be revoked. The hearing shall be conducted under the standards set forth in division (C) of this section.

(E) An anti-stalking protection order that is issued as a pretrial condition of release under this section:

28

(1) Is in addition to, but shall not be construed as a part of, any bail set under Criminal Rule 46;

(2) Is effective only until the disposition of the criminal proceeding arising out of the complaint upon which it is based;

(3) Shall not be construed as a finding that the alleged offender committed the alleged offense, and shall not be introduced as evidence of the commission of the offense at the trial of the alleged offender on the complaint upon which the order is based.

(F) A person who meets the criteria for bail under Criminal Rule 46 and who, if required to do so pursuant to that rule, executes or posts bond or deposits cash or securities as bail, shall not be held in custody pending a hearing before the court on a motion requesting an anti-stalking protection order.

(G)(1) A copy of any anti-stalking protection order that is issued under this section shall be issued by the court to the complainant, to the defendant, and to all law enforcement agencies that have jurisdiction to enforce the order. The court shall direct that a copy of the order be delivered to the defendant on the same day that the order is entered.

(2) All law enforcement agencies shall establish and maintain an index for the anti-stalking protection orders delivered to the agencies pursuant to division (G)(1) of this section. With respect to each order delivered, each agency shall note on the index, the date and time of the receipt of the order by the agency.

(3) Any officer of a law enforcement agency shall enforce an anti-stalking protection order in accordance with the provisions of the order.

(H) Upon a violation of an anti-stalking protection order, the court may issue another anti-stalking protection order, as a pretrial condition of release, that modifies the terms of the order that was violated.

(I) Notwithstanding any provision of law to the contrary, no court shall charge a fee for the filing of a motion pursuant to this section.

(1993 S 31, eff. 9–27–93; 1992 H 536)

2903.214   Violating anti-stalking protection order

(A) No person shall recklessly violate any terms of an anti-stalking protection order issued pursuant to section 2903.213 of the Revised Code.

(B) Whoever violates this section is guilty of violating an anti-stalking protection order. If the offender previously has not been convicted of or pleaded guilty to a violation of this section or a violation of section 2903.21, 2903.211, 2903.22, or 2911.211 of the Revised Code that involves the same person who is the subject of the anti-stalking protection order, violating an anti-stalking protection order is a misdemeanor of the fourth degree. If the offender previously has been convicted of or pleaded guilty to one violation of this section or one violation of section 2903.21, 2903.211, 2903.22, or 2911.211 of the Revised Code that involves the same person who is the subject of the anti-stalking protection order, violating an anti-stalking protection order is a misdemeanor of the first degree. If the offender previously has been convicted of or pleaded guilty to two or more violations of this section or to two or more violations of section 2903.21, 2903.211, 2903.22, or 2911.211 of the Revised Code that involve the same person who is the subject of the anti-stalking protection order, violating an anti-stalking protection order is a felony of the fourth degree.

(1992 H 536, eff. 11–5–92)

2903.215   Mental evaluations

(A) If a defendant is charged with a violation of section 2903.214 of the Revised Code or of a municipal ordinance that is substantially similar to that section, and if the court determines that the violation of the anti-stalking protection order allegedly involves conduct by the defendant that caused physical harm to the person or property of the person covered by the order or conduct by the defendant that caused the person covered by the order to believe that the defendant would cause physical harm to that person or his property, the court may order an evaluation of the mental condition of the defendant. The evaluation shall be completed no later than thirty days from the date the order is entered. In that order, the court shall do one of the following:

(1) Order that the evaluation of the mental condition of the defendant be preceded by an examination conducted either by a forensic center that is designated by the department of mental health to conduct examinations and make evaluations of defendants charged with violations of section 2903.214 of the Revised Code or of substantially similar municipal ordinances in the area in which the court is located, or by any other program or facility that is designated by the department of mental health or the department of mental retardation and developmental disabilities to conduct examinations and make evaluations of defendants charged with violations of section 2903.214 of the Revised Code or of substantially similar municipal ordinances, and that is operated by either department or is certified by either department as being in compliance with the standards established under division (J) of section 5119.01 of the Revised Code or division (C) of section 5123.04 of the Revised Code.

(2) Designate a center, program, or facility other than one designated by the department of mental health or the department of mental retardation and developmental disabilities, as described in division (A)(1) of this section, to conduct the evaluation and preceding examination of the mental condition of the defendant.

(3) Designate examiners other than the personnel of the center, program, or facility designated by the department of mental health or department of mental retardation and developmental disabilities to make the evaluation and preceding examination of the mental condition of the defendant.

(B) If the court considers that additional evaluations of the mental condition of a defendant are necessary following the evaluation authorized by division (A) of this section, the court may order up to two additional similar evaluations. These evaluations shall be completed no later than thirty days from the date the applicable court order is entered. If more than one evaluation of the mental condition of the defendant is ordered under this division, the prosecutor and the defendant may recommend to the court an examiner whom each prefers to perform one of the evaluations and preceding examinations.

(C)(1) The court may order a defendant who has been released on bail to submit to an examination under division (A) or (B) of this section. The examination shall be conducted either at the detention facility in which the defendant would have been confined if he had not been released on bail, or, if so specified by the center, program, facility, or examiners involved, at the premises of the center, program, or facility. Additionally, the examination shall be conducted at the times established by the examiners involved. If such a defendant refuses to submit to an examination or a complete examination as required by the court or the center, program, facility, or examiners involved, the court may amend the conditions of the bail of the defendant and order the sheriff to take him into custody and deliver him to the detention facility in which he would have been confined if he had not been released on bail, or, if so specified by the center, program, facility, or examiners involved, to the premises of the center, program, or facility, for purposes of the examination.

(2) A defendant who has not been released on bail shall be examined at his detention facility or, if so specified by the center, program, facility, or examiners involved, at the premises of the center, program, or facility.

(D) The examiner of the mental condition of a defendant under division (A) or (B) of this section shall file a written report with the court within thirty days after the entry of an order for the evaluation of the mental condition of the defendant. The report shall contain the findings of the examiner; the facts in reasonable detail on which the findings are based; the opinion of the examiner as to the mental condition of the defendant; the opinion of the examiner as to whether the defendant represents a substantial risk of physical harm to other persons as manifested by evidence of recent homicidal or other violent behavior, evidence of recent threats that placed other persons in reasonable fear of violent behavior and serious physical harm, or evidence of present dangerousness; and the opinion of the examiner as to the types of treatment or counseling that the defendant needs. The court shall provide copies of the report to the prosecutor and defense counsel.

(E) The costs of any evaluation and preceding examination of a defendant that is ordered pursuant to division (A) or (B) of this section shall be taxed as court costs in the criminal case.

(F) If he considers it necessary in order to make an accurate evaluation of the mental condition of a defendant, an examiner under division (A) or (B) of this section may request any family or household member of the defendant to provide the examiner with information. A family or household member may, but is not required to, provide information to the examiner upon receipt of such a request.

(G) As used in this section:

(1) "Bail" includes a recognizance.

(2) "Examiner" means a psychiatrist, a licensed social worker at the independent practice level who is employed by a forensic center that is certified as being in compliance with the standards established under division (J) of section 5119.01 or division (C) of section 5123.04 of the Revised Code, a licensed counselor with clinical endorsement who is employed at a forensic center that is certified as being in compliance with such standards, or a licensed clinical psychologist, except that in order to be an examiner, a licensed clinical psychologist shall meet the criteria of division (I)(1) of section 5122.01 of the Revised Code or be employed to conduct examinations by the department of mental health or by a forensic center certified as being in compliance with the standards established under division (J) of section 5119.01 or division (C) of section 5123.04 of the Revised Code that is designated by the department of mental health.

(3) "Family or household member" has the same meaning as in section 2919.25 of the Revised Code.

(4) "Prosecutor" has the same meaning as in section 2935.01 of the Revised Code.

(5) "Psychiatrist" and "licensed clinical psychologist" have the same meaning as in section 5122.01 of the Revised Code.

(1992 H 536, eff. 11–5–92)

2903.22   Menacing

(A) No person shall knowingly cause another to believe that the offender will cause physical harm to the person or property of such other person or member of his immediate family.

(B) Whoever violates this section is guilty of menacing, a misdemeanor of the fourth degree.

(1972 H 511, eff. 1–1–74)

HAZING

2903.31   Hazing; recklessly participating or permitting

(A) As used in this section, "hazing" means doing any act or coercing another, including the victim, to do any act of initiation into any student or other organization that causes or creates a substantial risk of causing mental or physical harm to any person.

(B)(1) No person shall recklessly participate in the hazing of another.

(2) No administrator, employee, or faculty member of any primary, secondary, or post-secondary school or of any other educational institution, public or private, shall recklessly permit the hazing of any person.

(C) Whoever violates this section is guilty of hazing, a misdemeanor of the fourth degree.

(1982 H 444, eff. 3–3–83)

PATIENT ABUSE OR NEGLECT

2903.33   Definitions

As used in sections 2903.33 to 2903.36 of the Revised Code:

(A) "Care facility" means any of the following:

(1) Any "home" as defined in section 3721.10 or 5111.20 of the Revised Code;

(2) Any "residential facility" as defined in section 5123.19 of the Revised Code;

(3) Any institution or facility operated or provided by the department of mental health or by the department of mental retardation and developmental disabilities pursuant to sections 5119.02 and 5123.03 of the Revised Code;

(4) Any "residential facility" as defined in section 5119.22 of the Revised Code;

(5) Any unit of any hospital, as defined in section 3701.01 of the Revised Code, that provides the same services as a nursing home, as defined in section 3721.01 of the Revised Code;

(6) Any institution, residence, or facility that provides, for a period of more than twenty-four hours, whether for a consideration or not, accommodations to one individual or two unrelated individuals who are dependent upon the services of others;

(7) Any "adult care facility" as defined in section 3722.01 of the Revised Code;

(8) Any adult foster home certified by the department of aging or its designee under section 173.36 of the Revised Code;

(9) Any "community alternative home" as defined in section 3724.01 of the Revised Code.

(B)(1) "Gross abuse" means knowingly causing serious physical harm to a person by physical contact with the person.

(2) "Abuse" means knowingly causing physical harm or recklessly causing serious physical harm to a person by physical contact with the person or by the inappropriate use of a physical or chemical restraint, medication, or isolation on the person.

(C)(1) "Gross neglect" means knowingly failing to provide a person with any treatment, care, goods, or service that is necessary to maintain the health or safety of the person when the failure results in physical harm or serious physical harm to the person.

(2) "Neglect" means recklessly failing to provide a person with any treatment, care, goods, or service that is necessary to maintain the health or safety of the person when the failure results in serious physical harm to the person.

(D) "Inappropriate use of a physical or chemical restraint, medication, or isolation" means the use of physical or chemical restraint, medication, or isolation as punishment, for staff convenience, excessively, as a substitute for treatment, or in quantities which preclude habilitation and treatment.

(1993 S 21, eff. 10–29–93; 1993 H 152; 1989 H 253, S 2; 1988 S 156; 1986 H 566)

Historical and Statutory Notes

Ed. Note: A special endorsement by the Legislative Service Commission states, "Comparison of these amendments [1993 S 21, eff. 10–29–93 and 1993 H 152, eff. 7–1–93] in pursuance of section 1.52 of the Revised Code discloses that they are not irreconcilable, so that they are required by that section to be harmonized to give effect to each amendment." In recognition of this rule of construction, changes made by 1993 S 21, eff. 10–29–93, and 1993 H 152, eff. 7–1–93, have been incorporated in the above amendment. See *Baldwin's Ohio Legislative Service*, 1993 Laws of Ohio, pages 5–801 and 5–407, for original versions of these Acts.

2903.34 Patient abuse or neglect; spiritual treatment; defense

(A) No person who owns, operates, or administers, or who is an agent or employee of a care facility shall do any of the following:

(1) Commit gross abuse against a resident or patient of the facility;

(2) Commit abuse against a resident or patient of the facility;

(3) Commit gross neglect against a resident or patient of the facility;

(4) Commit neglect against a resident or patient of the facility.

(B)(1) A person who relies upon treatment by spiritual means through prayer alone, in accordance with the tenets of a recognized religious denomination, shall not be considered neglected under division (A)(4) of this section for that reason alone.

(2) It is an affirmative defense to a charge of gross neglect or neglect under this section that the actor's conduct was committed in good faith solely because the actor was ordered to commit the conduct by a person with supervisory authority over the actor.

(C) Whoever violates division (A)(1) of this section is guilty of gross patient abuse, an aggravated felony of the second degree.

(D) Whoever violates division (A)(2) of this section is guilty of patient abuse, a felony of the fourth degree. If the offender previously has been convicted of, or pleaded guilty to, any violation of this section, patient abuse is a felony of the third degree.

(E) Whoever violates division (A)(3) of this section is guilty of gross patient neglect, a misdemeanor of the first degree. If the offender previously has been convicted of, or pleaded guilty to, any violation of this section, gross patient neglect is a felony of the fourth degree.

(F) Whoever violates division (A)(4) of this section is guilty of patient neglect, a misdemeanor of the second degree. If the offender previously has been convicted of any violation of this section, patient neglect is a felony of the fourth degree.

(1986 H 566, eff. 9–17–86)

2903.35   False statements

(A) No person shall knowingly make a false statement, or knowingly swear or affirm the truth of a false statement previously made, alleging a violation of section 2903.34 of the Revised Code, when the statement is made with purpose to incriminate another.

(B) Whoever violates this section is guilty of filing a false patient abuse or neglect complaint, a misdemeanor of the first degree.

(1986 H 566, eff. 9–17–86)

2903.36   Retaliation against person reporting patient abuse or neglect

No care facility shall discharge or in any manner discriminate or retaliate against any person solely because such person, in good faith, filed a complaint, affidavit, or other document alleging a violation of section 2903.34 of the Revised Code.

(1986 H 566, eff. 9–17–86)

2903.37   Revocation of license

Any individual, who owns, operates, or administers, or who is an agent or employee of, a care facility, who is convicted of a felony violation of section 2903.34 of the Revised Code, and who is required to be licensed under any law of this state, shall have his license revoked in accordance with Chapter 119. of the Revised Code.

(1986 H 566, eff. 9–17–86)

CHAPTER 2905

KIDNAPPING AND EXTORTION

KIDNAPPING AND RELATED OFFENSES

EXTORTION

EXTORTIONATE EXTENSION OF CREDIT

KIDNAPPING AND RELATED OFFENSES

2905.01 Kidnapping

(A) No person, by force, threat, or deception, or, in the case of a victim under the age of thirteen or mentally incompetent, by any means, shall remove another from the place where he is found or restrain him of his liberty, for any of the following purposes:

(1) To hold for ransom, or as a shield or hostage;

(2) To facilitate the commission of any felony or flight thereafter;

(3) To terrorize, or to inflict serious physical harm on the victim or another;

(4) To engage in sexual activity, as defined in section 2907.01 of the Revised Code, with the victim against his will;

(5) To hinder, impede, or obstruct a function of government, or to force any action or concession on the part of governmental authority.

(B) No person, by force, threat, or deception, or, in the case of a victim under the age of thirteen or mentally incompetent, by any means, shall knowingly do any of the following, under circumstances which create a substantial risk of serious physical harm to the victim:

(1) Remove another from the place where he is found;

(2) Restrain another of his liberty;

(3) Hold another in a condition of involuntary servitude.

(C) Whoever violates this section is guilty of kidnapping, an aggravated felony of the first degree. If the offender releases the victim in a safe place unharmed, kidnapping is an aggravated felony of the second degree.

(1982 H 269, § 4, eff. 7–1–83; 1982 S 199; 1972 H 511)

2905.02 Abduction

(A) No person, without privilege to do so, shall knowingly do any of the following:

(1) By force or threat, remove another from the place where he is found;

(2) By force or threat, restrain another of his liberty, under circumstances which create a risk of physical harm to the victim, or place him in fear;

(3) Hold another in a condition of involuntary servitude.

(B) Whoever violates this section is guilty of abduction, an aggravated felony of the third degree.

(1982 H 269, § 4, eff. 7–1–83; 1982 S 199; 1972 H 511)

2905.03 Unlawful restraint

(A) No person, without privilege to do so, shall knowingly restrain another of his liberty.

(B) Whoever violates this section is guilty of unlawful restraint, a misdemeanor of the third degree.

(1972 H 511, eff. 1–1–74)

2905.031 Rape of female under fourteen—Repealed

(1972 H 511, eff. 1–1–74; 129 v 998)

2905.04 Child stealing

(A) No person, by any means and with purpose to withhold a minor from the legal custody of his parent, guardian, or custodian, shall remove the minor from the place where he is found.

(B) It is an affirmative defense to a charge under this section that the actor reasonably believed that his conduct was necessary to preserve the minor's health or welfare.

(C) Whoever violates this section is guilty of child stealing.

(1) If the offender is a natural or adoptive parent, or a stepparent of the minor, but not entitled to legal custody of the minor when the offense is committed, child stealing is a misdemeanor of the first degree unless:

(a) The offender removes the child from this state or the offender previously has been convicted of child stealing or of kidnapping or abduction involving a minor, in which case child stealing is a felony of the fourth degree;

(b) Physical harm is done to the minor, in which case child stealing is a felony of the second degree.

(2) If the offender is not a natural or adoptive parent, or a stepparent of the minor, child stealing is an aggravated felony of the second degree, unless physical harm is done to the minor, in which case child stealing is an aggravated felony of the first degree.

(1984 S 321, eff. 4–9–85; 1972 H 511)

2905.041   Attempted rape of female person under fourteen—Repealed

(1972 H 511, eff. 1–1–74; 129 v 998)

2905.05   Criminal child enticement

(A) No person, by any means and without privilege to do so, shall knowingly solicit, coax, entice, or lure any child under fourteen years of age to enter into any vehicle, as defined in section 4501.01 of the Revised Code, whether or not the offender knows the age of the child, if both of the following apply:

(1) The actor does not have the express or implied permission of the parent, guardian, or other legal custodian of the child in undertaking the activity;

(2) The actor is not a law enforcement officer, medic, firefighter, or other person who regularly provides emergency services, and is not an employee or agent of, or a volunteer acting under the direction of any board of education, or the actor is any of such persons, but, at the time the actor undertakes the activity, he is not acting within the scope of his lawful duties in that capacity.

(B) It is an affirmative defense to a charge under division (A) of this section that the actor undertook the activity in response to a bona fide emergency situation or that the actor undertook the activity in a reasonable belief that it was necessary to preserve the health, safety, or welfare of the child.

(C) Whoever violates this section is guilty of criminal child enticement, a misdemeanor of the first degree. If the offender previously has been convicted of an offense under this section, criminal child enticement is a felony of the fourth degree.

(1984 S 321, eff. 4–9–85)

2905.06   Carnal knowledge of insane woman—Repealed

(1972 H 511, eff. 1–1–74; 1953 H 1; GC 13025)

2905.07   Incest—Repealed

(1972 H 511, eff. 1–1–74; 1953 H 1; GC 13023) ·

2905.08   Adultery or fornication—Repealed

(1972 H 511, eff. 1–1–74; 1953 H 1; GC 13024)

2905.09   Seduction under promise of marriage—Repealed

(1972 H 511, eff. 1–1–74; 126 v 575; 1953 H 1; GC 13026)

2905.10   Inducing illicit intercourse or permitting it upon the premises—Repealed

(1972 H 511, eff. 1–1–74; 1953 H 1; GC 13027)

EXTORTION

2905.11   Extortion

(A) No person, with purpose to obtain any valuable thing or valuable benefit or to induce another to do an unlawful act, shall do any of the following:

(1) Threaten to commit any felony;

(2) Threaten to commit any offense of violence;

(3) Violate section 2903.21 or 2903.22 of the Revised Code;

(4) Utter or threaten any calumny against any person;

(5) Expose or threaten to expose any matter tending to subject any person to hatred, contempt, or ridicule, or to damage his personal or business repute, or to impair his credit.

(B) Whoever violates this section is guilty of extortion, an aggravated felony of the third degree.

(C) As used in this section, "threat" includes a direct threat and a threat by innuendo.

(1982 H 269, § 4, eff. 7–1–83; 1982 S 199; 1972 H 511)

2905.12   Coercion

(A) No person, with purpose to coerce another into taking or refraining from action concerning which he has a legal freedom of choice, shall do any of the following:

(1) Threaten to commit any offense;

(2) Utter or threaten any calumny against any person;

(3) Expose or threaten to expose any matter tending to subject any person to hatred, contempt, or ridicule, or to damage his personal or business repute, or to impair his credit;

(4) Institute or threaten criminal proceedings against any person;

(5) Take or withhold, or threaten to take or withhold official action, or cause or threaten to cause official action to be taken or withheld.

(B) Divisions (A)(4) and (5) of this section shall not be construed to prohibit a prosecutor or court from doing any of the following in good faith and in the interests of justice:

(1) Offering or agreeing to grant, or granting immunity from prosecution pursuant to section 2945.44 of the Revised Code;

(2) In return for a plea of guilty to one or more offenses charged or to one or more other or lesser offenses, or in return for the testimony of the accused in a case to which he is not a party, offering or agreeing to dismiss, or dismissing one or more charges pending against an accused, or offering or agreeing to impose, or imposing a certain sentence or modification of sentence;

(3) Imposing probation on certain conditions, including without limitation requiring the offender to make restitution or redress to the victim of his offense.

(C) It is an affirmative defense to a charge under division (A)(3), (4), or (5) of this section that the actor's conduct was a reasonable response to the circumstances which occasioned it, and that his purpose was limited to:

(1) Compelling another to refrain from misconduct or to desist from further misconduct;

(2) Preventing or redressing a wrong or injustice;

(3) Preventing another from taking action for which the actor reasonably believed such other person to be disqualified;

(4) Compelling another to take action which the actor reasonably believed such other person to be under a duty to take.

(D) Whoever violates this section is guilty of coercion, a misdemeanor of the second degree.

(E) As used in this section, "threat" includes a direct threat and a threat by innuendo.

(1972 H 511, eff. 1–1–74)

2905.13 Sexual intercourse with female pupil—Repealed

(1972 H 511, eff. 1–1–74; 1953 H 1; GC 13030)

2905.14 Keeping house of ill fame or harboring child therein—Repealed

(1972 H 511, eff. 1–1–74; 1953 H 1; GC 13031)

2905.15 Pandering—Repealed

(1972 H 511, eff. 1–1–74; 1953 H 1; GC 13031–1)

2905.16 Placing or leaving female in house of assignation—Repealed

(1972 H 511, eff. 1–1–74; 1953 H 1; GC 13031–9)

2905.17 Forcing female to become a prostitute—Repealed

(1972 H 511, eff. 1–1–74; 1953 H 1; GC 13031–2)

2905.18 Procuring—Repealed

(1972 H 511, eff. 1–1–74; 1953 H 1; GC 13031–3)

2905.19 Procuring married woman—Repealed

(1972 H 511, eff. 1–1–74; 1953 H 1; GC 13031–4)

2905.20 Detention in a disorderly house—Repealed

(1972 H 511, eff. 1–1–74; 1953 H 1; GC 13031–5)

EXTORTIONATE EXTENSION OF CREDIT

2905.21 Definitions

As used in sections 2905.21 to 2905.24 of the Revised Code:

(A) "To extend credit" means to make or renew any loan, or to enter into any agreement, express or implied, for the repayment or satisfaction of any debt or claim, regardless of whether the extension of credit is acknowledged or disputed, valid or invalid, and however arising.

(B) "Creditor" means any person who extends credit, or any person claiming by, under, or through such a person.

(C) "Debtor" means any person who receives an extension of credit, any person who guarantees the repayment of an extension of credit, or any person who in any manner undertakes to indemnify the creditor against loss resulting from the failure of any recipient to repay an extension of credit.

(D) "Repayment" of an extension of credit means the repayment, satisfaction, or discharge in whole or in part of any debt or claim, acknowledged or disputed, valid or invalid, resulting from or in connection with that extension of credit.

(E) "Collect an extension of credit" means an attempt to collect from a debtor all or part of an amount due from the extension of credit.

(F) "Extortionate extension of credit" means any extension of credit with respect to which it is the understanding of the creditor and the debtor at the time it is made that delay in making repayment or failure to make repayment will result in the use of an extortionate means or if the debtor at a later time learns that failure to make repayment will result in the use of extortionate means.

(G) "Extortionate means" is any means that involves the use, or an express or implicit threat of use, of violence or other criminal means to cause harm to the person or property of the debtor or any member of his family.

(H) "Criminal usury" means illegally charging, taking, or receiving any money or other property as interest on an extension of credit at a rate exceeding twenty-five per cent per annum or the equivalent rate for a longer or shorter period, unless either:

(1) The rate of interest is otherwise authorized by law;

(2) The creditor and the debtor, or all the creditors and all the debtors are members of the same immediate family.

(I) "Immediate family" means a person's spouse residing in the person's household, brothers and sisters of the whole or of the half blood, and children, including adopted children.
(1978 H 88, eff. 10–9–78)

2905.22 Criminally usurious transactions prohibited

No person shall:

(A) Knowingly make or participate in an extortionate extension of credit;

(B) Knowingly engage in criminal usury;

(C) Possess any writing, paper, instrument, or article used to record criminally usurious transactions, knowing that the contents record a criminally usurious transaction;

(D) Whoever violates division (A) or (B) of this section is guilty of a felony of the third degree. Whoever violates division (C) of this section is guilty of a misdemeanor of the first degree.
(1978 H 88, eff. 10–9–78)

2905.23 Evidence establishing probable cause of extortionate intent

In any prosecution under sections 2905.21 to 2905.24 of the Revised Code, if it is shown that any of the following factors were present in connection with the extension of credit, there is probable cause to believe that the extension of credit was extortionate:

(A) The extension of credit was made at a rate of interest in excess of that established for criminal usury;

(B) At the time credit was extended, the debtor reasonably believed that:

(1) One or more extensions of credit by the creditor were collected or attempted to be collected by extortionate means, or the nonrepayment thereof was punished by extortionate means;

(2) The creditor had a reputation for the use of extortionate means to collect extensions of credit or punish the nonrepayment thereof.
(1978 H 88, eff. 10–9–78)

2905.24 Proof of implicit threat

In any prosecution under sections 2905.21 to 2905.24 of the Revised Code, for the purpose of showing an implicit threat as a means of collection, evidence may be introduced tending to show that one or more extensions of credit by the creditor were, to the knowledge of the person against whom the implicit threat is alleged to have been made, collected, or attempted to be collected by extortionate means or that the nonrepayment thereof was punished by extortionate means.
(1978 H 88, eff. 10–9–78)

2905.25 Competent evidence—Repealed

(1972 H 511, eff. 1–1–74; 1953 H 1; GC 13031–11)

2905.26 "Prostitution," "lewdness," and "assignation" defined—Repealed

(1972 H 511, eff. 1–1–74; 1953 H 1; GC 13031–14)

2905.27 Keeping a place for prostitution prohibited—Repealed

(1972 H 511, eff. 1–1–74; 130 v Pt 2, H 28; 1953 H 1; GC 13031–13; Source—GC 13031–16)

2905.28 Medical examination—Repealed

(1972 H 511, eff. 1–1–74; 130 v Pt 2, H 28; 1953 H 1; GC 13031–17)

2905.29 Prior conviction and testimony; admissible evidence—Repealed

(1972 H 511, eff. 1–1–74; 1953 H 1; GC 13031–15)

2905.30 Indecent exposure; solicitation of act of sex perversion—Repealed

(1972 H 511, eff. 1–1–74; 131 v S 284; 130 v S 60; 129 v 1670; 1953 H 1; GC 13032)

2905.301 Obscene language—Repealed

(1972 H 511, eff. 1–1–74)

2905.31 Nudism—Repealed

(1972 H 511, eff. 1–1–74; 1953 H 1; GC 13032–1)

2905.32 Selling, giving away, possessing, or advertising drugs for procuring abortion—Repealed

(1972 H 511, eff. 1–1–74; 1970 H 84; 131 v H 120; 1953 H 1; GC 13033)

2905.33 Advertising secret drugs—Repealed

(1972 H 511, eff. 1–1–74; 131 v H 20; 1953 H 1; GC 13034)

2905.34 Definitions—Repealed

(1972 H 511, eff. 1–1–74; 1970 H 84)

2905.341 Conditional sales or deliveries prohibited—Repealed

(1970 H 84, eff. 9–15–70; 126 v 1039)

2905.342 Exhibition of obscene movies prohibited; movies inciting disorder or violation of laws prohibited—Repealed

(1970 H 84, eff. 9–15–70; 126 v 1039)

2905.343 Enjoining sale or distribution of obscene matter—Repealed

(1970 H 84, eff. 9–15–70; 128 v 359)

2905.35 Obscenity prohibitions—Repealed

(1972 H 511, eff. 1–1–74; 1970 H 84)

2905.36 Forcing acceptance of objectionable materials for resale—Repealed

(1972 H 511, eff. 1–1–74; 1970 H 84)

2905.37 Enjoining objectionable materials or performances—Repealed

(1972 H 511, eff. 1–1–74; 1970 H 84)

2905.371 Printed matter which is immune; obscene matter defined—Repealed

(1970 H 84, eff. 9–15–70; 129 v 1400)

2905.38 Presumptions; defense—Repealed

(1972 H 511, eff. 1–1–74; 1973 S 62; 1970 H 84)

2905.39 Printing or posting immoral pictures—Repealed

(1970 H 84, eff. 9–15–70; 1953 H 1; GC 13039)

2905.40 Giving immoral exhibition—Repealed

(1970 H 84, eff. 9–15–70; 1953 H 1; GC 13040)

2905.41 Exhibiting lewd pictures in saloon—Repealed

(1970 H 84, eff. 9–15–70; 1953 H 1; GC 13041)

2905.42   Enticing married woman to join certain sects—Repealed

(1972 H 511, eff. 1–1–74; 1953 H 1; GC 13042)

2905.43   Bigamy—Repealed

(1972 H 511, eff. 1–1–74; 129 v 252; 1953 H 1; GC 13022)

2905.44   Sodomy—Repealed

(1972 H 511, eff. 1–1–74; 1953 H 1; GC 13043)

CHAPTER 2907

SEX OFFENSES

DEFINITIONS

DEFINITIONS

2907.01   Definitions

As used in sections 2907.01 to 2907.37 of the Revised Code:

(A) "Sexual conduct" means vaginal intercourse between a male and female, and anal intercourse, fellatio, and cunnilingus between persons regardless of sex. Penetration, however slight, is sufficient to complete vaginal or anal intercourse.

(B) "Sexual contact" means any touching of an erogenous zone of another, including without limitation the thigh, genitals, buttock, pubic region, or, if the person is a female, a breast, for the purpose of sexually arousing or gratifying either person.

(C) "Sexual activity" means sexual conduct or sexual contact, or both.

(D) "Prostitute" means a male or female who promiscuously engages in sexual activity for hire, regardless of whether the hire is paid to the prostitute or to another.

(E) Any material or performance is "harmful to juveniles," if it is offensive to prevailing standards in the adult community with respect to what is suitable for juveniles, and if any of the following apply:

(1) It tends to appeal to the prurient interest of juveniles;

(2) It contains a display, description, or representation of sexual activity, masturbation, sexual excitement, or nudity;

(3) It contains a display, description, or representation of bestiality or extreme or bizarre violence, cruelty, or brutality;

(4) It contains a display, description, or representation of human bodily functions of elimination;

(5) It makes repeated use of foul language;

(6) It contains a display, description, or representation in lurid detail of the violent physical torture, dismemberment, destruction, or death of a human being;

(7) It contains a display, description, or representation of criminal activity that tends to glorify or glamorize the activity, and that, with respect to juveniles, has a dominant tendency to corrupt.

(F) When considered as a whole, and judged with reference to ordinary adults or, if it is designed for sexual deviates or other specially susceptible group, judged with reference to that group, any material or performance is "obscene" if any of the following apply:

(1) Its dominant appeal is to prurient interest;

(2) Its dominant tendency is to arouse lust by displaying or depicting sexual activity, masturbation, sexual excitement, or nudity in a way that tends to represent human beings as mere objects of sexual appetite;

(3) Its dominant tendency is to arouse lust by displaying or depicting bestiality or extreme or bizarre violence, cruelty, or brutality;

(4) Its dominant tendency is to appeal to scatological interest by displaying or depicting human bodily functions of elimination in a way that inspires disgust or revulsion in persons with

ordinary sensibilities, without serving any genuine scientific, educational, sociological, moral, or artistic purpose;

(5) It contains a series of displays or descriptions of sexual activity, masturbation, sexual excitement, nudity, bestiality, extreme or bizarre violence, cruelty, or brutality, or human bodily functions of elimination, the cumulative effect of which is a dominant tendency to appeal to prurient or scatological interest, when the appeal to such an interest is primarily for its own sake or for commercial exploitation, rather than primarily for a genuine scientific, educational, sociological, moral, or artistic purpose.

(G) "Sexual excitement" means the condition of human male or female genitals when in a state of sexual stimulation or arousal.

(H) "Nudity" means the showing, representation, or depiction of human male or female genitals, pubic area, or buttocks with less than a full, opaque covering, or of a female breast with less than a full, opaque covering of any portion thereof below the top of the nipple, or of covered male genitals in a discernibly turgid state.

(I) "Juvenile" means an unmarried person under the age of eighteen.

(J) "Material" means any book, magazine, newspaper, pamphlet, poster, print, picture, figure, image, description, motion picture film, phonographic record, or tape, or other tangible thing capable of arousing interest through sight, sound, or touch.

(K) "Performance" means any motion picture, preview, trailer, play, show, skit, dance, or other exhibition performed before an audience.

(L) "Spouse" means a person married to an offender at the time of an alleged offense, except that such person shall not be considered the spouse when any of the following apply:

(1) When the parties have entered into a written separation agreement authorized by section 3103.06 of the Revised Code;

(2) During the pendency of an action between the parties for annulment, divorce, dissolution of marriage, or legal separation;

(3) In the case of an action for legal separation, after the effective date of the judgment for legal separation.

(M) "Minor" means a person under the age of eighteen.

(1990 H 514, eff. 1–1–91; 1988 H 51; 1975 S 144; 1972 H 511)

SEXUAL ASSAULTS

2907.02   Rape; evidence; marriage or cohabitation not defenses to rape charges

(A)(1) No person shall engage in sexual conduct with another who is not the spouse of the offender or who is the spouse of the offender but is living separate and apart from the offender, when any of the following applies:

(a) For the purpose of preventing resistance, the offender substantially impairs the other person's judgment or control by administering any drug or intoxicant to the other person, surreptitiously or by force, threat of force, or deception.

(b) The other person is less than thirteen years of age, whether or not the offender knows the age of the other person.

(c) The other person's ability to resist or consent is substantially impaired because of a mental or physical condition or because of advanced age, and the offender knows or has reasonable cause to believe that the other person's ability to resist or consent is substantially impaired because of a mental or physical condition or because of advanced age.

(2) No person shall engage in sexual conduct with another when the offender purposely compels the other person to submit by force or threat of force.

(B) Whoever violates this section is guilty of rape, an aggravated felony of the first degree. If the offender under division (A)(1)(b) of this section purposely compels the victim to submit by force or threat of force, whoever violates division (A)(1)(b) of this section shall be imprisoned for life.

(C) A victim need not prove physical resistance to the offender in prosecutions under this section.

(D) Evidence of specific instances of the victim's sexual activity, opinion evidence of the victim's sexual activity, and reputation evidence of the victim's sexual activity shall not be admitted under this section unless it involves evidence of the origin of semen, pregnancy, or disease, or the victim's past sexual activity with the offender, and only to the extent that the court finds that the evidence is material to a fact at issue in the case and that its inflammatory or prejudicial nature does not outweigh its probative value.

Evidence of specific instances of the defendant's sexual activity, opinion evidence of the defendant's sexual activity, and reputation evidence of the defendant's sexual activity shall not be admitted under this section unless it involves evidence of the origin of semen, pregnancy, or disease, the defendant's past sexual activity with the victim, or is admissible against the defendant under section 2945.59 of the Revised Code, and only to the extent that the court finds that the evidence is material to a fact at issue in the case and that its inflammatory or prejudicial nature does not outweigh its probative value.

(E) Prior to taking testimony or receiving evidence of any sexual activity of the victim or the defendant in a proceeding under this section, the court shall resolve the admissibility of the proposed evidence in a hearing in chambers, which shall be held at or before preliminary hearing and not less than three days before trial, or for good cause shown during the trial.

(F) Upon approval by the court, the victim may be represented by counsel in any hearing in chambers or other proceeding to resolve the admissibility of evidence. If the victim is indigent or otherwise unable to obtain the services of counsel, the court, upon request, may appoint counsel to represent the victim without cost to the victim.

(G) It is not a defense to a charge under division (A)(2) of this section that the offender and the victim were married or were cohabiting at the time of the commission of the offense.
(1993 S 31, eff. 9–27–93; 1985 H 475; 1982 H 269, § 4, S 199; 1975 S 144; 1972 H 511)

2907.021 Manufacture, distribution or possession of fire bombs—Repealed

(1972 H 511, eff. 1–1–74; 133 v H 1; 132 v H 179)

2907.03 Sexual battery

(A) No person shall engage in sexual conduct with another, not the spouse of the offender, when any of the following apply:

(1) The offender knowingly coerces the other person to submit by any means that would prevent resistance by a person of ordinary resolution.

(2) The offender knows that the other person's ability to appraise the nature of or control his or her own conduct is substantially impaired.

(3) The offender knows that the other person submits because he or she is unaware that the act is being committed.

(4) The offender knows that the other person submits because such person mistakenly identifies the offender as his or her spouse.

(5) The offender is the other person's natural or adoptive parent, or a stepparent, or guardian, custodian, or person in loco parentis.

(6) The other person is in custody of law or a patient in a hospital or other institution, and the offender has supervisory or disciplinary authority over such other person.

(7) The offender is a teacher, administrator, coach, or other person in authority employed by or serving in a school for which the state board of education prescribes minimum standards pursuant to division (D) of section 3301.07 of the Revised Code in which the other person is enrolled or that the other person attends, and the offender is not enrolled in and does not attend that school.

(8) The other person is a minor, and the offender is a teacher, administrator, coach, or other person in authority employed by or serving in an institution of higher education in which the other person is enrolled or that the other person attends.

(9) The other person is a minor, and the offender is the other person's athletic or other type of coach, is the other person's instructor, is the leader of a scouting troop of which the other person is a member, or is a person with temporary or occasional disciplinary control over the other person.

(B) Whoever violates this section is guilty of sexual battery, a felony of the third degree.

(C) As used in this section, "institution of higher education" means a state institution of higher education defined in section 3345.031 of the Revised Code, a private nonprofit college or university located in this state that possesses a certificate of authorization issued by the Ohio board of regents pursuant to Chapter 1713. of the Revised Code, or a school certified under Chapter 3332. of the Revised Code.

(1994 H 454, eff. 7–19–94; 1972 H 511, eff. 1–1–74)

2907.04   Corruption of a minor

(A) No person who is eighteen years of age or older shall engage in sexual conduct with another, who is not the spouse of the offender, when the offender knows such other person is thirteen years of age or older but less than sixteen years of age, or the offender is reckless in that regard.

(B) Whoever violates this section is guilty of corruption of a minor, a felony of the third degree. If the offender is less than four years older than the other person, corruption of a minor is a misdemeanor of the first degree.

(1990 H 44, eff. 7–24–90; 1972 H 511)

2907.05   Gross sexual imposition

(A) No person shall have sexual contact with another, not the spouse of the offender; cause another, not the spouse of the offender, to have sexual contact with the offender; or cause two or more other persons to have sexual contact when any of the following applies:

(1) The offender purposely compels the other person, or one of the other persons, to submit by force or threat of force.

(2) For the purpose of preventing resistance, the offender substantially impairs the judgment or control of the other person or of one of the other persons by administering any drug or intoxicant to the other person, surreptitiously or by force, threat of force, or deception.

(3) The offender knows that the judgment or control of the other person or of one of the other persons is substantially impaired as a result of the influence of any drug or intoxicant administered to the other person with his consent for the purpose of any kind of medical or dental examination, treatment, or surgery.

(4) The other person, or one of the other persons, is less than thirteen years of age, whether or not the offender knows the age of that person.

(5) The ability of the other person to resist or consent or the ability of one of the other persons to resist or consent is substantially impaired because of a mental or physical condition or because of advanced age, and the offender knows or has reasonable cause to believe that the ability to resist or consent of the other person or of one of the other persons is substantially impaired because of a mental or physical condition or because of advanced age.

(B) Whoever violates this section is guilty of gross sexual imposition. Violation of division (A)(1), (2), (3), or (5) of this section is a felony of the fourth degree. Violation of division (A)(4) of this section is a felony of the third degree.

(C) A victim need not prove physical resistance to the offender in prosecutions under this section.

(D) Evidence of specific instances of the victim's sexual activity, opinion evidence of the victim's sexual activity, and reputation evidence of the victim's sexual activity shall not be admitted under this section unless it involves evidence of the origin of semen, pregnancy, or disease, or the victim's past sexual activity with the offender, and only to the extent that the court finds that the evidence is material to a fact at issue in the case and that its inflammatory or prejudicial nature does not outweigh its probative value.

Evidence of specific instances of the defendant's sexual activity, opinion evidence of the defendant's sexual activity, and reputation evidence of the defendant's sexual activity shall not be admitted under this section unless it involves evidence of the origin of semen, pregnancy, or disease, the defendant's past sexual activity with the victim, or is admissible against the defendant under section 2945.59 of the Revised Code, and only to the extent that the court finds that the evidence is material to a fact at issue in the case and that its inflammatory or prejudicial nature does not outweigh its probative value.

(E) Prior to taking testimony or receiving evidence of any sexual activity of the victim or the defendant in a proceeding under this section, the court shall resolve the admissibility of the proposed evidence in a hearing in chambers, which shall be held at or before preliminary hearing and not less than three days before trial, or for good cause shown during the trial.

(F) Upon approval by the court, the victim may be represented by counsel in any hearing in chambers or other proceeding to resolve the admissibility of evidence. If the victim is indigent or otherwise is unable to obtain the services of counsel, the court, upon request, may appoint counsel to represent the victim without cost to the victim.

(1993 S 31, eff. 9–27–93; 1990 H 208; 1977 H 134; 1975 S 144; 1972 H 511)

2907.06 Sexual imposition

(A) No person shall have sexual contact with another, not the spouse of the offender; cause another, not the spouse of the offender, to have sexual contact with the offender; or cause two or more other persons to have sexual contact when any of the following applies:

(1) The offender knows that the sexual contact is offensive to the other person, or one of the other persons, or is reckless in that regard.

(2) The offender knows that the other person's, or one of the other person's, ability to appraise the nature of or control the offender's or touching person's conduct is substantially impaired.

(3) The offender knows that the other person, or one of the other persons, submits because of being unaware of the sexual contact.

(4) The other person, or one of the other persons, is thirteen years of age or older but less than sixteen years of age, whether or not the offender knows the age of such person, and the offender is at least eighteen years of age and four or more years older than such other person.

(B) No person shall be convicted of a violation of this section solely upon the victim's testimony unsupported by other evidence.

(C) Whoever violates this section is guilty of sexual imposition, a misdemeanor of the third degree.

(1990 H 44, eff. 7–24–90; 1977 H 134; 1972 H 511)

2907.07 Importuning

(A) No person shall solicit a person under thirteen years of age to engage in sexual activity with the offender, whether or not the offender knows the age of such person.

(B) No person shall solicit a person of the same sex to engage in sexual activity with the offender, when the offender knows such solicitation is offensive to the other person, or is reckless in that regard.

(C) No person shall solicit another, not the spouse of the offender, to engage in sexual conduct with the offender, when the offender is eighteen years of age or older and four or more years older that the other person, and the other person is over twelve but not over fifteen years of age, whether or not the offender knows the age of the other person.

(D) Whoever violates this section is guilty of importuning. Violation of division (A) or (B) of this section is a misdemeanor of the first degree. Violation of division (C) of this section is a misdemeanor of the fourth degree.

(1972 H 511, eff. 1–1–74)

2907.08   Voyeurism

(A) No person, for the purpose of sexually arousing or gratifying himself or herself, shall commit trespass or otherwise surreptitiously invade the privacy of another, to spy or eavesdrop upon another.

(B) Whoever violates this section is guilty of voyeurism, a misdemeanor of the third degree.

(1972 H 511, eff. 1–1–74)

2907.081   Malicious placing of bomb or explosive—Repealed

(1972 H 511, eff. 1–1–74; 129 v 562)

2907.082   Vandalism—Repealed

(1972 H 511, eff. 1–1–74; 131 v S 279)

2907.09   Public indecency

(A) No person shall recklessly do any of the following, under circumstances in which his or her conduct is likely to be viewed by and affront others, not members of his or her household:

(1) Expose his or her private parts, or engage in masturbation;

(2) Engage in sexual conduct;

(3) Engage in conduct which to an ordinary observer would appear to be sexual conduct or masturbation.

(B) Whoever violates this section is guilty of public indecency. If the offender previously has not been convicted of or pleaded guilty to a violation of this section, public indecency is a misdemeanor of the fourth degree. If the offender previously has been convicted of or pleaded guilty to one violation of this section, public indecency is a misdemeanor of the third degree. If the offender previously has been convicted of or pleaded guilty to two violations of this section, public indecency is a misdemeanor of the second degree. If the offender previously has been convicted of or pleaded guilty to three or more violations of this section, public indecency is a misdemeanor of the first degree.

(1990 H 214, eff. 4–13–90; 1972 H 511)

2907.10   Sentence of actual incarceration for subsequent offenders; transfer to mental institution—Repealed

(1982 H 269, § 4, eff. 7–1–83; 1982 S 199; 1980 H 900; 1978 H 565; 1975 S 144)

2907.11   Suppression of certain information

Upon the request of the victim or offender in a prosecution under sections 2907.02 to 2907.07 or section 2907.12 of the Revised Code, the judge before whom any person is brought on a charge of having committed an offense under sections 2907.02 to 2907.07 or section 2907.12 of the Revised Code shall order that the names of the victim and offender and the details of the alleged offense as obtained by any law enforcement officer be suppressed until the preliminary hearing, the accused is arraigned in the court of common pleas, the charge is dismissed, or the case is otherwise concluded, whichever occurs first. Nothing herein shall be construed to deny to either party in the case the name and address of the other party or the details of the alleged offense.

(1975 S 144, eff. 8–27–75)

2907.12   Felonious sexual penetration; marriage or cohabitation not defenses to charges

(A)(1) No person, without privilege to do so, shall insert any part of the body or any instrument, apparatus, or other object into the vaginal or anal cavity of another who is not the spouse of the offender or who is the spouse of the offender but is living separate and apart from the offender, when any of the following applies:

(a) For the purpose of preventing resistance, the offender substantially impairs the other person's judgment or control by administering any drug or intoxicant to the other person, surreptitiously or by force, threat of force, or deception.

(b) The other person is less than thirteen years of age, whether or not the offender knows the age of the other person.

(c) The other person's ability to resist or consent is substantially impaired because of a mental or physical condition or because of advanced age, and the offender knows or has reasonable cause to believe that the other person's ability to resist or consent is substantially impaired because of a mental or physical condition or because of advanced age.

(2) No person, without privilege to do so, shall insert any part of the body or any instrument, apparatus, or other object into the vaginal or anal cavity of another when the offender purposely compels the other person to submit by force or threat of force.

(B) Whoever violates this section is guilty of felonious sexual penetration, an aggravated felony of the first degree. If the offender under division (A)(1)(b) of this section purposely compels the victim to submit by force or threat of force, whoever violates division (A)(1)(b) of this section shall be imprisoned for life.

(C) It is not a defense to a charge under division (A)(2) of this section that the offender and the victim were married or were cohabiting at the time of the commission of the offense. (1993 S 31, eff. 9–27–93; 1989 S 94; 1985 H 475; 1982 H 269, § 4, S 199; 1975 S 144)

2907.121   Forcing entrance into coin-receiving device—Repealed

(1972 H 511, eff. 1–1–74; 132 v H 656)

2907.13   Malicious entry—Repealed

(1972 H 511, eff. 1–1–74; 129 v 1426; 1953 H 1; GC 12441)

2907.14   Definitions—Repealed

(1972 H 511, eff. 1–1–74; 130 v H 1; 129 v 1812; 1953 H 1; GC 12441)

2907.141   Robbery and unlawful entry—Repealed

(1972 H 511, eff. 1–1–74; 129 v 1812)

2907.142   Larceny—Repealed

(1972 H 511, eff. 1–1–74; 129 v 1812)

2907.143   Possession or receipt of stolen property—Repealed

(1972 H 511, eff. 1–1–74; 129 v 1812)

2907.144   Forcing person to accompany offender—Repealed

(1972 H 511, eff. 1–1–74; 129 v 1812)

2907.145   Assault during robbery or attempt—Repealed

(1972 H 511, eff. 1–1–74; 129 v 1812)

PROSTITUTION

2907.21   Compelling prostitution

(A) No person shall knowingly do any of the following:

(1) Compel another to engage in sexual activity for hire;

(2) Induce, procure, solicit, or request a minor to engage in sexual activity for hire, whether or not the offender knows the age of the minor;

(3) Pay or agree to pay a minor, either directly or through the minor's agent, so that the minor will engage in sexual activity, whether or not the offender knows the age of the minor;

(4) Pay a minor, either directly or through the minor's agent, for the minor having engaged in sexual activity, pursuant to a prior agreement, whether or not the offender knows the age of the minor.

(B) Whoever violates this section is guilty of compelling prostitution, a felony of the third degree.

(1988 H 51, eff. 3–17–89; 1972 H 511)

2907.22   Promoting prostitution

(A) No person shall knowingly:

(1) Establish, maintain, operate, manage, supervise, control, or have an interest in a brothel;

(2) Supervise, manage, or control the activities of a prostitute in engaging in sexual activity for hire;

(3) Transport another, or cause another to be transported across the boundary of this state or of any county in this state, in order to facilitate such other person's engaging in sexual activity for hire;

(4) For the purpose of violating or facilitating a violation of this section, induce or procure another to engage in sexual activity for hire.

(B) Whoever violates this section is guilty of promoting prostitution, a felony of the fourth degree. If any prostitute in the brothel involved in the offense, or the prostitute whose activities are supervised, managed, or controlled by the offender, or the person transported, induced, or procured by the offender to engage in sexual activity for hire, is a minor, whether or not the offender knows the age of the minor, then promoting prostitution is a felony of the second degree.

(1988 H 51, eff. 3–17–89; 1972 H 511)

2907.23   Procuring

(A) No person, knowingly and for gain, shall do either of the following:

(1) Entice or solicit another to patronize a prostitute or brothel;

(2) Procure a prostitute for another to patronize, or take or direct another at his or her request to any place for the purpose of patronizing a prostitute.

(B) No person, having authority or responsibility over the use of premises, shall knowingly permit such premises to be used for the purpose of engaging in sexual activity for hire.

(C) Whoever violates this section is guilty of procuring, a misdemeanor of the first degree.

(1972 H 511, eff. 1–1–74)

2907.24   Soliciting; solicitation after positive HIV test

(A) No person shall solicit another to engage with such other person in sexual activity for hire.

(B) No person, with knowledge that the person has tested positive as a carrier of a virus that causes acquired immunodeficiency syndrome, shall engage in conduct in violation of division (A) of this section.

(C)(1) Whoever violates division (A) of this section is guilty of soliciting, a misdemeanor of the third degree.

(2) Whoever violates division (B) of this section is guilty of engaging in solicitation after a positive HIV test. If the offender commits the violation prior to July 1, 1996, engaging in solicitation after a positive HIV test is a felony of the second degree. If the offender commits the violation on or after July 1, 1996, engaging in solicitation after a positive HIV test is a felony of the third degree.

(1996 H 40, eff. 5–30–96; 1972 H 511, eff. 1–1–74)

2907.241   Loitering to engage in solicitation; loitering to engage in solicitation after positive HIV test

(A) No person, with purpose to solicit another to engage in sexual activity for hire and while in or near a public place, shall do any of the following:

(1) Beckon to, stop, or attempt to stop another;

(2) Engage or attempt to engage another in conversation;

(3) Stop or attempt to stop the operator of a vehicle or approach a stationary vehicle;

(4) If the offender is the operator of or a passenger in a vehicle, stop, attempt to stop, beckon to, attempt to beckon to, or entice another to approach or enter the vehicle of which the offender is the operator or in which the offender is the passenger;

(5) Interfere with the free passage of another.

(B) No person, with knowledge that the person has tested positive as a carrier of a virus that causes acquired immunodeficiency syndrome, shall engage in conduct in violation of division (A) of this section.

(C) As used in this section:

(1) "Vehicle" has the same meaning as in section 4501.01 of the Revised Code.

(2) "Public place" means any of the following:

(a) A street, road, highway, thoroughfare, bikeway, walkway, sidewalk, bridge, alley, alley-way, plaza, park, driveway, parking lot, or transportation facility;

(b) A doorway or entrance way to a building that fronts on a place described in division (C)(2)(a) of this section;

(c) A place not described in division (C)(2)(a) or (b) of this section that is open to the public.

(D)(1) Whoever violates division (A) of this section is guilty of loitering to engage in solicitation, a misdemeanor of the third degree.

(2) Whoever violates division (B) of this section is guilty of loitering to engage in solicitation after a positive HIV test. If the offender commits the violation prior to July 1, 1996, loitering to engage in solicitation after a positive HIV test is a felony of the fourth degree. If the offender commits the violation on or after July 1, 1996, loitering to engage in solicitation after a positive HIV test is a felony of the fifth degree.

(1996 H 40, eff. 5–30–96)

2907.25   Prostitution; prostitution after positive HIV test

(A) No person shall engage in sexual activity for hire.

(B) No person, with knowledge that the person has tested positive as a carrier of a virus that causes acquired immunodeficiency syndrome, shall engage in sexual activity for hire.

(C)(1) Whoever violates division (A) of this section is guilty of prostitution, a misdemeanor of the third degree.

(2) Whoever violates division (B) of this section is guilty of engaging in prostitution after a positive HIV test. If the offender commits the violation prior to July 1, 1996, engaging in prostitution after a positive HIV test is a felony of the second degree. If the offender commits the violation on or after July 1, 1996, engaging in prostitution after a positive HIV test is a felony of the third degree.

(1996 H 40, eff. 5–30–96; 1972 H 511, eff. 1–1–74)

2907.26   Rules of evidence in prostitution cases

(A) In any case in which it is necessary to prove that a place is a brothel, evidence as to the reputation of such place and as to the reputation of the persons who inhabit or frequent it, is admissible on the question of whether such place is or is not a brothel.

(B) In any case in which it is necessary to prove that a person is a prostitute, evidence as to the reputation of such person is admissible on the question of whether such person is or is not a prostitute.

(C) In any prosecution for a violation of sections 2907.21 to 2907.25 of the Revised Code, proof of a prior conviction of the accused of any such offense or substantially equivalent offense is admissible in support of the charge.

(D) The prohibition contained in division (D) of section 2317.02 of the Revised Code against testimony by a husband or wife concerning communications between them does not apply, and the accused's spouse may testify concerning any such communication, in any of the following cases:

(1) When the husband or wife is charged with a violation of section 2907.21 of the Revised Code, and the spouse testifying was the victim of the offense;

(2) When the husband or wife is charged with a violation of section 2907.22 of the Revised Code, and the spouse testifying was the prostitute involved in the offense, or the person transported, induced, or procured by the offender to engage in sexual activity for hire;

(3) When the husband or wife is charged with a violation of section 2907.23 of the Revised Code, and the spouse testifying was the prostitute involved in the offense or the person who used the offender's premises to engage in sexual activity for hire;

(4) When the husband or wife is charged with a violation of section 2907.24 or 2907.25 of the Revised Code.

(1977 H 1, eff. 8–26–77; 1972 H 511)

2907.27 Examination and treatment for venereal disease and AIDS

(A)(1) If a person is charged with a violation of section 2907.02, 2907.03, 2907.04, 2907.24, 2907.241, or 2907.25 of the Revised Code or with a violation of a municipal ordinance that is substantially equivalent to any of those sections, the arresting authorities or a court, upon the request of the prosecutor in the case or upon the request of the victim, shall cause the accused to submit to one or more appropriate tests to determine if the accused is suffering from a venereal disease.

(2) If the accused is found to be suffering from a venereal disease in an infectious stage, the accused shall be required to submit to medical treatment for that disease. The cost of the medical treatment shall be charged to and paid by the accused who undergoes the treatment. If the accused is indigent, the court shall order the accused to report to a facility operated by a city health district or a general health district for treatment. If the accused is convicted of or pleads guilty to the offense with which the accused is charged and is placed on probation, a condition of probation shall be that the offender submit to and faithfully follow a course of medical treatment for the venereal disease. If the offender does not seek the required medical treatment, the court may revoke the offender's probation and order the offender to undergo medical treatment during the period of the offender's incarceration and to pay the cost of that treatment.

(B)(1)(a) Notwithstanding the requirements for informed consent in section 3701.242 of the Revised Code, if a person is charged with a violation of section 2907.02, 2907.03, 2907.04, 2907.05, 2907.12, 2907.24, 2907.241, or 2907.25 of the Revised Code or with a violation of a municipal ordinance that is substantially equivalent to any of those sections, the court, upon the request of the prosecutor in the case, upon the request of the victim, or upon the request of any other person whom the court reasonably believes had contact with the accused in circumstances related to the violation that could have resulted in the transmission to that person of a virus that causes acquired immunodeficiency syndrome, shall cause the accused to submit to one or more tests designated by the director of health under section 3701.241 of the Revised Code to determine if the accused is a carrier of a virus that causes acquired immunodeficiency syndrome. The court, upon the request of the prosecutor in the case, upon the request of the victim with the agreement of the prosecutor, or upon the request of any other person with the agreement of the prosecutor, may cause an accused who is charged with a violation of any other section of the Revised Code or with a violation of any other municipal ordinance to submit to one or more tests so designated by the director of health if the circumstances of the violation indicate probable cause to believe that the accused, if the accused is infected with the virus that causes acquired immunodeficiency syndrome, might have transmitted the virus to any of the following persons in committing the violation:

(i) In relation to a request made by the prosecuting attorney, to the victim or to any other person;

(ii) In relation to a request made by the victim, to the victim making the request;

(iii) In relation to a request made by any other person, to the person making the request.

(b) The results of a test performed under division (B)(1)(a) of this section shall be communicated in confidence to the court, and the court shall inform the accused of the result. The court shall inform the victim that the test was performed and that the victim has a right to receive the results on request. If the test was performed upon the request of a person other than the prosecutor in the case and other than the victim, the court shall inform the person who made the request that the test was performed and that the person has a right to receive the results upon request. Additionally, regardless of who made the request that was the basis of the test being performed, if the court reasonably believes that, in circumstances related to the violation, a person other than the victim had contact with the accused that could have resulted in the transmission of the virus to that person, the court may inform that person that the test was performed and that the person has a right to receive the results of the test on request. If the accused tests positive for a virus that causes acquired immunodeficiency syndrome, the test results shall be reported to the department of health in accordance with section 3701.24 of the Revised Code and to the sheriff, head of the state correctional institution, or other person in charge of any jail or prison in which the accused is incarcerated. If the accused tests positive for a virus that causes acquired immunodeficiency syndrome and the accused was charged with, and was convicted of or pleaded guilty to, a violation of section 2907.24, 2907.241, or 2907.25 of the Revised Code or a violation of a municipal ordinance that is substantially equivalent to any of those sections, the test results also shall be reported to the law enforcement agency that arrested the accused, and the law enforcement agency may use the test results as the basis for any future charge of a violation of division (B) of any of those sections or a violation of a municipal ordinance that is substantially equivalent to division (B) of any of those sections. No other disclosure of the test results or the fact that a test was performed shall be made, other than as evidence in a grand jury proceeding or as evidence in a judicial proceeding in accordance with the Rules of Evidence. If the test result is negative, and the charge has not been dismissed or if the accused has been convicted of the charge or a different offense arising out of the same circumstances as the offense charged, the court shall order that the test be repeated not earlier than three months nor later than six months after the original test.

(2) If an accused who is free on bond refuses to submit to a test ordered by the court pursuant to division (B)(1) of this section, the court may order that the accused's bond be revoked and that the accused be incarcerated until the test is performed. If an accused who is incarcerated refuses to submit to a test ordered by the court pursuant to division (B)(1) of this section, the court shall order the person in charge of the jail or prison in which the accused is incarcerated to take any action necessary to facilitate the performance of the test, including the forcible restraint of the accused for the purpose of drawing blood to be used in the test.

(3) A state agency, a political subdivision of the state, or an employee of a state agency or of a political subdivision of the state is immune from liability in a civil action to recover damages for injury, death, or loss to person or property allegedly caused by any act or omission in connection with the performance of the duties required under division (B)(2) of this section unless the acts or omissions are with malicious purpose, in bad faith, or in a wanton or reckless manner.

(1996 H 40, eff. 5–30–96; 1994 H 571, eff. 10–6–94; 1989 S 2, eff. 11–1–89; 1989 S 94; 1972 H 511)

ASSISTANCE TO VICTIMS OF SEXUAL ASSAULT

2907.28　Medical examination of victim;　costs

(A) Any cost incurred by a hospital or other emergency medical facility in conducting a medical examination of a victim of an offense under sections 2907.02 to 2907.06 or section 2907.12 of the Revised Code for the purpose of gathering physical evidence for a possible prosecution shall be charged to and paid by the appropriate local government as follows:

(1) Cost incurred by a county facility shall be charged to and paid by the county;

(2) Cost incurred by a municipal facility shall be charged to and paid by the municipal corporation;

(3) Cost incurred by a private facility shall be charged to and paid by the municipal corporation in which the alleged offense was committed, or charged to and paid by the county, if committed within an unincorporated area. If separate counts of an offense or separate offenses under sections 2907.02 to 2907.06 or section 2907.12 of the Revised Code took place in more than one municipal corporation or more than one unincorporated area, or both, the local governments shall share the cost of the examination.

(B) Any cost incurred by a hospital or other emergency medical facility in conducting a medical examination and test of any person who is charged with a violation of section 2907.02, 2907.03, 2907.04, 2907.05, 2907.12, 2907.24, 2907.241, or 2907.25 of the Revised Code or with a violation of a municipal ordinance that is substantially equivalent to any of those sections, pursuant to division (B) of section 2907.27 of the Revised Code, shall be charged to and paid by the accused who undergoes the examination and test, unless the court determines that the accused is unable to pay, in which case the cost shall be charged to and paid by the municipal corporation in which the offense allegedly was committed, or charged to and paid by the county if the offense allegedly was committed within an unincorporated area. If separate counts of an alleged offense or alleged separate offenses under section 2907.02, 2907.03, 2907.04, 2907.05, 2907.12, 2907.24, 2907.241, or 2907.25 of the Revised Code or under a municipal ordinance that is substantially equivalent to any of those sections took place in more than one municipal corporation or more than one unincorporated area, or both, the local governments shall share the cost of the examination and test. If a hospital or other emergency medical facility has submitted charges for the cost of a medical examination and test to an accused and has been unable to collect payment for the charges after making good faith attempts to collect for a period of six months or more, the cost shall be charged to and paid by the appropriate municipal corporation or county as specified in division (B) of this section.

(1996 H 40, eff. 5–30–96; 1989 S 2, eff. 11–1–89; 1975 S 144)

2907.29 Emergency medical services for victims; information to be given victim; consent of minor

Every hospital of this state which offers organized emergency services shall provide that a physician is available on call twenty-four hours each day for the examination of persons reported to any law enforcement agency to be victims of sexual offenses cognizable as violations of sections 2907.02 to 2907.06 or section 2907.12 of the Revised Code. The physician shall, upon the request of any peace officer or prosecuting attorney, and with the consent of the reported victim, or upon the request of the reported victim, examine such person for the purposes of gathering physical evidence. The public health council shall establish procedures for gathering evidence under this section.

Each reported victim shall be informed of available venereal disease, pregnancy, medical, and psychiatric services.

Notwithstanding any other provision of law, a minor may consent to examination under this section. Such consent is not subject to disaffirmance because of minority, and consent of the parent, parents, or guardian of the minor is not required for such examination. However, the hospital shall give written notice to the parent, parents, or guardian of a minor that such an examination has taken place. The parent, parents, or guardian of a minor giving consent under this section are not liable for payment for any services provided under this section without their consent.

(1975 S 144, eff. 8–27–75)

2907.30 Right to interview by one with crisis intervention training; notice to victim of accused sex offender's communicable disease

(A) A victim of a sexual offense cognizable as a violation of section 2907.02 or 2907.12 of the Revised Code who is interviewed by a law enforcement agency that shall be interviewed by a peace officer employed by the agency who has had crisis intervention training, if any of the peace officers employed by the agency who have had crisis intervention training is reasonably available.

(B) When a person is charged with a violation of section 2907.02, 2907.03, 2907.04, 2907.05, 2907.06, or 2907.12 of the Revised Code and the law enforcement agency that arrested the person or a court discovers that the person arrested or a person whom the person arrested caused to engage in sexual activity has a communicable disease, the law enforcement agency that arrested the person or the court immediately shall notify the victim of the nature of the disease.

(C) As used in this section, "crisis intervention training" has the same meaning as in section 109.71 of the Revised Code.

(1986 H 468, eff. 9–17–86; 1984 H 435)

OBSCENITY

2907.31 Disseminating matter harmful to juveniles

(A) No person, with knowledge of its character or content, shall recklessly do any of the following:

(1) Sell, deliver, furnish, disseminate, provide, exhibit, rent, or present to a juvenile any material or performance that is obscene or harmful to juveniles;

(2) Offer or agree to sell, deliver, furnish, disseminate, provide, exhibit, rent, or present to a juvenile any material or performance that is obscene or harmful to juveniles;

(3) Allow any juvenile to review or peruse any material or view any live performance that is harmful to juveniles.

(B) The following are affirmative defenses to a charge under this section that involves material or a performance that is harmful to juveniles but not obscene:

(1) The defendant is the parent, guardian, or spouse of the juvenile involved.

(2) The juvenile involved, at the time of the conduct in question, was accompanied by his parent or guardian who, with knowledge of its character, consented to the material or performance being furnished or presented to the juvenile.

(3) The juvenile exhibited to the defendant or his agent or employee a draft card, driver's license, birth record, marriage license, or other official or apparently official document purporting to show that such juvenile was eighteen years of age or over or married, and the person to whom such document was exhibited did not otherwise have reasonable cause to believe that such juvenile was under the age of eighteen and unmarried.

(C)(1) It is an affirmative defense to a charge under this section, involving material or a performance that is obscene or harmful to juveniles, that such material or performance was furnished or presented for a bona fide medical, scientific, educational, governmental, judicial, or other proper purpose, by a physician, psychologist, sociologist, scientist, teacher, librarian, clergyman, prosecutor, judge, or other proper person.

(2) Except as provided in division (B)(3) of this section, mistake of age is not a defense to a charge under this section.

(D) Whoever violates this section is guilty of disseminating matter harmful to juveniles. If the material or performance involved is harmful to juveniles but not obscene, violation of this section is a misdemeanor of the first degree. If the material or performance involved is obscene and the juvenile to whom it is sold, delivered, furnished, disseminated, provided, exhibited, rented, or presented, the juvenile to whom the offer is made or who is the subject of the agreement, or the juvenile who is allowed to review, peruse, or view it is thirteen years of age or older, violation of this section is a felony of the fourth degree. If the material or performance involved is obscene and the juvenile to whom it is sold, delivered, furnished, disseminated, provided, exhibited, rented, or presented, the juvenile to whom the offer is made or who is the subject of the agreement, or the juvenile who is allowed to review, peruse, or view it is under thirteen years of age, violation of this section is a felony of the third degree.

(1988 H 790, eff. 3–16–89; 1988 H 51; 1972 H 511)

Historical and Statutory Notes

Ed. Note: A special endorsement by the Legislative Service Commission states, "Comparison of these amendments [1988 H 790, eff. 3–16–89 and 1988 H 51, eff. 3–17–89] in pursuance of section 1.52 of the Revised Code discloses that they are not irreconcilable, so that they are required by that section to be harmonized to give effect to each amendment." In recognition of this rule of construction, changes made by 1988 H 790, eff. 3–16–89 and 1988 H 51, eff. 3–17–89 have been incorporated in the above amendment. See *Baldwin's Ohio Legislative Service*, 1988 Laws of Ohio, pages 5–1051 and 5–915, for original versions of these Acts.

2907.311 Displaying matter harmful to juveniles

(A) No person who has custody, control, or supervision of a commercial establishment, with knowledge of the character or content of the material involved, shall display at the establishment any material that is harmful to juveniles and that is open to view by juveniles as part of the invited general public.

(B) It is not a violation of division (A) of this section if the material in question is displayed by placing it behind "blinder racks" or similar devices that cover at least the lower two-thirds of the material, if the material in question is wrapped or placed behind the counter, or if the material in question otherwise is covered or located so that the portion that is harmful to juveniles is not open to the view of juveniles.

(C) Whoever violates this section is guilty of displaying matter harmful to juveniles, a misdemeanor of the first degree. Each day during which the offender is in violation of this section constitutes a separate offense.

(1988 H 51, eff. 3–17–89)

2907.32 Pandering obscenity

(A) No person, with knowledge of the character of the material or performance involved, shall do any of the following:

(1) Create, reproduce, or publish any obscene material, when the offender knows that such material is to be used for commercial exploitation or will be publicly disseminated or displayed, or when he is reckless in that regard;

(2) Promote or advertise for sale, delivery, or dissemination; sell, deliver, publicly disseminate, publicly display, exhibit, present, rent, or provide; or offer or agree to sell, deliver, publicly disseminate, publicly display, exhibit, present, rent, or provide, any obscene material;

(3) Create, direct, or produce an obscene performance, when the offender knows that it is to be used for commercial exploitation or will be publicly presented, or when he is reckless in that regard;

(4) Advertise or promote an obscene performance for presentation, or present or participate in presenting an obscene performance, when such performance is presented publicly, or when admission is charged;

(5) Buy, procure, possess, or control any obscene material with purpose to violate division (A)(2) or (4) of this section.

(B) It is an affirmative defense to a charge under this section, that the material or performance involved was disseminated or presented for a bona fide medical, scientific, educational, religious, governmental, judicial, or other proper purpose, by or to a physician, psychologist, sociologist, scientist, teacher, person pursuing bona fide studies or research, librarian, clergyman, prosecutor, judge, or other person having a proper interest in such material or performance.

(C) Whoever violates this section is guilty of pandering obscenity, a misdemeanor of the first degree. If the offender previously has been convicted of a violation of this section or of section 2907.31 of the Revised Code, then pandering obscenity is a felony of the fourth degree.

(1988 H 51, eff. 3–17–89; 1972 H 511)

2907.321 Pandering obscenity involving a minor

(A) No person, with knowledge of the character of the material or performance involved, shall do any of the following:

(1) Create, reproduce, or publish any obscene material that has a minor as one of its participants or portrayed observers;

(2) Promote or advertise for sale or dissemination; sell, deliver, disseminate, display, exhibit, present, rent, or provide; or offer or agree to sell, deliver, disseminate, display, exhibit, present, rent, or provide, any obscene material that has a minor as one of its participants or portrayed observers;

(3) Create, direct, or produce an obscene performance that has a minor as one of its participants;

(4) Advertise or promote for presentation, present, or participate in presenting an obscene performance that has a minor as one of its participants;

(5) Buy, procure, possess, or control any obscene material, that has a minor as one of its participants;

(6) Bring or cause to be brought into this state any obscene material that has a minor as one of its participants or portrayed observers.

(B)(1) This section does not apply to any material or performance that is sold, disseminated, displayed, possessed, controlled, brought or caused to be brought into this state, or presented for a bona fide medical, scientific, educational, religious, governmental, judicial, or other proper purpose, by or to a physician, psychologist, sociologist, scientist, teacher, person pursuing bona fide studies or research, librarian, clergyman, prosecutor, judge, or other person having a proper interest in the material or performance.

(2) Mistake of age is not a defense to a charge under this section.

(3) In a prosecution under this section, the trier of fact may infer that a person in the material or performance involved is a minor if the material or performance, through its title, text, visual representation, or otherwise, represents or depicts the person as a minor.

(C) Whoever violates this section is guilty of pandering obscenity involving a minor. Violation of division (A)(1), (2), (3), (4), or (6) of this section is a felony of the second degree. Violation of division (A)(5) of this section is a felony of the fourth degree. If the offender previously has been convicted of or pleaded guilty to a violation of this section or section 2907.322 or 2907.323 of the Revised Code, pandering obscenity involving a minor in violation of division (A)(5) of this section is a felony of the third degree.

(1988 H 51, eff. 3–17–89; 1984 H 44; 1977 S 243)

2907.322 Pandering sexually oriented matter involving a minor

(A) No person, with knowledge of the character of the material or performance involved, shall do any of the following:

(1) Create, record, photograph, film, develop, reproduce, or publish any material that shows a minor participating or engaging in sexual activity, masturbation, or bestiality;

(2) Advertise for sale or dissemination, sell, distribute, transport, disseminate, exhibit, or display any material that shows a minor participating or engaging in sexual activity, masturbation, or bestiality;

(3) Create, direct, or produce a performance that shows a minor participating or engaging in sexual activity, masturbation, or bestiality;

(4) Advertise for presentation, present, or participate in presenting a performance that shows a minor participating or engaging in sexual activity, masturbation, or bestiality;

(5) Solicit, receive, purchase, exchange, possess or control any material that shows a minor participating or engaging in sexual activity, masturbation, or bestiality;

(6) Bring or cause to be brought into this state any material that shows a minor participating or engaging in sexual activity, masturbation, or bestiality, or bring, cause to be brought, or

finance the bringing of any minor into or across this state with the intent that the minor engage in sexual activity, masturbation, or bestiality in a performance or for the purpose of producing material containing a visual representation depicting the minor engaged in sexual activity, masturbation, or bestiality.

(B)(1) This section does not apply to any material or performance that is sold, disseminated, displayed, possessed, controlled, brought or caused to be brought into this state, or presented for a bona fide medical, scientific, educational, religious, governmental, judicial, or other proper purpose, by or to a physician, psychologist, sociologist, scientist, teacher, person pursuing bona fide studies or research, librarian, clergyman, prosecutor, judge, or other person having a proper interest in the material or performance.

(2) Mistake of age is not a defense to a charge under this section.

(3) In a prosecution under this section, the trier of fact may infer that a person in the material or performance involved is a minor if the material or performance, through its title, text, visual representation, or otherwise, represents or depicts the person as a minor.

(C) Whoever violates this section is guilty of pandering sexually oriented matter involving a minor. Violation of division (A)(1), (2), (3), (4), or (6) of this section is a felony of the second degree. Violation of division (A)(5) of this section is a misdemeanor of the first degree. If the offender previously has been convicted of or pleaded guilty to a violation of this section or section 2907.321 or 2907.323 of the Revised Code, pandering sexually oriented matter involving a minor in violation of division (A)(5) of this section is a felony of the fourth degree.
(1988 H 51, eff. 3–17–89; 1984 H 44)

2907.323   Illegal use of a minor in nudity-oriented material or performance

(A) No person shall do any of the following:

(1) Photograph any minor who is not the person's child or ward in a state of nudity, or create, direct, produce, or transfer any material or performance that shows the minor in a state of nudity, unless both of the following apply:

(a) The material or performance is, or is to be, sold, disseminated, displayed, possessed, controlled, brought or caused to be brought into this state, or presented for a bona fide artistic, medical, scientific, educational, religious, governmental, judicial, or other proper purpose, by or to a physician, psychologist, sociologist, scientist, teacher, person pursuing bona fide studies or research, librarian, clergyman, prosecutor, judge, or other person having a proper interest in the material or performance;

(b) The minor's parents, guardian, or custodian consents in writing to the photographing of the minor, to the use of the minor in the material or performance, or to the transfer of the material and to the specific manner in which the material or performance is to be used.

(2) Consent to the photographing of his minor child or ward, or photograph his minor child or ward, in a state of nudity or consent to the use of his minor child or ward in a state of nudity in any material or performance, or use or transfer such material or performance, unless the material or performance is sold, disseminated, displayed, possessed, controlled, brought or caused to be brought into this state, or presented for a bona fide artistic, medical, scientific, educational, religious, governmental, judicial, or other proper purpose, by or to a physician, psychologist, sociologist, scientist, teacher, person pursuing bona fide studies or research, librarian, clergyman, prosecutor, judge, or other person having a proper interest in the material or performance;

(3) Possess or view any material or performance that shows a minor who is not the person's child or ward in a state of nudity, unless one of the following applies:

(a) The material or performance is sold, disseminated, displayed, possessed, controlled, brought or caused to be brought into this state, or presented for a bona fide artistic, medical, scientific, educational, religious, governmental, judicial, or other proper purpose, by or to a physician, psychologist, sociologist, scientist, teacher, person pursuing bona fide studies or research, librarian, clergyman, prosecutor, judge, or other person having a proper interest in the material or performance.

(b) The person knows that the parents, guardian, or custodian has consented in writing to the photographing or use of the minor in a state of nudity and to the manner in which the material or performance is used or transferred.

(B) Whoever violates this section is guilty of illegal use of a minor in a nudity-oriented material or performance. Whoever violates division (A)(1) or (2) of this section is guilty of a felony of the second degree. Whoever violates division (A)(3) of this section is guilty of a misdemeanor of the first degree. If the offender previously has been convicted of or pleaded guilty to a violation of this section or section 2907.321 or 2907.322 of the Revised Code, illegal use of a minor in a nudity-oriented material or performance in violation of division (A)(3) of this section is a felony of the fourth degree.

(1988 H 51, eff. 3–17–89; 1984 S 321, H 44)

2907.33   Deception to obtain matter harmful to juveniles

(A) No person, for the purpose of enabling a juvenile to obtain any material or gain admission to any performance which is harmful to juveniles, shall do either of the following:

(1) Falsely represent that he is the parent, guardian, or spouse of such juvenile;

(2) Furnish such juvenile with any identification or document purporting to show that such juvenile is eighteen years of age or over or married.

(B) No juvenile, for the purpose of obtaining any material or gaining admission to any performance which is harmful to juveniles, shall do either of the following:

(1) Falsely represent that he is eighteen years of age or over or married;

(2) Exhibit any identification or document purporting to show that he is eighteen years of age or over or married.

(C) Whoever violates this section is guilty of deception to obtain matter harmful to juveniles, a misdemeanor of the second degree. A juvenile who violates division (B) of this section shall be adjudged an unruly child, with such disposition of the case as may be appropriate under Chapter 2151. of the Revised Code.

(1972 H 511, eff. 1–1–74)

2907.34   Compelling acceptance of objectionable materials

(A) No person, as a condition to the sale, allocation, consignment, or delivery of any material or goods of any kind, shall require the purchaser or consignee to accept any other material reasonably believed to be obscene, or which if furnished or presented to a juvenile would be in violation of section 2907.31 of the Revised Code.

(B) No person shall deny or threaten to deny any franchise or impose or threaten to impose any financial or other penalty upon any purchaser or consignee because the purchaser or consignee failed or refused to accept any material reasonably believed to be obscene as a condition to the sale, allocation, consignment, or delivery of any other material or goods or because the purchaser or consignee returned any material believed to be obscene that he initially accepted.

(C) Whoever violates this section is guilty of compelling acceptance of objectionable materials, a felony of the fourth degree.

(1988 H 51, eff. 3–17–89; 1972 H 511)

2907.35   Presumptions; notice; defense

(A) An owner or manager, or his agent or employee, of a bookstore, newsstand, theater, or other commercial establishment engaged in selling materials or exhibiting performances, who, in the course of business:

(1) Possesses five or more identical or substantially similar obscene articles, having knowledge of their character, is presumed to possess them in violation of division (A)(5) of section 2907.32 of the Revised Code;

(2) Does any of the acts prohibited by section 2907.31 or 2907.32 of the Revised Code, is presumed to have knowledge of the character of the material or performance involved, if he has actual notice of the nature of such material or performance, whether or not he has precise knowledge of its contents.

(B) Without limitation on the manner in which such notice may be given, actual notice of the character of material or a performance may be given in writing by the chief legal officer of the jurisdiction in which the person to whom the notice is directed does business. Such notice, regardless of the manner in which it is given, shall identify the sender, identify the material or performance involved, state whether it is obscene or harmful to juveniles, and bear the date of such notice.

(C) Sections 2907.31 and 2907.32 of the Revised Code do not apply to a motion picture operator or projectionist acting within the scope of his employment as an employee of the owner or manager of a theater or other place for the showing of motion pictures to the general public, and having no managerial responsibility or financial interest in his place of employment, other than wages.

(1973 S 62, eff. 1–1–74; 1972 H 511)

2907.36   Declaratory judgment

(A) Without limitation on the persons otherwise entitled to bring an action for a declaratory judgment pursuant to sections 2721.01 to 2721.15 of the Revised Code, involving the same issue, the following persons have standing to bring such an action to determine whether particular materials or performances are obscene or harmful to juveniles:

(1) The chief legal officer of the jurisdiction in which there is reasonable cause to believe that section 2907.31 or 2907.32 of the Revised Code is being or is about to be violated;

(2) Any person who, pursuant to division (B) of section 2907.35 of the Revised Code, has received notice in writing from a chief legal officer stating that particular materials or performances are obscene or harmful to juveniles.

(B) Any party to an action for a declaratory judgment pursuant to division (A) of this section is entitled, upon his request, to trial on the merits within five days after joinder of the issues, and the court shall render judgment within five days after trial is concluded.

(C) An action for a declaratory judgment pursuant to division (A) of this section shall not be brought during the pendency of any civil action or criminal prosecution, when the character of the particular materials or performances involved is at issue in the pending case, and either of the following apply:

(1) Either of the parties to the action for a declaratory judgment is a party to the pending case;

(2) A judgment in the pending case will necessarily constitute res judicata as to the character of the materials or performances involved.

(D) A civil action or criminal prosecution in which the character of particular materials or performances is at issue, brought during the pendency of an action for a declaratory judgment involving the same issue, shall be stayed during the pendency of the action for a declaratory judgment.

(E) The fact that a violation of section 2907.31 or 2907.32 of the Revised Code occurs prior to a judicial determination of the character of the material or performance involved in the violation, does not relieve the offender of criminal liability for the violation, even though prosecution may be stayed pending the judicial determination.

(1972 H 511, eff. 1–1–74)

2907.37   Injunction

(A) Where it appears that section 2907.31 or 2907.32 of the Revised Code is being or is about to be violated, the chief legal officer of the jurisdiction in which the violation is taking place or is about to take place may bring an action to enjoin the violation. The defendant, upon his request, is entitled to trial on the merits within five days after joinder of the issues, and the court shall render judgment within five days after trial is concluded.

(B) Premises used or occupied for repeated violations of section 2907.31 or 2907.32 of the Revised Code constitute a nuisance subject to abatement pursuant to sections 3767.01 to 3767.99 of the Revised Code.

(1972 H 511, eff. 1–1–74)

2907.38 Embezzlement of textbooks—Repealed

(1972 H 511, eff. 1–1–74; 1953 H 1; GC 12471)

2907.39 Conversion of property by bailee—Repealed

(1972 H 511, eff. 1–1–74; 1953 H 1; GC 12475)

2907.40 Fraudulent conversion of grain or farm produce—Repealed

(1972 H 511, eff. 1–1–74; 1953 H 1; GC 12475–1)

2907.41 Deposition of child sex offense victim; presence of defendant; additional depositions; videotaped deposition; admissibility of deposition; televised or recorded testimony

(A)(1) In any proceeding in the prosecution of a charge of a violation of section 2907.02, 2907.03, 2907.04, 2907.05, 2907.06, 2907.12, 2907.21, 2907.31, 2907.32, 2907.321, 2907.322, or 2907.323, or division (B)(5) of section 2919.22 of the Revised Code in which an alleged victim was a child who was under eleven years of age when the complaint, indictment, or information was filed, whichever occurred earlier, the judge of the court in which the prosecution is being conducted, upon motion of an attorney for the prosecution, shall order that the testimony of the child victim be taken by deposition. The prosecution also may request that the deposition be videotaped in accordance with division (A)(2) of this section. The judge shall notify the child victim whose deposition is to be taken, the prosecution, and the defense of the date, time, and place for taking the deposition, which notice shall identify the child victim who is to be examined, and whether a request that the deposition be videotaped has been made. The defendant shall have the right to attend the deposition and the right to be represented by counsel. Depositions shall be taken in the manner provided in civil cases, except that the judge shall preside at the taking of the deposition and shall rule at that time on any objections of the prosecution or the attorney for the defense. The prosecution and the attorney for the defense shall have the right, as at trial, to full examination and cross-examination of the child victim whose deposition is to be taken. If a deposition taken under this division is intended to be offered as evidence in the proceeding it shall be filed in the court in which the action is pending, and is admissible in the manner described in division (B) of this section. If a deposition of a child victim taken under this division is admitted as evidence at the proceeding under division (B) of this section, the child victim shall not be required to testify in person at the proceeding. However, at any time before the conclusion of the proceeding, the attorney for the defense may file a motion with the judge requesting that another deposition of the child victim be taken because new evidence material to the defense has been discovered that the attorney for the defense could not with reasonable diligence have discovered prior to the taking of the admitted deposition. Any such motion shall be accompanied by supporting affidavits. Upon the filing of such a motion and affidavits, the court may order that additional testimony of the child victim relative to the new evidence be taken by another deposition. If the court orders the taking of another deposition under this provision, the deposition shall be taken in accordance with this division; if the admitted deposition was a videotaped deposition taken in accordance with division (A)(2) of this section, the new deposition also shall be videotaped in accordance with that division and in other cases, the new deposition may be videotaped in accordance with that division.

(2) If the prosecution requests that a deposition to be taken under division (A)(1) of this section be videotaped, the judge shall order that the deposition be videotaped in accordance with this division. If a judge issues such an order, the judge shall exclude from the room in which the deposition is to be taken every person except the child victim giving the testimony, the judge, one or more interpreters if needed, the attorneys for the prosecution and the defense, any person needed to operate the equipment to be used, one person chosen by the child victim giving the deposition, and any person whose presence the judge determines would contribute to the welfare and well-being of the child victim giving the deposition. The person

chosen by the child victim shall not himself be a witness in the proceeding, and both before and during the deposition shall not discuss the testimony of the child victim with any other witness in the proceeding. To the extent feasible, any person operating the recording equipment shall be restricted to a room adjacent to the room in which the deposition is being taken, or to a location in the room in which the deposition is being taken that is behind a screen or mirror so that any such person can see and hear, but cannot be seen or heard by, the child victim giving the deposition during his deposition. The defendant shall be permitted to observe and hear the testimony of the child victim giving the deposition on a monitor and shall be provided with an electronic means of immediate communication with his attorney during the testimony, but shall be restricted to a location that is such that he cannot be seen or heard by the child victim giving the deposition, except on a monitor provided for that purpose. The child victim giving the deposition shall be provided with a monitor on which he can observe, during his testimony, the defendant. The judge, at his discretion, may preside at the deposition by electronic means from outside the room in which the deposition is to be taken; if the judge presides in such a manner, the judge shall be provided with monitors on which he can see each person in the room in which the deposition is to be taken and with an electronic means of communication with each such person, and each person in the room shall be provided with a monitor on which he can see the judge and an electronic means of communication with the judge. A deposition that is videotaped under this division shall be taken and filed in the manner described in division (A)(1) of this section and is admissible in the manner described in this division and division (B) of this section, and if such a videotaped deposition is admitted as evidence at the proceeding, the child victim shall not be required to testify in person at the proceeding. No deposition videotaped under this division shall be admitted as evidence at any proceeding unless division (B) of this section is satisfied relative to the deposition and all of the following apply relative to the recording:

(a) The recording is both aural and visual and is recorded on film or videotape, or by other electronic means;

(b) The recording is authenticated under the Rules of Evidence and the Rules of Criminal Procedure as a fair and accurate representation of what occurred, and the recording is not altered other than at the direction and under the supervision of the judge in the proceeding;

(c) Each voice on the recording that is material to the testimony on the recording or the making of the recording, as determined by the judge, is identified;

(d) Both the prosecution and the defendant are afforded an opportunity to view the recording before it is shown in the proceeding.

(B)(1) At any proceeding in a prosecution in relation to which a deposition was taken under division (A) of this section, the deposition or a part of it is admissible in evidence upon motion of the prosecution if the testimony in the deposition or the part to be admitted is not excluded by the hearsay rule and if the deposition or the part to be admitted otherwise is admissible under the Rules of Evidence. For purposes of this division, testimony is not excluded by the hearsay rule if the testimony is not hearsay under Evidence Rule 801; if the testimony is within an exception to the hearsay rule set forth in Evidence Rule 803; if the child victim who gave the testimony is unavailable as a witness, as defined in Evidence Rule 804, and the testimony is admissible under that rule; or if both of the following apply:

(a) The defendant had an opportunity and similar motive at the time of the taking of the deposition to develop the testimony by direct, cross, or redirect examination;

(b) The judge determines that there is reasonable cause to believe that if the child victim who gave the testimony in the deposition were to testify in person at the proceeding, the child victim would experience serious emotional trauma as a result of his participation at the proceeding.

(2) Objections to receiving in evidence a deposition or a part of it under division (B) of this section shall be made as provided in civil actions.

(3) The provisions of divisions (A) and (B) of this section are in addition to any other provisions of the Revised Code, the Rules of Criminal Procedure, or the Rules of Evidence that pertain to the taking or admission of depositions in a criminal proceeding, and do not limit the admissibility under any such other provisions of any deposition taken under division (A) of this section or otherwise taken.

(C) In any proceeding in the prosecution of any charge of a violation listed in division (A)(1) of this section in which an alleged victim was a child who was under eleven years of age when the complaint, indictment, or information was filed, whichever occurred earlier, the prosecution may file a motion with the judge requesting the judge to order the testimony of the child victim to be taken in a room other than the room in which the proceeding is being conducted and be televised, by closed circuit equipment, into the room in which the proceeding is being conducted to be viewed by the jury, if applicable, the defendant, and any other persons who are not permitted in the room in which the testimony is to be taken but who would have been present during the testimony of the child victim had it been given in the room in which the proceeding is being conducted. Except for good cause shown, the prosecution shall file such a motion at least seven days before the date of the proceeding. The judge may issue such an order, upon motion of the prosecution, if the judge determines that the child victim is unavailable to testify in the room in which the proceeding is being conducted in the physical presence of the defendant, for one or more of the reasons set forth in division (E) of this section. If a judge issues such an order, the judge shall exclude from the room in which the testimony is to be taken every person except a person described in division (A)(2) of this section. The judge, at his discretion, may preside during the giving of the testimony by electronic means from outside the room in which it is being given, subject to the limitations set forth in division (A)(2) of this section. To the extent feasible, any person operating the televising equipment shall be hidden from the sight and hearing of the child victim giving the testimony, in a manner similar to that described in division (A)(2) of this section. The defendant shall be permitted to observe and hear the testimony of the child victim giving the testimony on a monitor and shall be provided with an electronic means of immediate communication with his attorney during the testimony, but shall be restricted to a location that is such that he cannot be seen or heard by the child victim giving the testimony, except on a monitor provided for that purpose. The child victim giving the testimony shall be provided with a monitor on which he can observe, during his testimony, the defendant.

(D) In any proceeding in the prosecution of any charge of a violation listed in division (A)(1) of this section in which an alleged victim was a child who was under eleven years of age when the complaint, indictment, or information was filed, whichever occurred earlier, the prosecution may file a motion with the judge requesting the judge to order the testimony of the child victim to be taken outside of the room in which the proceeding is being conducted and be recorded for showing in the room in which the proceeding is being conducted before the judge, the jury, if applicable, the defendant, and any other persons who would have been present during the testimony of the child victim had it been given in the room in which the proceeding is being conducted. Except for good cause shown, the prosecution shall file such a motion at least seven days before the date of the proceeding. The judge may issue such an order, upon motion of the prosecution, if the judge determines that the child victim is unavailable to testify in the room in which the proceeding is being conducted in the physical presence of the defendant, for one or more of the reasons set forth in division (E) of this section. If a judge issues such an order, the judge shall exclude from the room in which the testimony is to be taken every person except a person described in division (A)(2) of this section. To the extent feasible, any person operating the recording equipment shall be hidden from the sight and hearing of the child victim giving the testimony, in a manner similar to that described in division (A)(2) of this section. The defendant shall be permitted to observe and hear the testimony of the child victim who is giving the testimony on a monitor and shall be provided with an electronic means of immediate communication with his attorney during the testimony, but shall be restricted to a location that is such that he cannot be seen or heard by the child victim giving the testimony, except on a monitor provided for that purpose. The child victim giving the testimony shall be provided with a monitor on which he can observe, during his testimony, the defendant. No order for the taking of testimony by recording shall be issued under this division unless the provisions set forth in divisions (A)(2)(a), (b), (c), and (d) of this section apply to the recording of the testimony.

(E) For purposes of divisions (C) and (D) of this section, a judge may order the testimony of a child victim to be taken outside the room in which the proceeding is being conducted if the judge determines that the child victim is unavailable to testify in the room in the physical presence of the defendant due to one or more of the following:

(1) The persistent refusal of the child victim to testify despite judicial requests to do so;

(2) The inability of the child victim to communicate about the alleged violation because of extreme fear, failure of memory, or another similar reason;

(3) The substantial likelihood that the child victim will suffer serious emotional trauma from so testifying.

(F)(1) If a judge issues an order pursuant to division (C) or (D) of this section that requires the testimony of a child victim in a criminal proceeding to be taken outside of the room in which the proceeding is being conducted, the order shall specifically identify the child victim to whose testimony it applies, the order applies only during the testimony of the specified child victim, and the child victim giving the testimony shall not be required to testify at the proceeding other than in accordance with the order.

(2) A judge who makes any determination regarding the admissibility of a deposition under divisions (A) and (B) of this section, the videotaping of a deposition under division (A)(2) of this section, or the taking of testimony outside of the room in which a proceeding is being conducted under division (C) or (D) of this section, shall enter his determination and findings on the record in the proceeding.

(1986 H 108, eff. 10–14–86)

2907.42   Removal of buildings from mortgaged real estate—Repealed

(1972 H 511, eff. 1–1–74; 1953 H 1; GC 12476–2)

2907.43   Sale of unclaimed, stolen, or abandoned property in possession of officer—Repealed

(1972 H 511, eff. 1–1–74; 1953 H 1; GC 12465, 12466)

2907.44   Destroying trees—Repealed

(1972 H 511, eff. 1–1–74; 1953 H 1; GC 12490)

2907.45   Removal of serial numbers and brand names; penalties—Repealed

(1972 H 511, eff. 1–1–74; 125 v 535)

2907.46   Resale of apparatus from which brand name or serial number is removed, covered, altered, etc.; exception; penalty—Repealed

(1972 H 511, eff. 1–1–74; 125 v 535)

2907.47   Disposal of leased or rented personal property—Repealed

(1972 H 511, eff. 1–1–74; 131 v H 455)

2907.48   Shoplifting—Repealed

(1972 H 511, eff. 1–1–74; 1969 H 49)

CHAPTER 2909

ARSON AND RELATED OFFENSES

2909.01 Definitions

As used in sections 2909.01 to 2909.07 of the Revised Code:

(A) To "create a substantial risk of serious physical harm to any person" includes the creation of a substantial risk of serious physical harm to any emergency personnel.

(B) "Emergency personnel" means any of the following persons:

(1) A peace officer, as defined in section 2935.01 of the Revised Code;

(2) A member of a fire department or other firefighting agency of a municipal corporation, township, township fire district, joint fire district, other political subdivision, or combination of political subdivisions;

(3) A member of a private fire company, as defined in section 9.60 of the Revised Code, or a volunteer firefighter;

(4) A member of a joint ambulance district;

(5) An emergency medical technician-basic, emergency medical technician-intermediate, emergency medical technician-paramedic, ambulance operator, or other member of an emergency medical service that is owned or operated by a political subdivision or a private entity;

(6) The state fire marshal, an assistant state marshal, or an arson investigator of the office of the state fire marshal;

(7) A fire prevention officer of a political subdivision or an arson investigator or similar inspector of a political subdivision.

(C) "Occupied structure" means any house, building, outbuilding, watercraft, aircraft, railroad car, truck, trailer, tent, or other structure, vehicle, or shelter, or any portion thereof, to which any of the following applies:

(1) It is maintained as a permanent or temporary dwelling, even though it is temporarily unoccupied and whether or not any person is actually present.

(2) At the time, it is occupied as the permanent or temporary habitation of any person, whether or not any person is actually present.

(3) At the time, it is specially adapted for the overnight accommodation of any person, whether or not any person is actually present.

(4) At the time, any person is present or likely to be present in it.

(D) "Political subdivision" and "state" have the same meanings as in section 2744.01 of the Revised Code.

(1995 S 150, eff. 11–24–95; 1992 H 675, eff. 3–19–93; 1972 H 511)

ARSON

2909.02   Aggravated arson

(A) No person, by means of fire or explosion, shall knowingly:

(1) Create a substantial risk of serious physical harm to any person;

(2) Cause physical harm to any occupied structure;

(3) Create, through the offer or acceptance of an agreement for hire or other consideration, a substantial risk of serious physical harm to any person or of physical harm to any occupied structure.

(B) Whoever violates this section is guilty of aggravated arson, an aggravated felony of the first degree.

(1982 H 269, § 4, eff. 7–1–83; 1982 S 199; 1976 S 282; 1972 H 511)

2909.03   Arson

(A) No person, by means of fire or explosion, shall knowingly do any of the following:

(1) Cause, or create a substantial risk of, physical harm to any property of another without his consent;

(2) Cause, or create a substantial risk of, physical harm to any property of himself or another, with purpose to defraud;

(3) Cause, or create a substantial risk of, physical harm to the statehouse or a courthouse, school building, or other building or structure that is owned or controlled by the state, any political subdivision, or any department, agency, or instrumentality of the state or a political subdivision, and that is used for public purposes;

(4) Cause, or create a substantial risk of, physical harm, through the offer or the acceptance of an agreement for hire or other consideration, to any property of another without his consent or to any property of himself or another with purpose to defraud;

(5) Cause, or create a substantial risk of, physical harm to any park, preserve, wildlands, brush-covered land, cut-over land, forest, timberland, greenlands, woods, or similar real property that is owned or controlled by another person, the state, or a political subdivision without the consent of the other person, the state, or the political subdivision;

(6) With purpose to defraud, cause, or create a substantial risk of, physical harm to any park, preserve, wildlands, brush-covered land, cut-over land, forest, timberland, greenlands, woods, or similar real property that is owned or controlled by himself, another person, the state, or a political subdivision.

(B)(1) Whoever violates this section is guilty of arson.

(2) A violation of division (A)(1) of this section is one of the following:

(a) If the value of the property or the amount of the physical harm involved is less than three hundred dollars, a misdemeanor of the first degree;

(b) If the value of the property or the amount of the physical harm involved is three hundred dollars or more but less than five thousand dollars, a felony of the third degree;

(c) If the value of the property or the amount of the physical harm involved is five thousand dollars or more, a felony of the second degree.

(3) A violation of division (A)(2), (3), (5), or (6) of this section is one of the following:

(a) If the value of the property or the amount of physical harm involved is less than five thousand dollars, a felony of the third degree;

(b) If the value of the property or the amount of the physical harm involved is five thousand dollars or more, a felony of the second degree.

(4) A violation of division (A)(4) of this section is a felony of the second degree.

(1992 H 675, eff. 3–19–93; 1982 H 269, § 4, S 199; 1976 S 282; 1972 H 511)

DISRUPTION, VANDALISM, DAMAGING, AND ENDANGERING

2909.04   Disrupting public services

(A) No person, purposely by any means, or knowingly by damaging or tampering with any property, shall do any of the following:

(1) Interrupt or impair television, radio, telephone, telegraph, or other mass communications service, or police, fire, or other public service communications, or radar, loran, radio, or other electronic aids to air or marine navigation or communications, or amateur or citizens band radio communications being used for public service or emergency communications;

(2) Interrupt or impair public transportation, including without limitation school bus transportation, or water supply, gas, power, or other utility service to the public;

(3) Substantially impair the ability of law enforcement officers, firemen, or rescue personnel to respond to an emergency, or to protect and preserve any person or property from serious physical harm.

(B) Whoever violates this section is guilty of disrupting public services, a felony of the third degree.

(1972 H 511, eff. 1–1–74)

2909.05   Vandalism

(A) No person shall knowingly cause serious physical harm to an occupied structure or any of its contents.

(B)(1) No person shall knowingly cause serious physical harm to property that is owned or possessed by another, when either of the following applies:

(a) The property is used by its owner or possessor in his profession, business, trade, or occupation, and the value of the property or the amount of physical harm involved is three hundred dollars or more;

(b) Regardless of the value of the property or the amount of damage done, the property or its equivalent is necessary in order for its owner or possessor to engage in his profession, business, trade, or occupation.

(2) No person shall knowingly cause serious physical harm to property that is owned, leased, or controlled by a governmental entity. A governmental entity includes, but is not limited to, the state or a political subdivision of the state, a school district, the board of trustees of a public library or public university, or any other body corporate and politic responsible for governmental activities only in geographical areas smaller than that of the state.

(C) No person, without privilege to do so, shall knowingly cause serious physical harm to any tomb, monument, gravestone, or other similar structure that is used as a memorial for the dead; to any fence, railing, curb, or other property that is used to protect, enclose, or ornament any place of burial; or to a place of burial. For the purposes of this division, "serious physical harm" means that the amount of physical harm involved is three hundred dollars or more in value.

(D) No person, without privilege to do so, shall knowingly cause physical harm to a place of burial by breaking and entering into a tomb, crypt, casket, or other structure that is used as a memorial for the dead or as an enclosure for the dead.

(E) Whoever violates this section is guilty of vandalism. If the value of the property or the amount of physical harm involved is less than five thousand dollars, vandalism is a felony of the fourth degree that is punishable by a fine of up to two thousand five hundred dollars in addition to the penalties specified for a felony of the fourth degree in section 2929.11 of the Revised Code. If the value of the property or the amount of physical harm involved is five thousand dollars or more but less than one hundred thousand dollars, vandalism is a felony of the third degree. If the value of the property or the amount of physical harm involved is one hundred thousand dollars or more, vandalism is a felony of the second degree.

(1992 H 675, eff. 3–19–93; 1986 S 316; 1982 H 269, S 199; 1980 H 618; 1978 H 741; 1972 H 511)

2909.06 Criminal damaging or endangering

(A) No person shall cause, or create a substantial risk of physical harm to any property of another without his consent:

(1) Knowingly, by any means;

(2) Recklessly, by means of fire, explosion, flood, poison gas, poison, radioactive material, caustic or corrosive material, or other inherently dangerous agency or substance.

(B) Whoever violates this section is guilty of criminal damaging or endangering, a misdemeanor of the second degree. If violation of this section creates a risk of physical harm to any person, criminal damaging or endangering is a misdemeanor of the first degree. If the property involved in a violation of this section is an aircraft, an aircraft engine, propeller, appliance, spare part, or any other equipment or implement used or intended to be used in the operation of an aircraft and if the violation creates a risk of physical harm to any person or if the property involved in a violation of this section is an occupied aircraft, criminal damaging or endangering is a felony of the fourth degree.

(1984 H 570, eff. 3–28–85; 1972 H 511)

2909.07 Criminal mischief; safety device defined

(A) No person shall:

(1) Without privilege to do so, knowingly move, deface, damage, destroy, or otherwise improperly tamper with the property of another;

(2) With purpose to interfere with the use or enjoyment of property of another, employ a tear gas device, stink bomb, smoke generator, or other device releasing a substance which is harmful or offensive to persons exposed, or which tends to cause public alarm;

(3) Without privilege to do so, knowingly move, deface, damage, destroy, or otherwise improperly tamper with a bench mark, triangulation station, boundary marker, or other survey station, monument, or marker;

(4) Without privilege to do so, knowingly move, deface, damage, destroy, or otherwise improperly tamper with any safety device, the property of another, or the property of the offender when required or placed for the safety of others, so as to destroy or diminish its effectiveness or availability for its intended purpose;

(5) With purpose to interfere with the use or enjoyment of the property of another, set a fire on the land of another or place personal property that has been set on fire on the land of another, which fire or personal property is outside and apart from any building, other structure, or personal property that is on that land.

(B) As used in this section, "safety device" means any fire extinguisher, fire hose, or fire axe, or any fire escape, emergency exit, or emergency escape equipment, or any life line, life-saving ring, life preserver, or life boat or raft, or any alarm, light, flare, signal, sign, or notice intended to warn of danger or emergency, or intended for other safety purposes, or any guard railing or safety barricade, or any traffic sign or signal, or any railroad grade crossing sign, signal, or gate, or any first aid or survival equipment, or any other device, apparatus, or equipment intended for protecting or preserving the safety of persons or property.

(C) Whoever violates this section is guilty of criminal mischief, a misdemeanor of the third degree. If violation of this section creates a risk of physical harm to any person, criminal mischief is a misdemeanor of the first degree. If the property involved in violation of this section is an aircraft, an aircraft engine, propeller, appliance, spare part, fuel, lubricant, hydraulic fluid, any other equipment, implement, or material used or intended to be used in the operation of an aircraft, or any cargo carried or intended to be carried in an aircraft and if the violation creates a risk of physical harm to any person or if the property involved in a violation of this section is an occupied aircraft, criminal mischief is a felony of the fourth degree.

(1986 S 316, eff. 3–19–87; 1984 H 570; 1973 H 89; 1972 H 511)

2909.08 Endangering aircraft or airport operations

(A) As used in this section:

(1) "Air gun" means a hand pistol or rifle that propels its projectile by means of releasing compressed air, carbon dioxide, or other gas.

(2) "Firearm" has the same meaning as in section 2923.11 of the Revised Code.

(3) "Spring–operated gun" means a hand pistol or rifle that propels a projectile not less than four or more than five millimeters in diameter by means of a spring.

(4) "Airport operational surface" means any surface of land or water that is developed, posted, or marked so as to give an observer reasonable notice that the surface is designed and developed for the purpose of storing, parking, taxiing, or operating aircraft, or any surface of land or water that is actually being used for any of those purposes.

(B) No person shall do either of the following:

(1) Knowingly throw an object at, or drop an object upon, any moving aircraft;

(2) Knowingly shoot with a bow and arrow, or knowingly discharge a firearm, air gun, or spring-operated gun, at or toward any aircraft.

(C) No person shall knowingly or recklessly shoot with a bow and arrow, or shall knowingly or recklessly discharge a firearm, air gun, or spring-operated gun, upon or over any airport operational surface. This division does not apply to the following:

(1) An officer, agent, or employee of this or any other state or the United States, or a law enforcement officer, authorized to discharge firearms and acting within the scope of his duties;

(2) A person who, with the consent of the owner or operator of the airport operational surface or the authorized agent of either, is lawfully engaged in any hunting or sporting activity or is otherwise lawfully discharging a firearm.

(D) Whoever violates division (B) of this section is guilty of endangering aircraft, a misdemeanor of the first degree. If the violation creates a risk of physical harm to any person or if the aircraft that is the subject of the violation is occupied, endangering aircraft is a felony of the fourth degree.

(E) Whoever violates division (C) of this section is guilty of endangering airport operations, a misdemeanor of the second degree. If the violation creates a risk of physical harm to any person, endangering airport operations is a felony of the fourth degree. Whoever violates division (C) of this section while hunting shall additionally have his hunting license or permit suspended or revoked pursuant to section 1533.68 of the Revised Code.

(F) Any bow and arrow, air gun, spring-operated gun, or firearm that has been used in a felony violation of this section, shall be seized or forfeited, and shall be disposed of pursuant to section 2933.41 of the Revised Code.

(1984 H 570, eff. 3–28–85)

2909.09 Injuring and committing nuisances in buildings—Repealed

(1972 H 511, eff. 1–1–74; 131 v S 190; 1953 H 1; GC 12487)

2909.10 Destroying books or paintings—Repealed

(1972 H 511, eff. 1–1–74; 1953 H 1; GC 12488)

2909.11 Determining property value or amount of physical harm

(A) When a person is charged with a violation of division (A)(1), (2), (3), (5), or (6) of section 2909.03 or division (B)(1)(a) or (C) of section 2909.05 of the Revised Code, involving property value or amount of physical harm of three hundred dollars or more, the jury or court trying the accused shall determine the value of the property or amount of physical harm and, if a guilty verdict is returned, shall return the finding as part of the verdict. In any such case, it is unnecessary to find or return the exact value or amount of physical harm, and it is sufficient if the finding and return are to the effect that the value or amount of physical harm was either:

(1) In one of the following categories if the finding and return relate to a violation of division (A)(1) of section 2909.03 of the Revised Code:

(a) Five thousand dollars or more;

(b) Three hundred dollars or more but less than five thousand dollars;

(c) Less than three hundred dollars.

(2) In one of the following categories if the finding and return relate to a violation of division (A)(2), (3), (5), or (6) of section 2909.03 of the Revised Code:

(a) Five thousand dollars or more;

(b) Less than five thousand dollars.

(3) In one of the following categories if the finding and return relate to a violation of division (B)(1)(a) or (C) of section 2909.05 of the Revised Code:

(a) One hundred thousand dollars or more;

(b) Five thousand dollars or more but less than one hundred thousand dollars;

(c) Three hundred dollars or more but less than five thousand dollars;

(d) Less than three hundred dollars.

(B) The following criteria shall be used in determining the value of property or amount of physical harm involved in a violation of division (A)(1), (2), (3), (5), or (6) of section 2909.03 or division (B)(1)(a) or (C) of section 2909.05 of the Revised Code:

(1) If the property is an heirloom, memento, collector's item, antique, museum piece, manuscript, document, record, or other thing that is either irreplaceable or is replaceable only on the expenditure of substantial time, effort, or money, the value of the property or the amount of physical harm involved is the amount that would compensate the owner for its loss.

(2) If the property is not covered under division (B)(1) of this section, and the physical harm is such that the property can be restored substantially to its former condition, the amount of physical harm involved is the reasonable cost of restoring the property.

(3) If the property is not covered under division (B)(1) of this section, and the physical harm is such that the property cannot be restored substantially to its former condition, the value of the property, in the case of personal property, is the cost of replacing the property with new property of like kind and quality, and, in the case of real property or real property fixtures, is the difference in the fair market value of the property immediately before and immediately after the offense.

(C) As used in this section, "fair market value" has the same meaning as in section 2913.61 of the Revised Code.

(D) Prima–facie evidence of the value of property, as provided in division (E) of section 2913.61 of the Revised Code, may be used to establish the value of property pursuant to this section.

(1992 H 675, eff. 3–19–93; 1982 H 269, S 199; 1980 H 618; 1978 H 741; 1972 H 511)

2909.12 Throwing or shooting at train, motor vehicle or vessel—Repealed

(1972 H 511, eff. 1–1–74; 131 v H 146; 126 v 575; 1953 H 1; GC 12497)

2909.13   Posting bills on buildings without consent of owner—Repealed

(1972 H 511, eff. 1–1–74; 1953 H 1; GC 12492)

2909.14   Breaking open pounds—Repealed

(1972 H 511, eff. 1–1–74; 1953 H 1; GC 12493)

2909.15   Taking bicycle with intent to injure or use—Repealed

(1972 H 511, eff. 1–1–74; 1953 H 1; GC 12514)

2909.16   Altering, defacing, or removing number or name on bicycle—Repealed

(1972 H 511, eff. 1–1–74; 1953 H 1; GC 12515)

2909.17   Injuring, removing, or destroying part of bicycle—Repealed

(1972 H 511, eff. 1–1–74; 1953 H 1; GC 12516)

2909.18   Disposition of fines—Repealed

(1972 H 511, eff. 1–1–74; 1953 H 1; GC 12518)

2909.19   Entering ground of agricultural association or molesting property—Repealed

(1972 H 511, eff. 1–1–74; 1953 H 1; GC 12519)

2909.20   Prosecutions—Repealed

(1972 H 511, eff. 1–1–74; 129 v 582; 1953 H 1; GC 12520)

2909.21   Trespassing upon lands or premises of another—Repealed

(1972 H 511, eff. 1–1–74; 1953 H 1; GC 12522)

2909.22   Written consent of owner or presence required—Repealed

(1972 H 511, eff. 1–1–74; 1953 H 1; GC 12530)

2909.23   Violating rules of boards of county commissioners and township trustees as to roads—Repealed

(1972 H 511, eff. 1–1–74; 1953 H 1; GC 12532)

2909.24   Destruction of public utility facilities prohibited—Repealed

(1972 H 511, eff. 1–1–74; 127 v 810)

2909.25   Dumping on premises of another—Repealed

(1972 H 511, eff. 1–1–74; 128 v 467)

2909.26   Trespass upon damaged premises—Repealed

(1972 H 511, eff. 1–1–74; 132 v H 996)

CHAPTER 2911

ROBBERY, BURGLARY, AND TRESPASS

ROBBERY

BURGLARY

TRESPASS

SAFECRACKING

ROBBERY

2911.01   Aggravated robbery

(A) No person, in attempting or committing a theft offense, as defined in section 2913.01 of the Revised Code, or in fleeing immediately after such attempt or offense, shall do either of the following:

(1) Have a deadly weapon or dangerous ordnance, as defined in section 2923.11 of the Revised Code, on or about his person or under his control;

(2) Inflict, or attempt to inflict serious physical harm on another.

(B) Whoever violates this section is guilty of aggravated robbery, an aggravated felony of the first degree.

(1983 S 210, eff. 7–1–83; 1982 H 269, § 4, S 199; 1972 H 511)

2911.02   Robbery

(A) No person, in attempting or committing a theft offense, as defined in section 2913.01 of the Revised Code, or in fleeing immediately after such attempt or offense, shall use or threaten the immediate use of force against another.

(B) Whoever violates this section is guilty of robbery, an aggravated felony of the second degree.

(1982 H 269, § 4, eff. 7–1–83; 1982 S 199; 1972 H 511)

2911.03   False statements—Repealed

(1972 H 511, eff. 1–1–74; 126 v 575; 1953 H 1; GC 13105–1)

2911.04   Definition of "insolvent"—Repealed

(1972 H 511, eff. 1–1–74; 1953 H 1; GC 13108–1)

2911.05   Insolvent broker receiving money or securities—Repealed

(1972 H 511, eff. 1–1–74; 126 v 575; 1953 H 1; GC 13108)

2911.06   Disposing of securities without consent of owner—Repealed

(1972 H 511, eff. 1–1–74; 126 v 575; 1953 H 1; GC 13108–2)

2911.07   Reporting false transaction—Repealed

(1972 H 511, eff. 1–1–74; 1953 H 1; GC 13108–3)

2911.08   False statements concerning value of stocks, bonds, or notes—Repealed

(1972 H 511, eff. 1–1–74; 126 v 575; 1953 H 1; GC 13108–4)

2911.09   Delivering a false note of sale—Repealed

(1972 H 511, eff. 1–1–74; 1953 H 1; GC 13108–5)

2911.10   Aiders and abettors—Repealed

(1972 H 511, eff. 1–1–74; 1953 H 1; GC 13108–6)

BURGLARY

2911.11   Aggravated burglary

(A) No person, by force, stealth, or deception, shall trespass in an occupied structure, as defined in section 2909.01 of the Revised Code, or in a separately secured or separately

73

occupied portion thereof, with purpose to commit therein any theft offense, as defined in section 2913.01 of the Revised Code, or any felony, when any of the following apply:

(1) The offender inflicts, or attempts or threatens to inflict physical harm on another;

(2) The offender has a deadly weapon or dangerous ordnance, as defined in section 2923.11 of the Revised Code, on or about his person or under his control;

(3) The occupied structure involved is the permanent or temporary habitation of any person, in which at the time any person is present or likely to be present.

(B) Whoever violates this section is guilty of aggravated burglary, an aggravated felony of the first degree.

(1983 S 210, eff. 7–1–83; 1982 H 269, § 4, S 199; 1972 H 511)

2911.111   Fraudulent check, draft or order on bank or depository—Repealed

(1972 H 511, eff. 1–1–74; 132 v S 97)

2911.12   Burglary

(A) No person, by force, stealth, or deception, shall do any of the following:

(1) Trespass in an occupied structure or in a separately secured or separately occupied portion thereof, with purpose to commit therein any theft offense or any felony;

(2) Trespass in a permanent or temporary habitation of any person when any person is present or likely to be present, with purpose to commit in the habitation any misdemeanor that is not a theft offense;

(3) Trespass in a permanent or temporary habitation of any person when any person is present or likely to be present.

(B) As used in this section:

(1) "Occupied structure" has the same meaning as in section 2909.01 of the Revised Code.

(2) "Theft offense" has the same meaning as in section 2913.01 of the Revised Code.

(C) Whoever violates this section is guilty of burglary. A violation of division (A)(1) of this section is an aggravated felony of the second degree. A violation of division (A)(2) of this section is a felony of the third degree. A violation of division (A)(3) of this section is a felony of the fourth degree.

(1990 H 837, eff. 7–3–90; 1982 H 269, § 4, S 199; 1972 H 511)

2911.13   Breaking and entering

(A) No person by force, stealth, or deception, shall trespass in an unoccupied structure, with purpose to commit therein any theft offense as defined in section 2913.01 of the Revised Code, or any felony.

(B) No person shall trespass on the land or premises of another, with purpose to commit a felony.

(C) Whoever violates this section is guilty of breaking and entering, a felony of the fourth degree.

(1972 H 511, eff. 1–1–74)

2911.131   False motor vehicle repair estimates and fraudulent charges—Repealed

(1972 H 511, eff. 1–1–74; 1969 H 192)

2911.14   Defrauding innkeeper—Repealed

(1972 H 511, eff. 1–1–74; 1953 H 1; GC 13131)

2911.15   Frauds of owners on consignees—Repealed

(1972 H 511, eff. 1–1–74; 1953 H 1; GC 13143)

2911.16 Practicing astrology, fortune telling, clairvoyancy, or palmistry—Repealed

(1972 H 511, eff. 1–1–74; 1953 H 1; GC 13145)

2911.17 Performing dramatic composition without consent of owner—Repealed

(1972 H 511, eff. 1–1–74; 1953 H 1; GC 13148)

TRESPASS

2911.18 Taking or selling note for patent right—Repealed

(129 v 13, eff. 7–1–62; 1953 H 1; GC 13149)

2911.19 Misrepresentation by married man—Repealed

(1972 H 511, eff. 1–1–74; 1953 H 1; GC 13146)

2911.20 Furnishing false pedigree—Repealed

(1972 H 511, eff. 1–1–74; GC 13158)

2911.21 Criminal trespass

(A) No person, without privilege to do so, shall do any of the following:

(1) Knowingly enter or remain on the land or premises of another;

(2) Knowingly enter or remain on the land or premises of another, the use of which is lawfully restricted to certain persons, purposes, modes, or hours, when the offender knows he is in violation of any such restriction or is reckless in that regard;

(3) Recklessly enter or remain on the land or premises of another, as to which notice against unauthorized access or presence is given by actual communication to the offender, or in a manner prescribed by law, or by posting in a manner reasonably calculated to come to the attention of potential intruders, or by fencing or other enclosure manifestly designed to restrict access;

(4) Being on the land or premises of another, negligently fail or refuse to leave upon being notified to do so by the owner or occupant, or the agent or servant of either.

(B) It is no defense to a charge under this section that the land or premises involved was owned, controlled, or in custody of a public agency.

(C) It is no defense to a charge under this section that the offender was authorized to enter or remain on the land or premises involved, when such authorization was secured by deception.

(D) Whoever violates this section is guilty of criminal trespass, a misdemeanor of the fourth degree.

(E) As used in this section, "land or premises" includes any land, building, structure, or place belonging to, controlled by, or in custody of another, and any separate enclosure or room, or portion thereof.

(1972 H 511, eff. 1–1–74)

2911.211 Aggravated trespass

(A) No person shall enter or remain on the land or premises of another with purpose to commit on that land or those premises a misdemeanor, the elements of which involve causing physical harm to another person or causing another person to believe that the offender will cause physical harm to him.

(B) Whoever violates this section is guilty of aggravated trespass, a misdemeanor of the first degree.

(1992 H 536, eff. 11–5–92)

2911.22 Unlawful entries relative to milk or butterfat or purebred cattle—Repealed

(1972 H 511, eff. 1–1–74; 1953 H 1; GC 13162–1)

2911.23 Fraud in sale of grain or seed—Repealed

(1972 H 511, eff. 1–1–74; 1953 H 1; GC 13129)

2911.24 Placing in packages substance other than tobacco—Repealed

(1972 H 511, eff. 1–1–74; 1953 H 1; GC 13147)

2911.25 Unlawful sale of certain kinds of wool—Repealed

(1972 H 511, eff. 1–1–74; 1953 H 1; GC 13114)

2911.26 Wearing insignia of civic or religious society—Repealed

(1972 H 511, eff. 1–1–74; 1953 H 1; GC 13164)

2911.27 Display of emblem of certain orders, societies and organizations—Repealed

(1972 H 511, eff. 1–1–74; 131 v H 241; 1953 H 1; GC 13163)

2911.28 Wearing or displaying badge of United Veterans of Republic by nonmember prohibited—Repealed

(1972 H 511, eff. 1–1–74; 1953 H 1; GC 13163–1)

2911.29 Unlawful wearing of badge—Repealed

(1972 H 511, eff. 1–1–74; 130 v Pt 2, H 5; 129 v 582; 1953 H 1; GC 14867–21, 14867–22)

2911.30 Publishing fraudulent prospectus—Repealed

(1972 H 511, eff. 1–1–74; 1953 H 1; GC 13175)

SAFECRACKING

2911.31 Safecracking

(A) No person, with purpose to commit an offense, shall knowingly enter, force an entrance into, or tamper with any vault, safe, or strongbox.

(B) Whoever violates this section is guilty of safecracking, a felony of the third degree.

(1972 H 511, eff. 1–1–74)

2911.32 Tampering with coin machines

(A) No person, with purpose to commit theft or to defraud, shall knowingly enter, force an entrance into, tamper with, or insert any part of an instrument into any coin machine.

(B) Whoever violates this section is guilty of tampering with coin machines, a misdemeanor of the first degree. If the offender has previously been convicted of a violation of this section or of any theft offense as defined in section 2913.01 of the Revised Code, tampering with coin machines is a felony of the fourth degree.

(1972 H 511, eff. 1–1–74)

2911.33 Adulteration of materials used in the manufacture of crockery ware—Repealed

(1972 H 511, eff. 1–1–74; 1953 H 1; GC 13152)

2911.34 Sending letters to obtain money—Repealed

(1972 H 511, eff. 1–1–74; 1953 H 1; GC 13144)

2911.35 Fraudulent use of false coin or slug—Repealed

(1972 H 511, eff. 1–1–74; 1953 H 1; GC 13183)

2911.36 Possession of false coin or slug—Repealed

(1972 H 511, eff. 1–1–74; 1953 H 1; GC 13184)

2911.37   Tokens intended for unlawful use—Repealed

(1972 H 511, eff. 1–1–74; 1953 H 1; GC 13184–1)

2911.38   Sale of rebuilt storage batteries—Repealed

(1972 H 511, eff. 1–1–74; 1953 H 1; GC 13187)

2911.39   Lease or rental of batteries—Repealed

(1972 H 511, eff. 1–1–74; 1953 H 1; GC 13187–1)

2911.40   Use of terms "Army" or "Navy" by stores prohibited—Repealed

(1972 H 511, eff. 1–1–74; 1953 H 1; GC 13194–1)

2911.41   Fraudulent advertising—Repealed

(1972 H 511, eff. 1–1–74; 129 v 1305; 127 v 461; 1953 H 1; GC 13193–2)

2911.42   Prosecuting attorney may bring action for fraudulent advertising—Repealed

(1972 H 511, eff. 1–1–74; 1953 H 1; GC 13193–3)

2911.43   False statement in bill of lading or warehouse receipt—Repealed

(1972 H 511, eff. 1–1–74; 129 v 13)

2911.44   Control of goods—Repealed

(1972 H 511, eff. 1–1–74; 129 v 13)

2911.45   Duplicate or additional bill of lading or warehouse receipt—Repealed

(1972 H 511, eff. 1–1–74; 129 v 13)

2911.46   Deposit of goods without title—Repealed

(1972 H 511, eff. 1–1–74; 129 v 13)

2911.47   Falsifying receipt of goods—Repealed

(1972 H 511, eff. 1–1–74; 129 v 13)

2911.48   Fictitious warehouse receipt—Repealed

(1972 H 511, eff. 1–1–74; 129 v 13)

2911.49   Removal of property from state—Repealed

(1972 H 511, eff. 1–1–74; 129 v 13)

2911.71   Definitions—Repealed

(1972 H 511, eff. 1–1–74; 129 v 1023)

2911.72   Misrepresentation of picture tubes as being new—Repealed

(1972 H 511, eff. 1–1–74; 129 v 1023)

2911.73   Medical fraud and misrepresentation; exemptions—Repealed

(1972 H 511, eff. 1–1–74; 1969 S 6)

CHAPTER 2913

THEFT AND FRAUD

DEFINITIONS

DEFINITIONS

2913.01   Definitions

As used in this chapter:

(A) "Deception" means knowingly deceiving another or causing another to be deceived by any false or misleading representation, by withholding information, by preventing another from acquiring information, or by any other conduct, act, or omission that creates, confirms, or perpetuates a false impression in another, including a false impression as to law, value, state of mind, or other objective or subjective fact.

78

(B) "Defraud" means to knowingly obtain, by deception, some benefit for oneself or another, or to knowingly cause, by deception, some detriment to another.

(C) "Deprive" means to:

(1) Withhold property of another permanently, or for such period as to appropriate a substantial portion of its value or use, or with purpose to restore it only upon payment of a reward or other consideration;

(2) Dispose of property so as to make it unlikely that the owner will recover it;

(3) Accept, use, or appropriate money, property, or services, with purpose not to give proper consideration in return for the money, property, or services, and without reasonable justification or excuse for not giving proper consideration.

(D) "Owner" means any person, other than the actor, who is the owner of, or who has possession or control of, or any license or interest in property or services, even though the ownership, possession, control, license, or interest is unlawful.

(E) "Services" include labor, personal services, professional services, public utility services, common carrier services, and food, drink, transportation, entertainment, and cable television services.

(F) "Writing" means any computer software, document, letter, memorandum, note, paper, plate, data, film, or other thing having in or upon it any written, typewritten, or printed matter, and also means any token, stamp, seal, credit card, badge, trademark, label, or other symbol of value, right, privilege, license, or identification.

(G) "Forge" means to fabricate or create, in whole or in part and by any means, any spurious writing, or to make, execute, alter, complete, reproduce, or otherwise purport to authenticate any writing, when the writing in fact is not authenticated by that conduct.

(H) "Utter" means to issue, publish, transfer, use, put or send into circulation, deliver, or display.

(I) "Coin machine" means any mechanical or electronic device designed to do both of the following:

(1) Receive a coin or bill, or token made for that purpose;

(2) In return for the insertion or deposit of a coin, bill, or token, automatically dispense property, provide a service, or grant a license.

(J) "Slug" means an object that, by virtue of its size, shape, composition, or other quality, is capable of being inserted or deposited in a coin machine as an improper substitute for a genuine coin, bill, or token made for that purpose.

(K) "Theft offense" means any of the following:

(1) A violation of section 2911.01, 2911.02, 2911.11, 2911.12, 2911.13, 2911.31, 2911.32, 2913.02, 2913.03, 2913.04, 2913.11, 2913.21, 2913.31, 2913.32, 2913.33, 2913.40, 2913.41, 2913.42, 2913.43, 2913.44, 2913.45, 2913.47, former section 2913.47 or 2913.48, or section 2913.51, 2913.81, 2915.05, 2915.06, or 2921.41 of the Revised Code;

(2) A violation of an existing or former municipal ordinance or law of this or any other state, or of the United States, substantially equivalent to any section listed in division (K)(1) of this section;

(3) An offense under an existing or former municipal ordinance or law of this or any other state, or of the United States, involving robbery, burglary, breaking and entering, theft, embezzlement, wrongful conversion, forgery, counterfeiting, deceit, or fraud;

(4) A conspiracy or attempt to commit, or complicity in committing any offense under division (K)(1), (2), or (3) of this section.

(L) "Computer services" includes, but is not limited to, the use of a computer system, computer network, computer program, data that is prepared for computer use, or data that is contained within a computer system or computer network.

(M) "Computer" means an electronic device that performs logical, arithmetic, and memory functions by the manipulation of electronic or magnetic impulses. "Computer" includes, but is not limited to, all input, output, processing, storage, computer program, or communication facilities that are connected, or related, in a computer system or network to such an electronic device.

(N) "Computer system" means a computer and related devices, whether connected or unconnected, including, but not limited to, data input, output, and storage devices, data communications links, and computer programs and data that make the system capable of performing specified special purpose data processing tasks.

(O) "Computer network" means a set of related and remotely connected computers and communication facilities that includes more than one computer system that has the capability to transmit among the connected computers and communication facilities through the use of computer facilities.

(P) "Computer program" means an ordered set of data representing coded instructions or statements that, when executed by a computer, cause the computer to process data.

(Q) "Computer software" means computer programs, procedures, and other documentation associated with the operation of a computer system.

(R) "Data" means a representation of information, knowledge, facts, concepts, or instructions that are being or have been prepared in a formalized manner and that are intended for use in a computer system or computer network. For purposes of section 2913.47 of the Revised Code, "data" has the additional meaning set forth in division (A) of that section.

(S) "Cable television service" means any services provided by or through the facilities of any cable television system or other similar closed circuit coaxial cable communications system, or any microwave or similar transmission service used in connection with any cable television system or other similar closed circuit coaxial cable communications system.

(T) "Gain access" means to approach, instruct, communicate with, store data in, retrieve data from, or otherwise make use of any resources of a computer, computer system, or computer network.

(U) "Credit card" includes, but is not limited to, a card, code, device, or other means of access to a customer's account for the purpose of obtaining money, property, labor, or services on credit, or for initiating an electronic fund transfer at a point-of-sale terminal, an automated teller machine, or a cash dispensing machine.

(V) "Electronic fund transfer" has the same meaning as in 92 Stat. 3728, 15 U.S.C.A. 1693a, as amended.

(1990 H 347, eff. 7–18–90; 1987 H 182; 1986 H 49, H 340; 1984 S 183; 1983 H 97; 1982 H 437; 1972 H 511)

THEFT

2913.02   Theft; aggravated theft

(A) No person, with purpose to deprive the owner of property or services, shall knowingly obtain or exert control over either the property or services in any of the following ways:

(1) Without the consent of the owner or person authorized to give consent;

(2) Beyond the scope of the express or implied consent of the owner or person authorized to give consent;

(3) By deception;

(4) By threat.

(B) Whoever violates this section is guilty of theft. If the value of the property or services stolen is less than three hundred dollars, a violation of this section is petty theft, a misdemeanor of the first degree. If the value of the property or services stolen is three hundred dollars or more and is less than five thousand dollars, if the property stolen is any of the property listed in section 2913.71 of the Revised Code, or if the offender previously has been convicted of a theft offense, a violation of this section is theft, a felony of the fourth degree. If the value of the property or services stolen is five thousand dollars or more and is less than one hundred thousand dollars, if the property stolen is a firearm or dangerous ordnance, as defined in section 2923.11 of the Revised Code, or if the offender previously has been convicted of two or more theft offenses, a violation of this section is grand theft, a felony of the third degree. If the property stolen is a motor vehicle, as defined in section 4501.01 of the Revised Code, a violation of this section is grand theft of a motor vehicle, a felony of the third degree. If the value of the property or services stolen is one hundred thousand dollars or more, a violation of this section is aggravated theft, a felony of the second degree. If the property stolen is any dangerous drug, as defined in section 4729.02 of the Revised Code, a violation of this section is theft of drugs, a felony of the fourth degree, or, if the offender previously has been convicted of a felony drug abuse offense, as defined in section 2925.01 of the Revised Code, a felony of the third degree.

(1995 H 4, eff. 11–9–95; 1990 S 258, eff. 11–20–90; 1990 H 347; 1986 H 49; 1984 H 632; 1982 H 269, § 4, S 199; 1980 S 191; 1972 H 511)

2913.03 Unauthorized use of a vehicle

(A) No person shall knowingly use or operate an aircraft, motor vehicle, motorcycle, motorboat, or other motor-propelled vehicle without the consent of the owner or person authorized to give consent.

(B) No person shall knowingly use or operate an aircraft, motor vehicle, motorboat, or other motor-propelled vehicle without the consent of the owner or person authorized to give consent, and either remove it from this state, or keep possession of it for more than forty-eight hours.

(C) The following are affirmative defenses to a charge under this section:

(1) At the time of the alleged offense, the actor, though mistaken, reasonably believed that he was authorized to use or operate the property.

(2) At the time of the alleged offense, the actor reasonably believed that the owner or person empowered to give consent would authorize the actor to use or operate the property.

(D) Whoever violates this section is guilty of unauthorized use of a vehicle. Violation of division (A) of this section is a misdemeanor of the first degree. If the offender has previously been convicted of a violation of this section or of any other theft offense, violation of division (A) of this section is a felony of the fourth degree. Violation of division (B) of this section is a felony of the fourth degree.

(1972 H 511, eff. 1–1–74)

2913.04 Unauthorized use of property; unauthorized access to computer systems

(A) No person shall knowingly use or operate the property of another without the consent of the owner or person authorized to give consent.

(B) No person shall knowingly gain access to, attempt to gain access to, or cause access to be gained to any computer, computer system, or computer network without the consent of, or beyond the scope of the express or implied consent of, the owner of the computer, computer system, or computer network or other person authorized to give consent by the owner.

(C) The affirmative defenses contained in division (C) of section 2913.03 of the Revised Code are affirmative defenses to a charge under this section.

(D) Whoever violates this section is guilty of unauthorized use of property. If the offense involves a violation of division (A) of this section and does not involve any computer, computer system, computer network, computer software, or data, unauthorized use of property is a misdemeanor of the fourth degree. If the offense involves a violation of division (A) of this section and involves any computer, computer system, computer network, computer software, or data or if the offense involves a violation of division (B) of this section, unauthorized use of property is whichever of the following is applicable:

(1) If division (D)(2) or (3) of this section does not apply, a felony of the fourth degree;

(2) If division (D)(3) of this section does not apply and the offender previously has been convicted of a theft offense, a felony of the third degree;

(3) If the offense is committed for the purpose of devising or executing a scheme to defraud or to obtain property or services and the value of the property or services or the loss to the victim is one hundred thousand dollars or more, a felony of the second degree.

(1986 H 49, eff. 6–26–86; 1972 H 511)

2913.05 Obliterating or concealing cancellation of a token, ticket, transfer, or check—Repealed

(1972 H 511, eff. 1–1–74; 129 v 1594; 1953 H 1; GC 13087)

2913.06 Altering public documents—Repealed

(1972 H 511, eff. 1–1–74; 127 v 1039; 1953 H 1; GC 13088)

2913.07 Forging brand, stamp, label, or trade-mark—Repealed

(1972 H 511, eff. 1–1–74; 1953 H 1; GC 13089)

2913.08 Possessing label for fraudulent use—Repealed

(1972 H 511, eff. 1–1–74; 1953 H 1; GC 13091)

2913.09 Counterfeiting coins—Repealed

(1972 H 511, eff. 1–1–74; 1953 H 1; GC 13094)

2913.10 Counterfeiting issues of the United States—Repealed

(1972 H 511, eff. 1–1–74; 126 v 575; 1953 H 1; GC 13096)

PASSING BAD CHECKS

2913.11 Passing bad checks

(A) No person, with purpose to defraud, shall issue or transfer or cause to be issued or transferred a check or other negotiable instrument, knowing that it will be dishonored.

(B) For purposes of this section, a person who issues or transfers a check or other negotiable instrument is presumed to know that it will be dishonored, if either of the following occurs:

(1) The drawer had no account with the drawee at the time of issue or the stated date, whichever is later;

(2) The check or other negotiable instrument was properly refused payment for insufficient funds upon presentment within thirty days after issue or the stated date, whichever is later, and the liability of the drawer, indorser, or any party who may be liable thereon is not discharged by payment or satisfaction within ten days after receiving notice of dishonor.

(C) For purposes of this section, a person who issues or transfers a check, bill of exchange, or other draft is presumed to have the purpose to defraud if the drawer fails to comply with section 1349.16 of the Revised Code by doing any of the following when opening a checking account intended for personal, family, or household purposes at a financial institution:

(1) Falsely stating that he has not been issued a valid driver's or commercial driver's license or identification card issued under section 4507.50 of the Revised Code;

(2) Furnishing such license or card, or another identification document that contains false information;

(3) Making a false statement with respect to his current address or any additional relevant information reasonably required by the financial institution.

(D) Whoever violates this section is guilty of passing bad checks. If the check or other negotiable instrument is for the payment of less than three hundred dollars, passing bad checks is a misdemeanor of the first degree. If the check or other negotiable instrument is for payment of three hundred dollars or more and is for the payment of less than five thousand dollars, or if the offender previously has been convicted of a theft offense, passing bad checks is a felony of the fourth degree. If the check or other negotiable instrument is for the payment of five thousand dollars or more and is for the payment of less than one hundred thousand dollars, or if the offender previously has been convicted of two or more theft offenses, passing bad checks is a felony of the third degree. If the check or other negotiable instrument is for the payment of one hundred thousand dollars or more, passing bad checks is a felony of the second degree.

(1990 H 711, eff. 10–16–90; 1986 H 49; 1982 H 269, S 199; 1972 H 511)

2913.12 Counterfeiting county certificates—Repealed

(1972 H 511, eff. 1–1–74; 1953 H 1; GC 13097–2)

2913.13 Illegal printing from genuine plates—Repealed

(1972 H 511, eff. 1–1–74; 126 v 575; 1953 H 1; GC 13098)

2913.14 Engraving or keeping plate for counterfeiting or altering bank bills—Repealed

(1972 H 511, eff. 1–1–74; 1953 H 1; GC 13099)

2913.15 Possessing or disposing of counterfeit coin or fictitious bank notes—Repealed

(1972 H 511, eff. 1–1–74; 1953 H 1; GC 13100)

2913.16 Attempting to pass counterfeit coin or bank notes—Repealed

(1972 H 511, eff. 1–1–74; 1953 H 1; GC 13101)

2913.17 Altering or transferring certificate of disability—Repealed

(1972 H 511, eff. 1–1–74; 1953 H 1; GC 13093)

MISUSE OF CREDIT CARDS

2913.21 Misuse of credit cards

(A) No person shall do any of the following:

(1) Practice deception for the purpose of procuring the issuance of a credit card, when a credit card is issued in actual reliance thereon;

(2) Knowingly buy or sell a credit card from or to a person other than the issuer.

(B) No person, with purpose to defraud, shall do any of the following:

(1) Obtain control over a credit card as security for a debt;

(2) Obtain property or services by the use of a credit card, in one or more transactions, knowing or having reasonable cause to believe that such card has expired or been revoked, or was obtained, is retained, or is being used in violation of law;

(3) Furnish property or services upon presentation of a credit card, knowing that such card is being used in violation of law;

(4) Represent or cause to be represented to the issuer of a credit card that property or services have been furnished, knowing that such representation is false.

(C) No person, with purpose to violate this section, shall receive, possess, control, or dispose of a credit card.

(D)(1) Whoever violates this section is guilty of misuse of credit cards.

(2) Violation of division (A), (B)(1), or (C) of this section is a misdemeanor of the first degree. If the value of the property or services or the loss to the victim involved in a violation of division (A), (B)(1), or (C) of this section is one hundred thousand dollars or more, then misuse of credit cards is a felony of the second degree.

(3) If the cumulative retail value of the property and services involved in one or more violations of division (B)(2), (3), or (4) of this section, which violations involve one or more credit card accounts and occur within a period of ninety consecutive days commencing on the date of the first violation, is less than three hundred dollars, then misuse of credit cards is a misdemeanor of the first degree. If the cumulative retail value of the property and services

involved in one or more violations of division (B)(2), (3), or (4) of this section, which violations involve one or more credit card accounts and occur within a period of ninety consecutive days commencing on the date of the first violation, is three hundred dollars or more and is less than five thousand dollars, or if the offender previously has been convicted of a theft offense, then misuse of credit cards is a felony of the fourth degree. If the cumulative retail value of the property and services involved in one or more violations of division (B)(2), (3), or (4) of this section, which violations involve one or more credit card accounts and occur within a period of ninety consecutive days commencing on the date of the first violation, is five thousand dollars or more and is less than one hundred thousand dollars; or if the offender previously has been convicted of two or more theft offenses, then misuse of credit cards is a felony of the third degree. If the cumulative retail value of the property and services involved in one or more violations of division (B)(2), (3), or (4) of this section, which violations involve one or more credit card accounts and occur within a period of ninety consecutive days commencing on the date of the first violation, is one hundred thousand dollars or more, then misuse of credit cards is a felony of the second degree.

(1986 H 49, eff. 6–26–86; 1983 S 210; 1982 S 199, H 269; 1978 S 289; 1972 H 511)

FORGERY

2913.31   Forgery

(A) No person, with purpose to defraud, or knowing that he is facilitating a fraud, shall do any of the following:

(1) Forge any writing of another without his authority;

(2) Forge any writing so that it purports to be genuine when it is actually spurious, or to be the act of another who did not authorize that act, or to have been executed at a time or place or with terms different from what was in fact the case, or to be a copy of an original when no such original existed;

(3) Utter, or possess with purpose to utter, any writing which he knows to have been forged.

(B) No person shall knowingly do either of the following:

(1) Forge an identification card;

(2) Sell or otherwise distribute a card that purports to be an identification card, knowing it to have been forged.

As used in this division, "identification card" means a card that includes personal information or characteristics of an individual, a purpose of which is to establish the identity of the bearer described on the card, whether the words "identity," "identification," "identification card," or other similar words appear on the card.

(C)(1) Whoever violates division (A) of this section is guilty of forgery, a felony of the fourth degree.

(2) Whoever violates division (B) of this section is guilty of forging identification cards or selling or distributing forged identification cards, a misdemeanor of the first degree. If the offender previously has been convicted of a violation of such division, forging identification cards or selling or distributing forged identification cards is a misdemeanor of the first degree and, in addition, the court shall impose upon the offender a fine of not less than two hundred fifty dollars.

(1991 H 162, eff. 11–11–91; 1972 H 511)

2913.32   Criminal simulation

(A) No person, with purpose to defraud, or knowing that he is facilitating a fraud, shall do any of the following:

(1) Make or alter any object so that it appears to have value because of antiquity, rarity, curiosity, source, or authorship, which it does not in fact possess;

(2) Practice deception in making, retouching, editing, or reproducing any photograph, movie film, video tape, phonograph record, or recording tape;

(3) Utter, or possess with purpose to utter, any object which he knows to have been simulated as provided in division (A)(1) or (2) of this section.

(B) Whoever violates this section is guilty of criminal simulation, a felony of the fourth degree.

(1972 H 511, eff. 1–1–74)

2913.33 Making or using slugs

(A) No person shall do any of the following:

(1) Insert or deposit a slug in a coin machine, with purpose to defraud;

(2) Make, possess, or dispose of a slug, with purpose of enabling another to defraud by inserting or depositing it in a coin machine.

(B) Whoever violates this section is guilty of making or using slugs, a misdemeanor of the second degree.

(1972 H 511, eff. 1–1–74)

FRAUDS

2913.40 Medicaid fraud

(A) As used in this section:

(1) "Statement or representation" means any oral, written, electronic, electronic impulse, or magnetic communication that is used to identify an item of goods or a service for which reimbursement may be made under the medical assistance program or that states income and expense and is or may be used to determine a rate of reimbursement under the medical assistance program.

(2) "Medical assistance program" means the program established by the department of human services to provide medical assistance under section 5111.01 of the Revised Code and the medicaid program of Title XIX of the "Social Security Act," 49 Stat. 620 (1935), 42 U.S.C. 301, as amended.

(3) "Provider" means any person who has signed a provider agreement with the department of human services to provide goods or services pursuant to the medical assistance program or any person who has signed an agreement with a party to such a provider agreement under which the person agrees to provide goods or services that are reimbursable under the medical assistance program.

(4) "Provider agreement" means an oral or written agreement between the department of human services and a person in which the person agrees to provide goods or services under the medical assistance program.

(5) "Recipient" means any individual who receives goods or services from a provider under the medical assistance program.

(6) "Records" means any medical, professional, financial, or business records relating to the treatment or care of any recipient, to goods or services provided to any recipient, or to rates paid for goods or services provided to any recipient and any records that are required by the rules of the department of human services to be kept for the medical assistance program.

(B) No person shall knowingly make or cause to be made a false or misleading statement or representation for use in obtaining reimbursement from the medical assistance program.

(C) No person, with purpose to commit fraud or knowing that he is facilitating a fraud, shall do either of the following:

(1) Contrary to the terms of his provider agreement, charge, solicit, accept, or receive for goods or services that he provides under the medical assistance program any property, money, or other consideration in addition to the amount of reimbursement under the medical assistance program and his provider agreement for the goods or services and any deductibles or co-payments authorized by section 5111.02 of the Revised Code or by any rules adopted pursuant to that section.

(2) Solicit, offer, or receive any remuneration, other than any deductibles or co-payments authorized by section 5111.02 of the Revised Code or by any rules adopted pursuant to that section, in cash or in kind, including, but not limited to, a kickback or rebate, in connection with the furnishing of goods or services for which whole or partial reimbursement is or may be made under the medical assistance program.

(D) No person, having submitted a claim for or provided goods or services under the medical assistance program, shall do either of the following for a period of at least six years after a reimbursement pursuant to that claim, or a reimbursement for those goods or services, is received under the medical assistance program:

(1) Knowingly alter, falsify, destroy, conceal, or remove any records that are necessary to fully disclose the nature of all goods or services for which the claim was submitted, or for which reimbursement was received, by the person;

(2) Knowingly alter, falsify, destroy, conceal, or remove any records that are necessary to disclose fully all income and expenditures upon which rates of reimbursements were based for the person.

(E) Whoever violates this section is guilty of medicaid fraud, a felony of the fourth degree. If the value of the property, services, or funds obtained in violation of this section is five thousand dollars or more, medicaid fraud is a felony of the third degree.

(F) Upon application of the governmental agency, office, or other entity that conducted the investigation and prosecution in a case under this section, the court shall order any person, who is convicted of a violation of this section for receiving any reimbursement for furnishing goods or services under the medical assistance program to which he is not entitled, to pay to the applicant its cost of investigating and prosecuting the case. The costs of investigation and prosecution that a defendant is ordered to pay pursuant to this division shall be in addition to any other penalties for the receipt of that reimbursement that are provided in this section, section 5111.03 of the Revised Code, or any other provision of law.

(G) The provisions of this section are not intended to be exclusive remedies and do not preclude the use of any other criminal or civil remedy for any act that is in violation of this section.

(1989 H 672, eff. 11–14–89; 1986 H 340)

2913.41 Defrauding a livery or hostelry

(A) No person, with purpose to defraud or knowing that he is facilitating a fraud, shall do either of the following:

(1) Hire an aircraft, motor vehicle, motorcycle, motorboat, sailboat, camper, trailer, horse, or buggy, or keep or operate any of the same which has been hired;

(2) Engage accommodations at a hotel, motel, inn, campground, or other hostelry.

(B) It is prima-facie evidence of purpose to defraud if the offender does any of the following:

(1) Uses deception to induce the rental agency to furnish the offender with any of the property listed in division (A)(1) of this section, or uses deception to induce the hostelry to furnish him with accommodations;

(2) Hires any of the property named in division (A)(1) of this section, or engages accommodations, knowing he is without sufficient means to pay the hire or rental;

(3) Absconds without paying the hire or rental;

(4) Knowingly fails to pay the hire or rental as required by the contract of hire or rental, without reasonable excuse for such failure;

(5) Knowingly fails to return hired property as required by the contract of hire, without reasonable excuse for such failure.

(C) Whoever violates this section is guilty of defrauding a livery or hostelry, a misdemeanor of the first degree. If the offender has previously been convicted of an offense under this section or of any other theft offense, defrauding a livery or hostelry is a felony of the fourth degree.

(1972 H 511, eff. 1–1–74)

2913.42 Tampering with records

(A) No person, knowing he has no privilege to do so, and with purpose to defraud or knowing that he is facilitating a fraud, shall do any of the following:

(1) Falsify, destroy, remove, conceal, alter, deface, or mutilate any writing, data, or record;

(2) Utter any writing or record, knowing it to have been tampered with as provided in division (A)(1) of this section.

(B) No person, knowing he has no privilege to do so, shall falsify, destroy, remove, conceal, alter, deface, or mutilate any computer software or data.

(C)(1) Whoever violates this section is guilty of tampering with records.

(2) If the offense involves a violation of division (A) of this section and does not involve data, tampering with records is whichever of the following is applicable:

(a) If division (C)(2)(b) of this section does not apply, a misdemeanor of the first degree;

(b) If the writing or record is a will unrevoked at the time of the offense or a record kept by or belonging to a governmental agency, a felony of the fourth degree.

(3) If the offense involves a violation of division (A) of this section involving data, tampering with records is whichever of the following is applicable:

(a) If division (C)(3)(b) or (c) of this section does not apply, a felony of the fourth degree;

(b) If division (C)(3)(c) of this section does not apply and the writing or record is a record kept by or belonging to a governmental agency or the offender previously has been convicted of a theft offense, a felony of the third degree;

(c) If the value of the data involved in the offense or the loss to the victim is one hundred dollars or more, a felony of the second degree.

(4) If the offense involves a violation of division (B) of this section, tampering with records is whichever of the following is applicable:

(a) If division (C)(4)(b) or (c) of this section does not apply, a felony of the fourth degree;

(b) If division (C)(4)(c) of this section does not apply and the offender previously has been convicted of a theft offense, a felony of the third degree;

(c) If the offense is committed for the purpose of devising or executing a scheme to defraud or to obtain property or services and the value of the property or services or the loss to the victim is one hundred thousand dollars or more, a felony of the second degree.

(1986 H 428, eff. 12–23–86; 1986 H 49; 1972 H 511)

2913.43 Securing writings by deception

(A) No person, by deception, shall cause another to execute any writing which disposes of or encumbers property, or by which a pecuniary obligation is incurred.

(B) Whoever violates this section is guilty of securing writings by deception. If the value of the property or the obligation involved is less than three hundred dollars, securing writings by deception is a misdemeanor of the first degree. If the value of the property or the obligation involved is three hundred dollars or more and less than five thousand dollars, securing writings by deception is a felony of the fourth degree. If the value of the property or the obligation involved is five thousand dollars or more and is less than one hundred thousand dollars, securing writings by deception is a felony of the third degree. If the value of the property or the obligation involved is one hundred thousand dollars or more, securing writings by deception is a felony of the second degree.

(1986 H 49, eff. 6–26–86; 1982 H 269, S 199; 1972 H 511)

2913.44 Personating an officer

(A) No person, with purpose to defraud or knowing that he is facilitating a fraud, or with purpose to induce another to purchase property or services, shall personate a law enforcement officer, or an inspector, investigator, or agent of any governmental agency.

(B) Whoever violates this section is guilty of personating an officer, a misdemeanor of the first degree.

(1972 H 511, eff. 1–1–74)

2913.441 Unauthorized display of emblems related to law enforcement on motor vehicles

(A) No person who is not entitled to do so shall knowingly display on a motor vehicle the emblem of a law enforcement agency or an organization of law enforcement officers.

(B) Whoever violates this section is guilty of the unlawful display of the emblem of a law enforcement agency or an organization of law enforcement officers, a minor misdemeanor.

(1976 H 1363, eff. 1–11–77)

2913.45 Defrauding creditors

(A) No person, with purpose to defraud one or more of his creditors, shall do any of the following:

(1) Remove, conceal, destroy, encumber, convey, or otherwise deal with any of his property;

(2) Misrepresent or refuse to disclose to a fiduciary appointed to administer or manage his affairs or estate, the existence, amount, or location of any of his property, or any other information regarding such property which he is legally required to furnish to the fiduciary.

(B) Whoever violates this section is guilty of defrauding creditors, a misdemeanor of the first degree.

(1972 H 511, eff. 1–1–74)

2913.46 Trafficking in or illegal use of food stamps

(A) As used in this section:

(1) "Electronically transferred benefit" means the transfer of food stamp program benefits through the use of an access device, which may include an electronic debit card or other means authorized by section 5101.33 of the Revised Code.

(2) "Access device" means any card, plate, code, account number, or other means of access that can be used, alone or in conjunction with another access device, to obtain payments, allotments, benefits, money, goods, or other things of value or that can be used to initiate a transfer of funds pursuant to section 5101.33 of the Revised Code and the "Food Stamp Act of 1977," 91 Stat. 958, 7 U.S.C.A. 2011 et seq., or any supplemental food program administered by any department of this state or any county or local agency pursuant to the "Child Nutrition Act of 1966," 80 Stat. 885, 42 U.S.C.A. 1786, as amended.

(3) "Aggregate face value of the food stamp coupons plus coupons provided under the "Child Nutrition Act of 1966," 80 Stat. 885, 42 U.S.C.A. 1786, as amended, plus the aggregate value of the electronically transferred benefits involved in the violation" means the total face value of any food stamps plus such coupons, plus the total value of any electronically transferred benefit or other access devices, involved in the violation.

(4) "Total value of any electronically transferred benefit or other access device" means the total value of the payments, allotments, benefits, money, goods, or other things of value that may be obtained, or the total value of funds that may be transferred, by use of any electronically transferred benefit or other access device at the time of violation.

If food stamp coupons or electronically transferred benefits or other access devices of various values are used, transferred, bought, acquired, altered, purchased, possessed, presented for redemption, or transported in violation of this section over a period of twelve months, the course of conduct may be charged as one offense and the values of food stamp coupons or any electronically transferred benefits or other access devices may be aggregated in determining the degree of the offense.

(B) No individual shall knowingly possess, buy, sell, use, alter, accept, or transfer food stamp coupons, any electronically transferred benefit, or any women, infants, and children program coupon in any manner not authorized by the "Food Stamp Act of 1977," 91 Stat. 958, 7 U.S.C.A. 2011, as amended, or the "Child Nutrition Act of 1966," 80 Stat. 885, 42 U.S.C.A. 1786, as amended.

(C) No organization, as defined in division (D) of section 2901.23 of the Revised Code, shall:

(1) Knowingly allow an employee to sell, transfer, or trade items or services, the purchase of which is prohibited by the "Food Stamp Act of 1977," 91 Stat. 958, 7 U.S.C.A. 2011, as amended, or the "Child Nutrition Act of 1966," 80 Stat. 885, 42 U.S.C.A. 1786, as amended, in exchange for food stamp coupons, any electronically transferred benefit, or any women, infants, and children program coupon;

(2) Negligently allow an employee to sell, transfer, or exchange food stamp coupons, any electronically transferred benefit, or any women, infants, and children program coupon for anything of value.

(D) Whoever violates division (B) of this section is guilty of trafficking in food stamps or coupons. If the aggregate face value of the food stamp coupons plus coupons provided under the "Child Nutrition Act of 1966," 80 Stat. 885, 42 U.S.C.A. 1786, as amended, plus the aggregate value of the electronically transferred benefits involved in the violation is less than five hundred dollars, trafficking in food stamps or coupons is a felony of the third degree. If the aggregate face value of the food stamp coupons plus coupons provided under the "Child Nutrition Act of 1966," 80 Stat. 885, 42 U.S.C.A. 1786, as amended, plus the aggregate value of the electronically transferred benefits involved in the violation is five hundred dollars or more, or if the offender previously has been convicted of a theft offense or a violation of the "Food Stamp Act" or the "Child Nutrition Act," trafficking in food stamps or coupons is a felony of the second degree.

(E) Whoever violates division (C) of this section is guilty of illegal use of food stamps or coupons. If the aggregate face value of the food stamp coupons plus coupons provided under the "Child Nutrition Act of 1966," 80 Stat. 885, 42 U.S.C.A. 1786, as amended, plus the aggregate value of the electronically transferred benefits involved in the violation is less than two hundred dollars, illegal use of food stamps or coupons is a felony of the fourth degree. If the aggregate face value of the food stamp coupons plus coupons provided under the "Child Nutrition Act of 1966," 80 Stat. 885, 42 U.S.C.A. 1786, as amended, plus the aggregate value of the electronically transferred benefits involved in the violation is two hundred dollars or more, or if the offender previously has been convicted of a violation of the "Food Stamp Act" or the "Child Nutrition Act," then illegal use of food stamps or coupons is a felony of the second degree.

(1996 S 107, eff. 5–8–96; 1995 S 162, eff. 10–29–95; 1995 H 239, eff. 11–24–95; 1983 H 291, eff. 7–1–83)

2913.47 Insurance fraud

(A) As used in this section:

(1) "Data" has the same meaning as in section 2913.01 of the Revised Code and additionally includes any other representation of information, knowledge, facts, concepts, or instructions that are being or have been prepared in a formalized manner.

(2) "Deceptive" means that a statement, in whole or in part, would cause another to be deceived because it contains a misleading representation, withholds information, prevents the acquisition of information, or by any other conduct, act, or omission creates, confirms, or perpetuates a false impression, including, but not limited to, a false impression as to law, value, state of mind, or other objective or subjective fact.

(3) "Insurer" means any person that is authorized to engage in the business of insurance in this state under Title XXXIX of the Revised Code; any prepaid dental plan, medical care corporation, health care corporation, dental care corporation, or health maintenance organiza-

tion; and any legal entity that is self-insured and provides benefits to its employees or members.

(4) "Policy" means a policy, certificate, contract, or plan that is issued by an insurer.

(5) "Statement" includes, but is not limited to, any notice, letter, or memorandum; proof of loss; bill of lading; receipt for payment; invoice, account, or other financial statement; estimate of property damage; bill for services; diagnosis or prognosis; prescription; hospital, medical, or dental chart or other record; x–ray, photograph, videotape, or movie film; test result; other evidence of loss, injury, or expense; computer–generated document; and data in any form.

(B) No person, with purpose to defraud or knowing that he is facilitating a fraud, shall do either of the following:

(1) Present to, or cause to be presented to, an insurer any written or oral statement that is part of, or in support of, an application for insurance, a claim for payment pursuant to a policy, or a claim for any other benefit pursuant to a policy, knowing that the statement, or any part of the statement, is false or deceptive;

(2) Assist, aid, abet, solicit, procure, or conspire with another to prepare or make any written or oral statement that is intended to be presented to an insurer as part of, or in support of, an application for insurance, a claim for payment pursuant to a policy, or a claim for any other benefit pursuant to a policy, knowing that the statement, or any part of the statement, is false or deceptive.

(C) Whoever violates this section is guilty of insurance fraud. If the false or deceptive statement is presented or intended to be presented as part of, or in support of, an application for insurance or if the amount of the claim that is false or deceptive is less than three hundred dollars, insurance fraud is a misdemeanor of the first degree. If the amount of the claim that is false or deceptive is three hundred dollars or more and is less than five thousand dollars, or if the offender previously has been convicted of a theft offense, insurance fraud is a felony of the fourth degree. If the amount of the claim that is false or deceptive is five thousand dollars or more and is less than one hundred thousand dollars, or if the offender previously has been convicted of two or more theft offenses, insurance fraud is a felony of the third degree. If the amount of the claim that is false or deceptive is one hundred thousand dollars or more, insurance fraud is a felony of the second degree.

(D) This section shall not be construed to abrogate, waive, or modify division (A) of section 2317.02 of the Revised Code.

(1990 H 347, eff. 7–18–90)

2913.48 Workers' compensation fraud

(A) No person, with purpose to defraud or knowing that he is facilitating a fraud shall do any of the following:

(1) Receive workers' compensation benefits to which he is not entitled;

(2) Make or present or cause to be made or presented a false or misleading statement with the purpose to secure payment for goods or services rendered under Chapter 4121., 4123., 4127., or 4131. of the Revised Code or to secure workers' compensation benefits;

(3) Alter, falsify, destroy, conceal, or remove any record or document that is necessary to fully establish the validity of any claim filed with, or necessary to establish the nature and validity of all goods and services for which reimbursement or payment was received or is requested from, the bureau of workers' compensation, or a self-insuring employer under Chapter 4121., 4123., 4127., or 4131. of the Revised Code;

(4) Enter into an agreement or conspiracy to defraud the bureau or a self-insuring employer by making or presenting or causing to be made or presented a false claim for workers' compensation benefits.

(B) Whoever violates this section is guilty of workers' compensation fraud. If the value of the goods, services, property, or money stolen is less than three hundred dollars, a violation of this section is petty theft, a misdemeanor of the first degree. If the value of the goods, services, property, or money stolen is three hundred dollars or more and is less than five thousand dollars, or if the offender previously has been convicted of a theft offense under this section, a violation of this section is theft, a felony of the fourth degree. If the value of the goods, services, property, or money stolen is five thousand dollars or more and is less than one hundred thousand dollars, or if the offender previously has been convicted of two or more theft offenses under this section, a violation of this section is grand theft, a felony of the third degree. If the value of the goods, services, property, or money stolen is one hundred thousand dollars or more, a violation of this section is aggravated theft, a felony of the second degree.

(C) Upon application of the governmental body that conducted the investigation and prosecution of a violation of this section, the court shall order the person who is convicted of the violation to pay the governmental body its costs of investigating and prosecuting the case. These costs are in addition to any other costs or penalty provided in the Revised Code or any other section of law.

(D) The remedies and penalties provided in this section are not exclusive remedies and penalties and do not preclude the use of any other criminal or civil remedy or penalty for any act that is in violation of this section.

(E) As used in this section:

(1) "False" means wholly or partially untrue or deceptive.

(2) "Goods" includes, but is not limited to, medical supplies, appliances, rehabilitative equipment, and any other apparatus or furnishing provided or used in the care, treatment, or rehabilitation of a claimant for workers' compensation benefits.

(3) "Services" includes, but is not limited to, any service provided by any health care provider to a claimant for workers' compensation benefits.

(4) "Claim" means any attempt to cause the bureau, an independent third party with whom the administrator or an employer contracts under section 4121.44 of the Revised Code, or a self-insuring employer to make payment or reimbursement for workers' compensation benefits.

(5) "Employment" means participating in any trade, occupation, business, service, or profession for substantial gainful remuneration.

(6) "Employer," "employee," and "self–insuring employer" have the same meanings as in section 4123.01 of the Revised Code.

(7) "Remuneration" includes, but is not limited to, wages, commissions, rebates, and any other reward or consideration.

(8) "Statement" includes, but is not limited to, any oral, written, electronic, electronic impulse, or magnetic communication notice, letter, memorandum, receipt for payment, invoice, account, financial statement, bill for services; diagnosis, prognosis, prescription, hospital, medical, or dental chart or other record; and computer generated document.

(9) "Records" means any medical, professional, financial, or business record relating to the treatment or care of any person, to goods or services provided to any person, or to rates paid for goods or services provided to any person, or any record that the administrator of workers' compensation requires pursuant to rule.

(10) "Workers' compensation benefits" means any compensation or benefits payable under Chapter 4121., 4123., 4127., or 4131. of the Revised Code.

(1993 H 107, eff. 10–20–93)

MISCELLANEOUS PROVISIONS

2913.51 Receiving stolen property

(A) No person shall receive, retain, or dispose of property of another knowing or having reasonable cause to believe that the property has been obtained through commission of a theft offense.

(B) Whoever violates this section is guilty of receiving stolen property. If the value of the property involved is less than three hundred dollars, receiving stolen property is a misdemeanor of the first degree. If the value of the property involved is three hundred dollars or more and is less than five thousand dollars, if the property involved is any of the property listed in section 2913.71 of the Revised Code, or if the offender previously has been convicted of a theft offense, receiving stolen property is a felony of the fourth degree. If the property involved is a motor vehicle, as defined in section 4501.01 of the Revised Code, if the value of the property involved is five thousand dollars or more and is less than one hundred thousand dollars, if the property involved is a firearm or dangerous ordnance, as defined in section 2923.11 of the Revised Code, or if the offender previously has been convicted of two or more theft offenses, receiving stolen property is a felony of the third degree. If the value of the property involved is one hundred thousand dollars or more, receiving stolen property is a felony of the second degree.

(1995 H 4, eff. 11–9–95; 1986 H 49, eff. 6–26–86; 1983 S 210; 1982 S 199, H 269; 1980 S 191; 1972 H 511)

2913.61   Value of stolen property

(A) When a person is charged with a theft offense involving property or services valued at three hundred dollars or more, a violation of section 2913.02, 2913.11, 2913.21, 2913.43, 2913.51, or 4931.99 of the Revised Code involving property or services valued at three hundred dollars or more and less than five thousand dollars, or a violation of section 2913.02, 2913.11, 2913.21, 2913.43, 2913.51, or 4931.99 of the Revised Code involving property or services valued at five thousand dollars or more, the jury or court trying the accused shall determine the value of such property or services as of the time of the offense and, if a guilty verdict is returned, shall return the finding of value as part of the verdict. In any such case, it is unnecessary to find and return exact value, and it is sufficient if, in a case involving a theft offense other than a violation of section 2913.02, 2913.11, 2913.21, 2913.43, 2913.51, or 4931.99 of the Revised Code, the finding and return is to the effect that the value of the property or services involved was less than three hundred dollars or was three hundred dollars or more or, in a case involving a violation of section 2913.02, 2913.11, 2913.21, 2913.43, 2913.51, or 4931.99 of the Revised Code, the finding and return is to the effect that the value of the property or services involved was less than three hundred dollars, was three hundred dollars or more and less than five thousand dollars, or was five thousand dollars or more.

(B) Where more than one item of property or services is involved in a theft offense, the value of the property or services involved for the purpose of determining the value as required by division (A) of this section, is the aggregate value of all property or services involved in the offense.

(C) When a series of offenses under section 2913.02 of the Revised Code is committed by the offender in his same employment, capacity, or relationship to another, all such offenses shall be tried as a single offense, and the value of the property or services involved for the purpose of determining the value as required by division (A) of this section, is the aggregate value of all property and services involved in all offenses in the series. In prosecuting a single offense under this division, it is not necessary to separately allege and prove each offense in the series. It is sufficient to allege and prove that the offender, within a given span of time, committed one or more theft offenses in his same employment, capacity, or relationship to another.

(D) The following criteria shall be used in determining the value of property or services involved in a theft offense:

(1) The value of an heirloom, memento, collector's item, antique, museum piece, manuscript, document, record, or other thing which has intrinsic worth to its owner and which is either irreplaceable or is replaceable only on the expenditure of substantial time, effort, or money, is the amount which would compensate the owner for its loss.

(2) The value of personal effects and household goods, and of materials, supplies, equipment, and fixtures used in the profession, business, trade, occupation, or avocation of its owner, which property is not covered under division (D)(1) of this section, and which retains substantial utility for its purpose regardless of its age or condition, is the cost of replacing such property with new property of like kind and quality.

(3) The value of any property, real or personal, not covered under division (D)(1) or (2) of this section, and the value of services, is the fair market value of such property or services. As

used in this section, "fair market value" is the money consideration which a buyer would give and a seller would accept for property or services, assuming that the buyer is willing to buy and the seller is willing to sell, that both are fully informed as to all facts material to the transaction, and that neither is under any compulsion to act.

(E) Without limitation on the evidence that may be used to establish the value of property or services involved in a theft offense:

(1) When the property involved is personal property held for sale at wholesale or retail, the price at which such property was held for sale is prima-facie evidence of its value.

(2) When the property involved is a security or commodity traded on an exchange, the closing price or, if there is no closing price, the asked price, given in the latest market quotation prior to the offense, is prima-facie evidence of the value of such security or commodity.

(3) When the property involved is livestock, poultry, or raw agricultural products for which a local market price is available, the latest local market price prior to the offense is prima-facie evidence of the value of such livestock, poultry, or products.

(4) When the property involved is a negotiable instrument, the face value is prima-facie evidence of the value of such instrument.

(5) When the property involved is a warehouse receipt, bill of lading, pawn ticket, claim check, or other instrument entitling the holder or bearer to receive property, the face value or, if there is no face value, the value of the property covered by the instrument less any payment necessary to receive the property, is prima-facie evidence of the value of the instrument.

(6) When the property involved is a ticket of admission, ticket for transportation, coupon, token, or other instrument entitling the holder or bearer to receive property or services, the face value or, if there is no face value, the value of the property or services which may be received thereby, is prima-facie evidence of the value of such instrument.

(7) When the services involved are gas, electricity, water, telephone, transportation, shipping, or other services for which the rate is established by law, the duly established rate is prima-facie evidence of the value of such services.

(8) When the services involved are services for which the rate is not established by law, and the offender has been notified prior to the offense of the rate for such services, either in writing, or orally, or by posting in a manner reasonably calculated to come to the attention of potential offenders, the rate contained in such notice is prima-facie evidence of the value of such services.

(1982 H 269, eff. 12–17–82; 1982 S 199; 1972 H 511)

2913.71   Degree of offense when certain property involved

Regardless of the value of the property involved and regardless of whether the offender previously has been convicted of a theft offense, a violation of section 2913.02 or 2913.51 of the Revised Code is a felony of the fourth degree if the property involved is any of the following:

(A) A credit card;

(B) A printed form for a check or other negotiable instrument, that on its face identifies the drawer or maker for whose use it is designed or identifies the account on which it is to be drawn, and that has not been executed by the drawer or maker or on which the amount is blank;

(C) A motor vehicle identification license plate as prescribed by section 4503.22 of the Revised Code, a temporary license placard or windshield sticker as prescribed by section 4503.182 of the Revised Code, or any comparable license plate, placard, or sticker as prescribed by the applicable law of another state or the United States;

(D) A blank form for a certificate of title or a manufacturer's or importer's certificate to a motor vehicle, as prescribed by section 4505.07 of the Revised Code;

(E) A blank form for any license listed in section 4507.01 of the Revised Code.

(1995 H 4, eff. 11–9–95; 1984 H 632, eff. 3–28–85; 1980 S 191; 1977 H 1; 1972 H 511)

2913.81   Denying access to a computer

(A) No person, without privilege to do so, shall knowingly deny or cause the denial of a computer system or computer services to an authorized user of a computer system or computer services that, in whole or in part, are owned by, under contract to, operated for, or operated in conjunction with another person.

(B) Whoever violates this section is guilty of denying access to a computer, a felony of the fourth degree. If the offender previously has been convicted of a theft offense, denying access to a computer is a felony of the third degree. If the offense is committed for the purpose of devising or executing a scheme to defraud or to obtain property or services and the value of the property or services or the loss to the victim is one hundred thousand dollars or more, denying access to a computer is a felony of the second degree.

(1986 H 49, eff. 6–26–86)

2913.82   Theft involving motor vehicle; offender to pay towing and storage fees

If a person is convicted of a theft offense that involves a motor vehicle, as defined in section 4501.01 of the Revised Code, or any major part of a motor vehicle, and if a local authority, as defined in section 4511.01 of the Revised Code, the owner of the vehicle or major part, or a person, acting on behalf of the owner, was required to pay any towing or storage fees prior to recovering possession of the motor vehicle or major part, the court that sentences the offender, as a part of its sentence, shall require the offender to repay the fees to the local authority, the owner, or the person who paid the fees on behalf of the owner.

As used in this section, "major part" has the same meaning as in the "Motor Vehicle Theft Law Enforcement Act of 1984," 98 Stat. 2754, 15 U.S.C. 2021 (7), as amended.

(1986 H 546, eff. 3–25–87)

CHAPTER 2915

GAMBLING

GENERAL PROVISIONS

GENERAL PROVISIONS

2915.01   Definitions

As used in sections 2915.01 to 2915.12 of the Revised Code:

(A) "Bookmaking" means the business of receiving or paying off bets.

(B) "Bet" means the hazarding of anything of value upon the result of an event, undertaking, or contingency, but does not include a bona fide business risk.

(C) "Scheme of chance" means a lottery, numbers game, pool, or other scheme in which a participant gives a valuable consideration for a chance to win a prize.

(D) "Game of chance" means poker, craps, roulette, a slot machine, a punch board, or other game in which a player gives anything of value in the hope of gain, the outcome of which is determined largely or wholly by chance.

(E) "Scheme or game of chance conducted for profit" means any scheme or game of chance designed to produce income for the person who conducts or operates the scheme or game of chance, but does not include a charitable bingo game.

(F) "Gambling device" means:

(1) A book, totalizer, or other equipment for recording bets;

(2) A ticket, token, or other device representing a chance, share, or interest in a scheme of chance, except a charitable bingo game, or evidencing a bet;

(3) A deck of cards, dice, gaming table, roulette wheel, slot machine, punch board, or other apparatus designed for use in connection with a game of chance;

(4) Any equipment, device, apparatus, or paraphernalia specially designed for gambling purposes.

(G) "Gambling offense" means any of the following:

(1) A violation of section 2915.02, 2915.03, 2915.04, 2915.05, 2915.06, 2915.07, 2915.08, 2915.09, 2915.10, or 2915.11 of the Revised Code;

(2) A violation of an existing or former municipal ordinance or law of this or any other state or the United States substantially equivalent to any section listed in division (G) (1) of this section;

(3) An offense under an existing or former municipal ordinance or law of this or any other state or the United States, of which gambling is an element;

(4) A conspiracy or attempt to commit, or complicity in committing any offense under division (G)(1), (2), or (3) of this section.

(H) "Charitable organization" means any tax exempt religious, educational, veteran's, fraternal, service, nonprofit medical, volunteer rescue service, volunteer fire fighter's, senior citizen's, youth athletic, amateur athletic, or youth athletic park organization. An organization is tax exempt if the organization is, and has received from the internal revenue service a determination letter that currently is in effect stating that the organization is, exempt from federal income taxation under subsection 501(a) and described in subsection 501(c)(3), 501(c)(4), 501(c)(8), 501(c)(10), or 501(c)(19) of the Internal Revenue Code. To qualify as a charitable organization, an organization, except a volunteer rescue service or volunteer fire fighter's organization, shall have been in continuous existence as such in this state for a period of two years immediately preceding either the making of an application for a bingo license under section 2915.08 of the Revised Code or the conducting of any scheme of chance or game of chance as provided in division (C) of section 2915.02 of the Revised Code.

(I) "Religious organization" means any church, body of communicants, or group that is not organized or operated for profit, that gathers in common membership for regular worship and religious observances.

(J) "Educational organization" means any organization within this state that is not organized for profit, the primary purpose of which is to educate and develop the capabilities of individuals through instruction, and that operates or contributes to the support of a school, academy, college, or university.

(K) "Veteran's organization" means any individual post of a national veteran's association or an auxiliary unit of any individual post of a national veteran's association, which post or auxiliary unit has been incorporated as a nonprofit corporation for at least two years and has received a letter from the state headquarters of the national veteran's association indicating that the individual post or auxiliary unit is in good standing with the national veteran's association. As used in this division, "national veteran's association" means any veteran's association that has been in continuous existence as such for a period of at least ten years and either is incorporated by an act of the United States congress or has a national dues-paying membership of at least five thousand persons.

(L) "Volunteer fire fighter's organization" means any organization of volunteer fire fighters, as defined in section 146.01 of the Revised Code, that is organized and operated exclusively to provide financial support for a volunteer fire department or a volunteer fire company.

(M) "Fraternal organization" means any society, order, or association within this state, except a college or high school fraternity, that is not organized for profit, that is a branch, lodge, or chapter of a national or state organization, that exists exclusively for the common business or brotherhood of its members, and that has been in continuous existence in this state for a period of five years.

(N) "Volunteer rescue service organization" means any organization of volunteers organized to function as an emergency medical service organization as defined in section 4765.01 of the Revised Code.

(O) "Service organization" means any organization, not organized for profit, that is organized and operated exclusively to provide, or to contribute to the support of organizations or institutions organized and operated exclusively to provide, medical and therapeutic services for persons who are crippled, born with birth defects, or have any other mental or physical defect or those organized and operated exclusively to protect, or to contribute to the support of organizations or institutions organized and operated exclusively to protect, animals from inhumane treatment.

(P) "Nonprofit medical organization" means any organization that has been incorporated as a nonprofit corporation for at least five years and that has continuously operated and will be operated exclusively to provide, or to contribute to the support of organizations or institutions organized and operated exclusively to provide, hospital, medical, research, or therapeutic services for the public.

(Q) "Senior citizen's organization" means any private organization, not organized for profit, that is organized and operated exclusively to provide recreational or social services for persons who are fifty-five years of age or older and that is described and qualified under subsection 501(c)(3) of the Internal Revenue Code.

(R) "Charitable bingo game" means any bingo game that is conducted by a charitable organization that has obtained a bingo license pursuant to section 2915.08 of the Revised Code and the proceeds of which are used for a charitable purpose.

(S) "Bingo" means:

(1) A game with all of the following characteristics:

(a) The participants use bingo cards that are divided into twenty-five spaces arranged in five horizontal and five vertical rows of spaces, with each space, except the central space, being designated by a combination of a letter and a number and with the central space being designated as a free space.

(b) The participants cover the spaces on the bingo cards that correspond to combinations of letters and numbers that are announced by a bingo game operator.

(c) A bingo game operator announces combinations of letters and numbers that appear on objects that a bingo game operator selects by chance, either manually or mechanically, from a receptacle that contains seventy-five objects at the beginning of each game, each object marked by a different combination of a letter and a number that corresponds to one of the seventy-five possible combinations of a letter and a number that can appear on the bingo cards.

(d) The winner of the bingo game includes any participant who properly announces during the interval between the announcements of letters and numbers as described in division (S)(1)(c) of this section, that a predetermined and preannounced pattern of spaces has been covered on a bingo card being used by the participant.

(2) Any scheme or game other than a game as defined in division (S)(1) of this section with the following characteristics:

(a) The participants use cards, sheets, or other devices that are divided into spaces arranged in horizontal, vertical, or diagonal rows of spaces, with each space, except free spaces, being designated by a single letter, number, or symbol; by a combination of letters, numbers, or symbols; by a combination of a letter and a number, a letter and a symbol, or a number and a symbol; or by any combination of letters, numbers, and symbols, with some or none of the spaces being designated as a free, complimentary, or similar space.

(b) The participants cover the spaces on the cards, sheets, or devices that correspond to letters, numbers, symbols, or combinations of such that are announced by a bingo game operator or otherwise transmitted to the participants.

(c) A bingo game operator announces, or otherwise transmits to the participants, letters, numbers, symbols, or any combination of such as set forth in division (S)(2)(a) of this section that appear on objects that a bingo game operator selects by chance that correspond to one of the possible letters, numbers, symbols, or combinations of such that can appear on the bingo cards, sheets, or devices.

(d) The winner of the bingo game is any participant who properly announces that a predetermined and preannounced pattern of spaces has been covered on a card, sheet, or device being used by the participant.

(T) "Conduct" means to back, promote, organize, manage, carry on, or prepare for the operation of a scheme or game of chance but does not include any act performed by a bingo game operator.

(U) "Bingo game operator" means any person, except security personnel, who performs work or labor at the site of a bingo game including, but not limited to, collecting money from participants, handing out bingo cards or objects to cover spaces on the bingo cards, selecting from a receptacle the objects that contain the combination of letters and numbers that appear on the bingo cards, calling out the combinations of letters and numbers, distributing prizes to the winner of the bingo game, and preparing, selling, and serving food or beverages.

(V) "Participant" means any person who plays bingo by covering the spaces on a bingo card that correspond to combinations of letters and numbers that are announced by a bingo game operator.

(W) "Bingo session" means a period, not to exceed five continuous hours, during which a person conducts one or more bingo games.

(X) "Gross receipts" means all money or assets, including admission fees, that a person receives from a bingo session that the person conducts without the deduction of any amounts for prizes paid out during the session or for the expenses of conducting the bingo session. "Gross receipts" does not include any money directly taken in from the sale of food or beverages by a charitable organization conducting a bingo session, or by a bona fide auxiliary unit or society of a charitable organization, at a bingo session conducted by the charitable organization, provided all of the following apply:

(1) The auxiliary unit or society has been in existence as a bona fide auxiliary unit or society of the charitable organization for at least two years prior to the bingo session.

(2) The person who purchases the food or beverage receives nothing of value except the food or beverage and items customarily received with the purchase of that food or beverage.

(3) The food and beverages are sold at customary and reasonable prices.

(4) No person preparing, selling, or serving the food or beverages at the site of the bingo game receives directly or indirectly any form of compensation for the preparation, sale, or service of the food or beverages.

(Y) "Security personnel" includes any person who either is a sheriff, deputy sheriff, marshal, deputy marshal, township constable, or member of an organized police department of a municipal corporation or has successfully completed a peace officer's training course pursuant to sections 109.71 to 109.79 of the Revised Code and who is hired to provide security for the premises on which a bingo game is conducted.

(Z) "To use gross receipts for a charitable purpose" means that the proceeds of the bingo game are used by, or given, donated, or otherwise transferred to, any organization that is described in subsection 509(a)(1), 509(a)(2), or 509(a)(3) of the Internal Revenue Code and is either a governmental unit or an organization that is tax exempt under subsection 501(a) and described in subsection 501(c)(3) of the Internal Revenue Code; that the proceeds of the bingo game are used by, or given, donated, or otherwise transferred to a veteran's organization, as defined in division (K) of this section, that is a post, chapter, or organization of war veterans, or an auxiliary unit or society of, or a trust or foundation for, any such post, chapter, or organization organized in the United States or any of its possessions, at least seventy-five per cent of the members of which are war veterans and substantially all of the other members of which are individuals who are veterans (but not war veterans) or are cadets, or are spouses, widows or widowers of war veterans, or such individuals, provided that no part of the net earnings of such post or organization inures to the benefit of any private shareholder or individual, and further provided that the bingo game proceeds are used by the post or organization for the charitable purposes set forth in division (B)(12) of section 5739.02 of the

Revised Code, are used for awarding scholarships to or for attendance at an institution mentioned in division (B)(12) of section 5739.02 of the Revised Code, are donated to a governmental agency, or are used for nonprofit youth activities, the purchase of United States or Ohio flags that are donated to schools, youth groups, or other bona fide nonprofit organizations, promotion of patriotism, or disaster relief; that the proceeds of the bingo game are used by, or given, donated, or otherwise transferred to a fraternal organization that has been in continuous existence in this state for fifteen years for use exclusively for religious, charitable, scientific, literary, or educational purposes, or for the prevention of cruelty to children or animals and contributions for such use would qualify as a deductible charitable contribution under subsection 170 of the Internal Revenue Code; or that the proceeds of the bingo game are used by a volunteer fire fighter's organization and are used by the organization for the purposes set forth in division (L) of this section.

(AA) "Internal Revenue Code" means the "Internal Revenue Code of 1986," 100 Stat. 2085, 26 U.S.C. 1, as now or hereafter amended.

(BB) "Youth athletic organization" means any organization, not organized for profit, that is organized and operated exclusively to provide financial support to, or to operate, athletic activities for persons who are twenty-one years of age or younger by means of sponsoring, organizing, operating, or contributing to the support of an athletic team, club, league, or association.

(CC) "Youth athletic park organization" means any organization, not organized for profit, that satisfies both of the following:

(1) It owns, operates, and maintains playing fields that satisfy both of the following:

(a) The playing fields are used at least one hundred days per year for athletic activities by one or more organizations, not organized for profit, each of which is organized and operated exclusively to provide financial support to, or to operate, athletic activities for persons who are eighteen years of age or younger by means of sponsoring, organizing, operating, or contributing to the support of an athletic team, club, league, or association.

(b) The playing fields are not used for any profit-making activity at any time during the year.

(2) It uses the proceeds of the bingo games it conducts exclusively for the operation, maintenance, and improvement of its playing fields of the type described in division (CC)(1) of this section.

(DD) "Amateur athletic organization" means any organization, not organized for profit, that is organized and operated exclusively to provide financial support to, or to operate, athletic activities for persons who are training for amateur athletic competition that is sanctioned by a national governing body as defined in the "Amateur Sports Act of 1978," 90 Stat. 3045, 36 U.S.C.A. 373.

This is an interim section effective until July 1, 1996.

(1996 H 143, § 1, eff. 5–15–96; 1992 S 98, eff. 11–12–92; 1990 H 573; 1981 S 91; 1977 H 72; 1976 S 398, H 1547; 1975 H 1; 1972 H 511)

2915.02 Gambling; exceptions for charitable organizations

(A) No person shall do any of the following:

(1) Engage in bookmaking, or knowingly engage in conduct that facilitates bookmaking;

(2) Establish, promote, or operate or knowingly engage in conduct that facilitates any scheme or game of chance conducted for profit;

(3) Knowingly procure, transmit, exchange, or engage in conduct that facilitates the procurement, transmission, or exchange of information for use in establishing odds or determining winners in connection with bookmaking or with any scheme or game of chance conducted for profit;

(4) Engage in betting or in playing any scheme or game of chance, except a charitable bingo game, as a substantial source of income or livelihood;

(5) With purpose to violate division (A)(1), (2), (3), or (4) of this section, acquire, possess, control, or operate any gambling device.

(B) For purposes of division (A)(1) of this section, a person facilitates bookmaking if he in any way knowingly aids an illegal bookmaking operation, including, without limitation, placing a bet with a person engaged in or facilitating illegal bookmaking. For purposes of division (A)(2) of this section, a person facilitates a scheme or game of chance conducted for profit if he in any way knowingly aids in the conduct or operation of any such scheme or game, including, without limitation, playing any such scheme or game.

(C) This section does not prohibit conduct in connection with gambling expressly permitted by law.

(D) This section does not apply to any of the following:

(1) Schemes of chance conducted by a charitable organization that is, and has received from the internal revenue service a determination letter that is currently in effect stating that the organization is, exempt from federal income taxation under subsection 501(a) and described in subsection 501(c)(3) of the Internal Revenue Code, provided that all of the money or assets received from the scheme of chance after deduction only of prizes paid out during the conduct of the scheme of chance are used by, or given, donated, or otherwise transferred to, any organization that is described in subsection 509(a)(1), 509(a)(2), or 509(a)(3) of the Internal Revenue Code and is either a governmental unit or an organization that is tax exempt under subsection 501(a) and described in subsection 501(c)(3) of the Internal Revenue Code, and provided that the scheme of chance is not conducted during, or within ten hours of, a bingo game conducted for amusement purposes only pursuant to section 2915.12 of the Revised Code;

(2) Games of chance, if all of the following apply:

(a) The games of chance are not craps for money, roulette for money, or slot machines;

(b) The games of chance are conducted by a charitable organization that is, and has received from the internal revenue service a determination letter that is currently in effect, stating that the organization is, exempt from federal income taxation under subsection 501(a) and described in subsection 501(c)(3) of the Internal Revenue Code;

(c) The games of chance are conducted at festivals of the organization that are conducted either for a period of four consecutive days or less and not more than twice a year or for a period of five consecutive days not more than once a year, and are conducted on premises owned by the charitable organization for a period of no less than one year immediately preceding the conducting of the games of chance, on premises leased from a governmental unit, or on premises that are leased from a veteran's or fraternal organization and that have been owned by the lessor veteran's or fraternal organization for a period of no less than one year immediately preceding the conducting of the games of chance;

A charitable organization shall not lease premises from a veteran's or fraternal organization, or lease from a governmental unit premises located in a county with a population exceeding five hundred thousand, to conduct a festival described in division (D)(2)(c) of this section if the veteran's or fraternal organization or governmental unit already has leased the premises twice during the preceding year to charitable organizations for that purpose. If a charitable organization leases premises from a veteran's or fraternal organization to conduct a festival described in division (D)(2)(c) of this section, the charitable organization shall not pay a rental rate for the premises per day of the festival that exceeds the rental rate per bingo session that a charitable organization may pay under division (A)(3) of section 2915.09 of the Revised Code when it leases premises from another charitable organization to conduct bingo games.

(d) All of the money or assets received from the games of chance after deduction only of prizes paid out during the conduct of the games of chance are used by, or given, donated, or otherwise transferred to, any organization that is described in subsection 509(a)(1), 509(a)(2), or 509(a)(3) of the Internal Revenue Code and is either a governmental unit or an organization that is tax exempt under subsection 501(a) and described in subsection 501(c)(3) of the Internal Revenue Code;

(e) The games of chance are not conducted during, or within ten hours of, a bingo game conducted for amusement purposes only pursuant to section 2915.12 of the Revised Code.

No person shall receive any commission, wage, salary, reward, tip, donation, gratuity, or other form of compensation, directly or indirectly, for operating or assisting in the operation of any scheme or game of chance.

(3) Any tag fishing tournament operated under a permit issued under section 1533.92 of the Revised Code, as "tag fishing tournament" is defined in section 1531.01 of the Revised Code.

(E) Division (D) of this section shall not be construed to authorize the sale, lease, or other temporary or permanent transfer of the right to conduct schemes of chance or games of chance, as granted by division (D) of this section, by any charitable organization that is granted that right.

(F) Whoever violates this section is guilty of gambling, a misdemeanor of the first degree. If the offender has previously been convicted of any gambling offense, gambling is a felony of the fourth degree.

(1993 H 336, eff. 10–29–93; 1993 H 104; 1990 H 573, H 550; 1988 H 514; 1977 H 72; 1976 S 398, H 1547; 1972 H 511)

Historical and Statutory Notes

Ed. Note: "Comparison of these amendments [1993 H 336, eff. 10–29–93 and 1993 H 104, eff. 10–7–93] in pursuance of section 1.52 of the Revised Code discloses that they are not irreconcilable, so that they are required by that section to be harmonized to give effect to each amendment." In recognition of this rule of construction, changes made by 1993 H 336, eff. 10–29–93, and 1993 H 104, eff. 10–7–93, have been incorporated in the above amendment. See *Baldwin's Ohio Legislative Service*, 1993 Laws of Ohio, pages 5–855 and 5–251, for original versions of these Acts.

2915.03 Operating a gambling house

(A) No person, being the owner or lessee, or having custody, control, or supervision of premises, shall:

(1) Use or occupy such premises for gambling in violation of section 2915.02 of the Revised Code;

(2) Recklessly permit such premises to be used or occupied for gambling in violation of section 2915.02 of the Revised Code.

(B) Whoever violates this section is guilty of operating a gambling house, a misdemeanor of the first degree. If the offender has previously been convicted of a gambling offense, operating a gambling house is a felony of the fourth degree.

(C) Premises used or occupied in violation of this section constitute a nuisance subject to abatement pursuant to sections 3767.01 to 3767.99 of the Revised Code.

(1972 H 511, eff. 1–1–74)

2915.04 Public gaming

(A) No person, while at a hotel, restaurant, tavern, store, arena, hall, or other place of public accommodation, business, amusement, or resort shall make a bet or play any game of chance.

(B) No person, being the owner or lessee, or having custody, control, or supervision of a hotel, restaurant, tavern, store, arena, hall, or other place of public accommodation, business, amusement, or resort shall recklessly permit such premises to be used or occupied in violation of division (A) of this section.

(C) This section does not prohibit conduct in connection with gambling expressly permitted by law.

(D) Whoever violates this section is guilty of public gaming, a minor misdemeanor. If the offender has previously been convicted of any gambling offense, public gaming is a misdemeanor of the fourth degree.

(E) Premises used or occupied in violation of division (B) of this section constitute a nuisance subject to abatement pursuant to sections 3767.01 to 3767.99 of the Revised Code.

(1972 H 511, eff. 1–1–74)

2915.05 Cheating

(A) No person, with purpose to defraud or knowing that he is facilitating a fraud, shall engage in conduct designed to corrupt the outcome of:

(1) The subject of a bet;

(2) A contest of knowledge, skill, speed, strength, or endurance;

(3) A scheme or game of chance.

(B) Whoever violates this section is guilty of cheating, a misdemeanor of the first degree. If the potential gain from cheating is three hundred dollars or more, or if the offender has previously been convicted of any gambling offense or of any theft offense as defined in section 2913.01 of the Revised Code, then cheating is a felony of the fourth degree.

(1982 H 269, § 4, eff. 1–5–83; 1982 S 199; 1972 H 511)

2915.06 Corrupting sports

(A) No person shall knowingly:

(1) Offer, give, solicit, or accept anything of value to corrupt the outcome of any athletic or sporting event;

(2) Engage in conduct designed to corrupt the outcome of any athletic or sporting event.

(B) Whoever violates this section is guilty of corrupting sports, a felony of the fourth degree. If the offender has previously been convicted of any gambling offense or of any theft offense as defined in section 2913.01 of the Revised Code, corrupting sports is a felony of the third degree.

(1972 H 511, eff. 1–1–74)

CHARITABLE BINGO

2915.07 Conducting an illegal bingo game

(A) No person, except a charitable organization that has obtained a bingo license pursuant to section 2915.08 of the Revised Code, shall conduct or advertise a bingo game.

(B) Whoever violates this section is guilty of conducting an illegal bingo game, a felony of the third degree.

(1976 S 398, eff. 5–26–76)

2915.08 License of charitable organization to conduct bingo games; temporary renewal; notice of issuance; amendment of license; rules

(A) Annually before the first day of January a charitable organization that desires to conduct bingo games shall make out and deliver to the attorney general, upon a form to be furnished by the attorney general for that purpose, an application for a license to conduct bingo and a license fee of one hundred dollars or a reduced license fee established by the attorney general pursuant to division (G) of this section. The application shall be in the form prescribed by the attorney general and shall be signed and sworn to by the applicant.

The application shall contain the following:

(1) The name and post-office address of the applicant;

(2) A statement that the applicant is a charitable organization and that it has been in continuous existence as a charitable organization in this state for two years immediately preceding the making of the application or for five years in the case of a fraternal organization or a nonprofit medical organization;

(3) The location at which the organization will conduct the bingo game, which location shall be within the county in which the principal place of business of the applicant is located, the days of the week and the times on each of those days when a bingo session will be conducted, whether the organization owns, leases, or subleases the premises, and a copy of the rental agreement if it leases or subleases the premises;

(4) A statement of the applicant's previous history, record, and association that is sufficient to establish that the applicant is a charitable organization and a copy of a determination letter that is issued by the Internal Revenue Service and states that the organization is tax exempt under subsection 501(a) and described in subsection 501(c)(3), 501(c)(4), 501(c)(8), 501(c)(10), or 501(c)(19) of the Internal Revenue Code;

(5) A statement as to whether the applicant has ever had any previous application refused, whether it previously has had a license revoked or suspended, and the reason stated by the attorney general for the refusal, revocation, or suspension;

(6) A statement of the charitable purpose for which the bingo proceeds will be used;

(7) Other necessary and reasonable information that the attorney general may require by rule adopted pursuant to section 111.15 of the Revised Code;

(8) In the case of an applicant seeking to qualify as a youth athletic park organization under division (CC) of section 2915.01 of the Revised Code, a statement issued by a board or body vested with authority under Chapter 755. of the Revised Code for the supervision and maintenance of recreation facilities in the territory in which the organization is located, certifying that the playing fields owned by the organization were used for at least one hundred days during the year in which the statement is issued, and were open for use to all residents of that territory, regardless of race, color, creed, religion, sex, or national origin, for athletic activities by youth athletic organizations, as defined in division (BB) of section 2915.01 of the Revised Code, that do not discriminate on the basis of race, color, creed, religion, sex, or national origin, and that the fields were not used for any profit-making activity at any time during the year. That type of board or body is authorized to issue the statement upon request and shall issue the statement if it finds that the applicant's playing fields were so used.

The attorney general, within thirty days after receiving a timely filed application from a charitable organization that has been issued a bingo license that has not expired and has not been revoked or suspended, shall send a temporary permit to the applicant specifying the date on which the application was filed with the attorney general and stating that, pursuant to section 119.06 of the Revised Code, the applicant may continue to conduct bingo games until a new license is granted or, if the application is rejected, until fifteen days after notice of the rejection is mailed to the applicant. The temporary permit does not affect the validity of the applicant's application and does not grant any rights to the applicant except those rights specifically granted in section 119.06 of the Revised Code. The issuance of a temporary permit by the attorney general pursuant to this paragraph does not prohibit the attorney general from rejecting the applicant's application because of acts that the applicant committed, or actions that he failed to take, before or after the issuance of the temporary permit.

(B)(1) The attorney general shall adopt rules to enforce sections 2915.01, 2915.02, and 2915.07 to 2915.12 of the Revised Code, to ensure that bingo games are conducted in accordance with those sections, and to maintain proper control over the conduct of bingo games. The rules, except rules adopted pursuant to division (A)(7) of this section, shall be adopted pursuant to Chapter 119. of the Revised Code. The attorney general shall license charitable organizations to conduct bingo games in conformance with this chapter and with the licensing provisions of Chapter 119. of the Revised Code.

(2) The attorney general may refuse to grant a bingo license to any organization, or revoke or suspend the license of any organization, that does any of the following or to which any of the following applies:

(a) Fails or has failed at any time to meet any requirement of sections 2915.07 to 2915.11 of the Revised Code, or violates or has violated any provision of sections 2915.02 or 2915.07 to 2915.12 of the Revised Code or any rule adopted by the attorney general pursuant to this section;

(b) Makes or has made an incorrect or false statement that is material to the granting of the license in an application filed pursuant to division (A) of this section;

(c) Submits or has submitted any incorrect or false information relating to an application if the information is material to the granting of the license;

(d) Maintains or has maintained any incorrect or false information that is material to the granting of the license in the records required to be kept pursuant to division (A) of section 2915.10 of the Revised Code, if applicable;

(e) The attorney general has good cause to believe will not conduct its bingo games in accordance with sections 2915.02 and 2915.07 to 2915.12 of the Revised Code or with any rule adopted by the attorney general pursuant to this section.

(3) For the purposes of this division, any action of an officer, trustee, agent, representative, or bingo game operator of an organization is an action of the organization.

(C) The attorney general may grant bingo licenses to charitable organizations that are branches, lodges, or chapters of national charitable organizations.

(D) The attorney general shall send notice in writing to the prosecuting attorney and sheriff of the county in which the organization will conduct the bingo game, as stated in its application for a license or amended license, and to any other law enforcement agency in that county that so requests, of all of the following:

(1) The issuance of the license;

(2) The issuance of the amended license;

(3) The rejection of an application for and refusal to grant a license;

(4) The revocation of any license previously issued;

(5) The suspension of any license previously issued.

(E) A bingo license issued by the attorney general shall set forth the information contained on the application of the charitable organization that the attorney general determines is relevant, including, but not limited to, the location at which the organization will conduct the bingo game and the days of the week and the times on each of those days when a bingo session will be conducted. If the attorney general refuses to grant or revokes or suspends a bingo license, he shall notify the applicant in writing and specifically identify the reason for the refusal, revocation, or suspension in narrative form and, if applicable, by identifying the section of the Revised Code violated. The failure of the attorney general to give the written notice of the reasons for the refusal, revocation, or suspension or a mistake in the written notice does not affect the validity of the attorney general's refusal to grant, or the revocation or suspension of, a bingo license. If the attorney general fails to give the written notice or if there is a mistake in the written notice, the applicant may bring an action to compel the attorney general to comply with this division or to correct the mistake, but the attorney general's order refusing to grant, or revoking or suspending, a bingo license shall not be enjoined during the pendency of the action.

(F) A charitable organization that has been issued a bingo license pursuant to division (B) of this section but that cannot conduct bingo sessions at the location, or on the day of the week or the time, specified on the license due to circumstances beyond its control may apply, without charge, in writing to the attorney general for an amended bingo license. The application shall describe in detail the causes making it impossible for the organization to conduct its bingo sessions in conformity with its license and shall indicate the location, days of the week, and times on each of those days when it desires to conduct a bingo session. If the attorney general approves the application for the amended license, he shall issue the amended license in accordance with division (E) of this section, and the organization shall surrender its original license to the attorney general. The attorney general shall refuse to grant an application for an amended bingo license according to the terms of division (B) of this section.

(G) The attorney general, by rule adopted pursuant to section 111.15 of the Revised Code, shall establish a schedule of reduced license fees for charitable organizations that desire to conduct bingo games during fewer than twenty-six weeks in any calendar year.

(1993 H 104, eff. 10–7–93; 1983 H 291; 1982 S 550; 1981 S 91; 1977 H 72; 1976 S 398, H 1547)

2915.09 Methods of conducting a licensed bingo game; prohibitions

(A) A charitable organization that conducts a bingo game shall do all of the following:

(1) Own all of the equipment used to conduct the bingo game or lease that equipment from a charitable organization that is licensed to conduct a bingo game for a rental rate that is not more than is customary and reasonable for that equipment;

(2) Use all of the gross receipts from the bingo game for paying prizes, for the charitable purposes listed in its bingo license application, for purchasing or leasing bingo cards and other equipment used in conducting the bingo game, hiring security personnel for the bingo game, or advertising the bingo game, provided that the amount of the receipts so spent is not more than is customary and reasonable for a similar purchase, lease, hiring, or advertising, and for renting premises in which to conduct the bingo game, except that if the building in which the game is conducted is owned by the charitable organization conducting the game, the charitable organization may deduct from the total amount of the gross receipts from each session a sum equal to the lesser of six hundred dollars or forty-five per cent of the gross receipts from the session as consideration for the use of the premises;

(3) Conduct the bingo game on premises that are owned by the charitable organization, on premises that are owned by another charitable organization and leased from that charitable organization for a rental rate not in excess of four hundred fifty dollars per bingo session, on premises that are leased from a person other than a charitable organization for a rental rate that is not more than is customary and reasonable for premises that are similar in location, size, and quality but not in excess of four hundred fifty dollars per bingo session, or on premises that are owned by a person other than a charitable organization, that are leased from that person by another charitable organization, and that are subleased from that other charitable organization by the charitable organization for a rental rate not in excess of four hundred fifty dollars per bingo session. If the charitable organization leases from a person other than a charitable organization the premises on which it conducts bingo games, the lessor of the premises shall provide only the premises to the organization and shall not provide the organization with bingo game operators, security personnel, concessions or concession operators, bingo equipment, or any other type of service or equipment. A charitable organization shall not lease or sublease premises that it owns or leases to more than one other charitable organization per calendar week for the purpose of conducting bingo games on the premises. A person that is not a charitable organization shall not lease premises that it owns, leases, or otherwise is empowered to lease to more than one charitable organization per calendar week for conducting bingo games on the premises. In no case shall more than two bingo sessions be conducted on any premises in any calendar week.

(4) Display its bingo license conspicuously at the location where the bingo game is conducted;

(5) Conduct the bingo game in accordance with the definition of bingo set forth in division (S)(1) of section 2915.01 of the Revised Code.

(B) A charitable organization that conducts a bingo game shall not do any of the following:

(1) Pay any compensation to a bingo game operator for operating a bingo game that is conducted by the charitable organization or for preparing, selling, or serving food or beverages at the site of the bingo game, permit any auxiliary unit or society of the charitable organization to pay compensation to any bingo game operator who prepares, sells, or serves food or beverages at a bingo session conducted by the charitable organization, or permit any auxiliary unit or society of the charitable organization to prepare, sell, or serve food or beverages at a bingo session conducted by the charitable organization, if the auxiliary unit or society pays any compensation to the bingo game operators who prepare, sell, or serve the food or beverages;

(2) Pay consulting fees to any person for any services performed in relation to the bingo game;

(3) Pay concession fees to any person who provides refreshments to the participants in the bingo game;

(4) Conduct more than two bingo sessions in any seven-day period. Except that a volunteer fire fighter's organization or a volunteer rescue service organization that conducts not more than five bingo sessions in a calendar year may conduct more than two bingo sessions in a seven-day period after notifying the attorney general when it will conduct the sessions;

(5) Pay out more than three thousand five hundred dollars in prizes during any bingo session that is conducted by the charitable organization;

(6) Conduct a bingo session at any time during the ten-hour period between midnight and ten a.m., at any time during, or within ten hours of, a bingo game conducted for amusement only pursuant to section 2915.12 of the Revised Code, at any location not specified on its bingo license, or on any day of the week or during any time period not specified on its bingo license. If circumstances beyond its control make it impossible for the charitable organization to conduct a bingo session at the location specified on its bingo license or if a charitable organization wants to conduct bingo sessions on a day of the week or at a time other than the day or time specified on its bingo license, the charitable organization may apply in writing to the attorney general for an amended bingo license, pursuant to division (F) of section 2915.08 of the Revised Code. A charitable organization may apply only once in each calendar year for an amended license to conduct bingo sessions on a day of the week or at a time other than the day or time specified on its bingo license. If the amended license is granted, the organization may conduct bingo sessions at the location, on the day of the week, and at the time specified on its amended license.

(7) Permit any person whom the charitable organization knows, or should have known, is under the age of eighteen to work as a bingo game operator;

(8) Permit any person whom the charitable organization knows, or should have known, has been convicted of a felony or gambling offense in any jurisdiction to be a bingo game operator;

(9) Permit the lessor of the premises on which bingo is conducted, if the lessor is not a charitable organization, to provide the charitable organization with bingo game operators, security personnel, concessions, bingo equipment, or any other type of service or equipment.

(C) A bingo game operator shall not receive or accept any commission, wage, salary, reward, tip, donation, gratuity, or other form of compensation, directly or indirectly, regardless of the source, for operating a bingo game or providing other work or labor at the site of the bingo game.

(D) Notwithstanding division (A)(3) of this section, a charitable organization that, prior to December 6, 1977, has entered into written agreements for the lease of premises it owns to another charitable organization or other charitable organizations for the conducting of bingo sessions so that more than two bingo sessions are conducted per calendar week on the premises, and a person that is not a charitable organization and that, prior to December 6, 1977, has entered into written agreements for the lease of premises it owns to charitable organizations for the conducting of more than two bingo sessions per calendar week on the premises, may continue to lease the premises to those charitable organizations, provided that no more than four sessions are conducted per calendar week, that the lessor organization or person has notified the attorney general in writing of the organizations that will conduct the sessions and the days of the week and the times of the day on which the sessions will be conducted, that the initial lease entered into with each organization that will conduct the sessions was filed with the attorney general prior to December 6, 1977, and that each organization that will conduct the sessions was issued a license to conduct bingo games by the attorney general prior to December 6, 1977.

(E) Whoever violates division (A)(2) of this section is guilty of illegally conducting a bingo game, a felony of the third degree. Whoever violates division (A)(1), (3), (4), or (5), (B), or (C) of this section is guilty of a minor misdemeanor. If the offender previously has been convicted of a violation of division (A)(1), (3), (4), or (5), (B), or (C) of this section, a violation of division (A)(1), (3), (4), or (5), (B), or (C) of this section is a misdemeanor of the first degree.

(1995 S 70, eff. 3–5–96; 1993 H 104, eff. 10–7–93; 1990 H 573; 1981 S 91; 1977 H 72; 1976 S 398, H 1547)

2915.10   Records to be maintained; enforcement; prohibitions

(A) A charitable organization that conducts a bingo session or scheme or game of chance pursuant to division (D) of section 2915.02 of the Revised Code, shall maintain the following records for at least three years from the date on which the bingo session or scheme or game of chance is conducted:

(1) An itemized list of the gross receipts of each session or scheme or game of chance;

(2) An itemized list of all expenses other than prizes that are incurred in conducting the bingo session, the name of each person to whom the expenses are paid, and a receipt for all of the expenses;

(3) A list of all prizes awarded during the bingo session or scheme or game of chance conducted by the charitable organization and the name and address of all persons who are winners of prizes of one hundred dollars or more in value;

(4) An itemized list of the charitable recipients of the proceeds of the bingo session or scheme or game of chance, including the name and address of each recipient to whom the money is distributed, and if the organization uses the proceeds of a bingo session, or the money or assets received from a scheme or game of chance for any purpose set forth in division (Z) of section 2915.01 or division (D) of section 2915.02 of the Revised Code, a list of each purpose and an itemized list of each expenditure for each purpose;

(5) The number of persons who participate in any bingo session or scheme or game of chance that is conducted by the charitable organization;

(6) A list of receipts from the sale of food and beverages by the charitable organization or one of its auxiliary units or societies, if the receipts were excluded from the definition of "gross receipts" under division (X) of section 2915.01 of the Revised Code;

(7) An itemized list of all expenses incurred at each bingo session conducted by the charitable organization in the sale of food and beverages by the charitable organization or by an auxiliary unit or society of the charitable organization, the name of each person to whom the expenses are paid, and a receipt for all of the expenses.

(B) The attorney general, or any local law enforcement agency, may:

(1) Investigate any charitable organization or any officer, agent, trustee, member, or employee of the organization;

(2) Examine the accounts and records of the organization;

(3) Conduct inspections, audits, and observations of bingo games or schemes or games of chance while they are in session;

(4) Conduct inspections of the premises where bingo games or schemes or games of chance are operated;

(5) Take any other necessary and reasonable action to determine if a violation of any provision of sections 2915.01, 2915.02, and 2915.07 to 2915.12 of the Revised Code has occurred.

If any local law enforcement agency has reasonable grounds to believe that a charitable organization or an officer, agent, trustee, member, or employee of the organization has violated any provision of sections 2915.01 to 2915.12 of the Revised Code, the local law enforcement agency may proceed by action in the proper court to enforce sections 2915.01 to 2915.12 of the Revised Code, provided that the local law enforcement agency shall give written notice to the attorney general when commencing an action as described in this division.

(C) No person shall destroy, alter, conceal, withhold, or deny access to any accounts or records of a charitable organization that have been requested for examination, or obstruct, impede, or interfere with any inspection, audit, or observation of a bingo game or scheme or game of chance or premises where a bingo game or scheme or game of chance is operated, or refuse to comply with any reasonable request of, or obstruct, impede, or interfere with any other reasonable action undertaken by, the attorney general or a local law enforcement agency pursuant to division (B) of this section.

(D) Whoever violates division (A) or (C) of this section is guilty of a misdemeanor of the first degree.

(1981 S 91, eff. 10–20–81; 1977 H 72; 1976 S 398, H 1547)

2915.11 Minor and felon not to work at bingo session

(A) No person shall be a bingo game operator unless he is eighteen years of age or older.

(B) No person who has been convicted of a felony or a gambling offense in any jurisdiction shall be a bingo game operator.

(C) Whoever violates division (A) of this section is guilty of a misdemeanor of the third degree.

(D) Whoever violates division (B) of this section is guilty of a misdemeanor of the first degree.

(1977 H 72, eff. 12–15–77; 1976 S 398)

2915.111   Possession of "numbers" ticket—Repealed

(1972 H 511, eff. 1–1–74; 129 v 1409)

2915.12   Game for amusement only excepted; conditions; enforcement; offense

Sections 2915.07 to 2915.11 of the Revised Code do not apply to bingo games that are conducted for the purpose of amusement only. A bingo game is conducted for the purpose of amusement only if it complies with all of the requirements specified in either division (A) or (B) of this section:

(A)(1) The participants do not pay any money or any other thing of value including an admission fee, or any fee for bingo cards, sheets, objects to cover the spaces, or other devices used in playing bingo, for the privilege of participating in the bingo game, or to defray any costs of the game, or pay tips or make donations during or immediately before or after the bingo game;

(2) All prizes awarded during the course of the game are nonmonetary, and in the form of merchandise, goods, or entitlements to goods or services only, and the total value of all prizes awarded during the game is less than one hundred dollars;

(3) No commission, wages, salary, reward, tip, donation, gratuity, or other form of compensation, either directly or indirectly, and regardless of the source, is paid to any bingo game operator for work or labor performed at the site of the bingo game;

(4) The bingo game is not conducted either during or within ten hours of:

(a) A bingo session during which a charitable bingo game is conducted pursuant to sections 2915.07 to 2915.11 of the Revised Code;

(b) A scheme or game of chance other than a bingo game conducted pursuant to this section.

(5) The number of players participating in the bingo game does not exceed fifty.

(B)(1) The participants do not pay money or any other thing of value as an admission fee, and no participant is charged more than twenty-five cents to purchase a bingo card, sheet, objects to cover the spaces, or other devices used in playing bingo;

(2) The total amount of money paid by all of the participants for bingo cards, sheets, objects to cover the spaces, or other devices used in playing bingo does not exceed one hundred dollars;

(3) All of the money paid for bingo cards, sheets, objects to cover spaces, or other devices used in playing bingo are used only to pay winners monetary and nonmonetary prizes and to provide refreshments;

(4) The total value of all prizes awarded during the game does not exceed one hundred dollars;

(5) No commission, wages, salary, reward, tip, donation, gratuity, or other form of compensation, either directly or indirectly, and regardless of the source, is paid to any bingo game operator for work or labor performed at the site of the bingo game;

(6) The bingo game is not conducted during or within ten hours of either of the following:

(a) A bingo session during which a charitable bingo game is conducted pursuant to sections 2915.07 to 2915.11 of the Revised Code;

(b) A scheme of chance or game of chance other than a bingo game conducted pursuant to this section.

(7) All of the participants reside at the premises where the bingo game is conducted;

(8) The bingo games are conducted on different days of the week and not more than twice in a calendar week.

(C) The attorney general, or any local law enforcement agency, may investigate the conduct of amusement bingo if there is reason to believe that a purported amusement bingo game is operated in violation of this section. A local law enforcement agency may proceed by action in the proper court to enforce this section if the local law enforcement agency gives written notice to the attorney general when commencing the action.

(D) Whoever conducts a bingo game that is not a charitable bingo game and that does not conform to division (A) or (B) of this section is guilty of a misdemeanor of the first degree on the first offense, and is guilty of a felony of the fourth degree for each subsequent offense.
(1990 H 573, eff. 4–10–91; 1977 H 72; 1976 S 398)

2915.121   Manufacture or sale of pool ticket on sports or athletic event—Repealed

(1972 H 511, eff. 1–1–74; 129 v 1408)

Historical and Statutory Notes

Ed. Note: See now 2915.02 for provisions analogous to former 2915.121.

2915.122   Possession of pool ticket on sports or athletic event—Repealed

(1972 H 511, eff. 1–1–74; 129 v 1408)

Historical and Statutory Notes

Ed. Note: See now 2915.02 for provisions analogous to former 2915.122.

2915.13   Penalty for promoting a "numbers game"—Repealed

(1972 H 511, eff. 1–1–74; 129 v 1409; 1953 H 1; GC 13064–1)

2915.14   Common gambler—Repealed

(1972 H 511, eff. 1–1–74; 1953 H 1; GC 13065)

Historical and Statutory Notes

Ed. Note: See now 2915.02 for provisions analogous to former 2915.14.

Pre–1953 H 1 Amendments: RS 6934

2915.15   Exhibiting gambling devices for gain—Repealed

(1972 H 511, eff. 1–1–74; 1953 H 1; GC 13066)

Historical and Statutory Notes

Ed. Note: See now 2915.02 for provisions analogous to former 2915.15.

Pre–1953 H 1 Amendments: 124 v H 115;   RS 6934

2915.16   Definition of gambling device—Repealed

(1972 H 511, eff. 1–1–74; 1953 H 1; GC 13066–1)

Historical and Statutory Notes

Ed. Note: See now 2915.01 for provisions analogous to former 2915.16.

Pre–1953 H 1 Amendments: 124 v H 115

2915.17   Penalty for owning, possessing, or exhibiting gambling devices—Repealed

(1972 H 511, eff. 1–1–74; 1953 H 1; GC 13066–2; Source—GC 13066–4)

Historical and Statutory Notes

Ed. Note: See now 2915.02 for provisions analogous to former 2915.17.

Pre–1953 H 1 Amendments: 124 v H 115

2915.18   Penalty for transporting gambling devices—Repealed

(1972 H 511, eff. 1–1–74; 1953 H 1; GC 13066–3; Source—GC 13066–4)

Historical and Statutory Notes

Ed. Note: See now 2915.02 for provisions analogous to former 2915.18.

Pre–1953 H 1 Amendments: 124 v H 115

2915.19   Advertising lotteries; venue—Repealed

(1972 H 511, eff. 1–1–74; 1953 H 1; GC 13067, 13068)

Historical and Statutory Notes

Ed. Note: See now 2915.02 for provisions analogous to former 2915.19.

Pre–1953 H 1 Amendments: RS 6929

2915.20   Contract for option on grain; "cornering" the market—Repealed

(1972 H 511, eff. 1–1–74; 1953 H 1; GC 13069)

Historical and Statutory Notes

Ed. Note: See now federal securities laws for provisions analogous to former 2915.20.

Pre–1953 H 1 Amendments: RS 6934a

2915.21   Contracts void—Repealed

(1972 H 511, eff. 1–1–74; 1953 H 1; GC 13070)

Historical and Statutory Notes

Pre–1953 H 1 Amendments: RS 6934a

2915.31   Definitions—Repealed

(1972 H 511, eff. 1–1–74; 1953 H 1; GC 13079, 13080)

Historical and Statutory Notes

Ed. Note: See now federal securities laws for provisions analogous to former 2915.31.

Pre–1953 H 1 Amendments: 102 v 318; 86 v 14, § 4

2915.32   Keeping a bucket shop—Repealed

(1972 H 511, eff. 1–1–74; 1953 H 1; GC 13071, 13072)

Historical and Statutory Notes

Ed. Note: See now federal securities laws for provisions analogous to former 2915.32.

Pre–1953 H 1 Amendments: 102 v 317; 86 v 12, § 1

2915.33 Foreign affiliations of bucket shop—Repealed

(1972 H 511, eff. 1–1–74; 1953 H 1; GC 13073, 13074)

Historical and Statutory Notes

Ed. Note: See now federal securities laws for provisions analogous to former 2915.33.

Pre–1953 H 1 Amendments: 86 v 12

2915.34 When offense is complete—Repealed

(1972 H 511, eff. 1–1–74; 1953 H 1; GC 13075)

Historical and Statutory Notes

Ed. Note: See now federal securities laws for provisions analogous to former 2915.34.

Pre–1953 H 1 Amendments: 86 v 13, § 2

2915.35 Principal offender—Repealed

(1972 H 511, eff. 1–1–74; 1953 H 1; GC 13076)

Historical and Statutory Notes

Ed. Note: See now federal securities laws for provisions analogous to former 2915.35.

Pre–1953 H 1 Amendments: 86 v 13, § 2

2915.36 Broker shall give principal written statement concerning transactions—Repealed

(1972 H 511, eff. 1–1–74; 1953 H 1; GC 13077)

Historical and Statutory Notes

Ed. Note: See now federal securities laws for provisions analogous to former 2915.36.

Pre–1953 H 1 Amendments: 102 v 317; 86 v 14, § 3

2915.37 Permitting building to be used for bucket shop or grain gambling—Repealed

(1972 H 511, eff. 1–1–74; 1953 H 1; GC 13081)

Historical and Statutory Notes

Ed. Note: See now federal securities laws for provisions analogous to former 2915.37.

Pre–1953 H 1 Amendments: 86 v 14, § 5

2915.40 Coercion of retailer to conduct games—Repealed

(1972 H 511, eff. 1–1–74; 1970 S 284)

Historical and Statutory Notes

Ed. Note: See now 2915.02 for provisions analogous to former 2915.40.

CHAPTER 2917

OFFENSES AGAINST THE PUBLIC PEACE

INCITING, RIOT, AND RELATED OFFENSES

DISORDERLY CONDUCT

HARASSMENT

FALSE ALARMS

MISCELLANEOUS OFFENSES

INCITING, RIOT, AND RELATED OFFENSES

2917.01 Inciting to violence

(A) No person shall knowingly engage in conduct designed to urge or incite another to commit any offense of violence, when either of the following apply:

(1) Such conduct takes place under circumstances which create a clear and present danger that any offense of violence will be committed;

(2) Such conduct proximately results in the commission of any offense of violence.

(B) Whoever violates this section is guilty of inciting to violence, a felony of the third degree.

(1972 H 511, eff. 1–1–74)

2917.02 Aggravated riot

(A) No person shall participate with four or more others in a course of disorderly conduct in violation of section 2917.11 of the Revised Code:

(1) With purpose to commit or facilitate the commission of a felony;

(2) With purpose to commit or facilitate the commission of any offense of violence;

(3) When the offender or any participant to the knowledge of the offender has on or about his person or under his control, uses, or intends to use a deadly weapon or dangerous ordnance, as defined in section 2923.11 of the Revised Code.

(B) No person, being an inmate in a detention facility, as defined in section 2921.01 of the Revised Code, shall violate division (A) of this section, or section 2917.03 of the Revised Code.

(C) Whoever violates this section is guilty of aggravated riot. Violation of division (A) of this section is a felony of the fourth degree. Violation of division (B) of this section is a felony of the third degree, and sentence of confinement imposed shall be served consecutively to any other sentence of confinement imposed on such offender.

(1983 S 210, eff. 7–1–83; 1982 H 269, § 4, S 199; 1972 H 511)

2917.03 Riot

(A) No person shall participate with four or more others in a course of disorderly conduct in violation of section 2917.11 of the Revised Code:

(1) With purpose to commit or facilitate the commission of a misdemeanor, other than disorderly conduct;

(2) With purpose to intimidate a public official or employee into taking or refraining from official action, or with purpose to hinder, impede, or obstruct a function of government;

(3) With purpose to hinder, impede, or obstruct the orderly process of administration or instruction at an educational institution, or to interfere with or disrupt lawful activities carried on at such institution.

(B) No person shall participate with four or more others with purpose to do an act with unlawful force or violence, even though such act might otherwise be lawful.

(C) Whoever violates this section is guilty of riot, a misdemeanor of the first degree.

(1972 H 511, eff. 1–1–74)

2917.04 Failure to disperse

(A) Where five or more persons are participating in a course of disorderly conduct in violation of section 2917.11 of the Revised Code, and there are other persons in the vicinity whose presence creates the likelihood of physical harm to persons or property or of serious public inconvenience, annoyance, or alarm, a law enforcement officer or other public official may order the participants and such other persons to disperse. No person shall knowingly fail to obey such order.

(B) Nothing in this section requires persons to disperse who are peaceably assembled for a lawful purpose.

(C) Whoever violates this section is guilty of failure to disperse, a minor misdemeanor.

(1972 H 511, eff. 1–1–74)

2917.05   Justifiable use of force to suppress riot

A law enforcement officer or fireman, engaged in suppressing riot or in protecting persons or property during riot:

(A) Is justified in using force, other than deadly force, when and to the extent he has probable cause to believe such force is necessary to disperse or apprehend rioters;

(B) Is justified in using force, including deadly force, when and to the extent he has probable cause to believe such force is necessary to disperse or apprehend rioters whose conduct is creating a substantial risk of serious physical harm to persons.

(1972 H 511, eff. 1–1–74)

2917.06   Bribery of witness—Repealed

(1972 H 511, eff. 1–1–74; 1953 H 1; GC 12827)

2917.07   Intimidating witness, juror, or officer—Repealed

(1972 H 511, eff. 1–1–74; 1953 H 1; GC 12866)

2917.08   Juror before county court receiving excessive fees—Repealed

(1972 H 511, eff. 1–1–74; 129 v 582; 1953 H 1; GC 12828)

2917.09   Breaking into jail or attacking officer for the purpose of lynching— Repealed

(1972 H 511, eff. 1–1–74; 1953 H 1; GC 12831)

2917.10   Permitting prisoner to escape; rescuing prisoner by force—Repealed

(1972 H 511, eff. 1–1–74; 1953 H 1; GC 12832)

DISORDERLY CONDUCT

2917.11   Disorderly conduct

(A) No person shall recklessly cause inconvenience, annoyance, or alarm to another, by doing any of the following:

(1) Engaging in fighting, in threatening harm to persons or property, or in violent or turbulent behavior;

(2) Making unreasonable noise or offensively coarse utterance, gesture, or display, or communicating unwarranted and grossly abusive language to any person;

(3) Insulting, taunting, or challenging another, under circumstances in which such conduct is likely to provoke a violent response;

(4) Hindering or preventing the movement of persons on a public street, road, highway, or right-of-way, or to, from, within, or upon public or private property, so as to interfere with the rights of others, and by any act which serves no lawful and reasonable purpose of the offender;

(5) Creating a condition which is physically offensive to persons or which presents a risk of physical harm to persons or property, by any act which serves no lawful and reasonable purpose of the offender.

(B) No person, while voluntarily intoxicated shall do either of the following:

(1) In a public place or in the presence of two or more persons, engage in conduct likely to be offensive or to cause inconvenience, annoyance, or alarm to persons of ordinary sensibilities, which conduct the offender, if he were not intoxicated, should know is likely to have such effect on others;

(2) Engage in conduct or create a condition which presents a risk of physical harm to himself or another, or to the property of another.

(C) Violation of any statute or ordinance of which an element is operating a motor vehicle, locomotive, watercraft, aircraft, or other vehicle while under the influence of alcohol or any drug of abuse, is not a violation of division (B) of this section.

(D) When to an ordinary observer a person appears to be intoxicated, it is probable cause to believe such person is voluntarily intoxicated for purposes of division (B) of this section.

(E) Whoever violates this section is guilty of disorderly conduct, a minor misdemeanor, except that if the offender persists in disorderly conduct after reasonable warning or request to desist, or if the offender is within one thousand feet of the boundaries of any school, school premises, or school building, disorderly conduct is a misdemeanor of the fourth degree.

(F) As used in this section, "school," "school premises," and "school building" have the same meanings as in section 2925.01 of the Revised Code.

(1990 H 51, eff. 11–8–90; 1972 H 511)

2917.12   Disturbing a lawful meeting

(A) No person, with purpose to prevent or disrupt a lawful meeting, procession, or gathering, shall do either of the following:

(1) Do any act which obstructs or interferes with the due conduct of such meeting, procession, or gathering;

(2) Make any utterance, gesture, or display which outrages the sensibilities of the group.

(B) Whoever violates this section is guilty of disturbing a lawful meeting, a misdemeanor of the fourth degree.

(1972 H 511, eff. 1–1–74)

2917.13   Misconduct at an emergency

(A) No person shall knowingly:

(1) Hamper the lawful operations of any law enforcement officer, fireman, rescuer, medical person, or other authorized person, engaged in his duties at the scene of a fire, accident, disaster, riot, or emergency of any kind;

(2) Fail to obey the lawful order of any law enforcement officer engaged in his duties at the scene of or in connection with a fire, accident, disaster, riot, or emergency of any kind.

(B) Nothing in this section shall be construed to limit access or deny information to any news media representative in the lawful exercise of his duties.

(C) Whoever violates this section is guilty of misconduct at an emergency, a minor misdemeanor. If violation of this section creates a risk of physical harm to persons or property, misconduct at an emergency is a misdemeanor of the fourth degree.

(1973 H 716, eff. 1–1–74; 1972 H 511)

2917.14   Conveying articles into penitentiary to aid an escape—Repealed

(1972 H 511, eff. 1–1–74; 125 v 222; 1953 H 1; GC 12835)

2917.15   Conveying articles into jail to aid an escape—Repealed

(1972 H 511, eff. 1–1–74; 1953 H 1; GC 12835)

2917.16   Conveying letters into or from prison—Repealed

(1972 H 511, eff. 1–1–74; 1953 H 1; GC 12837)

2917.17   Conveying intoxicating liquors or drugs into prison—Repealed

(1972 H 511, eff. 1–1–74; 1972 H 494; 130 v Pt 2, H 28; 128 v 1040; 1953 H 1; GC 12836)

2917.18   Permitting prisoner to receive liquor in jail—Repealed

(1972 H 511, eff. 1–1–74; 1953 H 1; GC 12846)

2917.19   Enticing inmates to escape from state institutions—Repealed

(1972 H 511, eff. 1–1–74; 130 v H 40; 1953 H 1; GC 12838)

2917.191   Attempt to entice inmates to escape from state institutions—Repealed

(1972 H 511, eff. 1–1–74; 130 v H 40)

2917.20   Soliciting money from persons confined—Repealed

(1972 H 511, eff. 1–1–74; 1953 H 1; GC 12838–1)

HARASSMENT

2917.21   Telephone harassment

(A) No person shall knowingly make or cause to be made a telephone call, or knowingly permit a telephone call to be made from a telephone under his control, to another, if the caller does any of the following:

(1) Fails to identify himself to the recipient of the telephone call and makes the telephone call with purpose to harass, abuse, or annoy any person at the premises to which the telephone call is made, whether or not conversation takes place during the telephone call;

(2) Describes, suggests, requests, or proposes that the caller, recipient of the telephone call, or any other person engage in, any sexual activity as defined in division (C) of section 2907.01 of the Revised Code, and the recipient of the telephone call, or another person at the premises to which the telephone call is made, has requested, in a previous telephone call or in the immediate telephone call, the caller not to make a telephone call to the recipient of the telephone call or to the premises to which the telephone call is made;

(3) During the telephone call, violates section 2903.21 of the Revised Code;

(4) Knowingly states to the recipient of the telephone call that he intends to cause damage to or destroy public or private property, and the recipient of the telephone call, any member of the family of the recipient of the telephone call, or any other person who resides at the premises to which the telephone call is made owns, leases, resides, or works in, will at the time of the destruction or damaging be near or in, has the responsibility of protecting, or insures the property that will be destroyed or damaged;

(5) Knowingly makes the telephone call to the recipient of the telephone call, to another person at the premises to which the telephone call is made, or to the premises to which the telephone call is made, and the recipient of the telephone call, or another person at the premises to which the telephone call is made, has previously told the caller not to call the premises to which the telephone call is made or not to call any persons at the premises to which the telephone call is made.

(B) No person shall make or cause to be made a telephone call, or permit a telephone call to be made from a telephone under his control, with purpose to abuse, threaten, annoy, or harass another person.

(C) Whoever violates this section is guilty of telephone harassment, a misdemeanor of the first degree. If the offender has previously been convicted of a violation of this section, then telephone harassment is a felony of the fourth degree.

(1980 H 164, eff. 4–9–81; 1972 H 511)

2917.211   Trespassing or loitering in school buildings or grounds—Repealed

(1972 H 511, eff. 1–1–74; 131 v S 21)

2917.22   Harboring a felon—Repealed

(1972 H 511, eff. 1–1–74; 1953 H 1; GC 12841)

2917.23   Escape from workhouse—Repealed

(1972 H 511, eff. 1–1–74; 1953 H 1; GC 12840)

2917.24   Escape from workhouse of person in default of fine—Repealed

(1972 H 511, eff. 1–1–74; 1970 S 460; 1953 H 1; GC 12840–1)

2917.25   Perjury—Repealed

(1972 H 511, eff. 1–1–74; 1953 H 1; GC 12842)

2917.26   Witness refusing to appear, be sworn, or answer—Repealed

(1972 H 511, eff. 1–1–74; 1953 H 1; GC 12843)

2917.27   Proceedings for contempt—Repealed

(1972 H 511, eff. 1–1–74; 1953 H 1; GC 12844)

2917.28   Jailer permitting jail to become unclean—Repealed

(1972 H 511, eff. 1–1–74; 1953 H 1; GC 12849)

2917.29   Officers neglecting duty in criminal cases—Repealed

(1972 H 511, eff. 1–1–74; 1953 H 1; GC 12850)

2917.30   Officers neglecting duty in misdemeanor cases—Repealed

(1972 H 511, eff. 1–1–74; 1953 H 1; GC 12850)

FALSE ALARMS

2917.31   Inducing panic

(A) No person shall cause the evacuation of any public place, or otherwise cause serious public inconvenience or alarm, by doing any of the following:

(1) Initiating or circulating a report or warning of an alleged or impending fire, explosion, crime, or other catastrophe, knowing that such report or warning is false;

(2) Threatening to commit any offense of violence;

(3) Committing any offense, with reckless disregard of the likelihood that its commission will cause serious public inconvenience or alarm.

(B) Division (A)(1) of this section does not apply to any person conducting an authorized fire or emergency drill.

(C) Whoever violates this section is guilty of inducing panic, a misdemeanor of the first degree. If violation of this section results in physical harm to any person, inducing panic is a felony of the fourth degree.

(1972 H 511, eff. 1–1–74)

2917.32   Making false alarms

(A) No person shall do either of the following:

(1) Initiate or circulate a report or warning of an alleged or impending fire, explosion, crime, or other catastrophe, knowing that the report or warning is false and likely to cause public inconvenience or alarm;

(2) Knowingly cause a false alarm of fire or other emergency to be transmitted to or within any organization, public or private, for dealing with emergencies involving a risk of physical harm to persons or property;

(3) Report to any law enforcement agency an alleged offense or other incident within its concern, knowing that such offense did not occur.

(B) This section does not apply to any person conducting an authorized fire or emergency drill.

(C) Whoever violates this section is guilty of making false alarms, a misdemeanor of the first degree.

(1972 H 511, eff. 1–1–74)

2917.33 Resisting or abusing a judge or officer—Repealed

(1972 H 511, eff. 1-1-74; 127 v 1039; 1953 H 1; GC 12858)

2917.34 Falsely personating another—Repealed

(1972 H 511, eff. 1-1-74; 129 v 582; 1953 H 1; GC 12859)

2917.35 Impersonating an officer—Repealed

(1972 H 511, eff. 1-1-74; 1953 H 1; GC 12860)

2917.36 Compounding felonies—Repealed

(1972 H 511, eff. 1-1-74; 1953 H 1; GC 12861)

2917.37 Assignment of claim or debt for collection by attachment outside state— Repealed

(1972 H 511, eff. 1-1-74; 1953 H 1; GC 12862)

2917.38 Purchase of claim for purpose of collection outside state—Repealed

(1972 H 511, eff. 1-1-74; 1953 H 1; GC 12863)

2917.39 Transfer is prima-facie evidence of violation—Repealed

(1972 H 511, eff. 1-1-74; 1953 H 1; GC 12864)

MISCELLANEOUS OFFENSES

2917.40 Definitions; seating at certain performances; crowd control measures; exemption may be granted by police; contracts for performances; exceptions; offenses

(A) As used in this section:

(1) "Live entertainment performance" means any live speech; any live musical performance, including a concert; any live dramatic performance; any live variety show; and any other live performance with respect to which the primary intent of the audience can be construed to be viewing the performers. A "live entertainment performance" does not include any form of entertainment with respect to which the person purchasing a ticket routinely participates in amusements as well as views performers.

(2) "Restricted entertainment area" means any wholly or partially enclosed area, whether indoors or outdoors, that has limited access through established entrances, or established turnstyles [sic] or similar devices.

(3) "Concert" means a musical performance of which the primary component is a presentation by persons singing or playing musical instruments, that is intended by its sponsors mainly, but not necessarily exclusively, for the listening enjoyment of the audience, and that is held in a facility. A "concert" does not include any performance in which music is a part of the presentation and the primary component of which is acting, dancing, a motion picture, a demonstration of skills or talent other than singing or playing an instrument, an athletic event, an exhibition, or a speech.

(4) "Facility" means any structure that has a roof or partial roof and that has walls that wholly surround the area on all sides, including, but not limited to, a stadium, hall, arena, armory, auditorium, ballroom, exhibition hall, convention center, or music hall.

(5) "Person" includes, in addition to an individual or entity specified in division (C) of section 1.59 of the Revised Code, any governmental entity.

(B)(1) No person shall sell, offer to sell, or offer in return for a donation any ticket that is not numbered and that does not correspond to a specific seat for admission to either of the following:

(a) A live entertainment performance that is not exempted under division (D) of this section, that is held in a restricted entertainment area, and for which more than eight thousand tickets are offered to the public;

(b) A concert that is not exempted under division (D) of this section and for which more than three thousand tickets are offered to the public.

(2) No person shall advertise any live entertainment performance as described in division (B)(1)(a) of this section or any concert as described in division (B)(1)(b) of this section, unless the advertisement contains the words "Reserved Seats Only."

(C) Unless exempted by division (D)(1) of this section, no person who owns or operates any restricted entertainment area shall fail to open, maintain, and properly staff at least the number of entrances designated under division (E) of this section for a minimum of ninety minutes prior to the scheduled start of any live entertainment performance that is held in the restricted entertainment area and for which more than three thousand tickets are sold, offered for sale, or offered in return for a donation.

(D)(1) A live entertainment performance, other than a concert, is exempted from the provisions of divisions (B) and (C) of this section if both of the following apply:

(a) The restricted entertainment area in which the performance is held has at least eight entrances or, if both entrances and separate admission turnstyles [*sic*] or similar devices are used, has at least eight turnstyles [*sic*] or similar devices;

(b) The eight entrances or, if applicable, the eight turnstyles [*sic*] or similar devices are opened, maintained, and properly staffed at least one hour prior to the scheduled start of the performance.

(2)(a) The chief of the police department of a township police district in the case of a facility located within the district, the officer responsible for public safety within a municipal corporation in the case of a facility located within the municipal corporation, or the county sheriff in the case of a facility located outside the boundaries of a township police district or municipal corporation may, upon application of the sponsor of a concert covered by division (B) of this section, exempt the concert from the provisions of that division if the official finds that the health, safety, and welfare of the participants and spectators would not be substantially affected by failure to comply with the provisions of that division.

In determining whether to grant an exemption, the official shall consider the following factors:

(i) The size and design of the facility in which the concert is scheduled;

(ii) The size, age, and anticipated conduct of the crowd expected to attend the concert;

(iii) The ability of the sponsor to manage and control the expected crowd.

If the sponsor of any concert desires to obtain an exemption under this division, the sponsor shall apply to the appropriate official on a form prescribed by that official. The official shall issue an order that grants or denies the exemption within five days after receipt of the application. The sponsor may appeal any order that denies an exemption to the court of common pleas of the county in which the facility is located.

(b) If an official grants an exemption under division (D)(2)(a) of this section, the official shall designate an on-duty law enforcement officer to be present at the concert. The designated officer has authority to issue orders to all security personnel at the concert to protect the health, safety, and welfare of the participants and spectators.

(3) Notwithstanding division (D)(2) of this section, in the case of a concert held in a facility located on the campus of an educational institution covered by section 3345.04 of the Revised Code, a state university law enforcement officer appointed pursuant to sections 3345.04 and 3345.21 of the Revised Code shall do both of the following:

(a) Exercise the authority to grant exemptions provided by division (D)(2)(a) of this section in lieu of an official designated in that division;

(b) If the officer grants an exemption under division (D)(3)(a) of this section, designate an on-duty state university law enforcement officer to be present at the concert. The designated officer has authority to issue orders to all security personnel at the concert to protect the health, safety, and welfare of the participants and spectators.

(E)(1) Unless a live entertainment performance is exempted by division (D)(1) of this section, the chief of the police department of a township police district in the case of a restricted entertainment area located within the district, the officer responsible for public safety within a municipal corporation in the case of a restricted entertainment area located within the municipal corporation, or the county sheriff in the case of a restricted entertainment area located outside the boundaries of a township police district or municipal corporation shall designate, for purposes of division (C) of this section, the minimum number of entrances required to be opened, maintained, and staffed at each live entertainment performance so as to permit crowd control and reduce congestion at the entrances. The designation shall be based on such factors as the size and nature of the crowd expected to attend the live entertainment performance, the length of time prior to the live entertainment performance that crowds are expected to congregate at the entrances, and the amount of security provided at the restricted entertainment area.

(2) Notwithstanding division (E)(1) of this section, a state university law enforcement officer appointed pursuant to sections 3345.04 and 3345.21 of the Revised Code shall designate the number of entrances required to be opened, maintained, and staffed in the case of a live entertainment performance that is held at a restricted entertainment area located on the campus of an educational institution covered by section 3345.04 of the Revised Code.

(F) No person shall enter into any contract for a live entertainment performance, that does not permit or require compliance with this section.

(G)(1) This section does not apply to a live entertainment performance held in a restricted entertainment area if one admission ticket entitles the holder to view or participate in three or more different games, rides, activities, or live entertainment performances occurring simultaneously at different sites within the restricted entertainment area and if the initial admittance entrance to the restricted entertainment area, for which the ticket is required, is separate from the entrance to any specific live entertainment performance and an additional ticket is not required for admission to the particular live entertainment performance.

(2) This section does not apply to a symphony orchestra performance, a ballet performance, horse races, dances, or fairs.

(H) This section does not prohibit the legislative authority of any municipal corporation from imposing additional requirements, not in conflict with this section, for the promotion or holding of live entertainment performances.

(I) Whoever violates division (B), (C), or (F) of this section is guilty of a misdemeanor of the first degree. If any individual suffers physical harm to his person as a result of a violation of this section, the sentencing court shall consider this factor in favor of imposing a term of imprisonment upon the offender.

(1980 S 320, eff. 3–23–81)

2917.41 Misconduct involving a public transportation system

(A) No person shall evade the payment of the known fares of a public transportation system.

(B) No person shall alter any transfer, pass, ticket, or token of a public transportation system with the purpose of evading the payment of fares or of defrauding the system.

(C) No person shall do any of the following while in any facility or on any vehicle of a public transportation system:

(1) Play sound equipment without the proper use of a private earphone;

(2) Smoke, eat, or drink in any area where the activity is clearly marked as being prohibited;

(3) Expectorate upon a facility or vehicle.

(D) No person shall write, deface, draw, or otherwise mark on any facility or vehicle of a public transportation system.

(E) Whoever violates this section is guilty of misconduct involving a public transportation system.

(1) Violation of division (A) of this section is a misdemeanor of the fourth degree.

(2) Violation of division (B) of this section is a misdemeanor of the fourth degree.

(3) Violation of division (C) of this section is a misdemeanor of the fourth degree.

(4) Violation of division (D) of this section is a misdemeanor of the third degree.

(F) Notwithstanding any other provision of law, seventy-five per cent of each fine paid to satisfy a sentence imposed for a violation of this section shall be deposited into the treasury of the county in which the violation occurred and twenty-five per cent shall be deposited with the county transit board, regional transit authority, or regional transit commission that operates the public transportation system involved in the violation, unless the board of county commissioners operates the public transportation system, in which case one hundred per cent of each fine shall be deposited into the treasury of the county.

(G) As used in this section, "public transportation system" means a county transit system operated in accordance with sections 306.01 to 306.13 of the Revised Code, a regional transit authority operated in accordance with sections 306.30 to 306.71 of the Revised Code, or a regional transit commission operated in accordance with sections 306.80 to 306.90 of the Revised Code.

(1995 H 61, eff. 10–25–95; 1986 H 813, eff. 9–17–86; 1984 S 86)

2917.42 Refusing to testify before general assembly or a committee thereof—Repealed

(1972 H 511, eff. 1–1–74; 1953 H 1; GC 12845)

2917.43 Stirring up lawsuits and quarrels—Repealed

(1972 H 511, eff. 1–1–74; 127 v 1039; 1953 H 1; GC 12847)

2917.44 Report of wound with deadly weapon—Repealed

(1972 H 511, eff. 1–1–74; 130 v H 1; 129 v 1034)

2917.45 Wearing of masks prohibited; exceptions—Repealed

(1972 H 511, eff. 1–1–74; 131 v S 293)

2917.46 Misuse of block parent symbol

(A) No person shall, with intent to identify a building as a block parent home or building, display the block parent symbol adopted by the state board of education pursuant to section 3301.076 of the Revised Code unless authorized in accordance with that section or section 3313.206 of the Revised Code.

(B) No person shall, with intent to identify a building as a block parent home or building, display a symbol that falsely gives the appearance of being the block parent symbol adopted by the board of education.

(C) Whoever violates division (A) or (B) of this section is guilty of unauthorized use of a block parent symbol, a minor misdemeanor.

(1988 H 708, eff. 4–19–88; 1985 H 112)

CHAPTER 2919

OFFENSES AGAINST THE FAMILY

BIGAMY

BIGAMY

2919.01   Bigamy

(A) No married person shall marry another or continue to cohabit with such other person in this state.

(B) It is an affirmative defense to a charge under this section that the actor's spouse was continuously absent for five years immediately preceding the purported subsequent marriage, and was not known by the actor to be alive within that time.

(C) Whoever violates this section is guilty of bigamy, a misdemeanor of the first degree.

(1972 H 511, eff. 1–1–74)

2919.02   Deposit of certain fees and trust funds—Repealed

(1972 H 511, eff. 1–1–74; 1953 H 1; GC 12875)

2919.03   Embezzlement of public property; fraudulent conversion—Repealed

(1972 H 511, eff. 1–1–74; 1953 H 1; GC 12876)

2919.04 Embezzlement of negotiable instrument before delivery—Repealed

(1972 H 511, eff. 1–1–74; 1953 H 1; GC 12877)

2919.05 Embezzlement by municipal and school officers; fine is judgment against entire estate—Repealed

(1972 H 511, eff. 1–1–74; 1953 H 1; GC 12878, 12879)

2919.06 Selling public property with intent to defraud; fine is judgment against entire estate—Repealed

(1972 H 511, eff. 1–1–74; 1953 H 1; GC 12880, 12881)

2919.07 Neglect by jailer—Repealed

(1972 H 511, eff. 1–1–74; 1953 H 1; GC 12886)

2919.08 Officer or agent interested in contracts—Repealed

(1972 H 511, eff. 1–1–74; 1953 H 1; GC 12910)

2919.09 Officer interested in contract for another agency—Repealed

(1972 H 511, eff. 1–1–74; 1953 H 1; GC 12911)

2919.10 Officer of municipal corporation or township interested in contract—Repealed

(1972 H 511, eff. 1–1–74; 1953 H 1; GC 12912)

ABORTION

2919.11 Abortion defined; practice of medicine

As used in the Revised Code, "abortion" means the purposeful termination of a human pregnancy by any person, including the pregnant woman herself, with an intention other than to produce a live birth or to remove a dead fetus or embryo. Abortion is the practice of medicine or surgery for the purposes of section 4731.41 of the Revised Code.
(1974 H 989, eff. 9–16–74)

2919.12 Abortion without informed consent prohibited; unmarried minors

(A) No person shall perform or induce an abortion without the informed consent of the pregnant woman.

(B)(1)(a) No person shall knowingly perform or induce an abortion upon a woman who is pregnant, unmarried, under eighteen years of age, and unemancipated unless at least one of the following applies:

(i) Subject to division (B)(2) of this section, the person has given at least twenty-four hours actual notice, in person or by telephone, to one of the woman's parents, her guardian, or her custodian as to the intention to perform or induce the abortion, provided that if the woman has requested, in accordance with division (B)(1)(b) of this section, that notice be given to a specified brother or sister of the woman who is twenty-one years of age or older or to a specified stepparent or grandparent of the woman instead of to one of her parents, her guardian, or her custodian, and if the person is notified by a juvenile court that affidavits of the type described in that division have been filed with that court, the twenty-four hours actual notice described in this division as to the intention to perform or induce the abortion shall be given, in person or by telephone, to the specified brother, sister, stepparent, or grandparent instead of to the parent, guardian, or custodian;

(ii) One of the woman's parents, her guardian, or her custodian has consented in writing to the performance or inducement of the abortion;

(iii) A juvenile court pursuant to section 2151.85 of the Revised Code issues an order authorizing the woman to consent to the abortion without notification of one of her parents, her guardian, or her custodian;

(iv) A juvenile court or a court of appeals, by its inaction, constructively has authorized the woman to consent to the abortion without notification of one of her parents, her guardian, or her custodian under division (B)(1) of section 2151.85 or division (A) of section 2505.073 of the Revised Code.

(b) If a woman who is pregnant, unmarried, under eighteen years of age, and unemancipated desires notification as to a person's intention to perform or induce an abortion on the woman to be given to a specified brother or sister of the woman who is twenty-one years of age or older or to a specified stepparent or grandparent of the woman instead of to one of her parents, her guardian, or her custodian, the person who intends to perform or induce the abortion shall notify the specified brother, sister, stepparent, or grandparent instead of the parent, guardian, or custodian for purposes of division (A)(1)(a)(i) of this section if all of the following apply:

(i) The woman has requested the person to provide the notification to the specified brother, sister, stepparent, or grandparent, clearly has identified the specified brother, sister, stepparent, or grandparent and her relation to that person, and, if the specified relative is a brother or sister, has indicated the age of the brother or sister;

(ii) The woman has executed an affidavit stating that she is in fear of physical, sexual, or severe emotional abuse from the parent, guardian, or custodian who otherwise would be notified under division (B)(1)(a)(i) of this section, and that the fear is based on a pattern of physical, sexual, or severe emotional abuse of her exhibited by that parent, guardian, or custodian, has filed the affidavit with the juvenile court of the county in which the woman has a residence or legal settlement, the juvenile court of any county that borders to any extent the county in which she has a residence or legal settlement, or the juvenile court of the county in which the hospital, clinic, or other facility in which the abortion would be performed or induced is located, and has given the court written notice of the name and address of the person who intends to perform or induce the abortion;

(iii) The specified brother, sister, stepparent, or grandparent has executed an affidavit stating that the woman has reason to fear physical, sexual, or severe emotional abuse from the parent, guardian, or custodian who otherwise would be notified under division (B)(1)(a)(i) of this section, based on a pattern of physical, sexual, or severe emotional abuse of her by that parent, guardian, or custodian, and the woman or the specified brother, sister, stepparent, or grandparent has filed the affidavit with the juvenile court in which the affidavit described in division (B)(1)(b)(ii) of this section was filed;

(iv) The juvenile court in which the affidavits described in divisions (B)(1)(b)(ii) and (iii) of this section were filed has notified the person that both of those affidavits have been filed with the court.

(c) If an affidavit of the type described in division (B)(1)(b)(ii) of this section and an affidavit of the type described in division (B)(1)(b)(iii) of this section are filed with a juvenile court and the court has been provided with written notice of the name and address of the person who intends to perform or induce an abortion upon the woman to whom the affidavits pertain, the court promptly shall notify the person who intends to perform or induce the abortion that the affidavits have been filed. If possible, the notice to the person shall be given in person or by telephone.

(2) If division (B)(1)(a)(ii), (iii), or (iv) of this section does not apply, and if no parent, guardian, or custodian can be reached for purposes of division (B)(1)(a)(i) of this section after a reasonable effort, or if notification is to be given to a specified brother, sister, stepparent, or grandparent under that division and the specified brother, sister, stepparent, or grandparent cannot be reached for purposes of that division after a reasonable effort, no person shall perform or induce such an abortion without giving at least forty-eight hours constructive notice to one of the woman's parents, her guardian, or her custodian, by both certified and ordinary mail sent to the last known address of the parent, guardian, or custodian, or if notification for purposes of division (B)(1)(a)(i) of this section is to be given to a specified brother, sister, stepparent, or grandparent, without giving at least forty-eight hours constructive notice to that specified brother, sister, stepparent, or grandparent by both certified and ordinary mail sent to the last known address of that specified brother, sister, stepparent, or grandparent. The forty-eight hour period under this division begins when the certified mail notice is mailed. If a

parent, guardian, or custodian of the woman, or if notification under division (B)(1)(a)(i) of this section is to be given to a specified brother, sister, stepparent, or grandparent, the specified brother, sister, stepparent, or grandparent, is not reached within the forty-eight hour period, the abortion may proceed even if the certified mail notice is not received.

(3) If a parent, guardian, custodian, or specified brother, sister, stepparent, or grandparent who has been notified in accordance with division (B)(1) or (2) of this section clearly and unequivocally expresses that he or she does not wish to consult with a pregnant woman prior to her abortion, then the abortion may proceed without any further waiting period.

(4) For purposes of prosecutions for a violation of division (B)(1) or (2) of this section, it shall be a rebuttable presumption that a woman who is unmarried and under eighteen years of age is unemancipated.

(C)(1) It is an affirmative defense to a charge under division (B)(1) or (2) of this section that the pregnant woman provided the person who performed or induced the abortion with false, misleading, or incorrect information about her age, marital status, or emancipation, about the age of a brother or sister to whom she requested notice be given as a specified relative instead of to one of her parents, her guardian, or her custodian, or about the last known address of either of her parents, her guardian, her custodian, or a specified brother, sister, stepparent, or grandparent to whom she requested notice be given and the person who performed or induced the abortion did not otherwise have reasonable cause to believe the pregnant woman was under eighteen years of age, unmarried, or unemancipated, to believe that the age of a brother or sister to whom she requested notice be given as a specified relative instead of to one of her parents, her guardian, or her custodian was not twenty-one years of age, or to believe that the last known address of either of her parents, her guardian, her custodian, or a specified brother, sister, stepparent, or grandparent to whom she requested notice be given was incorrect.

(2) It is an affirmative defense to a charge under this section that compliance with the requirements of this section was not possible because an immediate threat of serious risk to the life or physical health of the pregnant woman from the continuation of her pregnancy created an emergency necessitating the immediate performance or inducement of an abortion.

(D) Whoever violates this section is guilty of unlawful abortion, a misdemeanor of the first degree. If the offender previously has been convicted of or pleaded guilty to a violation of this section, unlawful abortion is a felony of the fourth degree.

(E) Whoever violates this section is liable to the pregnant woman and her parents, guardian, or custodian for civil compensatory and exemplary damages.

(F) As used in this section "unemanicipated" [sic] means that a woman who is unmarried and under eighteen years of age has not entered the armed services of the United States, has not become employed and self-subsisting, or has not otherwise become independent from the care and control of her parent, guardian, or custodian.

(1985 H 319, eff. 3–24–86; 1974 H 989)

2919.13   Abortion manslaughter

(A) No person shall purposely take the life of a child born by attempted abortion who is alive when removed from the uterus of the pregnant woman.

(B) No person who performs an abortion shall fail to take the measures required by the exercise of medical judgment in light of the attending circumstances to preserve the life of a child who is alive when removed from the uterus of the pregnant woman.

(C) Whoever violates this section is guilty of abortion manslaughter, a felony of the first degree.

(1974 H 989, eff. 9–16–74)

2919.14   Abortion trafficking

(A) No person shall experiment upon or sell the product of human conception which is aborted. Experiment does not include autopsies pursuant to sections 313.13 and 2108.50 of the Revised Code.

(B) Whoever violates this section is guilty of abortion trafficking, a misdemeanor of the first degree.

(1974 H 989, eff. 9–16–74)

2919.15 Dilation and extraction procedure

(A) As used in this section, "dilation and extraction procedure" means the termination of a human pregnancy by purposely inserting a suction device into the skull of a fetus to remove the brain. "Dilation and extraction procedure" does not include either the suction curettage procedure of abortion or the suction aspiration procedure of abortion.

(B) No person shall knowingly perform or attempt to perform a dilation and extraction procedure upon a pregnant woman.

(C)(1) It is an affirmative defense to a charge under division (B) of this section that all other available abortion procedures would pose a greater risk to the health of the pregnant woman than the risk posed by the dilation and extraction procedure.

(2) Notwithstanding section 2901.05 of the Revised Code, if a person charged with a violation of division (B) of this section presents prima facie evidence relative to the affirmative defense set forth in division (C)(1) of this section, the prosecution, in addition to proving all elements of the violation by proof beyond a reasonable doubt, has the burden of proving by proof beyond a reasonable doubt that at least one other available abortion procedure would not pose a greater risk to the health of the pregnant woman than the risk posed by the dilation and extraction procedure performed or attempted to be performed by the person charged with the violation of division (B) of this section.

(D) Whoever violates division (B) of this section is guilty of performing an unlawful abortion procedure, a felony of the fourth degree.

(E) A pregnant woman upon whom a dilation and extraction procedure is performed or attempted to be performed in violation of division (B) of this section is not guilty of an attempt to commit, complicity in the commission of, or conspiracy in the commission of a violation of that division.

(1995 H 135, eff. 11–15–95)

2919.16 Definitions

As used in sections 2919.16 to 2919.18 of the Revised Code:

(A) "Fertilization" means the fusion of a human spermatozoon with a human ovum.

(B) "Gestational age" means the age of an unborn human as calculated from the first day of the last menstrual period of a pregnant woman.

(C) "Health care facility" means a hospital, clinic, ambulatory surgical treatment center, other center, medical school, office of a physician, infirmary, dispensary, medical training institution, or other institution or location in or at which medical care, treatment, or diagnosis is provided to a person.

(D) "Hospital" has the same meanings as in sections 2108.01, 3701.01, and 5122.01 of the Revised Code.

(E) "Live birth" has the same meaning as in division (A) of section 3705.01 of the Revised Code.

(F) "Medical emergency" means a condition that a pregnant woman's physician determines, in good faith and in the exercise of reasonable medical judgment, so complicates the woman's pregnancy as to necessitate the immediate performance or inducement of an abortion in order to prevent the death of the pregnant woman or to avoid a serious risk of the substantial and irreversible impairment of a major bodily function of the pregnant woman that delay in the performance or inducement of the abortion would create.

(G) "Physician" has the same meaning as in section 2305.11 of the Revised Code.

(H) "Pregnant" means the human female reproductive condition, that commences with fertilization, of having a developing fetus.

(I) "Premature infant" means a human whose live birth occurs prior to thirty-eight weeks of gestational age.

(J) "Serious risk of the substantial and irreversible impairment of a major bodily function" means any medically diagnosed condition that so complicates the pregnancy of the woman as to directly or indirectly cause the substantial and irreversible impairment of a major bodily function, including, but not limited to, the following conditions:

(1) Pre–eclampsia;

(2) Inevitable abortion;

(3) Prematurely ruptured membrane;

(4) Diabetes;

(5) Multiple sclerosis.

(K) "Unborn human" means an individual organism of the species homo sapiens from fertilization until live birth.

(L) "Viable" means the stage of development of a human fetus at which in the determination of a physician, based on the particular facts of a woman's pregnancy that are known to the physician and in light of medical technology and information reasonably available to the physician, there is a realistic possibility of the maintaining and nourishing of a life outside of the womb with or without temporary artificial life-sustaining support.

(1995 H 135, eff. 11–15–95)

2919.17 Terminating a human pregnancy after viability

(A) No person shall purposely perform or induce or attempt to perform or induce an abortion upon a pregnant woman if the unborn human is viable, unless either of the following applies:

(1) The abortion is performed or induced or attempted to be performed or induced by a physician, and that physician determines, in good faith and in the exercise of reasonable medical judgment, that the abortion is necessary to prevent the death of the pregnant woman or a serious risk of the substantial and irreversible impairment of a major bodily function of the pregnant woman.

(2) The abortion is performed or induced or attempted to be performed or induced by a physician and that physician determines, in good faith and in the exercise of reasonable medical judgment, after making a determination relative to the viability of the unborn human in conformity with division (a) of section 2919.18 of the Revised Code, that the unborn human is not viable.

(B)(1) Except as provided in division (B)(2) of this section, no physician shall purposely perform or induce or attempt to perform or induce an abortion upon a pregnant woman when the unborn human is viable and when the physician has determined, in good faith and in the exercise of reasonable medical judgment, that the abortion is necessary to prevent the death of the pregnant woman or a serious risk of the substantial and irreversible impairment of a major bodily function of the pregnant woman, unless each of the following conditions is satisfied:

(a) The physician who performs or induces or attempts to perform or induce the abortion certifies in writing that that physician has determined, in good faith and in the exercise of reasonable medical judgment, that the abortion is necessary to prevent the death of the pregnant woman or a serious risk of the substantial and irreversible impairment of a major bodily function of the pregnant woman.

(b) The determination of the physician who performs or induces or attempts to perform or induce the abortion that is described in division (B)(1)(a) of this section is concurred in by at least one other physician who certifies in writing that the concurring physician has determined, in good faith, in the exercise of reasonable medical judgment, and following a review of the available medical records of and any available tests results pertaining to the pregnant woman, that the abortion is necessary to prevent the death of the pregnant woman or a serious risk of the substantial and irreversible impairment of a major bodily function of the pregnant woman.

(c) The abortion is performed or induced or attempted to be performed or induced in a health care facility that has or has access to appropriate neonatal services for premature infants.

(d) The physician who performs or induces or attempts to perform or induce the abortion terminates or attempts to terminate the pregnancy in the manner that provides the best opportunity for the unborn human to survive, unless that physician determines, in good faith and in the exercise of reasonable medical judgment, that the termination of the pregnancy in that manner poses a significantly greater risk of the death of the pregnant woman or a serious risk of the substantial and irreversible impairment of a major bodily function of the pregnant woman than would other available methods of abortion.

(e) The physician who performs or induces or attempts to perform or induce the abortion has arranged for the attendance in the same room in which the abortion is to be performed or induced or attempted to be performed or induced of at least one other physician who is to take control of, provide immediate medical care for, and take all reasonable steps necessary to preserve the life and health of the unborn human immediately upon the unborn human's complete expulsion or extraction from the pregnant woman.

(2) Division (B)(1) of this section does not prohibit the performance or inducement or an attempted performance or inducement of an abortion without prior satisfaction of each of the conditions described in divisions (B)(1)(a) to (e) of this section if the physician who performs or induces or attempts to perform or induce the abortion determines, in good faith and in the exercise of reasonable medical judgment, that a medical emergency exists that prevents compliance with one or more of those conditions.

(C) For purposes of this section, it shall be rebuttably presumed that an unborn child of at least twenty-four weeks of gestational age is viable.

(D) Whoever violates this section is guilty of terminating or attempting to terminate a human pregnancy after viability, a felony of the fourth degree.

(E) A pregnant woman upon whom an abortion is performed or induced or attempted to be performed or induced in violation of division (A) or (B) of this section is not guilty of an attempt to commit, complicity in the commission of, or conspiracy in the commission of a violation of either of those divisions.

(1995 H 135, eff. 11–15–95)

2919.18   Failure to perform viability testing on fetus

(A)(1) Except as provided in division (A)(3) of this section, no physician shall perform or induce or attempt to perform or induce an abortion upon a pregnant woman after the beginning of her twenty-second week of pregnancy unless, prior to the performance or inducement of the abortion or the attempt to perform or induce the abortion, the physician determines, in good faith and in the exercise of reasonable medical judgment, that the unborn human is not viable, and the physician makes that determination after performing a medical examination of the pregnant woman and after performing or causing the performing of gestational age, weight, lung maturity, or other tests of the unborn human that a reasonable physician making a determination as to whether an unborn human is or is not viable would perform or cause to be performed.

(2) Except as provided in division (A)(3) of this section, no physician shall perform or induce or attempt to perform or induce an abortion upon a pregnant woman after the beginning of her twenty-second week of pregnancy without first entering the determination described in division (A)(1) of this section and the associated findings of the medical examination and tests described in that division in the medical record of the pregnant woman.

(3) Divisions (A)(1) and (2) of this section do not prohibit a physician from performing or inducing or attempting to perform or induce an abortion upon a pregnant woman after the beginning of her twenty-second week of pregnancy without making the determination described in division (A)(1) of this section or without making the entry described in division (A)(2) of this section if a medical emergency exists.

(B) Whoever violates this section is guilty of failure to perform viability testing, a misdemeanor of the fourth degree.

(1995 H 135, eff. 11–15–95)

2919.19   Hindering examination of state treasury—Repealed

(1972 H 511, eff. 1–1–74; 1953 H 1; GC 12934)

2919.20   Failure to prefer soldiers for appointments—Repealed

(1972 H 511, eff. 1–1–74; 1953 H 1; GC 12893)

NONSUPPORT; CHILD ENDANGERING; RELATED OFFENSES

2919.21   Nonsupport of dependents; assessment of court costs and attorney fees in some cases

(A) No person shall abandon, or fail to provide adequate support to:

(1) His or her spouse, as required by law;

(2) His or her legitimate or illegitimate child who is under age eighteen, or mentally or physically handicapped child who is under age twenty-one;

(3) His or her aged or infirm parent or adoptive parent, who from lack of ability and means is unable to provide adequately for his or her own support;

(4) Any person whom, by law or by court order or decree, the offender is legally obligated to support.

(B) No person shall aid, abet, induce, cause, encourage, or contribute to a child or a ward of the juvenile court becoming a dependent child, as defined in section 2151.04 of the Revised Code, or a neglected child, as defined in section 2151.03 of the Revised Code.

(C) It is an affirmative defense to a charge under division (A) of this section of failure to provide adequate support that the accused was unable to provide adequate support, but did provide such support as was within his ability and means.

(D) It is an affirmative defense to a charge under division (A)(3) of this section that the parent abandoned the accused or failed to support the accused as required by law, while the accused was under age eighteen, or was mentally or physically handicapped and under age twenty-one.

(E) Whoever violates division (A) of this section is guilty of nonsupport of dependents, a misdemeanor of the first degree. If the offender previously has been convicted of or pleaded guilty to a violation of division (A)(2) of this section or there has been a court finding that the offender has failed to provide support under division (A)(2) of this section for a total accumulated period of twenty-six weeks out of one hundred four consecutive weeks, whether or not the twenty-six weeks were consecutive, then a violation of division (A)(2) of this section is a felony of the fourth degree. If the offender is guilty of nonsupport of dependents by reason of failing to provide support to his or her child as required by a child support order issued on or after April 15, 1985, pursuant to section 2151.23, 3105.21, 3109.05, 3111.13, 3113.04, 3113.31, or 3115.22 of the Revised Code, the court, in addition to any other sentence imposed, shall assess all court costs arising out of the charge against the person and require the person to pay any reasonable attorney's fees of any adverse party other than the state, as determined by the court, that arose in relation to the charge. Whoever violates division (B) of this section is guilty of contributing to the nonsupport of dependents, a misdemeanor of the first degree. Each day of violation of division (B) of this section is a separate offense.

(1986 S 136, eff. 9–24–86; 1985 H 349; 1984 H 614; 1972 H 511)

2919.22   Endangering children

(A) No person, who is the parent, guardian, custodian, person having custody or control, or person in loco parentis of a child under eighteen years of age or a mentally or physically handicapped child under twenty-one years of age, shall create a substantial risk to the health or safety of the child, by violating a duty of care, protection, or support. It is not a violation of a duty of care, protection, or support under this division when the parent, guardian, custodian, or person having custody or control of a child treats the physical or mental illness or defect of the child by spiritual means through prayer alone, in accordance with the tenets of a recognized religious body.

(B) No person shall do any of the following to a child under eighteen years of age or a mentally or physically handicapped child under twenty-one years of age:

(1) Abuse the child;

(2) Torture or cruelly abuse the child;

(3) Administer corporal punishment or other physical disciplinary measure, or physically restrain the child in a cruel manner or for a prolonged period, which punishment, discipline, or restraint is excessive under the circumstances and creates a substantial risk of serious physical harm to the child;

(4) Repeatedly administer unwarranted disciplinary measures to the child, when there is a substantial risk that such conduct, if continued, will seriously impair or retard the child's mental health or development;

(5) Entice, coerce, permit, encourage, compel, hire, employ, use, or allow the child to act, model, or in any other way participate in, or be photographed for, the production, presentation, dissemination, or advertisement of any material or performance that he knows or reasonably should know is obscene, is sexually oriented matter, or is nudity-oriented matter;

(6) Allow, entice, encourage, or force the child to solicit for or engage in prostitution as a prostitute, or otherwise facilitate a child in soliciting for or engaging in prostitution as a prostitute. As used in this division, "prostitute" has the same meaning as in section 2907.01 of the Revised Code.

(C)(1) No person shall operate a vehicle, streetcar, or trackless trolley within this state and in violation of division (A) of section 4511.19 of the Revised Code when one or more children under eighteen years of age are in the vehicle, streetcar, or trackless trolley. Notwithstanding any other provision of law, a person may be convicted at the same trial or proceeding of a violation of this division and a violation of division (A) of section 4511.19 of the Revised Code that constitutes the basis of the charge of the violation of this division. For purposes of section 4511.191 of the Revised Code and all related provisions of law, a person arrested for a violation of this division shall be considered to be under arrest for operating a vehicle while under the influence of alcohol, a drug of abuse, or alcohol and a drug of abuse or for operating a vehicle with a prohibited concentration of alcohol in the blood, breath, or urine.

(2) As used in division (C)(1) of this section, "vehicle," "streetcar," and "trackless trolley" have the same meanings as in section 4511.01 of the Revised Code.

(D)(1) Division (B)(5) of this section does not apply to any material or performance that is produced, presented, or disseminated for a bona fide medical, scientific, educational, religious, governmental, judicial, or other proper purpose, by or to a physician, psychologist, sociologist, scientist, teacher, person pursuing bona fide studies or research, librarian, clergyman, prosecutor, judge, or other person having a proper interest in the material or performance.

(2) Mistake of age is not a defense to a charge under division (B)(5) or (6) of this section.

(3) In a prosecution under division (B)(5) of this section, the trier of fact may infer that an actor, model, or participant in the material or performance involved is a juvenile if the material or performance, through its title, text, visual representation, or otherwise, represents or depicts the actor, model, or participant as a juvenile.

(4) As used in this division and division (B)(5) of this section:

(a) "Material," "performance," "obscene," and "sexual activity" have the same meanings as in section 2907.01 of the Revised Code.

(b) "Nudity–oriented matter" means any material or performance that shows a minor in a state of nudity and that, taken as a whole by the average person applying contemporary community standards, appeals to prurient interest.

(c) "Sexually oriented matter" means any material or performance that shows a minor participating or engaging in sexual activity, masturbation, or bestiality.

(E)(1) Whoever violates this section is guilty of endangering children.

(2) If the offender violates division (A) or (B)(1) of this section, endangering children is a misdemeanor of the first degree, except that if the violation results in serious physical harm to the child involved, or if the offender previously has been convicted of an offense under this section or of any offense involving neglect, abandonment, contributing to the delinquency of, or physical abuse of a child, endangering children is a felony of the fourth degree.

(3) If the offender violates division (B)(2), (3), or (4) of this section, endangering children is a felony of the third degree, except that if the violation results in serious physical harm to the child involved, or if the offender has previously been convicted of an offense under this section or of any offense involving neglect, abandonment, contributing to the delinquency of, or physical abuse of a child, endangering children is a felony of the second degree.

(4) If the offender violates division (B)(5) or (6) of this section, endangering children is a felony of the second degree.

(5) If the offender violates division (C) of this section, the offender shall be punished as follows:

(a) If neither division (E)(5)(b) nor (c) of this section applies, endangering children in violation of division (C) of this section is a misdemeanor of the first degree;

(b) If division (E)(5)(c) of this section does not apply and if the violation results in serious physical harm to the child involved or the offender previously has been convicted of an offense under this section or any offense involving neglect, abandonment, contributing to the delinquency of, or physical abuse of a child, endangering children in violation of division (C) of this section is a felony of the fourth degree;

(c) If the violation results in serious physical harm to the child involved and if the offender previously has been convicted of a violation of division (C) of this section, section 2903.06, 2903.07, or 2903.08 of the Revised Code, or section 2903.04 of the Revised Code in a case in which the offender was subject to the sanctions described in division (D) of that section, endangering children in violation of division (C) of this section is a felony of the third degree.

(d) In addition to any term of imprisonment, fine, or other sentence, penalty, or sanction it imposes upon the offender pursuant to division (E)(5)(a), (b), or (c) of this section or pursuant to any other provision of law, the court also may impose upon the offender one or both of the following sanctions:

(i) It may require the offender, as part of his sentence and in the manner described in division (F) of this section, to perform not more than two hundred hours of supervised community service work under the authority of any agency, political subdivision, or charitable organization of the type described in division (H)(1) of section 2951.02 of the Revised Code, provided that the court shall not require the offender to perform supervised community service work under this division unless the offender agrees to perform the supervised community service work.

(ii) It may suspend the driver's or commercial driver's license or permit or nonresident operating privilege of the offender for up to ninety days, in addition to any suspension or revocation of the offender's driver's or commercial driver's license or permit or nonresident operating privilege under Chapter 4506., 4507., 4509., or 4511. of the Revised Code or under any other provision of law.

(e) In addition to any term of imprisonment, fine, or other sentence, penalty, or sanction imposed upon the offender pursuant to division (E)(5)(a), (b), (c), OR (d) of this section or pursuant to any other provision of law for the violation of division (C) of this section, if as part of the same trial or proceeding the offender also is convicted of or pleads guilty to a separate charge charging the violation of division (A) of section 4511.19 of the Revised Code that was the basis of the charge of the violation of division (C) of this section, the offender also shall be sentenced, in accordance with section 4511.99 of the Revised Code, for that violation of division (A) of section 4511.19 of the Revised Code and also shall be subject to all other sanctions that are required or authorized by any provision of law for that violation of division (A) of section 4511.19 of the Revised Code.

(F)(1)(a) If a court, pursuant to division (E)(5)(d)(i) of this section, requires an offender to perform supervised community service work under the authority of an agency, subdivision, or charitable organization, the requirement shall be part of the sentence of the offender, and the community service work shall be imposed in accordance with and subject to divisions (F)(1)(a) and (b) of this section. The court may require an offender whom it requires to perform supervised community service work as part of his sentence to pay the court a reasonable fee to cover the costs of his participation in the work, including, but not limited to, the costs of procuring a policy or policies of liability insurance to cover the period during which the offender will perform the work. If the court requires the offender to perform supervised community service work as part of his sentence, the court shall do so in accordance with the following limitations and criteria:

(i) The court shall require that the community service work be performed after completion of the term of imprisonment imposed upon the offender for the violation of division (C) of this section, if applicable.

(ii) The supervised community service work shall be subject to the limitations set forth in divisions (H)(1)(a) to (c) of section 2951.02 of the Revised Code.

(iii) The community service work shall be supervised in the manner described in division (H)(1)(d) of section 2951.02 of the Revised Code by an official or person with the qualifications described in that division. The official or person periodically shall report in writing to the court concerning the conduct of the offender in performing the work.

(iv) The court shall inform the offender in writing that if he does not adequately perform, as determined by the court, all of the required community service work, the court may order that he be committed to a jail or workhouse for a period of time that does not exceed the longest definite sentence or minimum term of imprisonment that the court could have imposed upon the offender for the violation of division (C) of this section, reduced by the total amount of time that the offender actually was imprisoned under the sentence or term that was imposed upon the offender for that violation and by the total amount of time that the offender was confined for any reason arising out of the offense for which he was convicted and sentenced as described in sections 2949.08 and 2967.191 of the Revised Code, and that, if the court orders that he be so committed, the court is authorized, but not required, to grant him credit upon the period of the commitment for the community service work that he adequately performed.

(b) If a court, pursuant to this division and division (E)(5)(d)(i) of this section, orders an offender to perform community service work as part of his sentence and if the offender does not adequately perform all of the required community service work, as determined by the court, the court may order that the offender be committed to a jail or workhouse for a period of time that does not exceed the longest definite sentence or minimum term of imprisonment that the court could have imposed upon the offender for the violation of division (C) of this section, reduced by the total amount of time that the offender actually was imprisoned under the sentence or term that was imposed upon the offender for that violation and by the total amount of time that the offender was confined for any reason arising out of the offense for which he was convicted and sentenced as described in sections 2949.08 and 2967.191 of the Revised Code. The court may order that a person committed pursuant to this division shall receive hour-for-hour credit upon the period of the commitment for the community service work that he adequately performed. No commitment pursuant to this division shall exceed the period of the longest definite sentence or minimum term of imprisonment that the sentencing court could have imposed upon the offender for the violation of division (C) of this section, reduced by the total amount of time that the offender actually was imprisoned under that sentence or term and by the total amount of time that the offender was confined for any reason arising out of the offense for which he was convicted and sentenced as described in sections 2949.08 and 2967.191 of the Revised Code.

(2) Divisions (E)(5)(d)(i) and (F)(1) of this section do not limit or affect the authority of the court to suspend the sentence imposed upon the offender and place the offender on probation or otherwise suspend the sentence pursuant to sections 2929.51 and 2951.02 of the Revised Code, or to require the offender, as a condition of the offender's probation or of otherwise suspending his sentence, to perform supervised community service work in accordance with division (H) of section 2951.02 of the Revised Code.

(G) If a court suspends an offender's driver's or commercial driver's license or permit or nonresident operating privilege under division (E)(5)(d)(ii) of this section, the period of the suspension shall be consecutive to, and commence after, the period of suspension or revocation of the offender's driver's or commercial driver's license or permit or nonresident operating privilege that is imposed under Chapter 4506., 4507., 4509., or 4511. of the Revised Code or under any other provision of law in relation to the violation of division (C) of this section that is the basis of the suspension under division (E)(5)(d)(ii) of this section or in relation to the violation of division (A) of section 4511.19 of the Revised Code that is the basis for that violation of division (C) of this section.

If an offender's license, permit, or privilege has been suspended under division (E)(5)(d)(ii) of this section and the offender, within the preceding seven years, has been convicted of or pleaded guilty to three or more violations of division (C) of this section, division (A) or (B) of section 4511.19 of the Revised Code, a municipal ordinance relating to operating a vehicle while under the influence of alcohol, a drug of abuse, or alcohol and a drug of abuse, a municipal ordinance relating to operating a vehicle with a prohibited concentration of alcohol in the blood, breath, or urine, section 2903.04 of the Revised Code in a case in which the person was subject to the sanctions described in division (D) of that section, or section 2903.06, 2903.07, or 2903.08 of the Revised Code or a municipal ordinance that is substantially similar to section 2903.07 of the Revised Code in a case in which the jury or judge found that the person was under the influence of alcohol, a drug of abuse, or alcohol and a drug of abuse, the offender is not entitled to request, and the court shall not grant to the offender, occupational driving privileges under this division. Any other offender whose license, permit, or nonresident operating privilege has been suspended under division (E)(5)(d)(ii) of this section may file with the court that sentenced him a petition alleging that the suspension would seriously affect his ability to continue his employment. Upon satisfactory proof that there is reasonable cause to believe that the suspension would seriously affect the offender's ability to continue his employment, the court may grant the offender occupational driving privileges during the period during which the suspension otherwise would be imposed, except that the court shall not grant occupational driving privileges to any offender who, within seven years of the filing of the petition, has been convicted of or pleaded guilty to three or more violations of division (C) of this section, division (A) or (B) of section 4511.19 of the Revised Code, a municipal ordinance relating to operating a vehicle while under the influence of alcohol, a drug of abuse, or alcohol and a drug of abuse, a municipal ordinance relating to operating a vehicle with a prohibited concentration of alcohol in the blood, breath, or urine, section 2903.04 of the Revised Code in a case in which the person was subject to the sanctions described in division (D) of that section, or section 2903.06, 2903.07, or 2903.08 of the Revised Code or a municipal ordinance that is substantially similar to section 2903.07 of the Revised Code in a case in which the jury or judge found that the person was under the influence of alcohol, a drug of abuse, or alcohol and a drug of abuse and shall not grant occupational driving privileges for employment as a driver of commercial motor vehicles to any person who is disqualified from operating a commercial motor vehicle under section 4506.16 of the Revised Code.

(H)(1) If a person violates division (C) of this section and if, at the time of the violation, there were two or more children under eighteen years of age in the motor vehicle involved in the violation, the offender may be convicted of a violation of division (C) of this section for each of the children, but the court may sentence the offender for only one of the violations.

(2)(a) If a person is convicted of or pleads guilty to a violation of division (C) of this section but the person is not also convicted of and does not also plead guilty to a separate charge charging the violation of division (A) of section 4511.19 of the Revised Code that was the basis of the charge of the violation of division (C) of this section, both of the following apply:

(i) For purposes of the provisions of section 4511.99 of the Revised Code that set forth the penalties and sanctions for a violation of division (A) of section 4511.19 of the Revised Code, the conviction of or plea of guilty to the violation of division (C) of this section shall not constitute a violation of division (A) of section 4511.19 of the Revised Code;

(ii) For purposes of any provision of law that refers to a conviction of or plea of guilty to a violation of division (A) of section 4511.19 of the Revised Code and that is not described in division (H)(2)(a)(i) of this section, the conviction of or plea of guilty to the violation of division (C) of this section shall constitute a conviction of or plea of guilty to a violation of division (A) of section 4511.19 of the Revised Code.

(b) If a person is convicted of or pleads guilty to a violation of division (C) of this section and the person also is convicted of or pleads guilty to a separate charge charging the violation of division (A) of section 4511.19 of the Revised Code that was the basis of the charge of the violation of division (C) of this section, the conviction of or plea of guilty to the violation of division (C) of this section shall not constitute, for purposes of any provision of law that refers to a conviction of or plea of guilty to a violation of division (A) of section 4511.19 of the Revised Code, a conviction of or plea of guilty to a violation of division (A) of section 4511.19 of the Revised Code.

(1994 H 236, eff. 9–29–94; 1988 H 51, eff. 3–17–89; 1985 H 349; 1984 S 321, H 44; 1977 S 243; 1972 H 511)

2919.23 Interference with custody

(A) No person, knowing he is without privilege to do so or being reckless in that regard, shall entice, take, keep, or harbor any of the following persons from his parent, guardian, or custodian:

(1) A child under the age of eighteen, or a mentally or physically handicapped child under the age of twenty-one;

(2) A person committed by law to an institution for delinquent, unruly, neglected, abused, or dependent children;

(3) A person committed by law to an institution for the mentally ill or mentally retarded.

(B) No person shall aid, abet, induce, cause, or encourage a child or a ward of the juvenile court who has been committed to the custody of any person, department, or public or private institution to leave the custody of that person, department, or institution without legal consent.

(C) It is an affirmative defense to a charge of enticing or taking under division (A)(1) of this section, that the actor reasonably believed that his conduct was necessary to preserve the child's health or safety. It is an affirmative defense to a charge of keeping or harboring under division (A) of this section, that the actor in good faith gave notice to law enforcement or judicial authorities within a reasonable time after the child or committed person came under his shelter, protection, or influence.

(D)(1) Whoever violates this section is guilty of interference with custody.

(2) If the child who is the subject of a violation of division (A)(1) of this section is not kept or harbored in a foreign country, a violation of division (A)(1) of this section is a misdemeanor of the third degree. If the child who is the subject of a violation of division (A)(1) of this section is kept or harbored in a foreign country, a violation of division (A)(1) of this section is a felony of the fourth degree.

(3) A violation of division (A)(2) or (3) of this section is a misdemeanor of the third degree.

(4) A violation of division (B) of this section is a misdemeanor of the first degree. Each day of violation of division (B) of this section is a separate offense.

(1990 S 3, eff. 4–11–91; 1985 H 349; 1975 H 85; 1972 H 511)

2919.231 Interfering with action to issue or modify support order

(A) No person, by using physical harassment or threats of violence against another person, shall interfere with the other person's initiation or continuance of, or attempt to prevent the other person from initiating or continuing, an action to issue or modify a support order under Chapter 3115. or under section 2151.23, 2151.231, 2151.36, 2151.49, 3105.18, 3105.21, 3109.05, 3109.19, 3111.13, 3113.04, 3113.07, or 3113.31 of the Revised Code.

(B) Whoever violates this section is guilty of interfering with an action to issue or modify a support order, a misdemeanor of the first degree. If the offender previously has been convicted of or pleaded guilty to a violation of this section or of section 3111.25 [1] of the

Revised Code, interfering with an action to issue or modify a support order is a felony of the fourth degree.

(1995 H 167, eff. 11–15–95; 1992 S 10, eff. 7–15–92)

¹ So in original; should this read "3111.29"?

2919.24 Contributing to unruliness or delinquency

(A) No person shall do either of the following:

(1) Aid, abet, induce, cause, encourage, or contribute to a child or a ward of the juvenile court becoming an unruly child, as defined in section 2151.022 of the Revised Code, or a delinquent child, as defined in section 2151.02 of the Revised Code;

(2) Act in a way tending to cause a child or a ward of the juvenile court to become an unruly child, as defined in section 2151.022 of the Revised Code, or a delinquent child, as defined in section 2151.02 of the Revised Code.

(B) Whoever violates this section is guilty of contributing to the unruliness or delinquency of a child, a misdemeanor of the first degree. Each day of violation of this section is a separate offense.

(1985 H 349, eff. 3–6–86)

DOMESTIC VIOLENCE

2919.25 Domestic violence

(A) No person shall knowingly cause or attempt to cause physical harm to a family or household member.

(B) No person shall recklessly cause serious physical harm to a family or household member.

(C) No person, by threat of force, shall knowingly cause a family or household member to believe that the offender will cause imminent physical harm to the family or household member.

(D) Whoever violates this section is guilty of domestic violence. A violation of division (C) of this section is a misdemeanor of the fourth degree. A violation of division (A) or (B) of this section is a misdemeanor of the first degree. If the offender previously has been convicted of domestic violence or a violation of section 2903.11, 2903.12, 2903.13, 2903.211, or 2911.211 of the Revised Code involving a person who was a family or household member at the time of such violation, a violation of division (A) or (B) of this section is a felony of the fourth degree and a violation of division (C) of this section is a misdemeanor of the third degree.

(E) As used in this section and sections 2919.251 and 2919.26 of the Revised Code:

(1) "Family or household member" means any of the following:

(a) Any of the following who is residing or has resided with the offender:

(i) A spouse, a person living as a spouse, or a former spouse of the offender;

(ii) A parent or a child of the offender, or another person related by consanguinity or affinity to the offender;

(iii) A parent or a child of a spouse, person living as a spouse, or former spouse of the offender, or another person related by consanguinity or affinity to a spouse, person living as a spouse, or former spouse of the offender.

(b) The natural parent of any child of whom the offender is the other natural parent.

(2) "Person living as a spouse" means a person who is living or has lived with the offender in a common law marital relationship, who otherwise is cohabiting with the offender, or who otherwise has cohabited with the offender within one year prior to the date of the alleged commission of the act in question.

(1994 H 335, eff. 12–9–94; 1992 H 536, eff. 11–5–92; 1990 S 3; 1988 H 172; 1987 S 6; 1984 H 587; 1980 H 920; 1978 H 835)

2919.251   Factors to be considered when protection order or consent agreement violated; bail schedule

(A) If a person is charged with a violation of section 2919.25 of the Revised Code, a violation of a municipal ordinance that is substantially similar to that section, a violation of section 2903.11, 2903.12, 2903.13, 2903.211, or 2911.211 of the Revised Code involving a person who was a family or household member at the time of the violation, or a violation of a municipal ordinance substantially similar to section 2903.13, 2903.211, or 2911.211 of the Revised Code that involves a person who was a family or household member at the time of the violation and if the person, at the time of the alleged violation, was subject to the terms of a protection order issued or consent agreement approved pursuant to section 2919.26 or 3113.31 of the Revised Code or previously was convicted of or pleaded guilty to a violation of section 2919.25 or 2919.27 of the Revised Code, a violation of a municipal ordinance that is substantially similar to either section, a violation of section 2903.11, 2903.12, 2903.13, 2903.211, or 2911.211 of the Revised Code involving a person who was a family or household member at the time of the violation, or a violation of a municipal ordinance substantially similar to section 2903.13, 2903.211, or 2911.211 of the Revised Code that involves a person who was a family or household member at the time of the violation, the court shall consider all of the following, in addition to any other circumstances considered by the court and notwithstanding any provisions to the contrary contained in Criminal Rule 46, before setting bail for the person:

(1) Whether the person has a history of domestic violence or a history of other violent acts;

(2) The mental health of the person;

(3) Whether the person has a history of violating the orders of any court or governmental entity;

(4) Whether the person is potentially a threat to any other person;

(5) Whether setting bail at a high level will interfere with any treatment or counseling that the person or the family of the person is undergoing.

(B) Any court that has jurisdiction over violations of section 2919.25 of the Revised Code, violations of a municipal ordinance that is substantially similar to that section, violations of section 2903.13, 2903.211, or 2911.211 of the Revised Code that involve persons who are family or household members at the time of the violation, or violations of a municipal ordinance substantially similar to section 2903.13, 2903.211, or 2911.211 of the Revised Code that involve persons who are family or household members at the time of the violation, may set a schedule for bail to be used in cases involving those violations. The schedule shall require that a judge consider all of the factors listed in division (A) of this section and may require judges to set bail at a certain level if the history of the alleged offender or the circumstances of the alleged offense meet certain criteria in the schedule.

(1992 H 536, eff. 11–5–92; 1990 S 3; 1985 H 475)

2919.26   Temporary protection orders

(A)(1) Upon the filing of a complaint that alleges a violation of section 2919.25 of the Revised Code, a violation of a municipal ordinance substantially similar to that section, a violation of section 2903.11, 2903.12, 2903.13, 2903.211, or 2911.211 of the Revised Code that involves a person who was a family or household member at the time of the violation, or a violation of a municipal ordinance that is substantially similar to section 2903.13, 2903.211, or 2911.211 of the Revised Code that involves a person who was a family or household member at the time of the violation, the complainant may file, or, if in an emergency the complainant is unable to file, a person who made an arrest for the alleged violation under section 2935.03 of the Revised Code may file on behalf of the complainant, a motion that requests the issuance of a temporary protection order as a pretrial condition of release of the alleged offender, in addition to any bail set under Criminal Rule 46. The motion shall be filed with the clerk of the court that has jurisdiction of the case at any time after the filing of the complaint.

(2) For purposes of section 2930.09 of the Revised Code, all stages of a proceeding arising out of a violation specified in division (A)(1) of this section, including all proceedings on a motion for a temporary protection order, are critical stages of the case, and a complainant may

be accompanied by a victim advocate or another person to provide support to the victim as provided in that section.

(B) The motion shall be prepared on a form that is provided by the clerk of the court, which form shall be substantially as follows:

"MOTION FOR TEMPORARY PROTECTION ORDER

_____ Court

Name and address of court

State of Ohio

v. No. _____

_____

Name of Defendant

(name of person), the complainant in the above-captioned case, moves the court to issue a temporary protection order containing terms designed to ensure the safety and protection of the complainant and other family or household members, in relation to the named defendant, pursuant to its authority to issue such an order under section 2919.26 of the Revised Code.

A complaint, a copy of which has been attached to this motion, has been filed in this court charging the named defendant with at least one of the following violations of section 2919.25 of the Revised Code that constitutes "domestic violence" or a municipal ordinance that is substantially similar to that section: knowingly causing or attempting to cause physical harm to a family or household member; recklessly causing serious physical harm to a family or household member; or, by threat of force, knowingly causing a family or household member to believe that he would cause imminent physical harm to that family or household member; charging the named defendant with felonious assault, aggravated assault, or assault that involved a family or household member in violation of section 2903.11, 2903.12, or 2903.13 of the Revised Code; charging the named defendant with menacing by stalking or aggravated trespass that involves a family or household member in violation of section 2903.211 or 2911.211 of the Revised Code; or charging the named defendant with a violation of a municipal ordinance that is substantially similar to section 2903.13, 2903.211, or 2911.211 of the Revised Code that involves a family or household member.

I understand that I must appear before the court, at a time set by the court within twenty-four hours after the filing of this motion, for a hearing on the motion or that, if I am unable to appear because of hospitalization or a medical condition resulting from the offense alleged in the complaint, a person who can provide information about my need for a temporary protection order must appear before the court in lieu of my appearing in court. I understand that any temporary protection order granted pursuant to this motion is a pretrial condition of release and is effective only until the disposition of the criminal proceeding arising out of the attached complaint, or the issuance of a civil protection order or the approval of a consent agreement, arising out of the same activities as those that were the basis of the complaint, under section 3113.31 of the Revised Code.

_____

Signature of complainant

(or signature of the arresting officer who filed the motion on behalf of the complainant)

_____

Address of complainant (or office address of the arresting officer who filed the motion on behalf of the complainant)"

(C) As soon as possible after the filing of a motion that requests the issuance of a temporary protection order, but not later than twenty-four hours after the filing of the motion, the court shall conduct a hearing to determine whether to issue the order. The person who requested the order shall appear before the court and provide the court with the information that it requests concerning the basis of the motion. If the person who requested the order is unable to appear and if the court finds that the failure to appear is because of the person's hospitalization or medical condition resulting from the offense alleged in the complaint, another person who is able to provide the court with the information it requests may appear in lieu of the person who requested the order. If the court finds that the safety and protection of the complainant or other family or household member of the alleged offender may be impaired by the continued presence of the alleged offender, the court may issue a temporary protection order, as a pretrial condition of release, that contains terms designed to ensure the safety and protection of the complainant or family or household member, including a requirement that the alleged offender refrain from entering the residence, school, business, or place of employment of the complainant or family or household member.

(D)(1) Upon the filing of a complaint that alleges a violation of section 2919.25 of the Revised Code, a violation of a municipal ordinance that is substantially similar to that section, a violation of section 2903.11, 2903.12, 2903.13, 2903.211, or 2911.211 of the Revised Code that involves a person who was a family or household member at the time of the violation, or a violation of a municipal ordinance that is substantially similar to section 2903.13, 2903.211, or 2911.211 of the Revised Code that involves a person who was a family or household member at the time of the violation, the court, upon its own motion, may issue a temporary protection order as a pretrial condition of release if it finds that the safety and protection of the complainant or other family or household member of the alleged offender may be impaired by the continued presence of the alleged offender.

(2) If the court issues a temporary protection order under this section as an ex parte order, it shall conduct, as soon as possible after the issuance of the order, a hearing in the presence of the alleged offender not later than the next day on which the court is scheduled to conduct business after the day on which the alleged offender was arrested or at the time of the appearance of the alleged offender pursuant to summons to determine whether the order should remain in effect, be modified, or be revoked. The hearing shall be conducted under the standards set forth in division (C) of this section.

(3) An order issued under this division shall contain only those terms authorized in orders issued under division (C) of this section.

(E) A temporary protection order that is issued as a pretrial condition of release under this section:

(1) Is in addition to, but shall not be construed as a part of, any bail set under Criminal Rule 46;

(2) Is effective only until the disposition of the criminal proceeding arising out of the complaint upon which it is based, or the issuance of a protection order or the approval of a consent agreement, arising out of the same activities as those that were the basis of the complaint, under section 3113.31 of the Revised Code;

(3) Shall not be construed as a finding that the alleged offender committed the alleged offense, and shall not be introduced as evidence of the commission of the offense at the trial of the alleged offender on the complaint upon which the order is based.

(F) A person who meets the criteria for bail under Criminal Rule 46 and who, if required to do so pursuant to that rule, executes or posts bond or deposits cash or securities as bail, shall not be held in custody pending a hearing before the court on a motion requesting a temporary protection order.

(G)(1) A copy of any temporary protection order that is issued under this section shall be issued by the court to the complainant, to the defendant, and to all law enforcement agencies that have jurisdiction to enforce the order. The court shall direct that a copy of the order be delivered to the defendant on the same day that the order is entered.

(2) All law enforcement agencies shall establish and maintain an index for the temporary protection orders delivered to the agencies pursuant to division (G)(1) of this section. With respect to each order delivered, each agency shall note on the index, the date and time of the receipt of the order by the agency.

(3) A complainant who obtains a temporary protection order under this section may provide notice of the issuance of the temporary protection order to the judicial and law enforcement officials in any county other than the county in which the order is issued by registering that order in the other county in accordance with division (N) of section 3113.31 of the Revised Code and filing a copy of the registered protection order with a law enforcement agency in the other county in accordance with that division.

(4) Any officer of a law enforcement agency shall enforce a temporary protection order issued by any court in this state in accordance with the provisions of the order, including removing the defendant from the premises, regardless of whether the order is registered in the county in which the officer's agency has jurisdiction as authorized by division (G)(3) of this section.

(H) Upon a violation of a temporary protection order, the court may issue another temporary protection order, as a pretrial condition of release, that modifies the terms of the order that was violated.

(I)(1) As used in divisions (I)(1) and (2) of this section, "defendant" means a person who is alleged in a complaint to have committed a violation of the type described in division (A) of this section.

(2) If a complaint is filed that alleges that a person committed a violation of the type described in division (A) of this section, the court may not issue a temporary protection order under this section that requires the complainant or another family or household member of the defendant to do or refrain from doing an act that the court may require the defendant to do or refrain from doing under a temporary protection order unless both of the following apply:

(a) The defendant has filed a separate complaint that alleges that the complainant or other family or household member in question who would be required under the order to do or refrain from doing the act committed a violation of the type described in division (A) of this section.

(b) The court determines that both the complainant or other family or household member in question who would be required under the order to do or refrain from doing the act and the defendant acted primarily as aggressors, that neither the complainant or other family or household member in question who would be required under the order to do or refrain from doing the act nor the defendant acted primarily in self-defense, and, in accordance with the standards and criteria of this section as applied in relation to the separate complaint filed by the defendant, that it should issue the order to require the complainant or other family or household member in question to do or refrain from doing the act.

(J) Notwithstanding any provision of law to the contrary, no court shall charge a fee for the filing of a motion pursuant to this section.

(K) As used in this section, "victim advocate" means a person who provides support and assistance for a victim of an offense during court proceedings.

(1994 H 335, eff. 12–9–94; 1992 H 536, eff. 11–5–92; 1990 S 3; 1984 H 587; 1980 H 920; 1978 H 835)

2919.27   Violating a protection order or consent agreement

(A) No person shall recklessly violate any terms of a protection order issued or consent agreement approved pursuant to section 2919.26 or 3113.31 of the Revised Code.

(B) Whoever violates this section is guilty of violating a protection order or consent agreement. If the offender previously has not been convicted of or pleaded guilty to two or more violations of section 2903.211 or 2911.211 of the Revised Code that involve the same person who is the subject of the protection order or consent agreement and previously has not been convicted of or pleaded guilty to any violation of this section, violating a protection order or consent agreement is a misdemeanor of the first degree. If the offender previously has been convicted of or pleaded guilty to two or more violations of of [sic] section 2903.211 or 2911.211 of the Revised Code that involve the same person who is the subject of the protection order or consent agreement or previously has been convicted of or pleaded guilty to one or more violations of this section, violating a protection order or consent agreement is a felony of the fourth degree.

(1994 H 335, eff. 12–9–94; 1992 H 536, eff. 11–5–92; 1985 H 475; 1984 H 587)

2919.271   Mental evaluations

(A) If a defendant is charged with a violation of section 2919.27 of the Revised Code or of a municipal ordinance that is substantially similar to that section, and if the court determines that the violation of the protection order or consent agreement allegedly involves conduct by the defendant that caused physical harm to the person or property of a family or household member covered by the order or agreement or conduct by the defendant that caused a family or household member to believe that the defendant would cause physical harm to that member or his property, the court may order an evaluation of the mental condition of the defendant. The evaluation shall be completed no later than thirty days from the date the order is entered. In that order, the court shall do either of the following:

(1) Order that the evaluation of the mental condition of the defendant be preceded by an examination conducted either by a forensic center that is designated by the department of mental health to conduct examinations and make evaluations of defendants charged with violations of section 2919.27 of the Revised Code or of substantially similar municipal ordinances in the area in which the court is located, or by any other program or facility that is designated by the department of mental health or the department of mental retardation and developmental disabilities to conduct examinations and make evaluations of defendants charged with violations of section 2919.27 of the Revised Code or of substantially similar municipal ordinances, and that is operated by either department or is certified by either department as being in compliance with the standards established under division (J) of section 5119.01 of the Revised Code or division (C) of section 5123.04 of the Revised Code.

(2) Designate a center, program, or facility other than one designated by the department of mental health or the department of mental retardation and developmental disabilities, as described in division (A)(1) of this section, to conduct the evaluation and preceding examination of the mental condition of the defendant.

Whether the court acts pursuant to division (A)(1) or (2) of this section, the court may designate examiners other than the personnel of the center, program, facility, or department involved to make the evaluation and preceding examination of the mental condition of the defendant.

(B) If the court considers that additional evaluations of the mental condition of a defendant are necessary following the evaluation authorized by division (A) of this section, the court may order up to two additional similar evaluations. These evaluations shall be completed no later than thirty days from the date the applicable court order is entered. If more than one evaluation of the mental condition of the defendant is ordered under this division, the prosecutor and the defendant may recommend to the court an examiner whom each prefers to perform one of the evaluations and preceding examinations.

(C)(1) The court may order a defendant who has been released on bail to submit to an examination under division (A) or (B) of this section. The examination shall be conducted either at the detention facility in which the defendant would have been confined if he had not been released on bail, or, if so specified by the center, program, facility, or examiners involved, at the premises of the center, program, or facility. Additionally, the examination shall be conducted at the times established by the examiners involved. If such a defendant refuses to submit to an examination or a complete examination as required by the court or the center, program, facility, or examiners involved, the court may amend the conditions of the bail of the defendant and order the sheriff to take him into custody and deliver him to the detention facility in which he would have been confined if he had not been released on bail, or, if so specified by the center, program, facility, or examiners involved, to the premises of the center, program, or facility, for purposes of the examination.

(2) A defendant who has not been released on bail shall be examined at his detention facility or, if so specified by the center, program, facility, or examiners involved, at the premises of the center, program, or facility.

(D) The examiner of the mental condition of a defendant under division (A) or (B) of this section shall file a written report with the court within thirty days after the entry of an order for the evaluation of the mental condition of the defendant. The report shall contain the findings of the examiner; the facts in reasonable detail on which the findings are based; the opinion of the examiner as to the mental condition of the defendant; the opinion of the examiner as to whether the defendant represents a substantial risk of physical harm to other persons as manifested by evidence of recent homicidal or other violent behavior, evidence of recent threats that placed other persons in reasonable fear of violent behavior and serious physical harm, or evidence of present dangerousness; and the opinion of the examiner as to the types of treatment or counseling that the defendant needs. The court shall provide copies of the report to the prosecutor and defense counsel.

(E) The costs of any evaluation and preceding examination of a defendant that is ordered pursuant to division (A) or (B) of this section shall be taxed as court costs in the criminal case.

(F) If he considers it necessary in order to make an accurate evaluation of the mental condition of a defendant, an examiner under division (A) or (B) of this section may request any family or household member of the defendant to provide the examiner with information. A family or household member may, but is not required to, provide information to the examiner upon receipt of such a request.

(G) As used in this section:

(1) "Bail" includes a recognizance.

(2) "Examiner" means a psychiatrist, a licensed social worker at the independent practice level who is employed by a forensic center that is certified as being in compliance with the standards established under division (J) of section 5119.01 or division (C) of section 5123.04 of the Revised Code, a licensed counselor with clinical endorsement who is employed at a forensic center that is certified as being in compliance with such standards, or a licensed clinical psychologist, except that in order to be an examiner, a licensed clinical psychologist shall meet the criteria of division (I)(1) of section 5122.01 of the Revised Code or be employed to conduct examinations by the department of mental health or by a forensic center certified as being in compliance with the standards established under division (J) of section 5119.01 or division (C) of section 5123.04 of the Revised Code that is designated by the department of mental health.

(3) "Family or household member" has the same meaning as in section 2919.25 of the Revised Code.

(4) "Prosecutor" has the same meaning as in section 2935.01 of the Revised Code.

(5) "Psychiatrist" and "licensed clincial [sic] psychologist" have the same meaning as in section 5122.01 of the Revised Code.

(1985 H 475, eff. 3–7–86)

CHAPTER 2921

OFFENSES AGAINST JUSTICE AND PUBLIC ADMINISTRATION

DEFINITIONS

DEFINITIONS

2921.01 Definitions

As used in sections 2921.01 to 2921.45 of the Revised Code:

(A) "Public official" means any elected or appointed officer, or employee, or agent of the state or any political subdivision, whether in a temporary or permanent capacity, and including without limitation legislators, judges, and law enforcement officers.

(B) "Public servant" means any of the following:

(1) Any public official;

(2) Any person performing ad hoc a governmental function, including without limitation a juror, member of a temporary commission, master, arbitrator, advisor, or consultant;

(3) A candidate for public office, whether or not he is elected or appointed to the office for which he is a candidate. A person is a candidate for purposes of this division if he has been nominated according to law for election or appointment to public office, or if he has filed a petition or petitions as required by law to have his name placed on the ballot in a primary, general, or special election, or if he campaigns as a write-in candidate in any primary, general, or special election.

(C) "Party official" means any person who holds an elective or appointive post in a political party in the United States or this state, by virtue of which he directs, conducts, or participates in directing or conducting party affairs at any level of responsibility.

(D) "Official proceeding" means any proceeding before a legislative, judicial, administrative, or other governmental agency or official authorized to take evidence under oath, and includes any proceeding before a referee, hearing examiner, commissioner, notary, or other person taking testimony or a deposition in connection with an official proceeding.

(E) "Detention" means arrest; confinement in any vehicle subsequent to an arrest; confinement in any facility for custody of persons charged with or convicted of crime or alleged or found to be a delinquent child or unruly child; hospitalization, institutionalization, or confinement in any facility that is ordered pursuant to or under the authority of section 2945.37, 2945.371, 2945.38, 2945.39, or 2945.40 of the Revised Code; confinement in any vehicle for transportation to or from any such facility; detention for extradition or deportation; except as provided in this division, supervision by any employee of any such facility that is incidental to hospitalization, institutionalization, or confinement in the facility but that occurs outside the facility; or supervision by an employee of the department of rehabilitation and correction of a person on any type of release from a state correctional institution other than release on parole or shock probation. For a person confined in a county jail who participates in a county jail industry program pursuant to section 5147.30 of the Revised Code, "detention" includes time spent at an assigned work site and going to and from the work site. Detention does not include supervision of probation or parole, or constraint incidental to release on bail.

(F) "Detention facility" means any place used for the confinement of a person charged with or convicted of any crime or alleged or found to be a delinquent child or unruly child.

(G) "Valuable thing or valuable benefit" includes, but is not limited to, a contribution. This inclusion does not indicate or imply that a contribution was not included in those terms before September 17, 1986.

(H) "Campaign committee," "contribution," "political action committee," "legislative campaign fund," and "political party" have the same meanings as in section 3517.01 of the Revised Code.

(I) "Provider agreement" and "medical assistance program" have the same meanings as in section 2913.40 of the Revised Code.

(1995 S 8, eff. 8–23–95; 1994 H 571, eff. 10–6–94; 1993 H 42, eff. 2–9–94; 1992 S 37; 1990 H 51; 1988 H 708; 1986 H 428, H 300, H 340; 1972 H 511)

BRIBERY, INTIMIDATION, AND RETALIATION

2921.02 Bribery

(A) No person, with purpose to corrupt a public servant or party official, or improperly to influence him with respect to the discharge of his duty, whether before or after he is elected, appointed, qualified, employed, summoned, or sworn, shall promise, offer, or give any valuable thing or valuable benefit.

(B) No person, either before or after he is elected, appointed, qualified, employed, summoned, or sworn as a public servant or party official, shall knowingly solicit or accept for himself or another person any valuable thing or valuable benefit to corrupt or improperly influence him or another public servant or party official with respect to the discharge of his or the other public servant's or party official's duty.

(C) No person, with purpose to corrupt a witness or improperly to influence him with respect to his testimony in an official proceeding, either before or after he is subpoenaed or sworn, shall promise, offer, or give him or another person any valuable thing or valuable benefit.

(D) No person, either before or after he is subpoenaed or sworn as a witness, shall knowingly solicit or accept for himself or another person any valuable thing or valuable benefit to corrupt or improperly influence him with respect to his testimony in an official proceeding.

(E) Whoever violates this section is guilty of bribery, a felony of the third degree.

(F) A public servant or party official who is convicted of bribery is forever disqualified from holding any public office, employment, or position of trust in this state.

(1986 H 300, eff. 9–17–86; 1972 H 511)

2921.03 Intimidation

(A) No person, knowingly and by force or by unlawful threat of harm to any person or property, shall attempt to influence, intimidate, or hinder a public servant, party official, or witness in the discharge of his duty.

(B) Whoever violates this section is guilty of intimidation, a felony of the third degree.

(1984 S 172, eff. 9–26–84; 1972 H 511)

2921.04 Intimidation of crime victim or witness

(A) No person shall knowingly attempt to intimidate or hinder the victim of a crime in the filing or prosecution of criminal charges, or a witness in a criminal case in the discharge of his duty.

(B) No person, knowingly and by force or by unlawful threat of harm to any person or property, shall attempt to influence, intimidate, or hinder the victim of a crime in the filing or prosecution of criminal charges, or a witness in a criminal case in the discharge of his duty.

(C) Division (A) of this section does not apply to any person who is attempting to resolve a dispute pertaining to the alleged commission of a criminal offense, either prior to or subsequent to the filing of a complaint, or who is attempting to arbitrate or assist in the conciliation of any such dispute, either prior to or subsequent to the filing of a complaint.

(D) Whoever violates this section is guilty of intimidation of a crime victim or witness. Violation of division (A) of this section is a misdemeanor of the first degree. Violation of division (B) of this section is a felony of the third degree.

(1984 S 172, eff. 9–26–84)

2921.05 Desecrating flag of this state or the United States—Repealed

(1972 H 511, eff. 1–1–74; 132 v H 664; 1953 H 1; GC 12396, 12397)

2921.06 Printing of flag design permitted—Repealed

(1972 H 511, eff. 1–1–74; 1953 H 1; GC 12398)

2921.07   Carrying and displaying certain flags prohibited—Repealed

(1972 H 511, eff. 1–1–74; 1953 H 1; GC 12398–1, 12398–2)

2921.08   Abducting inmates from state institutions—Repealed

(1972 H 511, eff. 1–1–74; 1953 H 1; GC 12426)

2921.09   Stealing water from the state—Repealed

(1972 H 511, eff. 1–1–74; 1953 H 1; GC 12461)

2921.10   Lessee shall provide proper water gauges—Repealed

(1972 H 511, eff. 1–1–74; 1953 H 1; GC 12462)

PERJURY

2921.11   Perjury

(A) No person, in any official proceeding, shall knowingly make a false statement under oath or affirmation, or knowingly swear or affirm the truth of a false statement previously made, when either statement is material.

(B) A falsification is material, regardless of its admissibility in evidence, if it can affect the course or outcome of the proceeding. It is no defense to a charge under this section that the offender mistakenly believed a falsification to be immaterial.

(C) It is no defense to a charge under this section that the oath or affirmation was administered or taken in an irregular manner.

(D) Where contradictory statements relating to the same material fact are made by the offender under oath or affirmation and within the period of the statute of limitations for perjury, it is not necessary for the prosecution to prove which statement was false, but only that one or the other was false.

(E) No person shall be convicted of a violation of this section where proof of falsity rests solely upon contradiction by testimony of one person other than the defendant.

(F) Whoever violates this section is guilty of perjury, a felony of the third degree.

(1972 H 511, eff. 1–1–74)

2921.12   Tampering with evidence

(A) No person, knowing that an official proceeding or investigation is in progress, or is about to be or likely to be instituted, shall do any of the following:

(1) Alter, destroy, conceal, or remove any record, document, or thing, with purpose to impair its value or availability as evidence in such proceeding or investigation;

(2) Make, present, or use any record, document, or thing, knowing it to be false and with purpose to mislead a public official who is or may be engaged in such proceeding or investigation, or with purpose to corrupt the outcome of any such proceeding or investigation.

(B) Whoever violates this section is guilty of tampering with evidence, a felony of the third degree.

(1972 H 511, eff. 1–1–74)

2921.13   Falsification

(A) No person shall knowingly make a false statement, or knowingly swear or affirm the truth of a false statement previously made, when any of the following applies:

(1) The statement is made in any official proceeding.

(2) The statement is made with purpose to incriminate another.

(3) The statement is made with purpose to mislead a public official in performing the public official's official function.

(4) The statement is made with purpose to secure the payment of unemployment compensation, aid to dependent children, disability assistance, retirement benefits, economic development assistance, as defined in section 9.66 of the Revised Code, or other benefits administered by a governmental agency or paid out of a public treasury.

(5) The statement is made with purpose to secure the issuance by a governmental agency of a license, permit, authorization, certificate, registration, release, or provider agreement.

(6) The statement is sworn or affirmed before a notary public or another person empowered to administer oaths.

(7) The statement is in writing on or in connection with a report or return that is required or authorized by law.

(8) The statement is in writing and is made with purpose to induce another to extend credit to or employ the offender, to confer any degree, diploma, certificate of attainment, award of excellence, or honor on the offender, or to extend to or bestow upon the offender any other valuable benefit or distinction, when the person to whom the statement is directed relies upon it to that [1] person's detriment.

(9) The statement is made with purpose to commit or facilitate the commission of a theft offense involving a motor vehicle.

(10) The statement is made with purpose to commit or facilitate the commission of a theft offense involving the proceeds of an insurance policy.

(11) The statement is knowingly made to a probate court in connection with any action, proceeding, or other matter within its jurisdiction, either orally or in a written document, including, but not limited to, an application, petition, complaint, or other pleading, or an inventory, account, or report.

(12) The statement is made on an application for a marriage license under section 3101.05 of the Revised Code.

(13) The statement is made, either orally or in writing, in connection with an application for legal representation submitted to a court, the state public defender, a county public defender, or a joint county public defender by a defendant in a criminal case for the purpose of a determination of indigency and eligibility for legal representation by the state public defender, a county public defender, a joint county public defender, or court-appointed counsel.

(14) The statement is made in connection with the purchase of a firearm, as defined in section 2923.11 of the Revised Code, and in conjunction with the furnishing to the seller of the firearm of a fictitious or altered driver's or commercial driver's license or permit, a fictitious or altered identification card, or any other document that contains false information about the purchaser's identity.

(B) No person, in connection with the purchase of a firearm, as defined in section 2923.11 of the Revised Code, shall knowingly furnish to the seller of the firearm a fictitious or altered driver's or commercial driver's license or permit, a fictitious or altered identification card, or any other document that contains false information about the purchaser's identity.

(C) It is no defense to a charge under division (A)(4) of this section that the oath or affirmation was administered or taken in an irregular manner.

(D) Where contradictory statements relating to the same fact are made by the offender within the period of the statute of limitations for falsification, it is not necessary for the prosecution to prove which statement was false but only that one or the other was false.

(E)(1) Whoever violates division (A)(1), (2), (3), (4), (5), (6), (7), (8), (11), or (12) of this section is guilty of falsification, a misdemeanor of the first degree.

(2) Whoever violates division (A)(9) of this section is guilty of falsification of a report of a motor vehicle theft, a felony of the third degree.

(3) Whoever violates division (A)(10) of this section is guilty of falsification of an insurance claim. If the amount of the claim is less than three hundred dollars, falsification of an insurance claim is a misdemeanor of the first degree. If the amount of the claim is three hundred dollars or more and is less than five thousand dollars or if the offender previously has been convicted of a theft offense, falsification of an insurance claim is a felony of the fourth

degree. If the amount of the claim is five thousand dollars or more and is less than one hundred thousand dollars, or if the claim is made for the theft of a motor vehicle, or if the offender previously has been convicted of two or more theft offenses, falsification of an insurance claim is a felony of the third degree. If the amount of the claim is one hundred thousand dollars or more, falsification of an insurance claim is a felony of the second degree.

(4) Whoever violates division (A)(13) of this section is guilty of falsification, a misdemeanor of the first degree. If, as a result of the false statement that is the basis of the conviction under division (A)(13) of this section the offender received legal representation to which the offender was not entitled from the state public defender, a county public defender, a joint county public defender, or court-appointed counsel, the court shall order the offender to make restitution, in an amount equal to the value of the legal representation provided by the state public defender, county public defender, joint county public defender, or court-appointed counsel, to the public entity that paid for the legal representation.

(5) Whoever violates division (A)(14) or (B) of this section is guilty of falsification to purchase a firearm, a felony of the fourth degree.

(1995 S 46, eff. 11–15–95; 1995 H 4, eff. 11–9–95; 1995 H 249, eff. 7–17–95; 1993 H 107, eff. 10–20–93; 1993 H 152; 1991 H 298; 1990 S 3, H 347; 1989 S 46; 1988 H 708; 1986 H 340; 1984 H 632; 1976 S 545; 1972 H 511)

1 Language appears as the result of the harmonization of 1995 S 46 and 1995 H 4.

Historical and Statutory Notes

Ed. Note: Comparison of these amendments [1995 S 46, eff. 11–15–95 and 1995 H 4, eff. 11–9–95] in pursuance of section 1.52 of the Revised Code discloses that they are not substantively irreconcilable, so that they are required by that section to be harmonized to give effect to each amendment. In recognition of this rule of construction, changes made by 1995 S 46, eff. 11–15–95, and 1995 H 4, eff. 11–9–95, have been incorporated in the above amendment. See *Baldwin's Ohio Legislative Service*, 1995, pages 7/L–1602 and 7/L–1481, for original versions of these Acts.

2921.14   False report of child abuse or neglect

(A) No person shall knowingly make or cause another person to make a false report under division (B) of section 2151.421 of the Revised Code alleging that any person has committed an act or omission that resulted in a child being an abused child as defined in section 2151.031 of the Revised Code or a neglected child as defined in section 2151.03 of the Revised Code.

(B) Whoever violates this section is guilty of making or causing a false report of child abuse or child neglect, a misdemeanor of the first degree.

(1990 S 3, eff. 4–11–91)

2921.15   Prosecution by attorney general; special grand jury—Repealed

(1972 H 511, eff. 1–1–74; 1953 H 1; GC 13116–2)

2921.16   Compensation of jurors—Repealed

(1972 H 511, eff. 1–1–74; 1953 H 1; GC 13116–3)

2921.17   Injuring property of United States along navigable streams—Repealed

(1972 H 511, eff. 1–1–74; 1953 H 1; GC 12506)

2921.18   Prison riots—Repealed

(1972 H 511, eff. 1–1–74; 1972 H 494; 1969 H 1; 132 v H 65; 130 v H 802)

COMPOUNDING

2921.21   Compounding a crime

(A) No person shall knowingly demand, accept, or agree to accept anything of value in consideration of abandoning or agreeing to abandon a pending criminal prosecution.

(B) It is an affirmative defense to a charge under this section when both of the following apply:

(1) The pending prosecution involved is for a violation of section 2913.02 or 2913.11, division (B)(2) of section 2913.21, or section 2913.47 of the Revised Code, of which the actor under this section was the victim.

(2) The thing of value demanded, accepted, or agreed to be accepted, in consideration of abandoning or agreeing to abandon the prosecution, did not exceed an amount that the actor reasonably believed due him as restitution for the loss caused him by the offense.

(C) When a prosecuting witness abandons or agrees to abandon a prosecution under division (B) of this section, the abandonment or agreement in no way binds the state to abandoning the prosecution.

(D) Whoever violates this section is guilty of compounding a crime, a misdemeanor of the first degree.

(1990 H 347, eff. 7–18–90; 1973 H 716; 1972 H 511)

2921.22 Reporting felony; medical personnel to report gunshot, stabbing, and burn injuries and suspected domestic violence

(A) No person, knowing that a felony has been or is being committed, shall knowingly fail to report such information to law enforcement authorities.

(B) Except for conditions that are within the scope of division (E) of this section, no physician, limited practitioner, nurse, or person giving aid to a sick or injured person, shall negligently fail to report to law enforcement authorities any gunshot or stab wound treated or observed by him, or any serious physical harm to persons that he knows or has reasonable cause to believe resulted from an offense of violence.

(C) No person who discovers the body or acquires the first knowledge of the death of any person shall fail to report the death immediately to any physician whom the person knows to be treating the deceased for a condition from which death at such time would not be unexpected, or to a law enforcement officer, ambulance service, emergency squad, or the coroner in a political subdivision in which the body is discovered, the death is believed to have occurred, or knowledge concerning the death is obtained.

(D) No person shall fail to provide upon request of the person to whom he has made a report required by division (C) of this section, or to any law enforcement officer who has reasonable cause to assert the authority to investigate the circumstances surrounding the death, any facts within his knowledge that may have a bearing on the investigation of the death.

(E)(1) As used in this division, "burn injury" means any of the following:

(a) Second or third degree burns;

(b) Any burns to the upper respiratory tract or laryngeal edema due to the inhalation of superheated air;

(c) Any burn injury or wound that may result in death.

(2) No physician, nurse, or limited practitioner who, outside a hospital, sanitarium, or other medical facility, attends or treats a person who has sustained a burn injury inflicted by an explosion or other incendiary device, or that shows evidence of having been inflicted in a violent, malicious, or criminal manner, shall fail to report the burn injury immediately to the local arson bureau, if there is such a bureau in the jurisdiction in which the person is attended or treated, or otherwise to local law enforcement authorities.

(3) No manager, superintendent, or other person in charge of a hospital, sanitarium, or other medical facility in which a person is attended or treated for any burn injury inflicted by an explosion or other incendiary device, or that shows evidence of having been inflicted in a violent, malicious, or criminal manner, shall fail to report the burn injury immediately to the local arson bureau, if there is such a bureau in the jurisdiction in which the person is attended or treated, or otherwise to local law enforcement authorities.

(4) No person who is required to report any burn injury under division (E)(2) or (3) of this section shall fail to file, within three working days after attending or treating the victim, a written report of the burn injury with the office of the state fire marshal. The report shall be made on a form provided by the state fire marshal.

(5) Anyone participating in the making of reports under division (E) of this section or anyone participating in a judicial proceeding resulting from the reports shall be immune from any civil or criminal liability that otherwise might be incurred or imposed as a result of such actions. Notwithstanding section 4731.22 of the Revised Code, the physician-patient relationship is not a ground for excluding evidence regarding a person's burn injury or the cause of the burn injury in any judicial proceeding resulting from a report submitted pursuant to division (E) of this section.

(F)(1) Any doctor of medicine or osteopathic medicine, hospital intern or resident, registered or licensed practical nurse, psychologist, social worker, independent social worker, social work assistant, licensed professional clinical counselor, licensed professional counselor, or licensed counselor's assistant who knows or has reasonable cause to believe that a patient or client has been the victim of domestic violence, as defined in section 3113.31 of the Revised Code, shall note that knowledge or belief and the basis for it in the patient's or client's records.

(2) Notwithstanding section 4731.22 of the Revised Code, the doctor-patient privilege shall not be a ground for excluding any information regarding the report containing the knowledge or belief noted pursuant to division (F)(1) of this section, and the information may be admitted as evidence in accordance with the Rules of Evidence.

(G) Division (A) or (D) of this section does not require disclosure of information, when any of the following applies:

(1) The information is privileged by reason of the relationship between attorney and client, doctor and patient, licensed psychologist or licensed school psychologist and client, clergyman or rabbi or minister or priest and any person communicating information confidentially to him for a religious counseling purpose in his professional character, husband and wife, or a communications assistant and those who are a party to a telecommunications relay service call.

(2) The information would tend to incriminate a member of the actor's immediate family.

(3) Disclosure of the information would amount to revealing a news source, privileged under section 2739.04 or 2739.12 of the Revised Code.

(4) Disclosure of the information would amount to disclosure by an ordained clergyman of an organized religious body of a confidential communication made to him in his capacity as such by a person seeking his aid or counsel.

(5) Disclosure would amount to revealing information acquired by the actor in the course of his duties in connection with a bona fide program of treatment or services for drug dependent persons or persons in danger of drug dependence, which program is maintained or conducted by a hospital, clinic, person, agency, or organization certified pursuant to section 3793.06 of the Revised Code.

(6) Disclosure would amount to revealing information acquired by the actor in the course of his duties in connection with a bona fide program for providing counseling services to victims of crimes that are violations of section 2907.02, 2907.05, or 2907.12 of the Revised Code. As used in this division, "counseling services" include services provided in an informal setting by a person who, by education or experience, is competent to provide such services.

(H) No disclosure of information pursuant to this section gives rise to any liability or recrimination for a breach of privilege or confidence.

(I) Whoever violates division (A) or (B) of this section is guilty of failure to report a crime. Violation of division (A) of this section is a misdemeanor of the fourth degree. Violation of division (B) of this section is a misdemeanor of the second degree.

(J) Whoever violates division (C) or (D) of this section is guilty of failure to report knowledge of a death, a misdemeanor of the fourth degree.

(K)(1) Whoever negligently violates division (E) of this section is guilty of a minor misdemeanor.

(2) Whoever knowingly violates division (E) of this section is guilty of a misdemeanor of the second degree.

(1994 H 335, eff. 12–9–94; 1992 S 343, eff. 3–24–93; 1989 H 317; 1987 H 273; 1980 H 284; 1977 H 1, S 203; 1975 S 283, H 750; 1972 H 511)

2921.23 Failure to aid a law enforcement officer

(A) No person shall negligently fail or refuse to aid a law enforcement officer, when called upon for assistance in preventing or halting the commission of an offense, or in apprehending or detaining an offender, when such aid can be given without a substantial risk of physical harm to the person giving it.

(B) Whoever violates this section is guilty of failure to aid a law enforcement officer, a minor misdemeanor.

(1972 H 511, eff. 1–1–74)

DISCLOSURE OF CONFIDENTIAL INFORMATION

2921.24 Home address of peace officer not to be disclosed during criminal case

(A) No officer or employee of a law enforcement agency or court, or of the office of the clerk of any court, shall disclose during the pendency of any criminal case the home address of any peace officer, as defined in section 2935.01 of the Revised Code, who is a witness or arresting officer in the case.

(B) Division (A) of this section does not prohibit a peace officer from disclosing his own home address, and does not apply to any person who discloses the home address of a peace officer pursuant to a court-ordered disclosure under division (C) of this section.

(C) The court in which any criminal case is pending may order the disclosure of the home address of any peace officer who is a witness or arresting officer in the case, if the court determines after a written request for the disclosure that good cause exists for disclosing the home address of the peace officer.

(D) Whoever violates division (A) of this section is guilty of disclosure of confidential information, a misdemeanor of the fourth degree.

(1984 H 403, eff. 9–26–84)

2921.25 Judge not to order disclosure; exception

No judge of a court of record, or mayor presiding over a mayor's court, shall order a peace officer, as defined in section 2935.01 of the Revised Code, who is a witness in a criminal case, to disclose his home address during his examination in the case, unless the judge or mayor determines that the defendant has a right to the disclosure.

(1984 H 403, eff. 9–26–84)

2921.26 Judge to charge grand jury, when—Repealed

(1972 H 511, eff. 1–1–74; 125 v 813)

2921.27 Records confidential; exceptions—Repealed

(1972 H 511, eff. 1–1–74; 125 v 813)

OBSTRUCTING AND ESCAPE

2921.31 Obstructing official business

(A) No person, without privilege to do so and with purpose to prevent, obstruct, or delay the performance by a public official of any authorized act within his official capacity, shall do any act which hampers or impedes a public official in the performance of his lawful duties.

(B) Whoever violates this section is guilty of obstructing official business, a misdemeanor of the second degree.

(1972 H 511, eff. 1–1–74)

2921.32 Obstructing justice

(A) No person, with purpose to hinder the discovery, apprehension, prosecution, conviction, or punishment of another for crime, or to assist another to benefit from the commission of a crime, shall do any of the following:

(1) Harbor or conceal such other person;

(2) Provide such other person with money, transportation, a weapon, a disguise, or other means of avoiding discovery or apprehension;

(3) Warn such other person of impending discovery or apprehension;

(4) Destroy or conceal physical evidence of the crime, or induce any person to withhold testimony or information or to elude legal process summoning him to testify or supply evidence;

(5) Communicate false information to any person.

(B) Whoever violates this section is guilty of obstructing justice, a misdemeanor of the first degree. If the crime committed by the person aided is a felony, obstructing justice is a felony of the fourth degree.

(1972 H 511, eff. 1–1–74)

2921.321 Assaulting police dog, horse, or handicapped assistance dog

(A) No person shall knowingly cause, or attempt to cause, physical harm to a police dog or horse in either of the following circumstances:

(1) The police dog or horse is assisting a law enforcement officer in the performance of his official duties at the time the physical harm is caused or attempted.

(2) The police dog or horse is not assisting a law enforcement officer in the performance of his official duties at the time the physical harm is caused or attempted, but the offender has actual knowledge that the dog or horse is a police dog or horse.

(B) No person shall knowingly cause, or attempt to cause, physical harm to a handicapped assistance dog in either of the following circumstances:

(1) The handicapped assistance dog is assisting a blind, deaf, or mobility impaired person at the time the physical harm is caused or attempted.

(2) The handicapped assistance dog is not assisting a blind, deaf, or mobility impaired person at the time the physical harm is caused or attempted, but the offender has actual knowledge that the dog is a handicapped assistance dog.

(C)(1) Whoever violates division (A) of this section is guilty of assaulting a police dog or horse. If the violation results in the death of the dog or horse, assaulting a police dog or horse is a felony of the third degree. If the violation results in serious physical harm to the police dog or horse other than its death, assaulting a police dog or horse is a felony of the fourth degree. If the violation results in physical harm to the police dog or horse other than death or serious physical harm, assaulting a police dog or horse is a misdemeanor of the first degree. If the violation does not result in death, serious physical harm, or physical harm to the police dog or horse, assaulting a police dog or horse is a misdemeanor of the second degree.

(2) Whoever violates division (B) of this section is guilty of assaulting a handicapped assistance dog. If the violation results in the death of the dog, assaulting a handicapped assistance dog is a felony of the third degree. If the violation results in serious physical harm to the dog other than its death, assaulting a handicapped assistance dog is a felony of the fourth degree. If the violation results in physical harm to the dog other than death or serious physical harm, assaulting a handicapped assistance dog is a misdemeanor of the first degree. If the violation does not result in death, serious physical harm, or physical harm to the dog, assaulting a handicapped assistance dog is a misdemeanor of the second degree.

(D) This section does not apply to a licensed veterinarian whose conduct is in accordance with Chapter 4741. of the Revised Code.

(E) As used in this section:

(1) "Physical harm" means any injury, illness, or other physiological impairment, regardless of its gravity or duration.

(2) "Police dog or horse" means a dog or horse that has been trained, and may be used, to assist law enforcement officers in the performance of their official duties.

(3) "Serious physical harm" means any of the following:

(a) Any physical harm that carries a substantial risk of death;

(b) Any physical harm that causes permanent maiming or that involves some temporary, substantial maiming;

(c) Any physical harm that causes acute pain of a duration that results in substantial suffering.

(4) "Handicapped assistance dog" means a dog that serves as a guide or leader for a blind person or as a listener for a deaf person or that provides support or assistance for a mobility impaired person.

(5) "Blind" and "mobility impaired person" have the same meanings as in section 955.011 of the Revised Code.

(1994 S 116, eff. 9–29–94)

2921.33   Resisting arrest

(A) No person, recklessly or by force, shall resist or interfere with a lawful arrest of himself or another.

(B) Whoever violates this section is guilty of resisting arrest, a misdemeanor of the second degree.

(1972 H 511, eff. 1–1–74)

2921.331   Failure to comply with order or signal of police officer

(A) No person shall fail to comply with any lawful order or direction of any police officer invested with authority to direct, control, or regulate traffic.

(B) No person shall operate a motor vehicle so as willfully to elude or flee a police officer after receiving a visible or audible signal from a police officer to bring his motor vehicle to a stop.

(C) Whoever violates this section is guilty of failure to comply with an order or signal of a police officer. A violation of division (A) of this section is a misdemeanor of the first degree. A violation of division (B) of this section is a misdemeanor of the first degree, except that a violation of division (B) of this section is a felony of the fourth degree if the jury or judge as trier of fact finds any one of the following by proof beyond a reasonable doubt:

(1) In committing the offense, the offender was fleeing immediately after the commission of a felony;

(2) The operation of the motor vehicle by the offender was a proximate cause of serious physical harm to persons or property;

(3) The operation of the motor vehicle by the offender caused a substantial risk of serious physical harm to persons or property.

(D) As used in this section, "police officer" has the same meaning as in section 4511.01 of the Revised Code.

(1989 S 49, eff. 11–3–89)

2921.34   Escape

(A) No person, knowing he is under detention or being reckless in that regard, shall purposely break or attempt to break the detention, or purposely fail to return to detention, either following temporary leave granted for a specific purpose or limited period, or at the time required when serving a sentence in intermittent confinement.

(B) Irregularity in bringing about or maintaining detention, or lack of jurisdiction of the committing or detaining authority, is not a defense to a charge under this section if the detention is pursuant to judicial order or in a detention facility. In the case of any other detention, irregularity or lack of jurisdiction is an affirmative defense only if either of the following occurs:

(1) The escape involved no substantial risk of harm to the person or property of another.

(2) The detaining authority knew or should have known there was no legal basis or authority for the detention.

(C) Whoever violates this section is guilty of escape.

(1) If the offender, at the time of the commission of the offense, was under detention as an alleged or adjudicated delinquent child or unruly child and if the act for which the offender was under detention would not be a felony if committed by an adult, escape is a misdemeanor of the first degree.

(2) If the offender, at the time of the commission of the offense, was under detention in any other manner, escape is one of the following:

(a) An aggravated felony of the first degree, when the most serious offense for which the person was under detention is aggravated murder or murder or, if the person was under detention as an alleged or adjudicated delinquent child, when the most serious act for which the person was under detention would be aggravated murder or murder if committed by an adult;

(b) An aggravated felony of the next lesser aggravated degree than the most serious offense for which the person was under detention, when the most serious offense for which the person was under detention is an aggravated felony of the first or second degree or, if the person was under detention as an alleged or adjudicated delinquent child, when the most serious act for which the person was under detention would be an aggravated felony of the first or second degree if committed by an adult;

(c) A felony of the next lesser degree than the most serious offense for which the person was under detention, when the most serious offense for which the person was under detention is a felony of the first or second degree or, if the person was under detention as an alleged or adjudicated delinquent child, when the most serious act for which the person was under detention would be a felony of the first or second degree if committed by an adult;

(d) A felony of the fourth degree, when any of the following applies:

(i) The most serious offense for which the person was under detention is an aggravated felony of the third degree, a felony of the third or fourth degree, an unclassified felony, or a misdemeanor, or, if the person was under detention as an alleged or adjudicated delinquent child, the most serious act for which the person was under detention would be an aggravated felony of the third degree, a felony of the third or fourth degree, or an unclassified felony if committed by an adult.

(ii) The person's detention consisted of hospitalization, institutionalization, or confinement in a facility under an order made pursuant to or under authority of section 2945.40 of the Revised Code.

(3) Sentence of confinement imposed for escape shall be served consecutively to any other sentence of confinement imposed on the offender.

(1993 H 42, eff. 2–9–94; 1992 H 725, S 37; 1991 H 298; 1972 H 511)

2921.35 Aiding escape or resistance to authority

(A) No person, with purpose to promote or facilitate an escape or resistance to lawful authority, shall convey into a detention facility, or provide anyone confined therein with any instrument or thing which may be used for such purposes.

(B) No person who is confined in a detention facility, and with purpose to promote or facilitate an escape or resistance to lawful authority, shall make, procure, conceal, unlawfully possess, or give to another inmate, any instrument or thing which may be used for such purposes.

(C) Whoever violates this section is guilty of aiding escape or resistance to lawful authority, a felony of the fourth degree. Sentence of confinement imposed for a violation of division (B) of this section shall be served consecutively to any other sentence of confinement imposed on such offender.

(1972 H 511, eff. 1–1–74)

CONVEYANCE OF PROHIBITED ITEMS

2921.36 Prohibition of conveyance of certain items onto grounds of detention facility or mental health or mental retardation and developmental disabilities facility

(A) No person shall knowingly convey, or attempt to convey, onto the grounds of a detention facility or of an institution that is under the control of the department of mental health or the department of mental retardation and developmental disabilities, any of the following items:

(1) Any deadly weapon or dangerous ordnance, as defined in section 2923.11 of the Revised Code, or any part of or ammunition for use in such a deadly weapon or dangerous ordnance;

(2) Any drug of abuse, as defined in section 3719.011 of the Revised Code;

(3) Any intoxicating liquor, as defined in section 4301.01 of the Revised Code.

(B) Division (A) of this section does not apply to any person who conveys or attempts to convey an item onto the grounds of a detention facility or of an institution under the control of the department of mental health or the department of mental retardation and developmental disabilities pursuant to the written authorization of the person in charge of the detention facility or the institution and in accordance with the written rules of the detention facility or the institution.

(C) No person shall knowingly deliver, or attempt to deliver, to any person who is confined in a detention facility or to any patient in an institution under the control of the department of mental health or the department of mental retardation and developmental disabilities, any item listed in division (A)(1), (2), or (3) of this section.

(D) No person shall knowingly deliver, or attempt to deliver, cash to any person who is confined in a detention facility.

(E) It is an affirmative defense to a charge under division (C) of this section that the actor was not otherwise prohibited by law from delivering the item to the confined person or the patient and that either of the following applies:

(1) The actor was permitted by the written rules of the detention facility or the institution to deliver the item to the confined person or the patient.

(2) The actor was given written authorization by the person in charge of the detention facility or the institution to deliver the item to the confined person or the patient.

(F)(1) Whoever violates division (A)(1) of this section or commits a violation of division (C) of this section involving an item listed in division (A)(1) of this section is guilty of illegal conveyance of weapons onto the grounds of a detention facility or a mental health or mental retardation and developmental disabilities institution, a felony of the third degree.

(2) Whoever violates division (A)(2) of this section or commits a violation of division (C) of this section involving any drug of abuse is guilty of illegal conveyance of drugs of abuse onto the grounds of a detention facility or a mental health or mental retardation and developmental disabilities institution, a felony of the third degree if the offender is an officer or employee of the facility or institution or a felony of the fourth degree if the offender is not such an officer or employee.

(3) Whoever violates division (A)(3) of this section or commits a violation of division (C) of this section involving any intoxicating liquor is guilty of illegal conveyance of intoxicating liquor onto the grounds of a detention facility or a mental health or mental retardation and developmental disabilities institution, a misdemeanor of the second degree.

(4) Whoever violates division (D) of this section is guilty of illegal conveyance of cash onto the grounds of a detention facility, a misdemeanor of the first degree. If the offender previously has been convicted of or pleaded guilty to a violation of division (D) of this section, illegal conveyance of cash onto the grounds of a detention facility is a felony of the fourth degree.

(1994 H 571, eff. 10–6–94; 1990 S 258, eff. 11–20–90; 1980 H 900; 1978 H 630)

2921.37 Person in charge of detention facility to have powers of peace officer as to prohibited items

The person in charge of a detention facility shall, on the grounds of the detention facility, have the same power as a peace officer, as defined in section 2935.01 of the Revised Code, to arrest a person who violates section 2921.36 of the Revised Code.

(1978 H 630, eff. 5–23–78)

PECULATION AND DERELICTION

2921.41 Theft in office; restitution order against public or party official; withholding from payments by retirement system; procedures

(A) No public official or party official shall commit any theft offense, as defined in division (K) of section 2913.01 of the Revised Code, when either of the following applies:

(1) The offender uses his office in aid of committing the offense or permits or assents to its use in aid of committing the offense;

(2) The property or service involved is owned by this state, any other state, the United States, a county, a municipal corporation, a township, or any political subdivision, department, or agency of any of them, is owned by a political party, or is part of a political campaign fund.

(B) Whoever violates this section is guilty of theft in office, a felony of the third degree.

(C)(1) A public official or party official who is convicted of or pleads guilty to, theft in office is forever disqualified from holding any public office, employment, or position of trust in this state.

(2)(a) A court that imposes sentence for a violation of this section based on conduct described in division (A)(2) of this section shall require the public official or party official who is convicted of or pleads guilty to the offense to make restitution for all of the property or the service that is the subject of the offense, in addition to the term of imprisonment and any fine imposed. A court that imposes sentence for a violation of this section based on conduct described in division (A)(1) of this section and that determines at trial that this state or a political subdivision of this state if the offender is a public official, or a political party in the United States or this state if the offender is a party official, suffered actual loss as a result of the offense shall require the offender to make restitution to the state, political subdivision, or political party for all of the actual loss experienced, in addition to the term of imprisonment and any fine imposed.

(b)(i) In any case in which a sentencing court is required to order restitution under division (C)(2)(a) of this section and in which the offender, at the time of the commission of the offense or at any other time, was a member of the public employees retirement system, the police and firemen's disability and pension fund, the state teachers retirement system, the school employees retirement system, or the state highway patrol retirement system, was a participating employee or continuing member, as defined in section 145.71 of the Revised Code, in a deferred compensation program offered by the Ohio public employees deferred compensation board, was an officer or employee of a municipal corporation who was a participant in a deferred compensation program offered by that municipal corporation, was an officer or employee of a government unit, as defined in section 145.74 of the Revised Code, who was a participant in a deferred compensation program offered by that government unit, or was a participating employee, continuing member, or participant in any deferred compensation program described in this division and a member of a retirement system specified in this division or a retirement system of a municipal corporation, the entity to which restitution is to be made may file a motion with the sentencing court specifying any retirement system and any deferred compensation program of which the offender was a member, participating employee, continuing member, or participant and requesting the court to issue an order requiring the specified retirement system, specified deferred compensation program, or, if both are specified in the motion, the specified retirement system and deferred compensation program to withhold the amount required as restitution from any payment that is to be made under a pension, annuity, or allowance, under a participant account, as defined in section 145.71 of the Revised Code, or under any other type of benefit, other than a survivorship benefit, that has been or is in the future granted to the offender, from any payment of accumulated employee contributions standing to the offender's credit with that retirement system, that deferred compensation program, or, if both are specified in the motion, that retirement system and deferred compensation program, and from any payment of any other amounts to be paid to the offender upon his withdrawal of his contributions pursuant to Chapter 145., 742., 3307., 3309., or 5505. of the Revised Code. A motion described in this division may be filed at any time subsequent to the conviction of the offender or his entry of a guilty plea. Upon the filing of the motion, the clerk of the court in which the motion is filed shall notify the offender, the specified retirement system, the specified deferred compensation program, or, if both are specified in the motion, the specified retirement system and deferred compensation program, in writing, of all of the following: that the motion was filed; that the offender will be granted a hearing on the issuance of the requested order if the offender files a written request for a hearing with the clerk prior to the expiration of thirty days after the offender receives the notice; that, if a hearing is requested, the court will schedule a hearing as soon as possible and notify the offender, any specified retirement system, and any specified deferred compensation program of the date, time, and place of the hearing; that, if a hearing is conducted, it will be limited only to a consideration of whether the offender can show good cause why the requested order should not be issued; that, if a hearing is conducted, the court will not issue the requested order if the court determines, based on evidence presented at the hearing by the offender, that there is good cause for the requested order not to be issued; that the court will issue the requested order if a hearing is not requested or if a hearing is conducted but the court does not determine, based on evidence presented at the hearing by the offender, that there is good cause for the requested order not to be issued; and that, if the requested order is issued, any retirement system and any deferred compensation program specified in the motion will be required to withhold the amount required as restitution from payments to the offender.

(ii) In any case in which a sentencing court is required to order restitution under division (C)(2)(a) of this section and in which a motion requesting the issuance of a withholding order as described in division (C)(2)(b)(i) of this section is filed, the offender may receive a hearing on the motion by delivering a written request for a hearing to the court prior to the expiration of thirty days after the offender's receipt of the notice provided pursuant to division (C)(2)(b)(i) of this section. If a request for a hearing is made by the offender within the prescribed time, the court shall schedule a hearing as soon as possible after the request is made and shall notify the offender, the specified retirement system, the specified deferred compensation program, or, if both are specified in the motion, the specified retirement system and deferred compensation program of the date, time, and place of the hearing. A hearing scheduled under this division shall be limited to a consideration of whether there is good cause, based on evidence presented by the offender, for the requested order not to be issued. If the court determines, based on evidence presented by the offender, that there is good cause for the order not to be issued, the court shall deny the motion and shall not issue the requested order. If the offender does not request a hearing within the prescribed time or if the court conducts a hearing but does not determine, based on evidence presented by the offender, that there is good cause for the order not to be issued, the court shall order the specified retirement system, the specified deferred compensation program, or, if both are specified in the motion, the specified retirement system and deferred compensation program to withhold the amount required as restitution under division (C)(2)(a) of this section from any payments to be made under a pension, annuity, or allowance, under a participant account, as defined in section 145.71 of the Revised Code, or under any other type of benefit, other than a survivorship benefit, that has been or is in the future granted to the offender, from any payment of accumulated employee contributions standing to the offender's credit with that retirement system, that deferred compensation program, or, if both are specified in the motion, that retirement system and deferred compensation program and from any payment of any other amounts to be paid to the offender upon his withdrawal of his contributions pursuant to Chapter 145., 742., 3307., 3309., or 5505. of the Revised Code, and to continue the withholding for that purpose, in accordance with the order, out of each payment to be made on or after the date of issuance of the order, until further order of the court. Upon receipt of an order issued under this division, the public employees retirement system, the police and firemen's disability and pension fund, the state teachers retirement system, the school employees retirement system, the state highway patrol retirement system, a municipal corporation retirement system, and the deferred compensation program offered by the Ohio public employees deferred compensation board, a municipal corporation, or a government unit, as defined in section 145.74 of the Revised Code, whichever are applicable, shall withhold the amount required as restitution, in accordance with the order, from any such payments and immediately shall forward the amount withheld to the clerk of the court in which the order was issued for payment to the entity to which restitution is to be made.

(iii) Service of a notice required by division (C)(2)(b)(i) or (ii) of this section shall be effected in the same manner as provided in the Rules of Civil Procedure for the service of process.

(D) Upon the filing of charges against a person under this section, the prosecutor, as defined in section 2935.01 of the Revised Code, who is assigned the case shall send written notice that charges have been filed against that person to the public employees retirement system, the police and firemen's disability and pension fund, the state teachers retirement system, the school employees retirement system, the state highway patrol retirement system, any municipal corporation retirement system in this state, and the deferred compensation program offered by the Ohio public employees deferred compensation board, a municipal corporation, or a government unit, as defined in section 145.74 of the Revised Code. The written notice shall specifically identify the person charged.

(1992 S 300, eff. 11–5–92; 1984 H 265; 1972 H 511)

2921.42 Having an unlawful interest in a public contract

(A) No public official shall knowingly do any of the following:

(1) Authorize, or employ the authority or influence of his office to secure authorization of any public contract in which he, a member of his family, or any of his business associates has an interest;

(2) Authorize, or employ the authority or influence of his office to secure the investment of public funds in any share, bond, mortgage, or other security, with respect to which he, a member of his family, or any of his business associates either has an interest, is an underwriter, or receives any brokerage, origination, or servicing fees;

(3) During his term of office or within one year thereafter, occupy any position of profit in the prosecution of a public contract authorized by him or by a legislative body, commission, or board of which he was a member at the time of authorization, unless the contract was let by competitive bidding to the lowest and best bidder;

(4) Have an interest in the profits or benefits of a public contract entered into by or for the use of the political subdivision or governmental agency or instrumentality with which he is connected;

(5) Have an interest in the profits or benefits of a public contract that is not let by competitive bidding if required by law and that involves more than one hundred fifty dollars.

(B) In the absence of bribery or a purpose to defraud, a public official, member of his family, or any of his business associates shall not be considered as having an interest in a public contract or the investment of public funds, if all of the following apply:

(1) The interest of that person is limited to owning or controlling shares of the corporation, or being a creditor of the corporation or other organization, that is the contractor on the public contract involved, or that is the issuer of the security in which public funds are invested;

(2) The shares owned or controlled by that person do not exceed five per cent of the outstanding shares of the corporation, and the amount due that person as creditor does not exceed five per cent of the total indebtedness of the corporation or other organization;

(3) That person, prior to the time the public contract is entered into, files with the political subdivision or governmental agency or instrumentality involved, an affidavit giving his exact status in connection with the corporation or other organization.

(C) This section does not apply to a public contract in which a public official, member of his family, or one of his business associates has an interest, when all of the following apply:

(1) The subject of the public contract is necessary supplies or services for the political subdivision or governmental agency or instrumentality involved;

(2) The supplies or services are unobtainable elsewhere for the same or lower cost, or are being furnished to the political subdivision or governmental agency or instrumentality as part of a continuing course of dealing established prior to the public official's becoming associated with the political subdivision or governmental agency or instrumentality involved;

(3) The treatment accorded the political subdivision or governmental agency or instrumentality is either preferential to or the same as that accorded other customers or clients in similar transactions;

(4) The entire transaction is conducted at arm's length, with full knowledge by the political subdivision or governmental agency or instrumentality involved, of the interest of the public official, member of his family, or business associate, and the public official takes no part in the deliberations or decision of the political subdivision or governmental agency or instrumentality with respect to the public contract.

(D) Division (A)(4) of this section does not prohibit participation by a public employee in any housing program funded by public moneys if the public employee otherwise qualifies for the program and does not use the authority or influence of his office or employment to secure benefits from the program and if the moneys are to be used on the primary residence of the public employee. Such participation does not constitute an unlawful interest in a public contract in violation of this section.

(E) Whoever violates this section is guilty of having an unlawful interest in a public contract. Violation of division (A)(1) or (2) of this section is a felony of the fourth degree. Violation of division (A)(3), (4), or (5) of this section is a misdemeanor of the first degree.

(F) It is not a violation of this section for a prosecuting attorney to appoint assistants and employees in accordance with sections 309.06 and 2921.421 of the Revised Code, for a chief legal officer of a municipal corporation or an official designated as prosecutor in a municipal corporation to appoint assistants and employees in accordance with sections 733.621 and 2921.421 of the Revised Code, or for a township law director appointed under section 504.15 of the Revised Code to appoint assistants and employees in accordance with sections 504.151 and 2921.421 of the Revised Code.

(F) [1] This section does not apply to a public contract in which a township trustee in a township with a population of five thousand or less in its unincorporated area, a member of the township trustee's family, or one of his business associates has an interest, if all of the following apply:

(1) The subject of the public contract is necessary supplies or services for the township and the amount of the contract is less than five thousand dollars per year;

(2) The supplies or services are being furnished to the township as part of a continuing course of dealing established before the township trustee held that office with the township;

(3) The treatment accorded the township is either preferential to or the same as that accorded other customers or clients in similar transactions;

(4) The entire transaction is conducted with full knowledge by the township of the interest of the township trustee, member of his family, or his business associate.

(G) As used in this section:

(1) "Public contract" means any of the following:

(a) The purchase or acquisition, or a contract for the purchase or acquisition, of property or services by or for the use of the state, any of its political subdivisions, or any agency or instrumentality of either, including the employment of an individual by the state, any of its political subdivisions, or any agency or instrumentality of either;

(b) A contract for the design, construction, alteration, repair, or maintenance of any public property.

(2) "Chief legal officer" has the same meaning as in section 733.621 of the Revised Code.

(1994 H 150, eff. 6–23–94; 1994 H 285, eff. 3–2–94; 1993 H 152, eff. 7–1–93; 1992 S 359; 1972 H 511)

[1] Paragraph designation appears as a result of the harmonization of 1994 H 285 and 1994 H 150.

Historical and Statutory Notes

Ed. Note: A special endorsement by the Legislative Service Commission states, "Comparison of these amendments [1994 H 150, eff. 6–23–94 and 1994 H 285, eff. 3–2–94] in pursuance of section 1.52 of the Revised Code discloses that they are not irreconcilable, so that they are required by that section to be harmonized to give effect to each amendment." In recognition of this rule of construction, changes made by 1994 H 150, eff. 6–23–94, and 1994 H 285, eff. 3–2–94, have been incorporated in the above amendment. See *Baldwin's Ohio Legislative Service*, 1994 Laws of Ohio, pages 5–85 and 5–37, for original versions of these Acts.

2921.421   Assistants and employees of prosecutors, law directors, and solicitors

(A) As used in this section:

(1) "Chief legal officer" has the same meaning as in section 733.621 of the Revised Code.

(2) "Political subdivision" means a county, a municipal corporation, or a township that adopts the limited self-government form of government under Chapter 504. of the Revised Code.

(B) A prosecuting attorney may appoint assistants and employees, except a member of the family of the prosecuting attorney, in accordance with division (B) of section 309.06 of the Revised Code, a chief legal officer of a municipal corporation or an official designated as prosecutor in a municipal corporation may appoint assistants and employees, except a member of the family of the chief legal officer or official designated as prosecutor, in accordance with section 733.621 of the Revised Code, and a township law director appointed under section 504.15 of the Revised Code may appoint assistants and employees, except a member of the family of the township law director, in accordance with section 504.151 of the Revised Code, if all of the following apply:

(1) The services to be furnished by the appointee or employee are necessary services for the political subdivision or are authorized by the legislative authority, governing board, or other contracting authority of the political subdivision.

(2) The treatment accorded the political subdivision is either preferential to or the same as that accorded other clients or customers of the appointee or employee in similar transactions, or the legislative authority, governing board, or other contracting authority of the political subdivision, in its sole discretion, determines that the compensation and other terms of appointment or employment of the appointee or employee are fair and reasonable to the political subdivision.

(3) The appointment or employment is made after prior written disclosure to the legislative authority, governing board, or other contracting authority of the political subdivision of the business relationship between the prosecuting attorney, the chief legal officer or official designated as prosecutor in a municipal corporation, or the township law director and his appointee or employee. In the case of a municipal corporation, the disclosure may be made or evidenced in an ordinance, resolution, or other document that does either or both of the following:

(a) Authorizes the furnishing of services as required under division (B)(1) of this section;

(b) Determines that the compensation and other terms of appointment or employment of the appointee or employee are fair and reasonable to the political subdivision as required under division (B)(2) of this section.

(4) The prosecuting attorney, the elected chief legal officer, or the township law director does not receive any distributive share or other portion, in whole or in part, of the earnings of his business associate, partner, or employee paid by the political subdivision to the business associate, partner, or employee for services rendered for the political subdivision.

(C) It is not a violation of this section or of section 102.03 or 2921.42 of the Revised Code for the legislative authority, the governing board, or other contracting authority of a political subdivision to engage the services of any firm that practices the profession of law upon the terms approved by the legislative authority, the governing board, or the contracting authority, or to designate any partner, officer, or employee of that firm as a nonelected public official or

employee of the political subdivision, whether the public office or position of employment is created by statute, charter, ordinance, resolution, or other legislative or administrative action.
(1994 H 285, eff. 3–2–94)

2921.43   Soliciting or receiving improper compensation

(A) No public servant shall knowingly solicit or accept and no person shall knowingly promise or give to a public servant either of the following:

(1) Any compensation, other than as allowed by divisions (G), (H), and (I) of section 102.03 of the Revised Code or other provisions of law, to perform his official duties, to perform any other act or service in the public servant's public capacity, for the general performance of the duties of the public servant's public office or public employment, or as a supplement to the public servant's public compensation;

(2) Additional or greater fees or costs than are allowed by law to perform his official duties.

(B) No public servant for his own personal or business use and no person for his own personal or business use or for the personal or business use of a public servant or party official, shall solicit or accept anything of value in consideration of either of the following:

(1) Appointing or securing, maintaining, or renewing the appointment of any person to any public office, employment, or agency;

(2) Preferring, or maintaining the status of, any public employee with respect to his compensation, duties, placement, location, promotion, or other material aspects of his employment.

(C) No person for the benefit of a political party, campaign committee, legislative campaign fund, or political action committee shall coerce any contribution in consideration of either of the following:

(1) Appointing or securing, maintaining, or renewing the appointment of any person to any public office, employment, or agency;

(2) Preferring, or maintaining the status of, any public employee with respect to his compensation, duties, placement, location, promotion, or other material aspects of his employment.

(D) Whoever violates this section is guilty of soliciting improper compensation, a misdemeanor of the first degree.

(E) A public servant who is convicted of a violation of this section is disqualified from holding any public office, employment, or position of trust in this state for a period of seven years from the date of conviction.

(F) Divisions (A), (B), and (C) of this section do not prohibit a person from making voluntary contributions to a political party, campaign committee, legislative campaign fund, or political action committee or prohibit a political party, campaign committee, legislative campaign fund, or political action committee from accepting voluntary contributions.
(1995 S 8, eff. 8–23–95; 1986 H 300, eff. 9–17–86; 1974 S 46; 1972 H 511)

2921.431   Soliciting political contributions from public employees—Repealed
(1995 S 8, eff. 8–23–95; 1976 H 784, eff. 12–6–76)

2921.44   Dereliction of duty

(A) No law enforcement officer shall negligently do any of the following:

(1) Fail to serve a lawful warrant without delay;

(2) Fail to prevent or halt the commission of an offense or to apprehend an offender, when it is in his power to do so alone or with available assistance.

(B) No law enforcement, ministerial, or judicial officer shall negligently fail to perform a lawful duty in a criminal case or proceeding.

(C) No officer, having charge of a detention facility, shall negligently do any of the following:

(1) Allow the detention facility to become littered or unsanitary;

(2) Fail to provide persons confined in the detention facility with adequate food, clothing, bedding, shelter, and medical attention;

(3) Fail to control an unruly prisoner, or to prevent intimidation of or physical harm to a prisoner by another;

(4) Allow a prisoner to escape;

(5) Fail to observe any lawful and reasonable regulation for the management of the detention facility.

(D) No public official of the state shall recklessly create a deficiency, incur a liability, or expend a greater sum than is appropriated by the general assembly for the use in any one year of the department, agency, or institution of the state with which the public official is connected.

(E) No public servant shall recklessly fail to perform a duty expressly imposed by law with respect to his office, or recklessly do any act expressly forbidden by law with respect to his office.

(F) Whoever violates this section is guilty of dereliction of duty, a misdemeanor of the second degree.

(1972 H 511, eff. 1–1–74)

2921.45   Interfering with civil rights

(A) No public servant, under color of his office, employment, or authority, shall knowingly deprive, or conspire or attempt to deprive any person of a constitutional or statutory right.

(B) Whoever violates this section is guilty of interfering with civil rights, a misdemeanor of the first degree.

(1972 H 511, eff. 1–1–74)

IMPERSONATION OF OFFICERS

2921.51   Impersonation of certain officers

(A) As used in this section:

(1) "Peace officer" means a sheriff, deputy sheriff, marshal, deputy marshal, member of the organized police department of a municipal corporation, or township constable, who is employed by a political subdivision of this state, a member of a police force employed by a metropolitan housing authority under division (D) of section 3735.31 of the Revised Code, a state university law enforcement officer appointed under section 3345.04 of the Revised Code, an Ohio veterans' home policeman appointed under section 5907.02 of the Revised Code, or a state highway patrol trooper and whose primary duties are to preserve the peace, to protect life and property, and to enforce the laws, ordinances, or rules of the state or any of its political subdivisions.

(2) "Private policeman" means any security guard, special policeman, private detective, or other person who is privately employed in a police capacity.

(3) "Impersonate" means to act the part of, assume the identity of, wear the uniform or any part of the uniform of, or display the identification of a particular person or of a member of a class of persons with purpose to make another person believe that the actor is that particular person or is a member of that class of persons.

(B) No person shall impersonate a peace officer or a private policeman.

(C) No person, by impersonating a peace officer or a private policeman, shall arrest or detain any person, search any person, or search the property of any person.

(D) No person, with purpose to commit or facilitate the commission of an offense, shall impersonate a peace officer, a private policeman, or an officer, agent, or employee of the state.

(E) No person shall commit a felony while impersonating a peace officer, a private policeman, or an officer, agent, or employee of the state.

(F) It is an affirmative defense to a charge under division (B) of this section that the impersonation of the peace officer was for a lawful purpose.

(G) Whoever violates division (B) of this section is guilty of a misdemeanor of the fourth degree. Whoever violates division (C) or (D) of this section is guilty of a misdemeanor of the first degree. If the purpose of a violation of division (D) of this section is to commit or facilitate the commission of a felony, a violation of division (D) is a felony of the third degree. Whoever violates division (E) of this section is guilty of a felony of the second degree.

(1991 S 144, eff. 8–8–91; 1988 H 708, § 1)

CHAPTER 2923

CONSPIRACY, ATTEMPT, AND COMPLICITY; WEAPONS CONTROL

CONSPIRACY, ATTEMPT, AND COMPLICITY

WEAPONS CONTROL

CORRUPT ACTIVITY

CONSPIRACY, ATTEMPT, AND COMPLICITY

2923.01   Conspiracy

(A) No person, with purpose to commit or to promote or facilitate the commission of aggravated murder, murder, kidnapping, compelling prostitution, promoting prostitution, aggravated arson, arson, aggravated robbery, robbery, aggravated burglary, burglary, engaging in a pattern of corrupt activity, corrupting another with drugs, aggravated trafficking, trafficking in drugs, theft of drugs, or illegal processing of drug documents, the commission of a felony offense of unauthorized use of a vehicle or trafficking in marihuana, or the commission of a violation of any provision of Chapter 3734. of the Revised Code, other than section 3734.18 of the Revised Code, that relates to hazardous wastes, shall do either of the following:

(1) With another person or persons, plan or aid in planning the commission of any such offense;

(2) Agree with another person or persons that one or more of them will engage in conduct that facilitates the commission of any such offense.

(B) No person shall be convicted of conspiracy unless a substantial overt act in furtherance of the conspiracy is alleged and proved to have been done by him or a person with whom he conspired, subsequent to the accused's entrance into the conspiracy. For purposes of this section, an overt act is substantial when it is of such character as to manifest a purpose on the part of the actor that the object of the conspiracy should be completed.

(C) When the offender knows or has reasonable cause to believe that a person with whom he conspires has also conspired or is conspiring with another to commit the same offense, then the offender is guilty of conspiring with that other person, even though his identity may be unknown to the offender.

(D) It is no defense to a charge under this section that, in retrospect, commission of the offense that was the object of the conspiracy was impossible under the circumstances.

(E) A conspiracy terminates when the offense or offenses that are its objects are committed, or when it is abandoned by all conspirators. In the absence of abandonment, it is no defense to a charge under this section that no offense that was the object of the conspiracy was committed.

(F) A person who conspires to commit more than one offense is guilty of only one conspiracy, when such offenses are the object of the same agreement or continuous conspiratorial relationship.

(G) When a person is convicted of committing or attempting to commit a specific offense or of complicity in the commission of or attempt to commit the specific offense, he shall not be convicted of conspiracy involving the same offense.

(H)(1) No person shall be convicted of conspiracy upon the testimony of a person with whom he conspired, unsupported by other evidence.

(2) If a person with whom the defendant allegedly has conspired testifies against the defendant in a case in which the defendant is charged with conspiracy and if the testimony is supported by other evidence, the court, when it charges the jury, shall state substantially the following:

"The testimony of an accomplice that is supported by other evidence does not become inadmissible because of his complicity, moral turpitude, or self-interest, but the admitted or claimed complicity of a witness may affect his credibility and make his testimony subject to grave suspicion, and require that it be weighed with great caution.

It is for you, as jurors, in the light of all the facts presented to you from the witness stand, to evaluate such testimony and to determine its quality and worth or its lack of quality and worth."

(3) "Conspiracy," as used in division (H)(1) of this section, does not include any conspiracy that results in an attempt to commit an offense or in the commission of an offense.

(I) The following are affirmative defenses to a charge of conspiracy:

(1) After conspiring to commit an offense, the actor thwarted the success of the conspiracy under circumstances manifesting a complete and voluntary renunciation of his criminal purpose.

(2) After conspiring to commit an offense, the actor abandoned the conspiracy prior to the commission of or attempt to commit any offense that was the object of the conspiracy, either by advising all other conspirators of his abandonment, or by informing any law enforcement authority of the existence of the conspiracy and of his participation in the conspiracy.

(J) Whoever violates this section is guilty of conspiracy, which is:

(1) A felony of the first degree, when one of the objects of the conspiracy is aggravated murder or murder;

(2) An aggravated felony of the next lesser aggravated degree than the most serious offense that is the object of the conspiracy, when the most serious offense that is the object of the conspiracy is an aggravated felony of the first or second degree;

(3) A felony of the fourth degree, when the most serious offense that is the object of the conspiracy is an aggravated felony of the third degree;

(4) A felony of the next lesser degree than the most serious offense that is the object of the conspiracy, when the most serious offense that is the object of the conspiracy is a felony of the first, second, or third degree;

(5) A felony punishable by a fine of not more than twenty-five thousand dollars or imprisonment for not more than eighteen months, or both, when the offense that is the object of the conspiracy is a violation of any provision of Chapter 3734. of the Revised Code, other than section 3734.18 of the Revised Code, that relates to hazardous wastes;

(6) A misdemeanor of the first degree, when the most serious offense that is the object of the conspiracy is a felony of the fourth degree.

(K) This section does not define a separate conspiracy offense or penalty where conspiracy is defined as an offense by one or more sections of the Revised Code, other than this section. In such case, however:

(1) With respect to the offense specified as the object of the conspiracy in the other section or sections, division (A) of this section defines the voluntary act or acts and culpable mental state necessary to constitute the conspiracy;

(2) Divisions (B) to (I) of this section are incorporated by reference in the conspiracy offense defined by the other section or sections of the Revised Code.

(L) In addition to the penalties that are otherwise imposed for conspiracy, a person who is found guilty of conspiracy to engage in a pattern of corrupt activity is subject to divisions (B)(2), (3), (4), and (5) of section 2923.32 of the Revised Code.

(1986 H 428, eff. 12–23–86; 1986 H 338; 1985 H 5; 1984 H 651; 1983 S 210; 1982 H 269, § 4, S 199, H 108; 1975 H 300; 1972 H 511)

2923.011   Carrying firearms or explosives on an aircraft—Repealed

(1972 H 511, eff. 1–1–74; 132 v H 1; 131 v H 788)

2923.012   Carrying other concealed weapons—Repealed

(1972 H 511, eff. 1–1–74; 1969 H 288)

2923.02   Attempt

(A) No person, purposely or knowingly, and when purpose or knowledge is sufficient culpability for the commission of an offense, shall engage in conduct which, if successful, would constitute or result in the offense.

(B) It is no defense to a charge under this section that, in retrospect, commission of the offense which was the object of the attempt was either factually or legally impossible under the attendant circumstances, if that offense could have been committed had the attendant circumstances been as the actor believed them to be.

(C) No person who is convicted of committing a specific offense, of complicity in the commission of an offense, or of conspiracy to commit an offense shall be convicted of an attempt to commit the same offense in violation of this section.

(D) It is an affirmative defense to a charge under this section that the actor abandoned his effort to commit the offense or otherwise prevented its commission, under circumstances manifesting a complete and voluntary renunciation of his criminal purpose.

(E) Whoever violates this section is guilty of an attempt to commit an offense. An attempt to commit aggravated murder or murder is an aggravated felony of the first degree. An attempt to commit an aggravated felony of the first or second degree is an aggravated felony of the next lesser aggravated degree than the aggravated felony attempted. An attempt to commit an aggravated felony of the third degree is a felony of the fourth degree. An attempt to commit any other offense is an offense of the next lesser degree than the offense attempted. In the case of an attempt to commit an offense other than a violation of Chapter 3734. of the Revised Code that is not specifically classified, an attempt is a misdemeanor of the first degree if the offense attempted is a felony, and a misdemeanor of the fourth degree if the offense attempted is a misdemeanor. In the case of an attempt to commit a violation of any provision of Chapter 3734. of the Revised Code, other than section 3734.18 of the Revised Code, that relates to hazardous wastes, an attempt is a felony punishable by a fine of not more than twenty-five thousand dollars or imprisonment for not more than eighteen months, or both. An attempt to commit a minor misdemeanor, or to engage in conspiracy, is not an offense under this section.

(1991 H 225, eff. 10–23–91; 1984 H 651; 1983 S 210; 1972 H 511)

2923.021   Switch blade knives—Repealed

(1972 H 511, eff. 1–1–74; 125 v 125)

2923.03   Complicity

(A) No person, acting with the kind of culpability required for the commission of an offense, shall do any of the following:

(1) Solicit or procure another to commit the offense;

(2) Aid or abet another in committing the offense;

(3) Conspire with another to commit the offense in violation of section 2923.01 of the Revised Code;

(4) Cause an innocent or irresponsible person to commit the offense.

(B) It is no defense to a charge under this section that no person with whom the accused was in complicity has been convicted as a principal offender.

(C) No person shall be convicted of complicity under this section unless an offense is actually committed, but a person may be convicted of complicity in an attempt to commit an offense in violation of section 2923.02 of the Revised Code.

(D) If an alleged accomplice of the defendant testifies against the defendant in a case in which the defendant is charged with complicity in the commission of or an attempt to commit an offense, an attempt to commit an offense, or an offense, the court, when it charges the jury, shall state substantially the following:

"The testimony of an accomplice does not become inadmissible because of his complicity, moral turpitude, or self-interest, but the admitted or claimed complicity of a witness may affect his credibility and make his testimony subject to grave suspicion, and require that it be weighed with great caution.

It is for you, as jurors, in the light of all the facts presented to you from the witness stand, to evaluate such testimony and to determine its quality and worth or its lack of quality and worth."

(E) It is an affirmative defense to a charge under this section that, prior to the commission of or attempt to commit the offense, the actor terminated his complicity, under circumstances manifesting a complete and voluntary renunciation of his criminal purpose.

(F) Whoever violates this section is guilty of complicity in the commission of an offense, and shall be prosecuted and punished as if he were a principal offender. A charge of complicity may be stated in terms of this section, or in terms of the principal offense.

(1986 H 338, eff. 9–17–86; 1972 H 511)

2923.04 Engaging in organized crime—Repealed

(1985 H 5, eff. 1–1–86; 1973 H 716; 1972 H 511)

2923.05 Transfer of machine gun or sawed-off firearm; record of transaction—Repealed

(1972 H 511, eff. 1–1–74; 132 v H 43; 1953 H 1; GC 12819–6)

2923.06 War trophies—Repealed

(1972 H 511, eff. 1–1–74; 1953 H 1; GC 12819–7)

2923.07 Grave robbing—Repealed

(1972 H 511, eff. 1–1–74; 1953 H 1; GC 13391)

2923.08 Mutilation or destruction of a dead human body—Repealed

(1972 H 511, eff. 1–1–74; 126 v 575; 1953 H 1; GC 13391–1)

2923.09 Anatomical demonstration upon a corpse—Repealed

(1972 H 511, eff. 1–1–74; 1953 H 1; GC 13392)

2923.10 Corpse, nuisance—Repealed

(1972 H 511, eff. 1–1–74; 129 v 582; 1953 H 1; GC 12684)

WEAPONS CONTROL

2923.11 Definitions

As used in sections 2923.11 to 2923.24 of the Revised Code:

(A) "Deadly weapon" means any instrument, device, or thing capable of inflicting death, and designed or specially adapted for use as a weapon, or possessed, carried, or used as a weapon.

(B)(1) "Firearm" means any deadly weapon capable of expelling or propelling one or more projectiles by the action of an explosive or combustible propellant. "Firearm" includes an unloaded firearm, and any firearm which is inoperable but which can readily be rendered operable.

(2) When determining whether a firearm is capable of expelling or propelling one or more projectiles by the action of an explosive or combustible propellant, the trier of fact may rely upon circumstantial evidence, including, but not limited to, the representations and actions of the individual exercising control over the firearm.

(C) "Handgun" means any firearm designed to be fired while being held in one hand.

(D) "Semi–automatic firearm" means any firearm designed or specially adapted to fire a single cartridge and automatically chamber a succeeding cartridge ready to fire, with a single function of the trigger.

(E) "Automatic firearm" means any firearm designed or specially adapted to fire a succession of cartridges with a single function of the trigger. "Automatic firearm" also means any semi-automatic firearm designed or specially adapted to fire more than thirty-one cartridges without reloading, other than a firearm chambering only .22 caliber short, long, or long-rifle cartridges.

(F) "Sawed–off firearm" means a shotgun with a barrel less than eighteen inches long, or a rifle with a barrel less than sixteen inches long, or a shotgun or rifle less than twenty-six inches long overall.

(G) "Zip–gun" means any of the following:

(1) Any firearm of crude and extemporized manufacture;

(2) Any device, including without limitation a starter's pistol, not designed as a firearm, but which is specially adapted for use as a firearm;

(3) Any industrial tool, signalling device, or safety device, not designed as a firearm, but which as designed is capable of use as such, when possessed, carried, or used as a firearm.

(H) "Explosive device" means any device designed or specially adapted to cause physical harm to persons or property by means of an explosion, and consisting of an explosive substance or agency and a means to detonate it. "Explosive device" includes without limitation any bomb, any explosive demolition device, any blasting cap or detonator containing an explosive charge, and any pressure vessel which has been knowingly tampered with or arranged so as to explode.

(I) "Incendiary device" means any firebomb, and any device designed or specially adapted to cause physical harm to persons or property by means of fire, and consisting of an incendiary substance or agency and a means to ignite it.

(J) "Ballistic knife" means a knife with a detachable blade that is propelled by a spring-operated mechanism.

(K) "Dangerous ordnance" means any of the following, except as provided in division (L) of this section:

(1) Any automatic or sawed-off firearm, zip-gun, or ballistic knife;

(2) Any explosive device or incendiary device;

(3) Nitroglycerin, nitrocellulose, nitrostarch, PETN, cyclonite, TNT, picric acid, and other high explosives; amatol, tritonal, tetrytol, pentolite, pecretol, cyclotol, and other high explosive compositions; plastic explosives; dynamite, blasting gelatin, gelatin dynamite, sensitized ammonium nitrate, liquid-oxygen blasting explosives, blasting powder, and other blasting agents; and any other explosive substance having sufficient brisance or power to be particularly suitable for use as a military explosive, or for use in mining, quarrying, excavating, or demolitions;

(4) Any firearm, rocket launcher, mortar, artillery piece, grenade, mine, bomb, torpedo, or similar weapon, designed and manufactured for military purposes, and the ammunition for that weapon;

(5) Any firearm muffler or silencer;

(6) Any combination of parts that is intended by the owner for use in converting any firearm or other device into a dangerous ordnance.

(L) "Dangerous ordnance" does not include any of the following:

(1) Any firearm, including a military weapon and the ammunition for that weapon, and regardless of its actual age, which employs a percussion cap or other obsolete ignition system, or which is designed and safe for use only with black powder;

(2) Any pistol, rifle, or shotgun, designed or suitable for sporting purposes, including a military weapon as issued or as modified, and the ammunition for that weapon, unless the firearm is an automatic or sawed-off firearm;

(3) Any cannon or other artillery piece which, regardless of its actual age, is of a type in accepted use prior to 1887, has no mechanical, hydraulic, pneumatic, or other system for absorbing recoil and returning the tube into battery without displacing the carriage, and is designed and safe for use only with black powder;

(4) Black powder, priming quills, and percussion caps possessed and lawfully used to fire a cannon of a type defined in division (L)(3) of this section during displays, celebrations, organized matches or shoots, and target practice, and smokeless and black powder, primers, and percussion caps possessed and lawfully used as a propellant or ignition device in small-arms or small-arms ammunition;

(5) Dangerous ordnance which is inoperable or inert and cannot readily be rendered operable or activated, and which is kept as a trophy, souvenir, curio, or museum piece.

(6) Any device which is expressly excepted from the definition of a destructive device pursuant to the "Gun Control Act of 1968," 82 Stat. 1213, 18 U.S.C. 921 (a) (4), as amended, and regulations issued under that act.

(1990 S 96, eff. 6–13–90; 1987 H 24; 1986 H 51; 1978 H 728; 1972 H 511)

2923.12   Carrying concealed weapons

(A) No person shall knowingly carry or have, concealed on his person or concealed ready at hand, any deadly weapon or dangerous ordnance.

(B) This section does not apply to officers, agents, or employees of this or any other state or the United States, or to law enforcement officers, authorized to carry concealed weapons or dangerous ordnance, and acting within the scope of their duties.

(C) It is an affirmative defense to a charge under this section of carrying or having control of a weapon other than dangerous ordnance, that the actor was not otherwise prohibited by law from having the weapon, and that any of the following apply:

(1) The weapon was carried or kept ready at hand by the actor for defensive purposes, while he was engaged in or was going to or from his lawful business or occupation, which business or occupation was of such character or was necessarily carried on in such manner or at such a time or place as to render the actor particularly susceptible to criminal attack, such as would justify a prudent man in going armed.

(2) The weapon was carried or kept ready at hand by the actor for defensive purposes, while he was engaged in a lawful activity, and had reasonable cause to fear a criminal attack upon himself or a member of his family, or upon his home, such as would justify a prudent man in going armed.

(3) The weapon was carried or kept ready at hand by the actor for any lawful purpose and while in his own home.

(4) The weapon was being transported in a motor vehicle for any lawful purpose, and was not on the actor's person, and, if the weapon was a firearm, was carried in compliance with the applicable requirements of division (C) of section 2923.16 of the Revised Code.

(D) Whoever violates this section is guilty of carrying concealed weapons, a misdemeanor of the first degree. If the offender previously has been convicted of a violation of this section or of any offense of violence, if the weapon involved is a firearm and the violation of this section is committed at premises for which a D permit has been issued under Chapter 4303. of the Revised Code, if the weapon involved is a firearm which is either loaded or for which the offender has ammunition ready at hand, or if the weapon involved is dangerous ordnance, then carrying concealed weapons is a felony of the third degree. If the offense is committed aboard an aircraft, or with purpose to carry a concealed weapon aboard an aircraft, regardless of the weapon involved, carrying concealed weapons is a felony of the second degree.

(1986 H 51, eff. 7–30–86; 1973 H 716; 1972 H 511)

2923.121   Possessing firearm in liquor permit premises; privileges; defenses

(A) No person shall possess a firearm in any room in which liquor is being dispensed in premises for which a D permit has been issued under Chapter 4303. of the Revised Code.

(B)(1) This section does not apply to officers, agents, or employees of this or any other state or the United States, or to law enforcement officers, authorized to carry firearms, and acting within the scope of their duties.

(2) This section does not apply to any room used for the accommodation of guests of a hotel, as defined in section 4301.01 of the Revised Code.

(3) This section does not prohibit any person who is a member of a veteran's organization, as defined in section 2915.01 of the Revised Code, from possessing a rifle in any room in any premises owned, leased, or otherwise under the control of the veteran's organization, if the rifle is not loaded with live ammunition and if the person otherwise is not prohibited by law from having the rifle.

(4) This section does not apply to any person possessing or displaying firearms in any room used to exhibit unloaded firearms for sale or trade in a soldiers' memorial established pursuant to Chapter 345. of the Revised Code, in a convention center, or in any other public meeting place, if the person is an exhibitor, trader, purchaser, or seller of firearms and is not otherwise prohibited by law from possessing, trading, purchasing, or selling the firearms.

(C) It is an affirmative defense to a charge under this section of illegal possession of a firearm in liquor permit premises, that the actor was not otherwise prohibited by law from having the firearm, and that any of the following apply:

(1) The firearm was carried or kept ready at hand by the actor for defensive purposes, while he was engaged in or was going to or from his lawful business or occupation, which business or occupation was of such character or was necessarily carried on in such manner or at such a time or place as to render the actor particularly susceptible to criminal attack, such as would justify a prudent man in going armed.

(2) The firearm was carried or kept ready at hand by the actor for defensive purposes, while he was engaged in a lawful activity, and had reasonable cause to fear a criminal attack upon himself or a member of his family, or upon his home, such as would justify a prudent man in going armed.

(D) Whoever violates this section is guilty of illegal possession of a firearm in liquor permit premises, a felony. If the offender previously has not been convicted of or pleaded guilty to illegal possession of a firearm in liquor permit premises, he shall be sentenced to a term of actual incarceration, as defined in section 2929.01 of the Revised Code, of one year. If the offender previously has been convicted of or pleaded guilty to illegal possession of a firearm in liquor permit premises, he shall be sentenced to a term of actual incarceration, as defined in section 2929.01 of the Revised Code, of two years.

(1986 H 39, eff. 2–21–87; 1986 H 51)

2923.122   Conveyance or possession of deadly weapons or dangerous ordnance on school premises

(A) No person shall knowingly convey, or attempt to convey, any deadly weapon or dangerous ordnance onto any property owned or controlled by, or to any activity held under the auspices of, a board of education of a city, local, exempted village, or joint vocational school district or of a governing body of a school for which the state board of education prescribes minimum standards under section 3301.07 of the Revised Code.

(B) No person shall knowingly possess a deadly weapon or dangerous ordnance on property owned or controlled by, or at any activity held under the auspices of, a board of education of a city, local, exempted village, or joint vocational school district or of a governing body of a school for which the state board of education prescribes minimum standards under section 3301.07 of the Revised Code.

(C) This section does not apply to officers, agents, or employees of this or any other state or the United States, or to law enforcement officers, authorized to carry deadly weapons or dangerous ordnance and acting within the scope of their duties, to any security officer employed by a board of education or governing body of a school during the time that the security officer is on duty pursuant to that contract of employment, or to any other person who has written authorization from the board of education or governing body of a school to convey deadly weapons or dangerous ordnance onto school property or to possess a deadly weapon or dangerous ordnance on school property and who conveys or possesses the deadly weapon or dangerous ordnance in accordance with that authorization.

(D) Whoever violates this section is guilty of illegal conveyance or possession of deadly weapons or dangerous ordnance on school premises. If the offender previously has not been convicted of a violation of this section, illegal conveyance or possession of deadly weapons or dangerous ordnance on school premises is a felony of the fourth degree. If the offender previously has been convicted of a violation of this section, illegal conveyance or possession of deadly weapons or dangerous ordnance on school premises is a felony of the third degree.
(1992 H 154, eff. 7–31–92)

2923.13 Having weapons while under disability

(A) Unless relieved from disability as provided in section 2923.14 of the Revised Code, no person shall knowingly acquire, have, carry, or use any firearm or dangerous ordnance, if any of the following apply:

(1) Such person is a fugitive from justice;

(2) Such person is under indictment for or has been convicted of any felony of violence, or has been adjudged a juvenile delinquent for commission of any such felony;

(3) Such person is under indictment for or has been convicted of any offense involving the illegal possession, use, sale, administration, distribution, or trafficking in any drug of abuse, or has been adjudged a juvenile delinquent for commission of any such offense;

(4) Such person is drug dependent or in danger of drug dependence, or is a chronic alcoholic;

(5) Such person is under adjudication of mental incompetence.

(B) Whoever violates this section is guilty of having weapons while under disability, a felony of the fourth degree.
(1972 H 511, eff. 1–1–74)

2923.14 Relief from disability

(A) Any person who, solely by reason of his disability under division (A)(2) or (3) of section 2923.13 of the Revised Code, is prohibited from acquiring, having, carrying, or using firearms, may apply to the court of common pleas in the county where he resides for relief from such prohibition.

(B) The application shall recite the following:

(1) All indictments, convictions, or adjudications upon which the applicant's disability is based, the sentence imposed and served, and probation, parole, or partial or conditional pardon granted, or other disposition of each case;

(2) Facts showing the applicant to be a fit subject for relief under this section.

(C) A copy of the application shall be served on the county prosecutor, who shall cause the matter to be investigated, and shall raise before the court such objections to granting relief as the investigation reveals.

(D) Upon hearing, the court may grant the applicant relief pursuant to this section, if all of the following apply:

(1) The applicant has been fully discharged from imprisonment, probation, and parole, or, if he is under indictment, has been released on bail or recognizance;

(2) The applicant has led a law-abiding life since his discharge or release, and appears likely to continue to do so;

(3) The applicant is not otherwise prohibited by law from acquiring, having, or using firearms.

(E) Costs of the proceeding shall be charged as in other civil cases, and taxed to the applicant.

(F) Relief from disability granted pursuant to this section:

(1) Applies only with respect to indictments, convictions, or adjudications recited in the application;

(2) Applies only with respect to firearms lawfully acquired, possessed, carried, or used by the applicant;

(3) Does not apply with respect to dangerous ordnance;

(4) May be revoked by the court at any time for good cause shown and upon notice to the applicant;

(5) Is automatically void upon commission by the applicant of any offense embraced by division (A)(2) or (3) of section 2923.13 of the Revised Code, or upon the applicant's becoming one of the class of persons named in division (A)(1), (4), or (5) of such section.

(1972 H 511, eff. 1–1–74)

2923.15 Using weapons while intoxicated

(A) No person, while under the influence of alcohol or any drug of abuse, shall carry or use any firearm or dangerous ordnance.

(B) Whoever violates this section is guilty of using weapons while intoxicated, a misdemeanor of the first degree.

(1972 H 511, eff. 1–1–74)

2923.16 Improperly handling firearms in a motor vehicle

(A) No person shall knowingly discharge a firearm while in or on a motor vehicle.

(B) No person shall knowingly transport or have a loaded firearm in a motor vehicle, in such manner that the firearm is accessible to the operator or any passenger without leaving the vehicle.

(C) No person shall knowingly transport or have a firearm in a motor vehicle, unless it is unloaded, and is carried in one of the following ways:

(1) In a closed package, box, or case;

(2) In a compartment which can be reached only by leaving the vehicle;

(3) In plain sight and secured in a rack or holder made for the purpose;

(4) In plain sight with the action open or the weapon stripped, or, if the firearm is of a type on which the action will not stay open or which cannot easily be stripped, in plain sight.

(D) This section does not apply to officers, agents, or employees of this or any other state or the United States, or to law enforcement officers, authorized to carry or have loaded or accessible firearms in motor vehicles, and acting within the scope of their duties.

(E) The affirmative defenses contained in division (C)(1) and (2) of section 2923.12 of the Revised Code are affirmative defenses to a charge under division (B) or (C) of this section.

(F) Whoever violates this section is guilty of improperly handling firearms in a motor vehicle. Violation of division (A) or (B) of this section is a misdemeanor of the first degree. Violation of division (C) of this section is a misdemeanor of the fourth degree.

(G) As used in this section, "unloaded" means, with respect to a firearm employing a percussion cap, flintlock, or other obsolete ignition system, when the weapon is uncapped, or when the priming charge is removed from the pan.

(1973 H 716, eff. 1–1–74; 1972 H 511)

2923.161 Improperly discharging firearm at or into habitation or school

(A) No person, without privilege to do so, shall knowingly discharge a firearm at or into an occupied structure that is a permanent or temporary habitation of any individual or a school.

(B) This section does not apply to any officer, agent, or employee of this or any other state or the United States, or to any law enforcement officer, who discharges the firearm while acting within the scope of his duties.

(C) Whoever violates this section is guilty of improperly discharging a firearm at or into a habitation or school. If the offender previously has not been convicted of or pleaded guilty to a violation of this section, improperly discharging a firearm at or into a habitation or school is a felony of the third degree. If the offender previously has been convicted of or pleaded guilty to a violation of this section, improperly discharging a firearm at or into a habitation or school is a felony of the second degree.

(D) As used in this section, "occupied structure" has the same meaning as in section 2909.01 of the Revised Code.

(1990 S 258, eff. 11–20–90)

2923.17   Unlawful possession of dangerous ordnance

(A) No person shall knowingly acquire, have, carry, or use any dangerous ordnance.

(B) This section does not apply to:

(1) Officers, agents, or employees of this or any other state or the United States, members of the armed forces of the United States or the organized militia of this or any other state, and law enforcement officers, to the extent that any such person is authorized to acquire, have, carry, or use dangerous ordnance and is acting within the scope of his duties;

(2) Importers, manufacturers, dealers, and users of explosives, having a license or user permit issued and in effect pursuant to the "Organized Crime Control Act of 1970," 84 Stat. 952, 18 U.S.C. 843, and any amendments or additions thereto or reenactments thereof, with respect to explosives and explosive devices lawfully acquired, possessed, carried, or used under the laws of this state and applicable federal law;

(3) Importers, manufacturers, and dealers having a license to deal in destructive devices or their ammunition, issued and in effect pursuant to the "Gun Control Act of 1968," 82 Stat. 1213, 18 U.S.C. 923, and any amendments or additions thereto or reenactments thereof, with respect to dangerous ordnance lawfully acquired, possessed, carried, or used under the laws of this state and applicable federal law;

(4) Persons to whom surplus ordnance has been sold, loaned, or given by the secretary of the army pursuant to 70A Stat. 262 and 263, 10 U.S.C. 4684, 4685, and 4686, and any amendments or additions thereto or reenactments thereof, with respect to dangerous ordnance when lawfully possessed and used for the purposes specified in such sections;

(5) Owners of dangerous ordnance registered in the national firearms registration and transfer record pursuant to the act of October 22, 1968, 82 Stat. 1229, 26 U.S.C. 5841, and any amendments or additions thereto or reenactments thereof, and regulations issued thereunder.

(6) Carriers, warehousemen, and others engaged in the business of transporting or storing goods for hire, with respect to dangerous ordnance lawfully transported or stored in the usual course of their business and in compliance with the laws of this state and applicable federal law;

(7) The holders of a license or temporary permit issued and in effect pursuant to section 2923.18 of the Revised Code, with respect to dangerous ordnance lawfully acquired, possessed, carried, or used for the purposes and in the manner specified in such license or permit.

(C) Whoever violates this section is guilty of unlawful possession of dangerous ordnance, a felony of the fourth degree.

(1978 H 728, eff. 8–22–78; 1972 H 511)

2923.18   License or permit to possess dangerous ordnance

(A) Upon application to the sheriff of the county or safety director or police chief of the municipality where the applicant resides or has his principal place of business, and upon payment of the fee specified in division (B) of this section, a license or temporary permit shall be issued to qualified applicants to acquire, possess, carry, or use dangerous ordnance, for the following purposes:

(1) Contractors, wreckers, quarrymen, mine operators, and other persons regularly employing explosives in the course of a legitimate business, with respect to explosives and explosive devices acquired, possessed, carried, or used in the course of such business;

(2) Farmers, with respect to explosives and explosive devices acquired, possessed, carried, or used for agricultural purposes on lands farmed by them;

(3) Scientists, engineers, and instructors, with respect to dangerous ordnance acquired, possessed, carried, or used in the course of bona fide research or instruction;

(4) Financial institution and armored car company guards, with respect to automatic firearms lawfully acquired, possessed, carried, or used by any such person while acting within the scope of his duties;

(5) In the discretion of the issuing authority, any responsible person, with respect to dangerous ordnance lawfully acquired, possessed, carried, or used for a legitimate research, scientific, educational, industrial, or other proper purpose.

(B) Application for a license or temporary permit under this section shall be in writing under oath to the sheriff of the county or safety director or police chief of the municipality where the applicant resides or has his principal place of business. The application shall be accompanied by an application fee of fifty dollars when the application is for a license, and an application fee of five dollars when the application is for a temporary permit. The fees shall be paid into the general revenue fund of the county or municipality. The application shall contain the following information:

(1) The name, age, address, occupation, and business address of the applicant, if he is a natural person, or the name, address, and principal place of business of the applicant, if the applicant is a corporation;

(2) A description of the dangerous ordnance for which a permit is requested;

(3) A description of the place or places where and the manner in which the dangerous ordnance is to be kept, carried, and used;

(4) A statement of the purposes for which the dangerous ordnance is to be acquired, possessed, carried, or used;

(5) Such other information, as the issuing authority may require in giving effect to this section.

(C) Upon investigation, the issuing authority shall issue a license or temporary permit only if all of the following apply:

(1) The applicant is not otherwise prohibited by law from acquiring, having, carrying or using dangerous ordnance;

(2) The applicant is age twenty-one or over, if he is a natural person;

(3) It appears that the applicant has sufficient competence to safely acquire, possess, carry, or use the dangerous ordnance, and that proper precautions will be taken to protect the security of the dangerous ordnance and ensure the safety of persons and property;

(4) It appears that the dangerous ordnance will be lawfully acquired, possessed, carried, and used by the applicant for a legitimate purpose.

(D) The license or temporary permit shall identify the person to whom it is issued, identify the dangerous ordnance involved and state the purposes for which the license or temporary permit is issued, state the expiration date, if any, and list such restrictions on the acquisition, possession, carriage, or use of the dangerous ordnance as the issuing authority considers advisable to protect the security of the dangerous ordnance and ensure the safety of persons and property.

(E) A temporary permit shall be issued for the casual use of explosives and explosive devices, and other consumable dangerous ordnance, and shall expire within thirty days of its issuance. A license shall be issued for the regular use of consumable dangerous ordnance, or for any noncomsumable [*sic*] dangerous ordnance, which license need not specify an expiration date, but the issuing authority may specify such expiration date, not earlier than one year from the date of issuance, as it considers advisable in view of the nature of the dangerous ordnance and the purposes for which the license is issued.

(F) The dangerous ordnance specified in a license or temporary permit may be obtained by the holder anywhere in the state. The holder of a license may use such dangerous ordnance anywhere in the state. The holder of a temporary permit may use such dangerous ordnance only within the territorial jurisdiction of the issuing authority.

(G) The issuing authority shall forward to the state fire marshal a copy of each license or temporary permit issued pursuant to this section, and a copy of each record of a transaction in dangerous ordnance and of each report of lost or stolen dangerous ordnance, given to the local law enforcement authority as required by divisions (A)(4) and (5) of section 2923.20 of the Revised Code. The state fire marshal shall keep a permanent file of all licenses and temporary permits issued pursuant to this section, and of all records of transactions in, and losses or thefts of dangerous ordnance forwarded by local law enforcement authorities pursuant to this section.
(1978 H 590, eff. 7–1–79; 1972 H 511)

2923.19   Failure to secure dangerous ordnance

(A) No person, in acquiring, possessing, carrying, or using any dangerous ordnance, shall negligently fail to take proper precautions:

(1) To secure the dangerous ordnance against theft, or against its acquisition or use by any unauthorized or incompetent person;

(2) To insure the safety of persons and property.

(B) Whoever violates this section is guilty of failure to secure dangerous ordnance, a misdemeanor of the second degree.
(1972 H 511, eff. 1–1–74)

2923.20   Unlawful transactions in weapons

(A) No person shall:

(1) Recklessly sell, lend, give, or furnish any firearm to any person prohibited by section 2923.13 or 2923.15 of the Revised Code from acquiring or using any firearm, or recklessly sell, lend, give, or furnish any dangerous ordnance to any person prohibited by section 2923.13, 2923.15, or 2923.17 of the Revised Code from acquiring or using any dangerous ordnance;

(2) Possess any firearm or dangerous ordnance with purpose to dispose of it in violation of division (A) of this section;

(3) Manufacture, possess for sale, sell, or furnish to any person other than a law enforcement agency for authorized use in police work, any brass knuckles, cestus, billy, blackjack, sandbag, switchblade knife, springblade knife, gravity knife, or similar weapon;

(4) When transferring any dangerous ordnance to another, negligently fail to require the transferee to exhibit such identification, license, or permit showing him to be authorized to acquire dangerous ordnance pursuant to section 2923.17 of the Revised Code, or negligently fail to take a complete record of the transaction and forthwith forward a copy of such record to the sheriff of the county or safety director or police chief of the municipality where the transaction takes place;

(5) Knowingly fail to report to law enforcement authorities forthwith the loss or theft of any firearm or dangerous ordnance in such person's possession or under his control.

(B) Whoever violates this section is guilty of unlawful transactions in weapons. Violation of division (A)(1) or (2) of this section is a felony of the third degree. Violation of division (A)(3) or (4) of this section is a misdemeanor of the second degree. Violation of division (A)(5) of this section is a misdemeanor of the fourth degree.
(1978 H 728, eff. 8–22–78; 1972 H 511)

2923.21   Improperly furnishing firearms to a minor

(A) No person shall do any of the following:

(1) Sell any firearm to a person who is under eighteen years of age;

(2) Sell any handgun to a person who is under twenty-one years of age;

(3) Furnish any firearm to a person who is under eighteen years of age or any handgun to a person who is under twenty-one years of age, except for lawful hunting, sporting, or educational

purposes, including, but not limited to, instruction in firearms or handgun safety, care, handling, or marksmanship under the supervision or control of a responsible adult;

(4) Sell or furnish a firearm to a person who is eighteen years of age or older if the seller or furnisher knows, or has reason to know, that the person is purchasing or receiving the firearm for the purpose of selling the firearm in violation of division (A)(1) of this section to a person who is under eighteen years of age or for the purpose of furnishing the firearm in violation of division (A)(3) of this section to a person who is under eighteen years of age;

(5) Sell or furnish a handgun to a person who is twenty-one years of age or older if the seller or furnisher knows, or has reason to know, that the person is purchasing or receiving the handgun for the purpose of selling the handgun in violation of division (A)(2) of this section to a person who is under twenty-one years of age or for the purpose of furnishing the handgun in violation of division (A)(3) of this section to a person who is under twenty-one years of age;

(6) Purchase or attempt to purchase any firearm with the intent to sell the firearm in violation of division (A)(1) of this section to a person who is under eighteen years of age or with the intent to furnish the firearm in violation of division (A)(3) of this section to a person who is under eighteen years of age;

(7) Purchase or attempt to purchase any handgun with the intent to sell the handgun in violation of division (A)(2) of this section to a person who is under twenty-one years of age or with the intent to furnish the handgun in violation of division (A)(3) of this section to a person who is under twenty-one years of age.

(B) Whoever violates this section is guilty of improperly furnishing firearms to a minor, a felony of the fourth degree.

(1995 H 4, eff. 11–9–95; 1972 H 511, eff. 1–1–74)

2923.211   Underage purchase of firearm or handgun

(A) No person under eighteen years of age shall purchase or attempt to purchase a firearm.

(B) No person under twenty-one years of age shall purchase or attempt to purchase a handgun.

(C) Whoever violates division (A) of this section is guilty of underage purchase of a firearm, is a delinquent child, and is subject to an order of disposition as provided in section 2151.355 of the Revised Code.   Whoever violates division (B) of this section is guilty of underage purchase of a handgun, a misdemeanor of the second degree.

(1995 H 4, eff. 11–9–95)

2923.22   Permitted interstate transactions in firearms

(A) Any resident of Ohio age eighteen or over, and not prohibited by section 2923.13 or 2923.15 of the Revised Code or any applicable law of another state or the United States from acquiring or using firearms, may purchase or obtain a rifle, shotgun, or ammunition therefor in Indiana, Kentucky, Michigan, Pennsylvania, or West Virginia.

(B) Any resident of Indiana, Kentucky, Michigan, Pennsylvania, or West Virginia, age eighteen or over, and not prohibited by section 2923.13 or 2923.15 of the Revised Code or the laws of his domicile or the United States from acquiring or using firearms, may purchase or obtain a rifle, shotgun, or ammunition therefor in Ohio.

(C) Any purchase and sale pursuant to this section shall be for such purposes and under such circumstances and upon such conditions as are prescribed by the "Gun Control Act of 1968," 82 Stat. 1213, 18 U.S.C. 922(b)(3), and any amendments or additions thereto or reenactments thereof.

(1972 H 511, eff. 1–1–74)

2923.23   Immunity from prosecution

(A) No person who acquires, possesses, or carries a firearm or dangerous ordnance in violation of section 2923.13 or 2923.17 of the Revised Code shall be prosecuted for such violation, if he reports his possession of firearms or dangerous ordnance to any law enforcement authority, describes the firearms of [1] dangerous ordnance in his possession and where they may be found, and voluntarily surrenders the firearms or dangerous ordnance to the law enforcement authority. A surrender is not voluntary if it occurs when the person is taken into custody or during a pursuit or attempt to take the person into custody, under circumstances indicating that the surrender is made under threat of force.

(B) No person in violation of section 2923.13 of the Revised Code solely by reason of his being under indictment shall be prosecuted for such violation if, within ten days after service of the indictment, he voluntarily surrenders the firearms and dangerous ordnance in his possession to any law enforcement authority pursuant to division (A) of this section, for safekeeping pending disposition of the indictment or of an application for relief under section 2923.14 of the Revised Code.

(C) Evidence obtained from or by reason of an application or proceeding under section 2923.14 of the Revised Code for relief from disability, shall not be used in a prosecution of the applicant for any violation of section 2923.13 of the Revised Code.

(D) Evidence obtained from or by reason of an application under section 2923.18 of the Revised Code for a permit to possess dangerous ordnance, shall not be used in a prosecution of the applicant for any violation of section 2923.13 or 2923.17 of the Revised Code.

(1972 H 511, eff. 1–1–74)

[1] So in original; should this read "or"?

2923.24 Possessing criminal tools

(A) No person shall possess or have under his control any substance, device, instrument, or article, with purpose to use it criminally.

(B) Each of the following constitutes prima-facie evidence of criminal purpose:

(1) Possession or control of any dangerous ordnance, or the materials or parts for making dangerous ordnance, in the absence of circumstances indicating such dangerous ordnance, materials, or parts are intended for legitimate use;

(2) Possession or control of any substance, device, instrument, or article designed or specially adapted for criminal use;

(3) Possession or control of any substance, device, instrument, or article commonly used for criminal purposes, under circumstances indicating such item is intended for criminal use.

(C) Whoever violates this section is guilty of possessing criminal tools, a felony of the fourth degree.

(1972 H 511, eff. 1–1–74)

2923.25 Burners giving off obnoxious gases—Repealed

(1972 H 511, eff. 1–1–74; 1953 H 1; GC 12798–6)

2923.251 Unvented gas heaters—Repealed

(1972 H 511, eff. 1–1–74; 129 v 582; 127 v 459)

2923.26 Making a false alarm of fire—Repealed

(1972 H 511, eff. 1–1–74; 1953 H 1; GC 13396)

2923.27 Unlawful camping on public highways or adjacent lands—Repealed

(1972 H 511, eff. 1–1–74; 1953 H 1; GC 13397)

2923.28 Tramps—Repealed

(1972 H 511, eff. 1–1–74; 129 v 582; 1953 H 1; GC 13408)

2923.29 Improper use of stenographer's notes or transcripts thereof—Repealed

(1972 H 511, eff. 1–1–74; 1953 H 1; GC 13410)

**2923.30   False statements affecting solvency of banks or value of stocks or bonds—
Repealed**

(1972 H 511, eff. 1–1–74;   126 v 575;   1953 H 1;   GC 13383–1)

CORRUPT ACTIVITY

2923.31   Definitions

As used in sections 2923.31 to 2923.36 of the Revised Code:

(A) "Beneficial interest" means any of the following:

(1) The interest of a person as a beneficiary under a trust in which the trustee holds title to personal or real property;

(2) The interest of a person as a beneficiary under any other trust arrangement under which any other person holds title to personal or real property for the benefit of such person;

(3) The interest of a person under any other form of express fiduciary arrangement under which any other person holds title to personal or real property for the benefit of such person.

"Beneficial interest" does not include the interest of a stockholder in a corporation or the interest of a partner in either a general or limited partnership.

(B) "Costs of investigation and prosecution" and "costs of investigation and litigation" mean all of the costs incurred by the state or a county or municipal corporation under sections 2923.31 to 2923.36 of the Revised Code in the prosecution and investigation of any criminal action or in the litigation and investigation of any civil action, and includes, but is not limited to, the costs of resources and personnel.

(C) "Enterprise" includes any individual, sole proprietorship, partnership, limited partnership, corporation, trust, union, government agency, or other legal entity, or any organization, association, or group of persons associated in fact although not a legal entity. "Enterprise" includes illicit as well as licit enterprises.

(D) "Innocent person" includes any bona fide purchaser of property that is allegedly involved in a violation of section 2923.32 of the Revised Code, including any person who establishes a valid claim to or interest in the property in accordance with division (E) of section 2923.32 of the Revised Code, and any victim of an alleged violation of that section or of any underlying offense involved in an alleged violation of that section.

(E) "Pattern of corrupt activity" means two or more incidents of corrupt activity, whether or not there has been a prior conviction, that are related to the affairs of the same enterprise, are not isolated, and are not so closely related to each other and connected in time and place that they constitute a single event.

At least one of the incidents forming the pattern shall occur on or after January 1, 1986. Unless any incident was an aggravated murder or murder, the last of the incidents forming the pattern shall occur within six years after the commission of any prior incident forming the pattern, excluding any period of imprisonment served by any person engaging in the corrupt activity.

For the purposes of the criminal penalties that may be imposed pursuant to section 2923.32 of the Revised Code, at least one of the incidents forming the pattern shall constitute a felony under the laws of this state or, if committed in violation of the laws of the United States or of any other state, would constitute a felony under the law of this state if committed in this state.

(F) "Pecuniary value" means money, a negotiable instrument, a commercial interest, or anything of value, as defined in section 1.03 of the Revised Code, or any other property or service that has a value in excess of one hundred dollars.

(G) "Person" means any person, as defined in section 1.59 of the Revised Code, and any governmental officer, employee, or entity.

(H) "Personal property" means any personal property, any interest in personal property, or any right, including, but not limited to, bank accounts, debts, corporate stocks, patents, or copyrights.   Personal property and any beneficial interest in personal property are deemed to be located where the trustee of the property, the personal property, or the instrument evidencing the right is located.

(I) "Corrupt activity" means engaging in, attempting to engage in, conspiring to engage in, or soliciting, coercing, or intimidating another person to engage in any of the following:

(1) Conduct defined as "racketeering activity" under the "Organized Crime Control Act of 1970," 84 Stat. 941, 18 U.S.C. 1961(1)(B), (1)(C), (1)(D), and (1)(E), as amended;

(2) Conduct constituting any of the following:

(a) Any violation of section 1322.02, 2903.01, 2903.02, 2903.03, 2903.04, 2903.11, 2903.12, 2905.01, 2905.02, 2905.11, 2905.22, 2907.321, 2907.322, 2907.323, 2909.02, 2909.03, 2911.01, 2911.02, 2911.11, 2911.12, 2911.13, 2911.31, 2921.02, 2921.03, 2921.04, 2921.11, 2921.12, 2921.32, 2921.41, 2921.42, 2921.43, 2923.12, 2923.17, 3769.11, 3769.15, 3769.16, or 3769.19, or of division (A)(1) or (2) of section 1707.042, or of division (B), (C)(4), (D), (E), or (F) of section 1707.44, or of division (A)(1) or (2) of section 2923.20, or of division (J)(1) of section 4712.02 of the Revised Code.

(b) Any violation of section 2907.21, 2907.22, 2907.31, 2913.02, 2913.11, 2913.21, 2913.31, 2913.32, 2913.42, 2913.47, 2913.51, 2915.02, 2915.03, 2915.06, 2925.03, or 2925.37 of the Revised Code when the proceeds of the violation, the payments made in the violation, the amount of a claim for payment or for any other benefit that is false or deceptive and that is involved in the violation, or the value of the contraband or other property illegally possessed, sold, or purchased in the violation exceeds five hundred dollars, or any combination of violations of those sections when the total proceeds of the combination of violations, payments made in the combination of violations, amount of the claims for payment or for other benefits that is false or deceptive and that is involved in the combination of violations, or value of the contraband or other property illegally possessed, sold, or purchased in the combination of violations exceeds five hundred dollars;

(c) Any violation of section 5743.112 of the Revised Code when the amount of unpaid tax exceeds one hundred dollars;

(d) Any violation or combination of violations of section 2907.32 of the Revised Code involving any material or performance containing a display of bestiality or of sexual conduct, as defined in section 2907.01 of the Revised Code, that is explicit and depicted with clearly visible penetration of the genitals or clearly visible penetration by the penis of any orifice when the total proceeds of the violation or combination of violations, the payments made in the violation or combination of violations, or the value of the contraband or other property illegally possessed, sold, or purchased in the violation or combination of violations exceeds five hundred dollars;

(e) Any combination of violations of the sections listed in division (I)(2)(b) of this section and violations of section 2907.32 of the Revised Code involving any material or performance containing a display of bestiality or of sexual conduct, as defined in section 2907.01 of the Revised Code, that is explicit and depicted with clearly visible penetration of the genitals or clearly visible penetration by the penis of any orifice when the total proceeds of the combination of violations, payments made in the combination of violations, amount of the claims for payment or for other benefits that is false or deceptive and that is involved in the combination of violations, or value of the contraband or other property illegally possessed, sold, or purchased in the combination of violations exceeds five hundred dollars.

(3) Conduct constituting a violation of any law of any state other than this state that is substantially similar to the conduct described in division (I)(2) of this section, provided the defendant was convicted of such conduct in a criminal proceeding in the other state.

(J) "Real property" means any real property or any interest in real property, including, but not limited to, any lease of, or mortgage upon, real property. Real property and any beneficial interest in it is deemed to be located where the real property is located.

(K) "Trustee" means any of the following:

(1) Any person acting as trustee under a trust in which the trustee holds title to personal or real property;

(2) Any person who holds title to personal or real property for which any other person has a beneficial interest;

(3) Any successor trustee.

"Trustee" does not include an assignee or trustee for an insolvent debtor or an executor, administrator, administrator with the will annexed, testamentary trustee, guardian, or committee, appointed by, or under the control of, or accountable to, a court.

(L) "Unlawful debt" means any money or other thing of value constituting principal or interest of a debt that is legally unenforceable in this state in whole or in part because the debt was incurred or contracted in violation of any federal or state law relating to the business of gambling activity or relating to the business of lending money at an usurious rate unless the creditor proves, by a preponderance of the evidence, that the usurious rate was not intentionally set and that it resulted from a good faith error by the creditor, notwithstanding the maintenance of procedures that were adopted by the creditor to avoid such an error.

(1992 S 323, eff. 4–16–93; 1990 H 347; 1988 H 624, H 708; 1986 S 74; 1985 H 5)

2923.32 Engaging in a pattern of corrupt activity; fines; penalties; forfeiture; records and reports; third–party claims to property subject to forfeiture

(A)(1) No person employed by, or associated with, any enterprise shall conduct or participate in, directly or indirectly, the affairs of the enterprise through a pattern of corrupt activity or the collection of an unlawful debt.

(2) No person, through a pattern of corrupt activity or the collection of an unlawful debt, shall acquire or maintain, directly or indirectly, any interest in, or control of, any enterprise or real property.

(3) No person, who knowingly has received any proceeds derived, directly or indirectly, from a pattern of corrupt activity or the collection of any unlawful debt, shall use or invest, directly or indirectly, any part of those proceeds, or any proceeds derived from the use or investment of any of those proceeds, in the acquisition of any title to, or any right, interest, or equity in, real property or in the establishment or operation of any enterprise.

A purchase of securities on the open market with intent to make an investment, without intent to control or participate in the control of the issuer, and without intent to assist another to do so is not a violation of this division, if the securities of the issuer held after the purchase by the purchaser, the members of his immediate family, and his or their accomplices in any pattern of corrupt activity or the collection of an unlawful debt do not aggregate one per cent of the outstanding securities of any one class of the issuer and do not confer, in law or in fact, the power to elect one or more directors of the issuer.

(B)(1) Whoever violates this section is guilty of engaging in a pattern of corrupt activity, a felony of the first degree. Notwithstanding any other provision of law, a person may be convicted of violating the provisions of this section as well as of a conspiracy to violate one or more of those provisions under section 2923.01 of the Revised Code.

(2) Notwithstanding the fine authorized by section 2929.11 of the Revised Code, the court may do all of the following with respect to any person who derives pecuniary value or causes property damage, personal injury other than pain and suffering, or other loss through or by the violation of this section:

(a) Impose a fine not exceeding the greater of three times the gross value gained or three times the gross loss caused and order the clerk of the court to pay the fine into the corrupt activity investigation and prosecution fund created in section 2923.35 of the Revised Code;

(b) Order the person to pay court costs;

(c) Order the person to pay to the state, municipal, or county law enforcement agencies that handled the investigation and prosecution the costs of investigation and prosecution that are reasonably incurred.

The court shall hold a hearing to determine the amount of fine, court costs, and other costs to be imposed under this division.

(3) In addition to any other penalty or disposition authorized or required by law, the court shall order any person who is convicted of or pleads guilty to a violation of this section or who is adjudicated delinquent by reason of a violation of this section to criminally forfeit to the state any personal or real property in which he has an interest and that was used in the course of or intended for use in the course of a violation of this section, or that was derived from or realized through conduct in violation of this section, including any property constituting an interest in, means of control over, or influence over the enterprise involved in the violation and any property constituting proceeds derived from the violation, including all of the following:

(a) Any position, office, appointment, tenure, commission, or employment contract of any kind acquired or maintained by the person in violation of this section, through which he, in violation of this section, conducted or participated in the conduct of an enterprise, or that afforded him a source of influence or control over an enterprise that he exercised in violation of this section;

(b) Any compensation, right, or benefit derived from a position, office, appointment, tenure, commission, or employment contract described in division (B)(3)(a) of this section that accrued to him in violation of this section during the period of the pattern of corrupt activity;

(c) Any interest in, security of, claim against, or property or contractual right affording him a source of influence or control over the affairs of an enterprise that the person exercised in violation of this section;

(d) Any amount payable or paid under any contract for goods or services that was awarded or performed in violation of this section.

(4)(a) A sentence or disposition of criminal forfeiture pursuant to division (B)(3) of this section shall not be entered unless either of the following applies:

(i) The indictment, count in the indictment, or information charging the offense, or the complaint filed in juvenile court charging the violation as a delinquent act alleges the extent of the property subject to forfeiture;

(ii) The criminal sentence or delinquency disposition requires the forfeiture of property that was not reasonably foreseen to be subject to forfeiture at the time of the indictment, count in the indictment, or information charging the offense, or the complaint filed in juvenile court charging the violation as a delinquent act, provided that the prosecuting attorney gave prompt notice to the defendant or the alleged or adjudicated delinquent child of such property not reasonably foreseen to be subject to forfeiture when it is discovered to be forfeitable.

(b) A special verdict shall be returned as to the extent of the property, if any, subject to forfeiture. When the special verdict is returned, a judgment of forfeiture shall be entered.

(5) If any property included in a special verdict of forfeiture returned pursuant to division (B)(4) of this section cannot be located, has been sold to a bona fide purchaser for value, placed beyond the jurisdiction of the court, substantially diminished in value by the conduct of the defendant or adjudicated delinquent child, or commingled with other property that cannot be divided without difficulty or undue injury to innocent persons, or otherwise is unreachable without undue injury to innocent persons, the court shall order forfeiture of any other reachable property of the defendant or adjudicated delinquent child up to the value of the property that is unreachable.

(6) All property ordered forfeited pursuant to this section shall be held by the law enforcement agency that seized it for distribution or disposal pursuant to section 2923.35 of the Revised Code. The agency shall maintain an accurate record of each item of property so seized and held, which record shall include the date on which each item was seized, the manner and date of disposition by the agency, and if applicable, the name of the person who received the item; however, the record shall not identify or enable the identification of the individual officer who seized the property. The record is a public record open for inspection under section 149.43 of the Revised Code. Each law enforcement agency that seizes and holds in any calendar year any item of property that is ordered forfeited pursuant to this section shall prepare a report covering the calendar year that cumulates all of the information contained in all of the records kept by the agency pursuant to this division for that calendar year, and shall send the cumulative report, no later than the first day of March in the calendar year following the calendar year covered by the report, to the attorney general. Each such report so received

by the attorney general is a public record open for inspection under section 149.43 of the Revised Code. The attorney general shall make copies of each such report so received, and, no later than the fifteenth day of April in the calendar year in which the reports were received, shall send a copy of each such report to the office of the president of the senate and the office of the speaker of the house of representatives.

(C) Notwithstanding the notice and procedure prescribed by division (E) of this section, an order of criminal forfeiture entered under division (B)(3) of this section shall authorize an appropriate law enforcement agency to seize the property declared forfeited under this section upon the terms and conditions, relating to the time and manner of seizure, that the court determines proper.

(D) Criminal penalties under this section are not mutually exclusive, unless otherwise provided, and do not preclude the application of any other criminal or civil remedy under this or any other section of the Revised Code. A disposition of criminal forfeiture ordered pursuant to division (B)(3) of this section in relation to a child who was adjudicated delinquent by reason of a violation of this section does not preclude the application of any other order of disposition under section 2151.355 of the Revised Code or any other civil remedy under this or any other section of the Revised Code.

(E)(1) Upon the entry of a judgment of forfeiture pursuant to division (B)(3) of this section, the court shall cause notice of the judgment to be sent by certified mail, return receipt requested, to all persons known to have, or appearing to have, an interest in the property that was acquired prior to the filing of a corrupt activity lien notice or a lis pendens as authorized by section 2923.36 of the Revised Code. If the notices cannot be given to those persons in that manner, the court shall cause publication of the notice of the judgment of forfeiture pursuant to the Rules of Civil Procedure.

(2) Within thirty days after receipt of a notice or after the date of publication of a notice under division (E)(1) of this section, any person, other than the defendant or the adjudicated delinquent child, who claims an interest in the property that is subject to forfeiture may petition the court for a hearing to determine the validity of the claim. The petition shall be signed and sworn to by the petitioner and shall set forth the nature and extent of the petitioner's interest in the property, the date and circumstances of the petitioner's acquisition of the interest, any additional allegations supporting the claim, and the relief sought. The petitioner shall furnish the prosecuting attorney with a copy of the petition.

(3) The court, to the extent practicable and consistent with the interests of justice, shall hold the hearing described under division (E)(2) of this section within thirty days from the filing of the petition. The court may consolidate the hearings on all petitions filed by third party claimants under this section. At the hearing, the petitioner may testify and present evidence on his own behalf and cross-examine witnesses. The prosecuting attorney may present evidence and witnesses in rebuttal and in defense of the claim of the state to the property and cross-examine witnesses. The court, in making its determination, shall consider the testimony and evidence presented at the hearing and the relevant portions of the record of the criminal proceeding that resulted in the judgment of forfeiture.

(4) If at a hearing held under division (E)(3) of this section, the court, by a preponderance of the evidence, determines either that the petitioner has a legal right, title, or interest in the property that, at the time of the commission of the acts giving rise to the forfeiture of the property, was vested in the petitioner and not in the defendant or the adjudicated delinquent child or was superior to the right, title, or interest of the defendant or the adjudicated delinquent child, or that the petitioner is a bona fide purchaser for value of the right, title, or interest in the property and was at the time of the purchase reasonably without cause to believe that the property was subject to forfeiture under this section, it shall amend, in accordance with its determination, the judgment of forfeiture to protect the rights of innocent persons.

(F) Except as provided in division (E) of this section, no person claiming an interest in property that is subject to forfeiture under this section shall do either of the following:

(1) Intervene in a trial or appeal of a criminal case or a delinquency case that involves the forfeiture of the property;

(2) File an action against the state concerning the validity of his alleged interest in the property subsequent to the filing of the indictment, count in the indictment, or information, or

the filing of the complaint in juvenile court, that alleges that the property is subject to forfeiture under this section.

(G) As used in this section, "law enforcement agency" includes, but is not limited to, the state board of pharmacy.

(1990 H 266, eff. 9–6–90; 1990 H 215; 1988 H 708; 1986 S 74; 1985 H 5)

2923.33 Property subject to forfeiture; restraining orders

(A) At any time after an indictment is filed alleging a violation of section 2923.32 of the Revised Code or a conspiracy to violate that section or after a complaint is filed in juvenile court alleging a violation of that section or a conspiracy to violate that section as a delinquent act, the prosecuting attorney may file a motion requesting the court to issue an order to preserve the reachability of any property that may be subject to forfeiture. Upon the filing of the motion, the court, after giving notice to any person who will be affected by any order issued by the court pursuant to the motion, shall hold a hearing on the motion at which all affected persons have an opportunity to be heard and, upon a showing by the prosecuting attorney by a preponderance of the evidence that the particular action is necessary to preserve the reachability of any property that may be subject to forfeiture and based upon the indictment, may enter a restraining order or injunction, require the execution of a satisfactory performance bond, or take any other necessary action, including the appointment of a receiver. The prosecuting attorney is not required to show special or irreparable injury to obtain any court action pursuant to this division. Notwithstanding the Rules of Evidence, the court's order or injunction may be based on hearsay testimony.

(B) If no indictment has been filed alleging a violation of section 2923.32 of the Revised Code or a conspiracy to violate that section and no complaint has been filed in juvenile court alleging a violation of that section or a conspiracy to violate that section as a delinquent act, the court may take any action specified in division (A) of this section if the prosecuting attorney for the county, in addition to the showing that would be required pursuant to division (A) of this section, also shows both of the following by a preponderance of the evidence:

(1) There is probable cause to believe that the property with respect to which the order is sought, in the event of a conviction or a delinquency adjudication, would be subject to criminal forfeiture under section 2923.32 of the Revised Code;

(2) The requested order would not result in irreparable harm to the party against whom the order is to be entered that outweighs the need to preserve the reachability of the property.

No order entered pursuant to this division shall be effective for more than ninety days, unless it is extended pursuant to the procedure provided in this division by the court for good cause shown or an indictment is returned alleging that the property is subject to forfeiture.

(C) Upon application by the prosecuting attorney, the court may grant a temporary restraining order to preserve the reachability of property subject to criminal forfeiture under section 2923.32 of the Revised Code without notice to any party, if all of the following occur:

(1) Either an indictment or a juvenile delinquency complaint alleging that property is subject to criminal forfeiture has been filed, or the court determines that there is probable cause to believe that property with respect to which the order is sought would be subject, in the event of a conviction or a delinquency adjudication, to criminal forfeiture;

(2) The property is in the possession or control of the party against whom the order is to be entered;

(3) The court determines that the nature of the property is such that it can be concealed, disposed of, or placed beyond the jurisdiction of the court before any party may be heard in opposition to the order.

A temporary restraining order granted without notice to any party under this division shall expire within the time, not to exceed ten days, that the court fixes, unless extended for good cause shown or unless the party against whom it is entered consents to an extension for a longer period. If a temporary restraining order is granted under this division without notice to any party, the court shall hold a hearing concerning the entry of an order under this division at the earliest practicable time prior to the expiration of the temporary order.

(D) Following sentencing and the entry of a judgment against an offender that includes a fine or an order of criminal forfeiture, or both, under section 2923.32 of the Revised Code, or following the entry of a judgment against a delinquent child that includes an order of criminal forfeiture under that section, the court may enter a restraining order or injunction, require the execution of a satisfactory performance bond, or take any other action, including the appointment of a receiver, that the court determines to be proper to protect the interests of the state or an innocent person.

(1990 H 266, eff. 9–6–90; 1985 H 5)

2923.34 Civil proceedings

(A) The prosecuting attorney of the county in which a violation of section 2923.32 of the Revised Code, or a conspiracy to violate that section, occurs may institute a civil proceeding as authorized by this section in an appropriate court seeking relief from any person whose conduct violated section 2923.32 of the Revised Code or who conspired to violate that section.

(B) Any person who is injured or threatened with injury by a violation of section 2923.32 of the Revised Code may institute a civil proceeding in an appropriate court seeking relief from any person whose conduct violated or allegedly violated section 2923.32 of the Revised Code or who conspired or allegedly conspired to violate that section, except that the pattern of corrupt activity alleged by an injured person or person threatened with injury shall include at least one incident other than a violation of division (A)(1) or (2) of section 1707.042 or division (B), (C)(4), (D), (E), or (F) of section 1707.44 of the Revised Code, of 18 U.S.C. 1341, 18 U.S.C. 1343, 18 U.S.C. 2314, or any other offense involving fraud in the sale of securities.

(C) If the plaintiff in a civil action instituted pursuant to this section proves the violation by a preponderance of the evidence, the court, after making due provision for the rights of innocent persons, may grant relief by entering any appropriate orders to ensure that the violation will not continue or be repeated. The orders may include, but are not limited to, orders that:

(1) Require any defendant in the action to divest himself of any interest in any enterprise or in any real property;

(2) Impose reasonable restrictions upon the future activities or investments of any defendant in the action, including, but not limited to, restrictions that prohibit the defendant from engaging in the same type of endeavor as the enterprise in which he was engaged in violation of section 2923.32 of the Revised Code;

(3) Order the dissolution or reorganization of any enterprise;

(4) Order the suspension or revocation of a license, permit, or prior approval granted to any enterprise by any department or agency of the state;

(5) Order the dissolution of a corporation organized under the laws of this state, or the revocation of the authorization of a foreign corporation to conduct business within this state, upon a finding that the board of directors or an agent acting on behalf of the corporation, in conducting the affairs of the corporation, has authorized or engaged in conduct in violation of section 2923.32 of the Revised Code, and that, for the prevention of future criminal conduct, the public interest requires the corporation to be dissolved or its license revoked.

(D) Relief pursuant to division (C)(3), (4), or (5) of this section shall not be granted in any civil proceeding instituted by an injured person unless the attorney general intervenes in the civil action pursuant to this division.

Upon the filing of a civil proceeding for relief under division (C)(3), (4), or (5) of this section by an allegedly injured person other than a prosecuting attorney, the allegedly injured person immediately shall notify the attorney general of the filing. The attorney general, upon timely application, may intervene in any civil proceeding for relief under division (C)(3), (4), or (5) if the attorney general certifies that, in his opinion, the proceeding is of general public interest. In any proceeding brought by an injured person under division (C)(3), (4), or (5) of this section, the attorney general is entitled to the same relief as if the attorney general instituted the proceeding.

(E) In a civil proceeding under division (C) of this section, the court may grant injunctive relief without a showing of special or irreparable injury.

Pending final determination of a civil proceeding initiated under this section, the court may issue a temporary restraining order or a preliminary injunction upon a showing of immediate danger or significant injury to the plaintiff, including the possibility that any judgment for money damages might be difficult to execute, and, in a proceeding initiated by an aggrieved person, upon the execution of proper bond against injury for an improvidently granted injunction.

(F) In a civil proceeding under division (B) of this section, any person directly or indirectly injured by conduct in violation of section 2923.32 of the Revised Code or a conspiracy to violate that section, other than a violator of that section or a conspirator to violate that section, in addition to relief under division (C) of this section, shall have a cause of action for triple the actual damages he sustained. To recover triple damages, the plaintiff shall prove the violation or conspiracy to violate that section and actual damages by clear and convincing evidence. Damages under this division may include, but are not limited to, competitive injury and injury distinct from the injury inflicted by corrupt activity.

(G) In a civil action in which the plaintiff prevails under division (C) or (F) of this section, he shall recover reasonable attorney fees in the trial and appellate courts, and the court shall order the defendant to pay to the state, municipal, or county law enforcement agencies that handled the investigation and litigation the costs of investigation and litigation that reasonably are incurred and that are not ordered to be paid pursuant to division (B)(2) of section 2923.32 of the Revised Code or division (I) of this section.

(H) Upon application, based on the evidence presented in the case by the plaintiff, as the interests of justice may require, the trial court may grant a defendant who prevails in a civil action brought pursuant to this section all or part of his costs, including the costs of investigation and litigation reasonably incurred, and all or part of his reasonable attorney fees, unless the court finds that special circumstances, including the relative economic position of the parties, make an award unjust.

(I) If a person, other than an individual, is not convicted of a violation of section 2923.32 of the Revised Code, the prosecuting attorney may institute proceedings against the person to recover a civil penalty for conduct that the prosecuting attorney proves by clear and convincing evidence is in violation of section 2923.32 of the Revised Code. The civil penalty shall not exceed one hundred thousand dollars and shall be paid into the state treasury to the credit of the corrupt activity investigation and prosecution fund created in section 2923.35 of the Revised Code. If a civil penalty is ordered pursuant to this division, the court shall order the defendant to pay to the state, municipal, or county law enforcement agencies that handled the investigation and litigation the costs of investigation and litigation that are reasonably incurred and that are not ordered to be paid pursuant to this section.

(J) A final judgment, decree, or delinquency adjudication rendered against the defendant or the adjudicated delinquent child in a civil action under this section or in a criminal or delinquency action or proceeding for a violation of section 2923.32 of the Revised Code shall estop the defendant or the adjudicated delinquent child in any subsequent civil proceeding or action brought by any person as to all matters as to which the judgment, decree, or adjudication would be an estoppel as between the parties to the civil, criminal, or delinquency proceeding or action.

(K) Notwithstanding any other provision of law providing a shorter period of limitations, a civil proceeding or action under this section may be commenced at any time within five years after the unlawful conduct terminates or the cause of action accrues or within any longer statutory period of limitations that may be applicable. If a criminal proceeding, delinquency proceeding, civil action, or other proceeding is brought or intervened in by the state to punish, prevent, or restrain any activity that is unlawful under section 2923.32 of the Revised Code, the running of the period of limitations prescribed by this division with respect to any civil action brought under this section by a person who is injured by a violation or threatened violation of section 2923.32 of the Revised Code, based in whole or in part upon any matter complained of in the state prosecution, action, or proceeding, shall be suspended during the pendency of the state prosecution, action, or proceeding and for two years following its termination.

(L) Personal service of any process in a proceeding under this section may be made upon any person outside this state if the person was involved in any conduct constituting a violation of section 2923.32 of the Revised Code in this state. The person is deemed by his conduct in violation of section 2923.32 of the Revised Code to have submitted himself to the jurisdiction of the courts of this state for the purposes of this section.

(M) The application of any civil remedy under this section shall not preclude the application of any criminal remedy or criminal forfeiture under section 2923.32 of the Revised Code or any other provision of law, or the application of any delinquency disposition under section 2151.355 of the Revised Code or any other provision of law.

(N) As used in this section, "law enforcement agency" includes, but is not limited to, the state board of pharmacy.

(1990 H 266, eff. 9–6–90; 1986 H 428; 1985 H 5)

2923.35   Court orders; rights of prevailing party in civil action; disposal of property; records and reports; funds; written internal control policy on use and disposition of proceeds

(A)(1) With respect to property ordered forfeited under section 2923.32 of the Revised Code, with respect to any fine or civil penalty imposed in any criminal or civil proceeding under section 2923.32 or 2923.34 of the Revised Code, and with respect to any fine imposed for a violation of section 2923.01 of the Revised Code for conspiracy to violate section 2923.32 of the Revised Code, the court, upon petition of the prosecuting attorney, may do any of the following:

(a) Authorize the prosecuting attorney to settle claims;

(b) Award compensation to persons who provide information that results in a forfeiture, fine, or civil penalty under section 2923.32 or 2923.34 of the Revised Code;

(c) Grant petitions for mitigation or remission of forfeiture, fines, or civil penalties, or restore forfeited property, imposed fines, or imposed civil penalties to persons injured by the violation;

(d) Take any other action to protect the rights of innocent persons that is in the interest of justice and that is consistent with the purposes of sections 2923.31 to 2923.36 of the Revised Code.

(2) The court shall maintain an accurate record of the actions it takes under division (A)(1) of this section with respect to the property ordered forfeited or the fine or civil penalty. The record is a public record open for inspection under section 149.43 of the Revised Code.

(B)(1) After the application of division (A) of this section, any person who prevails in a civil action pursuant to section 2923.34 of the Revised Code has a right to any property, or the proceeds of any property, criminally forfeited to the state pursuant to section 2923.32 of the Revised Code or against which any fine under that section or civil penalty under division (I) of section 2923.34 of the Revised Code may be imposed.

The right of any person who prevails in a civil action pursuant to section 2923.34 of the Revised Code, other than a prosecuting attorney performing official duties under that section, to forfeited property, property against which fines and civil penalties may be imposed, and the proceeds of that property is superior to any right of the state, a municipal corporation, or a county to the property or the proceeds of the property, if the civil action is brought within one hundred eighty days after the entry of a sentence of forfeiture or a fine pursuant to section 2923.32 of the Revised Code or the entry of a civil penalty pursuant to division (I) of section 2923.34 of the Revised Code.

The right is limited to the total value of the treble damages, civil penalties, attorney's fees, and costs awarded to the prevailing party in an action pursuant to section 2923.34 of the Revised Code, less any restitution received by the person.

(2) If the aggregate amount of claims of persons who have prevailed in a civil action pursuant to section 2923.34 of the Revised Code against any one defendant is greater than the total value of the treble fines, civil penalties, and forfeited property paid by the person against whom the actions were brought, all of the persons who brought their actions within one

hundred eighty days after the entry of a sentence or disposition of forfeiture or a fine pursuant to section 2923.32 of the Revised Code or the entry of a civil penalty pursuant to division (I) of section 2923.34 of the Revised Code, first shall receive a pro rata share of the total amount of the fines, civil penalties, and forfeited property. After the persons who brought their actions within the specified one hundred eighty-day period have satisfied their claims out of the fines, civil penalties, and forfeited property, all other persons who prevailed in civil actions pursuant to section 2923.34 of the Revised Code shall receive a pro rata share of the total amount of the fines, civil penalties, and forfeited property that remains in the custody of the law enforcement agency or in the corrupt activity investigation and prosecution fund.

(C)(1) Subject to divisions (A) and (B) of this section and notwithstanding any contrary provision of section 2933.41 of the Revised Code, the prosecuting attorney shall order the disposal of property ordered forfeited in any proceeding under sections 2923.32 and 2923.34 of the Revised Code as soon as feasible, making due provisions for the rights of innocent persons, by any of the following methods:

(a) Transfer to any person who prevails in a civil action pursuant to section 2923.34 of the Revised Code, subject to the limit set forth in division (B)(1) of this section;

(b) Public sale;

(c) Transfer to a state governmental agency for official use;

(d) Sale or transfer to an innocent person;

(e) If the property is contraband and is not needed for evidence in any pending criminal or civil proceeding, pursuant to section 2933.41 or any other applicable section of the Revised Code.

(2) Any interest in personal or real property not disposed of pursuant to this division and not exercisable by, or transferable for value to, the state shall expire and shall not revert to the person found guilty of or adjudicated a delinquent child for a violation of section 2923.32 of the Revised Code. No person found guilty of or adjudicated a delinquent child for a violation of that section and no person acting in concert with a person found guilty of or adjudicated a delinquent child for a violation of that section is eligible to purchase forfeited property from the state.

(3) Upon application of a person, other than the defendant, the adjudicated delinquent child, or a person acting in concert with or on behalf of either the defendant or the adjudicated delinquent child, the court may restrain or stay the disposal of the property pursuant to this division pending the conclusion of any appeal of the criminal case or delinquency case giving rise to the forfeiture or pending the determination of the validity of a claim to or interest in the property pursuant to division (E) of section 2923.32 of the Revised Code, if the applicant demonstrates that proceeding with the disposal of the property will result in irreparable injury, harm, or loss to the applicant.

(4) The prosecuting attorney shall maintain an accurate record of each item of property disposed of pursuant to this division, which record shall include the date on which each item came into the prosecuting attorney's custody, the manner and date of disposition, and, if applicable, the name of the person who received the item. The record shall not identify or enable the identification of the individual officer who seized the property, and the record is a public record open for inspection under section 149.43 of the Revised Code.

Each prosecuting attorney who disposes in any calendar year of any item of property pursuant to this division shall prepare a report covering the calendar year that cumulates all of the information contained in all of the records kept by the prosecuting attorney pursuant to this division for that calendar year and shall send the cumulative report, no later than the first day of March in the calendar year following the calendar year covered by the report, to the attorney general. Each report received by the attorney general is a public record open for inspection under section 149.43 of the Revised Code. The attorney general shall send a copy of the cumulative report, no later than the fifteenth day of April in the calendar year following the calendar year covered by the report, to the president of the senate and the speaker of the house of representatives.

(D)(1)(a) Ten per cent of the proceeds of all property ordered forfeited by a juvenile court pursuant to section 2923.32 of the Revised Code shall be applied to one or more alcohol and drug addiction treatment programs that are certified by the department of alcohol and drug addiction services under section 3793.06 of the Revised Code and that are specified in the order of forfeiture. A juvenile court shall not specify an alcohol or drug addiction treatment program in the order of forfeiture unless the program is a certified alcohol and drug addiction treatment program and, except as provided in division (D)(1)(a) of this section, unless the program is located in the county in which the court that orders the forfeiture is located or in a contiguous county. If no certified alcohol and drug addiction treatment program is located in any of those counties, the juvenile court may specify in the order a certified alcohol and drug addiction treatment program located anywhere within this state. The remaining ninety per cent of the proceeds shall be disposed of as provided in divisions (D)(1)(b) and (D)(2) of this section.

All of the proceeds of all property ordered forfeited by a court other than a juvenile court pursuant to section 2923.32 of the Revised Code shall be disposed of as provided in divisions (D)(1)(b) and (D)(2) of this section.

(b) The remaining proceeds of all property ordered forfeited pursuant to section 2923.32 of the Revised Code, after compliance with division (D)(1)(a) of this section when that division is applicable, and all fines and civil penalties imposed pursuant to sections 2923.32 and 2923.34 of the Revised Code shall be deposited into the state treasury and credited to the corrupt activity investigation and prosecution fund, which is hereby created.

(2) The proceeds, fines, and penalties credited to the corrupt activity investigation and prosecution fund pursuant to division (D)(1) of this section shall be disposed of in the following order:

(a) To a civil plaintiff in an action brought within the one hundred eighty-day time period specified in division (B)(1) of this section, subject to the limit set forth in that division;

(b) To the payment of the fees and costs of the forfeiture and sale, including expenses of seizure, maintenance, and custody of the property pending its disposition, advertising, and court costs;

(c) Except as otherwise provided in division (D)(2)(c) of this section, the remainder shall be paid to the law enforcement trust fund of the prosecuting attorney that is established pursuant to division (D)(1)(c) of section 2933.43 of the Revised Code and to the law enforcement trust fund of the county sheriff that is established pursuant to that division if the county sheriff substantially conducted the investigation, to the law enforcement trust fund of a municipal corporation that is established pursuant to that division if its police department substantially conducted the investigation, to the law enforcement trust fund of a township that is established pursuant to that division if the investigation was substantially conducted by a township police department, township police district police force, or office of a township constable, or to the law enforcement trust fund of a park district created pursuant to section 511.18 or 1545.01 of the Revised Code that is established pursuant to that division if the investigation was substantially conducted by its park district police force or law enforcement department. The prosecuting attorney may decline to accept any of the remaining proceeds, fines, and penalties, and, if the prosecuting attorney so declines, they shall be applied to the fund described in division (D)(2)(c) of this section that relates to the appropriate law enforcement agency that substantially conducted the investigation.

If the state highway patrol substantially conducted the investigation, the director of budget and management shall transfer the remaining proceeds, fines, and penalties to the state highway patrol for deposit into the state highway patrol contraband, forfeiture, and other fund that is created by division (D)(1)(c) of section 2933.43 of the Revised Code. If the state board of pharmacy substantially conducted the investigation, the director shall transfer the remaining proceeds, fines, and penalties to the board for deposit into the board of pharmacy drug law enforcement fund that is created by division (B)(1) of section 4729.65 of the Revised Code. If a state law enforcement agency, other than the state highway patrol or the board, substantially conducted the investigation, the director shall transfer the remaining proceeds, fines, and penalties to the treasurer of state for deposit into the peace officer training council fund that is created by division (D)(1)(c) of section 2933.43 of the Revised Code.

The remaining proceeds, fines, and penalties that are paid to a law enforcement trust fund or that are deposited into the state highway patrol contraband, forfeiture, and other fund, the board of pharmacy drug law enforcement fund, or the peace officer training council fund pursuant to division (D)(2)(c) of this section shall be allocated, used, and expended only in accordance with division (D)(1)(c) of section 2933.43 of the Revised Code, only in accordance with a written internal control policy adopted under division (D)(3) of that section, and, if applicable, only in accordance with division (B) of section 4729.65 of the Revised Code. The annual reports that pertain to the funds and that are required by divisions (D)(1)(c) and (3)(b) of section 2933.43 of the Revised Code also shall address the remaining proceeds, fines, and penalties that are paid or deposited into the funds pursuant to division (D)(2)(c) of this section.

(3) If more than one law enforcement agency substantially conducted the investigation, the court ordering the forfeiture shall equitably divide the remaining proceeds, fines, and penalties among the law enforcement agencies that substantially conducted the investigation, in the manner described in division (D)(2) of section 2933.43 of the Revised Code for the equitable division of contraband proceeds and forfeited moneys. The equitable shares of the proceeds, fines, and penalties so determined by the court shall be paid or deposited into the appropriate funds specified in division (D)(2)(c) of this section.

(E) As used in this section, "law enforcement agency" includes, but is not limited to, the state board of pharmacy.

(1995 H 1, eff. 1–1–96; 1993 H 152, eff. 7–1–93; 1992 S 174; 1990 S 258, H 266, H 261, H 215; 1986 S 74; 1985 H 5)

2923.36 Corrupt activity lien notice

(A) Upon the institution of any criminal proceeding charging a violation of section 2923.32 of the Revised Code, the filing of any complaint in juvenile court alleging a violation of that section as a delinquent act, or the institution of any civil proceeding under section 2923.32 or 2923.34 of the Revised Code, the state, at any time during the pendency of the proceeding, may file a corrupt activity lien notice with the county recorder of any county in which property subject to forfeiture may be located. No fee shall be required for filing the notice. The recorder immediately shall record the notice pursuant to section 317.08 of the Revised Code.

(B) A corrupt activity lien notice shall be signed by the prosecuting attorney who files the lien. The notice shall set forth all of the following information:

(1) The name of the person against whom the proceeding has been brought. The prosecuting attorney may specify in the notice any aliases, names, or fictitious names under which the person may be known. The prosecuting attorney also may specify any corporation, partnership, or other entity in which the person has an interest subject to forfeiture under section 2923.32 of the Revised Code and shall describe in the notice the person's interest in the corporation, partnership, or other entity.

(2) If known to the prosecuting attorney, the present residence and business addresses of the person or names set forth in the notice;

(3) A statement that a criminal or delinquency proceeding for a violation of section 2923.32 of the Revised Code or a civil proceeding under section 2923.32 or 2923.34 of the Revised Code has been brought against the person named in the notice, the name of the county in which the proceeding has been brought, and the case number of the proceeding;

(4) A statement that the notice is being filed pursuant to this section;

(5) The name and address of the prosecuting attorney filing the notice;

(6) A description of the real or personal property subject to the notice and of the interest in that property of the person named in the notice, to the extent the property and the interest of the person in it reasonably is known at the time the proceeding is instituted or at the time the notice is filed.

(C) A corrupt activity lien notice shall apply only to one person and, to the extent applicable, any aliases, fictitious names, or other names, including names of corporations, partnerships, or other entities, to the extent permitted in this section. A separate corrupt activity lien notice is required to be filed for any other person.

(D) Within seven days after the filing of each corrupt activity lien notice, the prosecuting attorney who files the notice shall furnish to the person named in the notice by certified mail, return receipt requested, to the last known business or residential address of the person, a copy of the recorded notice with a notation on it of any county in which the notice has been recorded. The failure of the prosecuting attorney to furnish a copy of the notice under this section shall not invalidate or otherwise affect the corrupt activity lien notice when the prosecuting attorney did not know and could not reasonably ascertain the address of the person entitled to notice.

After receipt of a copy of the notice under this division, the person named in the notice may petition the court to authorize the person to post a surety bond in lieu of the lien or to otherwise modify the lien as the interests of justice may require. The bond shall be in an amount equal to the value of the property reasonably known to be subject to the notice and conditioned on the payment of any judgment and costs ordered in an action pursuant to section 2923.32 or 2923.34 of the Revised Code up to the value of the bond.

(E) From the date of filing of a corrupt activity lien notice, the notice creates a lien in favor of the state on any personal or real property or any beneficial interest in the property located in the county in which the notice is filed that then or subsequently is owned by the person named in the notice or under any of the names set forth in the notice.

The lien created in favor of the state is superior and prior to the interest of any other person in the personal or real property or beneficial interest in the property, if the interest is acquired subsequent to the filing of the notice.

(F)(1) Notwithstanding any law or rule to the contrary, in conjunction with any civil proceeding brought pursuant to section 2923.34 of the Revised Code, the prosecuting attorney may file in any county, without prior court order, a lis pendens pursuant to sections 2703.26 and 2703.27 of the Revised Code. In such a case, any person acquiring an interest in the subject property or beneficial interest in the property, if the property interest is acquired subsequent to the filing of the lis pendens, shall take the property or interest subject to the civil proceeding and any subsequent judgment.

(2) If a corrupt activity lien notice has been filed, the prosecuting attorney may name as a defendant in the lis pendens, in addition to the person named in the notice, any person acquiring an interest in the personal or real property or beneficial interest in the property subsequent to the filing of the notice. If a judgment of forfeiture is entered in the criminal or delinquency proceeding pursuant to section 2923.32 of the Revised Code in favor of the state, the interest of any person in the property that was acquired subsequent to the filing of the notice shall be subject to the notice and judgment of forfeiture.

(G) Upon a final judgment of forfeiture in favor of the state pursuant to section 2923.32 of the Revised Code, title of the state to the forfeited property shall do either of the following:

(1) In the case of real property, or a beneficial interest in it, relate back to the date of filing of the corrupt activity lien notice in the county where the property or interest is located. If no corrupt activity lien notice was filed, title of the state relates back to the date of the filing of any lis pendens under division (F) of this section in the records of the county recorder of the county in which the real property or beneficial interest is located. If no corrupt activity lien notice or lis pendens was filed, title of the state relates back to the date of the recording of the final judgment of forfeiture in the records of the county recorder of the county in which the real property or beneficial interest is located.

(2) In the case of personal property or a beneficial interest in it, relate back to the date on which the property or interest was seized by the state, or the date of filing of a corrupt activity lien notice in the county in which the property or beneficial interest is located. If the property was not seized and no corrupt activity lien notice was filed, title of the state relates back to the date of the recording of the final judgment of forfeiture in the county in which the personal property or beneficial interest is located.

(H) If personal or real property, or a beneficial interest in it, that is subject to forfeiture pursuant to section 2923.32 of the Revised Code is conveyed, alienated, disposed of, or otherwise rendered unavailable for forfeiture after the filing of either a corrupt activity lien notice, or a criminal or delinquency proceeding for a violation of section 2923.32 or a civil proceeding under section 2923.32 or 2923.34 of the Revised Code, whichever is earlier, the state may bring an action in any court of common pleas against the person named in the corrupt activity lien notice or the defendant in the criminal, delinquency, or civil proceeding to recover the value of the property or interest. The court shall enter final judgment against the person named in the notice or the defendant for an amount equal to the value of the property or interest together with investigative costs and attorney's fees incurred by the state in the action. If a civil proceeding is pending, an action pursuant to this section shall be filed in the court in which the proceeding is pending.

(I) If personal or real property, or a beneficial interest in it, that is subject to forfeiture pursuant to section 2923.32 of the Revised Code is alienated or otherwise transferred or disposed of after either the filing of a corrupt activity lien notice, or the filing of a criminal or delinquency proceeding for a violation of section 2923.32 or a civil proceeding under section 2923.32 or 2923.34 of the Revised Code, whichever is earlier, the transfer or disposal is fraudulent as to the state and the state shall have all the rights granted a creditor under Chapter 1336. of the Revised Code.

(J) No trustee, who acquires actual knowledge that a corrupt activity lien notice, a criminal or delinquency proceeding for a violation of section 2923.32 or a civil proceeding under section 2923.32 or 2923.34 of the Revised Code has been filed against any person for whom he holds legal or record title to personal or real property, shall recklessly fail to furnish promptly to the prosecuting attorney all of the following:

(1) The name and address of the person, as known to the trustee;

(2) The name and address, as known to the trustee, of all other persons for whose benefit the trustee holds title to the property;

(3) If requested by the prosecuting attorney, a copy of the trust agreement or other instrument under which the trustee holds title to the property.

Any trustee who fails to comply with this division is guilty of failure to provide corrupt activity lien information, a misdemeanor of the first degree.

(K) If a trustee transfers title to personal or real property after a corrupt activity lien notice is filed against the property, the lien is filed in the county in which the property is located, and the lien names a person who holds a beneficial interest in the property, the trustee if he has actual notice of the notice, shall be liable to the state for the greater of the following:

(1) The proceeds received directly by the person named in the notice as a result of the transfer;

(2) The proceeds received by the trustee as a result of the transfer and distributed to the person named in the notice;

(3) The fair market value of the interest of the person named in the notice in the property transferred.

However, if the trustee transfers property for at least its fair market value and holds the proceeds that otherwise would be paid or distributed to the beneficiary, or at the direction of the beneficiary or his designee, the liability of the trustee shall not exceed the amount of the proceeds held by the trustee.

(L) The filing of a corrupt activity lien notice does not constitute a lien on the record title to personal or real property owned by the trustee, except to the extent the trustee is named in the notice.

The prosecuting attorney for the county may bring a civil action in any court of common pleas to recover from the trustee the amounts set forth in division (H) of this section. The county may recover investigative costs and attorney's fees incurred by the prosecuting attorney.

(M)(1) This section does not apply to any transfer by a trustee under a court order, unless the order is entered in an action between the trustee and the beneficiary.

(2) Unless the trustee has actual knowledge that a person owning a beneficial interest in the trust is named in a corrupt activity lien notice or otherwise is a defendant in a civil proceeding brought pursuant to section 2923.34 of the Revised Code, this section does not apply to either of the following:

(a) Any transfer by a trustee required under the terms of any trust agreement, if the agreement is a matter of public record before the filing of any corrupt activity lien notice;

(b) Any transfer by a trustee to all of the persons who own a beneficial interest in the trust.

(N) The filing of a corrupt activity lien notice does not affect the use to which personal or real property, or a beneficial interest in it, that is owned by the person named in the notice may be put or the right of the person to receive any proceeds resulting from the use and ownership, but not the sale, of the property, until a judgment of forfeiture is entered.

(O) The term of a corrupt activity lien notice is five years from the date the notice is filed, unless a renewal notice has been filed by the prosecuting attorney of the county in which the property or interest is located. The term of any renewal of a corrupt activity lien notice granted by the court is five years from the date of its filing. A corrupt activity lien notice may be renewed any number of times while a criminal or civil proceeding under section 2923.32 or 2923.34 of the Revised Code, or an appeal from either type of proceeding, is pending.

(P) The prosecuting attorney who files the corrupt activity lien notice may terminate, in whole or part, any corrupt activity lien notice or release any personal or real property or beneficial interest in the property upon any terms that he determines are appropriate. Any termination or release shall be filed by the prosecuting attorney with each county recorder with whom the notice was filed. No fee shall be imposed for the filing.

(Q)(1) If no civil proceeding has been brought by the prosecuting attorney pursuant to section 2923.34 of the Revised Code against the person named in the corrupt activity lien notice, the acquittal in a criminal or delinquency proceeding for a violation of section 2923.32 of the Revised Code of the person named in the notice or the dismissal of a criminal or delinquency proceeding for such a violation against the person named in the notice terminates the notice. In such a case, the filing of the notice has no effect.

(2) If a civil proceeding has been brought pursuant to section 2923.34 of the Revised Code with respect to any property that is the subject of a corrupt activity lien notice and if the criminal or delinquency proceeding brought against the person named in the notice for a violation of section 2923.32 of the Revised Code has been dismissed or the person named in the notice has been acquitted in the criminal or delinquency proceeding for such a violation, the notice shall continue for the duration of the civil proceeding and any appeals from the civil proceeding, except that it shall not continue any longer than the term of the notice as determined pursuant to division (O) of this section.

(3) If no civil proceeding brought pursuant to section 2923.34 of the Revised Code then is pending against the person named in a corrupt activity lien notice, any person so named may bring an action against the prosecuting attorney who filed the notice, in the county where it was filed, seeking a release of the property subject to the notice or termination of the notice. In such a case, the court of common pleas promptly shall set a date for hearing, which shall be not less than five nor more than ten days after the action is filed. The order and a copy of the complaint shall be served on the prosecuting attorney within three days after the action is filed. At the hearing, the court shall take evidence as to whether any personal or real property, or beneficial interest in it, that is owned by the person bringing the action is covered by the notice or otherwise is subject to forfeiture. If the person bringing the action shows by a preponderance of the evidence that the notice does not apply to him or that any personal or real property, or beneficial interest in it, that is owned by him is not subject to forfeiture, the court shall enter a judgment terminating the notice or releasing the personal or real property or beneficial interest from the notice.

At a hearing, the court may release from the notice any property or beneficial interest upon the posting of security, by the person against whom the notice was filed, in an amount equal to the value of the property or beneficial interest owned by the person.

(4) The court promptly shall enter an order terminating a corrupt activity lien notice or releasing any personal or real property or beneficial interest in the property, if a sale of the property or beneficial interest is pending and the filing of the notice prevents the sale. However, the proceeds of the sale shall be deposited with the clerk of the court, subject to the further order of the court.

(R) Notwithstanding any provision of this section, any person who has perfected a security interest in personal or real property or a beneficial interest in the property for the payment of an enforceable debt or other similar obligation prior to the filing of a corrupt activity lien notice or a lis pendens in reference to the property or interest may foreclose on the property or interest as otherwise provided by law. The foreclosure, insofar as practical, shall be made so that it otherwise will not interfere with a forfeiture under section 2923.32 of the Revised Code.

(1990 H 506, eff. 9–28–90; 1990 H 266; 1989 H 190; 1985 H 5)

Historical and Statutory Notes

Ed. Note: A special endorsement by the Legislative Service Commission states, "Comparison of these amendments [1990 H 506, eff. 9–28–90 and 1990 H 266, eff. 9–6–90] in pursuance of section 1.52 of the Revised Code discloses that they are not irreconcilable, so that they are required by that section to be harmonized to give effect to each amendment." In recognition of this rule of construction, changes made by 1990 H 506, eff. 9–28–90 and 1990 H 266, eff. 9–6–90 have been incorporated in the above amendment. See *Baldwin's Ohio Legislative Service*, 1990 Laws of Ohio, pages 5–649 and 5–639, for original versions of these Acts.

2923.41 Disturbing the peace; penalties—Repealed

(1972 H 511, eff. 1–1–74; 1971 H 344; 125 v 211)

2923.42 Giving false information to officials—Repealed

(1972 H 511, eff. 1–1–74; 129 v 376, 582; 128 v 623)

2923.43 Interference with authorized persons at emergency scenes—Repealed

(1972 H 511, eff. 1–1–74; 132 v H 332)

2923.51 Disbursing of riotous group—Repealed

(1972 H 511, eff. 1–1–74; 132 v H 996)

2923.52 Riot, second degree—Repealed

(1972 H 511, eff. 1–1–74; 132 v H 996)

2923.53 Riot, first degree—Repealed

(1972 H 511, eff. 1–1–74; 132 v H 996)

2923.54 Inciting to riot—Repealed

(1972 H 511, eff. 1–1–74; 132 v H 996)

2923.55 Liability of law enforcement officer for use of force during riot—Repealed

(1972 H 511, eff. 1–1–74; 132 v H 996)

2923.56 Persons prohibited from obtaining or having firearms—Repealed

(1972 H 511, eff. 1–1–74; 1969 H 484)

2923.57 Transactions in firearms permitted between Ohio and contiguous states—Repealed

(1972 H 511, eff. 1–1–74; 1969 H 484)

2923.61 Disrupting orderly conduct of a college or university—Repealed

(1972 H 511, eff. 1–1–74; 1970 H 1219)

2923.99 Penalties—Repealed

(129 v 582, eff. 1–10–61; 127 v 460)

CHAPTER 2925

DRUG OFFENSES

DEFINITIONS

DEFINITIONS

2925.01 Definitions

As used in this chapter:

(A) "Administer," "controlled substance," "dispense," "distribute," "federal drug abuse control laws," "hypodermic," "manufacturer," "marihuana," "official written order," "person," "pharmacist," "pharmacy," "practitioner," "prescription," "sale," "schedule I," "schedule II," "schedule III," "schedule IV," "schedule V," and "wholesaler" have the same meanings as in section 3719.01 of the Revised Code.

(B) "Drug dependent person" and "drug of abuse" have the same meanings as in section 3719.011 of the Revised Code.

(C) "Drug," "dangerous drug," and "Federal Food, Drug, and Cosmetic Act" have the same meanings as in section 4729.02 of the Revised Code.

(D) "Actual incarceration" has the same meaning as in division (C) of section 2929.01 of the Revised Code.

(E) "Bulk amount" of a controlled substance means any of the following:

(1) An amount equal to or exceeding ten grams or twenty-five unit doses of a compound, mixture, preparation, or substance that is or contains any amount of a schedule I opiate or opium derivative, or cocaine;

194

(2) An amount equal to or exceeding ten grams of a compound, mixture, preparation, or substance that is or contains any amount of raw or gum opium;

(3) An amount equal to or exceeding two hundred grams of marihuana, or an amount equal to or exceeding ten grams of the resin contained in marihuana or of any extraction or preparation of the resin contained in marihuana, or equal to or exceeding two grams of the resin contained in marihuana in a liquid concentrate, liquid extract, or liquid distillate form;

(4) An amount equal to or exceeding thirty grams or ten unit doses of a compound, mixture, preparation, or substance that is or contains any amount of a schedule I hallucinogen other than tetrahydrocannabinol, lysergic acid diethylamide, lysergic acid amide, or marihuana, or a schedule I stimulant or depressant;

(5) An amount equal to or exceeding twenty grams or five times the maximum daily dose in the usual dose range specified in a standard pharmaceutical reference manual of a compound, mixture, preparation, or substance that is or contains any amount of a schedule II opiate or opium derivative;

(6) An amount equal to or exceeding one gram or ten unit doses of a compound, mixture, preparation, or substance that is or contains any amount of lysergic acid diethylamide, lysergic acid amide, or tetrahydrocannabinol;

(7) An amount equal to or exceeding five grams or ten unit doses of a compound, mixture, preparation, or substance that is or contains any amount of phencyclidine;

(8) An amount equal to or exceeding one hundred twenty grams or thirty times the maximum daily dose in the usual dose range specified in a standard pharmaceutical reference manual of a compound, mixture, preparation, or substance that is or contains any amount of a schedule II stimulant that is in a final dosage form manufactured by a person authorized by the Federal Food, Drug, and Cosmetic Act and the federal drug abuse control laws, that is or contains any amount of a schedule II depressant substance or a schedule II hallucinogenic substance, of [*sic*] that is or contains any amount of a schedule III or IV substance other than an anabolic steroid;

(9) An amount equal to or exceeding three grams of a compound, mixture, preparation, or substance that is or contains any amount of a schedule II stimulant, or any of its salts or isomers, that is not in a final dosage form manufactured by a person authorized by the Federal Food, Drug, and Cosmetic Act and the federal drug abuse control laws;

(10) An amount equal to or exceeding two hundred fifty milliliters or two hundred fifty grams of a compound, mixture, preparation, or substance that is or contains any amount of a schedule V substance;

(11) An amount equal to or exceeding two hundred solid dosage units, sixteen grams, or sixteen milliliters of a compound, mixture, preparation, or substance that is or contains any amount of a schedule III anabolic steroid.

(F) "Unit dose" means an amount or unit of a compound, mixture, or preparation containing a controlled substance, such amount or unit being separately identifiable and in such form as to indicate that it is the amount or unit by which the controlled substance is separately administered to or taken by an individual.

(G) "Cultivate" includes planting, watering, fertilizing, or tilling.

(H) "Drug abuse offense" means any of the following:

(1) A violation of division (B) of section 2913.02 that constitutes theft of drugs, or a violation of section 2925.02, 2925.03, 2925.11, 2925.12, 2925.13, 2925.22, 2925.23, 2925.31, 2925.32, 2925.36, or 2925.37 of the Revised Code;

(2) A violation of an existing or former law of this or any other state or of the United States that is substantially equivalent to any section listed in division (H)(1) of this section;

(3) An offense under an existing or former law of this or any other state, or of the United States, of which planting, cultivating, harvesting, processing, making, manufacturing, producing, shipping, transporting, delivering, acquiring, possessing, storing, distributing, dispensing, selling, inducing another to use, administering to another, using, or otherwise dealing with a controlled substance is an element;

(4) A conspiracy or attempt to commit, or complicity in committing or attempting to commit, any offense under division (H)(1), (2), or (3) of this section.

(I) "Felony drug abuse offense" means any drug abuse offense that would constitute a felony under the laws of this state, except a violation of section 2925.11 of the Revised Code.

(J) "Harmful intoxicant" does not include beer or intoxicating liquor, but means any compound, mixture, preparation, or substance the gas, fumes, or vapor of which when inhaled can induce intoxication, excitement, giddiness, irrational behavior, depression, stupefaction, paralysis, unconsciousness, asphyxiation, or other harmful physiological effects, and includes, but is not limited to, any of the following:

(1) Any volatile organic solvent, plastic cement, model cement, fingernail polish remover, lacquer thinner, cleaning fluid, gasoline, and any other preparation containing a volatile organic solvent;

(2) Any aerosol propellant;

(3) Any fluorocarbon refrigerant;

(4) Any anesthetic gas.

(K) "Manufacture" means to plant, cultivate, harvest, process, make, prepare, or otherwise engage in any part of the production of a drug, by propagation, extraction, chemical synthesis, or compounding, or any combination of the same, and includes packaging, repackaging, labeling, and other activities incident to production.

(L) "Possess" or "possession" means having control over a thing or substance but may not be inferred solely from mere access to the thing or substance through ownership or occupation of the premises upon which the thing or substance is found.

(M) "Sample drug" means a drug or pharmaceutical preparation that would be hazardous to health or safety if used without the supervision of a practitioner, or a drug of abuse, and that, at one time, had been placed in a container plainly marked as a sample by a manufacturer.

(N) "Standard pharmaceutical reference manual" means the current edition, with cumulative changes if any, of any of the following reference works:

(1) "The National Formulary";

(2) "The United States Pharmacopeia," prepared by authority of the United States Pharmacopeial Convention, Inc.;

(3) Other standard references that are approved by the state board of pharmacy.

(O) "Juvenile" means a person under eighteen years of age.

(P) "Counterfeit controlled substance" means any of the following:

(1) Any drug that bears, or whose container or label bears, a trademark, trade name, or other identifying mark used without authorization of the owner of rights to such trademark, trade name, or identifying mark;

(2) Any unmarked or unlabeled substance that is represented to be a controlled substance manufactured, processed, packed, or distributed by a person other than the person that manufactured, processed, packed, or distributed it;

(3) Any substance that is represented to be a controlled substance but is not a controlled substance or is a different controlled substance;

(4) Any substance other than a controlled substance that a reasonable person would believe to be a controlled substance because of its similarity in shape, size, and color, or its markings, labeling, packaging, distribution, or the price for which it is sold or offered for sale.

(Q) "School" means any school operated by a board of education or any school for which the state board of education prescribes minimum standards under section 3301.07 of the Revised Code, whether or not any instruction, extracurricular activities, or training provided by the school is being conducted at the time a criminal offense is committed.

(R) "School premises" means either of the following:

(1) The parcel of real property on which any school is situated, whether or not any instruction, extracurricular activities, or training provided by the school is being conducted on the premises at the time a criminal offense is committed;

(2) Any other parcel of real property that is owned or leased by a board of education of a school or the governing body of a school for which the state board of education prescribes minimum standards under section 3301.07 of the Revised Code and on which some of the instruction, extracurricular activities, or training of the school is conducted, whether or not any instruction, extracurricular activities, or training provided by the school is being conducted on the parcel of real property at the time a criminal offense is committed.

(S) "School building" means any building in which any of the instruction, extracurricular activities, or training provided by a school is conducted, whether or not any instruction, extracurricular activities, or training provided by the school is being conducted in the school building at the time a criminal offense is committed.

(T) "Disciplinary counsel" means the disciplinary counsel appointed by the board of commissioners on grievances and discipline of the supreme court under the Rules for the Government of the Bar of Ohio.

(U) "Certified grievance committee" means a duly constituted and organized committee of the Ohio state bar association or of one or more local bar associations of the state of Ohio that complies with the criteria set forth in Rule V, section 6 of the Rules for the Government of the Bar of Ohio.

(V) "Professional license" means any license, permit, certificate, registration, qualification, admission, temporary license, temporary permit, temporary certificate, or temporary registration that is described in divisions (W)(1) to (35) of this section and that qualifies a person as a professionally licensed person.

(W) "Professionally licensed person" means any of the following:

(1) A person who has obtained a license as a manufacturer of controlled substances or a wholesaler of controlled substances under Chapter 3719. of the Revised Code;

(2) A person who has received a certificate or temporary certificate as a certified public accountant or who has registered as a public accountant under Chapter 4701. of the Revised Code and who holds a live permit issued under that chapter;

(3) A person who holds a certificate of qualification to practice architecture issued or renewed and registered under Chapter 4703. of the Revised Code;

(4) A person who is registered as a landscape architect under Chapter 4703. of the Revised Code or who holds a permit as a landscape architect issued under that chapter;

(5) A person licensed as an auctioneer or apprentice auctioneer or licensed to operate an auction company under Chapter 4707. of the Revised Code;

(6) A person who has been issued a certificate of registration as a registered barber under Chapter 4709. of the Revised Code;

(7) A person licensed and regulated to engage in the business of a debt pooling company by a legislative authority, under authority of Chapter 4710. of the Revised Code;

(8) A person who has been issued a cosmetologist's license, manicurist's license, esthetician's license, managing cosmetologist's license, managing manicurist's license, managing esthetician's license, cosmetology instructor's license, manicurist instructor's license, esthetician instructor's license, or tanning facility permit under Chapter 4713. of the Revised Code;

(9) A person who has been issued a license to practice dentistry, a general anesthesia permit, a conscious intravenous sedation permit, a limited resident's license, a limited teaching license, a dental hygienist's license, or a dental hygienist's teacher's certificate under Chapter 4715. of the Revised Code;

(10) A person who has been issued an embalmer's license, a funeral director's license, or a funeral home license, or who has been registered for a funeral director's apprenticeship under Chapter 4717. of the Revised Code;

(11) A person who has been licensed as a registered nurse or practical nurse, or who has been issued a certificate for the practice of nurse-midwifery under Chapter 4723. of the Revised Code;

(12) A person who has been licensed to practice optometry or to engage in optical dispensing under Chapter 4725. of the Revised Code;

(13) A person licensed to act as a pawnbroker under Chapter 4727. of the Revised Code;

(14) A person licensed to act as a precious metals dealer under Chapter 4728. of the Revised Code;

(15) A person registered as a pharmacist, a pharmacy intern, a wholesale distributor of dangerous drugs, or a terminal distributor of dangerous drugs under Chapter 4729. of the Revised Code;

(16) A person who is authorized to practice as a physician assistant under Chapter 4730. of the Revised Code;

(17) A person who has been issued a certificate to practice medicine and surgery, osteopathic medicine and surgery, a limited branch of medicine or surgery, or podiatry under Chapter 4731. of the Revised Code;

(18) A person licensed as a psychologist or school psychologist under Chapter 4732. of the Revised Code;

(19) A person registered to practice the profession of engineering or surveying under Chapter 4733. of the Revised Code;

(20) A person who has been issued a certificate to practice chiropractic under Chapter 4734. of the Revised Code;

(21) A person licensed to act as a real estate broker, real estate salesman, limited real estate broker, or limited real estate salesman under Chapter 4735. of the Revised Code;

(22) A person registered as a registered sanitarian under Chapter 4736. of the Revised Code;

(23) A person licensed to operate or maintain a junkyard under Chapter 4737. of the Revised Code;

(24) A person who has been issued a motor vehicle salvage dealer's license under Chapter 4738. of the Revised Code;

(25) A person who has been licensed to act as a steam engineer under Chapter 4739. of the Revised Code;

(26) A person who has been issued a license or temporary permit to practice veterinary medicine or any of its branches, or who is registered as a graduate animal technician under Chapter 4741. of the Revised Code;

(27) A person who has been issued a hearing aid dealer's or fitter's license or trainee permit under Chapter 4747. of the Revised Code;

(28) A person who has been issued a class A, class B, or class C license or who has been registered as an investigator or security guard employee under Chapter 4749. of the Revised Code;

(29) A person licensed and registered to practice as a nursing home administrator under Chapter 4751. of the Revised Code;

(30) A person licensed to practice as a speech pathologist or audiologist under Chapter 4753. of the Revised Code;

(31) A person issued a license as an occupational therapist or physical therapist under Chapter 4755. of the Revised Code;

(32) A person who is licensed as a professional counselor, registered as a counselor assistant, licensed as a social worker or independent social worker, or registered as a social work assistant under Chapter 4757. of the Revised Code;

(33) A person issued a license to practice dietetics under Chapter 4759. of the Revised Code;

(34) A person who has been issued a license or temporary permit to practice respiratory therapy under Chapter 4761. of the Revised Code;

(35) A person who has been issued a real estate appraiser certificate under Chapter 4763. of the Revised Code.

This is an interim section effective until July 1, 1996.

(1995 S 143, § 1, eff. 3–5–96; 1993 H 156, eff. 5–19–93; 1991 H 322, H 62; 1990 S 258, H 215; 1985 H 281; 1982 H 269, § 4, S 199, H 535; 1980 S 378, H 900; 1978 H 565; 1976 S 414; 1975 H 300)

CORRUPTION WITH DRUGS; TRAFFICKING

2925.02 Corrupting another with drugs

(A) No person shall knowingly do any of the following:

(1) By force, threat, or deception, administer to another or induce or cause another to use a controlled substance;

(2) By any means, administer or furnish to another or induce or cause another to use a controlled substance with purpose to cause serious physical harm to the other person, or with purpose to cause the other person to become drug dependent;

(3) By any means, administer or furnish to another or induce or cause another to use a controlled substance, and thereby cause serious physical harm to the other person, or cause the other person to become drug dependent;

(4) By any means, do any of the following:

(a) Furnish or administer a controlled substance to a juvenile who is at least two years his junior, when the offender knows the age of the juvenile or is reckless in that regard;

(b) Induce or cause a juvenile who is at least two years his junior to use a controlled substance, when the offender knows the age of the juvenile or is reckless in that regard;

(c) Induce or cause a juvenile who is at least two years his junior to commit a felony drug abuse offense, when the offender knows the age of the juvenile or is reckless in that regard;

(d) Use a juvenile, whether or not the offender knows the age of the juvenile, to perform any surveillance activity that is intended to prevent the detection of the offender or any other person in the commission of a felony drug abuse offense or to prevent the arrest of the offender or any other person for the commission of a felony drug abuse offense.

(B) Division (A)(1), (3), or (4) of this section does not apply to manufacturers, wholesalers, practitioners, pharmacists, owners of pharmacies, and other persons whose conduct is in accordance with Chapters 3719., 4715., 4729., 4731., and 4741. of the Revised Code or section 4723.56 of the Revised Code.

(C) Whoever violates this section is guilty of corrupting another with drugs:

(1) If the drug involved is any compound, mixture, preparation, or substance included in schedule I or II, with the exception of marihuana, corrupting another with drugs is a felony of the first degree, and the court shall impose a sentence of actual incarceration of seven years, except that if the offender commits the offense on school premises, in a school building, or within one thousand feet of the boundaries of any school premises or if the offender previously has been convicted of a felony drug abuse offense, the court shall impose a sentence of actual incarceration of twelve years.

(2) If the drug involved is any compound, mixture, preparation, or substance included in schedule III, IV, or V, corrupting another with drugs is one of the following:

(a) If the offender did not commit the offense on school premises, in a school building, or within one thousand feet of the boundaries of any school premises, a felony of the second degree, and the court shall impose a sentence of actual incarceration of three years, except that, if the offender previously has been convicted of a felony drug abuse offense, the court shall impose a sentence of actual incarceration of five years.

(b) If the offender did commit the offense on school premises, in a school building, or within one thousand feet of the boundaries of any school premises, a felony of the first degree, and the court shall impose a sentence of actual incarceration of seven years, except that, if the offender previously has been convicted of a felony drug abuse offense, the court shall impose a sentence of actual incarceration of twelve years.

(3) If the drug involved is marihuana, corrupting another with drugs is one of the following:

(a) If the offender did not commit the offense on school premises, in a school building, or within one thousand feet of the boundaries of any school premises, a felony of the fourth degree, and the court shall impose a sentence of actual incarceration of three months, except that, if the offender previously has been convicted of a felony drug abuse offense, the court shall impose a sentence of actual incarceration of six months.

(b) If the offender did commit the offense on school premises, in a school building, or within one thousand feet of the boundaries of any school premises, a felony of the third degree, and the court shall impose a sentence of actual incarceration of one year, except that, if the offender previously has been convicted of a felony drug abuse offense, the court shall impose a sentence of actual incarceration of two years.

(D)(1) Notwithstanding the fines otherwise required to be imposed pursuant to section 2929.11 or 2929.31 of the Revised Code for violations of this section and notwithstanding section 2929.14 of the Revised Code, the court shall impose a mandatory fine of five thousand dollars if the violation of this section was a felony of the first degree, a mandatory fine of three thousand five hundred dollars if the violation of this section was a felony of the second degree, a mandatory fine of two thousand five hundred dollars if the violation of this section was a felony of the third degree, and a mandatory fine of one thousand five hundred dollars if the violation of this section was a felony of the fourth degree.

(2) The court may impose a fine in addition to a mandatory fine imposed pursuant to division (D)(1) of this section if the total of the additional and mandatory fines does not exceed the maximum fine that could be imposed pursuant to section 2929.11 or 2929.31 of the Revised Code.

(3) Notwithstanding any contrary provision of section 3719.21 of the Revised Code, fifty per cent of any mandatory fine imposed pursuant to division (D)(1) of this section shall be paid by the clerk of the court in accordance with and subject to the requirements of, and shall be used as specified in, division (J) of section 2925.03 of the Revised Code, and fifty per cent shall be disbursed as provided in section 3719.21 of the Revised Code. Any additional fine imposed pursuant to division (D)(2) of this section shall be disbursed by the clerk of the court as otherwise provided by law.

(4) If a person is charged with any violation of this section and posts bail pursuant to sections 2937.22 to 2937.46 of the Revised Code or Criminal Rule 46, and if the person forfeits the bail, the forfeited bail shall be paid by the clerk of the court in accordance with and subject to the requirements of, and shall be used as specified in, division (D)(3) of this section.

(5) No court shall impose a mandatory fine pursuant to division (D)(1) of this section upon an offender who alleges, in an affidavit filed with the court prior to his sentencing, that he is indigent and is unable to pay any mandatory fine imposed pursuant to that division, if the court determines the offender is an indigent person and is unable to pay the fine.

(E) In addition to any other penalty imposed for a violation of this section, the court may revoke, and, if it does not revoke the license, shall suspend for not less than six months nor more than five years, the driver's or commercial driver's license of any person who is convicted of or pleads guilty to a violation of this section that is a felony of the first degree and shall suspend for not less than six months nor more than five years the driver's or commercial driver's license of any person who is convicted of or pleads guilty to any other violation of this section. If an offender's driver's or commercial driver's license is revoked pursuant to this division, the offender, at any time after the expiration of two years from the day on which his sentence was imposed or from the day on which he finally was released from imprisonment under the sentence, whichever is later, may file a motion with the sentencing court requesting termination of the revocation; upon the filing of such a motion and the court's finding of good cause for the termination, the court may terminate the revocation.

If the offender is a professionally licensed person or a person who has been admitted to the bar by order of the supreme court in compliance with its prescribed and published rules, in addition to any other penalty imposed for a violation of this section, the court forthwith shall comply with section 2925.38 of the Revised Code.

(1994 H 391, eff. 7–21–94; 1993 H 377, eff. 9–30–93; 1992 H 591; 1990 S 258, H 215; 1975 H 300)

2925.03 Trafficking offenses; sentences; mandatory fines; written internal control policy on use and disposition of fines; records and reports

(A) No person shall knowingly do any of the following:

(1) Sell or offer to sell a controlled substance in an amount less than the minimum bulk amount;

(2) Prepare for shipment, ship, transport, deliver, prepare for distribution, or distribute a controlled substance, when the offender knows or has reasonable cause to believe the controlled substance is intended for sale or resale by the offender or another;

(3) Cultivate, manufacture, or otherwise engage in any part of the production of a controlled substance;

(4) Possess a controlled substance in an amount equal to or exceeding the bulk amount, but in an amount less than three times that amount;

(5) Sell or offer to sell a controlled substance in an amount equal to or exceeding the bulk amount, but in an amount less than three times that amount;

(6) Possess a controlled substance in an amount equal to or exceeding three times the bulk amount, but in an amount less than one hundred times that amount;

(7) Sell or offer to sell a controlled substance in an amount equal to or exceeding three times the bulk amount, but in an amount less than one hundred times that amount;

(8) Provide money or other items of value to another person with the purpose that the recipient of the money or items of value would use them to obtain controlled substances for the purpose of selling or offering to sell the controlled substances in amounts exceeding a bulk amount or for the purpose of violating division (A)(3) of this section;

(9) Possess a controlled substance in an amount equal to or exceeding one hundred times the bulk amount;

(10) Sell or offer to sell a controlled substance in an amount equal to or exceeding one hundred times the bulk amount;

(11) Administer to a human being, or prescribe or dispense for administration to a human being, any anabolic steroid not approved by the United States food and drug administration for administration to human beings.

(B) This section does not apply to the following:

(1) Manufacturers, practitioners, pharmacists, owners of pharmacies, and other persons whose conduct is in accordance with Chapters 3719., 4715., 4729., 4731., and 4741. of the Revised Code or section 4723.56 of the Revised Code;

(2) If the offense involves an anabolic steroid, any person who is conducting or participating in a research project involving the use of an anabolic steroid if the project has been approved by the United States food and drug administration;

(3) Any person who sells, offers for sale, prescribes, dispenses, or administers for livestock or other nonhuman species an anabolic steroid that is expressly intended for administration through implants to livestock or other nonhuman species and approved for that purpose under the "Federal Food, Drug, and Cosmetic Act," 52 Stat. 1040 (1938), 21 U.S.C.A. 301, as amended, and is sold, offered for sale, prescribed, dispensed, or administered for that purpose in accordance with that act.

(C) If the drug involved is any compound, mixture, preparation, or substance included in schedule I, with the exception of marihuana, or in schedule II, whoever violates this section is guilty of aggravated trafficking.

(1) Where the offender has violated division (A)(1) of this section, aggravated trafficking is a felony of the third degree, except that aggravated trafficking is a felony of the second degree, if any of the following apply:

(a) The offender commits the offense on school premises, in a school building, or within one thousand feet of the boundaries of any school premises;

(b) The offender commits the offense within one hundred feet of any juvenile or within the view of any juvenile, whether or not the offender knows the age of the juvenile, the offender knows the juvenile is within one hundred feet or within view of the commission of the offense, or the juvenile views the commission of the offense;

(c) The offender previously has been convicted of a felony drug abuse offense.

(2) Where the offender has violated division (A)(2) of this section, aggravated trafficking is a felony of the third degree, except that, if the offender previously has been convicted of a felony drug abuse offense, aggravated trafficking is a felony of the second degree.

(3) Where the offender has violated division (A)(3) of this section, aggravated trafficking is a felony of the second degree, and the court shall impose a sentence of actual incarceration of three years, except that, if the offender previously has been convicted of a felony drug abuse offense, aggravated trafficking is a felony of the first degree, and the court shall impose a sentence of actual incarceration of five years.

(4) Where the offender has violated division (A)(4) of this section, aggravated trafficking is a felony of the third degree, and the court shall impose a sentence of actual incarceration of eighteen months, except that, if the offender previously has been convicted of a felony drug abuse offense, aggravated trafficking is a felony of the second degree, and the court shall impose a sentence of actual incarceration of three years.

(5) Where the offender has violated division (A)(5) of this section, aggravated trafficking is a felony of the second degree, and the court shall impose a sentence of actual incarceration of three years, except that aggravated trafficking is a felony of the first degree and the court shall impose a sentence of actual incarceration of five years, if any of the following apply:

(a) The offender commits the offense on school premises, in a school building, or within one thousand feet of the boundaries of any school premises;

(b) The offender commits the offense within one hundred feet of any juvenile or within the view of any juvenile, whether or not the offender knows the age of the juvenile, the offender knows the juvenile is within one hundred feet or within view of the commission of the offense, or the juvenile views the commission of the offense;

(c) The offender previously has been convicted of a felony drug abuse offense.

(6) Where the offender has violated division (A)(6) of this section, aggravated trafficking is a felony of the second degree, and the court shall impose a sentence of actual incarceration of three years, except that, if the offender previously has been convicted of a felony drug abuse offense, aggravated trafficking is a felony of the first degree, and the court shall impose a sentence of actual incarceration of five years.

(7) Where the offender has violated division (A)(7) of this section, aggravated trafficking is a felony of the first degree, and the court shall impose a sentence of actual incarceration of five years, except that the court shall impose a sentence of actual incarceration of at least seven years, if any of the following apply:

(a) The offender commits the offense on school premises, in a school building, or within one thousand feet of the boundaries of any school premises;

(b) The offender commits the offense within one hundred feet of any juvenile or within the view of any juvenile, whether or not the offender knows the age of the juvenile, the offender knows the juvenile is within one hundred feet or within view of the commission of the offense, or the juvenile views the commission of the offense;

(c) The offender previously has been convicted of a felony drug abuse offense.

(8) Where the offender has violated division (A)(8) of this section, aggravated trafficking is a felony of the first degree, and the court shall impose a sentence of actual incarceration of

seven years, except that, if the offender previously has been convicted of a felony drug abuse offense, the court shall impose a sentence of actual incarceration of ten years.

(9) Where the offender has violated division (A)(9) of this section, aggravated trafficking is a felony of the first degree, and the court shall impose an indefinite term of imprisonment of fifteen years to life for the offense, with the minimum term of fifteen years being a sentence of actual incarceration.

(10) Where the offender has violated division (A)(10) of this section, aggravated trafficking is a felony of the first degree, and the court shall impose an indefinite term of imprisonment of fifteen years to life for the offense, with the minimum term of fifteen years being a sentence of actual incarceration, except that the court shall impose an indefinite term of imprisonment of twenty years to life for the offense, with the minimum term of twenty years being a sentence of actual incarceration, if any of the following apply:

(a) The offender commits the offense on school premises, in a school building, or within one thousand feet of the boundaries of any school premises;

(b) The offender commits the offense within one hundred feet of any juvenile or within the view of any juvenile, whether or not the offender knows the age of the juvenile, the offender knows the juvenile is within one hundred feet or within view of the commission of the offense, or the juvenile views the commission of the offense;

(c) The offender previously has been convicted of a felony drug abuse offense.

(D) If the drug involved is any compound, mixture, preparation, or substance included in schedule III, IV, or V, whoever violates this section is guilty of trafficking in drugs.

(1) Where the offender has violated division (A)(1) of this section, trafficking in drugs is a felony of the fourth degree, except that trafficking in drugs is a felony of the third degree, if any of the following apply:

(a) The offender commits the offense on school premises, in a school building, or within one thousand feet of the boundaries of any school premises;

(b) The offender commits the offense within one hundred feet of any juvenile or within the view of any juvenile, whether or not the offender knows the age of the juvenile, the offender knows the juvenile is within one hundred feet or within view of the commission of the offense, or the juvenile views the commission of the offense;

(c) The offender previously has been convicted of a drug abuse offense.

(2) Where the offender has violated division (A)(2) or (11) of this section, trafficking in drugs is a felony of the fourth degree, except that, if the offender previously has been convicted of a drug abuse offense, trafficking in drugs is a felony of the third degree.

(3) Where the offender has violated division (A)(3) of this section, trafficking in drugs is a felony of the third degree, and the court shall impose a sentence of actual incarceration of one year, except that, if the offender previously has been convicted of a felony drug abuse offense, trafficking in drugs is a felony of the second degree, and the court shall impose a sentence of actual incarceration of two years.

(4) Where the offender has violated division (A)(4) of this section, trafficking in drugs is a felony of the fourth degree, and the court shall impose a sentence of actual incarceration of six months, except that, if the offender previously has been convicted of a felony drug abuse offense, trafficking in drugs is a felony of the third degree, and the court shall impose a sentence of actual incarceration of eighteen months.

(5) Where the offender has violated division (A)(5) of this section, trafficking in drugs is a felony of the third degree, and the court shall impose a sentence of actual incarceration of one year, except that trafficking in drugs is a felony of the second degree, and the court shall impose a sentence of actual incarceration of two years, if any of the following apply:

(a) The offender commits the offense on school premises, in a school building, or within one thousand feet of the boundaries of any school premises;

(b) The offender commits the offense within one hundred feet of any juvenile or within the view of any juvenile, whether or not the offender knows the age of the juvenile, the offender knows the juvenile is within one hundred feet or within view of the commission of the offense, or the juvenile views the commission of the offense;

(c) The offender previously has been convicted of a felony drug abuse offense.

(6) Where the offender has violated division (A)(6) or (9) of this section, trafficking in drugs is a felony of the third degree, and the court shall impose a sentence of actual incarceration of eighteen months, except that, if the offender previously has been convicted of a felony drug abuse offense, trafficking in drugs is a felony of the second degree, and the court shall impose a sentence of actual incarceration of three years.

(7) Where the offender has violated division (A)(7) or (10) of this section, trafficking in drugs is a felony of the second degree, and the court shall impose a sentence of actual incarceration of two years, except that trafficking in drugs is a felony of the first degree, and the court shall impose a sentence of actual incarceration of four years, if any of the following apply:

(a) The offender commits the offense on school premises, in a school building, or within one thousand feet of the boundaries of any school premises;

(b) The offender commits the offense within one hundred feet of any juvenile or within the view of any juvenile, whether or not the offender knows the age of the juvenile, the offender knows the juvenile is within one hundred feet or within view of the commission of the offense, or the juvenile views the commission of the offense;

(c) The offender previously has been convicted of a felony drug abuse offense.

(8) Where the offender has violated division (A)(8) of this section, trafficking in drugs is a felony of the first degree, and the court shall impose a sentence of actual incarceration of five years, except that, if the offender previously has been convicted of a felony drug abuse offense, the court shall impose a sentence of actual incarceration of seven years.

(E) If the drug involved is marihuana, whoever violates this section is guilty of trafficking in marihuana.

(1) Where the offender has violated division (A)(1) of this section, trafficking in marihuana is a felony of the fourth degree, except that trafficking in marihuana is a felony of the third degree, if any of the following apply:

(a) The offender commits the offense on school premises, in a school building, or within one thousand feet of the boundaries of any school premises;

(b) The offender commits the offense within one hundred feet of any juvenile or within the view of any juvenile, whether or not the offender knows the age of the juvenile, the offender knows the juvenile is within one hundred feet or within view of the commission of the offense, or the juvenile views the commission of the offense;

(c) The offender previously has been convicted of a felony drug abuse offense.

(2) Where the offender has violated division (A)(2), (3), or (4) of this section, trafficking in marihuana is a felony of the fourth degree, except that, if the offender previously has been convicted of a felony drug abuse offense, trafficking in marihuana is a felony of the third degree.

(3) Where the offender has violated division (A)(5) of this section, trafficking in marihuana is a felony of the third degree, except that trafficking in marihuana is a felony of the second degree, if any of the following apply:

(a) The offender commits the offense on school premises, in a school building, or within one thousand feet of the boundaries of any school premises;

(b) The offender commits the offense within one hundred feet of any juvenile or within the view of any juvenile, whether or not the offender knows the age of the juvenile, the offender knows the juvenile is within one hundred feet or within view of the commission of the offense, or the juvenile views the commission of the offense;

(c) The offender previously has been convicted of a felony drug abuse offense.

(4) Where the offender has violated division (A)(6) or (9) of this section, trafficking in marihuana is a felony of the third degree, except that, if the offender previously has been

convicted of a felony drug abuse offense, trafficking in marihuana is a felony of the second degree.

(5) Where the offender has violated division (A)(7) or (10) of this section, trafficking in marihuana is a felony of the second degree, and the court shall impose a sentence of actual incarceration of six months, except that the court shall impose a sentence of actual incarceration of one year, if any of the following apply:

(a) The offender commits the offense on school premises, in a school building, or within one thousand feet of the boundaries of any school premises;

(b) The offender commits the offense within one hundred feet of any juvenile or within the view of any juvenile, whether or not the offender knows the age of the juvenile, the offender knows the juvenile is within one hundred feet or within view of the commission of the offense, or the juvenile views the commission of the offense;

(c) The offender previously has been convicted of a felony drug abuse offense.

(6) Where the offender has violated division (A)(8) of this section, trafficking in marihuana is a felony of the second degree, and the court shall impose a sentence of actual incarceration of one year, except that, if the offender previously has been convicted of a felony drug abuse offense, the court shall impose a sentence of actual incarceration of two years.

(7) If the offense involves a gift of twenty grams or less of marihuana and the offense does not involve a violation of division (A)(1), (5), (7), or (10) of this section that was committed on school premises, in a school building, or within one thousand feet of the boundaries of any school premises or that was committed within one hundred feet of any juvenile or within the view of any juvenile, whether or not the offender knows the age of the juvenile, the offender knows the juvenile is within one hundred feet or within view of the commission of the offense, or the juvenile views the commission of the offense, trafficking in marihuana is a minor misdemeanor for the first offense, and, for any subsequent offense, it is a misdemeanor of the third degree. If the offense involves a gift of twenty grams or less of marihuana and the offense involves a violation of division (A)(1), (5), (7), or (10) of this section that was committed on school premises, in a school building, or within one thousand feet of the boundaries of any school premises or that was committed within one hundred feet of any juvenile or within the view of any juvenile, whether or not the offender knows the age of the juvenile, the offender knows the juvenile is within one hundred feet or within view of the commission of the offense, or the juvenile views the commission of the offense, trafficking in marihuana is a misdemeanor of the third degree.

(F) It shall be an affirmative defense, as provided in section 2901.05 of the Revised Code, to a charge under this section for possessing a bulk amount of a controlled substance or for cultivating marihuana that the substance that gave rise to the charge is in such amount, in such form, or is prepared, compounded, or mixed with substances that are not controlled substances in such a manner, or is possessed or cultivated in any other circumstances whatsoever as to indicate that the substance was solely for personal use.

(G) When a person is charged with possessing a bulk amount or a multiple of a bulk amount, the jury, or the court trying the accused, shall determine the amount of the controlled substance involved at the time of the offense and, if a guilty verdict is returned, shall return the findings as part of the verdict. In any such case, it is unnecessary to find and return the exact amount of the controlled substance, and it is sufficient if the finding and return is to the effect that the amount of the controlled substance involved is a bulk amount or the requisite multiple of a bulk amount, or that the amount of the controlled substance involved is less than a bulk amount or the requisite multiple of a bulk amount.

(H) Notwithstanding the fines otherwise required to be imposed pursuant to section 2929.11 or 2929.31 of the Revised Code for violations of this section and notwithstanding section 2929.14 of the Revised Code, the court shall impose the following mandatory fines upon a person convicted of aggravated trafficking, trafficking in drugs, or trafficking in marihuana:

(1) If the offense is trafficking in marihuana and a violation of division (A)(1) of this section, the court shall impose a mandatory fine of one thousand dollars, and if the offender has previously been convicted of a felony drug abuse offense, the court shall impose a mandatory fine of two thousand dollars.

(2) If the offense is trafficking in drugs and a violation of division (A)(1) of this section, the court shall impose a mandatory fine of one thousand five hundred dollars, and if the offender has previously been convicted of a felony drug abuse offense, the court shall impose a mandatory fine of three thousand dollars.

(3) If the offense is trafficking in marihuana and a violation of division (A)(2), (3), or (4) of this section, or if the offense is trafficking in drugs and a violation of division (A)(2) of this section, the court shall impose a mandatory fine of two thousand dollars, and if the offender has previously been convicted of a felony drug abuse offense, the court shall impose a mandatory fine of four thousand dollars.

(4) If the offense is aggravated trafficking and a violation of division (A)(1) of this section, or if the offense is trafficking in drugs and a violation of division (A)(3) of this section, the court shall impose a mandatory fine of two thousand five hundred dollars, and if the offender has previously been convicted of a felony drug abuse offense, the court shall impose a mandatory fine of five thousand dollars.

(5) If the offense is trafficking in marihuana and a violation of division (A)(5), (6), or (9) of this section, or if the offense is trafficking in drugs and a violation of division (A)(4), (5), (6), or (9) of this section, the court shall impose a mandatory fine of three thousand dollars, and if the offender has previously been convicted of a felony drug abuse offense, the court shall impose a mandatory fine of six thousand dollars.

(6) If the offense is trafficking in marihuana and a violation of division (A)(7) or (10) of this section, if the offense is trafficking in drugs and a violation of division (A)(7), (10), or (11) of this section, or if the offense is aggravated trafficking and a violation of division (A)(2), (4), (5), (6), or (9) of this section, the court shall impose a mandatory fine of five thousand dollars, and if the offender has previously been convicted of a felony drug abuse offense, the court shall impose a mandatory fine of ten thousand dollars.

(7) If the offense is aggravated trafficking and a violation of division (A)(3), (7), or (10) of this section, the court shall impose a mandatory fine of seven thousand five hundred dollars, and if the offender has previously been convicted of a felony drug abuse offense, the court shall impose a mandatory fine of fifteen thousand dollars.

(8) If the offense is trafficking in marihuana and a violation of division (A)(8) of this section or if the offense is trafficking in drugs and a violation of division (A)(8) of this section, the court shall impose a mandatory fine of ten thousand dollars, and if the offender has previously been convicted of a felony drug abuse offense, the court shall impose a mandatory fine of twenty thousand dollars.

(9) If the offense is aggravated trafficking and a violation of division (A)(8) of this section, the court shall impose a mandatory fine of twenty-five thousand dollars, and if the offender has previously been convicted of a felony drug abuse offense, the court shall impose a mandatory fine of fifty thousand dollars.

(I) When the mandatory fine imposed pursuant to division (H) of this section does not exceed the maximum fine that could be imposed pursuant to section 2929.11 or 2929.31 of the Revised Code, the court may impose an additional fine if the total of the mandatory and additional fines together does not exceed the maximum fine that could be imposed pursuant to section 2929.11 or 2929.31 of the Revised Code. When the mandatory fine exceeds the maximum fine that could be imposed pursuant to section 2929.11 or 2929.31 of the Revised Code, the court shall not impose an additional fine.

(J)(1) Notwithstanding any contrary provision of section 3719.21 of the Revised Code, any mandatory fine imposed pursuant to this section shall be paid by the clerk of the court to the county, township, municipal corporation, park district, as created pursuant to section 511.18 or 1545.04 of the Revised Code, or state law enforcement agencies in this state that primarily were responsible for or involved in making the arrest of, and in prosecuting, the offender. However, no mandatory fine so imposed shall be paid to a law enforcement agency unless the agency has adopted a written internal control policy under division (J)(2) of this section that addresses the use of the fine moneys that it receives. The mandatory fines so paid shall be used to subsidize each agency's law enforcement efforts that pertain to drug offenses, in accordance with the written internal control policy adopted by the recipient agency under division (J)(2) of this section. Any additional fine imposed pursuant to division (I) of this section shall be disbursed by the clerk of the court as otherwise provided by law.

(2)(a) Prior to receiving any fine moneys under division (J)(1) of this section or division (B)(5) of section 2925.42 of the Revised Code, a law enforcement agency shall adopt a written internal control policy that addresses the agency's use and disposition of all fine moneys so received and that provides for the keeping of detailed financial records of the receipts of those fine moneys, the general types of expenditures made out of those fine moneys, and the specific amount of each general type of expenditure. The policy shall not provide for or permit the identification of any specific expenditure that is made in an ongoing investigation. All financial records of the receipts of those fine moneys, the general types of expenditures made out of those fine moneys, and the specific amount of each general type of expenditure by an agency are public records open for inspection under section 149.43 of the Revised Code. Additionally, a written internal control policy adopted under this division is such a public record, and the agency that adopted it shall comply with it.

(b) Each law enforcement agency that receives in any calendar year any fine moneys under division (J)(1) of this section or division (B)(5) of section 2925.42 of the Revised Code shall prepare a report covering the calendar year that cumulates all of the information contained in all of the public financial records kept by the agency pursuant to division (J)(2)(a) of this section for that calendar year, and shall send a copy of the cumulative report, no later than the first day of March in the calendar year following the calendar year covered by the report, to the attorney general. Each report received by the attorney general is a public record open for inspection under section 149.43 of the Revised Code. The attorney general shall make copies of each report received, and, no later than the fifteenth day of April in the calendar year in which the report is received, shall send a copy of it to the president of the senate and the speaker of the house of representatives.

(3) As used in divisions (J) and (N) of this section:

(a) "Law enforcement agencies" includes, but is not limited to, the state board of pharmacy and the office of a prosecutor.

(b) "Prosecutor" has the same meaning as in section 2935.01 of the Revised Code.

(K) If a person is charged with any violation of this section and posts bail pursuant to sections 2937.22 to 2937.46 of the Revised Code or Criminal Rule 46, and if the person forfeits the bail, the forfeited bail shall be paid pursuant to division (J) of this section.

(L) No court shall impose a mandatory fine pursuant to division (H) of this section upon an offender who alleges, in an affidavit filed with the court prior to his sentencing, that he is indigent and is unable to pay any mandatory fine imposed pursuant to that division, if the court determines that the offender is an indigent person and is unable to pay the fine.

(M) In addition to any other penalty imposed for a violation of this section, the court may revoke, and, if it does not revoke the license, shall suspend for not less than six months nor more than five years, the driver's or commercial driver's license of any person who is convicted of or pleads guilty to a violation of this section that is a felony of the first degree and shall suspend for not less than six months nor more than five years the driver's or commercial driver's license of any person who is convicted of or pleads guilty to any other violation of this section. If an offender's driver's or commercial driver's license is revoked pursuant to this division, the offender, at any time after the expiration of two years from the day on which his sentence was imposed or from the day on which he finally was released from imprisonment under the sentence, whichever is later, may file a motion with the sentencing court requesting termination of the revocation; upon the filing of such a motion and the court's finding of good cause for the termination, the court may terminate the revocation.

If the offender is a professionally licensed person or a person who has been admitted to the bar by order of the supreme court in compliance with its prescribed and published rules, in addition to any other penalty imposed for a violation of this section, the court forthwith shall comply with section 2925.38 of the Revised Code.

(N) If a person commits any act that violates division (A)(11) of this section and also violates any other provision of the Revised Code, the prosecutor, using customary prosecutorial discretion, may prosecute the person for a violation of the appropriate provision of the Revised Code.

(1994 H 391, eff. 7–21–94; 1993 H 377, eff. 9–30–93; 1992 H 591, S 174; 1991 H 62; 1990 S 258, H 266, H 261, H 215; 1986 S 67; 1975 H 300)

2925.04 Sale or use of drugs not approved by Food and Drug Administration

(A) No person shall administer, dispense, distribute, manufacture, possess, sell, or use any drug, other than a controlled substance, that is not approved by the United States food and drug administration, or the United States department of agriculture, unless one of the following applies:

(1) The United States food and drug administration has approved an application for investigational use in accordance with the Federal Food, Drug, and Cosmetic Act," 52 Stat. 1040 (1938), 21 U.S.C.A. 301, as amended, and the drug is used only for the approved investigational use;

(2) The United States department of agriculture has approved an application for investigational use in accordance with the federal "Virus-Serum-Toxin Act," 37 Stat. 832 (1913), 21 U.S.C.A. as amended, 151, as amended, and the drug is used only for the approved investigational use;

(3) A practitioner, other than a veterinarian, prescribes or combines two or more drugs as a single product for medical purposes;

(4) A pharmacist, pursuant to a prescription, compounds and dispenses two or more drugs as a single product for medical purposes.

(B)(1) As used in this division, "dangerous drug," "prescription," "sale at retail," "wholesale distributor of dangerous drugs," and "terminal distributor of dangerous drugs," have the meanings set forth in section 4729.02 of the Revised Code.

(2) Except as provided in division (B)(3) of this section, no person shall administer, dispense, distribute, manufacture, possess, sell, or use any dangerous drug to or for livestock or any animal that is generally used for food or in the production of food, unless the drug is prescribed by a licensed veterinarian by prescription or other written order and the drug is used in accordance with the veterinarian's order or direction.

(3) Division (B)(2) of this section does not apply to a registered wholesale distributor of dangerous drugs, a licensed terminal distributor of dangerous drugs, or a person who possesses, possesses for sale, or sells, at retail, a drug in accordance with Chapters 3719., 4729., or 4741. of the Revised Code.

(C) Whoever violates division (A) or (B)(2) of this section is guilty of a felony of the fourth degree on a first offense. On each subsequent offense, the offender is guilty of a felony of the third degree.

(1995 H 202, eff. 6–14–95)

2925.11 Drug abuse; certain violations do not constitute criminal record

(A) No person shall knowingly obtain, possess, or use a controlled substance.

(B) This section does not apply to the following:

(1) Manufacturers, practitioners, pharmacists, owners of pharmacies, and other persons whose conduct was in accordance with Chapters 3719., 4715., 4729., 4731., and 4741. of the Revised Code or section 4723.56 of the Revised Code;

(2) If the offense involves an anabolic steroid, any person who is conducting or participating in a research project involving the use of an anabolic steroid if the project has been approved by the United States food and drug administration;

(3) Any person who sells, offers for sale, prescribes, dispenses, or administers for livestock or other nonhuman species an anabolic steroid that is expressly intended for administration through implants to livestock or other nonhuman species and approved for that purpose under the "Federal Food, Drug, and Cosmetic Act," 52 Stat. 1040 (1938), 21 U.S.C.A. 301, as

amended, and is sold, offered for sale, prescribed, dispensed, or administered for that purpose in accordance with that act;

(4) Any person who obtained the controlled substance pursuant to a prescription issued by a practitioner, where the drug is in the original container in which it was dispensed to such person.

(C) Whoever violates this section is guilty of drug abuse, and shall be sentenced as follows:

(1) If the drug involved is a compound, mixture, preparation, or substance included in schedule I or II, with the exception of marihuana, drug abuse is a felony of the fourth degree, and, if the offender previously has been convicted of a drug abuse offense, drug abuse is a felony of the third degree.

(2) If the drug involved is a compound, mixture, preparation, or substance included in schedule III, IV, or V, with the exception of an anabolic steroid, drug abuse is a misdemeanor of the third degree, and if the offender previously has been convicted of a drug abuse offense, drug abuse is a misdemeanor of the second degree.

(3) If the drug involved is marihuana, drug abuse is a misdemeanor of the fourth degree, unless the amount of marihuana involved is less than one hundred grams, the amount of marihuana resin, or extraction or preparation of such resin, is less than five grams, and the amount of such resin in a liquid concentrate, liquid extract, or liquid distillate form, is less than one gram, in which case drug abuse is a minor misdemeanor.

(4) If the drug involved is an anabolic steroid included in schedule III, drug abuse is a misdemeanor of the third degree and, in lieu of sentencing an offender to a definite or indefinite term of imprisonment in a detention facility, the court may place the offender on conditional probation pursuant to division (G) of this section or division (H) of section 2951.02 of the Revised Code, unless the offender previously has been convicted of a drug abuse offense, in which case drug abuse is a misdemeanor of the second degree.

(D) Arrest or conviction for a minor misdemeanor violation of this section does not constitute a criminal record and need not be reported by the person so arrested or convicted in response to any inquiries about the person's criminal record, including any inquiries contained in any application for employment, license, or other right or privilege, or made in connection with the person's appearance as a witness.

(E)(1) Notwithstanding the fines otherwise required to be imposed pursuant to section 2929.11, 2929.21, or 2929.31 of the Revised Code for violations of this section and notwithstanding section 2929.14 or 2929.22 of the Revised Code, the court shall impose a mandatory fine of two thousand five hundred dollars if the violation of this section was a felony of the third degree, a mandatory fine of one thousand five hundred dollars if the violation of this section was a felony of the fourth degree, a mandatory fine of seven hundred fifty dollars if the violation of this section was a misdemeanor of the second degree, a mandatory fine of five hundred dollars if the violation of this section was a misdemeanor of the third degree, a mandatory fine of two hundred fifty dollars if the violation of this section was a misdemeanor of the fourth degree, and a mandatory fine of one hundred dollars if the violation of this section was a minor misdemeanor.

(2) The court may impose a fine in addition to a mandatory fine imposed pursuant to division (E)(1) of this section if the total of the additional and mandatory fines does not exceed the maximum fine that could be imposed pursuant to section 2929.11, 2929.21, or 2929.31 of the Revised Code.

(3) Notwithstanding any contrary provision of section 3719.21 of the Revised Code, fifty per cent of any mandatory fine imposed pursuant to division (E)(1) of this section shall be paid by the clerk of the court in accordance with and subject to the requirements of, and shall be used as specified in, division (J) of section 2925.03 of the Revised Code, and fifty per cent shall be disbursed as provided in section 3719.21 of the Revised Code. Any additional fine imposed pursuant to division (E)(2) of this section shall be disbursed by the clerk of the court as otherwise provided by law.

(4) If a person is charged with any violation of this section and posts bail pursuant to sections 2937.22 to 2937.46 of the Revised Code or Criminal Rule 46, and if the person forfeits

the bail, the forfeited bail shall be paid by the clerk of the court in accordance with and subject to the requirements of, and shall be used as specified in, division (E)(3) of this section.

(5) No court shall impose a mandatory fine pursuant to division (E)(1) of this section upon an offender who alleges, in an affidavit filed with the court prior to his sentencing, that he is indigent and is unable to pay any mandatory fine imposed pursuant to that division, if the court determines the offender is an indigent person and is unable to pay the fine.

(F)(1) In addition to any other penalty imposed for a violation of this section, the court shall suspend for not less than six months nor more than five years the driver's or commercial driver's license of any person who is convicted of or has pleaded guilty to a violation of this section. Division (F)(1) of this section does not apply if the court is required to suspend a pregnant woman's sentence of imprisonment and place her on probation under the circumstances described in division (H) of this section, unless, at any time, the pregnant woman fails to comply with the condition of probation described in that division and her probation is revoked.

(2) If the offender is a professionally licensed person or a person who has been admitted to the bar by order of the supreme court in compliance with its prescribed and published rules, in addition to any other penalty imposed for a violation of this section, the court forthwith shall comply with section 2925.38 of the Revised Code. Division (F)(2) of this section does not apply if the court is required to suspend the sentence of imprisonment of, and to place on probation under the circumstances described in division (H) of this section, a pregnant woman who is a professionally licensed person or is a person who has been admitted to the bar by order of the supreme court, except that, if the pregnant woman at any time fails to comply with the condition of probation described in that division and if the court revokes her probation, the court then shall comply with section 2925.38 of the Revised Code.

(G)(1)(a) In lieu of sentencing an offender, who has pleaded guilty to a violation of this section prior to the commencement of the trial in the criminal action, to a definite or indefinite term of imprisonment in a detention facility, the court may place the offender on conditional probation under this division, with the terms of his probation including the following requirements in addition to any terms of probation that can be imposed pursuant to section 2951.02 of the Revised Code:

(i) The offender shall enter into an alternative residential diversion program as described in division (G)(2) of this section and submit to drug abuse treatment and counseling in the program for the period specified by the court, which period shall be at least ninety days.

(ii) Upon his release from the alternative residential diversion program, the offender shall continue to submit for a period specified by the court, which period shall be at least nine months, to drug abuse outpatient treatment and counseling as specified by the court.

(b) If, at any time, the offender fails to comply with the conditions set forth in division (G)(1)(a) of this section and any other conditions of his probation imposed pursuant to section 2951.02 of the Revised Code, the offender shall be arrested pursuant to section 2951.08 of the Revised Code. The court immediately shall hold a hearing to determine if the offender has failed to comply with the conditions set forth in division (G)(1)(a) of this section and any other conditions of his probation imposed pursuant to section 2951.02 of the Revised Code. If the court determines that the offender has so failed, it immediately shall revoke the offender's conditional probation under this division, impose upon the offender any definite or indefinite term of imprisonment that the court previously could have imposed, and order the offender to commence serving that definite or indefinite term of imprisonment.

(c) If the offender complies with the conditions set forth in division (G)(1)(a) of this section and all other conditions of his probation imposed pursuant to section 2951.02 of the Revised Code, the court shall relieve the offender of the condition of drug abuse treatment and counseling and the other conditions of the probation, enter on its journal a dismissal of the charges against the offender, and discharge the offender.

(2) Each court of common pleas, by local rule, may provide for one or more alternative residential diversion programs that are designed to provide drug abuse treatment and counseling for adults and juveniles who commit violations of this section. The rule shall be consistent with divisions (G)(1) and (3) of this section and all of the following:

(a) The rule shall design the programs so as to reduce the number of future violations of this section in the county by rehabilitating persons who have committed violations of this section, to provide persons who have committed violations of this section and who are not dangerous offenders with residential treatment and counseling alternatives to incarceration in a detention facility, to reduce overcrowding conditions in detention facilities in the county and elsewhere in the state, and to provide, at the same time, for the safety of residents of this state during the period the persons who have committed violations of this section are receiving treatment and counseling as described in division (G)(1) of this section.

(b) The rule shall require that the programs be used for qualified persons who commit violations of this section and who the trial courts in the county have reason to believe are drug dependent persons or persons in danger of becoming drug dependent persons.

(c) The rule shall require that persons who commit violations of this section, other than indigent persons, persons in danger of becoming indigent persons because of their violations of this section, and persons receiving aid to dependent children or disability assistance, are liable for the expenses associated with the treatment and counseling that they receive pursuant to the programs.

(3) Nothing in this division affects, or shall be construed as affecting, the ability of the courts of this state to grant conditional probation under section 2951.04 of the Revised Code or to grant treatment in lieu of conviction under section 2951.041 of the Revised Code.

(4) As used in this division:

(a) "Dangerous offender" has the same meaning as in section 2929.01 of the Revised Code.

(b) "Detention facility" has the same meaning as in section 2921.01 of the Revised Code.

(c) "Drug dependent person" and "person in danger of becoming a drug dependent person" have the same meanings as in section 3719.011 of the Revised Code.

(H) If a person who has been convicted of or pleaded guilty to a violation of this section is a woman who is pregnant at the time of sentencing for the violation of this section, and if the offender agrees both to receive prenatal care as ordered by the court and to participate in and successfully complete rehabilitation at an appropriate drug treatment facility or program as described in division (B) of section 2951.04 of the Revised Code in connection with the use of any controlled substance, then, in lieu of requiring the offender to serve a term of imprisonment pursuant to division (C) of this section, the court shall suspend the offender's sentence of imprisonment and place her on probation pursuant to section 2951.02 of the Revised Code, with at least one of the conditions of her probation being that she receive prenatal care as ordered by the court until the birth of her child and participate in and successfully complete rehabilitation at an appropriate drug treatment facility or program as described in division (B) of section 2951.04 of the Revised Code in connection with the use of any controlled substance until she is rehabilitated and released from this requirement by an order of the court.

(1995 H 249, eff. 7–17–95; 1994 H 391, eff. 7–21–94; 1993 H 377, eff. 9–30–93; 1991 H 298, H 62; 1990 S 258; 1980 S 184, § 5)

2925.12   Possessing drug abuse instruments

(A) No person shall knowingly make, obtain, possess, or use any instrument, article, or thing whose customary and primary purpose is for the administration or use of a dangerous drug, other than marihuana, when the instrument involved is a hypodermic or syringe, whether or not of crude or extemporized manufacture or assembly, and the instrument, article, or thing involved has been used by the offender to unlawfully administer or use a dangerous drug, other than marihuana, or to prepare a dangerous drug, other than marihuana, for unlawful administration or use.

(B) This section does not apply to manufacturers, practitioners, pharmacists, owners of pharmacies, and other persons whose conduct was in accordance with Chapters 3719., 4715., 4729., 4731., and 4741. of the Revised Code or section 4723.56 of the Revised Code.

(C) Whoever violates this section is guilty of possessing drug abuse instruments, a misdemeanor of the second degree. If the offender previously has been convicted of a drug abuse offense, a violation of this section is a misdemeanor of the first degree.

(D)(1) Notwithstanding the fines otherwise required to be imposed pursuant to section 2929.21 or 2929.31 of the Revised Code for violations of this section and notwithstanding section 2929.22 of the Revised Code, the court shall impose a mandatory fine of one thousand dollars if the violation of this section was a misdemeanor of the first degree and a mandatory fine of seven hundred fifty dollars if the violation of this section was a misdemeanor of the second degree.

(2) The court may impose a fine in addition to a mandatory fine imposed pursuant to division (D)(1) of this section if the total of the additional and mandatory fines does not exceed the maximum fine that could be imposed pursuant to section 2929.21 or 2929.31 of the Revised Code.

(3) Notwithstanding any contrary provision of section 3719.21 of the Revised Code, fifty per cent of any mandatory fine imposed pursuant to division (D)(1) of this section shall be paid by the clerk of the court in accordance with and subject to the requirements of, and shall be used as specified in, division (J) of section 2925.03 of the Revised Code, and fifty per cent shall be disbursed as provided in section 3719.21 of the Revised Code. Any additional fine imposed pursuant to division (D)(2) of this section shall be disbursed by the clerk of the court as otherwise provided by law.

(4) If a person is charged with any violation of this section and posts bail pursuant to sections 2937.22 to 2937.46 of the Revised Code or Criminal Rule 46, and if the person forfeits the bail, the forfeited bail shall be paid by the clerk of the court in accordance with and subject to the requirements of, and shall be used as specified in, division (D)(3) of this section.

(5) No court shall impose a mandatory fine pursuant to division (D)(1) of this section upon an offender who alleges, in an affidavit filed with the court prior to his sentencing, that he is indigent and is unable to pay any mandatory fine imposed pursuant to that division, if the court determines the offender is an indigent person and is unable to pay the fine.

(E) In addition to any other penalty imposed for a violation of this section, the court shall suspend for not less than six months nor more than five years the driver's or commercial driver's license of any person who is convicted of or has pleaded guilty to a violation of this section. If the offender is a professionally licensed person or a person who has been admitted to the bar by order of the supreme court in compliance with its prescribed and published rules, in addition to any other penalty imposed for a violation of this section, the court forthwith shall comply with section 2925.38 of the Revised Code.

(1994 H 391, eff. 7–21–94; 1993 H 377, eff. 9–30–93; 1990 S 258; 1975 H 300)

2925.13 Permitting drug abuse

(A) No person who is the owner, operator, or person in charge of a locomotive, watercraft, aircraft, or other vehicle as defined in division (A) of section 4501.01 of the Revised Code, shall knowingly permit the vehicle to be used for the commission of a felony drug abuse offense.

(B) No person who is the owner, lessee, or occupant, or who has custody, control, or supervision, of premises or real estate, including vacant land, shall knowingly permit the premises or real estate, including vacant land, to be used for the commission of a felony drug abuse offense by another person.

(C) Whoever violates this section is guilty of permitting drug abuse, a misdemeanor of the first degree, except that permitting drug abuse is a felony of the fourth degree, if any of the following apply:

(1) The offender previously has been convicted of a drug abuse offense;

(2) The felony drug abuse offense in question is a violation of section 2925.02 or division (A)(1), (5), (7), or (10) of section 2925.03 of the Revised Code that was committed in either of the following ways:

(a) On school premises, in a school building, or within one thousand feet of the boundaries of any school premises;

(b) Within one hundred feet of any juvenile or within the view of any juvenile, whether or not the offender knows the age of the juvenile, the offender knows the juvenile is within one hundred feet or within view of the commission of the offense, or the juvenile views the commission of the offense.

(D)(1) Notwithstanding the fines otherwise required to be imposed pursuant to section 2929.11 or 2929.31 of the Revised Code for violations of this section and notwithstanding section 2929.14 of the Revised Code, the court shall impose a mandatory fine of one thousand five hundred dollars if the violation of this section was a felony of the fourth degree and a mandatory fine of one thousand dollars if the violation of this section was a misdemeanor of the first degree.

(2) The court may impose a fine in addition to a mandatory fine imposed pursuant to division (D)(1) of this section if the total of the additional and mandatory fines does not exceed the maximum fine that could be imposed pursuant to section 2929.11 or 2929.31 of the Revised Code.

(3) Notwithstanding any contrary provision of section 3719.21 of the Revised Code, fifty per cent of any mandatory fine imposed pursuant to division (D)(1) of this section shall be paid by the clerk of the court in accordance with and subject to the requirements of, and shall be used as specified in, division (J) of section 2925.03 of the Revised Code, and fifty per cent shall be disbursed as provided in section 3719.21 of the Revised Code. Any additional fine imposed pursuant to division (D)(2) of this section shall be disbursed by the clerk of the court as otherwise provided by law.

(4) If a person is charged with any violation of this section and posts bail pursuant to sections 2937.22 to 2937.46 of the Revised Code or Criminal Rule 46, and if the person forfeits the bail, the forfeited bail shall be paid by the clerk of the court in accordance with and subject to the requirements of, and shall be used as specified in, division (D)(3) of this section.

(5) No court shall impose a mandatory fine pursuant to division (D)(1) of this section upon an offender who alleges, in an affidavit filed with the court prior to his sentencing, that he is indigent and is unable to pay any mandatory fine imposed pursuant to that division, if the court determines the offender is an indigent person and is unable to pay the fine.

(E) In addition to any other penalty imposed for a violation of this section, the court shall suspend for not less than six months nor more than five years the driver's or commercial driver's license of any person who is convicted of or has pleaded guilty to a violation of this section. If the offender is a professionally licensed person or a person who has been admitted to the bar by order of the supreme court in compliance with its prescribed and published rules, in addition to any other penalty imposed for a violation of this section, the court forthwith shall comply with section 2925.38 of the Revised Code.

(1993 H 377, eff. 9-30-93; 1992 H 591; 1990 S 258, H 215; 1975 H 300)

2925.14 Use, possession, or sale of drug paraphernalia; exemptions; forfeiture

(A) As used in this section, "drug paraphernalia" means any equipment, product, or material of any kind that is used by the offender, intended by the offender for use, or designed for use, in propagating, cultivating, growing, harvesting, manufacturing, compounding, converting, producing, processing, preparing, testing, analyzing, packaging, repackaging, storing, containing, concealing, injecting, ingesting, inhaling, or otherwise introducing into the human body, a controlled substance in violation of this chapter. "Drug paraphernalia" includes, but is not limited to, any of the following equipment, products, or materials that are used by the offender, intended by the offender for use, or designed by the offender for use, in any of the following manners:

(1) A kit for propagating, cultivating, growing, or harvesting any species of a plant that is a controlled substance or from which a controlled substance can be derived;

(2) A kit for manufacturing, compounding, converting, producing, processing, or preparing a controlled substance;

(3) An isomerization device for increasing the potency of any species of a plant that is a controlled substance;

(4) Testing equipment for identifying, or analyzing the strength, effectiveness, or purity of, a controlled substance;

(5) A scale or balance for weighing or measuring a controlled substance;

(6) A diluent or adulterant, such as quinine hydrochloride, mannitol, mannite, dextrose, or lactose, for cutting a controlled substance;

(7) A separation gin or sifter for removing twigs and seeds from, or otherwise cleaning or refining, marihuana;

(8) A blender, bowl, container, spoon, or mixing device for compounding a controlled substance;

(9) A capsule, balloon, envelope, or container for packaging small quantities of a controlled substance;

(10) A container or device for storing or concealing a controlled substance;

(11) A hypodermic syringe, needle, or instrument for parenterally injecting a controlled substance into the human body;

(12) An object, instrument, or device for ingesting, inhaling, or otherwise introducing into the human body, marihuana, cocaine, hashish, or hashish oil, such as a metal, wooden, acrylic, glass, stone, plastic, or ceramic pipe, with or without a screen, permanent screen, hashish head, or punctured metal bowl; water pipe; carburetion tube or device; smoking or carburetion mask; roach clip or similar object used to hold burning material, such as a marihuana cigarette, that has become too small or too short to be held in the hand; miniature cocaine spoon, or cocaine vial; chamber pipe; carburetor pipe; electric pipe; air driver pipe; chillum; bong; or ice pipe or chiller.

(B) In determining if an object is drug paraphernalia, a court or law enforcement officer shall consider, in addition to other relevant factors, the following:

(1) Any statement by the owner, or by anyone in control, of the object, concerning its use;

(2) The proximity in time or space of the object, or of the act relating to the object, to a violation of any provision of this chapter;

(3) The proximity of the object to any controlled substance;

(4) The existence of any residue of a controlled substance on the object;

(5) Direct or circumstantial evidence of the intent of the owner, or of anyone in control, of the object, to deliver it to any person whom he knows intends to use the object to facilitate a violation of any provision of this chapter. A finding that the owner, or anyone in control, of the object, is not guilty of a violation of any other provision of this chapter, does not prevent a finding that the object was intended or designed by the offender for use as drug paraphernalia.

(6) Any oral or written instruction provided with the object concerning its use;

(7) Any descriptive material accompanying the object and explaining or depicting its use;

(8) National or local advertising concerning the use of the object;

(9) The manner and circumstances in which the object is displayed for sale;

(10) Direct or circumstantial evidence of the ratio of the sales of the object to the total sales of the business enterprise;

(11) The existence and scope of legitimate uses of the object in the community;

(12) Expert testimony concerning the use of the object.

(C)(1) No person shall knowingly use, or possess with purpose to use, drug paraphernalia.

(2) No person shall knowingly sell, or possess or manufacture with purpose to sell, drug paraphernalia, if he knows or reasonably should know that the equipment, product, or material will be used as drug paraphernalia.

(3) No person shall place an advertisement in any newspaper, magazine, handbill, or other publication that is published and printed and circulates primarily within this state, if he knows that the purpose of the advertisement is to promote the illegal sale in this state of the equipment, product, or material that the offender intended or designed for use as drug paraphernalia.

(D) This section does not apply to manufacturers, practitioners, pharmacists, owners of pharmacies, and other persons whose conduct is in accordance with Chapter 3719., 4715., 4729., 4731., or 4741. of the Revised Code or section 4723.56 of the Revised Code. This section shall not be construed to prohibit the possession or use of a hypodermic as authorized by section 3719.172 of the Revised Code.

(E) Notwithstanding sections 2933.42 and 2933.43 of the Revised Code, any drug paraphernalia that was used, possessed, sold, or manufactured in a violation of this section shall be seized, after a conviction for that violation shall be forfeited, and upon forfeiture shall be disposed of pursuant to division (D)(8) of section 2933.41 of the Revised Code.

(F)(1) Whoever violates division (C)(1) of this section is guilty of illegal use or possession of drug paraphernalia, a misdemeanor of the fourth degree.

(2) Except as provided in division (F)(3) of this section, whoever violates division (C)(2) of this section is guilty of dealing in drug paraphernalia, a misdemeanor of the second degree.

(3) Whoever violates division (C)(2) of this section by selling drug paraphernalia to a juvenile is guilty of selling drug paraphernalia to juveniles, a misdemeanor of the first degree.

(4) Whoever violates division (C)(3) of this section is guilty of illegal advertising of drug paraphernalia, a misdemeanor of the second degree.

(G)(1) Notwithstanding the fines otherwise required to be imposed pursuant to section 2929.21 or 2929.31 of the Revised Code for violations of this section and notwithstanding section 2929.22 of the Revised Code, the court shall impose a mandatory fine of one thousand dollars if the violation of this section was a misdemeanor of the first degree, a mandatory fine of seven hundred fifty dollars if the violation of this section was a misdemeanor of the second degree, and a mandatory fine of two hundred fifty dollars if the violation of this section was a misdemeanor of the fourth degree.

(2) The court may impose a fine in addition to a mandatory fine imposed pursuant to division (G)(1) of this section if the total of the additional and mandatory fines does not exceed the maximum fine that could be imposed pursuant to section 2929.21 or 2929.31 of the Revised Code.

(3) Notwithstanding any contrary provision of section 3719.21 of the Revised Code, fifty per cent of any mandatory fine imposed pursuant to division (G)(1) of this section shall be paid by the clerk of the court in accordance with and subject to the requirements of, and shall be used as specified in, division (J) of section 2925.03 of the Revised Code, and fifty per cent shall be disbursed as provided in section 3719.21 of the Revised Code. Any additional fine imposed pursuant to division (G)(2) of this section shall be disbursed by the clerk of the court as otherwise provided by law.

(4) If a person is charged with any violation of this section and posts bail pursuant to sections 2937.22 to 2937.46 of the Revised Code or Criminal Rule 46, and if the person forfeits the bail, the forfeited bail shall be paid by the clerk of the court in accordance with and subject to the requirements of, and shall be used as specified in, division (G)(3) of this section.

(5) No court shall impose a mandatory fine pursuant to division (G)(1) of this section upon an offender who alleges, in an affidavit filed with the court prior to his sentencing, that he is indigent and is unable to pay any mandatory fine imposed pursuant to that division, if the court determines the offender is an indigent person and is unable to pay the fine.

(H) In addition to any other penalty imposed for a violation of this section, the court shall suspend for not less than six months nor more than five years the driver's or commercial driver's license of any person who is convicted of or has pleaded guilty to a violation of this section. If the offender is a professionally licensed person or a person who has been admitted to the bar by order of the supreme court in compliance with its prescribed and published rules, in addition to any other penalty imposed for a violation of this section, the court forthwith shall comply with section 2925.38 of the Revised Code.

(1994 H 391, eff. 7–21–94; 1993 H 377, eff. 9–30–93; 1990 S 258; 1989 H 182)

2925.21 Theft of drugs—Repealed

(1990 S 258, eff. 11–20–90; 1975 H 300)

2925.22 Deception to obtain a dangerous drug

(A) No person, by deception as defined in section 2913.01 of the Revised Code, shall procure the administration of, a prescription for, or the dispensing of, a dangerous drug, or possess an uncompleted preprinted prescription blank used for writing a prescription for a dangerous drug.

(B) Whoever violates this section is guilty of deception to obtain a dangerous drug, a felony of the fourth degree. If the offender previously has been convicted of a drug abuse offense, deception to obtain drugs is a felony of the third degree. If the drug involved is a compound, mixture, preparation, or substance included in schedule I or II, with the exception of marihuana, deception to obtain drugs is a felony of the third degree. If the offender previously has been convicted of a felony drug abuse offense and the drug involved is a compound, mixture, preparation, or substance included in schedule I or II with the exception of marihuana, deception to obtain drugs is a felony of the second degree.

(C)(1) Notwithstanding the fines otherwise required to be imposed pursuant to section 2929.11 or 2929.31 of the Revised Code for violations of this section and notwithstanding section 2929.14 of the Revised Code, the court shall impose a mandatory fine of three thousand five hundred dollars if the violation of this section was a felony of the second degree, a mandatory fine of two thousand five hundred dollars if the violation of this section was a felony of the third degree, and a mandatory fine of one thousand five hundred dollars if the violation of this section was a felony of the fourth degree.

(2) The court may impose a fine in addition to a mandatory fine imposed pursuant to division (C)(1) of this section if the total of the additional and mandatory fines does not exceed the maximum fine that could be imposed pursuant to section 2929.11 or 2929.31 of the Revised Code.

(3) Notwithstanding any contrary provision of section 3719.21 of the Revised Code, fifty per cent of any mandatory fine imposed pursuant to division (C)(1) of this section shall be paid by the clerk of the court in accordance with and subject to the requirements of, and shall be used as specified in, division (J) of section 2925.03 of the Revised Code, and fifty per cent shall be disbursed as provided in section 3719.21 of the Revised Code. Any additional fine imposed pursuant to division (C)(2) of this section shall be disbursed by the clerk of the court as otherwise provided by law.

(4) If a person is charged with any violation of this section and posts bail pursuant to sections 2937.22 to 2937.46 of the Revised Code or Criminal Rule 46, and if the person forfeits the bail, the forfeited bail shall be paid by the clerk of the court in accordance with and subject to the requirements of, and shall be used as specified in, division (C)(3) of this section.

(5) No court shall impose a mandatory fine pursuant to division (C)(1) of this section upon an offender who alleges, in an affidavit filed with the court prior to his sentencing, that he is indigent and is unable to pay any mandatory fine imposed pursuant to that division, if the court determines the offender is an indigent person and is unable to pay the fine.

(D) In addition to any other penalty imposed for a violation of this section, the court shall suspend for not less than six months nor more than five years the driver's or commercial driver's license of any person who is convicted of or has pleaded guilty to a violation of this section. If the offender is a professionally licensed person or a person who has been admitted to the bar by order of the supreme court in compliance with its prescribed and published rules, in addition to any other penalty imposed for a violation of this section, the court forthwith shall comply with section 2925.38 of the Revised Code.

(1993 H 377, eff. 9–30–93; 1990 H 615, S 258; 1975 H 300)

2925.23 Illegal processing of drug documents

(A) No person shall knowingly make a false statement in any prescription, order, report, or record required by Chapter 3719. of the Revised Code.

(B) No person shall intentionally make, utter, or sell, or knowingly possess a false or forged:

(1) Prescription;

(2) Uncompleted preprinted prescription blank used for writing a prescription;

(3) Official written order;

(4) License for a terminal distributor of dangerous drugs as required in section 4729.60 of the Revised Code;

(5) Registration certificate for a wholesale distributor of dangerous drugs as required in section 4729.60 of the Revised Code.

(C) No person, by theft as defined in section 2913.02 of the Revised Code, shall acquire any of the following:

(1) A prescription;

(2) An uncompleted preprinted prescription blank used for writing a prescription;

(3) An official written order;

(4) A blank official written order;

(5) A license or blank license for a terminal distributor of dangerous drugs as required in section 4729.60 of the Revised Code;

(6) A registration certificate or blank registration certificate for a wholesale distributor of dangerous drugs as required in section 4729.60 of the Revised Code.

(D) No person shall knowingly make or affix any false or forged label to a package or receptacle containing any dangerous drugs.

(E) Divisions (A) and (D) of this section do not apply to practitioners, pharmacists, owners of pharmacies, and other persons whose conduct is in accordance with Chapters 3719., 4715., 4725., 4729., 4731., and 4741. of the Revised Code or section 4723.56 of the Revised Code.

(F) Whoever violates this section is guilty of illegal processing of drug documents, a felony of the fourth degree. If the offender previously has been convicted of a felony drug abuse offense, illegal processing of drug documents is a felony of the third degree. If the drug involved is a compound, mixture, preparation, or substance included in schedule I or II with the exception of marihuana, illegal processing of drug documents is a felony of the third degree. If the drug involved is a compound, mixture, preparation, or substance included in schedule I or II with the exception of marihuana, and the offender previously has been convicted of a felony drug abuse offense, illegal processing of drug documents is a felony of the second degree.

(G)(1) Notwithstanding the fines otherwise required to be imposed pursuant to section 2929.11 or 2929.31 of the Revised Code for violations of this section and notwithstanding section 2929.14 of the Revised Code, the court shall impose a mandatory fine of three thousand five hundred dollars if the violation of this section was a felony of the second degree, a mandatory fine of two thousand five hundred dollars if the violation of this section was a felony of the third degree, and a mandatory fine of one thousand five hundred dollars if the violation of this section was a felony of the fourth degree.

(2) The court may impose a fine in addition to a mandatory fine imposed pursuant to division (G)(1) of this section if the total of the additional and mandatory fines does not exceed the maximum fine that could be imposed pursuant to section 2929.11 or 2929.31 of the Revised Code.

(3) Notwithstanding any contrary provision of section 3719.21 of the Revised Code, fifty per cent of any mandatory fine imposed pursuant to division (G)(1) of this section shall be paid by the clerk of the court in accordance with and subject to the requirements of, and shall be used as specified in, division (J) of section 2925.03 of the Revised Code, and fifty per cent shall be disbursed as provided in section 3719.21 of the Revised Code. Any additional fine imposed pursuant to division (G)(2) of this section shall be disbursed by the clerk of the court as otherwise provided by law.

(4) If a person is charged with any violation of this section and posts bail pursuant to sections 2937.22 to 2937.46 of the Revised Code or Criminal Rule 46, and if the person forfeits the bail, the forfeited bail shall be paid by the clerk of the court in accordance with and subject to the requirements of, and shall be used as specified in, division (G)(3) of this section.

(5) No court shall impose a mandatory fine pursuant to division (G)(1) of this section upon an offender who alleges, in an affidavit filed with the court prior to his sentencing, that he is indigent and is unable to pay any mandatory fine imposed pursuant to that division, if the court determines the offender is an indigent person and is unable to pay the fine.

(H) In addition to any other penalty imposed for a violation of this section, the court shall suspend for not less than six months nor more than five years the driver's or commercial driver's license of any person who is convicted of or has pleaded guilty to a violation of this section. If the offender is a professionally licensed person or a person who has been admitted to the bar by order of the supreme court in compliance with its prescribed and published rules, in addition to any other penalty imposed for a violation of this section, the court forthwith shall comply with section 2925.38 of the Revised Code.

(1994 H 391, eff. 7–21–94; 1993 H 377, eff. 9–30–93; 1992 S 110; 1990 S 258; 1975 H 300)

2925.31   Abusing harmful intoxicants

(A) Except for lawful research, clinical, medical, dental, or veterinary purposes, no person, with purpose to induce intoxication or similar physiological effects, shall obtain, possess, or use a harmful intoxicant.

(B) Whoever violates this section is guilty of abusing harmful intoxicants, a misdemeanor of the fourth degree. If the offender previously has been convicted of a drug abuse offense, abusing harmful intoxicants is a misdemeanor of the first degree.

(C)(1) Notwithstanding the fines otherwise required to be imposed pursuant to section 2929.21 or 2929.31 of the Revised Code for violations of this section and notwithstanding section 2929.22 of the Revised Code, the court shall impose a mandatory fine of one thousand dollars if the violation of this section was a misdemeanor of the first degree and a mandatory fine of two hundred fifty dollars if the violation of this section was a misdemeanor of the fourth degree.

(2) The court may impose a fine in addition to a mandatory fine imposed pursuant to division (C)(1) of this section if the total of the additional and mandatory fines does not exceed the maximum fine that could be imposed pursuant to section 2929.21 or 2929.31 of the Revised Code.

(3) Notwithstanding any contrary provision of section 3719.21 of the Revised Code, fifty per cent of any mandatory fine imposed pursuant to division (C)(1) of this section shall be paid by the clerk of the court in accordance with and subject to the requirements of, and shall be used as specified in, division (J) of section 2925.03 of the Revised Code, and fifty per cent shall be disbursed as provided in section 3719.21 of the Revised Code. Any additional fine imposed pursuant to division (C)(2) of this section shall be disbursed by the clerk of the court as otherwise provided by law.

(4) If a person is charged with any violation of this section and posts bail pursuant to sections 2937.22 to 2937.46 of the Revised Code or Criminal Rule 46, and if the person forfeits the bail, the forfeited bail shall be paid by the clerk of the court in accordance with and subject to the requirements of, and shall be used as specified in, division (C)(3) of this section.

(5) No court shall impose a mandatory fine pursuant to division (C)(1) of this section upon an offender who alleges, in an affidavit filed with the court prior to his sentencing, that he is indigent and is unable to pay any mandatory fine imposed pursuant to that division, if the court determines the offender is an indigent person and is unable to pay the fine.

(D) In addition to any other penalty imposed for a violation of this section, the court shall suspend for not less than six months nor more than five years the driver's or commercial driver's license of any person who is convicted of or has pleaded guilty to a violation of this section. If the offender is a professionally licensed person or a person who has been admitted to the bar by order of the supreme court in compliance with its prescribed and published rules, in addition to any other penalty imposed for a violation of this section, the court forthwith shall comply with section 2925.38 of the Revised Code.

(1993 H 377, eff. 9–30–93; 1990 S 258; 1975 H 300)

2925.32 Trafficking in harmful intoxicants

(A) No person shall knowingly dispense or distribute any harmful intoxicant, except gasoline, to any juvenile, if the person who dispenses or distributes it knows or has reason to believe that the harmful intoxicant will be used in violation of section 2925.31 of the Revised Code, unless a written order from the parent or guardian is provided to the dispenser or distributor. Six months after the board of pharmacy has designated the noxious additive, as defined in section 3719.01 of the Revised Code, that is to be included in any product containing toluene, the gas, fumes, or vapor of which when inhaled can induce intoxication, excitement, giddiness, irrational behavior, depression, stupefaction, paralysis, unconsciousness, asphyxiation, or other harmful physiological effects, no person shall dispense or distribute a product that is required to include a noxious additive unless such product includes the noxious additive in the amounts and proportions prescribed by the board.

(B) Any product that is required by division (A) of this section to include a noxious additive shall have such contents clearly stated on the label.

(C) The prohibitions of this section shall not apply after a prescribed noxious additive has been added to the harmful intoxicant or upon determination by the board of pharmacy that addition of a noxious additive is not required.

(D) Whoever violates this section is guilty of trafficking in harmful intoxicants, a misdemeanor of the fourth degree. If the offender previously has been convicted of a drug abuse offense, trafficking in harmful intoxicants is a misdemeanor of the third degree.

(E) This section does not apply to products used in making, fabricating, assembling, transporting, or constructing a product or structure by manual labor or machinery for sale or lease to another person, or to the mining, refining, or processing of natural deposits.

(F)(1) Notwithstanding the fines otherwise required to be imposed pursuant to section 2929.21 or 2929.31 of the Revised Code for violations of this section and notwithstanding section 2929.22 of the Revised Code, the court shall impose a mandatory fine of five hundred dollars if the violation of this section was a misdemeanor of the third degree and a mandatory fine of two hundred fifty dollars if the violation of this section was a misdemeanor of the fourth degree.

(2) The court may impose a fine in addition to a mandatory fine imposed pursuant to division (F)(1) of this section if the total of the additional and mandatory fines does not exceed the maximum fine that could be imposed pursuant to section 2929.21 or 2929.31 of the Revised Code.

(3) Notwithstanding any contrary provision of section 3719.21 of the Revised Code, fifty per cent of any mandatory fine imposed pursuant to division (F)(1) of this section shall be paid by the clerk of the court in accordance with and subject to the requirements of, and shall be used as specified in, division (J) of section 2925.03 of the Revised Code, and fifty per cent shall be disbursed as provided in section 3719.21 of the Revised Code. Any additional fine imposed pursuant to division (F)(2) of this section shall be disbursed by the clerk of the court as otherwise provided by law.

(4) If a person is charged with any violation of this section and posts bail pursuant to sections 2937.22 to 2937.46 of the Revised Code or Criminal Rule 46, and if the person forfeits the bail, the forfeited bail shall be paid by the clerk of the court in accordance with and subject to the requirements of, and shall be used as specified in, division (F)(3) of this section.

(5) No court shall impose a mandatory fine pursuant to division (F)(1) of this section upon an offender who alleges, in an affidavit filed with the court prior to his sentencing, that he is indigent and is unable to pay any mandatory fine imposed pursuant to that division, if the court determines the offender is an indigent person and is unable to pay the fine.

(G) In addition to any other penalty imposed for a violation of this section, the court shall suspend for not less than six months nor more than five years the driver's or commercial driver's license of any person who is convicted of or has pleaded guilty to a violation of this section. If the offender is a professionally licensed person or a person who has been admitted to the bar by order of the supreme court in compliance with its prescribed and published rules,

fine of three thousand five hundred dollars if the violation of this section was a felony of the second degree, a mandatory fine of two thousand five hundred dollars if the violation of this section was a felony of the third degree, a mandatory fine of one thousand five hundred dollars if the violation of this section was a felony of the fourth degree, and a mandatory fine of one thousand dollars if the violation of this section was a misdemeanor of the first degree.

(2) The court may impose a fine in addition to a mandatory fine imposed pursuant to division (L)(1) of this section if the total of the additional and mandatory fines does not exceed the maximum fine that could be imposed pursuant to section 2929.11, 2929.21, or 2929.31 of the Revised Code.

(3) Notwithstanding any contrary provision of section 3719.21 of the Revised Code, fifty per cent of any mandatory fine imposed pursuant to division (L)(1) of this section shall be paid by the clerk of the court in accordance with and subject to the requirements of, and shall be used as specified in, division (J) of section 2925.03 of the Revised Code, and fifty per cent shall be disbursed as provided in section 3719.21 of the Revised Code. Any additional fine imposed pursuant to division (L)(2) of this section shall be disbursed by the clerk of the court as otherwise provided by law.

(4) If a person is charged with any violation of this section and posts bail pursuant to sections 2937.22 to 2937.46 of the Revised Code or Criminal Rule 46, and if the person forfeits the bail, the forfeited bail shall be paid by the clerk of the court in accordance with and subject to the requirements of, and shall be used as specified in, division (L)(3) of this section.

(5) No court shall impose a mandatory fine pursuant to division (L)(1) of this section upon an offender who alleges, in an affidavit filed with the court prior to his sentencing, that he is indigent and is unable to pay any mandatory fine imposed pursuant to that division, if the court determines the offender is an indigent person and is unable to pay the fine.

(M) In addition to any other penalty imposed for a violation of this section, the court shall suspend for not less than six months nor more than five years the driver's or commercial driver's license of any person who is convicted of or has pleaded guilty to any other violation of this section. If the offender is a professionally licensed person or a person who has been admitted to the bar by order of the supreme court in compliance with its prescribed and published rules, in addition to any other penalty imposed for a violation of this section, the court forthwith shall comply with section 2925.38 of the Revised Code.

(1993 H 377, eff. 9–30–93; 1990 S 258; 1982 H 535)

2925.38 Convictions of professionally licensed persons

If a person who is convicted of or pleads guilty to a violation of section 2925.02, 2925.03, 2925.11, 2925.12, 2925.13, 2925.14, 2925.22, 2925.23, 2925.31, 2925.32, 2925.36, or 2925.37 of the Revised Code is a professionally licensed person, in addition to any other penalty imposed for a violation of the section, the court forthwith shall transmit a certified copy of the judgment entry of conviction to the regulatory or licensing board or agency that has the administrative authority to suspend or revoke the offender's professional license. If a person who is convicted of or pleads guilty to a violation of any such section is a person who has been admitted to the bar by order of the supreme court in compliance with its prescribed and published rules, in addition to any other penalties imposed for a violation of the section, the court forthwith shall transmit a certified copy of the judgment entry of conviction to the secretary of the board of commissioners on grievances and discipline of the supreme court and to either the disciplinary counsel or the president, secretary, and chairman of each certified grievance committee.

(1990 S 258, eff. 11–20–90)

FORFEITURE OF PROPERTY

2925.41 Definitions

As used in sections 2925.42 to 2925.45 of the Revised Code:

(A) "Financial institution" means a bank, credit union, savings and loan association, or a licensee or registrant under Chapter 1321. of the Revised Code.

(B) "Property" includes both of the following:

(1) Real property, including, but not limited to, things growing on, affixed to, and found in the real property;

(2) Tangible and intangible personal property, including, but not limited to, rights, privileges, interests, claims, and securities.

(1990 S 258, eff. 11–20–90)

2925.42 Criminal forfeiture of property

(A)(1) In accordance with division (B) of this section, a person who is convicted of or pleads guilty to a felony drug abuse offense, and any juvenile who is found by a juvenile court to be a delinquent child for an act that, if committed by an adult, would be a felony drug abuse offense, loses any right to the possession of property and forfeits to the state any right, title, and interest he may have in that property if either of the following applies:

(a) The property constitutes, or is derived directly or indirectly from, any proceeds that the person obtained directly or indirectly from the commission of the felony drug abuse offense or act.

(b) The property was used or intended to be used in any manner to commit, or to facilitate the commission of, the felony drug abuse offense or act.

(2) All right, title, and interest of a person in property described in division (A)(1) of this section vests in the state upon the person's commission of the felony drug abuse offense of which he is convicted or to which he pleads guilty and that is the basis of the forfeiture, or upon the juvenile's commission of the act that, if committed by an adult, would be a felony drug abuse offense, that is the basis of his being found to be a delinquent child, and that is the basis of the forfeiture. Subject to divisions (F)(3)(b) and (5)(b) and (G)(2) of this section, if any right, title, or interest in property is vested in this state under this division and subsequently is transferred to a person other than the offender who forfeits the right, title, or interest under division (A)(1) of this section, then, in accordance with division (B) of this section, the right, title, or interest in the property may be the subject of a special verdict of forfeiture and, after any special verdict of forfeiture, shall be ordered forfeited to this state, unless the transferee establishes in a hearing held pursuant to division (F) of this section that he is a bona fide purchaser for value of the right, title, or interest in the property and that, at the time of its purchase, he was reasonably without cause to believe that it was subject to forfeiture under this section.

(3) The provisions of section 2925.43 of the Revised Code that relate to the forfeiture of any right, title, or interest in property associated with a felony drug abuse offense pursuant to a civil action to obtain a civil forfeiture do not apply to the forfeiture of any right, title, or interest in property described in division (A)(1) of this section that occurs pursuant to division (B) of this section upon a person's conviction of or guilty plea to a felony drug abuse offense or upon a juvenile being found by a juvenile court to be a delinquent child for an act that, if committed by an adult, would be a felony drug abuse offense.

(4) Nothing in this section precludes a financial institution that has or purports to have a security interest in or lien on property described in division (A)(1) of this section from commencing a civil action or taking other appropriate legal action in connection with the property, prior to its disposition in accordance with section 2925.44 of the Revised Code, for the purpose of obtaining possession of the property in order to foreclose or otherwise enforce the security interest or lien. A financial institution may commence a civil action or take other appropriate legal action for that purpose prior to the disposition of the property in accordance with section 2925.44 of the Revised Code, even if a felony drug abuse offense prosecution or a delinquent child proceeding for an act that, if committed by an adult, would be a felony drug abuse offense has been or could be commenced, even if the property is or could be the subject of an order of forfeiture issued under division (B)(5) of this section, and even if the property has been seized or is subject to seizure pursuant to division (D) or (E) of this section.

If a financial institution commences a civil action or takes any other appropriate legal action as described in this division, if the financial institution subsequently causes the sale of the property prior to its seizure pursuant to division (D) or (E) of this section and its disposition pursuant to section 2925.44 of the Revised Code, and if the person responsible for the conduct of the sale has actual knowledge of the commencement of a felony drug abuse offense prosecution or of a delinquent child proceeding for an act that, if committed by an adult, would be a felony drug abuse offense, actual knowledge of a pending forfeiture proceeding under division (B) of this section, or actual knowledge of an order of forfeiture issued under division (B)(5) of this section, then the person responsible for the conduct of the sale shall dispose of the proceeds of the sale in the following order:

(a) First, to the payment of the costs of the sale and to the payment of the costs incurred by law enforcement agencies and financial institutions in connection with the seizure of, storage of, maintenance of, and provision of security for the property. As used in this division, "costs" of a financial institution do not include attorney's fees incurred by that institution in connection with the property.

(b) Second, the remaining proceeds of the sale after compliance with division (A)(4)(a) of this section, to the payment of valid security interests and liens pertaining to the property that, at the time of the vesting of the right, title, or interest of the adult or juvenile in the state under division (A)(2) of this section, are held by known secured parties and lienholders, in the order of priority of those security interests and liens;

(c) Third, the remaining proceeds of the sale after compliance with division (A)(4)(b) of this section, to the court that has or would have jurisdiction in a felony drug abuse offense prosecution or a delinquent child proceeding for an act that, if committed by an adult, would be a felony drug abuse offense, for disposition in accordance with section 2925.44 of the Revised Code.

(B)(1) A criminal forfeiture of any right, title, or interest in property described in division (A)(1) of this section is precluded unless one of the following applies:

(a) The indictment, count in the indictment, or information charging the felony drug abuse offense specifies the nature of the right, title, or interest of the alleged offender in the property described in division (A)(1) of this section that is potentially subject to forfeiture under this section, or a description of the property of the alleged offender that is potentially subject to forfeiture under this section, to the extent the right, title, or interest in the property or the property reasonably is known at the time of the filing of the indictment or information; or the complaint charging a juvenile with being a delinquent child for the commission of an act that, if committed by an adult, would be a felony drug abuse offense specifies the nature of the right, title, or interest of the juvenile in the property described in division (A)(1) of this section that is potentially subject to forfeiture under this section, or a description of the property of the juvenile that is potentially subject to forfeiture under this section, to the extent the right, title, or interest in the property or the property reasonably is known at the time of the filing of the complaint.

(b) The property in question was not reasonably foreseen to be subject to forfeiture under this section at the time of the filing of the indictment, information, or complaint, the prosecuting attorney gave prompt notice to the alleged offender or juvenile of that property when it was discovered to be subject to forfeiture under this section, and a verdict of forfeiture described in division (B)(3) of this section requires the forfeiture of that property.

(2) The specifications described in division (B)(1) of this section shall be stated at the end of the body of the indictment, count in the indictment, information, or complaint.

(3)(a) If a person is convicted of or pleads guilty to a felony drug abuse offense, or a juvenile is found to be a delinquent child for an act that, if committed by an adult, would be a felony drug abuse offense, then a special proceeding shall be conducted in accordance with this division to determine whether any property described in division (B)(1)(a) or (b) of this section will be the subject of an order of forfeiture under this section. Except as otherwise provided in division (B)(3)(b) of this section, the jury in the felony drug abuse offense criminal action or in the delinquent child action or, if that action was a nonjury action, the judge in that action shall hear and consider testimony and other evidence in the proceeding relative to whether any property described in division (B)(1)(a) or (b) of this section is subject to forfeiture under this section. If the jury or judge determines that the prosecuting attorney has established, by a preponderance of the evidence, that any property so described is subject to forfeiture under this section, the judge or juvenile judge shall render a verdict of forfeiture that specifically describes the right, title, or interest in property or the property that is subject to forfeiture under this section. The Rules of Evidence shall apply in the proceeding.

(b) If the trier of fact in a felony drug abuse offense criminal action or in a delinquent child action was a jury, then, upon the filing of a motion by the person who was convicted of or pleaded guilty to the felony drug abuse offense or upon the filing of a motion by the juvenile who was found to be a delinquent child for an act that, if committed by an adult, would be a felony drug abuse offense, the determinations in the proceeding described in this division instead shall be made by the judge in the felony drug abuse offense criminal action or the juvenile judge.

(4) In a felony drug abuse offense criminal action or in a delinquent child action, if the trier of fact is a jury, the jury shall not be informed of any specification described in division (B)(1)(a) of this section or of any property described in that division or division (B)(1)(b) of this section prior to the alleged offender being convicted of or pleading guilty to the felony drug abuse offense or prior to the juvenile being found to be a delinquent child for the commission of an act that, if committed by an adult, would be a felony drug abuse offense.

(5)(a) If a verdict of forfeiture is entered pursuant to division (B)(3) of this section, then the court that imposes sentence upon a person who is convicted of or pleads guilty to a felony drug abuse offense, or the juvenile court that finds a juvenile to be a delinquent child for an act that, if committed by an adult, would be a felony drug abuse offense, in addition to any other sentence imposed upon the offender or order of disposition imposed upon the delinquent child, shall order that he forfeit to the state all of his right, title, and interest in the property described in division (A)(1) of this section. If a person is convicted of or pleads guilty to a felony drug abuse offense, or a juvenile is found by a juvenile court to be a delinquent child for an act that, if committed by an adult, would be a felony drug abuse offense, and derives profits or other proceeds from the offense or act, the court that imposes sentence or an order of disposition upon him, in lieu of any fine that the court is otherwise authorized or required to impose, may impose a fine upon him of not more than twice the gross profits or other proceeds so derived.

(b) Notwithstanding any contrary provision of section 3719.21 of the Revised Code, all fines imposed pursuant to this division shall be paid by the clerk of the court to the county, municipal corporation, township, park district, as created pursuant to section 511.18 or 1545.01 of the Revised Code, or state law enforcement agencies in this state that were primarily responsible for or involved in making the arrest of, and in prosecuting, the offender. However, no fine so imposed shall be paid to a law enforcement agency unless the agency has adopted a written internal control policy under division (J)(2) of section 2925.03 of the Revised Code that addresses the use of the fine moneys that it receives under this division and division (J)(1) of section 2925.03 of the Revised Code. The fines imposed and paid pursuant to this division shall be used by the law enforcement agencies to subsidize their efforts pertaining to drug offenses, in accordance with the written internal control policy adopted by the recipient agency under division (J)(2) of section 2925.03 of the Revised Code.

(c) As used in division (B)(5) of this section:

(i) "Law enforcement agencies" includes, but is not limited to, the state board of pharmacy and the office of a prosecutor.

(ii) "Prosecutor" has the same meaning as in section 2935.01 of the Revised Code.

(6) If any of the property that is described in division (A)(1) of this section and that is the subject of an order of forfeiture issued under division (B)(5) of this section, because of an act or omission of the person who is convicted of or pleads guilty to the felony drug abuse offense that is the basis of the order of forfeiture, or an act or omission of the juvenile found by a juvenile court to be a delinquent child for an act that, if committed by an adult, would be a felony drug abuse offense and that is the basis of the forfeiture, cannot be located upon the exercise of due diligence, has been transferred to, sold to, or deposited with a third party, has been placed beyond the jurisdiction of the court, has been substantially diminished in value, or has been commingled with other property that cannot be divided without difficulty, the court that issues the order of forfeiture shall order the forfeiture of any other property of the offender up to the value of any forfeited property described in this division.

(C) There shall be a rebuttable presumption that any right, title, or interest of a person in property described in division (A)(1) of this section is subject to forfeiture under division (B) of this section, if the state proves both of the following by a preponderance of the evidence:

(1) The right, title, or interest in the property was acquired by the offender during the period of the commission of the felony drug abuse offense or act that, if committed by an adult, would be a felony drug abuse offense, or within a reasonable time after that period.

(2) There is no likely source for the right, title, or interest in the property other than proceeds obtained from the commission of the felony drug abuse offense or act.

(D)(1) Upon the application of the prosecuting attorney who is prosecuting or has jurisdiction to prosecute the felony drug abuse offense or act, the court of common pleas or juvenile court of the county in which property subject to forfeiture under division (B) of this section is located, whichever is applicable, may issue a restraining order or injunction, an order requiring the execution of a satisfactory performance bond, or an order taking any other reasonable action necessary to preserve the availability of the property, at either of the following times:

(a) Upon the filing of an indictment, complaint, or information charging a person who has any right, title, or interest in the property with the commission of a felony drug abuse offense and alleging that the property with respect to which the order is sought will be subject to forfeiture under division (B) of this section if the person is convicted of or pleads guilty to the offense, or upon the filing of a complaint alleging that a juvenile who has any right, title, or interest in the property is a delinquent child because of the commission of an act that, if committed by an adult, would be a felony drug abuse offense and alleging that the property with respect to which the order is sought will be subject to forfeiture under division (B) of this section if the juvenile is found to be a delinquent child because of the commission of that act;

(b) Except as provided in division (D)(3) of this section, prior to the filing of an indictment, complaint, or information charging a person who has any right, title, or interest in the property with the commission of a felony drug abuse offense, or prior to the filing of a complaint alleging that a juvenile who has any right, title, or interest in the property is a delinquent child because of the commission of an act that, if committed by an adult, would be a felony drug abuse offense, if, after notice is given to all persons known to have any right, title, or interest in the property and an opportunity to have a hearing on the order is given to those persons, the court determines both of the following:

(i) There is a substantial probability that the state will prevail on the issue of forfeiture and that failure to enter the order will result in the property subject to forfeiture being destroyed, removed from the jurisdiction of the court, or otherwise being made unavailable for forfeiture.

(ii) The need to preserve the availability of the property subject to forfeiture through the entry of the requested order outweighs the hardship on any party against whom the order is to be entered.

(2) Except as provided in division (D)(3) of this section, an order issued under division (D)(1) of this section is effective for not more than ninety days, unless extended by the court for good cause shown or unless an indictment, complaint, or information charging the commission of a felony drug abuse offense or a complaint alleging that a juvenile is a delinquent child because of the commission of an act that, if committed by an adult, would be a felony drug abuse offense, is filed against any alleged adult offender or alleged delinquent child with any right, title, or interest in the property that is the subject of the order.

(3) A court may issue an order under division (D)(1)(b) of this section without giving notice or an opportunity for a hearing to persons known to have any right, title, or interest in property, if the prosecuting attorney who is prosecuting or has jurisdiction to prosecute the felony drug abuse offense or act demonstrates that there is probable cause to believe that the property will be subject to forfeiture under division (B) of this section if a person with any right, title, or interest in the property is convicted of or pleads guilty to a felony drug abuse offense or a juvenile with any right, title, or interest in the property is found by a juvenile court to be a delinquent child for an act that, if committed by an adult, would be a felony drug abuse offense, and that giving notice or an opportunity for a hearing to persons with any right, title, or interest in the property will jeopardize its availability for forfeiture. The order shall be a temporary order and expire not more than ten days after the date on which it is entered, unless it is extended for good cause shown or unless a person with any right, title, or interest in the

property that is the subject of the order consents to an extension for a longer period. A hearing concerning an order issued under this division may be requested, and, if it is requested, the court shall hold the hearing at the earliest possible time prior to the expiration of the order.

(4) At any hearing held under division (D) of this section, the court may receive and consider evidence and information that is inadmissible under the Rules of Evidence. However, each hearing held under division (D) of this section shall be recorded by shorthand, by stenotype, or by any other mechanical, electronic, or video recording device. If, as a result of a hearing under division (D) of this section, property would be seized, the recording of and any transcript of the recording of that hearing shall not be a public record for purposes of section 149.43 of the Revised Code until that property has been seized pursuant to division (D) of this section. Division (D)(4) of this section shall not be construed as requiring, authorizing, or permitting, and does not require, authorize, or permit, the making available for inspection, or the copying, under section 149.43 of the Revised Code of any confidential law enforcement investigatory record or trial preparation record, as defined in that section.

(5) A prosecuting attorney or other law enforcement officer may request the court of common pleas of the county in which property subject to forfeiture under this section is located to issue a warrant authorizing the seizure of that property. The request shall be made in the same manner as provided for a search warrant. If the court determines that there is probable cause to believe that the property to be seized will be subject to forfeiture under this section when a person with any right, title, or interest in the property is convicted of or pleads guilty to a felony drug abuse offense or when a juvenile with any right, title, or interest in the property is found by a juvenile court to be a delinquent child for an act that, if committed by an adult, would be a felony drug abuse offense, and if the court determines that any order issued under division (D)(1), (2), or (3) of this section may not be sufficient to ensure the availability of the property for forfeiture, the court shall issue a warrant authorizing the seizure of the property.

(E)(1) Upon the entry of an order of forfeiture under this section, the court shall order an appropriate law enforcement officer to seize all of the forfeited property upon the terms and conditions that the court determines are proper. In addition, upon the request of the prosecuting attorney who prosecuted the felony drug abuse offense or act, the court shall enter any appropriate restraining orders or injunctions, require the execution of satisfactory performance bonds, appoint receivers, conservators, appraisers, accountants, or trustees, or take any other action to protect the interest of the state in the forfeited property. Any income accruing to or derived from property ordered forfeited under this section may be used to offset ordinary and necessary expenses related to the property that are required by law or that are necessary to protect the interest of the state or third parties.

After forfeited property is seized, the prosecuting attorney who prosecuted the felony drug abuse offense or act shall direct its disposition in accordance with section 2925.44 of the Revised Code, making due provision for the rights of any innocent persons. Any right, title, or interest in property not exercisable by, or transferable for value to, the state shall expire and shall not revert to the offender whose conviction or plea of guilty or act as a delinquent child is the basis of the order of forfeiture. Neither the adult offender or delinquent child nor any person acting in concert with him or on his behalf is eligible to purchase forfeited property at any sale held pursuant to section 2925.44 of the Revised Code.

Upon the application of any person other than the adult offender or delinquent child whose right, title, or interest in the property is the subject of the order of forfeiture or any person acting in concert with him or on his behalf, the court may restrain or stay the sale or other disposition of the property pursuant to section 2925.44 of the Revised Code pending the conclusion of any appeal of the felony drug abuse offense conviction or of the delinquent child adjudication that is the basis of the order of forfeiture, if the applicant demonstrates that proceeding with the sale or other disposition of the property will result in irreparable injury or loss to him.

(2) With respect to property that is the subject of an order of forfeiture issued under this section, the court that issued the order, upon the petition of the prosecuting attorney who prosecuted the felony drug abuse offense or act, may do any of the following:

(a) Grant petitions for mitigation or remission of forfeiture, restore forfeited property to victims of a felony drug abuse offense, or take any other action to protect the rights of innocent persons that is in the interest of justice and that is not inconsistent with this section;

(b) Compromise claims that arise under this section;

(c) Award compensation to persons who provide information resulting in a forfeiture under this section;

(d) Direct the disposition by the prosecuting attorney who prosecuted the felony drug abuse offense or act, in accordance with section 2925.44 of the Revised Code, of all property ordered forfeited under this section, making due provision for the rights of innocent persons;

(e) Pending the disposition of any property that is the subject of an order of forfeiture under this section, take any appropriate measures that are necessary to safeguard and maintain the property.

(3) To facilitate the identification and location of property that is the subject of an order of forfeiture under this section and to facilitate the disposition of petitions for remission or mitigation issued under division (E)(2) of this section, after the issuance of an order of forfeiture under this section and upon application by the prosecuting attorney who prosecuted the felony drug abuse offense or act, the court may order that the testimony of any witness relating to the forfeited property be taken by deposition, and that any designated book, paper, document, record, recording, or other material that is not privileged be produced at the same time and place as the testimony, in the same manner as provided for the taking of depositions under the Rules of Civil Procedure.

(F)(1) Except as provided in divisions (F)(2) to (5) of this section, no person claiming any right, title, or interest in property subject to forfeiture under this section or section 2925.43 of the Revised Code may intervene in a criminal trial or appeal, or a delinquent child proceeding or appeal, involving the forfeiture of the property under this section or in a civil action for a civil forfeiture under section 2925.43 of the Revised Code, or may commence an action at law or equity against the state concerning the validity of his alleged right, title, or interest in the property subsequent to the filing of an indictment, complaint, or information alleging that the property is subject to forfeiture under this section or subsequent to the filing of a complaint alleging that a juvenile who has any right, title, or interest in the property is a delinquent child because of the commission of an act that, if committed by an adult, would be a felony drug abuse offense and alleging that the property is subject to forfeiture under this section.

(2) After the entry of an order of forfeiture under this section, the prosecuting attorney who prosecuted the felony drug abuse offense or act shall conduct or cause to be conducted a search of the appropriate public records that relate to the property, and make or cause to be made reasonably diligent inquiries, for the purpose of identifying persons who have any right, title, or interest in the property. The prosecuting attorney then shall cause a notice of the order of forfeiture, of his intent to dispose of the property in accordance with section 2925.44 of the Revised Code, and of the manner of the proposed disposal, to be given to each person who is known, because of the conduct of the search, the making of the inquiries, or otherwise, to have any right, title, or interest in the property, by certified mail, return receipt requested, or by personal service. Additionally, the prosecuting attorney shall cause a similar notice to be published once a week for two consecutive weeks in a newspaper of general circulation in the county in which the property was seized.

(3)(a) Any person, other than the adult offender whose conviction or guilty plea or the delinquent child whose adjudication is the basis of the order of forfeiture, who asserts a legal right, title, or interest in the property that is the subject of the order may petition the court that issued the order, within thirty days after the earlier of the final publication of notice or his receipt of notice under division (F)(2) of this section, for a hearing to adjudicate the validity of his alleged right, title, or interest in the property. The petition shall be signed by the petitioner under the penalties for falsification as specified in section 2921.13 of the Revised Code and shall set forth the nature and extent of the petitioner's right, title, or interest in the property, the time and circumstances of his acquisition of that right, title, or interest, any additional facts supporting his claim, and the relief sought.

(b) In lieu of filing a petition as described in division (F)(3)(a) of this section, a secured party or other lienholder of record that asserts a legal right, title, or interest in the property that is the subject of the order, including, but not limited to, a mortgage, security interest, or other type of lien, may file an affidavit as described in this division to establish the validity of the alleged right, title, or interest in the property. The affidavit shall be filed within thirty days after the earlier of the final publication of notice or the receipt of notice under division (F)(2) of this section and, except as otherwise provided in this section, shall constitute prima-facie evidence of the validity of the secured party's or other lienholder's alleged right, title, or interest in the property. Unless the prosecuting attorney files a motion challenging the affidavit within ten days after its filing and unless the prosecuting attorney establishes, by a preponderance of the evidence, at a subsequent hearing before the court that issued the forfeiture order, that the secured party or other lienholder does not possess the alleged right, title, or interest in the property or that the secured party or other lienholder had actual knowledge of facts pertaining to the felony drug abuse offense or act that was the basis of the forfeiture order, the affidavit shall constitute conclusive evidence of the validity of the secured party's or other lienholder's right, title, or interest in the property and shall have the legal effect described in division (G)(2) of this section. To the extent practicable and consistent with the interests of justice, any such hearing shall be held within thirty days after the prosecuting attorney files the motion. At any such hearing, the prosecuting attorney and the secured party or other lienholder may present evidence and witnesses and cross-examine witnesses.

In order to be valid for the purposes of this division and division (G)(2) of this section, the affidavit of a secured party or other lienholder shall contain averments that the secured party or other lienholder acquired its alleged right, title, or interest in the property in the regular course of its business, for a specified valuable consideration, without actual knowledge of any facts pertaining to the felony drug abuse offense or act that was the basis of the forfeiture order, in good faith and without the intent to prevent or otherwise impede the state from seizing or obtaining a forfeiture of the property under sections 2925.41 to 2925.45 of the Revised Code, and prior to the seizure or forfeiture of the property under those sections.

(4) Upon receipt of a petition filed under division (F)(3) of this section, the court shall hold a hearing to determine the validity of the petitioner's right, title, or interest in the property that is the subject of the order of forfeiture. To the extent practicable and consistent with the interests of justice, the hearing shall be held within thirty days after the filing of the petition. The court may consolidate the hearing on the petition with a hearing on any other petition filed by a person other than the offender whose conviction or guilty plea or adjudication as a delinquent child is the basis of the order of forfeiture. At the hearing, the petitioner may testify, present evidence and witnesses on his behalf, and cross-examine witnesses for the state. The state may present evidence and witnesses in rebuttal and in defense of its claim to the property and cross-examine witnesses for the petitioner. In addition to evidence and testimony presented at the hearing, the court shall consider the relevant portions of the record in the felony drug abuse offense or delinquent child case that resulted in the order of forfeiture.

(5)(a) The court shall amend its order of forfeiture in accordance with its determination if it determines, at the hearing, that the petitioner has established either of the following by a preponderance of the evidence:

(i) The petitioner has a legal right, title, or interest in the property that renders the order of forfeiture completely or partially invalid because it was vested in the petitioner, rather than the adult offender whose conviction or guilty plea or the delinquent child whose adjudication is the basis of the order, or was superior to any right, title, or interest of that offender, at the time of the commission of the felony drug abuse offense or act that is the basis of the order.

(ii) The petitioner is a bona fide purchaser for value of the right, title, or interest in the property and was at the time of the purchase reasonably without cause to believe that it was subject to forfeiture under this section.

(b) The court also shall amend its order of forfeiture to reflect any right, title, or interest of a secured party or other lienholder of record in the property subject to the order that was established pursuant to division (F)(3)(b) of this section by means of an affidavit, or that was established pursuant to that division by the failure of a prosecuting attorney to establish, in a hearing as described in that division, that the secured party or other lienholder did not possess the alleged right, title, or interest in the property or that the secured party or other lienholder had actual knowledge of facts pertaining to the felony drug abuse offense or act that was the basis of the order.

(G)(1) Subject to division (G)(2) of this section, if the court has disposed of all petitions filed under division (F) of this section or if no petitions are filed under that division and the time for filing petitions under that division has expired, the state shall have clear title to all property that is the subject of an order of forfeiture issued under this section and may warrant good title to any subsequent purchaser or other transferee.

(2) If an affidavit as described in division (F)(3)(b) of this section is filed in accordance with that division, if the affidavit constitutes, under the circumstances described in that division, conclusive evidence of the validity of the right, title, or interest of a secured party or other lienholder of record in the property subject to a forfeiture order, and if any mortgage, security interest, or other type of lien possessed by the secured party or other lienholder in connection with the property is not satisfied prior to a sale or other disposition of the property pursuant to section 2925.44 of the Revised Code, then the right, title, or interest of the secured party or other lienholder in the property remains valid for purposes of sections 2925.41 to 2925.45 of the Revised Code and any subsequent purchaser or other transferee of the property pursuant to section 2925.44 of the Revised Code shall take the property subject to the continued validity of the right, title, or interest of the secured party or other lienholder in the property.
(1992 S 174, eff. 7–31–92; 1990 S 258)

2925.43   Civil forfeiture of property

(A) The following property is subject to forfeiture to the state in a civil action as described in division (E) of this section, and no person has any right, title, or interest in the following property:

(1) Any property that constitutes, or is derived directly or indirectly from, any proceeds that a person obtained directly or indirectly from the commission of an act that, upon the filing of an indictment, complaint, or information, could be prosecuted as a felony drug abuse offense or that, upon the filing of a complaint, could be the basis for finding a juvenile to be a delinquent child for committing an act that, if committed by an adult, would be a felony drug abuse offense;

(2) Any property that was used or intended to be used in any manner to commit, or to facilitate the commission of, an act that, upon the filing of an indictment, complaint, or information, could be prosecuted as a felony drug abuse offense or that, upon the filing of a complaint, could be the basis for finding a juvenile to be a delinquent child for committing an act that, if committed by an adult, would be a felony drug abuse offense.

(B)(1) All right, title, and interest in property described in division (A) of this section shall vest in the state upon the commission of the act giving rise to a civil forfeiture under this section.

(2) The provisions of section 2933.43 of the Revised Code relating to the procedures for the forfeiture of contraband do not apply to a civil action to obtain a civil forfeiture under this section.

(3) Any property taken or detained pursuant to this section is not subject to replevin and is deemed to be in the custody of the head of the law enforcement agency that seized the property.

This section does not preclude the head of a law enforcement agency that seizes property from seeking the forfeiture of that property pursuant to federal law. However, if the head of a law enforcement agency that seizes property does not seek the forfeiture of that property pursuant to federal law and if the property is subject to forfeiture under this section, the property is subject only to the orders of the court of common pleas of the county in which the property is located, and it shall be disposed of in accordance with section 2925.44 of the Revised Code.

(4) Nothing in this section precludes a financial institution that has or purports to have a security interest in or lien on property described in division (A) of this section from commencing a civil action or taking other appropriate legal action in connection with the property, prior to its disposition in accordance with section 2925.44 of the Revised Code, for

the purpose of obtaining possession of the property in order to foreclose or otherwise enforce the security interest or lien. A financial institution may commence a civil action or take other appropriate legal action for that purpose prior to the disposition of the property in accordance with section 2925.44 of the Revised Code, even if a civil action to obtain a civil forfeiture has been or could be commenced under this section, even if the property is or could be the subject of an order of civil forfeiture issued under this section, and even if the property has been seized or is subject to seizure pursuant to this section.

If a financial institution commences a civil action or takes any other appropriate legal action as described in this division, if the financial institution subsequently causes the sale of the property prior to its seizure pursuant to this section and its disposition pursuant to section 2925.44 of the Revised Code, and if the person responsible for the conduct of the sale has actual knowledge of the commencement of a civil action to obtain a civil forfeiture under this section or actual knowledge of an order of civil forfeiture issued under this section, then the person responsible for the conduct of the sale shall dispose of the proceeds of the sale in the following order:

(a) First, to the payment of the costs of the sale and to the payment of the costs incurred by law enforcement agencies and financial institutions in connection with the seizure of, storage of, maintenance of, and provision of security for the property. As used in this division, "costs" of a financial institution do not include attorney's fees incurred by that institution in connection with the property;

(b) Second, the remaining proceeds of the sale after compliance with division (B)(4)(a) of this section, to the payment of valid security interests and liens pertaining to the property that, at the time of the vesting of the right, title, or interest of the adult or juvenile in the state under division (B)(1) of this section, are held by known secured parties and lienholders, in the order of priority of those security interests and liens;

(c) Third, the remaining proceeds of the sale after compliance with division (B)(4)(b) of this section, to the court that has or would have jurisdiction in a civil action to obtain a civil forfeiture under this section, for disposition in accordance with section 2925.44 of the Revised Code.

(C)(1) Any property that is subject to civil forfeiture under this section may be seized by a law enforcement officer upon process, or a warrant as described in division (C)(2) of this section, issued by a court of common pleas that has jurisdiction over the property. Additionally, a seizure of the property, without process or a warrant being so issued, may be made by a law enforcement officer when any of the following applies:

(a) The seizure is incident to an arrest, a search under a search warrant, a lawful search without a search warrant, or an inspection under an administrative inspection warrant.

(b) The property is the subject of a prior judgment in favor of the state in a restraining order, injunction, or other preservation order proceeding under section 2925.42 of the Revised Code, or is the subject of a forfeiture order issued pursuant to that section.

(c) The law enforcement officer has probable cause to believe that the property is directly or indirectly dangerous to the public health or safety.

(d) The initial intrusion by the law enforcement officer afforded him with plain view of personal property that is subject to civil forfeiture in a civil action under this section, the initial intrusion by the law enforcement officer was lawful, the discovery of the personal property by the law enforcement officer was inadvertent, and the incriminating nature of the personal property was immediately apparent to the law enforcement officer.

(2) For purposes of division (C)(1) of this section, the state may request a court of common pleas to issue a warrant that authorizes the seizure of property that is subject to civil forfeiture under this section, in the same manner as provided in Criminal Rule 41 and Chapter 2933. of the Revised Code for the issuance of a search warrant. Additionally, for purposes of division (C)(1) of this section, any proceeding before a court of common pleas that involves a request for the issuance of process, or a warrant as described in this division, authorizing the seizure of any property that is subject to civil forfeiture under this section shall be recorded by shorthand, by stenotype, or by any other mechanical, electronic, or video recording device. The recording of and any transcript of the recording of such a proceeding shall not be a public record for

purposes of section 149.43 of the Revised Code until the property has been seized pursuant to the process or warrant. This division shall not be construed as requiring, authorizing, or permitting, and does not require, authorize, or permit, the making available for inspection, or the copying, under section 149.43 of the Revised Code of any confidential law enforcement investigatory record or trial preparation record, as defined in that section.

(3) If property is seized pursuant to division (C)(1) of this section and if a civil action to obtain a civil forfeiture under this section, a criminal action that could result in a criminal forfeiture under section 2925.42 of the Revised Code, or a delinquent child proceeding that could result in a criminal forfeiture under that section is not pending at the time of the seizure or previously did not occur in connection with the property, then the prosecuting attorney of the county in which the seizure occurred promptly shall commence a civil action to obtain a civil forfeiture under this section in connection with the property, unless an indictment, complaint, or information alleging the commission of a felony drug abuse offense or a complaint alleging that a juvenile is a delinquent child because of the commission of an act that, if committed by an adult, would be a felony drug abuse offense is filed prior to the commencement of the civil action. Nothing in this division precludes, or shall be construed as precluding, the filing of an indictment, complaint, or information alleging the commission of a felony drug abuse offense or the filing of a complaint alleging that a juvenile is a delinquent child because of the commission of an act that, if committed by an adult, would be a felony drug abuse offense, after the commencement of a civil action to obtain a civil forfeiture under this section.

(D)(1) The filing of an indictment, complaint, or information alleging the commission of a felony drug abuse offense that also is the basis of a civil action for a civil forfeiture under this section, or the filing of a complaint alleging that a juvenile is a delinquent child because of the commission of an act that, if committed by an adult, would be a felony drug abuse offense, and that also is the basis of a civil action for a civil forfeiture under this section, upon the motion of the prosecuting attorney of the county in which the indictment, complaint, or information or the complaint in the delinquent child proceeding is filed, shall stay the civil action.

(2) A civil action to obtain a civil forfeiture under this section may be commenced as described in division (E) of this section whether or not the adult or juvenile who committed a felony drug abuse offense or an act that, if committed by an adult, would be a felony drug abuse offense has been charged by an indictment, complaint, or information with the commission of such an offense or such an act, has pleaded guilty to or been found guilty of such an offense, has been determined to be a delinquent child for the commission of such an act, has been found not guilty of committing such an offense, or has not been determined to be a delinquent child for the alleged commission of such an act.

(E)(1) The prosecuting attorney of the county in which property described in division (A) of this section is located may commence a civil action to obtain a civil forfeiture under this section by filing, in the court of common pleas of that county, a complaint that requests the issuance of an order of civil forfeiture of the property to the state. Notices of the action shall be served and published in accordance with division (E)(2) of this section.

(2) Prior to or simultaneously with the commencement of the civil action as described in division (E)(1) of this section, the prosecuting attorney shall conduct or cause to be conducted a search of the appropriate public records that relate to the property subject to civil forfeiture, and make or cause to be made reasonably diligent inquiries, for the purpose of identifying persons who have any right, title, or interest in the property. The prosecuting attorney then shall cause a notice of the commencement of the civil action, together with a copy of the complaint filed in it, to be given to each person who is known, because of the conduct of the search, the making of the inquiries, or otherwise, to have any right, title, or interest in the property, by certified mail, return receipt requested, or by personal service. Additionally, the prosecuting attorney shall cause a similar notice to be published once a week for two consecutive weeks in a newspaper of general circulation in the county in which the property is located.

(3) The procedures specified in divisions (F)(3) to (5) of section 2925.42 of the Revised Code apply to persons claiming any right, title, or interest in property subject to civil forfeiture under this section. The references in those divisions to the adult offender whose conviction or guilty plea, or the delinquent child whose adjudication, is the basis of an order of criminal

forfeiture shall be construed for purposes of this section to mean the adult or juvenile who committed the act that could be the basis of an order of civil forfeiture under this section, and the references in those divisions to an issued order of criminal forfeiture shall be inapplicable.

(4) A hearing shall be held in the civil action described in division (E)(1) of this section at least thirty days after the final publication of notice as required by division (E)(2) of this section and after the date of completion of the service of notice by personal service or certified mail, return receipt requested, as required by that division. Following the hearing, the court shall issue the requested order of civil forfeiture if the court determines that the prosecuting attorney has proven, by clear and convincing evidence, that the property in question is property as described in division (A)(1) or (2) of this section, and if the court has disposed of all petitions filed under division (E)(3) of this section or no petitions have been so filed and the time for filing them has expired. An order of civil forfeiture so issued shall state that all right, title, and interest in the property in question of the adult or juvenile who committed the act that is the basis of the order, is forfeited to the state and shall make due provision for the right, title, or interest in that property of any other person in accordance with any determinations made by the court under division (E)(3) of this section and in accordance with divisions (F)(5)(b) and (G)(2) of section 2925.42 of the Revised Code.

(5) Subject to division (G)(2) of section 2925.42 of the Revised Code, if a court of common pleas enters an order of civil forfeiture in accordance with division (E) of this section, the state shall have clear title to the property that is the subject of the order and may warrant good title to any subsequent purchaser or other transferee.

(1990 S 258, eff. 11–20–90)

2925.44 Disposition of forfeited property

(A) If property is seized pursuant to section 2925.42 or 2925.43 of the Revised Code, it is deemed to be in the custody of the head of the law enforcement agency that seized it, and the head of that agency may do any of the following with respect to that property prior to its disposition in accordance with division (A)(4) or (B) of this section:

(1) Place the property under seal;

(2) Remove the property to a place that the head of that agency designates;

(3) Request the issuance of a court order that requires any other appropriate municipal corporation, county, township, park district created pursuant to section 511.18 or 1545.01 of the Revised Code, or state law enforcement officer or other officer to take custody of the property and, if practicable, remove it to an appropriate location for eventual disposition in accordance with division (B) of this section;

(4)(a) Seek forfeiture of the property pursuant to federal law. If the head of that agency seeks its forfeiture pursuant to federal law, the law enforcement agency shall deposit, use, and account for proceeds from a sale of the property upon its forfeiture, proceeds from another disposition of the property upon its forfeiture, or forfeited moneys it receives, in accordance with the applicable federal law and otherwise shall comply with that law.

(b) If the state highway patrol seized the property and if the superintendent of the state highway patrol seeks its forfeiture pursuant to federal law, the appropriate governmental officials shall deposit into the state highway patrol contraband, forfeiture, and other fund all interest or other earnings derived from the investment of the proceeds from a sale of the property upon its forfeiture, the proceeds from another disposition of the property upon its forfeiture, or the forfeited moneys. The state highway patrol shall use and account for that interest or other earnings in accordance with the applicable federal law.

(c) Division (B) of this section and divisions (D)(1) to (3) of section 2933.43 of the Revised Code do not apply to proceeds or forfeited moneys received pursuant to federal law or to the interest or other earnings that are derived from the investment of proceeds or forfeited moneys received pursuant to federal law and that are described in division (A)(4)(b) of this section.

(B) In addition to complying with any requirements imposed by a court pursuant to section 2925.42 or 2925.43 of the Revised Code, and the requirements imposed by those sections, in relation to the disposition of property forfeited to the state under either of those sections, the prosecuting attorney who is responsible for its disposition shall dispose of the property as follows:

(1) Any vehicle, as defined in section 4501.01 of the Revised Code, that was used in a felony drug abuse offense or in an act that, if committed by an adult, would be a felony drug abuse offense shall be given to the law enforcement agency of the municipal corporation or county in which the offense occurred if that agency desires to have the vehicle, except that, if the offense occurred in a township or in a park district created pursuant to section 511.18 or 1545.01 of the Revised Code and a law enforcement officer employed by the township or the park district was involved in the seizure of the vehicle, the vehicle may be given to the law enforcement agency of that township or park district if that agency desires to have the vehicle, and except that, if the state highway patrol made the seizure of the vehicle, the vehicle may be given to the state highway patrol if it desires to have the vehicle.

(2) Any drug paraphernalia that was used, possessed, sold, or manufactured in a violation of section 2925.14 of the Revised Code that would be a felony drug abuse offense or in a violation of that section committed by a juvenile that, if committed by an adult, would be a felony drug abuse offense, may be given to the law enforcement agency of the municipal corporation or county in which the offense occurred if that agency desires to have and can use the drug paraphernalia, except that, if the offense occurred in a township or in a park district created pursuant to section 511.18 or 1545.01 of the Revised Code and a law enforcement officer employed by the township or the park district was involved in the seizure of the drug paraphernalia, the drug paraphernalia may be given to the law enforcement agency of that township or park district if that agency desires to have and can use the drug paraphernalia. If the drug paraphernalia is not so given, it shall be disposed of by sale pursuant to division (B)(8) of this section or disposed of in another manner that the court that issued the order of forfeiture considers proper under the circumstances.

(3) Drugs shall be disposed of pursuant to section 3719.11 of the Revised Code or placed in the custody of the secretary of the treasury of the United States for disposal or use for medical or scientific purposes under applicable federal law.

(4) Firearms and dangerous ordnance suitable for police work may be given to a law enforcement agency for that purpose. Firearms suitable for sporting use, or as museum pieces or collectors' items, may be disposed of by sale pursuant to division (B)(8) of this section. Other firearms and dangerous ordnance shall be destroyed by a law enforcement agency or shall be sent to the bureau of criminal identification and investigation for destruction by it. As used in this division, "firearms" and "dangerous ordnance" have the same meanings as in section 2923.11 of the Revised Code.

(5) Computers, computer networks, computer systems, and computer software suitable for police work may be given to a law enforcement agency for that purpose. Other computers, computer networks, computer systems, and computer software shall be disposed of by sale pursuant to division (B)(8) of this section or disposed of in another manner that the court that issued the order of forfeiture considers proper under the circumstances. As used in this division, "computers," "computer networks," "computer systems," and "computer software" have the same meanings as in section 2913.01 of the Revised Code.

(6) Obscene materials shall be destroyed.

(7) Beer, intoxicating liquor, and alcohol shall be disposed of in accordance with division (D)(4) of section 2933.41 of the Revised Code.

(8) In the case of property not described in divisions (B)(1) to (7) of this section and of property described in those divisions but not disposed of pursuant to them, the property shall be sold in accordance with division (B)(8) of this section or, in the case of forfeited moneys, disposed of in accordance with division (B)(8) of this section. If the property is to be sold, the prosecuting attorney shall cause a notice of the proposed sale of the property to be given in accordance with law, and the property shall be sold, without appraisal, at a public auction to the highest bidder for cash. The proceeds of a sale and forfeited moneys shall be applied in the following order:

(a) First, to the payment of the costs incurred in connection with the seizure of, storage of, maintenance of, and provision of security for the property, the forfeiture proceeding or civil action, and, if any, the sale;

(b) Second, the remaining proceeds or forfeited moneys after compliance with division (B)(8)(a) of this section, to the payment of the value of any legal right, title, or interest in the property that is possessed by a person who, pursuant to division (F) of section 2925.42 of the Revised Code or division (E) of section 2925.43 of the Revised Code, established the validity of and consequently preserved that legal right, title, or interest, including, but not limited to, any mortgage, perfected or other security interest, or other lien in the property. The value of these rights, titles, or interests shall be paid according to their record or other order of priority.

(c) Third, the remaining proceeds or forfeited moneys after compliance with divisions (B)(8)(a) and (b) of this section, as follows:

(i) If the forfeiture was ordered in a juvenile court, ten per cent to one or more alcohol and drug addiction treatment programs that are certified by the department of alcohol and drug addiction services under section 3793.06 of the Revised Code and that are specified in the order of forfeiture. A juvenile court shall not specify an alcohol or drug addiction treatment program in the order of forfeiture unless the program is a certified alcohol and drug addiction treatment program and, except as provided in division (B)(8)(c)(i) of this section, unless the program is located in the county in which the court that orders the forfeiture is located or in a contiguous county. If no certified alcohol and drug addiction treatment program is located in any of those counties, the juvenile court may specify in the order a certified alcohol and drug addiction treatment program located anywhere within this state.

(ii) If the forfeiture was ordered in a juvenile court, ninety per cent, and if the forfeiture was ordered in a court other than a juvenile court, one hundred per cent to appropriate funds in accordance with divisions (D)(1)(c) and (2) of section 2933.43 of the Revised Code. The remaining proceeds or forfeited moneys so deposited shall be used only for the purposes authorized by those divisions and division (D)(3)(a)(ii) of that section.

(C)(1) Sections 2925.41 to 2925.45 of the Revised Code do not preclude a financial institution that possessed a valid mortgage, security interest, or lien that is not satisfied prior to a sale under division (B)(8) of this section or following a sale by application of division (B)(8)(b) of this section, from commencing a civil action in any appropriate court in this or another state to obtain a deficiency judgment against the debtor if the financial institution otherwise would have been entitled to do so in this or another state.

(2) Any law enforcement agency that obtains any vehicle pursuant to division (B)(1) of this section shall take the vehicle subject to the outstanding amount of any security interest or lien that attaches to the vehicle.

(3) Nothing in this section impairs a mortgage, security interest, lien, or other interest of a financial institution in property that was the subject of a forfeiture order under section 2925.42 or 2925.43 of the Revised Code and that was sold or otherwise disposed of in a manner that does not conform to the requirements of division (B) of this section, or any right of a financial institution of that nature to commence a civil action in any appropriate court in this or another state to obtain a deficiency judgment against the debtor.

(4) Following the sale under division (B)(8) of this section of any property that is required to be titled or registered under the law of this state, the prosecuting attorney responsible for the disposition of the property shall cause the state to issue an appropriate certificate of title or registration to the purchaser of the property. Additionally, if, in a disposition of property pursuant to division (B) of this section, the state or a political subdivision is given any property that is required to be titled or registered under the law of this state, the prosecuting attorney responsible for the disposition of the property shall cause the state to issue an appropriate certificate of title or registration to itself or to the political subdivision.

(D) Property that has been forfeited to the state pursuant to an order of criminal forfeiture under section 2925.42 of the Revised Code or an order of civil forfeiture under section 2925.43 of the Revised Code shall not be available for use to pay any fine imposed upon a person who is convicted of or pleads guilty to a felony drug abuse offense or upon any juvenile who is found by a juvenile court to be a delinquent child for an act that, if committed by an adult, would be a felony drug abuse offense.

(E) Sections 2925.41 to 2925.45 of the Revised Code do not prohibit a law enforcement officer from seeking the forfeiture of contraband associated with a felony drug abuse offense pursuant to section 2933.43 of the Revised Code.

(1995 H 1, eff. 1–1–96; 1995 H 107, eff. (See Historical and Statutory Notes); 1992 S 174, eff. 7–31–92; 1991 S 218; 1990 S 258)

Historical and Statutory Notes

Ed. Note: 1995 H 107 Effective Date—The Secretary of State assigned a general effective date of 6–30–95 for 1995 H 107. Pursuant to O Const Art II § 1c and 1d, and RC 1.471, sections of 1995 H 107 that are, or depend for their implementation upon, current expense appropriations are effective 3–31–95; sections of 1995 H 107 that are not, and do not depend for their implementation upon, current expense appropriations are effective 6–30–95. See Uncodified Law, 1995 H 107, § 16.

2925.45 Motion for possession of unlawfully seized property

(A) Any person who is aggrieved by an alleged unlawful seizure of property that potentially is subject to forfeiture under section 2925.42 or 2925.43 of the Revised Code may file a motion as described in division (B) of this section with whichever of the following courts is appropriate under the circumstances, within the time described in division (C) of this section:

(1) The court of common pleas in which a criminal prosecution for a felony drug abuse offense is pending;

(2) The juvenile court in which a delinquent child action for an act that, if committed by an adult, would be a felony drug abuse offense is pending;

(3) The court of common pleas in which a civil action as described in division (E) of section 2925.43 of the Revised Code is pending;

(4) The court of common pleas of the county in which the property was seized.

(B) The motion shall specify that the seizure of specified property was unlawful, state the reasons why the movant believes the seizure was unlawful, state that the movant is lawfully entitled to possession of the seized property, and request the court of common pleas to issue an order that mandates the law enforcement agency having custody of the seized property to return it to the movant. For purposes of this division, an unlawful seizure of property includes, but is not limited to, a seizure in violation of the Fourth Amendment to the Constitution of the United States or of Section 14 of Article I, Ohio Constitution, and a seizure pursuant to sections 2925.41 to 2925.44 of the Revised Code of property other than potentially forfeitable property as described in division (A)(1) of section 2925.42 or division (A) of section 2925.43 of the Revised Code.

(C)(1) If a motion as described in division (A) of this section is filed prior to the entry of an order of forfeiture under section 2925.42 or 2925.43 of the Revised Code, the court of common pleas promptly shall schedule a hearing on the motion and cause notice of the date and time of the hearing to be given to the movant and the prosecuting attorney of the county in which the property was seized. At the hearing, the movant and the prosecuting attorney may present witnesses and evidence relative to the issues of whether the property in question was unlawfully seized and whether the movant is lawfully entitled to possession of it. If, after the hearing, the court of common pleas determines that the movant has established, by a preponderance of the evidence, that the property in question was unlawfully seized and that the movant is lawfully entitled to possession of it, the court shall issue an order that requires the law enforcement agency having custody of the seized property to return it to the movant.

(2)(a) If a motion is filed in accordance with division (C)(1) of this section and, at the time of filing or of the hearing on the motion, a criminal prosecution for a felony drug abuse offense or a delinquent child action for an act that, if committed by an adult, would be a felony drug abuse offense has been commenced by the filing of an indictment, information, or complaint, then the court of common pleas shall treat the motion as a motion to suppress evidence.

(b) If an order to return seized property is issued pursuant to division (C)(1) of this section, the returned property shall not be admissible in evidence in any pending or subsequently commenced criminal prosecution for a felony drug abuse offense if the prosecution arose or arises out of the unlawful seizure of the property, or in any pending or subsequently commenced delinquent child action for an act that, if committed by an adult, would be a felony drug abuse offense if the action arose or arises out of the unlawful seizure of the property. (1990 S 258, eff. 11–20–90)

MISCELLANEOUS PROVISIONS

2925.50 Federal prosecution acts as bar

If a violation of this chapter is a violation of federal narcotic laws, as defined in section 3719.01 of the Revised Code, a conviction or acquittal under federal narcotic laws for the same act is a bar to prosecution in this state.

(1975 H 300, eff. 7–1–76)

2925.51 Laboratory report as prima-facie evidence of content; weight and identity of substance; rights of accused

(A) In any criminal prosecution for a violation of this chapter or Chapter 3719. of the Revised Code, a laboratory report from the bureau of criminal identification and investigation, a laboratory operated by another law enforcement agency, or a laboratory established by or under the authority of an institution of higher education that has its main campus in this state and that is accredited by the association of American universities or the north central association of colleges and secondary schools, primarily for the purpose of providing scientific services to law enforcement agencies and signed by the person performing the analysis, stating that the substance which is the basis of the alleged offense has been weighed and analyzed and stating the findings as to the content, weight, and identity of the substance and that it contains any amount of a controlled substance and the number and description of unit dosages, is prima-facie evidence of the content, identity, and weight or the existence and number of unit dosages of the substance.

Attached to that report shall be a copy of a notarized statement by the signer of the report giving the name of the signer and stating that he is an employee of the laboratory issuing the report and that performing the analysis is a part of his regular duties, and giving an outline of his education, training, and experience for performing an analysis of materials included under this section. The signer shall attest that scientifically accepted tests were performed with due caution, and that the evidence was handled in accordance with established and accepted procedures while in the custody of the laboratory.

(B) The prosecuting attorney shall serve a copy of the report on the attorney of record for the accused, or on the accused if he has no attorney, prior to any proceeding in which the report is to be used against the accused other than at a preliminary hearing or grand jury proceeding where the report may be used without having been previously served upon the accused.

(C) The report shall not be prima-facie evidence of the contents, identity, and weight or the existence and number of unit dosages of the substance if the accused or his attorney demands the testimony of the person signing the report, by serving the demand upon the prosecuting attorney within seven days from the accused or his attorney's receipt of the report. The time may be extended by a trial judge in the interests of justice.

(D) Any report issued for use under this section shall contain notice of the right of the accused to demand, and the manner in which the accused shall demand, the testimony of the person signing the report.

(E) Any person who is accused of a violation of this chapter or of Chapter 3719. of the Revised Code is entitled, upon written request made to the prosecuting attorney, to have a portion of the substance that is the basis of the alleged violation preserved for the benefit of independent analysis performed by a laboratory analyst employed by the accused person, or, if he is indigent, by a qualified laboratory analyst appointed by the court. Such portion shall be a representative sample of the entire substance that is the basis of the alleged violation and shall be of sufficient size, in the opinion of the court, to permit the accused's analyst to make a thorough scientific analysis concerning the identity of the substance. The prosecuting attorney shall provide the accused's analyst with the sample portion at least fourteen days prior to trial, unless the trial is to be held in a court not of record or unless the accused person is charged with a minor misdemeanor, in which case the prosecuting attorney shall provide the accused's analyst with the sample portion at least three days prior to trial. If the prosecuting attorney determines that such a sample portion cannot be preserved and given to the accused's analyst, the prosecuting attorney shall so inform the accused person or his attorney. In such a circumstance, the accused person is entitled, upon written request made to the prosecuting attorney, to have his privately employed or court appointed analyst present at an analysis of the substance that is the basis of the alleged violation, and, upon further written request, to receive copies of all recorded scientific data that result from the analysis and that can be used by an analyst in arriving at conclusions, findings, or opinions concerning the identity of the substance subject to the analysis.

(F) In addition to the rights provided under division (E) of this section, any person who is accused of a violation of this chapter or of Chapter 3719. of the Revised Code that involves a bulk amount of a controlled substance, or any multiple thereof, or who is accused of a violation of section 2925.11 of the Revised Code, other than a minor misdemeanor violation, that involves marihuana, is entitled, upon written request made to the prosecuting attorney, to have a laboratory analyst of his choice, or, if the accused is indigent, a qualified laboratory analyst appointed by the court present at a measurement or weighing of the substance that is the basis of the alleged violation. Also, the accused person is entitled, upon further written request, to receive copies of all recorded scientific data that result from the measurement or weighing and that can be used by an analyst in arriving at conclusions, findings, or opinions concerning the weight, volume, or number of unit doses of the substance subject to the measurement or weighing.

(1977 S 201, eff. 11–16–77; 1976 S 541; 1975 H 300)

CHAPTER 2927

MISCELLANEOUS OFFENSES

2927.01 Offenses against human corpse

(A) No person, except as authorized by law, shall treat a human corpse in a way that he knows would outrage reasonable family sensibilities.

(B) No person, except as authorized by law, shall treat a human corpse in a way that would outrage reasonable community sensibilities.

(C) Whoever violates division (A) of this section is guilty of abuse of a corpse, a misdemeanor of the second degree. Whoever violates division (B) of this section is guilty of gross abuse of a corpse, a felony of the fourth degree.

(1978 H 741, eff. 10-9-78; 1972 H 511)

2927.02 Illegal distribution of cigarettes or other tobacco products; vending machines

(A) No manufacturer, producer, distributor, wholesaler, or retailer of cigarettes or other tobacco products, or any agent, employee, or representative of a manufacturer, producer, distributor, wholesaler, or retailer of cigarettes or other tobacco products shall do any of the following:

(1) Give, sell, or otherwise distribute cigarettes or other tobacco products to any person under eighteen years of age;

(2) Give away, sell, or distribute cigarettes or other tobacco products in any place that does not have posted in a conspicuous place a sign stating that giving, selling, or otherwise distributing cigarettes or other tobacco products to a person under eighteen years of age is prohibited by law.

(B) No person shall sell or offer to sell cigarettes or other tobacco products by or from a vending machine except in the following locations:

(1) An area either:

(a) Within a factory, business, office, or other place not open to the general public; or

(b) To which persons under the age of eighteen years are not generally permitted access;

(2) In any other place not identified in division (B)(1) of this section, upon all of the following conditions:

(a) The vending machine is located within the immediate vicinity, plain view, and control of the person who owns or operates the place, or an employee of such person, so that all cigarettes and other tobacco product purchases from the vending machine will be readily observed by the person who owns or operates the place or an employee of such person. For the purpose of this section, a vending machine located in any unmonitored area, including an unmonitored coatroom, restroom, hallway, or outer waiting area, shall not be considered located within the immediate vicinity, plain view, and control of the person who owns or operates the place, or an employee of such person.

239

(b) The vending machine is inaccessible to the public when the place is closed.

(C) As used in this section, "vending machine" has the same meaning as "coin machine" as defined in section 2913.01 of the Revised Code.

(D) Whoever violates this section is guilty of illegal distribution of cigarettes or other tobacco products, a misdemeanor of the fourth degree. If the offender previously has been convicted of a violation of this section, then illegal distribution of cigarettes or other tobacco products is a misdemeanor of the third degree.

(1991 S 40, eff. 10–23–91; 1984 H 152)

2927.03   Injuring, intimidating, or interfering with housing

(A) No person, whether or not acting under color of law, shall by force or threat of force willfully injure, intimidate, or interfere with, or attempt to injure, intimidate, or interfere with any of the following:

(1) Any person because of race, color, religion, sex, familial status, as defined in section 4112.01 of the Revised Code, national origin, handicap, as defined in that section, or ancestry and because that person is or has been selling, purchasing, renting, financing, occupying, contracting, or negotiating for the sale, purchase, rental, financing, or occupation of any housing accommodations, or applying for or participating in any service, organization, or facility relating to the business of selling or renting housing accommodations;

(2) Any person because that person is or has been, or in order to intimidate that person or any other person or any class of persons from doing either of the following:

(a) Participating, without discrimination on account of race, color, religion, sex, familial status, as defined in section 4112.01 of the Revised Code, national origin, handicap, as defined in that section, or ancestry, in any of the activities, services, organizations, or facilities described in division (A)(1) of this section;

(b) Affording another person or class of persons opportunity or protection so to participate.

(3) Any person because that person is or has been, or in order to discourage that person or any other person from, lawfully aiding or encouraging other persons to participate, without discrimination on account of race, color, religion, sex, familial status, as defined in section 4112.01 of the Revised Code, national origin, handicap, as defined in that section, or ancestry, in any of the activities, services, organizations, or facilities described in division (A)(1) of this section, or participating lawfully in speech or peaceful assembly opposing any denial of the opportunity to so participate.

(B) Whoever violates division (A) of this section is guilty of a misdemeanor of the first degree, except that whoever violates division (A) of this section and causes bodily injury is guilty of a felony of the third degree, and whoever violates division (A) of this section and causes death is guilty of a felony of the first degree and subject to life imprisonment.

(1992 H 321, eff. 6–30–92; 1987 H 5)

2927.11   Desecration; fine

(A) No person, without privilege to do so, shall purposely deface, damage, pollute, or otherwise physically mistreat any of the following:

(1) The flag of the United States or of this state;

(2) Any public monument;

(3) Any historical or commemorative marker, or any structure, Indian mound or earthwork, thing, or site of great historical or archaeological interest;

(4) A place of worship, its furnishings, or religious artifacts or sacred texts within the place of worship;

(5) A work of art or museum piece;

(6) Any other object of reverence or sacred devotion.

(B) Whoever violates this section is guilty of desecration. Violation of division (A)(1), (2), (3), (5), or (6) of this section is a misdemeanor of the second degree. Violation of division

(A)(4) of this section is a misdemeanor of the first degree that is punishable by a fine of up to four thousand dollars in addition to the penalties specified for a misdemeanor of the first degree in section 2929.21 of the Revised Code.

(1986 S 316, eff. 3–19–87; 1978 H 741; 1976 H 418; 1972 H 511)

2927.12   Ethnic intimidation

(A) No person shall violate section 2903.21, 2903.22, 2909.06, or 2909.07, or division (A)(3), (4), or (5) of section 2917.21 of the Revised Code by reason of the race, color, religion, or national origin of another person or group of persons.

(B) Whoever violates this section is guilty of ethnic intimidation. Ethnic intimidation is an offense of the next higher degree than the offense the commission of which is a necessary element of ethnic intimidation.

(1986 S 316, eff. 3–19–87)

2927.13   Sale or donation of blood by AIDS carrier

(A) No person, with knowledge that he is a carrier of a virus that causes acquired immune deficiency syndrome, shall sell or donate his blood, plasma, or a product of his blood, if he knows or should know the blood, plasma, or product of his blood is being accepted for the purpose of transfusion to another individual.

(B) Whoever violates this section is guilty of selling or donating contaminated blood, a felony of the third degree.

(1988 H 571, eff. 3–17–89)

2927.21   Escape of exotic or dangerous animal; report

(A) The owner or keeper of any member of a species of the animal kingdom that escapes from his custody or control and that is not indigenous to this state or presents a risk of serious physical harm to persons or property, or both, shall, within one hour after he discovers or reasonably should have discovered the escape, report it to:

(1) A law enforcement officer of the municipal corporation or township and the sheriff of the county where the escape occurred; and

(2) The clerk of the municipal legislative authority or the township clerk of the township where the escape occurred.

(B) If the office of the clerk of a legislative authority or township clerk is closed to the public at the time a report is required by division (A) of this section, then it is sufficient compliance with division (A)(2) of this section if the owner or keeper makes the report within one hour after the office is next open to the public.

(C) Whoever violates this section is guilty of a misdemeanor of the first degree.

(1985 H 32, eff. 9–11–85)

2927.24   Contaminating substance for human consumption or use; spreading false report of contamination

(A) As used in this section, "poison" and "drug" have the same meanings as in section 4729.02 of the Revised Code.

(B) Except as provided in division (D) of this section, no person shall knowingly mingle a poison or other harmful substance with a food, drink, nonprescription drug, prescription drug, or pharmaceutical product, or knowingly place a poison or other harmful substance in a spring, well, reservoir, or public water supply, if the person knows or has reason to know that the food, drink, nonprescription drug, prescription drug, pharmaceutical product, or water may be ingested or used by another person. For purposes of this division, a person does not know or have reason to know that water may be ingested or used by another person if it is disposed of as waste into a household drain including the drain of a toilet, sink, tub, or floor.

(C) No person shall inform another person that a poison or other harmful substance has been or will be placed in a food, drink, nonprescription drug, prescription drug, or other pharmaceutical product, spring, well, reservoir, or public water supply, if the placement of the poison or other harmful substance would be a violation of division (B) of this section, and the person knows both that the information is false and that the information likely will be disseminated to the public.

(D)(1) A person may mingle a drug with a food or drink for the purpose of causing the drug to be ingested or used in the quantity described by its labeling or prescription.

(2) A person may place a poison or other harmful substance in a spring, well, reservoir, or public water supply in such quantity as is necessary to treat the spring, well, reservoir, or water supply to make it safe for human consumption and use.

(3) The provisions of division (A) of this section shall not be applied in a manner that conflicts with any other state or federal law or rule relating to substances permitted to be applied to or present in any food, raw or processed, any milk or milk product, any meat or meat product, any type of crop, water, or alcoholic or nonalcoholic beverage.

(E)(1) Whoever violates division (B) of this section is guilty of contaminating a substance for human consumption or use, a felony of the first degree. If the offense involved an amount of poison or other harmful substance sufficient to cause death if ingested or used by a person or if the offense resulted in serious physical harm to another person, whoever violates division (B) of this section is guilty of an aggravated felony of the first degree and shall be imprisoned for life.

(2) Whoever violates division (C) of this section is guilty of spreading a false report of contamination, a felony of the third degree.

(1994 H 280, eff. 6–29–94)

DEFINITIONS

DEFINITIONS

2929.01   Definitions

As used in sections 2929.01 to 2929.51 of the Revised Code:

(A) "Repeat offender" means a person who has a history of persistent criminal activity, and whose character and condition reveal a substantial risk that he will commit another offense. It is prima-facie evidence that a person is a repeat offender if any of the following apply:

(1) Having been convicted of one or more offenses of violence, and having been imprisoned pursuant to sentence for any such offense, he commits a subsequent offense of violence;

(2) Having been convicted of one or more sex offenses as defined in section 2950.01 of the Revised Code, and having been imprisoned pursuant to sentence for any such offense, he commits a subsequent sex offense;

(3) Having been convicted of one or more theft offenses as defined in section 2913.01 of the Revised Code, and having been imprisoned pursuant to sentence for any such offense, he commits a subsequent theft offense;

(4) Having been convicted of one or more felony drug abuse offenses as defined in Chapter 2925. of the Revised Code, and having been imprisoned pursuant to sentence for any such offense, he commits a subsequent felony drug abuse offense;

(5) Having been convicted of two or more felonies, and having been imprisoned pursuant to sentence for any such offense, he commits a subsequent offense;

(6) Having been convicted of three or more offenses of any type or degree other than traffic offenses, alcoholic intoxication offenses, or minor misdemeanors, and having been imprisoned pursuant to sentence for any such offense, he commits a subsequent offense.

(B) "Dangerous offender" means a person who has committed an offense, whose history, character, and condition reveal a substantial risk that he will be a danger to others, and whose conduct has been characterized by a pattern of repetitive, compulsive, or aggressive behavior with heedless indifference to the consequences.

(C) "Actual incarceration" means that an offender is required to be imprisoned for the stated period of time to which he is sentenced that is specified as a term of actual incarceration. If a person is sentenced to a term of actual incarceration, the court shall not suspend his term of actual incarceration, and shall not grant him probation or shock probation, pursuant to section 2929.51, 2947.061, 2951.02, or 2951.04 of the Revised Code, and the department of rehabilitation and correction or the adult parole authority shall not, pursuant to Chapter 2967. of the Revised Code or its rules adopted pursuant to Chapter 2967., 5120., or 5149. of the Revised Code, grant him a furlough for employment or education, a furlough for being a trustworthy prisoner other than a furlough pursuant to division (A)(1)(a) or (b) of section 2967.27 of the Revised Code, parole, emergency parole, or shock parole until after the expiration of his term of actual incarceration, diminished as provided in sections 2967.19, 2967.193, and 5145.11 of the Revised Code.

An offender who is sentenced to a term of actual incarceration may be transferred from an institution operated by the department of rehabilitation and correction to the custody of the department of mental health or the department of mental retardation and developmental disabilities, as provided in section 5120.17 of the Revised Code, and shall be credited with all time served in the custody of the department of mental health or the department of mental retardation and developmental disabilities against the term of actual incarceration.

(D) "Deadly weapon" has the same meaning as in section 2923.11 of the Revised Code.

(1994 S 186, eff. 10–12–94; 1994 H 571, eff. 10–6–94; 1987 H 261, eff. 11–1–87; 1983 S 210; 1982 H 269, § 4, S 199; 1978 H 565; 1975 H 300; 1972 H 511)

Historical and Statutory Notes

Ed. Note: A special endorsement by the Legislative Service Commission states, "Comparison of these amendments [1994 S 186, eff. 10–12–94 and 1994 H 571, eff. 10–6–94] in pursuance of section 1.52 of the Revised Code discloses that they are not irreconcilable, so that they are required by that section to be harmonized to give effect to each amendment." In recognition of this rule of construction, changes made by 1994 S 186, eff. 10–12–94, and 1994 H 571, eff. 10–6–94, have been incorporated in the above amendment. See *Baldwin's Ohio Legislative Service*, 1994 Laws of Ohio, pages 5–922 and 5–1153, for original versions of these Acts.

PENALTIES FOR MURDER

2929.02   Penalties for murder

(A) Whoever is convicted of, pleads guilty to, or pleads no contest and is found guilty of, aggravated murder in violation of section 2903.01 of the Revised Code shall suffer death or be imprisoned for life, as determined pursuant to sections 2929.022, 2929.03, and 2929.04 of the Revised Code, except that no person who raises the matter of age pursuant to section 2929.023 or division (C) of section 2929.05 of the Revised Code and who is not found to have been eighteen years of age or older at the time of the commission of the offense shall suffer death.

In addition, the offender may be fined an amount fixed by the court, but not more than twenty-five thousand dollars.

(B) Whoever is convicted of, pleads guilty to, or pleads no contest and is found guilty of, murder in violation of section 2903.02 of the Revised Code shall be imprisoned for an indefinite term of fifteen years to life. In addition, the offender may be fined an amount fixed by the court, but not more than fifteen thousand dollars.

(C) The court shall not impose a fine or fines for aggravated murder or murder which, in the aggregate and to the extent not suspended by the court, exceeds the amount which the offender is or will be able to pay by the method and within the time allowed without undue hardship to himself or his dependents, or will prevent him from making reparation for the victim's wrongful death.

(1981 S 1, eff. 10–19–81; 1972 H 511)

2929.021 Specifications of aggravating circumstance; clerk to notify supreme court of certain facts

(A) If an indictment or a count in an indictment charges the defendant with aggravated murder and contains one or more specifications of aggravating circumstances listed in division (A) of section 2929.04 of the Revised Code, the clerk of the court in which the indictment is filed, within fifteen days after the day on which it is filed, shall file a notice with the supreme court indicating that the indictment was filed. The notice shall be in the form prescribed by the clerk of the supreme court and shall contain, for each charge of aggravated murder with a specification, at least the following information pertaining to the charge:

(1) The name of the person charged in the indictment or count in the indictment with aggravated murder with a specification;

(2) The docket number or numbers of the case or cases arising out of the charge, if available;

(3) The court in which the case or cases will be heard;

(4) The date on which the indictment was filed.

(B) If an indictment or a count in an indictment charges the defendant with aggravated murder and contains one or more specifications of aggravating circumstances listed in division (A) of section 2929.04 of the Revised Code and if the defendant pleads guilty or no contest to any offense in the case or if the indictment or any count in the indictment is dismissed, the clerk of the court in which the plea is entered or the indictment or count is dismissed shall file a notice with the supreme court indicating what action was taken in the case. The notice shall be filed within fifteen days after the plea is entered or the indictment or count is dismissed, shall be in the form prescribed by the clerk of the supreme court, and shall contain at least the following information:

(1) The name of the person who entered the guilty or no contest plea or who is named in the indictment or count that is dismissed;

(2) The docket numbers of the cases in which the guilty or no contest plea is entered or in which the indictment or count is dismissed;

(3) The sentence imposed on the offender in each case.

(1981 S 1, eff. 10–19–81)

2929.022 Elections of defendant as to certain trial procedures

(A) If an indictment or count in an indictment charging a defendant with aggravated murder contains a specification of the aggravating circumstance of a prior conviction listed in division (A)(5) of section 2929.04 of the Revised Code, the defendant may elect to have the panel of three judges, if he waives trial by jury, or the trial judge, if he is tried by jury, determine the existence of that aggravating circumstance at the sentencing hearing held pursuant to divisions (C) and (D) of section 2929.03 of the Revised Code.

(1) If the defendant does not elect to have the existence of the aggravating circumstance determined at the sentencing hearing, the defendant shall be tried on the charge of aggravated

murder, on the specification of the aggravating circumstance of a prior conviction listed in division (A)(5) of section 2929.04 of the Revised Code, and on any other specifications of an aggravating circumstance listed in division (A) of section 2929.04 of the Revised Code in a single trial as in any other criminal case in which a person is charged with aggravated murder and specifications.

(2) If the defendant does elect to have the existence of the aggravating circumstance of a prior conviction listed in division (A)(5) of section 2929.04 of the Revised Code determined at the sentencing hearing, then, following a verdict of guilty of the charge of aggravated murder, the panel of three judges or the trial judge shall:

(a) Hold a sentencing hearing pursuant to division (B) of this section, unless required to do otherwise under division (A)(2)(b) of this section;

(b) If the offender raises the matter of age at trial pursuant to section 2929.023 of the Revised Code and is not found at trial to have been eighteen years of age or older at the time of the commission of the offense, conduct a hearing to determine if the specification of the aggravating circumstance of a prior conviction listed in division (A)(5) of section 2929.04 of the Revised Code is proven beyond a reasonable doubt. After conducting the hearing, the panel or judge shall proceed as follows:

(i) If that aggravating circumstance is proven beyond a reasonable doubt or if the defendant at trial was convicted of any other specification of an aggravating circumstance, the panel or judge shall impose sentence according to division (E) of section 2929.03 of the Revised Code;

(ii) If that aggravating circumstance is not proven beyond a reasonable doubt and the defendant at trial was not convicted of any other specification of an aggravating circumstance, the panel or judge shall impose sentence of life imprisonment with parole eligibility after serving twenty years of imprisonment on the offender.

(B) At the sentencing hearing, the panel of judges, if the defendant was tried by a panel of three judges, or the trial judge, if the defendant was tried by jury, shall, when required pursuant to division (A)(2) of this section, first determine if the specification of the aggravating circumstance of a prior conviction listed in division (A)(5) of section 2929.04 of the Revised Code is proven beyond a reasonable doubt. If the panel of judges or the trial judge determines that the specification of the aggravating circumstance of a prior conviction listed in division (A)(5) of section 2929.04 of the Revised Code is proven beyond a reasonable doubt or if they do not determine that the specification is proven beyond a reasonable doubt but the defendant at trial was convicted of a specification of any other aggravating circumstance listed in division (A) of section 2929.04 of the Revised Code, the panel of judges or the trial judge and trial jury shall impose sentence on the offender pursuant to division (D) of section 2929.03 and section 2929.04 of the Revised Code. If the panel of judges or the trial judge does not determine that the specification of the aggravating circumstance of a prior conviction listed in division (A)(5) of section 2929.04 of the Revised Code is proven beyond a reasonable doubt and the defendant at trial was not convicted of any other specification of an aggravating circumstance listed in division (A) of section 2929.04 of the Revised Code, the panel of judges or the trial judge shall terminate the sentencing hearing and impose a sentence of life imprisonment with parole eligibility after serving twenty years of imprisonment on the offender.

(1981 S 1, eff. 10–19–81)

2929.023 Defendant's age; raising issue; burdens relating to matter

A person charged with aggravated murder and one or more specifications of an aggravating circumstance may, at trial, raise the matter of his age at the time of the alleged commission of the offense and may present evidence at trial that he was not eighteen years of age or older at the time of the alleged commission of the offense. The burdens of raising the matter of age, and of going forward with the evidence relating to the matter of age, are upon the defendant. After a defendant has raised the matter of age at trial, the prosecution shall have the burden of proving, by proof beyond a reasonable doubt, that the defendant was eighteen years of age or older at the time of the alleged commission of the offense.

(1981 S 1, eff. 10–19–81)

2929.024 Indigency; services of investigation; experts; payment

If the court determines that the defendant is indigent and that investigation services, experts, or other services are reasonably necessary for the proper representation of a defendant charged with aggravated murder at trial or at the sentencing hearing, the court shall authorize the defendant's counsel to obtain the necessary services for the defendant, and shall order that payment of the fees and expenses for the necessary services be made in the same manner that payment for appointed counsel is made pursuant to Chapter 120. of the Revised Code. If the court determines that the necessary services had to be obtained prior to court authorization for payment of the fees and expenses for the necessary services, the court may, after the services have been obtained, authorize the defendant's counsel to obtain the necessary services and order that payment of the fees and expenses for the necessary services be made as provided in this section.

(1981 S 1, eff. 10–19–81)

2929.03 Imposing sentence for a capital offense; procedures; proof of relevant factors; alternative sentences

(A) If the indictment or count in the indictment charging aggravated murder does not contain one or more specifications of aggravating circumstances listed in division (A) of section 2929.04 of the Revised Code, then, following a verdict of guilty of the charge of aggravated murder, the trial court shall impose a sentence of life imprisonment with parole eligibility after serving twenty years of imprisonment on the offender.

(B) If the indictment or count in the indictment charging aggravated murder contains one or more specifications of aggravating circumstances listed in division (A) of section 2929.04 of the Revised Code, the verdict shall separately state whether the accused is found guilty or not guilty of the principal charge and, if guilty of the principal charge, whether the offender was eighteen years of age or older at the time of the commission of the offense, if the matter of age was raised by the offender pursuant to section 2929.023 of the Revised Code, and whether the offender is guilty or not guilty of each specification. The jury shall be instructed on its duties in this regard, which shall include an instruction that a specification shall be proved beyond a reasonable doubt in order to support a guilty verdict on the specification, but such instruction shall not mention the penalty which may be the consequence of a guilty or not guilty verdict on any charge or specification.

(C)(1) If the indictment or count in the indictment charging aggravated murder contains one or more specifications of aggravating circumstances listed in division (A) of section 2929.04 of the Revised Code, then, following a verdict of guilty of the charge but not guilty of each of the specifications, and regardless of whether the offender raised the matter of age pursuant to section 2929.023 of the Revised Code, the trial court shall impose a sentence of life imprisonment with parole eligibility after serving twenty years of imprisonment on the offender.

(2) If the indictment or count in the indictment contains one or more specifications of aggravating circumstances listed in division (A) of section 2929.04 of the Revised Code, and if the offender is found guilty of both the charge and one or more of the specifications, the penalty to be imposed on the offender shall be death, life imprisonment with parole eligibility after serving twenty full years of imprisonment, or life imprisonment with parole eligibility after serving thirty full years of imprisonment, shall be determined pursuant to divisions (D) and (E) of this section, and shall be determined by one of the following:

(a) By the panel of three judges that tried the offender upon the offender's waiver of the right to trial by jury;

(b) By the trial jury and the trial judge, if the offender was tried by jury.

(D)(1) Death may not be imposed as a penalty for aggravated murder if the offender raised the matter of age at trial pursuant to section 2929.023 of the Revised Code and was not found at trial to have been eighteen years of age or older at the time of the commission of the offense. When death may be imposed as a penalty for aggravated murder, the court shall proceed under this division. When death may be imposed as a penalty, the court, upon the request of the defendant, shall require a pre-sentence investigation to be made and, upon the request of the defendant, shall require a mental examination to be made, and shall require reports of the investigation and of any mental examination submitted to the court, pursuant to section 2947.06 of the Revised Code. No statement made or information provided by a defendant in a mental examination or proceeding conducted pursuant to this division shall be disclosed to any person, except as provided in this division, or be used in evidence against the defendant on the issue of guilt in any retrial. A pre-sentence investigation or mental examination shall not be made except upon request of the defendant. Copies of any reports prepared under this division shall be furnished to the court, to the trial jury if the offender was tried by a jury, to the prosecutor, and to the offender or the offender's counsel for use under this division. The court, and the trial jury if the offender was tried by a jury, shall consider any report prepared pursuant to this division and furnished to it and any evidence raised at trial that is relevant to the aggravating circumstances the offender was found guilty of committing or to any factors in mitigation of the imposition of the sentence of death, shall hear testimony and other evidence that is relevant to the nature and circumstances of the aggravating circumstances the offender was found guilty of committing, the mitigating factors set forth in division (B) of section 2929.04 of the Revised Code, and any other factors in mitigation of the imposition of the sentence of death, and shall hear the statement, if any, of the offender, and the arguments, if any, of counsel for the defense and prosecution, that are relevant to the penalty that should be imposed on the offender. The defendant shall be given great latitude in the presentation of evidence of the mitigating factors set forth in division (B) of section 2929.04 of the Revised Code and of any other factors in mitigation of the imposition of the sentence of death. If the offender chooses to make a statement, the offender is subject to cross-examination only if the offender consents to make the statement under oath or affirmation.

The defendant shall have the burden of going forward with the evidence of any factors in mitigation of the imposition of the sentence of death. The prosecution shall have the burden of proving, by proof beyond a reasonable doubt, that the aggravating circumstances the defendant was found guilty of committing are sufficient to outweigh the factors in mitigation of the imposition of the sentence of death.

(2) Upon consideration of the relevant evidence raised at trial, the testimony, other evidence, statement of the offender, arguments of counsel, and, if applicable, the reports submitted pursuant to division (D)(1) of this section, the trial jury, if the offender was tried by a jury, shall determine whether the aggravating circumstances the offender was found guilty of committing are sufficient to outweigh the mitigating factors present in the case. If the trial jury unanimously finds, by proof beyond a reasonable doubt, that the aggravating circumstances the offender was found guilty of committing outweigh the mitigating factors, the trial jury shall recommend to the court that the sentence of death be imposed on the offender. Absent such a finding, the jury shall recommend that the offender be sentenced to life imprisonment with parole eligibility after serving twenty full years of imprisonment or to life imprisonment with parole eligibility after serving thirty full years of imprisonment.

If the trial jury recommends that the offender be sentenced to life imprisonment with parole eligibility after serving twenty full years of imprisonment or to life imprisonment with parole eligibility after serving thirty full years of imprisonment, the court shall impose the sentence recommended by the jury upon the offender. If the trial jury recommends that the sentence of death be imposed upon the offender, the court shall proceed to impose sentence pursuant to division (D)(3) of this section.

(3) Upon consideration of the relevant evidence raised at trial, the testimony, other evidence, statement of the offender, arguments of counsel, and, if applicable, the reports submitted to the court pursuant to division (D)(1) of this section, if, after receiving pursuant to division (D)(2) of this section the trial jury's recommendation that the sentence of death be imposed, the court finds, by proof beyond a reasonable doubt, or if the panel of three judges unanimously finds, by proof beyond a reasonable doubt, that the aggravating circumstances the offender was found guilty of committing outweigh the mitigating factors, it shall impose sentence of death on the offender. Absent such a finding by the court or panel, the court or the panel shall impose one of the following sentences on the offender:

(a) Life imprisonment with parole eligibility after serving twenty full years of imprisonment;

(b) Life imprisonment with parole eligibility after serving thirty full years of imprisonment.

(E) If the offender raised the matter of age at trial pursuant to section 2929.023 of the Revised Code, was convicted of aggravated murder and one or more specifications of an aggravating circumstance listed in division (A) of section 2929.04 of the Revised Code, and was not found at trial to have been eighteen years of age or older at the time of the commission of the offense, the court or the panel of three judges shall not impose a sentence of death on the offender. Instead, the court or panel shall impose one of the following sentences on the offender:

(1) Life imprisonment with parole eligibility after serving twenty full years of imprisonment;

(2) Life imprisonment with parole eligibility after serving thirty full years of imprisonment.

(F) The court or the panel of three judges, when it imposes sentence of death, shall state in a separate opinion its specific findings as to the existence of any of the mitigating factors set forth in division (B) of section 2929.04 of the Revised Code, the existence of any other mitigating factors, the aggravating circumstances the offender was found guilty of committing, and the reasons why the aggravating circumstances the offender was found guilty of committing were sufficient to outweigh the mitigating factors. The court or panel, when it imposes life imprisonment under division (D) of this section, shall state in a separate opinion its specific findings of which of the mitigating factors set forth in division (B) of section 2929.04 of the Revised Code it found to exist, what other mitigating factors it found to exist, what aggravating circumstances the offender was found guilty of committing, and why it could not find that these aggravating circumstances were sufficient to outweigh the mitigating factors. For cases in which a sentence of death is imposed for an offense committed before January 1, 1995, the court or panel shall file the opinion required to be prepared by this division with the clerk of the appropriate court of appeals and with the clerk of the supreme court within fifteen days after the court or panel imposes sentence. For cases in which a sentence of death is imposed for an offense committed on or after January 1, 1995, the court or panel shall file the opinion required to be prepared by this division with the clerk of the supreme court within fifteen days after the court or panel imposes sentence. The judgment in a case in which a sentencing hearing is held pursuant to this section is not final until the opinion is filed.

(G)(1) Whenever the court or a panel of three judges imposes a sentence of death for an offense committed before January 1, 1995, the clerk of the court in which the judgment is rendered shall deliver the entire record in the case to the appellate court.

(2) Whenever the court or a panel of three judges imposes a sentence of death for an offense committed on or after January 1, 1995, the clerk of the court in which the judgment is rendered shall deliver the entire record in the case to the supreme court.

(1995 S 4, eff. 9–21–95; 1981 S 1, eff. 10–19–81; 1972 H 511)

2929.04 Criteria for imposing death or imprisonment for a capital offense

(A) Imposition of the death penalty for aggravated murder is precluded, unless one or more of the following is specified in the indictment or count in the indictment pursuant to section 2941.14 of the Revised Code and proved beyond a reasonable doubt:

(1) The offense was the assassination of the president of the United States or person in line of succession to the presidency, or of the governor or lieutenant governor of this state, or of the president-elect or vice president-elect of the United States, or of the governor-elect or lieutenant governor-elect of this state, or of a candidate for any of the foregoing offices. For purposes of this division, a person is a candidate if he has been nominated for election according to law, or if he has filed a petition or petitions according to law to have his name placed on the ballot in a primary or general election, or if he campaigns as a write-in candidate in a primary or general election.

(2) The offense was committed for hire.

(3) The offense was committed for the purpose of escaping detection, apprehension, trial, or punishment for another offense committed by the offender.

(4) The offense was committed while the offender was a prisoner in a detention facility as defined in section 2921.01 of the Revised Code.

(5) Prior to the offense at bar, the offender was convicted of an offense an essential element of which was the purposeful killing of or attempt to kill another, or the offense at bar was part of a course of conduct involving the purposeful killing of or attempt to kill two or more persons by the offender.

(6) The victim of the offense was a peace officer, as defined in section 2935.01 of the Revised Code, whom the offender had reasonable cause to know or knew to be such, and either the victim, at the time of the commission of the offense, was engaged in his duties, or it was the offender's specific purpose to kill a peace officer.

(7) The offense was committed while the offender was committing, attempting to commit, or fleeing immediately after committing or attempting to commit kidnapping, rape, aggravated arson, aggravated robbery, or aggravated burglary, and either the offender was the principal offender in the commission of the aggravated murder or, if not the principal offender, committed the aggravated murder with prior calculation and design.

(8) The victim of the aggravated murder was a witness to an offense who was purposely killed to prevent his testimony in any criminal proceeding and the aggravated murder was not committed during the commission, attempted commission, or flight immediately after the commission or attempted commission of the offense to which the victim was a witness, or the victim of the aggravated murder was a witness to an offense and was purposely killed in retaliation for his testimony in any criminal proceeding.

(B) If one or more of the aggravating circumstances listed in division (A) of this section is specified in the indictment or count in the indictment and proved beyond a reasonable doubt, and if the offender did not raise the matter of age pursuant to section 2929.023 of the Revised Code or if the offender, after raising the matter of age, was found at trial to have been eighteen years of age or older at the time of the commission of the offense, the court, trial jury, or panel of three judges shall consider, and weigh against the aggravating circumstances proved beyond a reasonable doubt, the nature and circumstances of the offense, the history, character, and background of the offender, and all of the following factors:

(1) Whether the victim of the offense induced or facilitated it;

(2) Whether it is unlikely that the offense would have been committed, but for the fact that the offender was under duress, coercion, or strong provocation;

(3) Whether, at the time of committing the offense, the offender, because of a mental disease or defect, lacked substantial capacity to appreciate the criminality of his conduct or to conform his conduct to the requirements of the law;

(4) The youth of the offender;

(5) The offender's lack of a significant history of prior criminal convictions and delinquency adjudications;

(6) If the offender was a participant in the offense but not the principal offender, the degree of the offender's participation in the offense and the degree of the offender's participation in the acts that led to the death of the victim;

(7) Any other factors that are relevant to the issue of whether the offender should be sentenced to death.

(C) The defendant shall be given great latitude in the presentation of evidence of the factors listed in division (B) of this section and of any other factors in mitigation of the imposition of the sentence of death.

The existence of any of the mitigating factors listed in division (B) of this section does not preclude the imposition of a sentence of death on the offender, but shall be weighed pursuant to divisions (D)(2) and (3) of section 2929.03 of the Revised Code by the trial court, trial jury, or the panel of three judges against the aggravating circumstances the offender was found guilty of committing.

(1981 S 1, eff. 10–19–81; 1972 H 511)

2929.05   Appeals; procedures

(A) Whenever sentence of death is imposed pursuant to sections 2929.03 and 2929.04 of the Revised Code, the court of appeals, in a case in which a sentence of death was imposed for an offense committed before January 1, 1995, and the supreme court shall upon appeal review the sentence of death at the same time that they review the other issues in the case. The court of appeals and the supreme court shall review the judgment in the case and the sentence of death imposed by the court or panel of three judges in the same manner that they review other criminal cases, except that they shall review and independently weigh all of the facts and other evidence disclosed in the record in the case and consider the offense and the offender to determine whether the aggravating circumstances the offender was found guilty of committing outweigh the mitigating factors in the case, and whether the sentence of death is appropriate. In determining whether the sentence of death is appropriate, the court of appeals, in a case in which a sentence of death was imposed for an offense committed before January 1, 1995, and the supreme court shall consider whether the sentence is excessive or disproportionate to the penalty imposed in similar cases. They shall also review all of the facts and other evidence to determine if the evidence supports the finding of the aggravating circumstances the trial jury or the panel of three judges found the offender guilty of committing, and shall determine whether the sentencing court properly weighed the aggravating circumstances the offender was found guilty of committing and the mitigating factors. The court of appeals, in a case in which a sentence of death was imposed for an offense committed before January 1, 1995, or the supreme court shall affirm a sentence of death only if the particular court is persuaded from the record that the aggravating circumstances the offender was found guilty of committing outweigh the mitigating factors present in the case and that the sentence of death is the appropriate sentence in the case.

A court of appeals that reviews a case in which the sentence of death is imposed for an offense committed before January 1, 1995, shall file a separate opinion as to its findings in the case with the clerk of the supreme court. The opinion shall be filed within fifteen days after the court issues its opinion and shall contain whatever information is required by the clerk of the supreme court.

(B) The court of appeals, in a case in which a sentence of death was imposed for an offense committed before January 1, 1995, and the supreme court shall give priority over all other cases to the review of judgments in which the sentence of death is imposed, and, except as otherwise provided in this section, shall conduct the review in accordance with the Appellate Rules.

(C) Whenever sentence of death is imposed pursuant to section 2929.022 or 2929.03 of the Revised Code, the court of common pleas that sentenced the offender shall, upon motion of the offender and after conducting a hearing on the motion, vacate the sentence if all of the following apply:

(1) The offender alleges in the motion and presents evidence at the hearing that the offender was not eighteen years of age or older at the time of the commission of the aggravated murder for which the offender was sentenced;

(2) The offender did not present evidence at trial pursuant to section 2929.023 of the Revised Code that the offender was not eighteen years of age or older at the time of the commission of the aggravated murder for which the offender was sentenced;

(3) The motion was filed at any time after the sentence was imposed in the case and prior to execution of the sentence;

(4) At the hearing conducted on the motion, the prosecution does not prove beyond a reasonable doubt that the offender was eighteen years of age or older at the time of the commission of the aggravated murder for which the offender was sentenced.

(1995 S 4, eff. 9–21–95; 1981 S 1, eff. 10–19–81)

2929.06   Resentencing after sentence of death is vacated

If the sentence of death that is imposed upon an offender is vacated upon appeal because the court of appeals, in a case in which a sentence of death was imposed for an offense committed before January 1, 1995, or the supreme court, in cases in which the supreme court reviews the sentence upon appeal, could not affirm the sentence of death under the standards imposed by section 2929.05 of the Revised Code, is vacated upon appeal for the sole reason that the statutory procedure for imposing the sentence of death that is set forth in sections 2929.03 and 2929.04 of the Revised Code is unconstitutional, or is vacated pursuant to division (C) of section 2929.05 of the Revised Code, the trial court that sentenced the offender shall conduct a hearing to resentence the offender. At the resentencing hearing, the court shall sentence the offender to life imprisonment with parole eligibility after serving twenty full years of imprisonment or to life imprisonment with parole eligibility after serving thirty full years of imprisonment.

(1995 S 4, eff. 9–21–95; 1981 S 1, eff. 10–19–81)

PENALTIES AND FINES FOR FELONY—CONSIDERATIONS

2929.11 Circumstances affecting types of sentences for felony

(A) Whoever is convicted of or pleads guilty to a felony other than aggravated murder or murder, except as provided in division (D), (E), or (H) of this section or section 2929.23 of the Revised Code, shall be imprisoned for an indefinite term and, in addition, may be fined or required to make restitution, or both. The indefinite term of imprisonment shall consist of a maximum term as provided in this section and a minimum term fixed by the court as provided in this section. The fine and restitution shall be fixed by the court as provided in this section.

Whoever is convicted of or pleads guilty to committing, attempting to commit, or complicity in committing a felony violation of section 2909.02 or 2909.03 of the Revised Code and is sentenced to an indefinite term of imprisonment shall be required to reimburse agencies for their investigation or prosecution costs in accordance with section 2929.28 of the Revised Code.

(B) Except as provided in division (D) or (H) of this section, sections 2929.71 and 2929.72, and Chapter 2925. of the Revised Code, terms of imprisonment for felony shall be imposed as follows:

(1) For an aggravated felony of the first degree:

(a) If the offender has not previously been convicted of or pleaded guilty to any aggravated felony of the first, second, or third degree, aggravated murder or murder, or any offense set forth in any existing or former law of this state, any other state, or the United States that is substantially equivalent to any aggravated felony of the first, second, or third degree or to aggravated murder or murder, the minimum term, which may be imposed as a term of actual incarceration, shall be five, six, seven, eight, nine, or ten years, and the maximum term shall be twenty-five years;

(b) If the offender has previously been convicted of or pleaded guilty to any aggravated felony of the first, second, or third degree, aggravated murder or murder, or any offense set forth in any existing or former law of this state, any other state, or the United States that is substantially equivalent to any aggravated felony of the first, second, or third degree or to aggravated murder or murder, the minimum term shall be imposed as a term of actual incarceration of ten, eleven, twelve, thirteen, fourteen, or fifteen years, and the maximum term shall be twenty-five years;

(2) For an aggravated felony of the second degree:

(a) If the offender has not previously been convicted of or pleaded guilty to any aggravated felony of the first, second, or third degree, aggravated murder or murder, or any offense set forth in any existing or former law of this state, any other state, or the United States that is substantially equivalent to any aggravated felony of the first, second, or third degree or to aggravated murder or murder, the minimum term, which may be imposed as a term of actual incarceration, shall be three, four, five, six, seven, or eight years, and the maximum term shall be fifteen years;

(b) If the offender has previously been convicted of or pleaded guilty to any aggravated felony of the first, second, or third degree, aggravated murder or murder, or any offense set forth in any existing or former law of this state, any other state, or the United States that is substantially equivalent to any aggravated felony of the first, second, or third degree or to aggravated murder or murder, the minimum term shall be imposed as a term of actual incarceration of eight, nine, ten, eleven, or twelve years, and the maximum term shall be fifteen years;

(3) For an aggravated felony of the third degree:

(a) If the offender has not previously been convicted of or pleaded guilty to any aggravated felony of the first, second, or third degree, aggravated murder or murder, or any offense set forth in any existing or former law of this state, any other state, or the United States that is substantially equivalent to any aggravated felony of the first, second, or third degree or to aggravated murder or murder, the minimum term, which may be imposed as a term of actual incarceration, shall be two, three, four, or five years, and the maximum term shall be ten years;

(b) If the offender has previously been convicted of or pleaded guilty to any aggravated felony of the first, second, or third degree, aggravated murder or murder, or any offense set forth in any existing or former law of this state, any other state, or the United States that is substantially equivalent to any aggravated felony of the first, second, or third degree or to aggravated murder or murder, the minimum term shall be imposed as a term of actual incarceration of five, six, seven, or eight years, and the maximum term shall be ten years;

(4) For a felony of the first degree, the minimum term shall be four, five, six, or seven years, and the maximum term shall be twenty-five years;

(5) For a felony of the second degree, the minimum term shall be two, three, four, or five years, and the maximum term shall be fifteen years;

(6) For a felony of the third degree, the minimum term shall be two years, thirty months, three years, or four years, and the maximum term shall be ten years;

(7) For a felony of the fourth degree, the minimum term shall be eighteen months, two years, thirty months, or three years, and the maximum term shall be five years.

(C) Fines for felony shall be imposed as follows:

(1) For an aggravated felony of the first degree or a felony of the first degree, not more than ten thousand dollars;

(2) For an aggravated felony of the second degree or a felony of the second degree, not more than seven thousand five hundred dollars;

(3) For an aggravated felony of the third degree or a felony of the third degree, not more than five thousand dollars;

(4) For a felony of the fourth degree, not more than two thousand five hundred dollars.

(D) Whoever is convicted of or pleads guilty to a felony of the third or fourth degree and did not, during the commission of that offense, cause physical harm to any person or make an actual threat of physical harm to any person with a deadly weapon, as defined in section 2923.11 of the Revised Code, and who has not previously been convicted of an offense of violence shall be imprisoned for a definite term, and, in addition, may be fined or required to make restitution. The restitution shall be fixed by the court as provided in this section. If a person is convicted of or pleads guilty to committing, attempting to commit, or complicity in committing a violation of section 2909.03 of the Revised Code that is a felony of the third or fourth degree and is sentenced pursuant to this division, he shall be required to reimburse agencies for their investigation or prosecution costs in accordance with section 2929.28 of the Revised Code.

The terms of imprisonment shall be imposed as follows:

(1) For a felony of the third degree, the term shall be one, one and one-half, or two years;

(2) For a felony of the fourth degree, the term shall be six months, one year, or eighteen months.

(E) The court shall require a person who is convicted of or pleads guilty to a violation of section 2921.41 of the Revised Code, in the circumstances described in division (C)(2)(a) of that section, to make restitution for all of the property that is the subject of the offense, in accordance with division (C)(2) of that section. The court shall require, if appropriate, a person who is convicted of or pleads guilty to arson under section 2909.03 or to aggravated arson under section 2909.02 of the Revised Code to make restitution for all or part of the property damage that is caused by his offense, which restitution shall be in addition to the penalties otherwise imposed by the court for a conviction or plea of guilty for arson or aggravated arson. The court, in any other case, may require a person who is convicted of or pleads guilty to a felony to make restitution for all or part of the property damage that is caused by his offense and for all or part of the value of the property that is the subject of any theft offense, as defined in division (K) of section 2913.01 of the Revised Code, that the person committed. If the court determines that the victim of the offense was sixty-five years of age or older or permanently and totally disabled at the time of the commission of the offense, the court shall, regardless of whether the offender knew the age of the victim, consider this fact in favor of imposing restitution, but this fact shall not control the decision of the court.

(F) No person shall be sentenced for an offense pursuant to division (B)(1)(b), (2)(b), or (3)(b) of this section because the offender has previously been convicted of or pleaded guilty to any aggravated felony of the first, second, or third degree, aggravated murder or murder, or any offense set forth in any existing or former law of this state, any other state, or the United States that is substantially equivalent to any aggravated felony of the first, second, or third degree or to aggravated murder or murder unless the indictment, count in the indictment, or information charging him with the offense contains a specification as set forth in section 2941.142 of the Revised Code.

(G) No person shall be sentenced pursuant to division (B)(6) or (7) of this section to an indefinite term of imprisonment for a felony of the third or fourth degree unless the indictment, count in the indictment, or information charging him with the offense contains a specification as set forth in section 2941.143 of the Revised Code.

(H) A person who has been convicted of or pleaded guilty to a felony of the third or fourth degree and who is an eligible offender may be permitted by the department of rehabilitation and correction to serve his term of imprisonment imposed for the offense under this section, under any section contained in Chapter 2925. of the Revised Code, or under any other provision of the Revised Code, as a sentence of shock incarceration, in accordance with section 5120.031 of the Revised Code. As used in this division, "eligible offender" and "shock incarceration" have the same meanings as in section 5120.031 of the Revised Code.

(1990 S 258, eff. 11–20–90; 1990 H 51; 1986 H 284; 1984 S 4, H 265; 1983 S 210; 1982 H 269, § 4, S 199; 1978 S 119; 1972 H 511)

Historical and Statutory Notes

Ed. Note: A special endorsement by the Legislative Service Commission states, "Comparison of these amendments [1990 S 258, eff. 11–20–90 and 1990 H 51, eff. 11–8–90] in pursuance of section 1.52 of the Revised Code discloses that they are not substantively irreconcilable, so that they are required by that section to be harmonized to give effect to each amendment." In recognition of this rule of construction, changes made by 1990 S 258, eff. 11–20–90 and 1990 H 51, eff. 11–8–90 have been incorporated in the above amendment. See *Baldwin's Ohio Legislative Service*, 1990 Laws of Ohio, pages 5–918 and 5–775, for original versions of these Acts.

2929.12   Imposing sentence for felony

(A) In determining the minimum term of imprisonment to be imposed for a felony for which an indefinite term of imprisonment is imposed, the court shall consider the risk that the offender will commit another crime and the need for protecting the public from the risk; the nature and circumstances of the offense; the victim impact statement prepared pursuant to section 2947.051 of the Revised Code, if a victim impact statement is required by that section; any statement by the victim pursuant to section 2930.14 of the Revised Code; and the history, character, and condition of the offender and his need for correctional or rehabilitative treatment.

(B) The following do not control the court's discretion, but shall be considered in favor of imposing a longer term of imprisonment for a felony for which an indefinite term of imprisonment is imposed:

(1) The offender is a repeat or dangerous offender;

(2) Regardless of whether the offender knew the age of the victim, the victim of the offense was sixty-five years of age or older, permanently and totally disabled, or less than eighteen years of age at the time of the commission of the offense;

(3) The victim of the offense has suffered severe social, psychological, physical, or economic injury as a result of the offense.

(C) The following do not control the court's discretion, but shall be considered in favor of imposing a shorter minimum term of imprisonment for a felony for which an indefinite term of imprisonment is imposed:

(1) The offense neither caused nor threatened serious physical harm to persons or property, or the offender did not contemplate that it would do so;

(2) The offense was the result of circumstances unlikely to recur;

(3) The victim of the offense induced or facilitated it;

(4) There are substantial grounds tending to excuse or justify the offense, though failing to establish a defense;

(5) The offender acted under strong provocation;

(6) The offender has no history of prior delinquency or criminal activity, or has led a law-abiding life for a substantial time before commission of the present offense;

(7) The offender is likely to respond quickly to correctional or rehabilitative treatment.

(D) The criteria listed in divisions (B) and (C) of this section do not limit the matters that may be considered in determining the minimum term of imprisonment to be imposed for a felony for which an indefinite term of imprisonment is imposed.

(1994 S 186, eff. 10–12–94; 1990 S 258, eff. 11–20–90; 1982 H 269, § 4; 1982 S 199; 1980 S 384; 1978 S 119; 1972 H 511)

2929.13 Factors to be considered in certain of court's sentencing decisions

(A) The following do not control the court's sentencing decision, but shall be considered in favor of imposing a shorter term of imprisonment when determining the term of imprisonment for a felony of the third or fourth degree for which a definite term of imprisonment is imposed:

(1) The offense was the result of circumstances unlikely to recur;

(2) The victim of the offense induced or facilitated it;

(3) There are substantial grounds tending to excuse or justify the offense, though not sufficient to establish a defense;

(4) The offender acted under strong provocation;

(5) The offender has no history of prior delinquency or criminal activity, or has led a law-abiding life for a substantial time before commission of the present offense;

(6) The offender is likely to respond quickly to correctional or rehabilitative treatment.

(B) The following do not control the court's sentencing decision, but shall be considered in favor of imposing a longer term of imprisonment when determining the term of imprisonment for a felony of the third or fourth degree for which a definite term of imprisonment is imposed:

(1) The defendant, by the duties of his office or by his position, was obliged to prevent the particular offense committed or to bring the offenders committing it to justice;

(2) The defendant held public office at the time of the offense, and the offense related to the conduct of that office;

(3) The defendant utilized his professional reputation or position in the community to commit the offense, or to afford him an easier means of committing it, in circumstances where his example probably would influence the conduct of others.

(C) The criteria listed in divisions (A) and (B) of this section do not limit the matters that may be considered in determining the term of imprisonment to be imposed for a felony of the third or fourth degree for which a definite term of imprisonment is imposed.

(1982 H 269, § 4, eff. 7–1–83; 1982 S 199)

2929.14 Factors to be considered in determining whether to impose a fine for a felony

(A) In determining whether to impose a fine for a felony and the amount and method of payment of a fine, the court shall consider the nature and circumstances of the offense; the victim impact statement prepared pursuant to section 2947.051 of the Revised Code; the history, character, and condition of the offender; any statement by the victim pursuant to section 2930.14 of the Revised Code; and the ability and resources of the offender and the nature of the burden that payment of a fine will impose on him.

(B) The court shall not impose a fine in addition to imprisonment for felony, unless a fine is specially adapted to deterrence of the offense or the correction of the offender, or the offense was a violation of section 2923.32 of the Revised Code, or the offense was committed for hire or for purpose of gain.

(C) The court shall not impose a fine or fines for felony that, in the aggregate and to the extent not suspended by the court, exceed the amount that the offender is or will be able to pay by the method and within the time allowed without undue hardship to himself or his dependents, or will prevent him from making restitution or reparation to the victim of his offense.

(D) At the time of imposing sentence, or as soon as possible after imposing sentence, for a felony, the court shall notify the victim of the offense of his right to file an application for an award of reparations pursuant to sections 2743.51 to 2743.72 of the Revised Code.

(1994 S 186, eff. 10–12–94; 1982 H 269, § 4, eff. 7–1–83; 1982 S 199)

2929.15 Prisoner's ability to reimburse for expenses of confinement; court to hold hearing; considerations

(A) If a judge in any jurisdiction in which the appropriate authority or board requires convicts to reimburse the costs of confinement pursuant to section 307.93, 341.14, 341.19, 341.23, 753.02, 753.04, 753.16., 2301.56, or 2947.19 of the Revised Code sentences a person to a term of imprisonment for an offense other than a minor misdemeanor, the judge also shall hold a hearing to determine whether the person has the ability to pay the reimbursement. The person whose ability to pay is being determined shall have an opportunity to be heard and may be represented by counsel at the hearing, at his option. A record shall be made of the hearing.

Reimbursable expenses shall include, but are not limited to, the expenses relating to the provision of food, clothing, and shelter to the person while he is imprisoned and during any time that the person is incarcerated before sentencing that is credited against his term of imprisonment. The reimbursement shall be made to the county or municipal corporation for expenses incurred by it during any time that the person serves in a local jail or workhouse.

(B) Before holding a hearing on reimbursement pursuant to division (A) of this section, the judge shall investigate or cause to be investigated the person's ability to pay the reimbursement and possible reimbursement schedules and methods. The amount of reimbursement shall be determined at the hearing in light of the sentence of imprisonment given and according to the person's ability to pay. However, the actual amount to be paid shall not exceed the actual cost of the confinement or forty dollars for each day of confinement, whichever is less. In determining the convicted person's ability to pay, all of the following shall be considered:

(1) His financial resources, excluding the funds saved from wages derived from his labor or employment during the period of incarceration;

(2) Any obligation to support his dependents;

(3) Any obligation to make restitution to the victim of the offense of which he is convicted;

(4) His income, assets, liabilities, ability to borrow, household expenses, and any other factor that may affect his financial ability to make reimbursement.

(1984 H 363, eff. 9–26–84)

2929.16 Participation in county jail industry program

If a person is sentenced to a term of imprisonment for a felony pursuant to section 2929.11 of the Revised Code and that term of imprisonment is to be served in a county jail in a county that has established a county jail industry program pursuant to section 5147.30 of the Revised Code, the court shall specify, as part of the sentence, whether the person may be considered by the county sheriff of that county for participation in the county jail industry program. The court shall retain jurisdiction to modify its specification made pursuant to this section during the person's term of imprisonment upon a reassessment of the person's qualifications for participation in the program.

(1990 H 51, eff. 11–8–90)

2929.17 Nonresidential sanctions

The prosecutor in any case against any person licensed, certified, registered, or otherwise authorized to practice under Chapter 3719., 4715., 4723., 4729., 4730., 4731., or 4741. of the Revised Code shall notify the appropriate licensing board, on forms provided by the board, of any of the following:

(A) A plea of guilty to, or a judicial finding of guilt of, a felony, or a court order dismissing a felony charge on technical or procedural grounds;

(B) A plea of guilty to, or a judicial finding of guilt of, a misdemeanor committed in the course of practice or in the course of business, or a court order dismissing such a misdemeanor charge on technical or procedural grounds;

(C) A plea of guilty to, or a judicial finding of guilt of, a misdemeanor involving moral turpitude, or a court order dismissing such a charge on technical or procedural grounds.

The report shall include the name and address of the person, the nature of the offense, and certified copies of court entries in the action.

This is an interim section effective until July 1, 1996.

(1995 S 143, eff. 3–5–96; 1990 H 615, eff. 3–27–91)

PENALTIES FOR MISDEMEANOR

2929.21 Penalties for misdemeanor; restitution

(A) Except as provided in section 2929.23 of the Revised Code, whoever is convicted of or pleads guilty to a misdemeanor other than a minor misdemeanor shall be imprisoned for a definite term or fined, or both, which term of imprisonment and fine shall be fixed by the court as provided in this section.

Whoever is convicted of or pleads guilty to committing, attempting to commit, or complicity in committing a violation of section 2909.03 of the Revised Code that is a misdemeanor, or a violation of division (A)(2) of section 2909.06 of the Revised Code when the means used are fire or explosion, shall be required to reimburse agencies for their investigation or prosecution costs in accordance with section 2929.28 of the Revised Code.

(B) Terms of imprisonment for misdemeanor shall be imposed as follows:

(1) For a misdemeanor of the first degree, not more than six months;

(2) For a misdemeanor of the second degree, not more than ninety days;

(3) For a misdemeanor of the third degree, not more than sixty days;

(4) For a misdemeanor of the fourth degree, not more than thirty days.

(C) Fines for misdemeanor shall be imposed as follows:

(1) For a misdemeanor of the first degree, not more than one thousand dollars;

(2) For a misdemeanor of the second degree, not more than seven hundred fifty dollars;

(3) For a misdemeanor of the third degree, not more than five hundred dollars;

(4) For a misdemeanor of the fourth degree, not more than two hundred fifty dollars.

(D) Whoever is convicted of or pleads guilty to a minor misdemeanor shall be fined not more than one hundred dollars.

(E) The court may require a person who is convicted of or pleads guilty to a misdemeanor to make restitution for all or part of the property damage that is caused by his offense and for all or part of the value of the property that is the subject of any theft offense, as defined in division (K) of section 2913.01 of the Revised Code, that the person committed. If the court determines that the victim of the offense was sixty-five years of age or older or permanently or totally disabled at the time of the commission of the offense, the court, regardless of whether the offender knew the age of victim, shall consider this fact in favor of imposing restitution, but this fact shall not control the decision of the court.

(F) If a person is sentenced to a term of imprisonment pursuant to this section and the term of imprisonment is to be served in a county jail in a county that has established a county jail industry program pursuant to section 5147.30 of the Revised Code, the court shall specify, as part of the sentence, whether the person may be considered by the county sheriff of that county for participation in the county jail industry program. The court shall retain jurisdiction to modify its specification made pursuant to this division during the person's term of imprisonment upon a reassessment of the person's qualifications for participation in the program.

(1990 H 51, eff. 11–8–90; 1990 S 131; 1986 H 284; 1978 S 119; 1972 H 511)

2929.22   Imposing sentence for misdemeanor

(A) In determining whether to impose imprisonment or a fine, or both, for a misdemeanor, and in determining the term of imprisonment and the amount and method of payment of a fine, the court shall consider the risk that the offender will commit another offense and the need for protecting the public from the risk; the nature and circumstances of the offense; the history, character, and condition of the offender and his need for correctional or rehabilitative treatment; any statement made by the victim, if the offense is a misdemeanor specified in division (A) of section 2930.01 of the Revised Code; and the ability and resources of the offender and the nature of the burden that payment of a fine will impose on him.

(B) The following do not control the court's discretion, but shall be considered in favor of imposing imprisonment for a misdemeanor:

(1) The offender is a repeat or dangerous offender;

(2) Regardless of whether or not the offender knew the age of the victim, the victim of the offense was sixty-five years of age or older, permanently and totally disabled, or less than eighteen years of age at the time of the commission of the offense.

(C) The criteria listed in section 2929.12 of the Revised Code, favoring shorter terms of imprisonment for felony, do not control the court's discretion, but shall be considered against imposing imprisonment for a misdemeanor.

(D) The criteria listed in divisions (B) and (C) of this section shall not be construed to limit the matters which may be considered in determining whether to impose imprisonment for a misdemeanor.

(E) The court shall not impose a fine in addition to imprisonment for a misdemeanor, unless a fine is specially adapted to deterrence of the offense or the correction of the offender, the offense has proximately resulted in physical harm to the person or property of another, or the offense was committed for hire or for purpose of gain.

(F) The court shall not impose a fine or fines which, in the aggregate and to the extent not suspended by the court, exceeds the amount which the offender is or will be able to pay by the method and within the time allowed without undue hardship to himself or his dependents, or will prevent him from making restitution or reparation to the victim of his offense.

(G) At the time of sentencing or as soon as possible after sentencing, the court shall notify the victim of the offense of his right to file an application for an award of reparations pursuant to sections 2743.51 to 2743.72 of the Revised Code.

(1994 S 186, eff. 10–12–94; 1990 S 258, eff. 11–20–90; 1978 S 119; 1972 H 511)

MISCELLANEOUS SENTENCING PROVISIONS

2929.221 Places of imprisonment according to offenses

(A) A person who pleads guilty to, pleads no contest to and is found guilty of, or is convicted of aggravated murder, murder, another offense punishable by life imprisonment, an aggravated felony of the first, second, or third degree, or a felony of the first or second degree and who is sentenced to a term of imprisonment pursuant to that conviction shall serve that term of imprisonment in an institution under the control of the department of rehabilitation and correction.

(B) A person who pleads guilty to, pleads no contest to and is found guilty of, or is convicted of a felony of the third or fourth degree and who is sentenced to a term of imprisonment pursuant to that conviction shall serve that term of imprisonment:

(1) In a county, multicounty, municipal, municipal-county, or multicounty-municipal jail or workhouse if the offense is a felony of the third or fourth degree and the person previously has not pleaded guilty to, pleaded no contest to and been found guilty of, or been convicted of a felony, if the offense is not an offense of violence, if the department of rehabilitation and correction and the local authority that operates the jail or workhouse have entered into an agreement pursuant to section 5120.161 of the Revised Code for the housing of such persons in the jail or workhouse, and if the department pursuant to that section designates the person to be imprisoned in the jail or workhouse;

(2) Except as provided in division (B)(1) of this section, in an institution under the control of the department of rehabilitation and correction.

(C) A person who pleads guilty to, pleads no contest to and is found guilty of, or is convicted of one or more misdemeanors and who is sentenced to a term of imprisonment pursuant to the conviction or convictions shall serve that term of imprisonment in a county, multicounty, municipal, municipal-county, or multicounty-municipal jail or workhouse, except that a person ordered to be imprisoned in a state correctional institution pursuant to division (F) of section 2929.41 of the Revised Code shall be imprisoned as ordered.

(D) Nothing in this section prohibits, or shall be construed as prohibiting, the commitment or referral of a person who pleads guilty to, pleads no contest to and is found guilty of, or is convicted of a felony to a community-based correctional facility and program or district community-based correctional facility and program in accordance with sections 2301.51 to 2301.56 of the Revised Code, or to prohibit the use of the probation split-sentencing provisions contained in division (A) of section 2929.51 of the Revised Code.

(1994 H 571, eff. 10–6–94; 1990 S 258, eff. 11–20–90; 1987 H 455; 1983 S 210; 1982 H 269, S 199)

2929.23 Electronically monitored house arrest, detention, and early release; funds

(A) As used in this section:

(1) "Electronic monitoring device" means either of the following:

(a) Any device that can be operated by electrical or battery power and that conforms with all of the following:

(i) The device has a transmitter that can be attached to a person, that will transmit a specified signal to a receiver of the type described in division (A)(1)(a)(ii) of this section if the transmitter is removed from the person, turned off, or altered in any manner without prior court approval in relation to electronically monitored house arrest or electronically monitored house detention or without prior approval of the department of rehabilitation and correction in relation to electronically monitored early release or otherwise is tampered with, that can transmit continuously and periodically a signal to that receiver when the person is within a specified distance from the receiver, and that can transmit an appropriate signal to that receiver if the person to whom it is attached travels a specified distance from that receiver.

(ii) The device has a receiver that can receive continuously the signals transmitted by a transmitter of the type described in division (A)(1)(a)(i) of this section, can transmit continuously those signals by telephone to a central monitoring computer of the type described in division (A)(1)(a)(iii) of this section, and can transmit continuously an appropriate signal to that central monitoring computer if the receiver is turned off or altered without prior court approval or otherwise tampered with.

(iii) The device has a central monitoring computer that can receive continuously the signals transmitted by telephone by a receiver of the type described in division (A)(1)(a)(ii) of this section and can monitor continuously the person to whom an electronic monitoring device of the type described in division (A)(1)(a) of this section is attached.

(b) Any device that is not a device of the type described in division (A)(1)(a) of this section and that conforms with all of the following:

(i) The device includes a transmitter and receiver that can monitor and determine the location of a subject person at any time, or at a designated point in time, through the use of a central monitoring computer or through other electronic means;

(ii) The device includes a transmitter and receiver that can determine at any time, or at a designated point in time, through the use of a central monitoring computer or other electronic means the fact that the transmitter is turned off or altered in any manner without prior approval of the court in relation to electronically monitored house arrest or electronically monitored house detention or without prior approval of the department of rehabilitation and correction in relation to electronically monitored early release or otherwise is tampered with.

(2) "Certified electronic monitoring device" means an electronic monitoring device that has been certified by the superintendent of the bureau of criminal identification and investigation pursuant to division (C)(1) of this section.

(3) "Eligible offender" means a person who has been convicted of or pleaded guilty to any offense, except that a person is not an "eligible offender" if any of the following apply in relation to the person, the offense, or the person and the offense:

(a) The person is prohibited by section 2951.02 of the Revised Code from being placed on probation for the offense.

(b) If the offense is a felony, the person has been convicted of or pleaded guilty to a specification charging him with having a firearm on or about his person or under his control while committing the offense.

(c) The offense is an offense of violence that is a felony.

(d) The offense is a violation of division (D)(2) of section 4507.02 of the Revised Code, and the person is sentenced for that offense under division (B)(3) of section 4507.99 of the Revised Code.

(4) "Electronically monitored house arrest" means a period of confinement of an eligible offender in his home or in other premises specified by the sentencing court, during which period of confinement all of the following apply:

(a) The eligible offender wears, otherwise has attached to his person, or otherwise is subject to monitoring by a certified electronic monitoring device, or he is subject to monitoring by a certified electronic monitoring system;

(b) The eligible offender is required to remain in his home or other premises specified by the sentencing court for the specified period of confinement, except for periods of time during which the person is at his place of employment or at other premises as authorized by the sentencing court;

(c) The eligible offender is subject to monitoring by a central system that monitors the certified electronic monitoring device that is attached to his person or that otherwise is being used to monitor him and that can monitor and determine his location at any time or at a designated point in time, or he is required to participate in monitoring by a certified electronic monitoring system;

(d) The eligible offender is required by the sentencing court to report periodically to a person designated by the court;

(e) The eligible offender is subject to any other restrictions and requirements that may be imposed by the sentencing court.

(5) "Electronic monitoring system" means a system by which the location of an eligible offender can be verified telephonically through the use of voice-activated voice response technology that conforms with all of the following:

(a) It can be programmed to call the telephone or telephones assigned to the person who is the subject of the monitoring as often as necessary;

(b) It is equipped with a voice recognition system that can work accurately and reliably under the anticipated conditions in which it will operate;

(c) It is equipped to perform an alarm function if the person who is the subject of monitoring does not respond to system commands in the manner required.

(6) "Certified electronic monitoring system" means an electronic monitoring system that has been certified by the superintendent of the bureau of criminal identification and investigation pursuant to division (C)(1) of this section.

(7) "Electronically monitored house detention" has the same meaning as in section 2151.355 of the Revised Code.

(8) "Electronically monitored early release" has the same meaning as in section 5120.071 of the Revised Code.

(B)(1) Any court may impose a period of electronically monitored house arrest upon an eligible offender in addition to or in lieu of any other sentence imposed or authorized for the offense, except that the total of any period of electronically monitored house arrest imposed upon an offender plus the period of any sentence of imprisonment imposed upon the same eligible offender shall not exceed the maximum term of imprisonment that could be imposed upon the eligible offender pursuant to section 2929.11 or 2929.21 of the Revised Code and except that, if the offense for which an eligible offender is being sentenced is a violation of division (A) of section 4511.19 or of division (D)(2) of section 4507.02 of the Revised Code, the court may impose a period of electronically monitored house arrest upon the eligible offender only when authorized by and only in the circumstances described in division (A) of section 4511.99 or division (B) of section 4507.99 of the Revised Code. If a court imposes a period of electronically monitored house arrest upon an eligible offender, it shall require him to wear, otherwise have attached to his person, or otherwise be subject to monitoring by a certified electronic monitoring device or to participate in the operation of and monitoring by a certified electronic monitoring system; to remain in his home or other specified premises for the entire period of electronically monitored house arrest except when the court permits him to leave those premises to go to his place of employment or to other specified premises; to be monitored by a central system that monitors the certified electronic monitoring device that is attached to his person or that otherwise is being used to monitor him and that can monitor and determine his location at any time or at a designated point in time or to be monitored by the certified electronic monitoring system; to report periodically to a person designated by the court; and, in return for receiving a sentence of electronically monitored house arrest, to enter into a written contract with the court agreeing to comply with all restrictions and requirements imposed by the court, agreeing to pay any fee imposed by the court for the costs of the electronically monitored house arrest imposed by the court pursuant to division (E) of this section, and agreeing to waive the right to receive credit for any time served on electronically monitored house arrest toward any sentence of imprisonment imposed upon him for the offense for which the sentence of electronically monitored house arrest was imposed if he violates any of the restrictions or requirements of the sentence of electronically monitored house arrest, and additionally, it may impose any other reasonable restrictions and requirements upon him.

(2) If an offender violates any of the restrictions or requirements imposed upon him as part of his sentence of electronically monitored house arrest, he shall not receive credit for any time served on electronically monitored house arrest toward any sentence of imprisonment imposed upon him for the offense for which the sentence of electronically monitored house arrest was imposed.

(C)(1) The superintendent of the bureau of criminal identification and investigation, in accordance with this section and rules adopted by him pursuant to division (C)(2) of this section, shall certify for use in cases of electronically monitored house arrest, electronically monitored house detention, and electronically monitored early release specific types and brands of electronic monitoring devices and electronic monitoring systems that comply with the requirements of this section, section 5120.073 of the Revised Code, and those rules. Any manufacturer that, pursuant to this division, seeks to obtain the certification of any type or brand of electronic monitoring device or electronic monitoring system shall submit to the superintendent an application for certification in accordance with those rules together with the application fee and costs of certification as required by those rules. The superintendent shall not certify any electronic monitoring device or electronic monitoring system pursuant to this division unless the application fee and costs have been paid to the superintendent.

(2) The superintendent, in accordance with Chapter 119. of the Revised Code, shall adopt rules for certifying specific types and brands of electronic monitoring devices and electronic monitoring systems for use in electronically monitored house arrest, electronically monitored house detention, and electronically monitored early release. The rules shall set forth the requirements for obtaining the certification, the application fee and other costs for obtaining the certification, the procedure for applying for certification, and any other requirements and procedures considered necessary by the superintendent. The rules shall require that no type or brand of electronic monitoring device or electronic monitoring system be certified unless the type or brand of device or system complies with whichever of the following is applicable, in addition to any other requirements specified by the superintendent:

(a) For electronic monitoring devices of the type described in division (A)(1)(a) of this section, the type or brand of device complies with all of the following:

(i) It has a transmitter of the type described in division (A)(1)(a)(i) of this section, a receiver of the type described in division (A)(1)(a)(ii) of this section, and a central monitoring computer of the type described in division (A)(1)(a)(iii) of this section;

(ii) Its transmitter can be worn by or attached to a person with a minimum of discomfort during normal activities, is difficult to remove, turn off, or otherwise alter without prior court approval in relation to electronically monitored house arrest or electronically monitored house detention or prior approval of the department of rehabilitation and correction in relation to electronically monitored early release, and will transmit a specified signal to the receiver if it is removed, turned off, altered, or otherwise tampered with;

(iii) Its receiver is difficult to turn off or alter and will transmit a signal to the central monitoring computer if it is turned off, altered, or otherwise tampered with;

(iv) Its central monitoring computer is difficult to circumvent;

(v) Its transmitter, receiver, and central monitoring computer work accurately and reliably under the anticipated conditions under which electronically monitored house arrest or electronically monitored house detention will be imposed by courts or under which electronically monitored early release will be used by the department of rehabilitation and correction;

(vi) It has a backup battery power supply that operates automatically when the main source of electrical or battery power for the device fails.

(b) For electronic monitoring devices of the type described in division (A)(1)(b) of this section, the type or brand of device complies with all of the following:

(i) It has a transmitter and receiver of the type described in divisions (A)(1)(b)(i) and (ii) of this section.

(ii) Its transmitter is difficult to turn off or alter without prior court approval in relation to electronically monitored house arrest or electronically monitored house detention or without prior approval of the department of rehabilitation and correction in relation to electronically monitored early release, and, if the transmitter is turned off or altered in any manner without prior approval of the court or department or otherwise is tampered with, the fact that it has been turned off, altered, or tampered with can be determined at any time, or at a designated point in time, through the use of a central monitoring computer or through other electronic means.

(iii) Its receiver is difficult to turn off or alter, and, if the receiver is turned off, altered, or otherwise tampered with, the fact that it has been turned off, altered, or tampered with can be determined at any time, or at a designated point in time, through the use of a central monitoring computer or through other electronic means.

(iv) Its central monitoring computer or other means of electronic monitoring is difficult to circumvent.

(v) Its transmitter, receiver, and central monitoring computer or other means of electronic monitoring work accurately and reliably under the anticipated conditions under which electronically monitored house arrest, electronically monitored house detention, or electronically monitored early release will be used.

(vi) If it operates on electrical or battery power, it has a backup battery power supply that operates automatically when the main source of electrical or battery power for the device fails, or, if it does not operate on electrical or battery power, it has a backup method of operation so that it will continue to operate if its main method of operation fails.

(c) For electronic monitoring systems, the type or brand of system complies with all of the following:

(i) It can be programmed to call the telephone or telephones assigned to the person who is the subject of the monitoring as often as necessary;

(ii) It is equipped with a voice recognition system that can work accurately and reliably under the anticipated conditions in which it will operate;

(iii) It is equipped to perform an alarm function if the person who is the subject of the monitoring does not respond to system commands in the manner required.

(3) The superintendent shall publish and make available to all courts and to the department of rehabilitation and correction, without charge, a list of all types and brands of electronic monitoring devices and electronic monitoring systems that have been certified by the superintendent pursuant to division (C)(1) of this section and information about the manufacturers of the certified devices and systems and places at which the devices and systems can be obtained.

(D) The superintendent of the bureau of criminal identification and investigation shall deposit all costs and fees collected by him pursuant to division (C) of this section into the general revenue fund.

(E)(1) Each county in which is located a court that imposes electronically monitored house arrest or electronically monitored house detention as a sentencing alternative may establish in the county treasury an electronically monitored house arrest and detention fund. The clerk of each court that uses that sentencing alternative may deposit in the fund all fees collected from eligible offenders upon whom electronically monitored house arrest or detention is imposed pursuant to this section, section 2151.355, or any other section of the Revised Code that specifically authorizes the imposition of electronically monitored house arrest or detention. Each court that imposes electronically monitored house arrest or detention, by local court rule may adopt a reasonable daily fee to be paid by each eligible offender sentenced to electronically monitored house arrest or detention. The fee may include the actual costs of providing house arrest or detention and an additional amount necessary to enable the court to provide electronically monitored house arrest or detention to indigent eligible offenders. The fund may be used only for the payment of the costs of electronically monitored house arrest or detention, including, but not limited to, the costs of electronically monitored house arrest or detention for indigent eligible offenders.

(2) If a fee is adopted pursuant to division (E)(1) of this section, it shall be in addition to any fine specifically authorized by any other section of the Revised Code for an eligible offender upon whom electronically monitored house arrest or detention is imposed as a sentencing alternative.

(1994 S 82, eff. 5–4–94; 1993 S 62, § 4, eff. 9–1–93; 1992 H 725, S 275, S 351; 1990 H 51, S 131)

2929.25 Crime victims recovery fund

(A) Notwithstanding the fines prescribed in section 2929.02 of the Revised Code for a person who is convicted of or pleads guilty to aggravated murder or murder, the fines prescribed in section 2929.11 of the Revised Code for a person who is convicted of or pleads guilty to a felony, the fines prescribed in section 2929.21 of the Revised Code for a person who is convicted of or pleads guilty to a misdemeanor, the fines prescribed in section 2929.31 of the Revised Code for an organization that is convicted of or pleads guilty to an offense, and the fines prescribed in any other section of the Revised Code for a person who is convicted of or pleads guilty to an offense, a sentencing court may impose upon the offender a fine of not more than one million dollars if any of the following applies to the offense and the offender:

(1) There are three or more victims, as defined in section 2969.11 of the Revised Code, of the offense for which the offender is being sentenced.

(2) The offender previously has been convicted of or pleaded guilty to one or more offenses, and, for the offense for which the offender is being sentenced and all of the other offenses, there is a total of three or more victims, as defined in section 2969.11 of the Revised Code.

(3) The offense for which the offender is being sentenced is aggravated murder, murder, or an aggravated felony of the first degree.

(B) If a sentencing court imposes a fine upon an offender pursuant to division (A) of this section, all moneys paid in satisfaction of the fine or collected pursuant to division (C) of this section in satisfaction of the fine shall be deposited into the crime victims recovery fund created by division (D) of this section and shall be distributed as described in that division.

(C) Notwithstanding any contrary provision of any section of the Revised Code, if a sentencing court imposes a fine upon an offender pursuant to division (A) of this section or pursuant to another section of the Revised Code, the fine shall be a judgment against the offender in favor of the state, and both of the following apply to that judgment:

(1) The state may collect the judgment by garnishing, attaching, or otherwise executing against any income, profits, or other real or personal property in which the offender has any right, title, or interest, including property acquired after the imposition of the fine, in the same manner as if the judgment had been rendered against the offender and in favor of the state in a civil action. If the fine is imposed pursuant to division (A) of this section, the moneys collected as a result of the garnishment, attachment, or other execution shall be deposited and distributed as described in divisions (B) and (D) of this section. If the fine is not imposed pursuant to division (A) of this section, the moneys collected as a result of the garnishment, attachment, or other execution shall be distributed as otherwise provided by law for the distribution of money paid in satisfaction of a fine.

(2) The provisions of Chapter 2329. of the Revised Code relative to the establishment of court judgments and decrees as liens and to the enforcement of those liens apply to the judgment.

(D) There is hereby created in the state treasury the crime victims recovery fund. If a sentencing court imposes a fine upon an offender pursuant to division (A) of this section, all moneys paid in satisfaction of the fine and all moneys collected in satisfaction of the fine pursuant to division (C) of this section shall be deposited into the fund. The fund shall be administered and the moneys in it shall be distributed in accordance with sections 2969.11 to 2969.14 of the Revised Code.

(1995 S 91, eff. 11–15–95)

2929.28   Convicted arsonist to make restitution to public agency; hearing

(A) As used in this section:

(1) "Agency" means any law enforcement agency, other public agency, or public official involved in the investigation or prosecution of the offender or in the investigation of the fire or explosion in an aggravated arson, arson, or criminal damaging or endangering case. An "agency" includes, but is not limited to, a sheriff's office, a municipal corporation, township, or township police district police department, the office of a prosecuting attorney, city director of law, village solicitor, or similar chief legal officer of a municipal corporation, the fire marshal's office, a municipal corporation, township, or township fire district fire department, the office of a fire prevention officer, and any state, county, or municipal corporation crime laboratory.

(2) "Assets" includes all forms of real or personal property.

(3) "Itemized statement" means the statement of costs described in division (B) of this section.

(4) "Offender" means the person who has been convicted of or pleaded guilty to committing, attempting to commit, or complicity in committing a violation of section 2909.02 or

2909.03 of the Revised Code, or, when the means used are fire or explosion, division (A)(2) of section 2909.06 of the Revised Code.

(5) "Costs" means the reasonable value of the time spent by an officer or employee of an agency on the aggravated arson, arson, or criminal damaging or endangering case, any moneys spent by the agency on that case, and the reasonable fair market value of resources used or expended by the agency on that case.

(B) Prior to the sentencing of an offender, the court shall enter an order that directs agencies that wish to be reimbursed by the offender for the costs they incurred in the investigation or prosecution of the offender or in the investigation of the fire or explosion involved in the case, to file with the court within a specified time an itemized statement of those costs. The order also shall require that a copy of the itemized statement be given to the offender or his attorney within the specified time. Only itemized statements so filed and given shall be considered at the hearing described in division (C) of this section.

(C) The court shall set a date for a hearing on all the itemized statements filed with it and given to the offender or his attorney in accordance with division (B) of this section. The hearing shall be held prior to the sentencing of the offender, but may be held on the same day as his sentencing. Notice of the hearing date shall be given to the offender or his attorney and to the agencies whose itemized statements are involved. At the hearing, each agency has the burden of establishing by a preponderance of the evidence that the costs set forth in its itemized statement were incurred in the investigation or prosecution of the offender or in the investigation of the fire or explosion involved in the case, and of establishing by a preponderance of the evidence that the offender has assets available for the reimbursement of all or a portion of the costs.

The offender may cross-examine all witnesses and examine all documentation presented by the agencies at the hearing, and he may present at the hearing witnesses and documentation he has obtained without a subpoena or a subpoena duces tecum or, in the case of documentation, that belongs to him. He also may issue subpoenas and subpoenas duces tecum for, and present and examine at the hearing, witnesses and documentation, subject to the following applying to the witnesses or documentation subpoenaed:

(1) The testimony of witnesses subpoenaed or documentation subpoenaed is material to the preparation or presentation by the offender of his defense to the claims of the agencies for a reimbursement of costs;

(2) If witnesses to be subpoenaed are personnel of an agency or documentation to be subpoenaed belongs to an agency, the personnel or documentation may be subpoenaed only if the agency involved has indicated, pursuant to this division, that it intends to present the personnel as witnesses or use the documentation at the hearing. The offender shall submit, in writing, a request to an agency as described in this division to ascertain whether the agency intends to present various personnel as witnesses or to use particular documentation. The request shall indicate that the offender is considering issuing subpoenas to personnel of the agency who are specifically named or identified by title or position, or for documentation of the agency that is specifically described or generally identified, and shall request the agency to indicate, in writing, whether it intends to present such personnel as witnesses or to use such documentation at the hearing. The agency shall promptly reply to the request of the offender. An agency is prohibited from presenting personnel as witnesses or from using documentation at the hearing if it indicates to the offender it does not intend to do so in response to a request of the offender under this division, or if it fails to reply or promptly reply to such a request.

(D) Following the hearing, the court shall determine which of the agencies established by a preponderance of the evidence that costs set forth in their itemized statements were incurred as described in division (C) of this section and that the offender has assets available for reimbursement purposes. The court also shall determine whether the offender has assets available to reimburse all such agencies, in whole or in part, for their established costs, and if it determines that the assets are available, it shall order the offender, as part of his sentence, to reimburse the agencies from his assets for all or a specified portion of their established costs.

(1986 H 284, eff. 3–6–86)

2929.31   Organizational penalties

(A) Regardless of the penalties provided in sections 2929.02, 2929.11, and 2929.21 of the Revised Code, an organization convicted of an offense pursuant to section 2901.23 of the Revised Code shall be fined, which fine shall be fixed by the court as follows:

(1) For aggravated murder, not more than one hundred thousand dollars;

(2) For murder, not more than fifty thousand dollars;

(3) For an aggravated felony of the first degree or a felony of the first degree, not more than twenty-five thousand dollars;

(4) For an aggravated felony of the second degree or a felony of the second degree, not more than twenty thousand dollars;

(5) For an aggravated felony of the third degree or a felony of the third degree, not more than fifteen thousand dollars;

(6) For a felony of the fourth degree, not more than ten thousand dollars;

(7) For a misdemeanor of the first degree, not more than five thousand dollars;

(8) For a misdemeanor of the second degree, not more than four thousand dollars;

(9) For a misdemeanor of the third degree, not more than three thousand dollars;

(10) For a misdemeanor of the fourth degree, not more than two thousand dollars;

(11) For a minor misdemeanor, not more than one thousand dollars;

(12) For a felony not specifically classified, not more than ten thousand dollars;

(13) For a misdemeanor not specifically classified, not more than two thousand dollars;

(14) For a minor misdemeanor not specifically classified, not more than one thousand dollars.

(B) When an organization is convicted of an offense not specifically classified, and the section defining the offense or penalty plainly indicates a purpose to impose the penalty provided for violation upon organizations, then such penalty shall be imposed in lieu of the penalty provided in this section.

(C) When an organization is convicted of an offense not specifically classified, and the penalty provided includes a higher fine than that provided in this section, then the penalty imposed shall be pursuant to the penalty provided for violation of the section defining the offense.

(D) This section does not prevent the imposition of available civil sanctions against an organization convicted of an offense pursuant to section 2901.23 of the Revised Code, either in addition to or in lieu of a fine imposed pursuant to this section.

(1982 H 269, § 4, eff. 7–1–83; 1982 S 199; 1972 H 511)

2929.41   Multiple sentences

(A) Except as provided in division (B) of this section, a sentence of imprisonment shall be served concurrently with any other sentence of imprisonment imposed by a court of this state, another state, or the United States. In any case, a sentence of imprisonment for misdemeanor shall be served concurrently with a sentence of imprisonment for felony served in a state or federal correctional institution.

(B) A sentence of imprisonment shall be served consecutively to any other sentence of imprisonment, in the following cases:

(1) When the trial court specifies that it is to be served consecutively;

(2) When it is imposed for a violation of division (A)(2), (3), or (4) of section 2907.21, division (B) of section 2917.02, section 2907.321, section 2907.322, division (B)(5) or (6) of section 2919.22, section 2921.34, or division (B) of section 2921.35 of the Revised Code, for a violation of section 2907.22 of the Revised Code that is a felony of the second degree, or for a violation of section 2903.13 of the Revised Code for which a sentence of imprisonment is imposed pursuant to division (C)(2) of that section;

(3) When it is imposed for a new felony committed by a probationer, parolee, or escapee;

(4) When a three-year term of actual incarceration is imposed pursuant to section 2929.71 of the Revised Code;

(5) When a six-year term of actual incarceration is imposed pursuant to section 2929.72 of the Revised Code.

(C) Subject to the maximums provided in division (E) of this section:

(1) When consecutive sentences of imprisonment are imposed for felony under division (B)(1) of this section, the minimum term to be served is the aggregate of the consecutive minimum terms imposed, and the maximum term to be served is the aggregate of the consecutive maximum terms imposed.

(2) When consecutive sentences of imprisonment are imposed for felony under division (B)(2) or (3) of this section, the minimum term to be served is the aggregate of the consecutive minimum terms imposed reduced by the time already served on any such minimum term, and the maximum term imposed is the aggregate of the consecutive maximum terms imposed.

(3) When consecutive sentences of imprisonment are imposed under division (B)(4) or (5) of this section, all of the three-year terms of actual incarceration imposed pursuant to section 2929.71 of the Revised Code and all of the six-year terms of actual incarceration imposed pursuant to section 2929.72 of the Revised Code shall be served first, and then the indefinite terms of imprisonment shall be served, with the aggregate minimum and maximum terms being determined in the same manner as aggregate minimum and maximum terms are determined pursuant to division (C)(2) of this section.

(4) When a person is serving definite terms of imprisonment consecutively to indefinite terms of imprisonment, to three-year terms of actual incarceration imposed pursuant to section 2929.71 of the Revised Code, to six-year terms of actual incarceration imposed pursuant to section 2929.72 of the Revised Code, or to both indefinite terms of imprisonment and the three-year or six-year terms of actual incarceration, the aggregate of all of the three-year or six-year terms of actual incarceration shall be served first, then the aggregate of the definite terms of imprisonment shall be served, and then the indefinite terms of imprisonment shall be served, with the aggregate minimum and maximum terms being determined in the same manner as aggregate minimum and maximum terms are determined pursuant to division (C)(2) of this section.

(D) Subject to the maximum provided in division (E) of this section, when consecutive sentences of imprisonment are imposed for misdemeanor, the term to be served is the aggregate of the consecutive terms imposed.

(E) Consecutive terms of imprisonment imposed shall not exceed:

(1) An aggregate minimum term of twenty years, when the consecutive terms imposed include a term of imprisonment for murder and do not include a term of imprisonment for aggravated murder;

(2) An aggregate minimum term of fifteen years, plus the sum of all three-year terms of actual incarceration imposed pursuant to section 2929.71 of the Revised Code and the sum of all six-year terms of actual incarceration imposed pursuant to section 2929.72 of the Revised Code, when the consecutive terms imposed are for felonies other than aggravated murder or murder;

(3) An aggregate term of eighteen months, when the consecutive terms imposed are for misdemeanors.

(F) When consecutive terms aggregating more than one year are imposed for misdemeanors under the Revised Code and at least one of the consecutive terms is for a misdemeanor of the first degree that is an offense of violence, the trial court may order the aggregate term imposed to be served in a state correctional institution.

(1994 H 571, eff. 10–6–94; 1992 H 561, eff. 4–9–93; 1990 S 258; 1988 H 51; 1983 S 210; 1982 H 269, § 4, S 199; 1981 S 1; 1978 H 202; 1972 H 511)

2929.51   Suspension of sentence; time; conditions; community based correctional program; domestic violence offenders

(A)(1) At any time after compliance with the procedures contained in division (C) of this section, if compliance with those procedures is required by that division, and before an offender is delivered into the custody of the institution in which he is to serve his sentence; or at any time between the time of sentencing, if compliance with the procedures contained in division (C) of this section is not required by that division, and the time at which an offender is delivered into the custody of the institution in which he is to serve his sentence, when a term of imprisonment for any felony is imposed, the court may suspend the sentence and place the offender on probation pursuant to section 2951.02 of the Revised Code. As one of the conditions of probation, the court may require the offender to serve a definite term of imprisonment of not more than six months in a county jail or workhouse, which term may be served in intermittent confinement as described in division (D)(3) of this section.

(2) At any time after compliance with the procedures contained in division (C) of this section, if compliance with those procedures is required by that division, and before an offender is delivered into the custody of the institution in which he is to serve his sentence; or at any time between the time of sentencing, if compliance with the procedures contained in division (C) of this section is not required by that division, and before an offender is delivered into the custody of the institution in which he is to serve his sentence, when a term of imprisonment for any felony is imposed, the court may require the offender to do either of the following:

(a) Serve a portion of his sentence, which may be served in a county jail or workhouse and may be served in intermittent confinement as described in division (D)(3) of this section, and suspend the balance of the sentence and place the offender on probation pursuant to section 2951.02 of the Revised Code, with at least one of the conditions of probation being that the offender perform supervised community service work as described in division (H) of section 2951.02 of the Revised Code;

(b) In accordance with division (A)(1) of this section, suspend the sentence of the offender and place him on probation pursuant to section 2951.02 of the Revised Code, with at least one of the conditions of probation being that the offender perform supervised community service work as described in division (H) of section 2951.02 of the Revised Code.

(B) After an offender is delivered into the custody of the institution in which he is to serve his sentence, when a term of imprisonment for felony is imposed, and during the period prescribed by section 2947.061 of the Revised Code, the court may suspend the balance of the sentence and place the offender on probation pursuant to that section.

(C) Between the time of sentencing and the time at which an offender who has been sentenced to a term of imprisonment for felony is delivered into the custody of the institution in which he is to serve his sentence, the court shall notify the intake officer of each community-based correctional facility and program or district community-based correctional facility and program that serves the county in which the court is located, if any facility and program has been established and is operating under sections 2301.51 to 2301.56 of the Revised Code, that the offender has been sentenced, and shall afford to the intake officer access to the offender for purposes of screening the offender and making a written recommendation to the court concerning the commitment or referral of the offender to the facility and program. The intake officer shall screen the offender and make his recommendation to the court within fourteen days after being notified that the offender has been sentenced. No offender who is subject to the terms of this division shall be delivered into the custody of the institution in which he is to serve his sentence until the intake officer for each facility and program that serves the county in which the court is located has screened the offender and has made his written recommendation to the court and until the court has acted upon the recommendation of each intake officer. If the intake officer for any facility and program recommends that the offender be committed or referred to the facility and program, the court may suspend the sentence and place the offender on probation pursuant to section 2951.02 of the Revised Code, with one of the conditions of probation being that the offender serve a term of not more than six months in the facility and program, the actual length of which term shall be determined by the court after considering the recommendation of staff of the facility and program with respect to the length of the term. When an offender's sentence is suspended and he is required to serve a term in a facility and program, a probation officer shall be assigned to the offender to work with the staff of the facility and program during the duration of the offender's term. The court is not required to suspend an offender's sentence and place him on probation under this division upon a recommendation to do so by any intake officer, and the court is not authorized to suspend an offender's sentence and place him on probation under this division unless it receives a recommendation to do so from an intake officer. An offender whose sentence is suspended and who is placed on probation under this division is subject to all terms, conditions, and laws that apply to offenders whose sentence is suspended and who are placed on probation otherwise than under this division.

(D) At the time of sentencing and after sentencing, when imprisonment for misdemeanor is imposed, the court may:

(1) Suspend the sentence and place the offender on probation pursuant to section 2951.02 of the Revised Code;

(2) Suspend the sentence pursuant to section 2951.02 of the Revised Code upon any terms that the court considers appropriate;

(3) Permit the offender to serve his sentence in intermittent confinement, overnight, or on weekends, or both, or at any other time or times that will allow him to continue at his occupation or care for his family;

(4) Require the offender to serve a portion of his sentence, which may be served in intermittent confinement, and suspend the balance of the sentence pursuant to section 2951.02 of the Revised Code upon any terms that the court considers appropriate, or suspend the balance of the sentence and place the offender on probation pursuant to that section.

(E) At the time of sentencing and after sentencing, when a term of imprisonment is imposed for a violation of section 2919.25 or 2919.27 of the Revised Code or a violation of a municipal ordinance that is substantially equivalent to either of those sections, and when the court has reason to believe, based on an evaluation performed pursuant to section 2919.271 of the Revised Code or on the advice of a chemical dependency professional, that the offender is a drug dependent person, is in danger of becoming a drug dependent person, is an alcoholic, or is suffering from acute alcohol intoxication, as defined in section 2935.33 of the Revised Code, the court may require the offender to serve a portion of his sentence and suspend the balance of the sentence and place the offender on probation pursuant to section 2951.02 of the Revised Code, with one of the conditions of probation being that the offender enter into an appropriate treatment program or facility and comply with the treatment prescribed at the program or facility. The court shall order a person to enter a particular program or facility under this division only if the court has received evidence that the program or facility has space available and that the treatment provided by the program or facility is appropriate. For purposes of this division, an appropriate treatment program or facility includes a program licensed by the director of alcohol and drug addiction services pursuant to section 3793.11 of the Revised Code, a program certified by the director of alcohol and drug addiction services pursuant to section 3793.06 of the Revised Code, a public or private hospital, the veterans administration or other agencies of the federal government, or private care or treatment rendered by a physician or a psychologist licensed in the state, a licensed independent social worker, a licensed professional counselor with endorsement, or a certified chemical dependency counselor. This division does not affect or limit, and is not affected or limited by, section 2951.04 of the Revised Code. For purposes of this division, the fact that an offender is a repeat offender, as defined in section 2929.01 of the Revised Code, shall not conclusively bar him from conditional probation under this division if the previous offenses for which he was imprisoned involved violations of section 2919.25 or 2919.27 of the Revised Code or violations of substantially equivalent municipal ordinances or would have been violations of either of those sections had they been in effect at the time of the violations.

(F) At the time of sentencing and after sentencing, when a fine is imposed, the court may:

(1) Suspend all or any portion of the fine, upon any conditions that the court imposes in the interests of justice and the correction and rehabilitation of the offender;

(2) Permit payment of all or any portion of the fine in installments, or by any other method and in any time and on any terms that the court considers just, except that the maximum time permitted for payment shall not exceed two years.

(1993 H 152, eff. 7–1–93; 1990 S 258; 1989 H 317; 1985 H 475; 1982 H 269, § 4, S 199; 1981 H 1; 1980 H 682, H 1000; 1972 H 511)

2929.61 Applicable law according to time of offense; may be chosen by person to be sentenced

(A) Persons charged with a capital offense committed prior to January 1, 1974, shall be prosecuted under the law as it existed at the time the offense was committed, and, if convicted, shall be imprisoned for life, except that whenever the statute under which any such person is prosecuted provides for a lesser penalty under the circumstances of the particular case, such lesser penalty shall be imposed.

(B) Persons charged with an offense, other than a capital offense, committed prior to January 1, 1974, shall be prosecuted under the law as it existed at the time the offense was committed. Persons convicted or sentenced on or after January 1, 1974, for an offense committed prior to January 1, 1974, shall be sentenced according to the penalty for commission of the substantially equivalent offense under Amended Substitute House Bill 511 of the 109th General Assembly. If the offense for which sentence is being imposed does not have a substantial equivalent under that act, or if that act provides a more severe penalty than that originally prescribed for the offense of which the person is convicted, then sentence shall be imposed under the law as it existed prior to January 1, 1974.

(C) Persons charged with an offense that is a felony of the third or fourth degree and that was committed on or after January 1, 1974, and before July 1, 1983, shall be prosecuted under the law as it existed at the time the offense was committed. Persons convicted or sentenced on or after July 1, 1983, for an offense that is a felony of the third or fourth degree and that was committed on or after January 1, 1974, and before July 1, 1983, shall be notified by the court sufficiently in advance of sentencing that they may choose to be sentenced pursuant to either the law in effect at the time of the commission of the offense or the law in effect at the time of sentencing. This notice shall be written and shall include the differences between and possible effects of the alternative sentence forms and the effect of the person's refusal to choose. The person to be sentenced shall then inform the court in writing of his choice, and shall be sentenced accordingly. Any person choosing to be sentenced pursuant to the law in effect at the time of the commission of an offense that is a felony of the third or fourth degree shall then be eligible for parole, and this person cannot at a later date have his sentence converted to a definite sentence. If the person refuses to choose between the two possible sentences, the person shall be sentenced pursuant to the law in effect at the time of the commission of the offense.

(D) Persons charged with an offense that was a felony of the first or second degree at the time it was committed, that was committed on or after January 1, 1974, and that was committed prior to July 1, 1983, shall be prosecuted for that offense and, if convicted, shall be sentenced under the law as it existed at the time the offense was committed.

(1983 S 210, eff. 7–1–83; 1982 H 269, S 199; 1975 H 1; 1972 H 511, § 3)

2929.71 Sentencing to term of actual incarceration for certain offenses

(A) The court shall impose a term of actual incarceration of three years in addition to imposing a life sentence pursuant to section 2907.02, 2907.12, or 2929.02 of the Revised Code or an indefinite term of imprisonment pursuant to section 2929.11 of the Revised Code, if all of the following apply:

(1) The offender is convicted of, or pleads guilty to, any felony other than a violation of section 2923.12 of the Revised Code.

(2) The offender also is convicted of, or pleads guilty to, a specification charging him with having a firearm on or about his person or under his control while committing the felony.

(3) Section 2929.72 of the Revised Code is inapplicable.

The three-year term of actual incarceration imposed pursuant to this section shall be served consecutively with, and prior to, the life sentence or the indefinite term of imprisonment.

(B) If an offender is convicted of, or pleads guilty to, two or more felonies and two or more specifications charging him with having a firearm on or about his person or under his control while committing the felonies, each of the three-year terms of actual incarceration imposed pursuant to this section shall be served consecutively with, and prior to, the life sentences or indefinite terms of imprisonment imposed pursuant to section 2907.02, 2907.12, 2929.02, or 2929.11 of the Revised Code, unless any of the felonies were committed as part of the same act or transaction. If any of the felonies were committed as part of the same act or transaction, only one three-year term of actual incarceration shall be imposed for those offenses, which three-year term shall be served consecutively with, and prior to, the life sentences or indefinite terms of imprisonment imposed pursuant to section 2907.02, 2907.12, 2929.02, or 2929.11 of the Revised Code.

(C) No person shall be sentenced pursuant to division (A) of this section unless the indictment, count in the indictment, or information charging him with the offense contains a specification as set forth in section 2941.141 of the Revised Code.

(D) As used in this section:

(1) "Firearm" has the same meaning as in section 2923.11 of the Revised Code;

(2) "Actual incarceration" has the same meaning as in division (C) of section 2929.01 of the Revised Code, except that a term of actual incarceration imposed pursuant to this section shall not be diminished pursuant to section 2967.19, 2967.193, or 5145.11 of the Revised Code.
(1994 H 571, eff. 10–6–94; 1990 S 258, eff. 11–20–90; 1987 H 261; 1983 S 210; 1982 H 269, § 4, S 199)

2929.72 Actual incarceration for persons committing felonies and having automatic firearm or firearm with silencer

(A) The court shall impose a term of actual incarceration of six years in addition to imposing a life sentence pursuant to section 2907.02, 2907.12, or 2929.02 of the Revised Code or an indefinite term of imprisonment pursuant to section 2929.11 of the Revised Code, if both of the following apply:

(1) The offender is convicted of, or pleads guilty to, any felony other than a violation of section 2923.12 of the Revised Code;

(2) The offender also is convicted of, or pleads guilty to, a specification charging him with having a firearm that is an automatic firearm or that was equipped with a firearm muffler or silencer on or about his person or under his control while committing the felony.

(B) A six-year term of actual incarceration imposed under division (A) of this section shall be served consecutively with, and prior to, the life sentence or indefinite term of imprisonment imposed pursuant to section 2907.02, 2907.12, 2929.02, or 2929.11 of the Revised Code.

(C) If an offender is convicted of or pleads guilty to two or more felonies other than a violation of section 2923.12 of the Revised Code and two or more specifications charging him with having an automatic firearm or a firearm that was equipped with a firearm muffler or silencer on or about his person or under his control while committing the felonies, each of the six-year terms of actual incarceration imposed pursuant to this section shall be served consecutively with, and prior to, the life sentences or indefinite terms of imprisonment imposed pursuant to section 2907.02, 2907.12, 2929.02, or 2929.11 of the Revised Code, unless any of the felonies were committed as part of the same act or transaction. If any of the felonies were committed as part of the same act or transaction, only one six-year term of actual incarceration shall be imposed for those offenses, which six-year term shall be served consecutively with, and prior to, the life sentences or indefinite terms of imprisonment imposed pursuant to section 2907.02, 2907.11, 2929.02, or 2929.11 of the Revised Code.

(D) No person shall be sentenced pursuant to division (A) of this section unless the indictment, count in the indictment, or information charging him with the offense contains a specification as set forth in section 2941.144 of the Revised Code.

(E) As used in this section:

(1) "Actual incarceration" has the same meaning as in section 2929.71 of the Revised Code;

(2) "Firearm" and "automatic firearm" have the same meanings as in section 2923.11 of the Revised Code.
(1990 S 258, eff. 11–20–90)

RIGHTS OF VICTIMS OF CRIMES

2930.01 Definitions

As used in this chapter:

(A) "Crime" means any felony or any violation of section 2903.13, 2903.21, 2903.22, 2919.25, or 2921.04 of the Revised Code.

(B) "Custodial agency" means the department of rehabilitation and correction, a county sheriff, the entity that administers a municipal jail or workhouse, or the entity that administers a multicounty, municipal-county, or multicounty-municipal jail or workhouse in which a defendant is incarcerated, or the department of mental health or other entity to which a defendant found incompetent to stand trial or not guilty by reason of insanity is committed.

(C) "Defendant" means a person who is charged with or convicted of a crime against a victim.

(D) "Member of the victim's family" means a spouse, child, stepchild, sibling, parent, stepparent, grandparent, or other relative designated by the victim or by a court pursuant to section 2930.02 of the Revised Code but does not include a person who is charged with or convicted of the crime against the victim or another crime arising from the same conduct, criminal episode, or plan.

(E) "Prosecutor" has the same meaning as in section 2935.01 of the Revised Code and also means the attorney general and, when appropriate, the employees of a prosecutor.

(F) "Public agency" means any office, agency, department, bureau, or other governmental entity of the state or of any political subdivision of the state.

(G) "Public official" has the same meaning as in section 2921.01 of the Revised Code.

(H) "Victim" means a person who is identified as the victim of a crime in a police report or in a complaint, indictment, or information charging the commission of a crime.
(1994 S 186, eff. 10–12–94)

2930.02 Representative of victim

(A)(1) A member of a victim's family or another person may exercise the rights of the victim under this chapter as the victim's representative if either of the following applies:

(a) The victim is a minor or is incapacitated, incompetent, or deceased.

(b) Division (A)(1)(a) of this section does not apply, and the victim authorizes the family member or other person to act as the victim's representative.

(2) If more than one person seeks to act as the victim's representative, the court in which the crime is prosecuted may designate one person as the victim's representative. A victim who, pursuant to division (A)(1)(b) of this section, has authorized a member of the victim's family or another person to exercise the rights of the victim as the victim's representative may revoke the authority of that family member or other person to act as the victim's representative.

(B) If a victim's representative is to exercise the rights of a victim, the victim or victim's representative shall notify the prosecutor that the victim's representative is to act for the victim. When a victim or victim's representative has so notified the prosecutor, all notice under this chapter shall be sent only to the victim's representative, all rights under this chapter shall be granted only to the victim's representative, and all references to a victim shall be interpreted to be references to the victim's representative unless the victim informs the notifying authority that the victim also wishes to receive the notices or exercise the rights or unless the victim has revoked the authority of the person who was the victim's representative to act in that capacity pursuant to division (A)(2) of this section and informs the notifying authority of the revocation.

(1994 S 186, eff. 10–12–94)

2930.03   Method of notice

(A) Notice under this chapter shall be given to a victim by any means reasonably calculated to provide prompt actual notice. Notice may be oral or written.

(B) A person or agency that is required to furnish notice under this chapter shall give the notice to the victim at the address or telephone number provided by the victim. The victim shall inform the person or agency of any change in the name, address, or telephone number of the victim.

(C) A person or agency that has furnished information to a victim in accordance with any requirement under this chapter shall notify the victim promptly of any significant changes to that information.

(1994 S 186, eff. 10–12–94)

2930.04   Information provided by law enforcement agency after initial contact with victim

(A) After the initial contact between a victim and the law enforcement agency responsible for investigating a crime, the law enforcement agency promptly shall give to the victim, in writing, all of the following information:

(1) An explanation of the victim's rights under this chapter;

(2) Information about medical, counseling, housing, and emergency services and about any other assistance that is available to a victim;

(3) Information about compensation for victims under the reparations program in sections 2743.51 to 2743.72 of the Revised Code and the name, street address, and telephone number of the agency to contact to apply for an award of reparations under those sections;

(4) Information about protection that is available to the victim, including protective orders issued by a court.

(B) A law enforcement agency, as soon as practicable after its initial contact with a victim in a case, shall give to the victim all of the following:

(1) The business telephone number of the law enforcement officer assigned to investigate the case;

(2) The name, office address, and telephone number of the prosecutor in the case;

(3) A statement that if the victim is not notified of the arrest of the offender in the case within a reasonable period of time, the victim may contact the law enforcement agency to learn the status of the case.

(C) To the extent that the information required by this section is provided in the pamphlet prepared pursuant to section 109.42 of the Revised Code or in the information card or other material prepared pursuant to section 2743.71 of the Revised Code, a law enforcement agency that is required to provide the information under this section may fulfill that portion of its obligations under this section by giving that pamphlet, information card, or other material to the victim.

(1994 S 186, eff. 10–12–94)

2930.05 Information provided by law enforcement agency after arrest of defendant

(A) Within a reasonable period of time after the arrest of a defendant for a crime, the law enforcement agency that investigates the crime shall give the victim of the crime notice of all of the following:

(1) The arrest;

(2) Whether the defendant is eligible for pretrial release;

(3) The telephone number of the law enforcement agency;

(4) The victim's right to telephone the agency to ascertain whether the defendant has been released from custody.

(B) Upon receiving the affidavit of a victim stating that the defendant, or someone acting at the defendant's direction, has committed or threatened to commit acts of violence or intimidation against the victim, the victim's family, or the victim's representative, the prosecutor in the case may file a motion asking the court to revoke the bond or personal recognizance granted to the defendant.

(1994 S 186, eff. 10–12–94)

2930.06 Information provided by prosecutor

(A) The prosecutor in a case, to the extent practicable, shall confer with the victim in the case before pretrial diversion is granted to the defendant in the case, before amending or dismissing a charge against that defendant, before agreeing to a negotiated plea for that defendant, or before a trial of that defendant by judge or jury. The court that tries a criminal case shall note on the record any failure of the prosecutor in the case to confer with the victim in the case at one of those times as well as the prosecutor's reasons for failing to confer with the victim. The prosecutor's failure to confer with the victim as required by this division does not affect the validity of an agreement between the prosecutor and the defendant in the case, a pretrial diversion of the defendant, an amendment or dismissal of a charge filed against the defendant, a plea entered by the defendant, or any other disposition in the case.

(B) After a prosecution in a case has been commenced, the prosecutor in the case, to the extent practicable, promptly shall give the victim all of the following information:

(1) The name of the offense with which the defendant in the case has been charged;

(2) The file number of the case;

(3) A brief statement regarding the procedural steps in a criminal case and the right of the victim to be present during all proceedings held throughout the prosecution of a case;

(4) A summary of the rights of a victim under this chapter;

(5) Procedures the victim may follow if the victim becomes subject to threats or intimidation from the defendant in the case or any other person;

(6) The name of a person to contact for further information with respect to the case;

(7) The right of the victim to have a representative exercise the victim's rights under this chapter in accordance with section 2930.02 of the Revised Code and the procedure by which a court will name a representative if the victim so requests.

(C) Upon the request of the victim in a case, the prosecutor in the case shall give the victim notice of any scheduled court proceedings in the case and notice of any changes in the schedule in the case.

(D) A victim who requests notice under this section and who elects to receive any other notice under this chapter shall keep the prosecutor informed of the victim's current address and telephone number until the case is dismissed or terminated, the defendant is acquitted or sentenced, or the appellate process is completed, whichever is the final disposition in the case.

(1994 S 186, eff. 10–12–94)

2930.07 Protection of victim

(A) If the prosecutor in a case determines that there are reasonable grounds for the victim in a case to be apprehensive regarding acts or threats of violence or intimidation by the defendant in the case or at the defendant's direction against the victim, the victim's family, or the victim's representative, the prosecutor may file a motion with the court requesting that the victim or other witnesses in the case not be compelled in any phase of the criminal proceeding to give testimony that would disclose the victim's address, place of employment, or similar identifying fact about the victim without the victim's consent. The court shall hold a hearing on the motion in chambers, and a court reporter shall make a record of the proceeding.

(B) The court file or court documents in a case shall not contain the address of the victim in the case or of the victim's representative unless the address is contained in a transcript of the trial or is used to identify the location of the crime. The court file or court documents in a case shall not contain the telephone number of the victim in a case or of the victim's representative unless the number is contained in a transcript of the trial.

(1994 S 186, eff. 10–12–94)

2930.08 Notice of potential delays in prosecution of defendant

If practicable, the prosecutor in a case shall inform the victim in the case of a motion, request, or agreement between counsel that may result in a substantial delay in the prosecution of the case. The prosecutor shall inform the court of the victim's objections to the delay, if any, and the court shall consider the victim's objections in ruling on the motion, request, or agreement.

(1994 S 186, eff. 10–12–94)

2930.09 Right of victim to be present

A victim in a case may be present whenever the defendant in the case is present during any critical stage of the case against the defendant that is conducted on the record, other than a grand jury proceeding, unless the court determines that exclusion of the victim is necessary to protect the defendant's right to a fair trial. At the victim's request, the court shall permit the victim to be accompanied by an individual to provide support to the victim unless the court determines that exclusion of the individual is necessary to protect the defendant's right to a fair trial.

(1994 S 186, eff. 10–12–94)

2930.10 Minimizing contact between victim and defendant

(A) The court that hears a criminal case shall make a reasonable effort to minimize any unwanted contact between the victim in the case, members of the victim's family, the victim's representative, or witnesses for the prosecution and the defendant in the case, members of the defendant's family, or witnesses for the defense before, during, and immediately after court proceedings.

(B) The court shall provide a waiting area for the victim, members of the victim's family, the victim's representative, or witnesses for the prosecution that is separate from the waiting area used by the defendant, members of the defendant's family, and defense witnesses if a separate waiting area is available and the use of the area is practical.

(1994 S 186, eff. 10–12–94)

2930.11   Property of victim

(A) The law enforcement agency that has responsibility for investigating a crime shall promptly return to the victim of the crime any property of the victim that was taken in the course of the investigation except as otherwise provided in sections 2933.41 to 2933.43 of the Revised Code. If the ownership of the property is in dispute, the agency shall not return the property until the dispute is resolved.

(B) The law enforcement agency that has responsibility for investigating a crime shall retain any property of the victim of the crime that is needed as evidence in the case, including any weapon used in the commission of the crime, upon the prosecutor's certification of a need to retain the property in lieu of a photograph of the property or of another evidentiary substitute for the property itself.

(C) If the defendant in a case files a motion for the law enforcement agency that has responsibility for investigating a crime to retain property of the victim in the case because the property is needed for the defense in the case, the agency shall retain the property until the court rules on the motion. The court, in making a determination on the motion, shall weigh the victim's need for the property against the defendant's assertion that the property has evidentiary value for the defense. The court shall rule on the motion in a timely fashion.

(1994 S 186, eff. 10–12–94)

2930.12   Notice of acquittal or conviction of defendant

At the victim's request, the prosecutor in a case shall give the victim in the case notice of the defendant's acquittal or conviction. If the defendant is convicted, the notice shall include all of the following:

(A) The crimes of which the defendant was convicted;

(B) The address and telephone number of the probation office that is to prepare a presentence investigation report pursuant to section 2951.03 of the Revised Code, and the address and telephone number of the person, if any, who is to prepare a victim impact statement pursuant to section 2947.051 of the Revised Code;

(C) Notice that the victim may make a statement about the impact of the offense to the probation officer who prepares the presentence investigation report or to the person who prepares a victim impact statement, that a statement included in the report will be made available to the defendant unless the court exempts it from disclosure, and that the court may make the victim impact statement available to the defendant;

(D) Notice of the victim's right to make a statement about the impact of the offense at sentencing;

(E) The date, time, and place of the sentencing hearing;

(F) Any sentence imposed upon the defendant and any modification of that sentence.

(1994 S 186, eff. 10–12–94)

2930.13   Victim impact statement;   presentence investigation report

(A) If the court orders the preparation of a victim impact statement pursuant to section 2947.051 of the Revised Code, the victim in the case may make a written or oral statement regarding the impact of the offense to the person whom the court orders to prepare the victim impact statement. A statement made by the victim under this section shall be included in the victim impact statement.

(B) If a probation officer is preparing a presentence investigation report concerning the defendant, the victim may make a written or oral statement regarding the impact of the offense to the probation officer for use by that officer in the presentence investigation report. Upon the victim's request, the probation officer shall include a written statement submitted by the victim in the presentence investigation report.

(C) A statement made by the victim under division (A) or (B) of this section may include the following:

(1) An explanation of the nature and extent of any physical, psychological, or emotional harm sufered [*sic*] by the victim as a result of the crime that is the basis of the case;

(2) An explanation of the extent of any property damage or other economic loss suffered by the victim as a result of the crime that is the basis of the case;

(3) An opinion regarding the extent to which, if any, the victim needs restitution for harm caused by the defendant and information about whether the victim has applied for or received any compensation for loss or damage caused by the crime that is the basis of the case;

(4) The victim's recommendation for an appropriate sanction for the defendant.

(D) The release of a statement made by a victim under division (A) of this section and included in a victim impact statement is governed by section 2947.051 of the Revised Code. The release of a statement made by a victim under division (B) of this section and included in a presentence investigation report is governed by section 2951.03 of the Revised Code.

(1994 S 186, eff. 10–12–94)

2930.14   Statement by victim prior to sentencing of defendant

(A) Before imposing sentence upon the defendant for the commission of a crime, the court shall permit the victim of the crime to make a statement concerning the effects of the crime upon the victim, the circumstances surrounding the crime, and the manner in which the crime was perpetrated.   At the judge's option, the victim may present the statement in writing prior to the sentencing hearing, orally at the hearing, or both.   The court shall give copies of any written statement by a victim to the prosecutor and the defendant.

(B) The court shall consider the victim's statement along with other factors that the court is required to consider in imposing sentence.   If the statement includes new material facts upon which the court intends to rely, the court shall continue the sentencing proceeding or take other appropriate action to allow the defendant an adequate opportunity to respond to the new material facts.

(1994 S 186, eff. 10–12–94)

2930.15   Notice of appeal by defendant

(A) If the victim of a crime requests notice of the filing of an appeal, the prosecutor in a case in which a defendant is convicted of committing that crime against the victim shall notify the victim if the defendant files an appeal of the conviction.   The prosecutor also shall give the victim all of the following information:

(1) A brief explanation of the appellate process, including the possible disposition of the case;

(2) Whether the defendant has been released on bail or other recognizance pending the disposition of the appeal;

(3) The time and place of appellate court proceedings and any subsequent changes in the time and place of those proceedings;

(4) The result of the appeal.

(B) If a defendant's conviction is reversed and the defendant's case is returned to the trial court for further proceedings, the victim of the crime of which the defendant was convicted may exercise all the rights that the victim previously requested in the case.

(1994 S 186, eff. 10–12–94)

2930.16   Notice of incarceration or release of defendant

(A) A victim in a case who pursuant to section 2930.06 of the Revised Code elected to receive any notice specified by this chapter shall be given notice of the incarceration of the defendant in the case.   Promptly after sentence is imposed upon the defendant, the prosecutor in the case shall notify the victim of the date on which the defendant will be released from confinement or the prosecutor's reasonable estimate of that date.   The prosecutor also shall notify the victim of the name of the custodial agency of the defendant and tell the victim how to contact that custodial agency. The victim shall keep the custodial agency informed of the victim's current address and telephone number.

(B) The prosecutor in a case promptly shall notify the victim in the case of any motion for early release of the defendant in the case, of any motion for modification of the defendant's sentence pursuant to section 2929.51 of the Revised Code, and of the court's ruling on each of those motions.

(C) Upon the victim's request, the custodial agency of a defendant shall give the victim of the defendant any of the following notices that is applicable:

(1) At least three weeks prior to a decision of the governor to grant a pardon or commutation of sentence to the defendant or at least three weeks prior to a hearing before the adult parole authority regarding a grant of parole to the defendant, notice of the victim's right to submit a statement regarding the impact of the defendant's release in accordance with section 2967.12 of the Revised Code;

(2) Notice to the victim at least thirty days before the defendant is granted a furlough under section 2967.26 of the Revised Code or as soon as practicable before the defendant is granted a furlough under 2967.27 of the Revised Code and notice to the victim of the victim's right to submit a statement regarding the impact of the release under those sections;

(3) Notice to the victim at least three weeks before the defendant is permitted to serve a portion of his sentence as a period of electronically monitored early release pursuant to section 5120.073 of the Revised Code;

(4) Prompt notice to the victim of the defendant's escape from a facility in which he was incarcerated or the defendant's absence without leave from a mental health facility or from other custody and of the capture of the defendant after an escape or absence;

(5) Notice to the victim of the defendant's death while in custody;

(6) Notice to the victim of the defendant's release from confinement and the conditions of the release.

(1994 S 186, eff. 10–12–94)

2930.17 Statement by victim prior to postsentence probation of defendant

(A) In determining whether to release a defendant from a term of incarceration pursuant to section 2947.061 of the Revised Code, the court shall permit a victim of the defendant to make an additional statement concerning the effects of the crime for which the defendant was incarcerated on the victim, the circumstances surrounding the crime, the manner in which the crime was perpetrated, and the victim's opinion whether the defendant should be released. The victim may make the statement in writing or orally, at the court's discretion. The court shall give the defendant and the adult parole authority a copy of any written impact statement made by the victim under this section.

(B) In deciding whether to release the defendant, the court shall consider a statement made by the victim under this section or section 2930.14 of the Revised Code.

(1994 S 186, eff. 10–12–94)

2930.18 Retaliation by employer against victim

No employer of a victim shall discharge, discipline, or otherwise retaliate against the victim, a member of the victim's family, or a victim's representative for participating, at the prosecutor's request, in preparation for a criminal justice proceeding or for attendance, pursuant to a subpoena, at a criminal justice proceeding if the attendance is reasonably necessary to protect the interests of the victim. An employer who knowingly violates this section is in contempt of court.

(1994 S 186, eff. 10–12–94)

2930.19 Miscellaneous provisions

(A) In a manner consistent with the duty of a prosecutor to represent the interests of the public as a whole, a prosecutor shall seek compliance with this chapter on behalf of a victim, a member of the victim's family, or the victim's representative.

(B) The failure of a public official, public employee, or public agency to comply with the requirements of this chapter does not give rise to a claim for damages against that public official, public employee, or public agency, except that a public agency as an employer may be held responsible for a violation of section 2930.18 of the Revised Code.

(C) The failure to provide a right, privilege, or notice to a victim under this chapter does not constitute grounds for declaring a mistrial or new trial, for setting aside a conviction or sentence, or for granting postconviction release to a defendant.

(D) If there is a conflict between a provision in this chapter and a specific statute governing the procedure in a capital case, the specific statute supersedes the provision in this chapter.

(E) If the victim is incarcerated in a state or local correctional facility, the victim's rights under this chapter may be modified by court order to prevent any security risk, hardship, or undue burden upon a public official, public employee, or public agency with a duty under this chapter.

(1994 S 186, eff. 10–12–94)

JURISDICTION

2931.01   Definition of magistrate

As used in Chapters 2931. to 2953. of the Revised Code:

(A) "Magistrate" includes county court judges, police justices, mayors of municipal corporation, and judges of other courts inferior to the court of common pleas.

(B) "Judge" does not include the probate judge.

(C) "Court" does not include the probate court.

(D) "Clerk" does not include the clerk of the probate court.

(1975 H 205, eff. 1–1–76; 127 v 1039; 1953 H 1; GC 13422–1)

2931.02   General jurisdiction of county court judge

A judge of a county court is a conservator of the peace and has jurisdiction in criminal cases throughout his area of jurisdiction. He may hear complaints of the peace and issue search warrants. Judges of county courts have jurisdiction on sworn complaint, to issue a warrant for the arrest of a person charged with the commission of a felony where it is made to appear that such person has fled or is outside this state and it is necessary or desirable to extradite such person. Judges of county courts have jurisdiction within their respective areas of jurisdiction in all cases of violation of any law relating to:

(A) Adulteration or deception in the sale of dairy products and other food, drink, drugs, and medicines;

(B) Prevention of cruelty to animals and children;

(C) The abandonment, nonsupport, or ill treatment of a child under eighteen years of age or a physically and mentally handicapped child under the age of eighteen years by its parents;

(D) The abandonment, or ill treatment of a child under eighteen years of age or a physically and mentally handicapped child under the age of eighteen years by its guardian;

(E) The employment of a child under fourteen years of age in public exhibitions or vocations injurious to health, life, or morals, or which will cause or permit him to suffer unnecessary physical or mental pain;

(F) The regulation, restriction, or prohibition of the employment of females and minors;

(G) The torturing, unlawfully punishing, ill treating, or depriving anyone of necessary food, clothing, or shelter;

(H) Any violation of Chapters 4301. and 4303. of the Revised Code, or keeping a place where intoxicating liquor is sold, given away, or furnished in violation of any law prohibiting such acts;

(I) The shipping, selling, using, permitting the use of, branding, or having unlawful quantities of illuminating oil for or in a mine;

(J) The sale, shipment, or adulteration of commercial feeds;

(K) The use of dust-creating machinery in workshops and factories;

(L) The conducting of a pharmacy, or retail drug or chemical store, or the dispensing or selling of drugs, chemicals, poisons, or pharmaceutical preparations therein;

(M) The failure to place and keep in a sanitary condition a bakery, confectionery, creamery, dairy barn, milk depot, laboratory, hotel, restaurant, eating house, packing house, slaughterhouse, ice cream factory, or place where a food product is manufactured, packed, stored, deposited, collected, prepared, produced, or sold for any purpose, or for the violation of any law relating to public health;

(N) Inspection of steam boilers, and of laws licensing steam engineers and boiler operators;

(O) Prevention of short weighing and measuring and all violations of the weights and measures laws;

(P) Laws relating to the practice of medicine or surgery, or any of its branches;

(Q) Laws relating to the filling or refilling of registered containers by other than the owner, or the defacing of the marks of ownership thereon;

(R) Offenses arising from or growing out of the violation of conservation laws.

(1973 S 1, eff. 1–1–74; 1969 H 1; 132 v S 65; 128 v 823; 127 v 1039; 1953 H 1; GC 13422–2)

2931.03 Jurisdiction of court of common pleas

The court of common pleas has original jurisdiction of all crimes and offenses, except in cases of minor offenses the exclusive jurisdiction of which is vested in courts inferior to the court of common pleas.

(1953 H 1, eff. 10–1–53; GC 13422–5)

2931.04 Jurisdiction of municipal courts not affected

Sections 2931.01 to 2931.03, inclusive, of the Revised Code, do not affect, modify, or limit the jurisdiction of municipal courts. All municipal court judges have jurisdiction within the territory for which they were elected or appointed in all cases of violation of Chapters 4301. and 4303. of the Revised Code and of prosecutions for keeping a place where intoxicating liquor is sold, given away, or furnished, in violation of any law prohibiting such acts.

(128 v 823, eff. 11–6–59; 1953 H 1; GC 13422–6)

2931.041   Criminal jurisdiction—Repealed

(1986 H 158, eff. 3–17–87; 129 v 582; 128 v 141)

PROCEDURE

2931.05   Bills of exception in summary convictions—Repealed

(128 v 97, eff. 1–1–60; 127 v 1039; 1953 H 1; GC 13423–1)

2931.06   Special constables in certain townships

When the constables in a township situated on and consisting in whole or in part of one or more islands in a lake in this state, or in a township adjoining or abutting on lands belonging to a state or national home for disabled volunteer soldiers or a disabled volunteer soldiers' home, are insufficient to maintain the peace and enforce the laws for the preservation of order therein, a judge of the county court having jurisdiction in township may appoint not more than ten special constables to be conservators of the peace within such township and with powers of constables in criminal causes. The appointing judge shall enter such appointments upon his docket and they shall continue in force for one year unless revoked by him. Such special constables shall receive like fees as are paid for similar services to regular constables.

(127 v 1039, eff. 1–1–58; 1953 H 1; GC 13423–2)

2931.07   Recognizance

Recognizances taken by a judge of a county court or other officer authorized to take them, may be returned to the court of common pleas.

Such recognizances shall be returned to such court forthwith after the commitment of the accused, or after the taking of a recognizance for his appearance before such court. The prosecuting attorney may proceed with the prosecution in such court, and the accused shall appear therein and answer to his recognizance.

(127 v 1039, eff. 1–1–58; 1953 H 1; GC 13423–2a, 13423–2b)

2931.08   County court fines to be paid into county general fund—Repealed

(1986 H 158, eff. 3–17–87; 1986 S 54; 127 v 1039; 125 v 903; 1953 H 1; GC 13423–3)

2931.09   Default of payment—Repealed

(1986 H 158, eff. 3–17–87; 127 v 1039; 1953 H 1; GC 13423–4)

2931.10   Annual statement of fines rendered county auditor—Repealed

(1986 H 158, eff. 3–17–87; 127 v 1039; 1953 H 1; GC 13423–5)

2931.11   Jury trial before magistrate—Repealed

(128 v 97, eff. 1–1–60; 1953 H 1; GC 13424–1)

2931.12   Venire of jurors in magistrate's court—Repealed

(128 v 97, eff. 1–1–60; 1953 H 1; GC 13424–2)

2931.13   Jury panel—Repealed

(128 v 97, eff. 1–1–60; 1953 H 1; GC 13424–3)

2931.14   Subsequent offense—Repealed

(128 v 97, eff. 1–1–60; 1953 H 1; GC 13424–4)

2931.15 New trial

In prosecutions before a magistrate, a defendant who has been found guilty upon the verdict of a jury or by the decision of the magistrate without the intervention of a jury may upon written application filed within three days after the verdict or decision, be granted a new trial in like manner and for like reasons as provided by sections 2945.79 to 2945.83, inclusive, of the Revised Code.

(128 v 141, eff. 1–1–60; 128 v 97; 1953 H 1; GC 13424–5)

2931.16 Mileage of jurors; payment—Repealed

(128 v 97, eff. 1–1–60; 1953 H 1; GC 13424–6)

2931.17 Security for costs—Repealed

(128 v 97, eff. 1–1–60; 1953 H 1; GC 13424–7)

2931.18 Humane society may employ attorney and assistants

A humane society or its agent may employ an attorney, and may also employ one or more assistant attorneys to prosecute violations of law relating to:

(A) Prevention of cruelty to animals or children;

(B) Abandonment, nonsupport, or ill-treatment of a child by its parent;

(C) Employment of a child under fourteen years of age in public exhibitions or vocations injurious to health, life, or morals or which cause or permit such child to suffer unnecessary physical or mental pain;

(D) Neglect or refusal of an adult to support destitute parent.

Such attorneys shall be paid out of the county treasury in an amount approved as just and reasonable by the board of county commissioners of that county.

(1988 H 246, eff. 12–12–88; 130 v S 4; 1953 H 1; GC 13424–8)

VENUE

2931.19 Death in one county from violence in another—Repealed

(1972 H 511, eff. 1–1–74; 126 v 812; 1953 H 1; GC 13426–3)

2931.20 Death in this state from violence without—Repealed

(1972 H 511, eff. 1–1–74; 1953 H 1; GC 13426–4)

2931.21 Violence in this state resulting in death without—Repealed

(1972 H 511, eff. 1–1–74; 1953 H 1; GC 13426–5)

2931.22 Stolen property brought into state—Repealed

(1972 H 511, eff. 1–1–74; 1953 H 1; GC 13426–6)

2931.23 Larceny; property stolen in one county taken into another—Repealed

(1972 H 511, eff. 1–1–74; 1953 H 1; GC 13426–7)

2931.24 Crime committed on board common carrier—Repealed

(1972 H 511, eff. 1–1–74; 1953 H 1; GC 13426–8)

2931.25 Prosecution for receiving stolen property—Repealed

(1972 H 511, eff. 1–1–74; 1953 H 1; GC 13426–9)

2931.26 Obtaining property by false pretenses—Repealed

(1972 H 511, eff. 1–1–74; 1953 H 1; GC 13426–10)

2931.27 Embezzlement—Repealed

(1972 H 511, eff. 1–1–74; 1953 H 1; GC 13426–11)

2931.28 Offenses against aircraft—Repealed

(1972 H 511, eff. 1–1–74; 1953 H 1; GC 13426–12)

2931.29 Procedure on change of venue

When a change of venue is ordered pursuant to section 2901.12 of the Revised Code, the clerk of the court in which the cause is pending shall make a certified transcript of the proceedings in the case, which, with the original affidavit, complaint, indictment, or information, he shall transmit to the clerk of the court to which said case is sent for trial, and the trial shall be conducted as if the cause had originated in the jurisdiction of the latter court. The prosecuting attorney, city director of law, or other officer who would have prosecuted the case in the court in which the cause originated shall take charge of and try the cause, and the court to which the cause is sent may on application appoint one or more attorneys to assist the prosecutor in the trial, and allow the appointed attorneys reasonable compensation.

(1977 H 219, eff. 11–1–77; 1972 H 511; 1953 H 1; GC 13427–1)

2931.30 Transfer of prisoner on change of venue

When a change of venue is ordered pursuant to section 2901.12 of the Revised Code, and the accused is in jail, a warrant shall be issued by the clerk of the court in which the cause originated, directed to the proper officer, commanding him to convey the prisoner to the jail of the county or municipal corporation where the prisoner is to be tried, there to be kept until discharged. If the accused is charged with a bailable offense, and at the date of the order changing the venue is under bond for his appearance at the court from which the venue is changed, the court may fix in said order the amount of recognizance which said accused shall give for his appearance at the time the court may designate, in the court to which the venue is changed, and the clerk shall take such recognizance as in other cases, and forward the same with the record. The court shall recognize the witnesses of the prosecution to appear before the court in which the accused is to be tried.

(1972 H 511, eff. 1–1–74; 1953 H 1; GC 13427–2)

2931.31 Payment of costs and expenses on change of venue

The reasonable expenses of the officer acting as prosecutor, incurred in consequence of a change of venue under section 2901.12 of the Revised Code, the fees of the clerk of the court to which the venue is changed, the sheriff or bailiff, and of the jury shall be allowed and paid out of the treasury of the county in which said cause originated.

(1972 H 511, eff. 1–1–74; 1953 H 1; GC 13427–3)

2931.32 Offenses on or near county boundaries—Repealed

(1972 H 511, eff. 1–1–74; 1953 H 1; GC 13426–2)

CHAPTER 2933

PEACE WARRANTS; SEARCH WARRANTS

PEACE WARRANTS

SEARCH WARRANTS

BODY CAVITY AND STRIP SEARCHES

DISPOSITION OF PROPERTY AND CONTRABAND

INTERCEPTION OF COMMUNICATIONS; WARRANTS

285

PEACE WARRANTS

2933.01   Definition of magistrate

The definition of "magistrate" set forth in section 2931.01 of the Revised Code applies to Chapter 2933. of the Revised Code.

(1953 H 1, eff. 10–1–53)

2933.02   Complaint to keep the peace

When a complaint is made in writing and upon oath, filed with a municipal or county court or a mayor sitting as the judge of a mayor's court, and states that the complainant has just cause to fear and fears that another individual will commit an offense against the person or property of the complainant or his ward or child, a municipal or county court judge or mayor shall issue to the sheriff or to any other appropriate peace officer, as defined in section 2935.01 of the Revised Code, within the territorial jurisdiction of the court, a warrant in the name of the state that commands him forthwith to arrest and take the individual complained of before the court to answer the complaint.

(1986 H 412, eff. 3–17–87; 1953 H 1; GC 13428–1)

2933.03   Form of warrant to keep the peace

Warrants issued under section 2933.02 of the Revised Code shall be substantially in the following form:

The State of Ohio, _____ County, ss:

To the sheriff or other appropriate peace officer, greeting:

Whereas, a complaint has been filed by one C.D., in writing and upon oath, stating that he has just cause to fear and does fear that one E.F. will (here state the threatened injury or violence according to the fact as sworn to).

These are therefore to command you to forthwith arrest E.F. and bring him before this court to show cause why he should not find surety to keep the peace and be of good behavior toward the citizens of the state generally, and C.D. especially, and for his appearance before the proper court.

Given under my hand, this _____ day of __

A. B., Judge, ...
County Court;

Judge, ...
Municipal Court;

Mayor, ...
Mayor's Court

(1986 H 412, eff. 3–17–87; 127 v 1039; 1953 H 1; GC 13428–2)

2933.04 Arraignment; detention

When the accused in [*sic*] brought before the municipal, county, or mayor's court pursuant to sections 2933.02 and 2933.03 of the Revised Code, he shall be heard in his defense. If it is necessary for just cause to adjourn the hearing, the municipal or county court judge or mayor involved may order such adjournment. The judge or mayor also may direct the sheriff or other peace officer having custody of the accused to detain him in the county jail or other appropriate detention facility until the cause of delay is removed, unless a bond in a sum fixed by the judge or mayor but not to exceed five hundred dollars, with sufficient surety, is given by the accused. A delay shall not exceed two days.

(1986 H 412, eff. 3–17–87; 1953 H 1; GC 13428–3)

2933.05 Hearing; discharge or bond; detention upon bond default

The municipal or county court judge or mayor sitting as the judge of a mayor's court, upon the appearance of the parties pursuant to sections 2933.02 to 2933.04 of the Revised Code, shall hear the witnesses under oath and do one of the following:

(A) Discharge the accused, render judgment against the complainant for costs, and award execution for the costs;

(B) Order the accused to enter into a bond of not less than fifty or more than five hundred dollars, with sufficient surety, to keep the peace and be of good behavior for such time as may be just, render judgment against him for costs, and award execution for the costs.

In default of such bond, the judge or mayor shall commit the accused to the county jail or other appropriate detention facility, until such order is complied with or he is discharged.

(1986 H 412, eff. 3–17–87; 1953 H 1; GC 13428–4, 13428–5)

2933.06 Appeal; bond; transcript

The accused under sections 2933.02 to 2933.05 of the Revised Code may appeal from the decision of a municipal or county court judge to the appropriate court of appeals or from the decision of a mayor sitting as the judge of a mayor's court to the appropriate municipal or county court. An appeal from the decision of a municipal or county court judge to the appropriate court of appeals shall be only as to questions of law and, to the extent that sections 2933.06 to 2933.09 of the Revised Code do not contain relevant provisions, shall be made and proceed in accordance with the Rules of Appellate Procedure. An appeal from the decision of a mayor sitting as the judge of a mayor's court to the appropriate municipal or county court shall be as to questions of law and fact, and shall be made and proceed in accordance with sections 2933.06 to 2933.09 of the Revised Code.

In connection with either type of appeal, the accused shall file with the clerk of the municipal, county, or mayor's court, within ten days after the decision is rendered, an appeal bond in a sum to be fixed by the judge or mayor at not less than fifty or more than five hundred dollars, with surety to be approved by the judge or mayor, conditioned that, pending the determination of the appeal, the accused will keep the peace and will be of good behavior generally and especially towards the person named in the complaint. Upon the filing of the appeal bond, the clerk of the municipal, county, or mayor's court forthwith shall make a certified transcript of the proceedings in the action, the appeal bond to be included. Upon the payment by the appellant of the fee for the transcript, the clerk immediately shall file the transcript and all the original papers in the action in the office of the clerk of the appellate court.

(1986 H 412, eff. 3–17–87; 1953 H 1; GC 13428–6)

2933.07 Discharge on failure to prosecute

In the case of an appeal from the decision of a mayor sitting as the judge of a mayor's court to the appropriate municipal or county court, no further pleadings shall be required. If the complainant fails to prosecute in such an appeal, the accused shall be discharged unless good cause to the contrary is shown, and the municipal or county court shall render judgment against the complainant for the costs of prosecution and award execution for the costs.

(1986 H 412, eff. 3–17–87; 1953 H 1; GC 13428–7)

2933.08 Hearing; judgment

In the case of an appeal from the decision of a mayor sitting as the judge of a mayor's court to the appropriate municipal or county court, the municipal or county court shall set a time for the hearing of that appeal and, at that time, shall hear the witnesses under oath, and either discharge the accused, render judgment against the complainant for costs, and award execution for the costs, or order the accused to enter into a bond, for such time as may be just, to keep the peace and be of good behavior, render judgment against him for costs, and award execution for the costs.

(1986 H 412, eff. 3–17–87; 1953 H 1; GC 13428–8)

2933.09 Commitment to jail

In the case of an appeal from the decision of a mayor sitting as the judge of a mayor's court to the appropriate municipal or county court, if the accused fails to enter into a bond ordered pursuant to section 2933.08 of the Revised Code, the municipal or county court shall commit the accused to jail until he enters into a bond or is discharged by law, and shall render judgment against him for costs and award execution for the costs. He shall not be imprisoned longer than one year.

After such a commitment following such an appeal, or after a commitment of not more than one year for not entering into a bond ordered pursuant to section 2933.05 of the Revised Code, if such an appeal was not taken, the court may at any time discharge the accused on his own recognizance.

(1986 H 412, eff. 3–17–87; 1953 H 1; GC 13428–9)

2933.10 Bond without process; commitment upon default

Whoever, in the presence of a municipal or county court judge, or a mayor sitting as the judge of a mayor's court, makes an affray, threatens to beat or kill another or to commit an offense against the person or property of another, or contends with angry words to the disturbance of the peace, may be ordered without process or other proof to enter into a bond under section 2933.05 of the Revised Code. In default of such a bond, the person may be committed under that section.

(1988 H 708, eff. 4–19–88; 1986 H 412; 1953 H 1; GC 13428–10)

2933.16 Probation conditioned upon treatment

Without limiting any other power of the court to grant or revoke probation, if an offender is convicted of, or pleads guilty to, a violation of division (B) of section 2919.22, or section 2919.25 of the Revised Code, the court may suspend execution of sentence and place the offender on probation conditioned upon the participation of the offender, to the satisfaction of the court, in a program of clinically appropriate psychiatric or psychological treatment.

(1978 H 835, eff. 3–27–79)

SEARCH WARRANTS

2933.21 Search warrant

A judge of a court of record may, within his jurisdiction, issue warrants to search a house or place:

(A) For property stolen, taken by robbers, embezzled, or obtained under false pretense;

(B) For weapons, implements, tools, instruments, articles or property used as a means of the commission of a crime, or when any of the objects or articles are in the possession of another person with the intent to use them as a means of committing crime;

(C) For forged or counterfeit coins, stamps, imprints, labels, trade-marks, bank bills, or other instruments of writing, and dies, plates, stamps, or brands for making them;

(D) For obscene materials and materials harmful to minors involved in a violation of section 2907.31 or 2907.32 of the Revised Code, but only so much of such materials shall be seized as are necessary for evidence in a prosecution of the violation;

(E) For gaming table, establishment, device, or apparatus kept or exhibited for unlawful gaming, or to win or gain money or other property, and for money or property won by unlawful gaming;

(F) For the existence of physical conditions which are or may become hazardous to the public health, safety, or welfare, when governmental inspections of property are authorized or required by law.

The enumeration of certain property and material [1] in this section shall not affect or modify other laws for search and seizure.

(1975 H 1, eff. 6–13–75; 1974 H 989; 1973 H 1; 1972 S 397; 1970 H 84; 1953 H 1; GC 13430–1)

[1] Prior and current versions differ; although no amendment to this language was indicated in 1975 H 1, "material" appeared as "materials" in 1974 H 989.

2933.22 Probable cause

(A) A warrant of search or seizure shall issue only upon probable cause, supported by oath or affirmation particularly describing the place to be searched and the property and things to be seized.

(B) A warrant of search to conduct an inspection of property shall issue only upon probable cause to believe that conditions exist upon such property which are or may become hazardous to the public health, safety, or welfare.

(1972 S 397, eff. 10–23–72; 1953 H 1; GC 13430–2)

2933.23 Affidavit for search warrant

A search warrant shall not be issued until there is filed with the judge or magistrate an affidavit that particularly describes the place to be searched, names or describes the person to be searched, and names or describes the property to be searched for and seized; that states substantially the offense in relation to the property and that the affiant believes and has good cause to believe that the property is concealed at the place or on the person; and that states the facts upon which the affiant's belief is based. The judge or magistrate may demand other and further evidence before issuing the warrant. If the judge or magistrate is satisfied that grounds for the issuance of the warrant exist or that there is probable cause to believe that they exist, he shall issue the warrant, identifying in it the property and naming or describing the person or place to be searched.

A search warrant issued pursuant to this chapter or Criminal Rule 41 also may contain a provision waiving the statutory precondition for nonconsensual entry, as described in division (C) of section 2933.231 of the Revised Code, if the requirements of that section are satisfied.

(1990 S 258, eff. 11–20–90; 130 v H 418; 1953 H 1; GC 13430–3)

2933.231 Waiver of statutory precondition for nonconsensual entry

(A) As used in this section:

(1) "Law enforcement officer" has the same meaning as in section 2901.01 of the Revised Code and in Criminal Rule 2.

(2) "Prosecutor" has the same meaning as in section 2935.01 of the Revised Code, and includes any prosecuting attorney as defined in Criminal Rule 2.

(3) "Statutory precondition for nonconsensual entry" means the precondition specified in section 2935.12 of the Revised Code that requires a law enforcement officer or other authorized individual executing a search warrant to give notice of his intention to execute the warrant and then be refused admittance to a dwelling house or other building before he legally may break down a door or window to gain entry to execute the warrant.

(B) A law enforcement officer, prosecutor, or other authorized individual who files an affidavit for the issuance of a search warrant pursuant to this chapter or Criminal Rule 41 may include in the affidavit a request that the statutory precondition for nonconsensual entry be waived in relation to the search warrant. A request for that waiver shall contain all of the following:

(1) A statement that the affiant has good cause to believe that there is a risk of serious physical harm to the law enforcement officers or other authorized individuals who will execute the warrant if they are required to comply with the statutory precondition for nonconsensual entry;

(2) A statement setting forth the facts upon which the affiant's belief is based, including, but not limited to, the names of all known persons who the affiant believes pose the risk of serious physical harm to the law enforcement officers or other authorized individuals who will execute the warrant at the particular dwelling house or other building;

(3) A statement verifying the address of the dwelling house or other building proposed to be searched as the correct address in relation to the criminal offense or other violation of law underlying the request for the issuance of the search warrant;

(4) A request that, based on those facts, the judge or magistrate waive the statutory precondition for nonconsensual entry.

(C) If an affidavit for the issuance of a search warrant filed pursuant to this chapter or Criminal Rule 41 includes a request for a waiver of the statutory precondition for nonconsensual entry, if the request conforms with division (B) of this section, if division (E) of this section is satisfied, and if the judge or magistrate issues the warrant, the judge or magistrate shall include in it a provision that waives the statutory precondition for nonconsensual entry for purposes of the search and seizure authorized under the warrant only if he determines there is probable cause to believe that, if the law enforcement officers or other authorized individuals who execute the warrant are required to comply with the statutory precondition for nonconsensual entry, they will be subjected to a risk of serious physical harm and to believe that the address of the dwelling house or other building to be searched is the correct address in relation to the criminal offense or other violation of law underlying the issuance of the warrant.

(D)(1) A waiver of the statutory precondition for nonconsensual entry by a judge or magistrate pursuant to division (C) of this section does not authorize, and shall not be construed as authorizing, a law enforcement officer or other authorized individual who executes a search warrant to enter a building other than a building described in the warrant.

(2) The state or any political subdivision associated with a law enforcement officer or other authorized officer who executes a search warrant that contains a provision waiving the statutory precondition for nonconsensual entry is liable in damages in a tort action for any injury, death, or loss to person or property that is proximately caused by the officer's execution of the warrant in accordance with the waiver at an address of a dwelling house or other building that is not described in the warrant.

(E) Any proceeding before a judge or magistrate that involves a request for a waiver of the statutory precondition for nonconsensual entry shall be recorded by shorthand, by stenotype, or by any other mechanical, electronic, or video recording device. The recording of and any transcript of the recording of such a proceeding shall not be a public record for purposes of section 149.43 of the Revised Code until the search warrant is returned by the law enforcement officer or other authorized officer who executes it. This division shall not be construed as requiring, authorizing, or permitting, and does not require, authorize, or permit, the making available for inspection, or the copying, under section 149.43 of the Revised Code of any confidential law enforcement investigatory record or trial preparation record, as defined in that section.

(1990 S 258, eff. 11–20–90)

2933.24 Contents of search warrant; report of inspection findings

(A) A search warrant shall be directed to the proper law enforcement officer or other authorized individual and, by a copy of the affidavit inserted in it or annexed and referred to in it, shall show or recite all the material facts alleged in the affidavit, and particularly name or describe the property to be searched for and seized, the place to be searched, and the person to be searched. If a waiver of the statutory precondition for nonconsensual entry, as defined in division (A) of section 2933.231 of the Revised Code, has been granted pursuant to that section, the warrant also shall contain a provision as described in division (C) of that section.

The warrant shall command the officer or individual to search the place or person named or described for the property, and to bring them, together with the person, before the judge or magistrate. The command of the warrant shall be that the search be made in the daytime, unless there is urgent necessity for a search in the night, in which case a search in the night may be ordered.

The warrant shall be returned by the officer or individual holding it not later than three days after its issuance. It shall designate the judge or magistrate to whom it shall be returned, if such judge or magistrate is available.

(B) When a search warrant commands a proper law enforcement officer or other authorized individual to inspect physical conditions relating to public health, safety, or welfare, such officer or individual, upon completion of the search, shall complete a report of the conditions and file a copy of such report with his agency headquarters.

(1990 S 258, eff. 11–20–90; 1972 S 397; 130 v H 418; 1953 H 1; GC 13430–4)

2933.241 Inventory of property taken

The officer taking property under a warrant for search shall give to the person from whom or from whose premises the property was taken a copy of the warrant and a receipt for the property taken or shall leave the copy and receipt at the place from which the property was taken. The return shall be made promptly and shall be accompanied by a written inventory of any property taken. The inventory shall be made in the presence of the applicant for the warrant and the person from whose possession or premises the property was taken, if they are present, or in the presence of at least one credible person other than the applicant for the warrant or the person from whose possession or premises the property was taken and shall be verified by the officer. The judge or magistrate shall upon request deliver a copy of the inventory to the person from whom or from whose premises the property was taken and to the applicant for the warrant.

(130 v H 418, eff. 10–14–63)

2933.25 Form of search warrant

Warrants issued under section 2933.21 of the Revised Code shall be substantially in the following form:

State of Ohio, _____ County, ss:

To the sheriff (or other officer) of said County, greeting:

Whereas there has been filed with me an affidavit, of which the following is a copy (here copy the affidavit).

These are, therefore, to command you in the name of the State of Ohio, with the necessary and proper assistance, to enter, in the daytime (or in the nighttime) into (here describe the house or place as in the affidavit) of the said _____ of the township of _____ in the County aforesaid, and there diligently search for the said goods and chattels, or articles, to wit: (here describe the articles as in the affidavit) and that you bring the same or any part thereof, found on such search, and also the body of E. F., forthwith before me, or some other judge or magistrate of the county having cognizance thereof to be disposed of and dealt with according to law.

Given under my hand, this _____ day of _____

A.B., Judge, County Court

(127 v 1039, eff. 1–1–58; 1953 H 1; GC 13430–5)

2933.26 Property seized to be kept by court

When a warrant is executed by the seizure of property or things described therein, such property or things shall be kept by the judge, clerk, or magistrate to be used as evidence.
(1953 H 1, eff. 10–1–53; GC 13430–6)

2933.27 Disposition of property before trial

If, upon examination, the judge or magistrate is satisfied that the offense charged with reference to the things seized under a search warrant has been committed, he shall keep such things or deliver them to the sheriff of the county, to be kept until the accused is tried or the claimant's right is otherwise ascertained.
(1953 H 1, eff. 10–1–53; GC 13430–7)

2933.28 Disposition of property after trial—Repealed

(1984 H 632, eff. 3–28–85; 1953 H 1; GC 13430–8)

2933.29 Property seized liable for fines

Upon conviction of a person for keeping a room or place to be used for gambling, or knowingly permitting gambling to be conducted therein, or permitting a game to be played for gain, or a gaming device for gain, money, or other property or for betting, or gambling, or permitting such device to be so used, or for being without a fixed residence and in the habit of gambling, if money or other property won in gaming is found in his possession, such money or other property is subject to seizure and payment of a judgment which may be rendered against him, growing out of such violation.
(1953 H 1, eff. 10–1–53; GC 13430–9)

2933.30 Search for dead bodies

When an affidavit is filed before a judge or magistrate, alleging that affiant has reason to believe and does believe that a dead human body, procured or obtained contrary to law, is secreted in a building or place in the county, therein particularly specified, such judge or magistrate, taking with him a judge of a county court, or if within a municipal corporation, two officers of such corporation, may enter, inspect, and search said building or place for such body. In making such search, they have the powers of officers executing warrants of search.
(127 v 1039, eff. 1–1–58; 1953 H 1; GC 13430–10)

2933.31 Search in case of animals

When complaint is made, on oath or affirmation to a judge or magistrate, that the complainant believes that the law relating to or affecting animals is being, or is about to be violated in a particular building or place, such judge or magistrate shall forthwith issue and deliver a warrant, directed to any sheriff, deputy sheriff, marshal, deputy marshal, watchman, police officer, or agent of a society for the prevention of cruelty to animals, authorizing him to enter and search such building or place and arrest all persons there violating, or attempting to violate, such law, and bring such persons before a judge or magistrate within the county within which such offense has been committed.

An attempt to violate such law relating to animals is a violation thereof.
(1953 H 1, eff. 10–1–53; GC 13430–11)

BODY CAVITY AND STRIP SEARCHES

2933.32 Conduct of body cavity search or strip search; conditions; methods; reports; offense

(A) As used in this section:

(1) "Body cavity search" means an inspection of the anal or vaginal cavity of a person that is conducted visually, manually, by means of any instrument, apparatus, or object, or in any other

manner while the person is detained or arrested for the alleged commission of a misdemeanor or traffic offense.

(2) "Strip search" means an inspection of the genitalia, buttocks, breasts, or undergarments of a person that is preceded by the removal or rearrangement of some or all of the person's clothing that directly covers the person's genitalia, buttocks, breasts, or undergarments and that is conducted visually, manually, by means of any instrument, apparatus, or object, or in any other manner while the person is detained or arrested for the alleged commission of a misdemeanor or traffic offense. "Strip search" does not mean the visual observation of a person who was afforded a reasonable opportunity to secure release on bail or recognizance, who fails to secure such release, and who is to be integrated with the general population of any detention facility, while the person is changing into clothing that is required to be worn by inmates in the facility.

(B)(1) Except as authorized by this division, no law enforcement officer, other employee of a law enforcement agency, physician, or registered nurse or licensed practical nurse shall conduct or cause to be conducted a body cavity search or a strip search.

(2) A body cavity search or strip search may be conducted if a law enforcement officer or employee of a law enforcement agency has probable cause to believe that the person is concealing evidence of the commission of a criminal offense, including fruits or tools of a crime, contraband, or a deadly weapon, as defined in section 2923.11 of the Revised Code, that could not otherwise be discovered. In determining probable cause for purposes of this section, a law enforcement officer or employee of a law enforcement agency shall consider the nature of the offense with which the person to be searched is charged, the circumstances of the person's arrest, and, if known, the prior conviction record of the person.

(3) A body cavity search or strip search may be conducted for any legitimate medical or hygienic reason.

(4) Unless there is a legitimate medical reason or medical emergency justifying a warrantless search, a body cavity search shall be conducted only after a search warrant is issued that authorizes the search. In any case, a body cavity search shall be conducted under sanitary conditions and only by a physician, or a registered nurse or licensed practical nurse, who is registered or licensed to practice in this state.

(5) Unless there is a legitimate medical reason or medical emergency that makes obtaining written authorization impracticable, a body cavity search or strip search shall be conducted only after a law enforcement officer or employee of a law enforcement agency obtains a written authorization for the search from the person in command of the law enforcement agency, or from a person specifically designated by the person in command to give a written authorization for either type of search.

(6) A body cavity search or strip search shall be conducted by a person or persons who are of the same sex as the person who is being searched and the search shall be conducted in a manner and in a location that permits only the person or persons who are physically conducting the search and the person who is being searched to observe the search.

(C)(1) Upon completion of a body cavity search or strip search pursuant to this section, the person or persons who conducted the search shall prepare a written report concerning the search that shall include all of the following:

(a) The written authorization for the search obtained from the person in command of the law enforcement agency or his designee, if required by division (B)(5) of this section;

(b) The name of the person who was searched;

(c) The name of the person or persons who conducted the search, the time and date of the search, and the place at which the search was conducted;

(d) A list of the items, if any, recovered during the search;

(e) The facts upon which the law enforcement officer or employee of the law enforcement agency based his probable cause for the search, including, but not limited to, the officer or employee's review of the nature of the offense with which the searched person is charged, the circumstances of his arrest, and, if known, his prior conviction record;

(f) If the body cavity search was conducted before or without the issuance of a search warrant pursuant to division (B)(4) of this section, or if the body cavity or strip search was conducted before or without the granting of written authorization pursuant to division (B)(5) of this section, the legitimate medical reason or medical emergency that justified the warrantless search or made obtaining written authorization impracticable.

(2) A copy of the written report required by division (C)(1) of this section shall be kept on file in the law enforcement agency, and another copy of it shall be given to the person who was searched.

(D)(1) This section does not preclude the prosecution of a law enforcement officer or employee of a law enforcement agency for the violation of any other section of the Revised Code.

(2) This section does not limit, and shall not be construed to limit, any statutory or common law rights of a person to obtain injunctive relief or to recover damages in a civil action.

(3) If a person is subjected to a body cavity search or strip search in violation of this section, any person may commence a civil action to recover compensatory damages for any injury, death, or loss to person or property or any indignity arising from the violation. In the civil action, the court may award punitive damages to the plaintiffs if they prevail in the action, and it may award reasonable attorney's fees to the parties who prevail in the action.

(4) This section does not apply to body cavity searches or strip searches of persons who have been sentenced to serve a term of imprisonment and who are serving that term in a detention facility, as defined in section 2921.01 of the Revised Code.

(E)(1) Whoever violates division (B) of this section is guilty of conducting an unauthorized search, a misdemeanor of the first degree.

(2) Whoever violates division (C) of this section is guilty of failure to prepare a proper search report, a misdemeanor of the fourth degree.

(1984 H 426, eff. 4–4–85; 1984 S 268)

DISPOSITION OF PROPERTY AND CONTRABAND

2933.41 Disposition of property held by law enforcement agency; written internal control policy; records and reports; funding citizens' reward programs

(A)(1) Any property, other than contraband that is subject to the provisions of section 2933.43 of the Revised Code, other than property that is subject to section 3719.141 of the Revised Code, other than property that is forfeited under sections 2925.41 to 2925.45 of the Revised Code, other than a vehicle that is criminally forfeited under an order issued under section 4503.233 or 4503.234 of the Revised Code and that is to be disposed of under section 4503.234 of the Revised Code, other than property that has been lawfully seized under sections 2933.71 to 2933.75 of the Revised Code in relation to a medicaid fraud offense, and other than property that has been lawfully seized in relation to a violation of section 2923.32 of the Revised Code, that has been lost, abandoned, stolen, seized pursuant to a search warrant, or otherwise lawfully seized or forfeited, and that is in the custody of a law enforcement agency, shall be kept safely pending the time it no longer is needed as evidence, and shall be disposed of pursuant to this section. Each law enforcement agency that has custody of any property that is subject to this section shall adopt a written internal control policy that addresses the keeping of detailed records as to the amount of property taken in by the agency, that addresses the agency's disposition of the property under this section, that provides for the keeping of detailed records of the disposition of the property, and that provides for the keeping of detailed financial records of the amount and disposition of any proceeds of a sale of the property under division (D)(8) of this section and of the general types of expenditures made out of the proceeds retained by the agency and the specific amount expended on each general type of expenditure. The policy shall not provide for or permit the identification of any specific expenditure that is made in an ongoing investigation. The policy is a public record open for inspection under section 149.43 of the Revised Code.

(2)(a) Every law enforcement agency that has any lost, abandoned, stolen, seized, or forfeited property as described in division (A)(1) of this section in its custody shall comply with its written internal control policy adopted under that division relative to the property. Each agency that has any such property in its custody, except for property to be disposed of under division (D)(4) of this section, shall maintain an accurate record, in accordance with its written internal control policy, of each item of the property. The record shall include the date on which each item of property came into the agency's custody, the manner in which it was disposed of, the date of its disposition, the name of the person who received the property if it was not destroyed, and all other information required by the agency's written internal control policy; however, the record shall not identify or enable the identification of the individual officer who seized any item of property. The record of any property that no longer is needed as evidence, and all financial records of the amount and disposition of any proceeds of a sale under division (D)(8) of this section and of the general types of expenditures made out of the proceeds retained by the agency and the specific amount of each general type of expenditure, shall be open to public inspection during the agency's regular business hours.

Each law enforcement agency that, during any calendar year, has any seized or forfeited property as described in division (A)(1) of this section in its custody shall prepare a report covering the calendar year that cumulates all of the information contained in all of the records kept by the agency pursuant to this division for that calendar year and shall send a copy of the cumulative report, no later than the first day of March in the calendar year following the calendar year covered by the report, to the attorney general. Each report received by the attorney general is a public record open for inspection under section 149.43 of the Revised Code. The attorney general shall make copies of each report received and, no later than the fifteenth day of April in the calendar year in which the report is received, shall send a copy of it to the president of the senate and the speaker of the house of representatives.

(b) Each law enforcement agency that receives in any calendar year any proceeds of a sale under division (D)(8) of this section shall prepare a report covering the calendar year that cumulates all of the information contained in all of the public financial records kept by the agency pursuant to division (D)(2)(a) of this section for that calendar year and shall send a copy of the cumulative report, no later than the first day of March in the calendar year following the calendar year covered by the report, to the attorney general. Each report received by the attorney general is a public record open for inspection under section 149.43 of the Revised Code. The attorney general shall make copies of each report received and, no later than the fifteenth day of April in the calendar year in which the report is received, shall send a copy of it to the president of the senate and the speaker of the house of representatives.

(B) A law enforcement agency that has property in its possession that is required to be disposed of pursuant to this section shall make a reasonable effort to locate the persons entitled to possession of the property in its custody, to notify them of when and where it may be claimed, and to return the property to them at the earliest possible time. In the absence of evidence identifying persons entitled to possession, it is sufficient notice to advertise in a newspaper of general circulation in the county, briefly describing the nature of the property in custody and inviting persons to view and establish their right to it.

(C) A person loses any right that the person may have to the possession, or the possession and ownership, of property if any of the following applies:

(1) The property was the subject, or was used in a conspiracy or attempt to commit, or in the commission, of an offense other than a traffic offense, and the person is a conspirator, accomplice, or offender with respect to the offense.

(2) A court determines that the property should be forfeited because, in light of the nature of the property or the circumstances of the person, it is unlawful for the person to acquire or possess the property.

(D) Unclaimed or forfeited property in the custody of a law enforcement agency, other than contraband that is subject to the provisions of section 2933.43 of the Revised Code, other than property forfeited under sections 2925.41 to 2925.45 of the Revised Code, and other than property that has been lawfully seized in relation to a violation of section 2923.32 of the Revised Code, shall be disposed of on application to and order of any court of record that has territorial jurisdiction over the political subdivision in which the law enforcement agency has jurisdiction to engage in law enforcement activities, as follows:

(1) Drugs shall be disposed of pursuant to section 3719.11 of the Revised Code or placed in the custody of the secretary of the treasury of the United States for disposal or use for medical or scientific purposes under applicable federal law.

(2) Firearms and dangerous ordnance suitable for police work may be given to a law enforcement agency for that purpose. Firearms suitable for sporting use, or as museum pieces or collectors' items, may be sold at public auction pursuant to division (D)(8) of this section. Other firearms and dangerous ordnance shall be destroyed by the agency or shall be sent to the bureau of criminal identification and investigation for destruction by the bureau.

(3) Obscene materials shall be destroyed.

(4) Beer, intoxicating liquor, or alcohol seized from a person who is not the holder of a permit issued under Chapters 4301. and 4303. of the Revised Code or is an offender and forfeited to the state under section 4301.45 or 4301.53 of the Revised Code shall be sold by the department of liquor control, if the department determines that the beer, intoxicating liquor, or alcohol is fit for sale. If any tax imposed under Title XLIII of the Revised Code has not been paid in relation to the beer, intoxicating liquor, or alcohol, the proceeds of the sale shall first be used to pay the tax. All other money collected under division (D)(4) of this section shall be paid into the state treasury. Any such beer, intoxicating liquor, or alcohol that the department determines to be unfit for sale shall be destroyed.

(5) Money received by an inmate of a correctional institution from an unauthorized source or in an unauthorized manner shall be returned to the sender, if known, or deposited in the inmates' industrial and entertainment fund if the sender is not known.

(6) Vehicles and vehicle parts forfeited under sections 4549.61 to 4549.63 of the Revised Code may be given to a law enforcement agency for use in the performance of its duties. Those parts may be incorporated into any other official vehicle. Parts that do not bear vehicle identification numbers or derivatives of them may be sold or disposed of as provided by rules of the director of public safety. Parts from which a vehicle identification number or derivative of it has been removed, defaced, covered, altered, or destroyed and that are not suitable for police work or incorporation into an official vehicle shall be destroyed and sold as junk or scrap.

(7)(a) Computers, computer networks, computer systems, and computer software suitable for police work may be given to a law enforcement agency for that purpose. Other computers, computer networks, computer systems, and computer software shall be disposed of pursuant to division (D)(8) of this section.

(b) As used in this section, "computers," "computer networks," "computer systems," and "computer software" have the same meanings as in section 2913.01 of the Revised Code.

(8) Other unclaimed or forfeited property, with the approval of the court, may be used by the law enforcement agency that has possession of it. If the other unclaimed or forfeited property is not used by the law enforcement agency, it may be sold, without appraisal, at a public auction to the highest bidder for cash, or, in the case of other unclaimed or forfeited moneys, disposed of in another manner that the court considers proper in the circumstances.

(E)(1)(a) If the property was in the possession of the law enforcement agency in relation to a delinquent child proceeding in a juvenile court, ten per cent of the proceeds from property disposed of pursuant to this section shall be applied to one or more alcohol and drug addiction treatment programs that are certified by the department of alcohol and drug addiction services under section 3793.06 of the Revised Code and that are specified by the court in its order issued under division (D) of this section. A juvenile court shall not specify an alcohol or drug addiction treatment program in the order unless the program is a certified alcohol and drug addiction treatment program and, except as provided in division (E)(1)(a) of this section, unless the program is located in the county in which the court that issues the orders is located or in a contiguous county. If no certified alcohol and drug addiction treatment program is located in any of those counties, the juvenile court may specify in the order a certified alcohol and drug addiction treatment program located anywhere within this state. The remaining ninety per cent of the proceeds shall be applied as provided in divisions (E)(1)(b) of this section.

If the property was in the possession of the law enforcement agency other than in relation to a delinquent child proceeding in a juvenile court, all of the proceeds from property disposed of pursuant to this section shall be applied as provided in division (E)(1)(b) of this section.

(b) Except as provided in divisions (D)(4), (5), and (E)(2) of this section and after compliance with division (E)(1)(a) of this section when that division is applicable, the proceeds from property disposed of pursuant to this section shall be placed in the general fund of the state, the county, the township, or the municipal corporation, of which the law enforcement agency involved is an agency.

(2) Each board of county commissioners that recognizes a citizens' reward program as provided in section 9.92 of the Revised Code shall notify each law enforcement agency of that county and each law enforcement agency of a township or municipal corporation wholly located in that county of the official recognition of the citizens' reward program by filing a copy of its resolution conferring that recognition with each of those law enforcement agencies. When the board of county commissioners of a county recognizes a citizens' reward program and the county includes a part, but not all, of the territory of a municipal corporation, the board shall so notify the law enforcement agency of that municipal corporation of the official recognition of the citizens' reward program only if the county contains the highest percentage of the municipal corporation's population. Upon receipt of a notice of that nature, each law enforcement agency shall pay twenty-five per cent of the proceeds from each sale of property disposed of pursuant to this section to the citizens' reward program for use exclusively for the payment of rewards. No part of those funds may be used to pay for the administrative expenses or any other expenses associated with a citizens' reward program. If a citizens' reward program that operates in more than one county or in another state or states in addition to this state receives funds pursuant to this section, the funds shall be used to pay rewards only for tips and information to law enforcement agencies concerning felonies, offenses of violence, or misdemeanors that have been committed in the county from which the funds were received.

(F) This section does not apply to the collection, storage, or disposal of abandoned junk motor vehicles. This section shall not be construed to rescind or restrict the authority of a municipal law enforcement agency to keep and dispose of lost, abandoned, stolen, seized, or forfeited property under an ordinance of the municipal corporation, provided that, when a municipal corporation that has received notice as provided in division (E)(2) of this section disposes of property under such an ordinance, it shall pay twenty-five per cent of the proceeds from any sale or auction to the citizens' reward program as provided under that division.

(G) The receipt of funds by a citizens' reward program pursuant to division (E) of this section does not make it a governmental unit for purposes of section 149.43 of the Revised Code and does not subject it to the disclosure provisions of that section.

(H) For purposes of this section, "law enforcement agency" includes correctional institutions. As used in this section, "citizens' reward program" has the same meaning as in section 9.92 of the Revised Code.

(1995 H 1, eff. 1–1–96; 1994 H 715, eff. 7–22–94; 1993 S 62, § 4, eff. 9–1–93; 1992 S 275, S 98; 1990 S 258, H 215; 1986 H 428, S 69, H 49; 1984 S 65, H 632; 1981 H 1; 1980 S 50; 1972 H 511)

2933.42 Possession or conveyance of contraband prohibited; when watercraft, motor vehicle, or aircraft considered contraband; property subject to seizure and forfeiture

(A) No person shall possess, conceal, transport, receive, purchase, sell, lease, rent, or otherwise transfer any contraband.

(B) For purposes of section 2933.43 of the Revised Code, if a watercraft, motor vehicle, aircraft, or other personal property that is not within the scope of the definition of contraband in section 2901.01 of the Revised Code is used in a violation of division (A) of this section, the watercraft, motor vehicle, aircraft, or personal property is contraband and, if the underlying offense involved in the violation of division (A) of this section is a felony, is subject to seizure and forfeiture pursuant to section 2933.43 of the Revised Code. It is rebuttably presumed that a watercraft, motor vehicle, aircraft, or other personal property in or on which contraband is found at the time of seizure has been, is being, or is intended to be used in a violation of division (A) of this section.

(C) For purposes of sections 2901.01 and 2933.41 to 2933.43 of the Revised Code, "offense," "criminal case," "criminal violation," "criminal offense," "felony," and similar terms shall be construed to include acts committed by persons under eighteen years of age that, if committed by an adult, would be within the meaning of those terms. This division shall be liberally construed to give effect to the intent of the general assembly in enacting this division that the forfeiture and contraband provisions of sections 2901.01 and 2933.41 to 2933.43 of the Revised Code apply to property that is possessed, or possessed and owned, by persons under eighteen years of age in the same manner as those provisions apply to property that is possessed, or possessed and owned, by adults.

(1990 S 258, eff. 8–22–90; 1986 S 69)

2933.43 Seizure of contraband; notice; holding period; records and reports; forfeiture proceeding; hearings; disposition; written internal control policy on use or disposition of proceeds

(A)(1) Except as provided in this division or sections 2925.41 to 2925.45 of the Revised Code, a law enforcement officer shall seize any contraband that has been, is being, or is intended to be used in violation of division (A) of section 2933.42 of the Revised Code. A law enforcement officer shall seize contraband that is a watercraft, motor vehicle, or aircraft and that has been, is being, or is intended to be used in violation of division (A) of section 2933.42 of the Revised Code only if the watercraft, motor vehicle, or aircraft is contraband because of its relationship to an underlying criminal offense that is a felony.

Additionally, a law enforcement officer shall seize any watercraft, motor vehicle, aircraft, or other personal property that is classified as contraband under division (B) of section 2933.42 of the Revised Code if the underlying offense involved in the violation of division (A) of that section that resulted in the watercraft, motor vehicle, aircraft, or personal property being classified as contraband, is a felony.

(2) If a law enforcement officer seizes property that is titled or registered under law, including a motor vehicle, pursuant to division (A)(1) of this section, the officer or the officer's employing law enforcement agency shall notify the owner of the seizure. The notification shall be given to the owner at the owner's last known address within seventy-two hours after the seizure, and may be given orally by any means, including telephone, or by certified mail, return receipt requested.

If the officer or the officer's agency is unable to provide the notice required by this division despite reasonable, good faith efforts to do so, the exercise of the reasonable, good faith efforts constitutes fulfillment of the notice requirement imposed by this division.

(B)(1) A motor vehicle seized pursuant to division (A)(1) of this section and the contents of the vehicle may be retained for a reasonable period of time, not to exceed seventy-two hours, for the purpose of inspection, investigation, and the gathering of evidence of any offense or illegal use.

At any time prior to the expiration of the seventy-two-hour period, the law enforcement agency that seized the motor vehicle may petition the court of common pleas of the county that has jurisdiction over the underlying criminal case or administrative proceeding involved in the forfeiture for an extension of the seventy-two-hour period if the motor vehicle or its contents are needed as evidence or if additional time is needed for the inspection, investigation, or gathering of evidence. Upon the filing of such a petition, the court immediately shall schedule a hearing to be held at a time as soon as possible after the filing, but in no event at a time later than the end of the next business day subsequent to the day on which the petition was filed, and upon scheduling the hearing, immediately shall notify the owner of the vehicle, at the address at which notification of the seizure was provided under division (A) of this section, of the date, time, and place of the hearing. If the court, at the hearing, determines that the vehicle or its contents, or both, are needed as evidence or that additional time is needed for the inspection, investigation, or gathering of evidence, the court may grant the petition and issue an order authorizing the retention of the vehicle or its contents, or both, for an extended period as specified by the court in its order. An order extending a period of retention issued under this division may be renewed.

If no petition for the extension of the initial seventy-two-hour period has been filed, prior to the expiration of that period, under this division, if the vehicle was not in the custody and control of the owner at the time of its seizure, and if, at the end of that seventy-two-hour period, the owner of the vehicle has not been charged with an offense or administrative violation that includes the use of the vehicle as an element and has not been charged with any other offense or administrative violation in the actual commission of which the motor vehicle was used, the vehicle and its contents shall be released to its owner or the owner's agent, provided that the law enforcement agency that seized the vehicle may require proof of ownership of the vehicle, proof of ownership or legal possession of the contents, and an affidavit of the owner that the owner neither knew of nor expressly or impliedly consented to the use of the vehicle that resulted in its forfeiture as conditions precedent to release. If a petition for the extension of the initial seventy-two-hour period has been filed, prior to the expiration of that period, under this division but the court does not grant the petition, if the vehicle was not in the custody and control of the owner at the time of its seizure, and if, at the end of that seventy-two-hour period, the owner of the vehicle has not been charged with an offense or administrative violation that includes the use of the vehicle as an element and has not been charged with any other offense or administrative violation in the actual commission of which the motor vehicle was used, the vehicle and its contents shall be released to its owner or the owner's agent, provided that the court may require the proof and affidavit described in the preceding sentence as conditions precedent to release. If the initial seventy-two-hour period has been extended under this division, the vehicle and its contents to which the extension applies may be retained in accordance with the extension order. If, at the end of that extended period, the owner of the vehicle has not been charged with an offense or administrative violation that includes the use of the vehicle as an element and has not been charged with any other offense or administrative violation in the actual commission of which the motor vehicle was used, and if the vehicle was not in the custody and control of the owner at the time of its seizure, the vehicle and its contents shall be released to its owner or the owner's agent, provided that the court may require the proof and affidavit described in the third preceding sentence as conditions precedent to release. In cases in which the court may require proof and affidavits as conditions precedent to release, the court also may require the posting of a bond, with sufficient sureties approved by the court, in an amount equal to the value of the property to be released, as determined by the court, and conditioned upon the return of the property to the court if it is forfeited under this section, as a further condition to release. If, at the end of the initial seventy-two-hour period or at the end of any extended period granted under this section, the owner has been charged with an offense or administrative violation that includes the use of the vehicle as an element or has been charged with another offense or administrative violation in the actual commission of which the motor vehicle was used, or if the vehicle was in the custody and control of the owner at the time of its seizure, the vehicle and its contents shall be retained pending disposition of the charge, provided that upon the filing of a motion for release by the owner, if the court determines that the motor vehicle or its contents, or both, are not needed as evidence in the underlying criminal case or administrative proceeding, the court may permit the release of the property that is not needed as evidence to the owner; as a condition precedent to a release of that nature, the court may require the owner to execute a bond with the court. Any bond so required shall be in an amount equal to the value of the property to be released, as determined by the court, shall have sufficient sureties approved by the court, and shall be conditioned upon the return of the property to the court to which it is forfeited under this section.

The final disposition of a motor vehicle seized pursuant to division (A)(1) of this section shall be determined in accordance with division (C) of this section.

(2) Pending a hearing pursuant to division (C) of this section, and subject to divisions (B)(1) and (C) of this section, any property lawfully seized pursuant to division (A) of this section because it was contraband of a type described in division (M)(2), (4), (5), (6), (7), (8), (9), or (10) of section 2901.01 of the Revised Code shall not be subject to replevin or other action in any court and shall not be subject to release upon request of the owner, and no judgment shall be enforced against the property. Pending the hearing, and subject to divisions (B)(1) and (C)

of this section, the property shall be kept in the custody of the law enforcement agency responsible for its seizure.

Pending a hearing pursuant to division (C) of this section, and notwithstanding any provisions of division (B)(1) or (C) of this section to the contrary, any property lawfully seized pursuant to division (A) of this section because it was contraband of a type described in division (M)(1) or (3) of section 2901.01 of the Revised Code shall not be subject to replevin or other action in any court and shall not be subject to release upon request of the owner, and no judgment shall be enforced against the property. Pending the hearing, and notwithstanding any provisions of division (B)(1) or (C) of this section to the contrary, the property shall be kept in the custody of the law enforcement agency responsible for its seizure.

A law enforcement agency that seizes property under division (A) of this section because it was contraband of any type described in division (M) of section 2901.01 or division (B) of section 2933.42 of the Revised Code shall maintain an accurate record of each item of property so seized, which record shall include the date on which each item was seized, the manner and date of its disposition, and if applicable, the name of the person who received the item; however, the record shall not identify or enable the identification of the individual officer who seized the item. The record of property of that nature that no longer is needed as evidence shall be open to public inspection during the agency's regular business hours. Each law enforcement agency that, during any calendar year, seizes property under division (A) of this section because it was contraband shall prepare a report covering the calendar year that cumulates all of the information contained in all of the records kept by the agency pursuant to this division for that calendar year, and shall send a copy of the cumulative report, no later than the first day of March in the calendar year following the calendar year covered by the report, to the attorney general. Each report received by the attorney general is a public record open for inspection under section 149.43 of the Revised Code. The attorney general shall make copies of each report received, and, no later than the fifteenth day of April in the calendar year in which the report is received, shall send a copy of it to the president of the senate and the speaker of the house of representatives.

(C) The prosecuting attorney, village solicitor, city director of law, or similar chief legal officer who has responsibility for the prosecution of the underlying criminal case or administrative proceeding, or the attorney general if the attorney general has that responsibility, shall file a petition for the forfeiture, to the seizing law enforcement agency of the contraband seized pursuant to division (A) of this section. The petition shall be filed in the court that has jurisdiction over the underlying criminal case or administrative proceeding involved in the forfeiture. If the property was seized on the basis of both a criminal violation and an administrative regulation violation, the petition shall be filed by the officer and in the court that is appropriate in relation to the criminal case.

The petitioner shall conduct or cause to be conducted a search of the appropriate public records that relate to the seized property for the purpose of determining, and shall make or cause to be made reasonably diligent inquiries for the purpose of determining, any person having an ownership or security interest in the property. The petitioner then shall give notice of the forfeiture proceedings by personal service or by certified mail, return receipt requested, to any persons known, because of the conduct of the search, the making of the inquiries, or otherwise, to have an ownership or security interest in the property, and shall publish notice of the proceedings once each week for two consecutive weeks in a newspaper of general circulation in the county in which the seizure occurred. The notices shall be personally served, mailed, and first published at least four weeks before the hearing. They shall describe the property seized; state the date and place of seizure; name the law enforcement agency that seized the property and, if applicable, that is holding the property; list the time, date, and place of the hearing; and state that any person having an ownership or security interest in the property may contest the forfeiture.

If the property seized was determined by the seizing law enforcement officer to be contraband because of its relationship to an underlying criminal offense or administrative violation, no forfeiture hearing shall be held under this section unless the person pleads guilty to or is convicted of the commission of, or an attempt or conspiracy to commit, the offense or a different offense arising out of the same facts and circumstances or unless the person admits or is adjudicated to have committed the administrative violation or a different violation arising out of the same facts and circumstances; a forfeiture hearing shall be held in a case of that nature no later than forty-five days after the conviction or the admission or adjudication of the violation, unless the time for the hearing is extended by the court for good cause shown. The owner of any property seized because of its relationship to an underlying criminal offense or administrative violation may request the court to release the property to the owner. Upon receipt of a request of that nature, if the court determines that the property is not needed as evidence in the underlying criminal case or administrative proceeding, the court may permit the release of the property to the owner. As a condition precedent to a release of that nature, the court may require the owner to execute a bond with the court. Any bond so required shall have sufficient sureties approved by the court, shall be in a sum equal to the value of the property, as determined by the court, and shall be conditioned upon the return of the property to the court if the property is forfeited under this section. Any property seized because of its relationship to an underlying criminal offense or administrative violation shall be returned to its owner if charges are not filed in relation to that underlying offense or violation within thirty days after the seizure, if charges of that nature are filed and subsequently are dismissed, or if charges of that nature are filed and the person charged does not plead guilty to and is not convicted of the offense or does not admit and is not found to have committed the violation.

If the property seized was determined by the seizing law enforcement officer to be contraband other than because of a relationship to an underlying criminal offense or administrative violation, the forfeiture hearing under this section shall be held no later than forty-five days after the seizure, unless the time for the hearing is extended by the court for good cause shown.

Where possible, a court holding a forfeiture hearing under this section shall follow the Rules of Civil Procedure. When a hearing is conducted under this section, property shall be forfeited upon a showing, by a preponderance of the evidence, by the petitioner that the person from which the property was seized was in violation of division (A) of section 2933.42 of the Revised Code. If that showing is made, the court shall issue an order of forfeiture. If an order of forfeiture is issued in relation to contraband that was released to the owner or the owner's agent pursuant to this division or division (B)(1) of this section, the order shall require the owner to deliver the property, by a specified date, to the law enforcement agency that employed the law enforcement officer who made the seizure of the property, and the court shall deliver a copy of the order to the owner or send a copy of it by certified mail, return receipt requested, to the owner at the address to which notice of the seizure was given under division (A)(2) of this section. Except as otherwise provided in this division, all rights, interest, and title to the forfeited contraband vests in the state, effective from the date of seizure.

No property shall be forfeited pursuant to this division if the owner of the property establishes, by a preponderance of the evidence, that the owner neither knew, nor should have known after a reasonable inquiry, that the property was used, or was likely to be used, in a crime or administrative violation. No bona fide security interest shall be forfeited pursuant to this division if the holder of the interest establishes, by a preponderance of the evidence, that the holder of the interest neither knew, nor should have known after a reasonable inquiry, that the property was used, or likely to be used, in a crime or administrative violation, that the holder of the interest did not expressly or impliedly consent to the use of the property in a crime or administrative violation, and that the security interest was perfected pursuant to law prior to the seizure. If the holder of the interest satisfies the court that these requirements are met, the interest shall be preserved by the court. In a case of that nature, the court shall either order that the agency to which the property is forfeited reimburse the holder of the interest to the extent of the preserved interest or order that the holder be paid for the interest from the proceeds of any sale pursuant to division (D) of this section.

(D)(1) Contraband ordered forfeited pursuant to this section shall be disposed of pursuant to divisions (D)(1) to (7) of section 2933.41 of the Revised Code or, if the contraband is not described in those divisions, may be used, with the approval of the court, by the law enforcement agency that has custody of the contraband pursuant to division (D)(8) of that section. In the case of contraband not described in any of those divisions and of contraband not disposed of pursuant to any of those divisions, the contraband shall be sold in accordance with this division or, in the case of forfeited moneys, disposed of in accordance with this division. If the contraband is to be sold, the prosecuting attorney shall cause a notice of the proposed sale of the contraband to be given in accordance with law, and the property shall be sold, without appraisal, at a public auction to the highest bidder for cash. The proceeds of a sale and forfeited moneys shall be applied in the following order:

(a) First, to the payment of the costs incurred in connection with the seizure of, storage of, maintenance of, and provision of security for the contraband, the forfeiture proceeding, and, if any, the sale;

(b) Second, the remaining proceeds or forfeited moneys after compliance with division (D)(1)(a) of this section, to the payment of the balance due on any security interest preserved pursuant to division (C) of this section;

(c) Third, the remaining proceeds or forfeited moneys after compliance with divisions (D)(1)(a) and (b) of this section, as follows:

(i) If the forfeiture was ordered in a juvenile court, ten per cent to one or more alcohol and drug addiction treatment programs that are certified by the department of alcohol and drug addiction services under section 3793.06 of the Revised Code and that are specified in the order of forfeiture. A juvenile court shall not certify an alcohol or drug addiction treatment program in the order of forfeiture unless the program is a certified alcohol and drug addiction treatment program and, except as provided in division (D)(1)(c)(i) of this section, unless the program is located in the county in which the court that orders the forfeiture is located or in a contiguous county. If no certified alcohol and drug addiction treatment program is located in any of those counties, the juvenile court may specify in the order a certified alcohol and drug addiction treatment program located anywhere within this state.

(ii) If the forfeiture was ordered in a juvenile court, ninety per cent, and if the forfeiture was ordered in a court other than a juvenile court, one hundred per cent to the law enforcement trust fund of the prosecuting attorney and to the law enforcement trust fund of the county sheriff if the county sheriff made the seizure, to the law enforcement trust fund of a municipal corporation if its police department made the seizure, to the law enforcement trust fund of a township if the seizure was made by a township police department, township police district police force, or office of a township constable, to the law enforcement trust fund of a park district created pursuant to section 511.18 or 1545.01 of the Revised Code if the seizure was made by the park district police force or law enforcement department, to the state highway patrol contraband, forfeiture, and other fund if the state highway patrol made the seizure, to the liquor enforcement contraband, forfeiture, and other fund if the liquor enforcement unit of the department of public safety made the seizure, to the food stamp contraband, forfeiture, and other fund if the food stamp trafficking unit of the department of public safety made the seizure, to the board of pharmacy drug law enforcement fund created by division (B)(1) of section 4729.65 of the Revised Code if the board made the seizure, or to the treasurer of state for deposit into the peace officer training council fund if a state law enforcement agency, other than the state highway patrol, the department of public safety, or the state board of pharmacy, made the seizure. The prosecuting attorney may decline to accept any of the remaining proceeds or forfeited moneys, and, if the prosecuting attorney so declines, the remaining proceeds or forfeited moneys shall be applied to the fund described in this division that relates to the law enforcement agency that made the seizure.

A law enforcement trust fund shall be established by the prosecuting attorney of each county who intends to receive any remaining proceeds or forfeited moneys pursuant to this division, by the sheriff of each county, by the legislative authority of each municipal corporation, by the board of township trustees of each township that has a township police department, township police district police force, or office of the constable, and by the board of park commissioners of each park district created pursuant to section 511.18 or 1545.01 of the Revised Code that has a park district police force or law enforcement department, for the purposes of this division. There is hereby created in the state treasury the state highway patrol contraband, forfeiture, and other fund, the liquor enforcement contraband, forfeiture, and other fund, the food stamp contraband, forfeiture, and other fund, and the peace officer training council fund, for the purposes described in this division.

Proceeds or forfeited moneys distributed to any municipal corporation, township, or park district law enforcement trust fund shall be allocated from the fund by the legislative authority only to the police department of the municipal corporation, by the board of township trustees only to the township police department, township police district police force, or office of the constable, and by the board of park commissioners only to the park district police force or law enforcement department.

Additionally, no proceeds or forfeited moneys shall be allocated to or used by the state highway patrol, the food stamp trafficking unit or liquor enforcement unit of the department of public safety, the state board of pharmacy, or a county sheriff, prosecuting attorney, municipal corporation police department, township police department, township police district police force, office of the constable, or park district police force or law enforcement department unless the state highway patrol, department of public safety, state board of pharmacy, sheriff, prosecuting attorney, municipal corporation police department, township police department, township police district police force, office of the constable, or park district police force or law enforcement department has adopted a written internal control policy under division (D)(3) of this section that addresses the use of moneys received from the state highway patrol contraband, forfeiture, and other fund, the liquor enforcement contraband, forfeiture, and other fund, the food stamp contraband, forfeiture, and other fund, the board of pharmacy drug law enforcement fund, or the appropriate law enforcement trust fund. The state highway patrol contraband, forfeiture, and other fund, the liquor enforcement contraband, forfeiture, and other fund, the food stamp contraband, forfeiture, and other fund, and a law enforcement trust fund shall be expended only in accordance with the written internal control policy so adopted by the recipient, and, subject to the requirements specified in division (D)(3)(a)(ii) of this section, only to pay the costs of protracted or complex investigations or prosecutions, to provide reasonable technical training or expertise, to provide matching funds to obtain federal grants to aid law enforcement, in the support of DARE programs or other programs designed to educate adults or children with respect to the dangers associated with the use of drugs of abuse, or for other law enforcement purposes that the superintendent of the state highway patrol, department of public safety, prosecuting attorney, county sheriff, legislative authority, board of township trustees, or board of park commissioners determines to be appropriate. The board of pharmacy drug law enforcement fund shall be expended only in accordance with the written internal control policy so adopted by the board and only in accordance with section 4729.65 of the Revised Code. The state highway patrol contraband, forfeiture, and other fund, the liquor enforcement contraband, seizure, and other fund, the food stamp contraband, forfeiture, and other fund, the board of pharmacy drug law enforcement fund, and a law enforcement trust fund shall not be used to meet the operating costs of the state highway patrol, of the food stamp trafficking unit or liquor enforcement unit of the department of public safety, of the state board of pharmacy, of any political subdivision, or of any office of a prosecuting attorney or county sheriff that are unrelated to law enforcement.

Proceeds and forfeited moneys that are paid into the state treasury to be deposited into the peace officer training council fund shall be used by the council only to pay the costs of peace officer training.

Any sheriff or prosecuting attorney who receives proceeds or forfeited moneys pursuant to this division during any calendar year shall file a report with the county auditor, no later than the thirty-first day of January of the next calendar year, verifying that the proceeds and forfeited moneys were expended only for the purposes authorized by this division and division (D)(3)(a)(ii) of this section and specifying the amounts expended for each authorized purpose. Any municipal corporation police department that is allocated proceeds or forfeited moneys from a municipal corporation law enforcement trust fund pursuant to this division during any calendar year shall file a report with the legislative authority of the municipal corporation, no later than the thirty-first day of January of the next calendar year, verifying that the proceeds and forfeited moneys were expended only for the purposes authorized by this division and division (D)(3)(a)(ii) of this section and specifying the amounts expended for each authorized purpose. Any township police department, township police district police force, or office of the constable that is allocated proceeds or forfeited moneys from a township law enforcement trust fund pursuant to this division during any calendar year shall file a report with the board of township trustees of the township, no later than the thirty-first day of January of the next calendar year, verifying that the proceeds and forfeited moneys were expended only for the purposes authorized by this division and division (D)(3)(a)(ii) of this section and specifying the amounts expended for each authorized purpose. Any park district police force or law enforcement department that is allocated proceeds or forfeited moneys from a park district law enforcement trust fund pursuant to this division during any calendar year shall file a report with the board of park commissioners of the park district, no later than the thirty-first day of January of the next calendar year, verifying that the proceeds and forfeited moneys were expended only for the purposes authorized by this division and division (D)(3)(a)(ii) of this section and specifying the amounts expended for each authorized purpose. The superintendent of the state highway patrol shall file a report with the attorney general, no later than the thirty-first day of January of each calendar year, verifying that proceeds and forfeited moneys paid into the state highway patrol contraband, forfeiture, and other fund pursuant to this division during the prior calendar year were used by the state highway patrol during the prior calendar year only for the purposes authorized by this division and specifying the amounts expended for each authorized purpose. The executive director of the state board of pharmacy shall file a report with the attorney general, no later than the thirty-first day of January of each calendar year, verifying that proceeds and forfeited moneys paid into the board of pharmacy drug law enforcement fund during the prior calendar year were used only in accordance with section 4729.65 of the Revised Code and specifying the amounts expended for each authorized purpose. The peace officer training council shall file a report with the attorney general, no later than the thirty-first day of January of each calendar year, verifying that proceeds and forfeited moneys paid into the peace officer training council fund pursuant to this division during the prior calendar year were used by the council during the prior calendar year only to pay the costs of peace officer training and specifying the amount used for that purpose.

(2) If more than one law enforcement agency is substantially involved in the seizure of contraband that is forfeited pursuant to this section, the court ordering the forfeiture shall equitably divide the proceeds or forfeited moneys, after calculating any distribution to the law enforcement trust fund of the prosecuting attorney pursuant to division (D)(1)(c) of this section, among any county sheriff whose office is determined by the court to be substantially involved in the seizure, any legislative authority of a municipal corporation whose police department is determined by the court to be substantially involved in the seizure, any board of township trustees whose law enforcement agency is determined by the court to be substantially involved in the seizure, any board of park commissioners of a park district whose police force or law enforcement department is determined by the court to be substantially involved in the seizure, the state board of pharmacy if it is determined by the court to be substantially involved in the seizure, the food stamp trafficking unit or liquor enforcement unit of the department of public safety if it is determined by the court to be substantially involved in the seizure, and the state highway patrol if it is determined by the court to be substantially involved in the seizure. The proceeds or forfeited moneys shall be deposited in the respective law enforcement trust funds of the county sheriff, municipal corporation, township, and park district, the board of pharmacy drug law enforcement fund, the liquor enforcement contraband, forfeiture, and other fund, the food stamp contraband, forfeiture, and other fund, or the state highway patrol contraband, forfeiture, and other fund, in accordance with division (D)(1)(c) of this section. If a state law enforcement agency, other than the state highway patrol, the food stamp trafficking unit or liquor enforcement unit of the department of public safety, or the state board of pharmacy, is determined by the court to be substantially involved in the seizure, the state agency's equitable share of the proceeds and forfeited moneys shall be paid to the treasurer of state for deposit into the peace officer training council fund.

(3)(a)(i) Prior to being allocated or using any proceeds or forfeited moneys out of the state highway patrol contraband, forfeiture, and other fund, the liquor enforcement contraband, forfeiture, and other fund, the food stamp contraband, seizure, and other fund, the board of pharmacy drug law enforcement fund, or a law enforcement trust fund under division (D)(1)(c) of this section, the state highway patrol, the department of public safety, the state board of pharmacy, and a county sheriff, prosecuting attorney, municipal corporation police department, township police department, township police district police force, office of the constable, or park district police force or law enforcement department shall adopt a written internal control policy that addresses the state highway patrol's, department of public safety's, state board of pharmacy's, sheriff's, prosecuting attorney's, police department's, police force's, office of the constable's, or law enforcement department's use and disposition of all the proceeds and forfeited moneys received and that provides for the keeping of detailed financial records of the receipts of the proceeds and forfeited moneys, the general types of expenditures made out of the proceeds and forfeited moneys, the specific amount of each general type of expenditure, and the amounts, portions, and programs described in division (D)(3)(a)(ii) of this section.

The policy shall not provide for or permit the identification of any specific expenditure that is made in an ongoing investigation.

All financial records of the receipts of the proceeds and forfeited moneys, the general types of expenditures made out of the proceeds and forfeited moneys, the specific amount of each general type of expenditure by the state highway patrol, by the department of public safety, by the state board of pharmacy, and by a sheriff, prosecuting attorney, municipal corporation police department, township police department, township police district police force, office of the constable, or park district police force or law enforcement department, and the amounts, portions, and programs described in division (D)(3)(a)(ii) of this section are public records open for inspection under section 149.43 of the Revised Code. Additionally, a written internal control policy adopted under this division is a public record of that nature, and the state highway patrol, the department of public safety, the state board of pharmacy, or the sheriff, prosecuting attorney, municipal corporation police department, township police department, township police district police force, office of the constable, or park district police force or law enforcement department that adopted it shall comply with it.

(ii) The written internal control policy of a county sheriff, prosecuting attorney, municipal corporation police department, township police department, township police district police force, office of the constable, or park district police force or law enforcement department shall provide that at least ten per cent of the first one hundred thousand dollars of proceeds and forfeited moneys deposited during each calendar year in the sheriff's, prosecuting attorney's, municipal corporation's, township's, or park district's law enforcement trust fund pursuant to division (B)(8)(c) of section 2925.44 of the Revised Code, and at least twenty per cent of the proceeds and forfeited moneys exceeding one hundred thousand dollars that are so deposited, shall be used in connection with community preventive education programs. The manner in which the described percentages are so used shall be determined by the sheriff, prosecuting attorney, department, police force, or office of the constable after the receipt and consideration of advice on appropriate community preventive education programs from the county's board of alcohol, drug addiction, and mental health services, from the county's alcohol and drug addiction services board, or through appropriate community dialogue. The financial records described in division (D)(3)(a)(i) of this section shall specify the amount of the proceeds and forfeited moneys deposited during each calendar year in the sheriff's, prosecuting attorney's, municipal corporation's, township's, or park district's law enforcement trust fund pursuant to division (B)(8)(c) of section 2925.44 of the Revised Code, the portion of that amount that was used pursuant to the requirements of this division, and the community preventive education programs in connection with which the portion of that amount was so used.

As used in this division, "community preventive education programs" includes, but is not limited to, DARE programs and other programs designed to educate adults or children with respect to the dangers associated with the use of drugs of abuse.

(b) Each sheriff, prosecuting attorney, municipal corporation police department, township police department, township police district police force, office of the constable, or park district police force or law enforcement department that receives in any calendar year any proceeds or forfeited moneys out of a law enforcement trust fund under division (D)(1)(c) of this section or uses any proceeds or forfeited moneys in its law enforcement trust fund in any calendar year shall prepare a report covering the calendar year that cumulates all of the information contained in all of the public financial records kept by the sheriff, prosecuting attorney, municipal corporation police department, township police department, township police district police force, office of the constable, or park district police force or law enforcement department pursuant to division (D)(3)(a) of this section for that calendar year, and shall send a copy of the cumulative report, no later than the first day of March in the calendar year following the calendar year covered by the report, to the attorney general.

The superintendent of the state highway patrol shall prepare a report covering each calendar year in which the state highway patrol uses any proceeds or forfeited moneys in the state highway patrol contraband, forfeiture, and other fund under division (D)(1)(c) of this section, that cumulates all of the information contained in all of the public financial records kept by the state highway patrol pursuant to division (D)(3)(a) of this section for that calendar year, and shall send a copy of the cumulative report, no later than the first day of March in the calendar year following the calendar year covered by the report, to the attorney general.

The department of public safety shall prepare a report covering each fiscal year in which the department uses any proceeds or forfeited moneys in the liquor enforcement contraband, seizure, and other fund and the food stamp contraband, forfeiture, and other fund under division (D)(1)(c) of this section that cumulates all of the information contained in all of the public financial records kept by the department pursuant to division (D)(3)(a) of this section for that fiscal year. The department shall send a copy of the cumulative report to the attorney general no later than the first day of August in the fiscal year following the fiscal year covered by the report. The director of public safety shall include in the report a verification that proceeds and forfeited moneys paid into the department of liquor enforcement contraband, seizure, and other fund and the food stamp contraband, forfeiture, and other fund under division (D)(1)(c) of this section during the preceding fiscal year were used by the department during that fiscal year only for the purposes authorized by that division and shall specify the amount used for each authorized purpose.

The executive director of the state board of pharmacy shall prepare a report covering each calendar year in which the board uses any proceeds or forfeited moneys in the board of pharmacy drug law enforcement fund under division (D)(1)(c) of this section, that cumulates all of the information contained in all of the public financial records kept by the board pursuant to division (D)(3)(a) of this section for that calendar year, and shall send a copy of the cumulative report, no later than the first day of March in the calendar year following the calendar year covered by the report, to the attorney general. Each report received by the attorney general is a public record open for inspection under section 149.43 of the Revised Code. The attorney general shall make copies of each report received, and, no later than the fifteenth day of April in the calendar year in which the report is received, shall send a copy of it to the president of the senate and the speaker of the house of representatives.

(4)(a) A law enforcement agency that receives pursuant to federal law proceeds from a sale of forfeited contraband, proceeds from another disposition of forfeited contraband, or forfeited contraband moneys shall deposit, use, and account for the proceeds or forfeited moneys in accordance with, and otherwise comply with, the applicable federal law.

(b) If the state highway patrol receives pursuant to federal law proceeds from a sale of forfeited contraband, proceeds from another disposition of forfeited contraband, or forfeited contraband moneys, the appropriate governmental officials shall deposit into the state highway patrol contraband, forfeiture, and other fund all interest or other earnings derived from the investment of the proceeds or forfeited moneys. The state highway patrol shall use and account for that interest or other earnings in accordance with the applicable federal law.

(c) Divisions (D)(1) to (3) of this section do not apply to proceeds or forfeited moneys received pursuant to federal law or to the interest or other earnings that are derived from the investment of proceeds or forfeited moneys received pursuant to federal law and that are described in division (D)(4)(b) of this section.

(E) Upon the sale pursuant to this section of any property that is required to be titled or registered under law, the state shall issue an appropriate certificate of title or registration to the purchaser. If the state is vested with title pursuant to division (C) of this section and elects to retain property that is required to be titled or registered under law, the state shall issue an appropriate certificate of title or registration.

(F) Notwithstanding any provisions of this section to the contrary, any property that is lawfully seized in relation to a violation of section 2923.32 of the Revised Code shall be subject to forfeiture and disposition in accordance with sections 2923.32 to 2923.36 of the Revised Code, and any property that is forfeited pursuant to section 2925.42 or 2925.43 of the Revised Code in relation to a felony drug abuse offense, as defined in section 2925.01 of the Revised Code, or in relation to an act that, if committed by an adult, would be a felony drug abuse offense of that nature, may be subject to forfeiture and disposition in accordance with sections 2925.41 to 2925.45 of the Revised Code or this section.

(G) Any failure of a law enforcement officer or agency, a prosecuting attorney, village solicitor, city director of law, or similar chief legal officer, a court, or the attorney general to comply with any duty imposed by this section in relation to any property seized or with any other provision of this section in relation to any property seized does not affect the validity of the seizure of the property, provided the seizure itself was made in accordance with law, and is not and shall not be considered to be the basis for the suppression of any evidence resulting from the seizure of the property, provided the seizure itself was made in accordance with law.

(H) Contraband that has been forfeited pursuant to division (C) of this section shall not be available for use to pay any fine imposed upon a person who is convicted of or pleads guilty to an underlying criminal offense or a different offense arising out of the same facts and circumstances.

(1995 H 1, eff. 1–1–96; 1995 S 162, eff. 10–29–95; 1995 H 107, eff. (See Historical and Statutory Notes); 1992 S 351, eff. 7–1–92; 1992 S 174; 1991 S 218; 1990 S 258, H 261, H 215; 1986 H 428, S 69)

Historical and Statutory Notes

Ed. Note: A special endorsement by the Legislative Service Commission states, "Comparison of these amendments [1995 H 1, eff. 1–1–96, 1995 S 162, eff. 10–29–95, and 1995 H 107, eff. (See Historical and Statutory Notes)] in pursuance of section 1.52 of the Revised Code discloses that they are not irreconcilable, so that they are required by that section to be harmonized to give effect to each amendment." In recognition of this rule of construction, changes made by 1995 H 1, eff. 1–1–96, 1995 S 162, eff. 10–29–95, and 1995 H 107, eff. (See Historical and Statutory Notes), have been incorporated in the above amendment. See *Bald-*

win's Ohio Legislative Service, 1995, pages 7/L–1540, 7/L–2225, and 3/L–19, for original versions of these Acts.

Ed. Note: 1995 H 107 Effective Date—The Secretary of State assigned a general effective date of 6–30–95 for 1995 H 107. Pursuant to O Const Art II § 1c and 1d, and RC 1.471, sections of 1995 H 107 that are, or depend for their implementation upon, current expense appropriations are effective 3–31–95; sections of 1995 H 107 that are not, and do not depend for their implementation upon, current expense appropriations are effective 6–30–95. See Uncodified Law, 1995 H 107, § 16.

2933.44 Reports regarding juvenile-related forfeiture orders by alcohol and drug addiction treatment programs

(A) As used in this section, "juvenile–related forfeiture order" means any order of forfeiture issued by a juvenile court under section 2923.32, 2925.42, 2925.43, or 2933.43 of the Revised Code and any order of disposition of property issued by a court under section 2933.41 of the Revised Code regarding property that was in the possession of a law enforcement agency in relation to a delinquent child proceeding in a juvenile court.

(B) Each certified alcohol and drug addiction treatment program that receives in any calendar year money under division (D)(1)(a) of section 2923.35, division (B)(8)(c)(i) of section 2925.44, division (E)(1)(a) of section 2933.41, or division (D)(1)(c)(i) of section 2933.43 of the Revised Code subsequent to the issuance of any juvenile-related forfeiture order shall file an annual report for that calendar year with the attorney general and with the court of common pleas and board of county commissioners of the county in which the program is located and of any other county from which the program received money under any of those divisions subsequent to the issuance of the juvenile-related forfeiture order. The program shall file the report on or before the first day of March in the calendar year following the calendar year in which the program received the money. The report shall include statistics on the number of persons the program served, identify the types of treatment services it provided to those persons, and include a specific accounting of the purposes for which it used the money so received. No information contained in the report shall identify, or enable a person to determine the identity of, any person served by the program.

(1995 H 1, eff. 1-1-96)

INTERCEPTION OF COMMUNICATIONS; WARRANTS

2933.51 Definitions

As used in sections 2933.51 to 2933.66 of the Revised Code:

(A) "Wire communication" means any aural transfer that is made in whole or in part through the use of facilities for the transmission of communications by the aid of wires or similar methods of connecting the point of origin of the communication and the point of reception of the communication, including the use of a method of connecting the point of origin and the point of reception of the communication in a switching station, if the facilities are furnished or operated by a person engaged in providing or operating the facilities for the transmission of communications. "Wire communication" includes an electronic storage of a wire communication.

(B) "Oral communication" means an oral communication uttered by a person exhibiting an expectation that the communication is not subject to interception under circumstances justifying that expectation. "Oral communication" does not include an electronic communication.

(C) "Intercept" means the aural or other acquisition of the contents of any wire, oral, or electronic communication through the use of an interception device.

(D) "Interception device" means an electronic, mechanical, or other device or apparatus that can be used to intercept a wire, oral, or electronic communication. "Interception device" does not mean any of the following:

(1) A telephone or telegraph instrument, equipment, or facility, or any of its components, if the instrument, equipment, facility, or component is any of the following:

(a) Furnished to the subscriber or user by a provider of wire or electronic communication service in the ordinary course of its business and being used by the subscriber or user in the ordinary course of its business;

(b) Furnished by a subscriber or user for connection to the facilities of a provider of wire or electronic communication service and used in the ordinary course of that subscriber's or user's business;

(c) Being used by a provider of wire or electronic communication service in the ordinary course of its business or by an investigative or law enforcement officer in the ordinary course of the officer's duties that do not involve the interception of wire, oral, or electronic communications.

(2) A hearing aid or similar device being used to correct subnormal hearing to not better than normal.

(E) "Investigative officer" means any of the following:

(1) An officer of this state or a political subdivision of this state, who is empowered by law to conduct investigations or to make arrests for a designated offense;

(2) A person described in divisions (K)(1) and (2) of section 2901.01 of the Revised Code;

(3) An attorney authorized by law to prosecute or participate in the prosecution of a designated offense;

(4) A secret service officer appointed pursuant to section 309.07 of the Revised Code;

(5) An officer of the United States, a state, or a political subdivision of a state who is authorized to conduct investigations pursuant to the "Electronic Communications Privacy Act of 1986," 100 Stat. 1848–1857, 18 U.S.C. 2510–2521 (1986), as amended.

(F) "Interception warrant" means a court order that authorizes the interception of wire, oral, or electronic communications and that is issued pursuant to sections 2933.53 to 2933.56 of the Revised Code.

(G) "Contents," when used with respect to a wire, oral, or electronic communication, includes any information concerning the substance, purport, or meaning of the communication.

(H) "Communications common carrier" means a person who is engaged as a common carrier for hire in intrastate, interstate, or foreign communications by wire, radio, or radio transmission of energy. "Communications common carrier" does not include, to the extent that the person is engaged in radio broadcasting, a person engaged in radio broadcasting.

(I) "Designated offense" means any of the following:

(1) A felony violation of section 2903.01, 2903.02, 2903.11, 2905.01, 2905.02, 2905.04, 2905.11, 2905.22, 2907.02, 2907.21, 2907.22, 2909.02, 2909.03, 2909.04, 2911.01, 2911.02, 2911.11, 2911.12, 2913.02, 2913.04, 2913.42, 2913.51, 2913.81, 2915.02, 2915.03, 2915.06, 2917.01, 2917.02, 2921.02, 2921.03, 2921.04, 2921.32, 2921.34, 2923.20, 2923.32, or 2925.03 of the Revised Code;

(2) Complicity in the commission of a felony violation of a section listed in division (I)(1) of this section;

(3) An attempt to commit, or conspiracy in the commission of, a felony violation of a section listed in division (I)(1) of this section, if the attempt or conspiracy is punishable by a term of imprisonment of more than one year.

(J) "Aggrieved person" means a person who was a party to an intercepted wire, oral, or electronic communication or a person against whom the interception of the communication was directed.

(K) "Person" means a person, as defined in section 1.59 of the Revised Code, or a governmental officer, employee, or entity.

(L) "Special need" means a showing that a licensed physician, licensed practicing psychologist, attorney, practicing clergyman, journalist, or either spouse is personally engaging in continuing criminal activity, was engaged in continuing criminal activity over a period of time, or is committing, has committed, or is about to commit, a designated offense, or a showing that specified public facilities are being regularly used by someone who is personally engaging in continuing criminal activity, was engaged in continuing criminal activity over a period of time, or is committing, has committed, or is about to commit, a designated offense.

(M) "Journalist" means a person engaged in, connected with, or employed by, any news media, including a newspaper, magazine, press association, news agency, or wire service, a radio or television station, or other similar media, for the purpose of gathering, processing, transmitting, compiling, editing, or disseminating news for the general public.

(N) "Electronic communication" means a transfer of a sign, signal, writing, image, sound, datum, or intelligence of any nature that is transmitted in whole or in part by a wire, radio, electromagnetic, photoelectronic, or photo-optical system. "Electronic communication" does not mean any of the following:

(1) A wire or oral communication;

(2) A communication made through a tone-only paging device;

(3) A communication from an electronic or mechanical tracking device that permits the tracking of the movement of a person or object.

(O) "User" means a person or entity that uses an electronic communication service and is duly authorized by the provider of the service to engage in the use of the electronic communication service.

(P) "Electronic communications system" means a wire, radio, electromagnetic, photoelectronic, or photo-optical facility for the transmission of electronic communications, and a computer facility or related electronic equipment for the electronic storage of electronic communications.

(Q) "Electronic communication service" means a service that provides to users of the service the ability to send or receive wire or electronic communications.

(R) "Readily accessible to the general public" means, with respect to a radio communication, that the communication is none of the following:

(1) Scrambled or encrypted;

(2) Transmitted using a modulation technique, the essential parameters of which have been withheld from the public with the intention of preserving the privacy of the communication;

(3) Carried on a subcarrier or other signal subsidiary to a radio transmission;

(4) Transmitted over a communications system provided by a communications common carrier, unless the communication is a tone-only paging system communication;

(5) Transmitted on a frequency allocated under part 25, subpart D, E, or F of part 74, or part 94 of the Rules of the Federal Communications Commission, as those provisions existed on the effective date of this amendment, unless, in the case of a communication transmitted on a frequency allocated under part 74 that is not exclusively allocated to broadcast auxiliary services, the communication is a two-way voice communication by radio.

(S) "Electronic Storage" means a temporary, intermediate storage of a wire or electronic communication that is incidental to the electronic transmission of the communication, and a storage of a wire or electronic communication by an electronic communication service for the purpose of backup protection of the communication.

(T) "Aural transfer" means a transfer containing the human voice at a point between and including the point of origin and the point of reception.

(U) "Pen register" means a device that records or decodes electronic impulses that identify the numbers dialed, pulsed, or otherwise transmitted on telephone lines to which the device is attached.

(V) "Trap and trace device" means a device or apparatus that connects to a telephone or telegraph instrument, equipment, or facility and determines the origin of a wire communication to a telephone or telegraph instrument, equipment, or facility but does not intercept the contents of a wire communication.

(W) "Judge of a court of common pleas" means a judge of that court who is elected or appointed as a judge of general jurisdiction or as a judge who exercises both general jurisdiction and probate, domestic relations, or juvenile jurisdiction. "Judge of a court of common pleas" does not mean a judge of that court who is elected or appointed specifically as a probate, domestic relations, or juvenile judge.

This is an interim section effective until July 1, 1996.

(1996 H 181, § 1, eff. 6–13–96; 1986 S 222, eff. 3–25–87)

2933.52 Prohibition against interception of communications; exceptions

(A) No person purposely shall do any of the following:

(1) Intercept, attempt to intercept, or procure another person to intercept or attempt to intercept a wire, oral, or electronic communication;

(2) Use, attempt to use, or procure another person to use or attempt to use an interception device to intercept a wire, oral, or electronic communication, if either of the following applies:

(a) The interception device is affixed to, or otherwise transmits a signal through, a wire, cable, satellite, microwave, or other similar method of connection used in wire communications;

(b) The interception device transmits communications by radio, or interferes with the transmission of communications by radio.

(3) Use, or attempt to use, the contents of a wire, oral, or electronic communication, knowing or having reason to know that the contents were obtained through the interception of a wire, oral, or electronic communication in violation of sections 2933.51 to 2933.66 of the Revised Code.

(B) This section does not apply to any of the following:

(1) The interception, disclosure, or use of the contents, or evidence derived from the contents, of an oral, wire, or electronic communication that is obtained through the use of an interception warrant issued pursuant to sections 2933.53 to 2933.56 of the Revised Code, that is obtained pursuant to an oral approval for an interception granted pursuant to section 2933.57 of the Revised Code, or that is obtained pursuant to an order that is issued or an interception that is made in accordance with section 802 of the "Omnibus Crime Control and Safe Streets Act of 1968," 82 Stat. 237, 254, 18 U.S.C. 2510 to 2520 (1968), as amended, the "Electronic Communications Privacy Act of 1986," 100 Stat. 1848–1857, 18 U.S.C. 2510–2521 (1986), as amended, or the "Foreign Intelligence Surveillance Act," 92 Stat. 1783, 50 U.S.C. 1801.11 (1978), as amended;

(2) An operator of a switchboard, or an officer, employee, or agent of a provider of wire or electronic communication service, whose facilities are used in the transmission of a wire or electronic communication to intercept, disclose, or use that communication in the normal course of employment while engaged in an activity that is necessary to the rendition of service or to the protection of the rights or property of the provider of that service, except that a provider of wire or electronic communication service to the public shall not utilize service observing or random monitoring except for mechanical or service quality control checks;

(3) A law enforcement officer who intercepts a wire, oral, or electronic communication, if the officer is a party to the communication or if one of the parties to the communication has given prior consent to the interception by the officer;

(4) A person who is not a law enforcement officer and who intercepts a wire, oral, or electronic communication, if the person is a party to the communication or if one of the parties to the communication has given the person prior consent to the interception, and if the communication is not intercepted for the purpose of committing a criminal offense or tortious act in violation of the laws or Constitution of the United States or this state or for the purpose of committing any other injurious act;

(5) An officer, employee, or agent of a communications common carrier providing information, facilities, or technical assistance to an investigative officer who is authorized to intercept a wire, oral, or electronic communication pursuant to sections 2933.51 to 2933.66 of the Revised Code;

(6) The use of a pen register in accordance with federal or state law;

(7) The use of a trap and trace device in accordance with federal or state law;

(8) A police, fire, or emergency communications system to intercept wire communications coming into and going out of the communications system of a police department, fire department, or emergency center, if both of the following apply:

(a) The telephone, instrument, equipment, or facility is limited to the exclusive use of the communication system for administrative purposes;

(b) At least one telephone, instrument, equipment, or facility that is not subject to interception is made available for public use at each police department, fire department, or emergency center.

(9) The interception or accessing of an electronic communication made through an electronic communication system that is configured so that the electronic communication is readily accessible to the general public.

(10) The interception of a radio communication that is transmitted by any of the following:

(a) A station for the use of the general public;

(b) A governmental, law enforcement, civil defense, private land mobile, or public safety communications system, including a police or fire system, that is readily accessible to the general public;

(c) A station operating on an authorized frequency within the bands allocated to the amateur, citizens band, or general mobile radio services;

(d) A marine or aeronautical communications system.

(11) The interception of a radio communication that relates to a ship, aircraft, vehicle, or person in distress.

(12) The interception of a wire or electronic communication the transmission of which is causing harmful interference to a lawfully operating station or consumer electronic equipment, to the extent necessary to identify the source of that interference.

(13) Other users of the same frequency to intercept a radio communication made through a system that utilizes frequencies monitored by individuals engaged in the provision or the use of that system, if the communication is not scrambled or encrypted.

(C) Whoever violates this section is guilty of interception of wire, oral, or electronic communications, a felony of the third degree.

(D) This is an interim section effective until July 1, 1996.

(1996 H 181, § 1, eff. 6–13–96; 1987 H 231, eff. 10–5–87; 1986 S 222)

2933.521 Divulging content of communication by provider of electronic communication service

(A) Except as provided in division (B) of this section, no person or entity that provides electronic communication service to the public shall purposely divulge the content of a communication, while it is in transmission on that service, to a person or entity other than an addressee or intended recipient of the communication or an agent of an addressee or intended recipient of the communication.

(B)(1) Division (A) of this section does not apply to a communication being transmitted to the person or entity providing the electronic communication service or to an agent of that person or entity.

(2) Notwithstanding division (A) of this section, a person or entity that provides electronic communication service to the public may divulge the content of a communication that is in transmission on that service in any of the following circumstances:

(a) The divulgence is authorized by division (B)(2) of section 2933.52, by section 2933.581, by division (C) of section 2933.55, or by division (F) or (G) of section 2933.59 of the Revised Code or by a provision of the "Electronic Communications Privacy Act of 1986," 100 Stat. 1848–1857, 18 U.S.C. 2510–2521 (1986), as amended.

(b) The originator or an addressee or intended recipient of the communication has lawfully consented to the divulgence.

(c) The divulgence is made to a person who is employed or authorized, or whose facilities are used, to forward the communication to its destination.

(d) The content of the communication divulged was inadvertently obtained by the provider of the service, the content appears to pertain to the commission of a crime, and the divulgence is made to a law enforcement agency.

(C) Neither division (A) of this section nor any other provision of sections 2933.51 to 2933.66 of the Revised Code prohibits a provider of electronic communication service from recording the fact that a wire or electronic communication was initiated or completed, in order to protect the provider, another provider furnishing service toward the completion of the wire or electronic communication, or a user of the electronic communication service from fraudulent, unlawful, or abusive use of the electronic communication service.

(1996 H 181, eff. 6–13–96)

2933.522 Authority of judges of courts of common pleas

A judge of a court of common pleas, in accordance with sections 2933.51 to 2933.66 of the Revised Code, may accept applications for interception warrants, may issue interception warrants, may accept applications for extensions of interception warrants, may order extensions of interception warrants, may accept applications for grants of oral orders for interceptions, may grant oral orders for interceptions, and may issue other orders, perform other functions, or engage in other activities authorized or required by sections 2933.51 to 2933.66 of the Revised Code.

(1996 H 181, eff. 6–13–96)

2933.53 Application for interception warrant; contents; exemptions

(A) The prosecuting attorney of the county in which an interception is to take place or in which an interception device is to be installed, or an assistant to the prosecuting attorney of that county who is specifically designated by the prosecuting attorney to exercise authority under this section, may authorize an application for an interception warrant to a judge of the court of common pleas of the county in which the interception is to take place or in which the interception device is to be installed. If the prosecuting attorney of a county in which an interception is to take place or in which an interception device is to be installed is the subject of an investigation, a special prosecutor appointed by a judge of the court of common pleas of the county served by the prosecuting attorney, without the knowledge of the prosecuting attorney, may apply the procedures of this section. If the subject of an investigation is employed in the office of the prosecuting attorney of the county in which an interception is to take place or in which an interception device is to be installed or the prosecuting attorney of that county believes that he or she has a conflict of interest, the approval of the prosecuting attorney shall be obtained before a special prosecutor is appointed to authorize the application for an interception warrant.

(B) Each application for an interception warrant shall be made in writing upon oath or affirmation to a judge of the court of common pleas of the county in which the interception is to take place or in which the interception device is to be installed, by a person who has received training that satisfies the minimum standards established by the attorney general and the Ohio peace officer training council under section 2933.64 of the Revised Code. Each application shall contain all of the following:

(1) The name and office of the applicant and the name and office of the prosecuting attorney or assistant prosecuting attorney authorizing the application;

(2) The identity of the investigative officers or law enforcement agency that will intercept the wire, oral, or electronic communications;

(3) A full and complete statement of the objective in seeking the warrant, and a full and complete statement of the facts and circumstances relied on by the applicant to justify the belief that the warrant should be issued, including, but not limited to the following:

(a) The details regarding the designated offense that has been, is being, or is about to be committed;

(b) The identity of the person, if known, who has committed, is committing, or is about to commit the designated offense and whose communications are to be intercepted and the location at which the communications are sought to be intercepted;

(c) Except as provided in division (G)(1) of this section, a particular description of the nature and location of the facilities from which, or the place at which, the communication is to be intercepted;

(d) A particular description of the type of communication sought to be intercepted, and the basis for believing that evidence relating to a designated offense will be obtained through the interception.

(4) A statement as to whether the applicant, or the prosecuting attorney or assistant prosecuting attorney authorizing the application for an interception warrant, knows or has reason to know that the communications sought to be intercepted are privileged under section 2317.02 of the Revised Code, the nature of any privilege that exists, and the basis of the knowledge of the applicant or authorizing prosecuting attorney or assistant prosecuting attorney of the privileged nature of the communications;

(5) A statement of the use to which the contents of an intercepted wire, oral, or electronic communication, or the evidence derived from the communication, will be put;

(6) A statement of the period of time for which the interception is required to be maintained, and, if the nature of the investigation requires that the authorization for interception not be terminated automatically when the described type of communication first has been intercepted, a particular description of the facts establishing probable cause to believe that additional communications of the same type will occur after the first intercepted communication;

(7) A full and complete statement indicating whether other investigative procedures have been tried and have failed to produce the required evidence or indicating the reason that other investigative procedures reasonably appear to be unlikely to succeed if tried or to be too dangerous to employ in order to obtain evidence;

(8) A full and complete statement of the particular facts concerning all previous applications known to the applicant or the prosecuting attorney or assistant prosecuting attorney authorizing the application for the interception warrant, that have been made to a judge for authorization to intercept wire, oral, or electronic communications involving any of the persons, facilities, or places specified in the application, and the action of the judge with respect to each previous application;

(9) Unless the attorney general is a subject of the investigation, a written statement, signed by the attorney general or an assistant attorney general designated by the attorney general, that the attorney general or assistant attorney general has reviewed the application and either agrees or disagrees with the submission of the application to a judge of the court of common pleas of the county in which the interception is to take place or in which the interception device is to be installed. A disagreement by the attorney general or assistant attorney general does

not preclude the making or consideration of an application that otherwise complies with divisions (B)(1) to (8) of this section.

(C) If an application for an interception warrant is for an extension of a warrant, the application shall include, in addition to the information and statements specified in division (B) of this section, a statement setting forth the results thus far obtained from the interceptions of wire, oral, or electronic communications, or a reasonable explanation of the failure to obtain results from the interceptions.

(D) An applicant may submit affidavits of persons other than the applicant in conjunction with the application if the affidavits support a fact or conclusion in the application. The accompanying affidavits shall be based on personal knowledge of the affiant or shall be based on information and belief and specify the source of the information and the reason for the belief. If the applicant or an affiant personally knows of the facts contained in the application or affidavit, the application or affidavit shall state the personal knowledge. If the application or affidavit states the facts based upon information and belief, the application or affidavit shall state that reliance upon information and belief and shall set forth fully the facts supporting the information and belief. If the facts contained in the application or affidavits are derived in whole or in part from the statement of a person other than the applicant or affiant, the application or affidavits shall disclose or describe the sources of the facts and shall contain facts establishing the existence and reliability of the other person or the reliability of the information supplied by the other person. The application also shall state, so far as possible, the basis of the other person's knowledge or belief. If the application or affidavit relies on hearsay to support a fact alleged on information and belief, the application or affidavit shall contain the underlying facts that establish the basis for the conclusions of the source of the hearsay and the factual basis upon which the applicant or the affiant concludes that the source of the hearsay is credible or reliable.

(E) A judge of a court of common pleas to whom an application is made under this section may require the applicant to furnish additional sworn testimony or documentary evidence in support of the application. All sworn testimony furnished shall be recorded and transcribed and shall be made part of the application.

(F) An interception warrant is not required for any of the following:

(1) A pen register used in accordance with federal or state law;

(2) The interception of a wire, oral, or electronic communication by a law enforcement officer if the officer is a party to the communication or if one of the parties to the communication has given prior consent to the interception by the officer;

(3) The interception of a wire, oral, or electronic communication by a person who is not a law enforcement officer if the person is a party to the communication or if one of the parties to the communication has given the person prior consent to the interception, and if the communication is not intercepted for the purpose of committing a criminal offense or tortious act in violation of the laws or constitution of the United States or this state or for the purpose of committing another injurious act.

(4) A trap and trace device used in accordance with federal or state law.

(G)(1) The requirements of division (B)(3)(c) of this section and of division (A)(5) of section 2933.54 of the Revised Code that relate to the specification of facilities from which or the place at which the communication is to be intercepted do not apply if either of the following applies:

(a) In the case of an application with respect to the interception of an oral communication, the application contains a full and complete statement indicating the reason that the specification is not practical and identifies the person committing the designated offense and whose communications are to be intercepted, and the judge of a court of common pleas to whom the application is made finds that the specification is not practical.

(b) In the case of an application with respect to a wire or electronic communication, the application identifies the person believed to be committing the designated offense and whose communications are to be intercepted, the applicant makes a showing of purpose on the part of that person to thwart interception by changing facilities, and the judge of a court of common pleas to whom the application is made finds that that purpose adequately has been shown.

(2) An interception of a communication under an interception warrant with respect to which the requirements of division (B)(3)(c) of this section and division (A)(5) of section 2933.54 of the Revised Code do not apply, due to the application of division (G)(1) of this section, shall not begin until the facilities from which or the place at which the communication is to be intercepted is ascertained by the person implementing the interception warrant.

A provider of wire or electronic communication service that has received an interception warrant that does not specify the facilities from which or the place at which the communication is to be intercepted, due to the application of division (G)(1)(b) of this section, may file a motion with the court requesting the court to modify or quash the interception warrant on the ground that the provider's assistance with respect to the interception cannot be performed in a timely or reasonable manner. The court, upon notice to the applicant for the interception warrant, shall decide the motion expeditiously.

(1996 H 181, eff. 6–13–96; 1986 S 222, eff. 3–25–87)

2933.54 Issuance of interception warrant; hearings

(A) A judge of a court of common pleas to whom an application for an interception warrant is made under section 2933.53 of the Revised Code may issue an interception warrant if the judge determines, on the basis of the facts submitted by the person who made the application and all affiants, that all of the following exist:

(1) The application and affidavits comply with section 2933.53 of the Revised Code.

(2) There is probable cause to believe that a particular person is committing, has committed, or is about to commit a designated offense.

(3) There is probable cause to believe that particular communications concerning the designated offense will be obtained through the interception of wire, oral, or electronic communications.

(4) Normal investigative procedures with respect to the designated offense have been tried and have failed or normal investigative procedures with respect to the designated offense reasonably appear to be unlikely to succeed if tried or to be too dangerous to employ in order to obtain evidence.

(5) Except as provided in division (G)(1) of section 2933.53 of the Revised Code, there is probable cause to believe that the communication facilities from which the communications are to be intercepted, or the place at which oral communications are to be intercepted, are being used or are about to be used in connection with the commission of the designated offense or are leased to, listed in the name of, or commonly used by a person who is the subject of the interception warrant.

(6) The investigative officer has received training that satisfies the minimum standards established by the attorney general and the Ohio peace officer training council under section 2933.64 of the Revised Code in order to intercept the wire, oral, or electronic communication and is able to execute the interception sought.

(B) If the communication facilities from which a wire or electronic communication is to be intercepted are public facilities, the judge of the court of common pleas to whom the application for an interception warrant is made shall not issue an interception warrant unless the judge, in addition to the findings specified in division (A) of this section, determines that there is a special need to intercept wire or electronic communications made from the facilities.

(C) If the facilities from which, or the place at which, the wire, oral, or electronic communications are to be intercepted are being used by, are about to be used by, are leased to, are listed in the name of, or are commonly used by a licensed physician, a licensed practicing psychologist, an attorney, a practicing clergyman, or a journalist or are used primarily for habitation by a husband and wife, the judge of the court of common pleas to whom the application is made shall not issue an interception warrant unless the judge, in addition to the findings specified in divisions (A) and (B) of this section, determines that there is a special need to intercept wire, oral, or electronic communications over the facilities or in those places. No otherwise privileged wire, oral, or electronic communication shall lose its privileged character because it is intercepted in accordance with or in violation of sections 2933.51 to 2933.66 of the Revised Code.

(D) If an application for an interception warrant does not comply with section 2933.53 of the Revised Code, or if the judge of a court of common pleas with whom an application is filed is not satisfied that grounds exist for issuance of an interception warrant, the judge shall deny the application.

(E) An interception warrant shall terminate when the objective of the warrant has been achieved or upon the expiration of thirty days after the date of commencement of the warrant as specified in this division, whichever occurs first, unless an extension is granted as described in this division. The date of commencement of an interception warrant is the day on which an investigative or law enforcement officer first begins to conduct an interception under the warrant, or the day that is ten days after the warrant is issued, whichever is earlier. A judge of a court of common pleas may grant extensions of a warrant pursuant to section 2933.55 of the Revised Code.

(F) If a judge of a court of common pleas issues an interception warrant, the judge shall make a finding as to the objective of the warrant.

(1996 H 181, eff. 6–13–96; 1988 H 708, eff. 4–19–88; 1986 S 222)

2933.55 Extension of interception warrant; approval of interceptions beyond scope of warrant

(A) At any time prior to the expiration of an interception warrant, the person who made the application for the warrant may apply for an extension of the warrant. The person shall file the application for extension with a judge of the court of common pleas of the county in which the interception under the warrant was to take place. An application for extension shall comply with section 2933.53 of the Revised Code.

(B) A judge of a court of common pleas with whom an application for extension of an interception warrant is filed shall determine whether to order an extension of the interception warrant in accordance with section 2933.54 of the Revised Code and shall order an extension for a period no longer than the judge considers necessary to achieve the purposes of the extension. The extension shall terminate upon the attainment of the authorized objective or thirty days after it is granted, whichever occurs first. All provisions of sections 2933.51 to 2933.66 of the Revised Code that apply to original interception warrants apply to extensions of interception warrants.

(C)(1) When an investigative officer, while intercepting communications pursuant to an interception warrant or pursuant to an oral order for an interception granted under section 2933.57 of the Revised Code, intercepts wire, oral, or electronic communications that pertain to a criminal offense that is other than the designated offense specified in the interception warrant or oral order and that is completely unrelated to the designated offense specified in the interception warrant or oral order, the prosecuting attorney, in order to permit the disclosure or use of the contents, or evidence derived from the contents, of the intercepted communications pursuant to division (G) of section 2933.59 of the Revised Code, may file a motion with the judge who issued the warrant or granted the oral order for an order approving the interception. The judge shall enter an order approving the interception if the judge finds that the communication otherwise was intercepted in accordance with sections 2933.53 to 2933.66 of the Revised Code.

A person may disclose or use the contents, and any evidence derived from the contents, of the intercepted communications dealing with the other, unrelated offense as set forth in division (F) of section 2933.59 of the Revised Code. The person may disclose or use those contents and the evidence derived from those contents as set forth in division (G) of section 2933.59 of the Revised Code only if the issuing judge issues an order approving the interception of the communications concerning the other, unrelated offense.

(2) When an investigative officer, while intercepting communications pursuant to an interception warrant or pursuant to an oral order for an interception granted under section 2933.57 of the Revised Code, intercepts wire, oral, or electronic communications that pertain to a criminal offense that is other than the designated offense specified in the interception warrant or oral order but that is not completely unrelated to the designated offense specified in the interception warrant or oral order, the wire, oral, or electronic communications intercepted

shall be treated for all purposes and without the need for further action as if the offense to which they pertain was a designated offense specified in the interception warrant or oral order. (1996 H 181, eff. 6–13–96; 1986 S 222, eff. 3–25–87)

2933.56 Contents of interception warrant; sealing of records

(A) Any interception warrant or extension of an interception warrant that is issued pursuant to sections 2933.53 to 2933.55 of the Revised Code shall contain all of the following:

(1) The name and court of the judge who issued the warrant and the jurisdiction of that court;

(2) If known, the identity of each person whose communications are to be intercepted or, if the identity is unascertainable, a detailed description of each known person whose communications are to be intercepted;

(3) The nature and location of the communications facilities from which or of the place at which the authority to intercept is granted and, in the case of telephone or telegraph communications, a designation of the particular lines involved;

(4) A statement of the objective of the warrant, as found by the issuing judge, and a statement of the designated offenses for which the authority to intercept is granted;

(5) A description of the particular type of communication sought to be intercepted;

(6) The identity of the investigative officer or law enforcement agency that is authorized to intercept communications pursuant to the interception warrant and the identity of the prosecuting attorney or assistant prosecuting attorney authorizing the application for the interception warrant;

(7) The period of time during which the interception is authorized, including a statement as to whether the interception shall terminate automatically when the described communication is first intercepted;

(8) A statement that the interception warrant shall be executed as soon as practicable;

(9) A statement that the interception shall be conducted in a way that minimizes the interception of communications that are not subject to the interception warrant, provided that if the intercepted communication is in a code or a foreign language and an expert in decoding or in that foreign language is not reasonably available during the interception period, minimization may be accomplished as soon as practicable after the interception;

(10) A statement that the interception shall terminate upon attainment of the authorized objective or upon the expiration of the thirty-day period described in division (E) of section 2933.54 of the Revised Code, whichever occurs first, unless an extension of the interception warrant is granted upon application by the judge who issued the original warrant;

(11) A statement that the person who made the application for the warrant or extension and the investigative officer or law enforcement agency authorized to intercept the communications shall provide oral or written progress reports at seven-day intervals to the judge who issued the warrant showing the progress made toward achievement of the authorized objective of the warrant and the need for continued interception;

(12) An authorization to enter private premises, other than the premises of a provider of wire or electronic communication service, for the sole purposes of installing, or of removing and permanently inactivating, interception devices and, if the entry is necessary to execute the interception warrant, a requirement that the time and date of the entry and name of the individual making the entry be reported to the court;

(13) If applicable, a statement directing a provider of wire or electronic communication service, landlord, custodian, or other person forthwith to furnish the applicant all information, facilities, and technical assistance necessary to accomplish the interception unobtrusively and with a minimum of interference with the services that the provider of wire or electronic communication service, landlord, custodian, or other person is providing to the person whose communications are to be intercepted. This assistance by a provider of wire or electronic communication service shall not include assistance in supplying, installing, or removing and permanently inactivating, interception devices. Any provider of wire or electronic communica-

tion service and any landlord, custodian, or other person furnishing the facilities or technical assistance shall be compensated for them at the prevailing rates.

(B) The judge of the court of common pleas to whom the application is made or who issued the warrant shall seal all applications for interception warrants that are made and all interception warrants that are issued pursuant to sections 2933.53 to 2933.55 of the Revised Code.

The judge of a court of common pleas who received the application or issued the warrant shall specify who shall have custody of the sealed application and interception warrant. Copies of the interception warrant, together with a copy of the application, shall be delivered to and retained by the person who made the application for the warrant or extension as authority for the interception authorized by the warrant.

Except as otherwise provided in sections 2933.51 to 2933.66 of the Revised Code, the application and interception warrants shall be disclosed only upon a showing of good cause before a judge who is authorized to issue interception warrants. Upon the termination of the authorized interception, the person who made the application for the warrant or extension shall return all applications made and interception warrants issued under sections 2933.53 to 2933.55 of the Revised Code that pertain to the interception to the issuing judge, and the applications and warrants shall be sealed under the issuing judge's direction.

The applications and warrants shall be kept for at least ten years. At the expiration of the ten-year period, the issuing or denying judge may order that the applications and warrants be destroyed.

(C) A violation of division (B) of this section may be punished as contempt of court.

(1996 H 181, eff. 6–13–96; 1986 S 222, eff. 3–25–87)

2933.57   Oral order for interception without warrant

(A) A judge of the court of common pleas may grant an oral order for an interception without a warrant of a wire, oral, or electronic communication. Upon receipt of an application under this division, the judge of the court of common pleas to whom the application is made may grant an oral order for an interception without a warrant, may include in the order a statement of the type described in division (A)(13) of section 2933.56 of the Revised Code, and shall condition the order upon the filing with the judge, within forty-eight hours, of an application for an interception warrant under section 2933.53 of the Revised Code and division (B) of this section, if the judge determines all of the following:

(1) There appear to be grounds upon which an interception warrant could be issued under section 2933.54 of the Revised Code.

(2) There is probable cause to believe that an emergency situation exists with respect to the investigation of a designated offense.

(3) There is probable cause to believe that the emergency situation involves an immediate danger of death or serious physical harm that justifies the authorization for immediate interception of a private wire, oral, or electronic communication before an application for an interception warrant could, with due diligence, be submitted to the judge and acted upon.

(B) No statement by the attorney general or the attorney general's designee pursuant to division (B)(9) of section 2933.53 is required prior to consideration of an application pursuant to this section.

(C) The judge of a court of common pleas to whom an application is made under division (A) of this section, the applicant, the prosecuting attorney or assistant prosecuting attorney who authorized the application, and any involved provider of wire or electronic communication service may tape record any telephone or other communications between any of them related to the application for, the approval of, and the implementation of an oral order for an interception. All of the provisions of sections 2933.51 to 2933.66 of the Revised Code concerning the sealing, distribution, use, and disclosure of an application for an interception warrant apply to any tape recording between the judge, the applicant, and the prosecuting attorney or the designated assistant concerning the application for and an oral order for an interception.

(D)(1) As soon as possible after granting an oral order for an interception without a warrant, a judge shall place upon the journal of the court an entry nunc pro tunc to record the granting of the oral order. If an interception warrant is issued pursuant to the filing of an application following the granting of an oral order for an interception under this section, the judge shall issue the warrant in accordance with section 2933.54 of the Revised Code, and the warrant shall recite the granting of the oral order and shall be retroactive to the time of the oral order.

(2) Interception pursuant to an oral order under this section shall be made in accordance with section 2933.59 of the Revised Code, except that the interception shall terminate immediately when the communication sought is obtained or when the application for a warrant is denied, whichever is earlier.

(3) If no application for a warrant is made in accordance with this section within forty-eight hours following a grant of an oral order or if an application for a warrant is made in accordance with this section following the grant of an oral order but the application is denied, the content of any private wire, oral, or electronic communication intercepted under the oral order shall be treated as having been obtained in violation of this chapter, and an inventory shall be served in accordance with section 2933.61 of the Revised Code upon the person named in the application. However, a provider of wire or electronic communication service that relies in good faith on the oral order in accordance with division (B) of section 2933.65 of the Revised Code is immune from civil or criminal liability in accordance with that section.

(4) If no application for a warrant is made within forty-eight hours following a grant of an oral order under this section or if an application for a warrant is made but is denied, the judge of a court of common pleas who granted an oral order for the interception shall prepare a journal entry reciting the grant of the oral order that includes as much of the information required to be included in an interception warrant that is practical to include. All of the provisions of sections 2933.51 to 2933.63 of the Revised Code concerning the sealing, distribution, use, and disclosure of an interception warrant apply to the journal entry required by this division. The judge who granted the oral order also shall order the person who received the oral order under this section to prepare an inventory of the recordings and resumes compiled under the oral order and shall require the tape or other recording of the intercepted communication to be delivered to, and sealed by, the judge in accordance with division (B) of section 2933.59 of the Revised Code. The court served by that judge shall retain the evidence, and no person shall use or disclose the evidence in a legal proceeding, other than a civil action brought by an aggrieved person or as otherwise authorized by the order of a judge of the court of common pleas of the county in which the interception took place. In addition to other remedies or penalties provided by law, a failure to deliver a tape or other recording to the judge in accordance with this division shall be punishable as contempt by the judge directing the delivery.

(1996 H 181, eff. 6–13–96; 1986 S 222, eff. 3–25–87)

2933.58 Instruction of investigative officers; privileged communications; validity of warrant

(A) Upon the issuance of an interception warrant pursuant to section 2933.54 of the Revised Code and prior to the execution of the warrant or upon a grant of an oral order for an interception under section 2933.57 of the Revised Code, the prosecuting attorney or assistant prosecuting attorney who authorized the application for the warrant or the oral approval shall instruct the investigative officers who are authorized to intercept the communications regarding the application and interpretation of divisions (A), (B), and (C) of section 2317.02 of the Revised Code. The prosecuting attorney or assistant prosecuting attorney who authorized the application or the oral order also shall instruct the officers to minimize the interception of communications that are not subject to the warrant or oral order and shall inform the officers of the procedures to be followed if communications concerning another offense are intercepted. If individuals operating under a contract to provide interception services as described in section 2933.59 of the Revised Code are involved in the interception, the prosecuting attorney or assistant prosecuting attorney who authorized the application for the warrant or the oral order also shall give the instructions and information under this division to those individuals.

(B) Investigative officers who are authorized to intercept communications pursuant to an interception warrant or pursuant to an oral order for an interception granted under section 2933.57 of the Revised Code and individuals who are operating under a contract to provide interception services as described in section 2933.59 of the Revised Code shall monitor the receiver of the interception device at all times during the time period for which the interception is authorized. All communications shall be intercepted only in accordance with the warrant or the oral order.

(C) An interception warrant issued pursuant to sections 2933.53 to 2933.55 of the Revised Code or an oral order for an interception granted under section 2933.57 of the Revised Code authorizes the interception of wire, oral, or electronic communications or the installation of an interception device within the jurisdiction of the court of common pleas served by the judge who issued the warrant or granted the oral order. The warrant or oral order is valid at any place if the interception device is installed within the jurisdiction of the judge who issued the warrant or granted the oral order and is then moved to another place by persons other than the investigative officers.

(1996 H 181, eff. 6–13–96; 1986 S 222, eff. 3–25–87)

2933.581   Assistance by provider of electronic communication service, landlord, or custodian; prohibition against disclosure of existence of interception

(A) Notwithstanding any other provision of law, a provider of wire or electronic communication service, an officer, employee, or agent of a provider of that type, and a landlord, custodian, or other person is authorized to provide information, facilities, or technical assistance to a person who is authorized by the law of this state or the United States to intercept wire, oral, or electronic communications if both of the following apply:

(1) The provider, officer, employee, agent, landlord, custodian, or person has been provided with either of the following:

(a) An interception warrant or extension of an interception warrant that contains a statement of the type described in division (A)(13) of section 2933.56 of the Revised Code;

(b) A written representation of a judge of a court of common pleas or of a prosecuting attorney or specifically designated assistant prosecuting attorney that an oral order for an interception has been granted pursuant to section 2933.57 of the Revised Code, that no interception warrant is required by law, that all applicable statutory requirements have been satisfied, and that the oral order contains a statement of the type described in division (A)(13) of section 2933.56 of the Revised Code that directs the provision of the specified information, facilities, or technical assistance.

(2) The warrant, extension, or representation sets forth the period of time during which the provision of the information, facilities, or technical assistance is authorized and specifies the information, facilities, or technical assistance required.

(B)(1) Except as provided in division (B)(2) of this section, no provider of wire or electronic communication service, no officer, employee, or agent of a provider of that type, and no landlord, custodian, or other person who is authorized to provide information, facilities, or technical assistance under division (A) of this section shall disclose the existence of an interception or the device used to accomplish the interception with respect to which the person has been furnished an interception warrant, an extension of an interception warrant, or a written representation pursuant to that division. A person that makes a disclosure in violation of this division is liable for civil damages of the type described in section 2933.65 of the Revised Code.

(2) Division (B)(1) of this section does not prohibit the disclosure of the existence of an interception or the disclosure of a device used to accomplish an interception when the disclosure is required by legal process, provided the person making the disclosure gives prior notification of the disclosure to the prosecuting attorney of the county in which the interception takes place or in which the interception device is installed.

(C) Except as provided in this section, a provider of wire or electronic communication service, an officer, employee, or agent of a provider of that type, and a landlord, custodian, or other specified person is immune from civil or criminal liability in any action that arises out of its providing information, facilities, or technical assistance in accordance with division (A) of this section and the terms of the interception warrant, extension of an interception warrant, or written representation provided under that division.

(1996 H 181, eff. 6–13–96)

2933.59 Execution of interception warrant; altering recordings or resumes; disclosure of information

(A) An investigative officer who is, or a member of the law enforcement agency that is, authorized by an interception warrant or a grant of an oral order for an interception pursuant to section 2933.57 of the Revised Code to intercept wire, oral, or electronic communications or an individual who is operating under a contract with that agency and is acting under the supervision of that officer or a member of that agency shall execute the interception warrant or the oral order in accordance with the terms of the warrant or oral order. The officer or member of the law enforcement agency who executes the warrant or oral order or who supervises the execution of the warrant or oral order shall have received training that satisfies the minimum standards established by the attorney general and the Ohio peace officer training council under section 2933.64 of the Revised Code. The contents of a wire, oral, or electronic communication intercepted pursuant to an interception warrant or pursuant to a grant of an oral order for an interception, if possible, shall be recorded on tape or another similar device. If it is not possible to record the intercepted communication, a detailed resume of that communication immediately shall be reduced to writing. The recording or transcribing of the contents of any wire, oral, or electronic communication pursuant to sections 2933.51 to 2933.66 of the Revised Code shall be done in a way that will protect the recording or transcription from editing or any other alteration.

(B) Immediately upon the expiration of the period of time for which an interception warrant was authorized, or any extensions of that time period, all wire, oral, or electronic communications interceptions shall cease, and any interception device installed pursuant to the interception warrant shall be removed or permanently inactivated as soon as is reasonably practicable. Entry to remove or inactivate an interception device is authorized by the granting of an interception warrant.

Immediately upon the expiration of that period of time or the extension, the recordings or resumes of intercepted communications shall be made available to the issuing judge and shall be sealed under the judge's direction. The issuing judge shall specify who shall have custody of the sealed recordings and resumes. The recordings and resumes shall be kept for at least ten years. At the expiration of the ten-year period, the recordings and resumes may be destroyed upon the order of a judge of the court of common pleas of the county in which the interception took place. Duplicate recordings or resumes may be made for use or disclosure pursuant to divisions (F) and (G) of this section.

(C) No person, with intent to present the altered recording or resume in any judicial proceeding or proceeding under oath or affirmation, shall purposely edit, alter, or tamper with any recording or resume of any intercepted wire, oral, or electronic communications, shall attempt to edit, alter, or tamper with any recording or resume of any intercepted wire, oral, or electronic communications, or shall present or permit the presentation of any altered recording or resume in any judicial proceeding or proceeding under oath or affirmation, without fully indicating the nature of the changes made in the original state of the recording or resume.

(D)(1) Any interception warrant, the existence of lawfully installed interception devices, the application, affidavits, and return prepared in connection with the warrant, and any information concerning the application for, the granting of, or the denial of an interception warrant shall remain secret until they have been disclosed in a criminal trial or in a proceeding that is open to the public or until they have been furnished to the defendant or unless otherwise provided in sections 2933.51 to 2933.66 of the Revised Code.

(2) Any person who violates division (D)(1) of this section may be punished for contempt of court.

(E) When an order for destruction of any documents dealing with an interception warrant is issued, the person directed in the order to destroy the applications, affidavits, interception warrants, any amendments or extensions of the warrants, or recordings or resumes made pursuant to the warrants shall do so in the presence of at least one witness who is not connected with a law enforcement agency. The person who destroys the documents and each witness shall execute affidavits setting forth the facts and circumstances of the destruction. The affidavits shall be filed with and approved by the court having custody of the original materials.

(F) An investigative officer who has obtained knowledge of the contents, or of evidence derived from the contents, of a wire, oral, or electronic communication pursuant to sections 2933.51 to 2933.66 of the Revised Code may disclose the contents or evidence to another investigative officer to the extent that the disclosure is appropriate to the proper performance of the official duties of the officer making or receiving the disclosure and may use the contents or evidence to the extent appropriate to the proper performance of his official duties.

(G) A person who has received, pursuant to sections 2933.51 to 2933.66 of the Revised Code, information concerning, or evidence derived from, a wire, oral, or electronic communication intercepted pursuant to an interception warrant may disclose the contents of that communication, or the evidence derived from the contents, while giving testimony under oath or affirmation in a proceeding held under the authority of the United States, this state, another state, or a political subdivision of this state or another state, except that the presence of the seal provided for in division (B) of section 2933.56 of the Revised Code and in division (B) of this section, or a satisfactory explanation of the absence of the seal, shall be a prerequisite for the use or disclosure of the contents of any wire, oral, or electronic communication or evidence derived from the contents. The contents, or evidence derived from the contents, of a wire, oral, or electronic communication intercepted pursuant to an interception warrant and in accordance with sections 2933.51 to 2933.66 of the Revised Code otherwise may be disclosed only upon a showing of good cause before a judge authorized to issue interception warrants.

(H) Whoever violates division (C) of this section is guilty of a felony of the third degree.

(1996 H 181, eff. 6–13–96; 1986 S 222, eff. 3–25–87)

2933.591 Giving warning of possible surveillance

(A) No person who knows that an application for an interception warrant has been authorized or made under section 2933.53 of the Revised Code, that an interception warrant has been issued under section 2933.54 of the Revised Code, that an application for an extension of an interception warrant has been filed under section 2933.53 of the Revised Code, that an extension of an interception warrant has been ordered under that section, that an application for a grant of an oral order for an interception has been made under section 2933.57 of the Revised Code, or that oral order for an interception has been granted under section 2933.57 of the Revised Code, with purpose to obstruct, impede, or prevent the interception in question, shall give notice or attempt to give notice of the possible interception to a person.

(B) Whoever violates division (A) of this section is guilty of giving warning of possible surveillance, a felony of the third degree.

(1996 H 181, eff. 6–13–96)

2933.60 Expiration or denial of interception warrant; reports

(A) Within thirty days after the expiration of an interception warrant, the expiration of an extension of an interception warrant, or the denial of an application for an interception warrant, the judge of a court of common pleas who issued the warrant or extension or denied the application shall report all of the following to the administrative office of the United States courts and to the attorney general of this state:

(1) The fact that an application was made for an interception warrant or extension of an interception warrant;

(2) The kind of interception warrant or extension for which application was made, including a statement of whether the warrant or extension was or was not one to which the requirements of division (B)(3)(c) of section 2933.53 and division (A)(5) of section 2933.54 of the Revised

Code did not apply due to the application of division (G)(1) of section 2933.53 of the Revised Code;

(3) The fact that the interception warrant or extension was granted as applied for or was denied;

(4) The period of interception authorized by the interception warrant, and the number and duration of any extensions of the warrant;

(5) The designated offenses specified in the interception warrant, application, or extension;

(6) The identity of the person who made the application, any person who executed any accompanying affidavit to an application, and the prosecuting attorney or assistant prosecuting attorney who authorized the application;

(7) The nature of the facilities from which, or the place at which, communications are to be intercepted.

(B) In January of each year, the prosecuting attorney of each county shall report to the administrative office of the United States courts and to the attorney general of this state all information that is required to be reported by subsection (2) of section 2519 of the "Omnibus Crime Control and Safe Streets Act of 1968," 82 Stat. 197, 18 U.S.C. 2519 (1968), as amended.

(1996 H 181, eff. 6–13–96; 1986 S 222, eff. 3–25–87)

2933.61   Notice to parties to intercepted communications

(A) Within a reasonable time not later than ninety days after the filing of an application for an interception warrant that is denied or after the termination of the period of an interception warrant or any extensions of an interception warrant, the judge of a court of common pleas who issued the warrant or extension or denied the application shall cause to be served on the persons named in the application or the interception warrant, and on any other parties to intercepted wire, oral, or electronic communications that the judge determines in the judge's discretion should be notified in the interest of justice, an inventory that shall include notice of all of the following:

(1) The fact that an interception warrant was issued or that application for one was made;

(2) The date the interception warrant was issued and the period of authorized, approved, or disapproved interception or the date of the denial of the application;

(3) The fact that during the stated period wire, oral, or electronic communications were or were not intercepted.

(B) A judge of the court of common pleas of the county, upon the filing of a motion for inspection, in the judge's discretion, may make available for inspection to the person filing the motion or the person's counsel any portions of intercepted wire, oral, or electronic communications, applications for interception warrants, or interception warrants that the judge determines to be in the interest of justice. Upon an ex parte showing of good cause to a judge of a court of common pleas who denied the issuance of or issued an interception warrant, the judge may postpone the serving of the inventory required by this section for a specified period of time.

(1996 H 181, eff. 6–13–96; 1986 S 222, eff. 3–25–87)

2933.62   Use of intercepted communication in evidence

(A) No part of the contents, and no evidence derived from the contents, of any intercepted wire, oral, or electronic communication shall be received in evidence in any trial, hearing, or other proceedings in or before any court, grand jury, department, officer, agency, regulatory body, legislative committee, or other authority of this state or of a political subdivision of this state, if the disclosure of that information is in violation of sections 2933.51 to 2933.66 of the Revised Code.

(B) The contents, or any evidence derived from the contents, of any wire, oral, or electronic communication intercepted pursuant to sections 2933.51 to 2933.66 of the Revised Code shall not be received in evidence or otherwise disclosed in any trial, hearing, or other proceeding held under the authority of this state, other than a proceeding or session of the grand jury, unless each party has been furnished not less than ten days before the trial, hearing, or proceeding, with a copy of the interception warrant and the related application, or a written representation of a judge of a court of common pleas or of a prosecuting attorney or specifically designated assistant prosecuting attorney that an oral order for an interception has been granted pursuant to section 2933.57 of the Revised Code, under which the interception was authorized or approved. The judge or other officer conducting the trial, hearing, or other proceeding may waive the ten-day period if the judge or officer finds that it was not possible to furnish the party with the above information at least ten days before the trial, hearing, or proceeding, and that the party will not be prejudiced by the delay in receiving the information.

(1996 H 181, eff. 6–13–96; 1986 S 222, eff. 3–25–87)

2933.63   Suppression of contents of intercepted communication

(A) Any aggrieved person in any trial, hearing, or proceeding in or before any court, department, officer, agency, regulatory body, or other authority of this state or of a political subdivision of this state, other than a grand jury, may request the involved court, department, officer, agency, body, or authority, by motion, to suppress the contents, or evidence derived from the contents, of a wire, oral, or electronic communication intercepted pursuant to sections 2933.51 to 2933.66 of the Revised Code for any of the following reasons:

(1) The communication was unlawfully intercepted.

(2) The interception warrant under which the communication was intercepted is insufficient on its face.

(3) The interception was not made in conformity with the interception warrant or an oral order for an interception granted under section 2933.57 of the Revised Code.

(4) The communications are of a privileged character and a special need for their interception is not shown or is inadequate as shown.

(B) Any motion filed pursuant to division (A) of this section shall be made before the trial, hearing, or proceeding at which the contents, or evidence derived from the contents, is to be used, unless there was no opportunity to make the motion or the aggrieved person was not aware of the intercepted communications or the grounds of the motion. Upon the filing of the motion by the aggrieved person, the judge or other officer conducting the trial, hearing, or proceeding may make available to the aggrieved person or the person's counsel for inspection any portions of the intercepted communication or evidence derived from the intercepted communication as the judge or other officer determines to be in the interest of justice. If the judge or other officer grants the motion to suppress evidence pursuant to this section, the contents, or the evidence derived from the contents, of the intercepted wire, oral, or electronic communications shall be treated as having been obtained in violation of the law, and the contents and evidence derived from the contents shall not be received in evidence in any trial, hearing, or proceeding.

(C) In addition to any other right to appeal, the state shall have an appeal as of right from an order granting a motion to suppress the contents, or evidence derived from the contents, of a wire, oral, or electronic communication that was intercepted pursuant to an interception warrant or an oral order for an interception granted under section 2933.57 of the Revised Code, or the denial of an application for an interception warrant, if the state's representative certifies to the judge or other official who granted the motion or denied the application that the appeal is not taken for purposes of delay. Any appeal shall be taken within thirty days after the date the order was entered and shall be diligently prosecuted.

(1996 H 181, eff. 6–13–96; 1986 S 222, eff. 3–25–87)

2933.64   Training of investigative officers

The attorney general and the Ohio peace officer training council, pursuant to Chapter 109. of the Revised Code, shall establish a course of training in the legal and technical aspects of wiretapping and electronic surveillance, shall establish regulations that they find necessary and proper for the training program, and shall establish minimum standards for certification and periodic recertification for investigative officers to be eligible to conduct wiretapping or electronic surveillance under sections 2933.51 to 2933.66 of the Revised Code. The council shall charge each investigative officer who enrolls in this training a reasonable enrollment fee to offset the cost of the training.

(1996 H 181, eff. 6–13–96; 1986 S 222, eff. 3–25–87)

2933.65 Civil liability for unlawful interceptions; defenses and immunities

(A) A person whose wire, oral, or electronic communications are intercepted, disclosed, or intentionally used in violation of sections 2933.51 to 2933.66 of the Revised Code may bring a civil action to recover from the person or entity that engaged in the violation any relief that may be appropriate and that includes, but is not limited to, the following:

(1) The preliminary and other equitable or declaratory relief that is appropriate;

(2) Whichever of the following is greater:

(a) Liquidated damages computed at a rate of two hundred dollars per day for each day of violation or liquidated damages of ten thousand dollars, whichever is greater;

(b) The sum of actual damages suffered by the plaintiff and the profits, if any, made as a result of the violation by the person or entity that engaged in the violation.

(3) Punitive damages, if appropriate;

(4) Reasonable attorney's fees and other litigation expenses that are reasonably incurred in bringing the civil action.

(B) Good faith reliance on an interception warrant, extension of an interception warrant, other court order, a grant of an oral order for an interception, a grand jury subpoena, a legislative or statutory authorization, or a good faith determination that divisions (A) and (B) of section 2933.521 of the Revised Code permitted the conduct that is the subject of a complaint is a complete defense to a civil action or criminal action that is brought under the laws of this state and that arises out of the execution of the warrant or the oral order.

(C) A claimant who brings a civil action under division (A) of this section shall commence the civil action within two years after the date on which the claimant first has a reasonable opportunity to discover the violation.

(D) The remedies and sanctions described in sections 2933.51 to 2933.66 of the Revised Code with respect to the interception of wire, oral, or electronic communications are the only judicial remedies and sanctions for violations of those sections involving those types of communications that are not violations of the constitution of the United States or of this state.

(1996 H 181, eff. 6–13–96; 1986 S 222, eff. 3–25–87)

2933.66 Proceedings to conform with constitutional provisions

Notwithstanding any provision of sections 2933.51 to 2933.65 of the Revised Code, a judge of a court of common pleas to whom an application for an interception warrant, an extension of an interception warrant, an oral order for an interception, or another purpose is made pursuant to sections 2933.51 to 2933.65 of the Revised Code may take evidence, make a finding, or issue an order to conform the proceedings or the issuance of an order to the constitution of the United States or of this state.

(1996 H 181, eff. 6–13–96; 1986 S 222, eff. 3–25–87)

MEDICAID FRAUD FORFEITURES

2933.71 Definitions

As used in sections 2933.71 to 2933.75 of the Revised Code:

(A) "Medicaid fraud offense" means any of the following:

(1) Any violation of section 2913.40 of the Revised Code;

(2) Any violation of section 2921.13 of the Revised Code that involves the making of a false statement in relation to the securement of benefits or payments under the medical assistance program established under section 5111.01 of the Revised Code or the swearing or affirming of

a false statement previously made in relation to the securement of any such benefits or payments;

(3) Any other criminal violation of law related to the medical assistance program established under section 5111.01 of the Revised Code;

(4) Any conspiracy to commit any violation described in division (A)(1), (2), or (3) of this section.

(B) "Forfeitable property" means any profit, money, or proceeds, and any property, real or personal, tangible, or intangible, including any interest in, security of, claim against, or property or contractual right of any kind affording a source of influence over any enterprise, that is derived from, or that is traceable to any profit, money, or proceeds obtained directly or indirectly from, any medicaid fraud offense.

(C) "Beneficial interest" means any of the following:

(1) The interest of a person as a beneficiary under a trust in which the trustee holds title to personal or real property;

(2) The interest of a person as a beneficiary under any other trust arrangement under which any other person holds title to personal or real property for the benefit of such person;

(3) The interest of a person under any other form of express fiduciary arrangement under which any other person holds title to personal or real property for the benefit of such person.

"Beneficial interest" does not include the interest of a stockholder in a corporation or the interest of a partner in either a general or limited partnership.

(D) "Costs of investigation and prosecution" and "costs of investigation and litigation" mean all of the costs incurred by the state or a county or municipal corporation in the prosecution and investigation of the medicaid fraud offense in question, and includes, but is not limited to, the costs of resources and personnel.

(E) "Innocent person" includes any bona fide purchaser of property that allegedly is forfeitable property, including any person who establishes a valid claim to or interest in the property in accordance with division (F) of section 2933.73 of the Revised Code.

(F) "Personal property" means any personal property, any interest in personal property, or any right, including, but not limited to, bank accounts, debts, corporate stocks, patents, or copyrights. Personal property and any beneficial interest in personal property are deemed to be located where the trustee of the property, the personal property, or the instrument evidencing the right is located.

(G) "Real property" means any real property or any interest in real property, including, but not limited to, any lease of, or mortgage upon, real property. Real property and any beneficial interest in it is deemed to be located where the real property is located.

(H) "Trustee" means any of the following:

(1) Any person acting as trustee under a trust in which the trustee holds title to personal or real property;

(2) Any person who holds title to personal or real property for which any other person has a beneficial interest;

(3) Any successor trustee.

"Trustee" does not include an assignee or trustee for an insolvent debtor or an executor, administrator, administrator with the will annexed, testamentary trustee, guardian, or committee, appointed by, or under the control of, or accountable to, a court.

(1993 H 152, eff. 7–1–93)

2933.72 Orders to preserve reachability of forfeitable property

(A) At any time after an indictment is filed alleging a medicaid fraud offense, the prosecuting attorney who is prosecuting the case or the attorney general, if the attorney general is prosecuting the case, may file a motion requesting the court to issue an order to preserve the reachability of any property that may be forfeitable property. Upon the filing of the motion, the court, after giving notice to any person who will be affected by any order issued by the court pursuant to the motion, shall hold a hearing on the motion at which all affected persons have an opportunity to be heard and, upon a showing by the prosecuting attorney or attorney general by a preponderance of the evidence that the particular action is necessary to preserve the reachability of any property that may be subject to forfeiture and based upon the indictment, may enter a restraining order or injunction, require the execution of a satisfactory performance bond, or take any other necessary action, including the attachment of the property or the appointment of a receiver. The prosecuting attorney or attorney general is not required to show special or irreparable injury to obtain any court action pursuant to this division. Notwithstanding the Rules of Evidence, the court's order or injunction may be based on hearsay testimony.

(B) If no indictment has been filed alleging a medicaid fraud offense, the court may take any action specified in division (A) of this section if the prosecuting attorney for the county or the attorney general, in addition to the showing that would be required pursuant to division (A) of this section, also shows both of the following by a preponderance of the evidence:

(1) There is probable cause to believe that the property with respect to which the order is sought, in the event of a conviction, would be forfeitable property subject to forfeiture under section 2933.73 of the Revised Code;

(2) The requested order would not result in irreparable harm to the party against whom the order is to be entered that outweighs the need to preserve the reachability of the property.

No order entered pursuant to division (B) of this section shall be effective for more than ninety days, unless it is extended pursuant to the procedure provided in division (B) of this section by the court for good cause shown or an indictment is returned alleging that the property is forfeitable property subject to forfeiture.

(C) Upon application by the prosecuting attorney or attorney general, the court may grant a temporary restraining order to preserve the reachability of forfeitable property that is subject to forfeiture under section 2933.73 of the Revised Code without notice to any party, if all of the following occur:

(1) An indictment alleging that property is forfeitable property has been filed, or the court determines that there is probable cause to believe that property with respect to which the order is sought would be forfeitable property subject, in the event of a conviction, to forfeiture under section 2933.73 of the Revised Code;

(2) The property is in the possession or control of the party against whom the order is to be entered;

(3) The court determines that the nature of the property is such that it can be concealed, disposed of, or placed beyond the jurisdiction of the court before any party may be heard in opposition to the order.

A temporary restraining order granted without notice to any party under division (C) of this section shall expire within the time, not to exceed ten days, that the court fixes, unless extended for good cause shown or unless the party against whom it is entered consents to an extension for a longer period. If a temporary restraining order is granted under division (C) of this section without notice to any party, the court shall hold a hearing concerning the entry of an order under division (C) of this section at the earliest practicable time prior to the expiration of the temporary order.

(D) Following sentencing and the entry of a judgment against an offender that includes an order of forfeiture under section 2933.73 of the Revised Code, the court may enter a restraining order or injunction, require the execution of a satisfactory performance bond, or take any other action, including the appointment of a receiver, that the court determines to be proper to protect the interests of the state or an innocent person.

(1994 H 715, eff. 7–22–94; 1993 H 152, eff. 7–1–93)

2933.73 Forfeiture of property

(A) In addition to any other penalty or disposition authorized or required by law, if a person is convicted of or pleads guilty to any medicaid fraud offense, the trial court shall conduct a civil forfeiture hearing to determine whether any property identified in division (B) of this section should be forfeited to the state in relation to the offense. At the hearing, the offender who was convicted of or pleaded guilty to the medicaid fraud offense has the burden of proving, by a preponderance of the evidence, that the property in question is not forfeitable property in relation to the offense. If the offender does not prove by a preponderance of the evidence that the property in question is not forfeitable property in relation to the offense, the court shall issue an order specifying that the forfeitable property is forfeited to the state. If the offender proves by a preponderance of the evidence that the property in question is not forfeitable property in relation to the offense, the court shall not issue an order specifying that the forfeitable property is forfeited to the state and, if the property has been seized, shall order that it be returned to the offender.

(B) A court shall not issue an order under division (A) of this section specifying that forfeitable property is forfeited to the state unless one of the following applies:

(1) The indictment, count in the indictment, or information charging the medicaid fraud offense specifically identified the property as forfeitable property;

(2) The property was not reasonably foreseen to be forfeitable property at the time of the indictment, count in the indictment, or information charging the offense, provided that the prosecuting attorney or attorney general who prosecuted the offense gave prompt notice to the defendant of such property not reasonably foreseen to be forfeitable property when it is discovered to be forfeitable property.

(C) If any forfeitable property included in a forfeiture order issued under division (A) of this section cannot be located, has been sold to a bona fide purchaser for value, placed beyond the jurisdiction of the court, substantially diminished in value by the conduct of the defendant, or commingled with other property that cannot be divided without difficulty or undue injury to innocent persons, or otherwise is unreachable without undue injury to innocent persons, the court shall order forfeiture of any other reachable property of the defendant up to the value of the property that is unreachable.

(D) All property ordered forfeited pursuant to this section shall be held by the law enforcement agency that seized it for distribution or disposal pursuant to section 2933.74 of the Revised Code. The agency shall maintain an accurate record of each item of property so seized and held, which record shall include the date on which each item was seized, the manner and date of disposition by the agency, and if applicable, the name of the person who received the item; however, the record shall not identify or enable the identification of the individual officer who seized the property. The record is a public record open for inspection under section 149.43 of the Revised Code. Each law enforcement agency that seizes and holds in any calendar year any item of property that is ordered forfeited pursuant to this section shall prepare a report covering the calendar year that cumulates all of the information contained in all of the records kept by the agency pursuant to this division for that calendar year, and shall send the cumulative report, no later than the first day of March in the calendar year following the calendar year covered by the report, to the attorney general. Each such report so received by the attorney general is a public record open for inspection under section 149.43 of the Revised Code. The attorney general shall make copies of each such report so received, and, no later than the fifteenth day of April in the calendar year in which the reports were received, shall send a copy of each such report to the office of the president of the senate and the office of the speaker of the house of representatives.

(E) Notwithstanding the notice and procedure prescribed by division (F) of this section, an order of forfeiture entered under division (A) of this section shall authorize an appropriate law enforcement agency to seize the forfeitable property declared forfeited under this section upon the terms and conditions, relating to the time and manner of seizure, that the court determines proper.

(F)(1) Upon the entry of a forfeiture order under division (A) of this section, the court shall cause notice of the issuance of the order to be sent by certified mail, return receipt requested, to all persons known to have, or appearing to have, an interest in the property that was acquired prior to the filing of a medicaid fraud lien notice as authorized by section 2933.75 of the Revised Code. If the notices cannot be given to those persons in that manner, the court shall cause publication of the notice of the forfeiture order pursuant to the Rules of Civil Procedure.

(2) Within thirty days after receipt of a notice or after the date of publication of a notice under division (F)(1) of this section, any person, other than the offender who was convicted of or pleaded guilty to the medicaid fraud offense, who claims an interest in the forfeitable property that is subject to forfeiture may petition the court for a hearing to determine the validity of the claim. The petition shall be signed and sworn to by the petitioner and shall set forth the nature and extent of the petitioner's interest in the property, the date and circumstances of the petitioner's acquisition of the interest, any additional allegations support-ing the claim, and the relief sought. The petitioner shall furnish a copy of the petition to the prosecuting attorney or attorney general who prosecuted the offense in relation to which the forfeiture order was issued.

(3) The court, to the extent practicable and consistent with the interests of justice, shall hold the hearing described under division (F)(2) of this section within thirty days from the filing of the petition. The court may consolidate the hearings on all petitions filed by third party claimants under this section. At the hearing, the petitioner may testify and present evidence on his own behalf and cross-examine witnesses. The prosecuting attorney or attorney general who prosecuted the offense may present evidence and witnesses in rebuttal and in defense of the claim of the state to the property and cross-examine witnesses. The court, in making its determination, shall consider the testimony and evidence presented at the hearing and the relevant portions of the record of the criminal proceeding that resulted in the forfeiture order.

(4) If at a hearing held under division (F)(3) of this section, the court, by a preponderance of the evidence, determines either that the petitioner has a legal right, title, or interest in the property that, at the time of the commission of the acts giving rise to the forfeiture of the property, was vested in the petitioner and not in the offender or was superior to the right, title, or interest of the offender, or that the petitioner is a bona fide purchaser for value of the right, title, or interest in the property and was at the time of the purchase reasonably without cause to believe that the property was subject to forfeiture under this section, it shall amend, in accordance with its determination, the order of forfeiture to protect the rights of innocent persons.

(G) Except as provided in division (F) of this section, no person claiming an interest in forfeitable property that is subject to forfeiture under this section shall do either of the following:

(1) Intervene in a trial or appeal of a criminal case that involves the forfeiture of the property;

(2) File an action against the state concerning the validity of his alleged interest in the property subsequent to the filing of the indictment, count in the indictment, or information, that alleges that the property is subject to forfeiture under this section.

(H) As used in this section, "law enforcement agency" includes the state board of pharmacy.
(1994 H 715, eff. 7–22–94; 1993 H 152, eff. 7–1–93)

2933.74   Disposition of forfeited property

(A)(1) With respect to forfeitable property ordered forfeited under section 2933.73 of the Revised Code, the court that issued the order, upon petition of the prosecuting attorney or attorney general who prosecuted the case, may do any of the following:

(a) Authorize the prosecuting attorney or the attorney general to settle claims;

(b) Award compensation to persons who provide information that results in a forfeiture under section 2933.73 of the Revised Code;

(c) Take any other action to protect the rights of innocent persons that is in the interest of justice and that is consistent with the purposes of sections 2933.71 to 2933.75 of the Revised Code.

(2) The court shall maintain an accurate record of the actions it takes under division (A)(1) of this section with respect to the forfeitable property ordered forfeited. The record is a public record open for inspection under section 149.43 of the Revised Code.

(B)(1) Subject to division (A) of this section and notwithstanding any contrary provision of section 2933.41 of the Revised Code, the prosecuting attorney or attorney general who prosecuted the case shall order the disposal of forfeitable property ordered forfeited in any proceeding under section 2933.73 of the Revised Code as soon as feasible, making due provisions for the rights of innocent persons, by any of the following methods:

(a) Public sale;

(b) Transfer to a state governmental agency for official use;

(c) Sale or transfer to an innocent person;

(d) If the property is contraband and is not needed for evidence in any pending criminal or civil proceeding, pursuant to section 2933.41 or any other applicable section of the Revised Code.

(2) Any interest in personal or real property not disposed of pursuant to division (B) of this section and not exercisable by, or transferable for value to, the state shall expire and shall not revert to the person who was convicted of or pleaded guilty to the medicaid fraud offense. No person who was convicted of or pleaded guilty to the medicaid fraud offense and no person acting in concert with a person who was convicted of or pleaded guilty to the medicaid fraud offense is eligible to purchase forfeited property from the state.

(3) Upon application of a person, other than the person who was convicted of or pleaded guilty to the medicaid fraud offense or a person acting in concert with or on behalf of the person who was convicted of or pleaded guilty to the medicaid fraud offense, the court may restrain or stay the disposal of the forfeitable property pursuant to this division pending the conclusion of any appeal of the criminal case giving rise to the forfeiture or pending the determination of the validity of a claim to or interest in the property pursuant to division (F) of section 2933.73 of the Revised Code, if the applicant demonstrates that proceeding with the disposal of the property will result in irreparable injury, harm, or loss to him.

(4) The prosecuting attorney or attorney general who prosecuted the case shall maintain an accurate record of each item of property disposed of pursuant to division (B) of this section, which record shall include the date on which each item came into his custody, the manner and date of disposition, and, if applicable, the name of the person who received the item. The record shall not identify or enable the identification of the individual officer who seized the property, and the record is a public record open for inspection under section 149.43 of the Revised Code.

Each prosecuting attorney who disposes in any calendar year of any item of property pursuant to division (B) of this section shall prepare a report covering the calendar year that cumulates all of the information contained in all of the records he kept pursuant to this division for that calendar year and shall send the cumulative report, no later than the first day of March in the calendar year following the calendar year covered by the report, to the attorney general. No later than the first day of March in the calendar year following the calendar year covered by the report, the attorney general shall prepare a report covering the calendar year that cumulates all of the records he kept pursuant to this division for that calendar year. Each report received or prepared by the attorney general is a public record open for inspection under section 149.43 of the Revised Code. The attorney general shall send a copy of each prosecuting attorney's cumulative report and of his own cumulative report, no later than the fifteenth day of April in the calendar year following the calendar year covered by the report, to the president of the senate and the speaker of the house of representatives.

(C)(1) The proceeds of the sale of all forfeitable property ordered forfeited pursuant to section 2933.73 of the Revised Code shall be deposited into the state treasury and credited to the medicaid fraud investigation and prosecution fund, which is hereby created.

(2) The proceeds credited to the medicaid fraud investigation and prosecution fund pursuant to division (C)(1) of this section shall be disposed of in the following order:

(a) To the payment of the fees and costs of the forfeiture and sale, including expenses of seizure, maintenance, and custody of the property pending its disposition, advertising, and court costs;

(b) Except as otherwise provided in division (C)(2)(b) of this section, the remainder shall be paid to the law enforcement trust fund of the prosecuting attorney that is established pursuant to division (D)(1)(c) of section 2933.43 of the Revised Code or to the attorney general, and to the law enforcement trust fund of the county sheriff that is established pursuant to that division if the county sheriff substantially conducted the investigation, to the law enforcement trust fund of a municipal corporation that is established pursuant to that division if its police department substantially conducted the investigation, to the law enforcement trust fund of a township that is established pursuant to that division if the investigation was substantially conducted by a township police department, township police district police force, or office of a township constable, or to the law enforcement trust fund of a park district created pursuant to section 511.18 or 1545.01 of the Revised Code that is established pursuant to that division if the investigation was substantially conducted by its park district police force or law enforcement department. The prosecuting attorney or attorney general may decline to accept any of the remaining proceeds, and, if he so declines, they shall be applied to the fund described in division (C)(2)(b) of this section that relates to the appropriate law enforcement agency that substantially conducted the investigation.

If the state highway patrol substantially conducted the investigation, the director of budget and management shall transfer the remaining proceeds to the state highway patrol for deposit into the state highway patrol contraband, forfeiture, and other fund that is created by division (D)(1)(c) of section 2933.43 of the Revised Code. If the state board of pharmacy substantially conducted the investigation, the director shall transfer the remaining proceeds to the board for deposit into the board of pharmacy drug law enforcement fund that is created by division (B)(1) of section 4729.65 of the Revised Code. If a state law enforcement agency, other than the state highway patrol, the board, or the attorney general, substantially conducted the investigation, the director shall transfer the remaining proceeds to the treasurer of state for deposit into the peace officer training council fund that is created by division (D)(1)(c) of section 2933.43 of the Revised Code.

The remaining proceeds that are paid to the attorney general shall be used and expended only in relation to the investigation and prosecution of medicaid fraud offenses or the activities identified in section 109.85 of the Revised Code, and those that are paid to a law enforcement trust fund or that are deposited into the state highway patrol contraband, forfeiture, and other fund, the board of pharmacy drug law enforcement fund, or the peace officer training council fund pursuant to division (C)(2)(b) of this section shall be allocated, used, and expended only in accordance with division (D)(1)(c) of section 2933.43 of the Revised Code, only in accordance with a written internal control policy adopted under division (D)(3) of that section, and, if applicable, only in accordance with division (B)(1) of section 4729.65 of the Revised Code. The annual reports that pertain to the funds and that are required by divisions (D)(1)(c) and (3)(b) of section 2933.43 of the Revised Code also shall address the remaining proceeds that are paid or deposited into the funds pursuant to division (C)(2)(b) of this section.

(3) If more than one law enforcement agency substantially conducted the investigation, the court ordering the forfeiture shall equitably divide the remaining proceeds among the law enforcement agencies that substantially conducted the investigation, in the manner described in division (D)(2) of section 2933.43 of the Revised Code for the equitable division of contraband proceeds and forfeited moneys. The equitable shares of the proceeds so determined by the court shall be paid or deposited into the appropriate funds specified in division (C)(2)(b) of this section.

(D) As used in this section, "law enforcement agency" includes, but is not limited to, the state board of pharmacy.

(1994 H 715, eff. 7–22–94; 1993 H 152, eff. 7–1–93)

2933.75   Medicaid fraud liens

(A) Upon the institution of any criminal proceeding charging a medicaid fraud offense, the state, at any time during the pendency of the proceeding, may file a medicaid fraud lien notice with the county recorder of any county in which forfeitable property subject to forfeiture may be located. No fee shall be required for filing the notice. The recorder immediately shall record the notice pursuant to section 317.08 of the Revised Code.

(B) A medicaid fraud lien notice shall be signed by the prosecuting attorney or attorney general who will prosecute the case and who files the lien. The notice shall set forth all of the following information:

(1) The name of the person against whom the proceeding has been brought. The prosecuting attorney or attorney general who will prosecute the case may specify in the notice any aliases, names, or fictitious names under which the person may be known.

(2) If known to the prosecuting attorney or attorney general who will prosecute the case, the present residence and business addresses of the person or names set forth in the notice;

(3) A statement that a criminal proceeding for a medicaid fraud offense has been brought against the person named in the notice, the name of the county in which the proceeding has been brought, and the case number of the proceeding;

(4) A statement that the notice is being filed pursuant to this section;

(5) The name and address of the prosecuting attorney or attorney general filing the notice;

(6) A description of the real or personal property subject to the notice and of the interest in that property of the person named in the notice, to the extent the property and the interest of the person in it reasonably is known at the time the proceeding is instituted or at the time the notice is filed.

(C) A medicaid fraud lien notice shall apply only to one person and, to the extent applicable, any aliases, fictitious names, or other names, including names of corporations, partnerships, or other entities, to the extent permitted in this section. A separate medicaid fraud lien notice is required to be filed for any other person.

(D) Within seven days after the filing of each medicaid fraud lien notice, the prosecuting attorney or attorney general who files the notice shall furnish to the person named in the notice by certified mail, return receipt requested, to the last known business or residential address of the person, a copy of the recorded notice with a notation on it of any county in which the notice has been recorded. The failure of the prosecuting attorney or attorney general to furnish a copy of the notice under this section shall not invalidate or otherwise affect the medicaid fraud lien notice when the prosecuting attorney or attorney general did not know and could not reasonably ascertain the address of the person entitled to notice.

After receipt of a copy of the notice under this division, the person named in the notice may petition the court to authorize the person to post a surety bond in lieu of the lien or to otherwise modify the lien as the interests of justice may require. The bond shall be in an amount equal to the value of the property reasonably known to be subject to the notice and conditioned on the payment of any judgment and costs ordered in an action pursuant to section 2933.73 of the Revised Code up to the value of the bond.

(E) From the date of filing of a medicaid fraud lien notice, the notice creates a lien in favor of the state on any personal or real property or any beneficial interest in the property located in the county in which the notice is filed that then or subsequently is owned by the person named in the notice or under any of the names set forth in the notice.

The lien created in favor of the state is superior and prior to the interest of any other person in the personal or real property or beneficial interest in the property, if the interest is acquired subsequent to the filing of the notice.

(F) If a medicaid fraud lien notice has been filed, and if a forfeiture order is entered subsequent to a conviction or guilty plea in the criminal proceeding pursuant to section 2933.73 of the Revised Code in favor of the state, the interest of any person in the property that was acquired subsequent to the filing of the notice shall be subject to the notice and order of forfeiture.

(G) Upon the issuance of an order of forfeiture in favor of the state pursuant to section 2933.73 of the Revised Code, title of the state to the forfeited property shall do either of the following:

(1) In the case of real property, or a beneficial interest in it, relate back to the date of filing of the medicaid fraud lien notice in the county where the property or interest is located. If no medicaid fraud lien notice was filed, title of the state relates back to the date of the recording

of the order of forfeiture in the records of the county recorder of the county in which the real property or beneficial interest is located.

(2) In the case of personal property or a beneficial interest in it, relate back to the date on which the property or interest was seized by the state, or the date of filing of a medicaid fraud lien notice in the county in which the property or beneficial interest is located. If the property was not seized and no medicaid fraud lien notice was filed, title of the state relates back to the date of the recording of the order of forfeiture in the county in which the personal property or beneficial interest is located.

(H) If personal or real property, or a beneficial interest in it, that is forfeitable property and is subject to forfeiture pursuant to section 2933.73 of the Revised Code is conveyed, alienated, disposed of, or otherwise rendered unavailable for forfeiture after the filing of either a medicaid fraud lien notice, or a criminal proceeding for a medicaid fraud offense, whichever is earlier, the state may bring an action in any court of common pleas against the person named in the medicaid fraud lien notice or the defendant in the criminal proceeding to recover the value of the property or interest. The court shall enter final judgment against the person named in the notice or the defendant for an amount equal to the value of the property or interest together with investigative costs and attorney's fees incurred by the state in the action.

(I) If personal or real property, or a beneficial interest in it, that is forfeitable property and is subject to forfeiture pursuant to section 2933.73 of the Revised Code is alienated or otherwise transferred or disposed of after either the filing of a medicaid fraud lien notice, or the filing of a criminal proceeding for a medicaid fraud offense, whichever is earlier, the transfer or disposal is fraudulent as to the state and the state shall have all the rights granted a creditor under Chapter 1336. of the Revised Code.

(J) No trustee, who acquires actual knowledge that a medicaid fraud lien notice or a criminal proceeding for a medicaid fraud offense has been filed against any person for whom he holds legal or record title to personal or real property, shall recklessly fail to furnish promptly to the prosecuting attorney or attorney general who is prosecuting the case all of the following:

(1) The name and address of the person, as known to the trustee;

(2) The name and address, as known to the trustee, of all other persons for whose benefit the trustee holds title to the property;

(3) If requested by the prosecuting attorney or attorney general who is prosecuting the case, a copy of the trust agreement or other instrument under which the trustee holds title to the property.

Any trustee who fails to comply with division (J) of this section is guilty of failure to provide medicaid fraud lien information, a misdemeanor of the first degree.

(K) If a trustee transfers title to personal or real property after a medicaid fraud lien notice is filed against the property, the lien is filed in the county in which the property is located, and the lien names a person who holds a beneficial interest in the property, the trustee, if he has actual notice of the notice, shall be liable to the state for the greater of the following:

(1) The proceeds received directly by the person named in the notice as a result of the transfer;

(2) The proceeds received by the trustee as a result of the transfer and distributed to the person named in the notice;

(3) The fair market value of the interest of the person named in the notice in the property transferred.

However, if the trustee transfers property for at least its fair market value and holds the proceeds that otherwise would be paid or distributed to the beneficiary, or at the direction of the beneficiary or his designee, the liability of the trustee shall not exceed the amount of the proceeds held by the trustee.

(L) The filing of a medicaid fraud lien notice does not constitute a lien on the record title to personal or real property owned by the trustee, except to the extent the trustee is named in the notice.

The prosecuting attorney for the county or the attorney general may bring a civil action in any court of common pleas to recover from the trustee the amounts set forth in division (H) of this section. The county or state may recover investigative costs and attorney's fees incurred by the prosecuting attorney or the attorney general.

(M)(1) This section does not apply to any transfer by a trustee under a court order, unless the order is entered in an action between the trustee and the beneficiary.

(2) Unless the trustee has actual knowledge that a person owning a beneficial interest in the trust is named in a medicaid fraud lien notice, this section does not apply to either of the following:

(a) Any transfer by a trustee required under the terms of any trust agreement, if the agreement is a matter of public record before the filing of any medicaid fraud lien notice;

(b) Any transfer by a trustee to all of the persons who own a beneficial interest in the trust.

(N) The filing of a medicaid fraud lien notice does not affect the use to which personal or real property, or a beneficial interest in it, that is owned by the person named in the notice may be put or the right of the person to receive any proceeds resulting from the use and ownership, but not the sale, of the property, until a judgment of forfeiture is entered.

(O) The term of a medicaid fraud lien notice is five years from the date the notice is filed, unless a renewal notice has been filed by the prosecuting attorney of the county in which the property or interest is located or by the attorney general. The term of any renewal of a medicaid fraud lien notice granted by the court is five years from the date of its filing. A medicaid fraud lien notice may be renewed any number of times while a criminal proceeding for a medicaid fraud offense, or an appeal from such a proceeding, is pending.

(P) The prosecuting attorney or attorney general who files the medicaid fraud lien notice may terminate, in whole or part, the notice or release any personal or real property or beneficial interest in the property upon any terms that he determines are appropriate. Any termination or release shall be filed by the prosecuting attorney or attorney general with each county recorder with whom the notice was filed. No fee shall be imposed for the filing.

(Q) The acquittal in a criminal proceeding for a medicaid fraud offense of the person named in the medicaid fraud lien notice or the dismissal of a criminal proceeding for such an offense against the person named in the notice terminates the notice. In such a case, the filing of the notice has no effect.

A person named in a medicaid fraud lien notice may bring an action against the prosecuting attorney or attorney general who filed the notice, in the county where it was filed, seeking a release of the property subject to the notice or termination of the notice. In such a case, the court of common pleas promptly shall set a date for hearing, which shall be not less than five nor more than ten days after the action is filed. The order and a copy of the complaint shall be served on the prosecuting attorney or attorney general within three days after the action is filed. At the hearing, the court shall take evidence as to whether any personal or real property, or beneficial interest in it, that is owned by the person bringing the action is covered by the notice or otherwise is subject to forfeiture. If the person bringing the action shows by a preponderance of the evidence that the notice does not apply to him or that any personal or real property, or beneficial interest in it, that is owned by him is not subject to forfeiture, the court shall enter a judgment terminating the notice or releasing the personal or real property or beneficial interest from the notice.

At a hearing, the court may release from the notice any property or beneficial interest upon the posting of security, by the person against whom the notice was filed, in an amount equal to the value of the property or beneficial interest owned by the person.

The court promptly shall enter an order terminating a medicaid fraud lien notice or releasing any personal or real property or beneficial interest in the property, if a sale of the property or beneficial interest is pending and the filing of the notice prevents the sale. However, the proceeds of the sale shall be deposited with the clerk of the court, subject to the further order of the court.

(R) Notwithstanding any provision of this section, any person who has perfected a security interest in personal or real property or a beneficial interest in the property for the payment of an enforceable debt or other similar obligation prior to the filing of a medicaid fraud lien notice in reference to the property or interest may foreclose on the property or interest as otherwise provided by law. The foreclosure, insofar as practical, shall be made so that it otherwise will not interfere with a forfeiture under section 2933.73 of the Revised Code.

(1994 H 715, eff. 7–22–94; 1993 H 152, eff. 7–1–93)

PEN REGISTERS; TRAP AND TRACE DEVICES

2933.76 Order authorizing installation and use of pen register or trap and trace device

(A) As used in this section and section 2933.77 of the Revised Code, "electronic communication," "electronic communication service," "pen register," "trap and trace device," and "wire communication" have the same meanings as in section 2933.51 of the Revised Code.

(B) A judge of a court of common pleas, in accordance with this section, may issue an order authorizing or approving the installation and use, within the jurisdiction of the court, of a pen register or a trap and trace device to obtain information in connection with a criminal investigation.

(C) A law enforcement officer may make an application to a judge of a court of common pleas for an order authorizing the installation and use, within the jurisdiction of the court, of a pen register or a trap and trace device to obtain information in connection with a criminal investigation. The application shall be in writing and shall be under oath or affirmation. Each application shall contain all of the following:

(1) The name of the law enforcement officer making the application and the name of the law enforcement agency conducting the criminal investigation to which the application relates;

(2) The name, if known, of the person to whom the telephone or other line to which the pen register or trap and trace device is to be attached is leased or in whose name that telephone or other line is listed;

(3) The name, if known, of the person who is the subject of the criminal investigation to which the application relates;

(4) The number and, if known, the physical location of the telephone or other line to which the pen register or the trap and trace device is to be attached;

(5) A statement of the offense to which the information that is likely to be obtained by the installation and use of the pen register or trap and trace device relates;

(6) A certification by the law enforcement officer making the application that the information that is likely to be obtained by the installation and use of the pen register or trap and trace device is relevant to an ongoing criminal investigation being conducted by the law enforcement agency identified under division (C)(1) of this section.

(D)(1) The judge to whom an application is made under division (C) of this section shall issue and enter an order authorizing the installation and use of a pen register or a trap and trace device if the judge finds that the information relating to an offense that is likely to be obtained by the installation and use of the pen register or trap and trace device is relevant to an ongoing criminal investigation being conducted by the law enforcement agency identified under division (C)(1) of this section. In the order, the judge shall specify a finding with respect to each of the items required by divisions (C)(1) to (6) of this section to be included in the application.

(2) If the law enforcement officer so requests, the order shall direct the appropriate provider of wire or electronic communication service, landlord, custodian, or other person to furnish the law enforcement officer with all information, facilities, and technical assistance necessary to accomplish the installation and operation of a pen register or trap and trace device unobtrusively and with a minimum of interference of service to the person with respect to whom the installation and operation are to take place. The order further shall direct the person who owns or leases the telephone or other line to which the pen register or trap and trace device is to be attached, or the provider of wire or electronic communication service, landlord, custodian, or other person who is ordered under division (D)(2) of this section to provide

information, facilities, or technical assistance, not to disclose the existence of the criminal investigation or of the installation and use of the pen register or trap and trace device to the listed subscriber of the telephone or other line or to another person unless or until otherwise ordered by the court. The order shall be sealed until otherwise ordered by the court.

(E) An order issued pursuant to division (D) of this section shall authorize the installation and use of a pen register or a trap and trace device for a period not to exceed sixty days. The court may grant an extension of the sixty-day period upon application for an order in accordance with division (C) of this section and upon the judicial findings required by division (D)(1) of this section. An extension of an order issued under this division shall be in effect for a period not to exceed sixty days. The court may order further extensions of the sixty-day extended period upon compliance with this division.

(F) A good faith reliance on a court order issued under this section, a legislative authorization, or a statutory authorization is a complete defense against any claim in a civil action or any charge in a criminal action alleging a violation of the requirements of this section or section 2933.77 of the Revised Code.

(1996 H 181, eff. 6–13–96)

2933.77 Assistance by provider of electronic communication service, landlord, or custodian

(A) If an order issued under section 2933.76 of the Revised Code authorizing the installation and use of a pen register or a trap and trace device directs a provider of wire or electronic communication service, landlord, custodian, or other person to furnish information, facilities, and technical assistance to accomplish the installation and operation of the pen register or trap and trace device, that provider, landlord, custodian, or other person, in accordance with the order, shall furnish the law enforcement officer with all information, facilities, and technical assistance necessary to accomplish the installation and operation of the pen register or trap and trace device unobtrusively and with a minimum of interference with the service accorded by the provider, landlord, custodian, or other person to the person with respect to whom the installation and operation are to take place.

(B) The law enforcement agency conducting the criminal investigation to which the order issued under section 2933.76 of the Revised Code for the installation and use of a pen register or a trap and trace device relates shall provide reasonable compensation to a provider of wire or electronic communication service, landlord, custodian, or other person who furnishes facilities or technical assistance in accordance with the order for any reasonable expenses the provider, landlord, custodian, or other person incurs in furnishing the facilities or technical assistance.

(C) A provider of wire or electronic communication service, an officer, employee, or agent of that provider, or a landlord, custodian, or other specified person is immune from civil or criminal liability in any action that arises from the provision of information, facilities, or technical assistance in accordance with the terms of an order of a court issued under section 2933.76 of the Revised Code.

(1996 H 181, eff. 6–13–96)

ARREST, CITATION, AND DISPOSITION ALTERNATIVES

DEFINITIONS

DEFINITIONS

2935.01 Definitions

As used in this chapter:

(A) "Magistrate" has the same meaning as in section 2931.01 of the Revised Code.

(B) "Peace officer" includes a sheriff, deputy sheriff, marshal, deputy marshal, member of the organized police department of any municipal corporation, including a member of the organized police department of a municipal corporation in an adjoining state serving in Ohio under a contract pursuant to section 737.04 of the Revised Code, member of a police force employed by a metropolitan housing authority under division (D) of section 3735.31 of the Revised Code, state university law enforcement officer appointed under section 3345.04 of the Revised Code, liquor control investigator or food stamp trafficking agent of the department of

337

public safety, Ohio veterans' home policeman appointed under section 5907.02 of the Revised Code, police constable of any township, and police officer of a township or joint township police district, and, for the purpose of arrests within those areas, and for the purposes of Chapter 5503. of the Revised Code, and the filing of and service of process relating to those offenses witnessed or investigated by them, includes the superintendent and troopers of the state highway patrol.

(C) "Prosecutor" includes the county prosecuting attorney, any assistant prosecutor designated to assist him, and, in the case of courts inferior to courts of common pleas, includes the village solicitor, city director of law, or similar chief legal officer of a municipal corporation, any such officer's assistants, or any attorney designated by the prosecuting attorney of the county to appear for the prosecution of a given case.

(D) "Offense," except where the context specifically indicates otherwise, includes felonies, misdemeanors, and violations of ordinances of municipal corporations and other public bodies authorized by law to adopt penal regulations.

(1995 S 162, eff. 10–29–95; 1991 S 144, eff. 8–8–91; 1991 H 77; 1988 H 708, § 1)

ARREST

2935.02   Accused may be arrested in any county

If an accused person flees from justice, or is not found in the county where a warrant for his arrest was issued, the officer holding the same may pursue and arrest him in any county in this state, and convey him before the magistrate or court of the county having cognizance of the case.

If such warrant directs the removal of the accused to the county in which the offense was committed, the officer holding the warrant shall deliver the accused to a court or magistrate of such county.

The necessary expense of such removal and reasonable compensation for his time and trouble, shall be paid to such officer out of the treasury of such county, upon the allowance and order of the county auditor.

(1953 H 1, eff. 10–1–53; GC 13432–10)

2935.03   Arrest and detention until warrant can be obtained

(A) A sheriff, deputy sheriff, marshal, deputy marshal, municipal police officer, township constable, police officer of a township or joint township police district, member of a police force employed by a metropolitan housing authority under division (D) of section 3735.31 of the Revised Code, state university law enforcement officer appointed under section 3345.04 of the Revised Code, or Ohio veterans' home policeman appointed under section 5907.02 of the Revised Code shall arrest and detain, until a warrant can be obtained, a person found violating, within the limits of the political subdivision, metropolitan housing authority housing project, college, university, or Ohio veterans' home in which the peace officer is appointed, employed, or elected, a law of this state, an ordinance of a municipal corporation, or a resolution of a township.

(B)(1) When there is reasonable ground to believe that an offense of violence, the offense of criminal child enticement as defined in section 2905.05 of the Revised Code, the offense of public indecency as defined in section 2907.09 of the Revised Code, the offense of domestic violence as defined in section 2919.25 of the Revised Code, the offense of violating a protection order or consent agreement as defined in section 2919.27 of the Revised Code, the offense of menacing by stalking as defined in section 2903.211 of the Revised Code, the offense of aggravated trespass as defined in section 2911.211 of the Revised Code, a theft offense as defined in section 2913.01 of the Revised Code, or a felony drug abuse offense as defined in section 2925.01 of the Revised Code, has been committed within the limits of the political subdivision, metropolitan housing authority housing project, college, university, or Ohio veterans' home in which the peace officer is appointed, employed, or elected, a sheriff, deputy sheriff, marshal, deputy marshal, municipal police officer, township constable, police officer of a township or joint township police district, member of a police force employed by a metropolitan housing authority under division (D) of section 3735.31 of the Revised Code, state university law enforcement officer appointed under section 3345.04 of the Revised Code, or Ohio veterans' home policeman appointed under section 5907.02 of the Revised Code may arrest and detain until a warrant can be obtained any person whom he has reasonable cause to believe is guilty of the violation.

(2) For purposes of division (B)(1) of this section, the execution of any of the following constitutes reasonable ground to believe that the offense alleged in the statement was committed and reasonable cause to believe that the person alleged in the statement to have committed the offense is guilty of the violation:

(a) A written statement by a person alleging that an alleged offender has committed the offense of menacing by stalking or aggravated trespass;

(b) A written statement by the administrator of the interstate compact on mental health appointed under section 5119.51 of the Revised Code alleging that a person who had been hospitalized, institutionalized, or confined in any facility under an order made pursuant to or under authority of section 2945.37, 2945.371, 2945.38, 2945.39, or 2945.40 of the Revised Code has escaped from the facility, from confinement in a vehicle for transportation to or from the facility, or from supervision by an employee of the facility that is incidental to hospitalization, institutionalization, or confinement in the facility and that occurs outside of the facility, in violation of section 2921.34 of the Revised Code;

(c) A written statement by the administrator of any facility in which a person has been hospitalized, institutionalized, or confined under an order made pursuant to or under authority of section 2945.37, 2945.371, 2945.38, 2945.39, or 2945.40 of the Revised Code alleging that the person has escaped from the facility, from confinement in a vehicle for transportation to or from the facility, or from supervision by an employee of the facility that is incidental to hospitalization, institutionalization, or confinement in the facility and that occurs outside of the facility, in violation of section 2921.34 of the Revised Code.

(3)(a) For purposes of division (B)(1) of this section, a peace officer described in that division has reasonable grounds to believe that the offense of domestic violence or the offense of violating a protection order or consent agreement has been committed and reasonable cause to believe that a particular person is guilty of committing the offense if any of the following occurs:

(i) A person executes a written statement alleging that the person in question has committed the offense of domestic violence or the offense of violating a protection order or consent agreement against the person who executes the statement or against a child of the person who executes the statement.

(ii) No written statement of the type described in division (B)(3)(a)(i) of this section is executed, but the peace officer, based upon his own knowledge and observation of the facts and circumstances of the alleged incident of the offense of domestic violence or the alleged incident of the offense of violating a protection order or consent agreement or based upon any other information, including, but not limited to, any reasonably trustworthy information given to him by the alleged victim of the alleged incident of the offense or any witness of the alleged incident of the offense, concludes that there are reasonable grounds to believe that the offense of domestic violence or the offense of violating a protection order or consent agreement has been committed and reasonable cause to believe that the person in question is guilty of committing the offense.

(iii) No written statement of the type described in division (B)(3)(a)(i) of this section is executed, but the peace officer witnessed the person in question commit the offense of domestic violence or the offense of violating a protection order or consent agreement.

(b) If pursuant to division (B)(3)(a) of this section a peace officer has reasonable grounds to believe that the offense of domestic violence or the offense of violating a protection order or consent agreement has been committed and reasonable cause to believe that a particular person is guilty of committing the offense, it is the preferred course of action in this state that the officer arrest and detain that person pursuant to division (B)(1) of this section until a warrant can be obtained.

If pursuant to division (B)(3)(a) of this section a peace officer has reasonable grounds to believe that the offense of domestic violence or the offense of violating a protection order or consent agreement has been committed and reasonable cause to believe that family or household members have committed the offense against each other, it is the preferred course of action in this state that the officer, pursuant to division (B)(1) of this section, arrest and detain until a warrant can be obtained the family or household member who committed the offense and whom the officer has reasonable cause to believe is the primary physical aggressor. There is no preferred course of action in this state regarding any other family or household member who committed the offense and whom the officer does not have reasonable cause to believe is the primary physical aggressor, but, pursuant to division (B)(1) of this section, the peace officer may arrest and detain until a warrant can be obtained any other family or household member who committed the offense and whom the officer does not have reasonable cause to believe is the primary physical aggressor.

(c) If a peace officer described in division (B)(1) of this section does not arrest and detain a person whom the officer has reasonable cause to believe committed the offense of domestic violence or the offense of violating a protection order or consent agreement when it is the preferred course of action in this state pursuant to division (B)(3)(b) of this section that the officer arrest that person, the officer shall articulate in his written report of the incident required by section 2935.032 of the Revised Code a clear statement of his reasons for not arresting and detaining that person until a warrant can be obtained.

(d) In determining for purposes of division (B)(3)(b) of this section which family or household member is the primary physical aggressor in a situation in which family or household members have committed the offense of domestic violence or the offense of violating a protection order or consent agreement against each other, a peace officer described in division (B)(1) of this section, in addition to any other relevant circumstances, should consider all of the following:

(i) Any history of domestic violence or of any other violent acts by either person involved in the alleged offense that the officer reasonably can ascertain;

(ii) Whether the alleged violence was caused by a person acting in self-defense;

(iii) Each person's fear of physical harm, if any, resulting from the other person's threatened use of force against any person or resulting from the other person's use or history of the use of force against any person, and the reasonableness of that fear;

(iv) The comparative severity of any injuries suffered by the persons involved in the alleged offense.

(e)(i) A peace officer described in division (B)(1) of this section shall not require, as a prerequisite to arresting or charging a person who has committed the offense of domestic violence or the offense of violating a protection order or consent agreement, that the victim of the offense specifically consent to the filing of charges against the person who has committed the offense or sign a complaint against the person who has committed the offense.

(ii) If a person is arrested for or charged with committing the offense of domestic violence or the offense of violating a protection order or consent agreement and if the victim of the offense does not cooperate with the involved law enforcement or prosecuting authorities in the prosecution of the offense or, subsequent to the arrest or the filing of the charges, informs the involved law enforcement or prosecuting authorities that the victim does not wish the prosecution of the offense to continue or wishes to drop charges against the alleged offender relative to the offense, the involved prosecuting authorities, in determining whether to continue with the prosecution of the offense or whether to dismiss charges against the alleged offender relative to the offense and notwithstanding the victim's failure to cooperate or the victim's wishes, shall consider all facts and circumstances that are relevant to the offense, including, but not limited to, the statements and observations of the peace officers who responded to the incident that resulted in the arrest or filing of the charges and of all witnesses to that incident.

(f) In determining pursuant to divisions (B)(3)(a) to (g) of this section whether to arrest a person pursuant to division (B)(1) of this section, a peace officer described in division (B)(1) of this section shall not consider as a factor any possible shortage of cell space at the detention facility to which the person will be taken subsequent to his arrest or any possibility that the person's arrest might cause, contribute to, or exacerbate overcrowding at that detention facility or at any other detention facility.

(g) If a peace officer described in division (A)(1) of this section intends to arrest a person pursuant to division (A)(2) of this section or a peace officer described in division (B)(1) of this section intends pursuant to divisions (B)(3)(a) to (g) of this section to arrest a person pursuant to division (B)(1) of this section and if in either case the officer is unable to do so because the person is not present, the officer promptly shall seek a warrant for the arrest of the person.

(h) If a peace officer described in division (B)(1) of this section responds to a report of an alleged incident of the offense of domestic violence or an alleged incident of the offense of violating a protection order or consent agreement and if the circumstances of the incident involved the use or threatened use of a deadly weapon or any person involved in the incident brandished a deadly weapon during or in relation to the incident, the deadly weapon that was used, threatened to be used, or brandished constitutes contraband, and, to the extent possible, the officer shall seize the deadly weapon as contraband pursuant to section 2933.43 of the Revised Code. Upon the seizure of a deadly weapon pursuant to this division, section 2933.43 of the Revised Code shall apply regarding the treatment and disposition of the deadly weapon. For purposes of that section, the "underlying criminal offense" that was the basis of the seizure of a deadly weapon under this division and to which the deadly weapon had a relationship is any of the following that is applicable:

(i) The alleged incident of the offense of domestic violence or the alleged incident of the offense of violating a protection order or consent agreement to which the officer who seized the deadly weapon responded;

(ii) Any offense that arose out of the same facts and circumstances as the report of the alleged incident of the offense of domestic violence or the alleged incident of the offense of violating a protection order or consent agreement to which the officer who seized the deadly weapon responded.

(4) If, in the circumstances described in divisions (B)(3)(a) to (g) of this section, a peace officer described in division (B)(1) of this section arrests and detains a person pursuant to division (B)(1) of this section, or if, pursuant to division (B)(3)(h) of this section, a peace officer described in division (B)(1) of this section seizes a deadly weapon, the officer, to the extent described in and in accordance with section 9.86 or 2744.03 of the Revised Code, is immune in any civil action for damages for injury, death, or loss to person or property that arises from or is related to the arrest and detention or the seizure.

(C) When there is reasonable ground to believe that a violation of division (A), (B), or (C) of section 4506.15 or a violation of section 4511.19 of the Revised Code has been committed by a person operating a motor vehicle subject to regulation by the public utilities commission of Ohio under Title XLIX of the Revised Code, a peace officer with authority to enforce that provision of law may stop or detain the person whom he has reasonable cause to believe was operating the motor vehicle in violation of the division or section and, after investigating the circumstances surrounding the operation of the vehicle, may arrest and detain the person.

(D) If a sheriff, deputy sheriff, marshal, deputy marshal, municipal police officer, member of a police force employed by a metropolitan housing authority under division (D) of section 3735.31 of the Revised Code, constable, police officer of a township or joint township police district, or state university law enforcement officer appointed under section 3345.04 of the Revised Code is authorized by division (A) or (B) of this section to arrest and detain, within the limits of the political subdivision, metropolitan housing authority housing project, college, or university in which he is appointed, employed, or elected, a person until a warrant can be obtained, the peace officer may, outside the limits of the political subdivision, metropolitan housing authority housing project, college, or university in which he is appointed, employed, or elected, pursue, arrest, and detain that person until a warrant can be obtained if all of the following apply:

(1) The pursuit takes place without unreasonable delay after the offense is committed.

(2) The pursuit is initiated within the limits of the political subdivision, metropolitan housing authority housing project, college, or university in which the peace officer is appointed, employed, or elected.

(3) The offense involved is a felony, a misdemeanor of the first degree or a substantially equivalent municipal ordinance, a misdemeanor of the second degree or a substantially equivalent municipal ordinance, or any offense for which points are chargeable pursuant to division (G) of section 4507.021 of the Revised Code.

(E) In addition to the authority granted under division (A) or (B) of this section:

(1) A sheriff or deputy sheriff may arrest and detain, until a warrant can be obtained, any person found violating section 4503.11, 4503.21, or 4549.01, sections 4549.08 to 4549.12, section 4549.62, or Chapter 4511. or 4513. of the Revised Code on the portion of any street or highway that is located immediately adjacent to the boundaries of the county in which the sheriff or deputy sheriff is elected or appointed.

(2) A member of the police force of a township police district created under section 505.48 of the Revised Code, a member of the police force of a joint township police district created under section 505.481 of the Revised Code, and a township constable appointed in accordance with section 509.01 of the Revised Code, who has received a certificate from the Ohio peace officer training council under section 109.75 of the Revised Code may arrest and detain, until a warrant can be obtained, any person found violating any section or chapter of the Revised Code listed in division (E)(1) of this section, other than sections 4513.33 and 4513.34 of the Revised Code, on the portion of any street or highway that is located immediately adjacent to the boundaries of the township police district or joint township police district, in the case of a member of a township police district or joint township police district police force, or the unincorporated territory of the township, in the case of a township constable. However, if the population of the township that created the township police district served by the member's police force, or the townships that created the joint township police district served by the member's police force, or the township that is served by the township constable, is sixty thousand or less, the member of the township police district or joint police district police force or the township constable may not make an arrest under this division on a state highway that is included as part of the interstate system.

(3) A police officer or village marshal appointed, elected, or employed by a municipal corporation may arrest and detain, until a warrant can be obtained, any person found violating any section or chapter of the Revised Code listed in division (E)(1) of this section on the portion of any street or highway that is located immediately adjacent to the boundaries of the municipal corporation in which the police officer or village marshal is appointed, elected, or employed.

(F)(1) A department of mental health special policeman or a department of mental retardation and developmental disabilities special policeman may arrest without a warrant and detain until a warrant can be obtained any person found committing on the premises of any institution under the jurisdiction of the particular department a misdemeanor under a law of the state.

A department of mental health special policeman or a department of mental retardation and developmental disabilities special policeman may arrest without a warrant and detain until a warrant can be obtained any person who has been hospitalized, institutionalized, or confined in an institution under the jurisdiction of the particular department pursuant to or under authority of section 2945.37, 2945.371, 2945.38, 2945.39, or 2945.40 of the Revised Code and who is found committing on the premises of any institution under the jurisdiction of the particular department a violation of section 2921.34 of the Revised Code that involves an escape from the premises of the institution.

(2)(a) If a department of mental health special policeman or a department of mental retardation and developmental disabilities special policeman finds any person who has been hospitalized, institutionalized, or confined in an institution under the jurisdiction of the particular department pursuant to or under authority of section 2945.37, 2945.371, 2945.38, 2945.39, or 2945.40 of the Revised Code committing a violation of section 2921.34 of the Revised Code that involves an escape from the premises of the institution, or if there is reasonable ground to believe that a violation of section 2921.34 of the Revised Code has been committed that involves an escape from the premises of an institution under the jurisdiction of the department of mental health or the department of mental retardation and developmental disabilities and if a department of mental health special policeman or a department of mental retardation and developmental disabilities special policeman has reasonable cause to believe that a particular person who has been hospitalized, institutionalized, or confined in the institution pursuant to or under authority of section 2945.37, 2945.371, 2945.38, 2945.39, or 2945.40 of the Revised Code is guilty of the violation, the special policeman, outside of the premises of the institution, may pursue, arrest, and detain that person for that violation of section 2921.34 of the Revised Code, until a warrant can be obtained, if both of the following apply:

(i) The pursuit takes place without unreasonable delay after the offense is committed.

(ii) The pursuit is initiated within the premises of the institution from which the violation of section 2921.34 of the Revised Code occurred.

(b) For purposes of division (F)(2)(a) of this section, the execution of a written statement by the administrator of the institution in which a person had been hospitalized, institutionalized, or confined pursuant to or under authority of section 2945.37, 2945.371, 2945.38, 2945.39, or 2945.40 of the Revised Code alleging that the person has escaped from the premises of the institution in violation of section 2921.34 of the Revised Code constitutes reasonable ground to believe that the violation was committed and reasonable cause to believe that the person alleged in the statement to have committed the offense is guilty of the violation.

(G) As used in this section:

(1) A "department of mental health special policeman" means a special policeman of the department of mental health designated under section 5119.14 of the Revised Code who is certified by the Ohio peace officer training council under section 109.77 of the Revised Code as having successfully completed an approved peace officer basic training program.

(2) A "department of mental retardation and developmental disabilities special policeman" means a special policeman of the department of mental retardation and developmental disabilities designated under section 5123.13 of the Revised Code who is certified by the Ohio peace officer training council under section 109.77 of the Revised Code as having successfully completed an approved peace officer basic training program.

(3) "Deadly weapon" has the same meaning as in section 2923.11 of the Revised Code.

(4) "Family or household member" has the same meaning as in section 2919.25 of the Revised Code.

(5) "Street" or "highway" has the same meaning as in section 4511.01 of the Revised Code.

(6) "Interstate system" has the same meaning as in section 5516.01 of the Revised Code.

(1994 H 335, eff. 12–9–94; 1994 S 82, eff. 5–4–94; 1993 H 42, eff. 2–9–94; 1992 H 536; 1991 H 77; 1990 H 669, H 88; 1988 H 708, § 1)

2935.031 Agencies employing persons with arrest authority to adopt motor vehicle pursuit policies

Any agency, instrumentality, or political subdivision of the state that employs a sheriff, deputy sheriff, constable, marshal, deputy marshal, police officer, member of a metropolitan housing authority police force, state university law enforcement officer, or Ohio veterans' home policeman with arrest authority under section 2935.03 of the Revised Code or that employs other persons with arrest authority under the Revised Code, shall adopt a policy for the pursuit in a motor vehicle of any person who violates a law of this state or an ordinance of a municipal corporation. The chief law enforcement officer or other chief official of the agency, instrumentality, or political subdivision shall formally advise each peace officer or other person with arrest authority it employs of the pursuit policy adopted by that agency, instrumentality, or political subdivision pursuant to this section.

(1989 S 49, eff. 11–3–89)

2935.032 Domestic violence arrest policies

(A) Not later than ninety days after the effective date of this section, each agency, instrumentality, or political subdivision that is served by any peace officer described in division (B)(1) of section 2935.03 of the Revised Code shall adopt, in accordance with division (E) of this section, written policies, written procedures implementing the policies, and other written procedures for the peace officers who serve it to follow in implementing division (B)(3) of section 2935.03 of the Revised Code and for their appropriate response to each report of an alleged incident of the offense of domestic violence or an alleged incident of the offense of violating a protection order or consent agreement. The policies and procedures shall conform to and be consistent with the provisions of divisions (B)(1) and (B)(3) of section 2935.03 of the Revised Code and divisions (B) to (D) of this section. Each policy adopted under this division shall include, but not be limited to, all of the following:

(1) Provisions specifying that, if a peace officer who serves the agency, instrumentality, or political subdivision responds to an alleged incident of the offense of domestic violence, an alleged incident of the offense of violating a protection order or consent agreement, or an alleged incident of any other offense, both of the following apply:

(a) If the officer determines that there are reasonable grounds to believe that a person knowingly caused serious physical harm to another or knowingly caused or attempted to cause physical harm to another by means of a deadly weapon or dangerous ordnance, as defined in section 2923.11 of the Revised Code, then, regardless of whether the victim of the offense was a family or household member of the offender, the officer shall treat the incident as felonious assault, shall consider the offender to have committed and the victim to have been the victim of felonious assault, shall consider the offense that was committed to have been felonious assault in determining the manner in which the offender should be treated, and shall comply with whichever of the following is applicable:

(i) Unless the officer has reasonable cause to believe that, during the incident, the offender who committed the felonious assault and one or more other persons committed offenses against each other, the officer shall arrest the offender who committed the felonious assault pursuant to section 2935.03 of the Revised Code and shall detain him pursuant to that section until a warrant can be obtained, and the arrest shall be for felonious assault.

(ii) If the officer has reasonable cause to believe that, during the incident, the offender who committed the felonious assault and one or more other persons committed offenses against each other, the officer shall determine in accordance with division (B)(3)(d) of section 2935.03 of the Revised Code which of those persons is the primary physical aggressor. If the offender who committed the felonious assault is the primary physical aggressor, the officer shall arrest that offender for felonious assault pursuant to section 2935.03 of the Revised Code and shall detain him pursuant to that section until a warrant can be obtained, and the officer is not required to arrest but may arrest pursuant to section 2935.03 of the Revised Code any other person who committed an offense but who is not the primary physical aggressor. If the offender who committed the felonious assault is not the primary physical aggressor, the officer is not required to arrest that offender or any other person who committed an offense during the incident but may arrest any of them pursuant to section 2935.03 of the Revised Code and detain them pursuant to that section until a warrant can be obtained.

(b) If the officer determines that there are reasonable grounds to believe that a person, while under the influence of sudden passion or in a sudden fit of rage, either of which is brought on by serious provocation occasioned by the victim that is reasonably sufficient to incite the person into using deadly force, knowingly caused serious physical harm to another or knowingly caused or attempted to cause physical harm to another by means of a deadly weapon or dangerous ordnance, as defined in section 2923.11 of the Revised Code, then, regardless of whether the victim of the offense was a family or household member of the offender, the officer shall treat the incident as aggravated assault, shall consider the offender to have committed and the victim to have been the victim of aggravated assault, shall consider the offense that was committed to have been aggravated assault in determining the manner in which the offender should be treated, and shall comply with whichever of the following is applicable:

(i) Unless the officer has reasonable cause to believe that, during the incident, the offender who committed the aggravated assault and one or more other persons committed offenses against each other, the officer shall arrest the offender who committed the aggravated assault pursuant to section 2935.03 of the Revised Code and shall detain him pursuant to that section until a warrant can be obtained, and the arrest shall be for aggravated assault.

(ii) If the officer has reasonable cause to believe that, during the incident, the offender who committed the aggravated assault and one or more other persons committed offenses against each other, the officer shall determine in accordance with division (B)(3)(d) of section 2935.03 of the Revised Code which of those persons is the primary physical aggressor. If the offender who committed the aggravated assault is the primary physical aggressor, the officer shall arrest that offender for aggravated assault pursuant to section 2935.03 of the Revised Code and shall detain him pursuant to that section until a warrant can be obtained, and the officer is not required to arrest but may arrest pursuant to section 2935.03 of the Revised Code any other person who committed an offense but who is not the primary physical aggressor. If the offender who committed the aggravated assault is not the primary physical aggressor, the officer is not required to arrest that offender or any other person who committed an offense during the incident but may arrest any of them pursuant to section 2935.03 of the Revised Code and detain them pursuant to that section until a warrant can be obtained.

(2) Provisions requiring the peace officers who serve the agency, instrumentality, or political subdivision to do all of the following:

(a) Respond without undue delay to a report of an alleged incident of the offense of domestic violence or the offense of domestic violence or the offense of violating a protection order or consent agreement;

(b) If the alleged offender has been granted pretrial release from custody on a prior charge of the offense of domestic violence or the offense of violating a protection order or consent agreement and has violated one or more conditions of that pretrial release, document the facts and circumstances of the violation in the report to the law enforcement agency he serves that he makes pursuant to division (D) of this section;

(c) Separate the victim of the offense of domestic violence or the offense of violating a protection order or consent agreement and the alleged offender, conduct separate interviews with the victim and the alleged offender in separate locations, and take a written statement from the victim that indicates the frequency and severity of any prior incidents of physical abuse of the victim by the alleged offender, the number of times the victim has called peace officers for assistance, and the disposition of those calls, if known;

(d) Comply with divisions (B)(1) and (B)(3) of section 2935.03 of the Revised Code and with divisions (B), (C), and (D) of this section.

(3) Sanctions to be imposed upon a peace officer who serves the agency, instrumentality, or political subdivision and who fails to comply with any provision in the policy or with division (B)(1) or (B)(3) of section 2935.03 of the Revised Code or division (B), (C), or (D) of this section.

(4) Examples of reasons that a peace officer may consider for not arresting and detaining until a warrant can be obtained a person who allegedly committed the offense of domestic violence or the offense of violating a protection order or consent agreement when it is the preferred course of action in this state that the officer arrest the alleged offender, as described in division (B)(3)(b) of section 2935.03 of the Revised Code.

(B)(1) Nothing in this section or in division (B)(1) or (B)(3) of section 2935.03 of the Revised Code precludes an agency, instrumentality, or political subdivision that is served by any peace officer described in division (B)(1) of section 2935.03 of the Revised Code from including in the policy it adopts under division (A) of this section either of the following types of provisions:

(a) A provision that requires the peace officers who serve it, if they have reasonable grounds to believe that the offense of domestic violence or the offense of violating a protection order or consent agreement has been committed within the limits of the jurisdiction of the agency, instrumentality, or political subdivision and reasonable cause to believe that a particular person committed the offense, to arrest the alleged offender;

(b) A provision that does not require the peace officers who serve it, if they have reasonable grounds to believe that the offense of domestic violence or the offense of violating a protection order or consent agreement has been committed within the limits of the jurisdiction of the agency, instrumentality, or political subdivision and reasonable cause to believe that a particular person committed the offense, to arrest the alleged offender, but that grants the officers less discretion in those circumstances in deciding whether to arrest the alleged offender than peace officers are granted by divisions (B)(1) and (B)(3) of section 2935.03 of the Revised Code.

(2) If an agency, instrumentality, or political subdivision that is served by any peace officer described in division (B)(1) of section 2935.03 of the Revised Code includes in the policy it adopts under division (A) of this section a provision of the type described in division (B)(1)(a) or (b) of this section, the peace officers who serve the agency, instrumentality, or political subdivision shall comply with the provision in making arrests authorized under division (B)(1) of section 2935.03 of the Revised Code.

(C) When a peace officer described in division (B)(1) of section 2935.03 of the Revised Code investigates a report of an alleged incident of the offense of domestic violence or an alleged incident of the offense of violating a protection order or consent agreement, the officer shall do all of the following:

(1) Complete a domestic violence report in accordance with division (D) of this section;

(2) Advise the victim of the availability of a temporary protection order pursuant to section 2919.26 of the Revised Code or a protection order or consent agreement pursuant to section 3113.31 of the Revised Code;

(3) Give the victim the officer's name, the officer's badge number if the officer has a badge and the badge has a number, the report number for the incident if a report number is available at the time of the officer's investigation, a telephone number that the victim can call for information about the case, the telephone number of a domestic violence shelter in the area, and information on any local victim advocate program.

(D) A peace officer who investigates a report of an alleged incident of the offense of domestic violence or an alleged incident of the offense of violating a protection order or consent agreement shall make a written report of the incident whether or not an arrest is made. The report shall document the officer's observations of the victim and the alleged offender, any visible injuries of the victim or alleged offender, any weapons at the scene, the actions of the alleged offender, any statements made by the victim or witnesses, and any other significant facts or circumstances. If the officer does not arrest and detain until a warrant can be obtained a person who allegedly committed the offense of domestic violence or the offense of violating a protection order or consent agreement when it is the preferred course of action in this state pursuant to division (B)(3)(b) of section 2935.03 of the Revised Code that the alleged offender be arrested, the officer must articulate in the report a clear statement of his reasons for not arresting and detaining that alleged offender until a warrant can be obtained. The officer shall submit the written report to the law enforcement agency to which he has been appointed, employed, or elected.

(E) Each agency, instrumentality, or political subdivision that is required to adopt policies and procedures under division (A) of this section shall adopt those policies and procedures in conjunction and consultation with shelters in the community for victims of domestic violence and private organizations, law enforcement agencies, and other public agencies in the community that have expertise in the recognition and handling of domestic violence cases.

(1994 H 335, eff. 12–9–94)

2935.04   When any person may arrest

When a felony has been committed, or there is reasonable ground to believe that a felony has been committed, any person without a warrant may arrest another whom he has reasonable cause to believe is guilty of the offense, and detain him until a warrant can be obtained.

(1953 H 1, eff. 10–1–53; GC 13432–2)

2935.041   Detention of shoplifters; rights of museums and libraries

(A) A merchant, or his employee or agent, who has probable cause to believe that items offered for sale by a mercantile establishment have been unlawfully taken by a person, may, for the purposes set forth in division (C) of this section, detain the person in a reasonable manner for a reasonable length of time within the mercantile establishment or its immediate vicinity.

(B) Any officer, employee, or agent of a library, museum, or archival institution may, for the purposes set forth in division (C) of this section or for the purpose of conducting a reasonable investigation of a belief that the person has acted in a manner described in divisions (B)(1) and (2) of this section, detain a person in a reasonable manner for a reasonable length of time within, or in the immediate vicinity of, the library, museum, or archival institution, if the officer, employee, or agent has probable cause to believe that the person has either:

(1) Without privilege to do so, knowingly moved, defaced, damaged, destroyed, or otherwise improperly tampered with property owned by or in the custody of the library, museum, or archival institution; or

(2) With purpose to deprive the library, museum, or archival institution of property owned by it or in its custody, knowingly obtained or exerted control over the property without the consent of the owner or person authorized to give consent, beyond the scope of the express or implied consent of the owner or person authorized to give consent, by deception, or by threat.

(C) An officer, agent, or employee of a library, museum, or archival institution pursuant to division (B) of this section or a merchant or his employee or agent pursuant to division (A) of this section may detain another person for any of the following purposes:

(1) To recover the property that is the subject of the unlawful taking, criminal mischief, or theft;

(2) To cause an arrest to be made by a peace officer;

(3) To obtain a warrant of arrest.

(D) The officer, agent, or employee of the library, museum, or archival institution, or the merchant or his employee or agent acting under division (A) or (B) of this section shall not search the person, search or seize any property belonging to the person detained without the person's consent, or use undue restraint upon the person detained.

(E) Any peace officer may arrest without a warrant any person that he has probable cause to believe has committed any act described in division (B)(1) or (2) of this section or that he has probable cause to believe has committed an unlawful taking in a mercantile establishment. An arrest under this division shall be made within a reasonable time after the commission of the act or unlawful taking.

(F) As used in this section:

(1) "Archival institution" means any public or private building, structure, or shelter in which are stored historical documents, devices, records, manuscripts, or items of public interest, which historical materials are stored to preserve the materials or the information in the materials, to disseminate the information contained in the materials, or to make the materials available for public inspection or for inspection by certain persons who have a particular interest in, use for, or knowledge concerning the materials.

(2) "Museum" means any public or private nonprofit institution that is permanently organized for primarily educational or aesthetic purposes, owns or borrows objects or items of public interest, and cares for and exhibits to the public the objects or items.

(1978 H 403, eff. 7–4–78; 1969 H 49; 131 v H 395; 127 v 765)

2935.05 Affidavit filed in case of arrest without warrant

When a person named in section 2935.03 of the Revised Code has arrested a person without a warrant, he shall, without unnecessary delay, take the person arrested before a court or magistrate having jurisdiction of the offense, and shall file or cause to be filed an affidavit describing the offense for which the person was arrested. Such affidavit shall be filed either with the court or magistrate, or with the prosecuting attorney or other attorney charged by law with prosecution of crimes before such court or magistrate and if filed with such attorney he shall forthwith file with such court or magistrate a complaint, based on such affidavit.

(128 v 97, eff. 1–1–60; 1953 H 1; GC 13432–3)

2935.06   Duty of private person making arrest

A private person who has made an arrest pursuant to section 2935.04 of the Revised Code or detention pursuant to section 2935.041 of the Revised Code shall forthwith take the person arrested before the most convenient judge or clerk of a court of record or before a magistrate, or deliver such person to an officer authorized to execute criminal warrants who shall, without unnecessary delay, take such person before the court or magistrate having jurisdiction of the offense. The officer may, but if he does not, the private person shall file or cause to be filed in such court or before such magistrate an affidavit stating the offense for which the person was arrested.

(128 v 97, eff. 1–1–60; 1953 H 1; GC 13432–4)

2935.07   Person arrested without warrant shall be informed of cause of arrest

When an arrest is made without a warrant by an officer, he shall inform the person arrested of such officer's authority to make the arrest and the cause of the arrest.

When an arrest is made by a private person, he shall, before making the arrest, inform the person to be arrested of the intention to arrest him and the cause of the arrest.

When a person is engaged in the commission of a criminal offense, it is not necessary to inform him of the cause of his arrest.

(1953 H 1, eff. 10–1–53; GC 13432–5)

2935.08   Issuance of warrant

Upon the filing of an affidavit or complaint as provided in sections 2935.05 or 2935.06 of the Revised Code such judge, clerk, or magistrate shall forthwith issue a warrant to the peace officer making the arrest, or if made by a private person, to the most convenient peace officer who shall receive custody of the person arrested. All further detention and further proceedings shall be pursuant to such affidavit or complaint and warrant.

(129 v 582, eff. 1–10–61; 128 v 97; 1953 H 1; GC 13432–6)

2935.09   Accusation by affidavit to cause arrest or prosecution

In all cases not provided by sections 2935.02 to 2935.08, inclusive, of the Revised Code, in order to cause the arrest or prosecution of a person charged with committing an offense in this state, a peace officer, or a private citizen having knowledge of the facts, shall file with the judge or clerk of a court of record, or with a magistrate, an affidavit charging the offense committed, or shall file such affidavit with the prosecuting attorney or attorney charged by law with the prosecution of offenses in court or before such magistrate, for the purpose of having a complaint filed by such prosecuting or other authorized attorney.

(128 v 97, eff. 1–1–60)

2935.10   Procedure upon filing of affidavit or complaint; withdrawal of unexecuted warrants

(A) Upon the filing of an affidavit or complaint as provided by section 2935.09 of the Revised Code, if it charges the commission of a felony, such judge, clerk, or magistrate, unless he has reason to believe that it was not filed in good faith, or the claim is not meritorious, shall forthwith issue a warrant for the arrest of the person charged in the affidavit, and directed to a peace officer; otherwise he shall forthwith refer the matter to the prosecuting attorney or other attorney charged by law with prosecution for investigation prior to the issuance of warrant.

(B) If the offense charged is a misdemeanor or violation of a municipal ordinance, such judge, clerk, or magistrate may:

(1) Issue a warrant for the arrest of such person, directed to any officer named in section 2935.03 of the Revised Code but in cases of ordinance violation only to a police officer or marshal or deputy marshal of the municipal corporation;

(2) Issue summons, to be served by a peace officer, bailiff, or court constable, commanding the person against whom the affidavit or complaint was filed to appear forthwith, or at a fixed

time in the future, before such court or magistrate. Such summons shall be served in the same manner as in civil cases.

(C) If the affidavit is filed by, or the complaint is filed pursuant to an affidavit executed by, a peace officer who has, at his discretion, at the time of commission of the alleged offense, notified the person to appear before the court or magistrate at a specific time set by such officer, no process need be issued unless the defendant fails to appear at the scheduled time.

(D) Any person charged with a misdemeanor or violation of a municipal ordinance may give bail as provided in sections 2937.22 to 2937.46 of the Revised Code, for his appearance, regardless of whether a warrant, summons, or notice to appear has been issued.

(E) Any warrant, summons, or any notice issued by the peace officer shall state the substance of the charge against the person arrested or directed to appear.

(F) When the offense charged is a misdemeanor, and the warrant or summons issued pursuant to this section is not served within two years of the date of issue, a judge or magistrate may order such warrant or summons withdrawn and the case closed, when it does not appear that the ends of justice require keeping the case open.

(1972 H 511, eff. 3–23–73; 129 v 582; 128 v 97)

2935.11 Failure of person summoned to appear

If the person summoned to appear as provided in division (B) of section 2935.10 of the Revised Code fails to appear without just cause and personal service of the summons was had upon him, he may be found guilty of contempt of court, and may be fined not to exceed twenty dollars for such contempt. Upon failure to appear the court or magistrate may forthwith issue a warrant for his arrest.

(128 v 97, eff. 1–1–60)

2935.12 Forcible entry in making arrest; execution of search warrant

(A) When making an arrest or executing an arrest warrant or summons in lieu of an arrest warrant, or when executing a search warrant, the peace officer, law enforcement officer, or other authorized individual making the arrest or executing the warrant or summons may break down an outer or inner door or window of a dwelling house or other building, if, after notice of his intention to make the arrest or to execute the warrant or summons, he is refused admittance, but the law enforcement officer or other authorized individual executing a search warrant shall not enter a house or building not described in the warrant.

(B) The precondition for nonconsensual, forcible entry established by division (A) of this section is subject to waiver, as it applies to the execution of a search warrant, in accordance with section 2933.231 of the Revised Code.

(1990 S 258, eff. 11–20–90; 128 v 97)

2935.13 Proceedings upon arrest

Upon the arrest of any person pursuant to warrant, he shall forthwith be taken before the court or magistrate issuing the same, if such court be in session or such magistrate available, and proceedings had as provided in sections 2937.01 to 2937.46, inclusive, of the Revised Code. If such court be not in session and a misdemeanor or ordinance violation is charged, he shall be taken before the clerk or deputy clerk of the court and let to bail, as provided in sections 2937.22 to 2937.46, inclusive, of the Revised Code, if the magistrate be not available, or if the defendant is arrested in a county other than that of the issuing court or magistrate he shall forthwith be taken before the most convenient magistrate, clerk, or deputy clerk of a court of record, and there let to bail for his appearance before the issuing court or magistrate within a reasonable time to be set by such clerk.

(128 v 97, eff. 1–1–60)

2935.14 Rights of person arrested

If the person arrested is unable to offer sufficient bail or, if the offense charged be a felony, he shall, prior to being confined or removed from the county of arrest, as the case may be, be speedily permitted facilities to communicate with an attorney at law of his own choice, or to communicate with at least one relative or other person for the purpose of obtaining counsel (or in cases of misdemeanors or ordinance violation for the purpose of arranging bail). He shall not thereafter be confined or removed from the county or from the situs of initial detention until such attorney has had reasonable opportunity to confer with him privately, or other person to arrange bail, under such security measures as may be necessary under the circumstances.

Whoever, being a police officer in charge of a prisoner, or the custodian of any jail or place of confinement, violates this section shall be fined not less than one hundred nor more than five hundred dollars or imprisoned not more than thirty days, or both.

(128 v 97, eff. 1–1–60)

2935.15 Amount and disposition of bail

Amount of bail, and nature of security therefor in misdemeanor cases may be set by a schedule fixed by the court or magistrate, or it may be endorsed on the warrant by the magistrate or clerk of the issuing court. If the amount be not endorsed on the warrant, the schedule set by the court or magistrate before whom bail is taken shall prevail. All recognizances taken, or cash received shall be promptly transmitted to the court issuing the warrant, and further proceedings thereon shall be the same as if taken by the issuing court.

(128 v 97, eff. 1–1–60)

WARRANT AND GENERAL PROVISIONS

2935.16 Prisoners held without process

When it comes to the attention of any judge or magistrate that a prisoner is being held in any jail or place of custody in his jurisdiction without commitment from a court or magistrate, he shall forthwith, by summary process, require the officer or person in charge of such jail or place of custody to disclose to such court or magistrate, in writing, whether or not he holds the person described or identified in the process and the court under whose process the prisoner is being held. If it appears from the disclosure that the prisoner is held solely under warrant of arrest from any court or magistrate, the judge or magistrate shall order the custodian to produce the prisoner forthwith before the court or magistrate issuing the warrant and if such be impossible for any reason, to produce him before the inquiring judge or magistrate. If it appears from the disclosure that the prisoner is held without process, such judge or magistrate shall require the custodian to produce the prisoner forthwith before him, there to be charged as provided in section 2935.06 of the Revised Code.

Whoever, being the person in temporary or permanent charge of any jail or place of confinement, violates this section shall be fined not less than one hundred nor more than five hundred dollars or imprisoned not more than ninety days, or both.

(128 v 97, eff. 1–1–60)

2935.17 Affidavit forms; authority of supreme court to prescribe

(A) An affidavit in either of the following forms is sufficient:

(1) State of Ohio,

_____ County, ss:

Before me, A.B., personally came C.D., who being duly sworn according to law deposes and says that on or about the day of _____, 19 ___, at the county of _____ one E.F. (here describe the offense as nearly according to the nature thereof as the case will admit, in ordinary concise language) C.D.

Sworn to and subscribed before me this _____ day of _____, 19 ___.

A.B., County Judge

Clerk of _____ Court

(2) State of Ohio,

_____ County, ss:

Before me, A.B., personally came C.D., who being duly sworn according to law says that on or about the _____ day of _____, 19 ___, one E.F. did: (here listing several common offenses, plainly but tersely described as: fail to stop at stop sign, pass at crest of grade, etc., with a ruled box before each, and then showing an X or distinctive mark in front of the offense claimed to be committed). C.D.

Sworn to before me and subscribed in my presence this _____ day of _____, 19 ___,

A.B., County Judge

Clerk of _____ Court

(B) A complaint in the following form is sufficient:

State of Ohio,

_____ County, ss:

The undersigned (assistant) prosecuting attorney of _____ County complains that on or about the _____ day of _____, 19 ___, one E.F. did (here describing the offense committed as above) based on affidavit of _____ filed with me.

Prosecuting Attorney

City Director of Law

Provided, that the supreme court of Ohio, may, by rule, provide for the uniform type and language to be used in any affidavit or complaint to be filed in any court inferior to the court of common pleas for violations of the motor vehicle and traffic acts and related ordinances and in any notice to violator to appear in such courts, and may require that such forms and no other, shall be received in such courts, and issued to violators.

(1977 H 219, eff. 11–1–77; 128 v 97)

2935.18   Contents of warrant, summons or notice

A warrant, summons, or notice of a peace officer shall either contain a copy of the affidavit, or recite the substance of the accusation. A warrant shall be directed to a specific officer or to a department designated by its chief, and shall command such officer or member of department to take the accused and bring him forthwith before the magistrate or court issuing such warrant, to be dealt with according to law. A summons shall be directed to the officer or department, and shall command him to notify the accused by serving a copy of such summons upon him. The following form of warrant is sufficient:

The State of Ohio,

_____ County, ss:

To the Sheriff (other Officer):

Greetings:

Whereas there has been filed with me an affidavit of which the following is a copy (here copy) or the substance, (here set forth the substance, omitting formal parts). These are therefore to command you to take the said E.F., if he is found in your county, or if he is not found in your county, that you pursue after him in any other county in this state and take and safely keep the said E.F. so that you have his body forthwith before me or some other magistrate of said county to answer the said complaint and be further dealt with according to law.

Given under my hand this ___ day of _____, 19 ___

A.B., Judge of _____ Court

Clerk of _____ Court

The following form of summons is sufficient:

The State of Ohio, _____ County, ss:

To the Bailiff or _____ Constable:

Whereas there has been filed before me an Affidavit (Complaint) of which the following is a copy (here copy) or the substance (here set forth the substance, omitting formal parts). You

351

are commanded to summon one said E.F. to appear before me on the _____ day of _____, 19 ___, at _____ o'clock, ___ M., at _____ Building, _____, Ohio, to answer to said charge.

You will make due return of this summons forthwith upon service.

A.B., Judge of _____ Court

Clerk of _____ Court

(128 v 97, eff. 1–1–60)

2935.19 Form of affidavit

An affidavit in the form following is sufficient:

The State of Ohio,

_____ County, ss:

Before me, A.B., personally came C.D., who being duly sworn according to law, deposes and says that on or about the _____ day of _____ at the county of _____, one E.F. (here describe the offense committed as nearly according to the nature thereof as the case will admit, in ordinary and concise language).

Sworn to and subscribed before me, this _____ day of _____, 19 ___

A.B., Judge

(127 v 1039, eff. 1–1–58; 1953 H 1; GC 13432–18)

2935.20 Right of one in custody to be visited by attorney

After the arrest, detention, or any other taking into custody of a person, with or without a warrant, such person shall be permitted forthwith facilities to communicate with an attorney at law of his choice who is entitled to practice in the courts of this state, or to communicate with any other person of his choice for the purpose of obtaining counsel. Such communication may be made by a reasonable number of telephone calls or in any other reasonable manner. Such person shall have a right to be visited immediately by any attorney at law so obtained who is entitled to practice in the courts of this state, and to consult with him privately. No officer or any other agent of this state shall prevent, attempt to prevent, or advise such person against the communication, visit, or consultation provided for by this section.

Whoever violates this section shall be fined not less than twenty-five nor more than one hundred dollars or imprisoned not more than thirty days, or both.

(131 v H 471, eff. 11–1–65)

2935.21 Security for costs

When the offense charged is a misdemeanor, the magistrate or court, before issuing the warrant, may require the complainant, or if the magistrate considers the complainant irresponsible, may require that said complainant procure a person to be liable for the costs if the complaint is dismissed, and the complainant or other person shall acknowledge himself so liable, and such court or magistrate shall enter such acknowledgment on his docket. Such bond shall not be required of an officer authorized to make arrests when in the discharge of his official duty, or other person or officer authorized to assist the prosecuting attorney in the prosecution of offenders.

(1953 H 1, eff. 10–1–53; GC 13432–20)

2935.22 Issuing subpoenas for witnesses—Repealed

(128 v 97, eff. 1–1–60; 1953 H 1; GC 13432–21)

2935.23 Felony investigation; examination of witnesses

After a felony has been committed, and before any arrest has been made, the prosecuting attorney of the county, or any judge or magistrate, may cause subpoenas to issue, returnable before any court or magistrate, for any person to give information concerning such felony.

The subpoenas shall require the witness to appear forthwith. Before such witness is required to give any information, he must be informed of the purpose of the inquiry, and that he is required to tell the truth concerning the same. He shall then be sworn and be examined under oath by the prosecuting attorney, or the court or magistrate, subject to the constitutional rights of the witness. Such examination shall be taken in writing in any form, and shall be filed with the court or magistrate taking the testimony. Witness fees shall be paid to such persons as in other cases.

(1972 H 511, eff. 1–1–74; 1953 H 1; GC 13432–22)

2935.24 Warrants transmitted by teletype or similar means

A judge of a court of record may, by an endorsement under his hand upon a warrant of arrest, authorize the service thereof by telegraph, teletype, wire photo, or other means whereby a written or facsimile copy may be transmitted, and thereafter a copy of such warrant may be sent by any such means to any law enforcement officer. Such copy is effectual in the hands of any law enforcement officer and he shall proceed in the same manner under it as though he held the orginal [*sic*] warrant issued by the court making the endorsement, except that a state university law enforcement officer shall not arrest for a minor misdemeanor on the basis of a written or facsimile copy of a warrant of arrest. Every officer causing copies of warrants to be sent pursuant to this section, shall certify as correct and file in the office from which such warrant was sent, a copy of such warrant and endorsement thereon, and shall return the original with a statement of his action thereunder.

(1978 H 588, eff. 6–19–78; 1972 H 511; 1953 H 1; GC 13432–23)

2935.25 Power of arrest

Sections 2935.02 to 2935.24, inclusive, of the Revised Code do not affect or modify the power of arrest vested by law in other persons or officers than those named in section 2935.03 of the Revised Code.

(1953 H 1, eff. 10–1–53; GC 13432–24)

2935.26 When citation must be used rather than arrest; exceptions; procedures

(A) Notwithstanding any other provision of the Revised Code, when a law enforcement officer is otherwise authorized to arrest a person for the commission of a minor misdemeanor, the officer shall not arrest the person, but shall issue a citation, unless one of the following applies:

(1) The offender requires medical care or is unable to provide for his own safety.

(2) The offender cannot or will not offer satisfactory evidence of his identity.

(3) The offender refuses to sign the citation.

(4) The offender has previously been issued a citation for the commission of that misdemeanor and has failed to do one of the following:

(a) Appear at the time and place stated in the citation;

(b) Comply with division (C) of this section.

(B) The citation shall contain all of the following:

(1) The name and address of the offender;

(2) A description of the offense and the numerical designation of the applicable statute or ordinance;

(3) The name of the person issuing the citation;

(4) An order for the offender to appear at a stated time and place;

(5) A notice that the offender may comply with division (C) of this section in lieu of appearing at the stated time and place;

(6) A notice that the offender is required to do one of the following and that he may be arrested if he fails to do one of them:

(a) Appear at the time and place stated in the citation;

(b) Comply with division (C) of this section.

(C) In lieu of appearing at the time and place stated in the citation, the offender may, within seven days after the date of issuance of the citation, do either of the following:

(1) Appear in person at the office of the clerk of the court stated in the citation, sign a plea of guilty and a waiver of trial provision that is on the citation, and pay the total amount of the fine and costs;

(2) Sign the guilty plea and waiver of trial provision of the citation, and mail the citation and a check or money order for the total amount of the fine and costs to the office of the clerk of the court stated in the citation.

Remittance by mail of the fine and costs to the office of the clerk of the court stated in the citation constitutes a guilty plea and waiver of trial whether or not the quilty plea and waiver of trial provision of the citation are signed by the defendant.

(D) A law enforcement officer who issues a citation shall complete and sign the citation form, serve a copy of the completed form upon the offender and, without unnecessary delay, file the original citation with the court having jurisdiction over the offense.

(E) Each court shall establish a fine schedule that shall list the fine for each minor misdemeanor, and state the court costs. The fine schedule shall be prominently posted in the place where minor misdemeanor fines are paid.

(F) If an offender fails to appear and does not comply with division (C) of this section, the court may issue a supplemental citation, or a summons or warrant for the arrest of the offender pursuant to the Criminal Rules. Supplemental citations shall be in the form prescribed by division (B) of this section, but shall be issued and signed by the clerk of the court at which the citation directed the offender to appear and shall be served in the same manner as a summons. (1978 S 351, eff. 10–25–78)

2935.27 Alternatives for security for appearance

(A)(1) If a law enforcement officer issues a citation to a person pursuant to section 2935.26 of the Revised Code and if the minor misdemeanor offense for which the citation is issued is an act prohibited by Chapter 4511., 4513., or 4549. of the Revised Code or an act prohibited by any municipal ordinance that is substantially similar to any section contained in Chapter 4511., 4513., or 4549. of the Revised Code, the officer shall inform the person, if he has a current valid Ohio driver's or commercial driver's license, of the possible consequences of his actions as required under division (E) of this section, and also shall inform him that he is required either to appear at the time and place stated in the citation or to comply with division (C) of section 2935.26 of the Revised Code.

(2) If the person does not have a current valid Ohio driver's or commercial driver's license, the officer shall bring the person before the court with which the citation is required to be filed for the setting of a reasonable security by the court pursuant to division (F) of this section.

(B) A person who appears before a court to have security set under division (A)(2) of this section shall be given a receipt or other evidence of the deposit of the security by the court.

(C) Upon compliance with division (C) of section 2935.26 of the Revised Code by a person who was issued a citation, the clerk of the court shall notify the court. The court shall immediately return any sum of money, license, or other security deposited in relation to the citation to the person, or to any other person who deposited the security.

(D) If a person who has a current valid Ohio driver's or commercial driver's license and who was issued a citation fails to appear at the time and place specified on the citation and fails to comply with division (C) of section 2935.26 of the Revised Code or fails to comply with or satisfy any judgment of the court within the time allowed by the court, the court shall declare the forfeiture of the person's license. Thirty days after the declaration of forfeiture, the court shall forward a copy of the declaration of forfeiture to the registrar of motor vehicles. The registrar shall cancel the person's driver's or commercial driver's license, send written notification of the cancellation to the person at his last known address, and order him to surrender his driver's or commercial driver's license to the registrar within forty-eight hours. No valid driver's or commercial driver's license shall be granted to the person for a period of one year after the cancellation, unless the court having jurisdiction of the offense that led to the cancellation orders that the forfeiture be terminated. The court shall so order the registrar if the person, after having failed to appear in court at the required time and place to answer the charge or after having pleaded guilty to or been found guilty of the violation and having failed within the time allowed by the court to pay the fine imposed by the court, thereafter appears to answer the charge and pays any fine imposed by the court or pays the fine originally imposed by the court.

If the person who was issued the citation fails to appear at the time and place specified on the citation and fails to comply with division (C) of section 2935.26 of the Revised Code and the person has deposited a sum of money or other security in relation to the citation under division (A)(2) of this section, the deposit shall immediately be forfeited to the court.

This section does not preclude further action as authorized by division (F) of section 2935.26 of the Revised Code.

(E) A law enforcement officer who issues a person a minor misdemeanor citation for an act prohibited by Chapter 4511., 4513., or 4549. of the Revised Code or an act prohibited by a municipal ordinance that is substantially similar to any section contained in Chapter 4511., 4513., or 4549. of the Revised Code shall inform the person that if he does not appear at the time and place stated on the citation or does not comply with division (C) of section 2935.26 of the Revised Code, the person's driver's or commercial driver's license will be canceled, the person will not be eligible for the reissuance of the license or the issuance of a new license for one year after cancellation, and the person is subject to any applicable criminal penalties.

(F) A court setting security under division (A)(2) of this section shall do so in conformity with sections 2937.22 and 2937.23 of the Revised Code and the Rules of Criminal Procedure.

(1994 H 687, eff. 10–12–94; 1993 S 62, § 4, eff. 9–1–93; 1992 S 275; 1990 S 338; 1989 H 381; 1986 S 356; 1978 S 351)

2935.28 Property owners to be provided with names of persons charged with damaging their property

(A) As used in this section, "motor vehicle" has the same meaning as in section 4501.01 of the Revised Code.

(B) If damage is caused to real property by the operation of a motor vehicle in, or during the, violation of any section of the Revised Code or of any municipal ordinance, the law enforcement agency that investigates the case, upon request of the real property owner, shall provide the owner with the names of the persons who are charged with the commission of the offense. If a request for the names is made, the agency shall provide the names as soon as possible after the persons are charged with the offense.

(C) The personnel of law enforcement agencies who act pursuant to division (B) of this section in good faith are not liable in damages in a civil action allegedly arising from their actions taken pursuant to that division. Political subdivisions and the state are not liable in damages in a civil action allegedly arising from the actions of personnel of their law enforcement agencies if the personnel have immunity under this division.

(1984 H 666, eff. 3–14–85)

2935.29 Definition of fresh pursuit and state

As used in sections 2935.30 and 2935.31 of the Revised Code:

(A) "Fresh pursuit" includes fresh pursuit as defined by the common law, and also the pursuit of a person who has committed a felony or who is reasonably suspected of having committed a felony. It includes the pursuit of a person suspected of having committed a supposed felony, though no felony has actually been committed, if there is reasonable ground for believing that a felony has been committed. Fresh pursuit does not necessarily imply instant pursuit, but pursuit without unreasonable delay.

(B) "State" includes the District of Columbia.

(1953 H 1, eff. 10–1–53; GC 13434–7, 13434–8)

2935.30 Authority of foreign police

Any member of an organized state, county, or municipal peace unit of another state of the United States who enters this state in fresh pursuit, and continues within this state in such fresh pursuit, of a person in order to arrest him on the ground that he is believed to have committed a felony in such other state has the same authority to arrest and hold such person in custody as has any member of any organized state, county, or municipal peace unit of this state to arrest and hold in custody a person on the ground that he is believed to have committed a felony in this state.

This section does not make unlawful any arrest in this state which would otherwise be lawful.
(1953 H 1, eff. 10–1–53; GC 13434–4, 13434–6)

2935.31 Hearing before magistrate in county of arrest

If an arrest is made in this state by an officer of another state under section 2935.30 of the Revised Code, he shall without unnecessary delay take the person arrested before a magistrate of the county in which the arrest was made, who shall conduct a hearing for the purpose of determining the lawfulness of the arrest. If the magistrate determines that the arrest was lawful be [1] shall commit the person arrested to await for a reasonable time the issuance of an extradition warrant by the governor of this state, or admit him to bail for such purposes. If the magistrate determines that the arrest was unlawful he shall discharge the person arrested.
(1953 H 1, eff. 10–1–53; GC 13434–5)

[1] So in original; should this read "he"?

2935.32 Broadcasting information of crime

The board of county commissioners or the prosecuting attorney of any county, with the consent of the court of common pleas, may contract with any company engaged in broadcasting by radio, for the purpose of immediate broadcasting of information concerning any violent felony, when the perpetrator thereof has escaped. The sheriff and heads of police departments, immediately upon the commission of any such felony and the escape of such perpetrator, shall furnish all information concerning said crime and the perpetrator thereof, to said company with which such contract may be made, for the purpose of broadcasting. The reasonable cost of such broadcasting shall be paid by the county, out of the county treasury, on the order of the board.
(1953 H 1, eff. 10–1–53; GC 13431–1)

2935.33 Commitment of alcoholics and intoxicated persons

(A) If it appears to a judge of a court of record before whom a person charged with a misdemeanor is taken, that the person is an alcoholic or is suffering from acute alcohol intoxication, as defined in division (D) of this section, and that the person would benefit from services provided by an alcohol and drug addiction program certified under Chapter 3793. of the Revised Code, the judge may place him temporarily in such a program in the area wherein the court has jurisdiction for inpatient care and treatment for an indefinite period not exceeding five days. Such commitment does not limit the right to release on bail. Any charge of a violation of division (B) of section 2917.11 of the Revised Code or a municipal ordinance substantially equivalent to that division may be dismissed by the judge if the defendant complies with all the conditions of treatment ordered by the court.

Any fines or court costs collected by the court from defendants who have received inpatient care from an alcohol and drug addiction program may be ordered to be paid, for the benefit of the program, to the board of alcohol, drug addiction, and mental health services of the alcohol, drug addiction, and mental health service district in which the program is located or to the director of alcohol and drug addiction services.

(B) If it appears to a judge at the time of sentencing for a violation of division (B) of section 2917.11 or section 4511.19, 2919.25, or 2919.27 of the Revised Code or for a violation of a municipal ordinance substantially equivalent to that division or any of those sections that the person convicted is an alcoholic or is suffering from acute alcohol intoxication and that, in lieu of imprisonment, the person would benefit from services provided by an alcohol and drug addiction program certified under Chapter 3793. of the Revised Code, the court may commit the person to close supervision in any facility in the area in which the court has jurisdiction that is, or is operated by, such a program. Any commitment to close supervision for violation of section 2919.25 or 2919.27 of the Revised Code or any substantially equivalent municipal ordinance shall be in accordance with division (E) of section 2929.51 of the Revised Code. Such close supervision may include outpatient services and part-time release, except that a person convicted of a violation of division (A) of section 4511.19 of the Revised Code shall be confined to the facility for at least three days and except that a person convicted of a violation of section 2919.25 or 2919.27 of the Revised Code or a substantially equivalent municipal ordinance shall be confined to the facility in accordance with the order of commitment. A commitment of a person to a facility for purposes of close supervision shall not exceed the maximum term for which the person could be imprisoned.

(C) A law enforcement officer who finds a person subject to prosecution for violation of division (B) of section 2917.11 of the Revised Code or a municipal ordinance substantially equivalent to that division and has reasonable cause to believe that the person is an alcoholic or is suffering from acute alcohol intoxication and that he would benefit from immediate treatment may immediately place him in an alcohol and drug addiction program certified under Chapter 3793. of the Revised Code in the area in which the person is found, for emergency treatment, in lieu of other arrest procedures, for a maximum period of forty-eight hours. During that time, if the person desires to leave such custody, he shall be released forthwith.

(D) As used in this section:

(1) "Alcoholic" has the same meaning as in section 3793.01 of the Revised Code;

(2) "Acute alcohol intoxication" means a heavy consumption of alcohol over a relatively short period of time, resulting in dysfunction of the brain centers controlling behavior, speech, and memory and causing characteristic withdrawal symptoms.

(1994 S 82, eff. 5–4–94; 1989 H 317, eff. 10–10–89; 1985 H 475; 1984 H 37; 1976 H 907; 1975 H 1; 1972 H 240)

2935.36 Pre–trial diversion programs for adult offenders; limits; procedure

(A) The prosecuting attorney may establish pre-trial diversion programs for adults who are accused of committing criminal offenses and whom he believes will probably not offend again. The programs shall be operated pursuant to written standards approved by journal entry by the presiding judge or, in courts with only one judge, the judge of the court of common pleas and shall not be applicable to any of the following:

(1) Repeat offenders or dangerous offenders, as defined in section 2929.01 of the Revised Code;

(2) Persons accused of an offense of violence or of a violation of section 2903.06, 2903.07, 2905.04, 2907.04, 2907.05, 2907.21, 2907.22, 2907.31, 2907.32, 2907.34, 2911.31, 2919.12, 2919.13, 2919.22, 2921.02, 2921.11, 2921.12, 2921.32, or 2923.20 of the Revised Code, with the exception that the prosecuting attorney may permit persons accused of such offenses to enter a pre-trial diversion program, if he finds any of the following:

(a) The accused did not cause, threaten, or intend serious physical harm to any person;

(b) The offense was the result of circumstances not likely to recur;

(c) The accused has no history of prior delinquency or criminal activity;

(d) The accused has led a law-abiding life for a substantial time before commission of the alleged offense;

(e) Substantial grounds tending to excuse or justify the alleged offense;

(3) Persons accused of a violation of Chapter 2925. or 3719. of the Revised Code;

(4) Drug dependent persons or persons in danger of becoming drug dependent persons, as defined in section 3719.011 of the Revised Code. However, this division does not affect the eligibility of such persons for treatment in lieu of conviction pursuant to section 2951.041 of the Revised Code.

(5) Persons accused of a violation of section 4511.19 of the Revised Code or a violation of any substantially similar municipal ordinance.

(B) An accused who enters a diversion program shall:

(1) Waive, in writing and contingent upon his successful completion of the program, his right to a speedy trial, the preliminary hearing, the time period within which the grand jury may consider an indictment against him, and arraignment, unless the hearing, indictment, or arraignment has already occurred;

(2) Agree, in writing, to the tolling while in the program of all periods of limitation established by statutes or rules of court, that are applicable to the offense with which he is charged and to the conditions of the diversion program established by the prosecuting attorney.

(C) The trial court, upon the application of the prosecuting attorney, shall order the release from confinement of any accused who has agreed to enter a pre-trial diversion program and shall discharge and release any existing bail and release any sureties on recognizances and shall release the accused on a recognizance bond conditioned upon the accused's compliance with the terms of the diversion program. The prosecuting attorney shall notify every victim of the crime and the arresting officers of his intent to permit the accused to enter a pre-trial diversion program. The victim of the crime and the arresting officers shall have the opportunity to file written objections with the prosecuting attorney prior to the commencement of the pre-trial diversion program.

(D) If the accused satisfactorily completes the diversion program, the prosecuting attorney shall recommend to the trial court that the charges against the accused be dismissed, and the court shall, upon the recommendation of the prosecuting attorney, dismiss the charges. If the accused chooses not to enter the prosecuting attorney's diversion program, or if the accused violates the conditions of the agreement pursuant to which he has been released, he may be brought to trial upon the charges in the manner provided by law, and the waiver executed pursuant to division (B)(1) of this section shall be void on the date the accused is removed from the program for the violation.

(1994 S 82, eff. 5–4–94; 1986 S 262, eff. 3–20–87; 1978 H 473)

CHAPTER 2937

PRELIMINARY EXAMINATION; BAIL

PRELIMINARY EXAMINATION

PRELIMINARY EXAMINATION

2937.01 Definitions

The definition of "magistrate" set forth in section 2931.01 of the Revised Code, and the definitions of "peace officer," "prosecutor," and "offense" set forth in section 2935.01 of the Revised Code apply to Chapter 2937. of the Revised Code.

(128 v 97, eff. 1–1–60; 1953 H 1)

2937.02 Announcement of charge and rights of accused by court

When, after arrest, the accused is taken before a court or magistrate, or when the accused appears pursuant to terms of summons or notice, the affidavit or complaint being first filed, the court or magistrate shall, before proceeding further:

(A) Inform the accused of the nature of the charge against him and the identity of the complainant and permit the accused or his counsel to see and read the affidavit or complaint or a copy thereof;

(B) Inform the accused of his right to have counsel and the right to a continuance in the proceedings to secure counsel;

(C) Inform the accused of the effect of pleas of guilty, not guilty, and no contest, of his right to trial by jury, and the necessity of making written demand therefor;

(D) If the charge be a felony, inform the accused of the nature and extent of possible punishment on conviction and of the right to preliminary hearing. Such information may be given to each accused individually or, if at any time there exists any substantial number of defendants to be arraigned at the same session, the judge or magistrate may, by general announcement or by distribution of printed matter, advise all those accused concerning those rights general in their nature, and informing as to individual matters at arraignment.

(128 v 97, eff. 1–1–60)

2937.03 Arraignment; counsel; bail

After the announcement, as provided by section 2937.02 of the Revised Code, the accused shall be arraigned by the magistrate, or clerk, or prosecutor of the court reading the affidavit or complaint, or reading its substance, omitting purely formal parts, to him unless such reading be waived. The judge or magistrate shall then inquire of the accused whether he understands the nature of the charge. If he does not indicate understanding, the magistrate shall give explanation in terms of the statute or ordinance claimed violated. If he is not represented by counsel and expresses desire to consult with an attorney at law, the judge or magistrate shall continue the case for a reasonable time to allow him to send for or consult with counsel and shall set bail for such later appearance if the offense is bailable. If the accused is not able to make bail, or the offense is not bailable, the court or magistrate shall require the officer having custody of accused forthwith to take a message to any attorney at law within the municipal corporation where accused is detained, or to make available to the accused forthwith use of telephone for calling to arrange for legal counsel or bail.

(129 v 582, eff. 1–10–61; 128 v 97)

2937.04 Motion for dismissal

If accused does not desire counsel or, having engaged counsel, appears at the end of granted continuance, he may then raise, by motion to dismiss the affidavit or complaint, any exception thereto which could be asserted against an indictment or information by motion to quash, plea in abatement, or demurrer. Such motion may be made orally and ruled upon by the court or magistrate at the time of presentation, with minute of motion and ruling made in the journal (if a court of record) or on the docket (if a court not of record) or such motion may be presented in writing and set down for argument at later time. Where the motion attacks a defect in the record by facts extrinsic thereto, proof may be offered by testimony or affidavit.

(128 v 97, eff. 1–1–60)

2937.05 Discharge on motion to dismiss; amendment of complaint

If the motion pursuant to section 2937.04 of the Revised Code be sustained, accused shall be discharged unless the court or magistrate finds that the defect can be corrected without changing the nature of the charge, in which case he may order the complaint amended or a proper affidavit filed forthwith and require the accused to plead thereto. The discharge of accused upon the sustaining of a motion to dismiss shall not be considered a bar to further prosecution either of felony or misdemeanor.

(128 v 97, eff. 1–1–60)

2937.06 Pleas

(A) After all motions are disposed of or if no motion is presented, the court or magistrate shall require the accused to plead to the charge.

(1) In cases of felony, only a plea of not guilty or a written plea of guilty shall be received and if the defendant declines to plead, a plea of not guilty shall be entered for him and further proceedings had as set forth in sections 2937.09 to 2937.12 of the Revised Code.

(2) In cases of misdemeanor, the following pleas may be received:

(a) Guilty;

(b) Not guilty;

(c) No contest;

(d) Once in jeopardy, which includes the defenses of former conviction or former acquittal.

(B) Prior to accepting a plea of guilty or a plea of no contest under division (A) of this section, the court shall comply with section 2943.031 of the Revised Code.

(C) Entry of any plea pursuant to this section shall constitute a waiver of any objection which could be taken advantage of by motion pursuant to section 2937.04 of the Revised Code.

(1989 S 95, eff. 10–2–89; 128 v 97)

2937.07 Action on pleas of "guilty" and "no contest" in misdemeanor cases

If the offense be a misdemeanor and the accused pleads guilty thereto, the court or magistrate shall receive and enter such plea unless he believes it made through fraud, collusion; or mistake in which case he shall enter a plea of not guilty and set the matter for trial pursuant to Chapter 2938. of the Revised Code. Upon a plea of guilty being received the court or magistrate shall call for explanation of circumstances of the offense from the affiant or complainant or his representatives, and after hearing the same, together with any statement of accused, shall proceed to pronounce sentence or continue the matter for the purpose of imposing sentence or admitting the defendant to probation.

If the plea be "no contest" or words of similar import in pleading to a misdemeanor, it shall constitute a stipulation that the judge or magistrate may make finding of guilty or not guilty from the explanation of circumstances, and if guilt be found, impose or continue for sentence accordingly. Such plea shall not be construed to import an admission of any fact at issue in the criminal charge in any subsequent action or proceeding, whether civil or criminal.

(128 v 97, eff. 1–1–60)

2937.08 Action on pleas of "not guilty" or "once in jeopardy" in misdemeanor cases

Upon a plea of not guilty or a plea of once in jeopardy, if the charge be a misdemeanor in a court of record, the court shall proceed to set the matter for trial at a future time, pursuant to Chapter 2938. of the Revised Code, and shall let accused to bail pending such trial. Or he may, but only if both prosecutor and accused expressly consent, set the matter for trial forthwith.

Upon the entry of such pleas to a charge of misdemeanor in a court not of record, the magistrate shall forthwith set the matter for future trial or, with the consent of both state and defendant may set trial forthwith, both pursuant to Chapter 2938. of the Revised Code, provided that if the nature of the offense is such that right to jury trial exists, such matter shall not be tried before him unless the accused, by writing subscribed by him, waives a jury and consents to be tried by the magistrate.

If the defendant in such event does not waive right to jury trial, then the magistrate shall require the accused to enter into recognizance to appear before a court of record in the county, set by such magistrate, and the magistrate shall thereupon certify all papers filed, together with transcript of proceedings and accrued costs to date, and such recognizance if given, to such designated court of record. Such transfer shall not require the filing of indictment or information and trial shall proceed in the transferee court pursuant to Chapter 2938. of the Revised Code.

(128 v 97, eff. 1–1–60)

2937.081 Duty of prosecutor to give victims of crime notice of certain facts concerning resulting prosecution; procedures; limits—Repealed

(1994 S 186, eff. 10–12–94; 1987 S 6, § 4, eff. 6–10–87; 1984 S 76, § 1, 2)

2937.09 Procedure in felony cases

If the charge is a felony, the court or magistrate shall, before receiving a plea of guilty, advise the accused that such plea constitutes an admission which may be used against him at a later trial. If the defendant enters a written plea of guilty or, pleading not guilty, affirmatively waives the right to have the court or magistrate take evidence concerning the offense, the court or magistrate forthwith and without taking evidence may find that the crime has been committed and that there is probable and reasonable cause to hold the defendant for trial pursuant to indictment by the grand jury, and, if the offense is bailable, require the accused to enter into recognizance in such amount as it determines to appear before the court of common pleas pursuant to indictment, otherwise to be confined until the grand jury has considered and reported the matter.

(129 v 582, eff. 1–10–61; 128 v 97)

2937.10 Hearing set in felony cases

If the charge be a felony and there be no written plea of guilty or waiver of examination, or the court or magistrate refuses to receive such waiver, the court or magistrate, with the consent of the prosecutor and the accused, may set the matter for hearing forthwith, otherwise he shall set the matter for hearing at a fixed time in the future and shall notify both prosecutor and defendant promptly of such time of hearing.

(128 v 97, eff. 1–1–60)

2937.11 Presentation of state's case; videotaped or recorded testimony of child victims

(A) At the preliminary hearing set pursuant to section 2937.10 of the Revised Code and the Criminal Rules, the prosecutor may, but is not required to, state orally the case for the state, and shall then proceed to examine witnesses and introduce exhibits for the state. The accused and the magistrate have full right of cross examination and the accused has the right of inspection of exhibits prior to their introduction. The hearing shall be conducted under the rules of evidence prevailing in criminal trials generally. On motion of either the state or the accused, witnesses shall be separated and not permitted in the hearing room except when called to testify.

(B) In a case involving an alleged felony violation of section 2907.02, 2907.03, 2907.04, 2907.05, 2907.06, 2907.12, 2907.21, 2907.31, 2907.32, 2907.321, 2907.322, or 2907.323, or division (B)(5) of section 2919.22 of the Revised Code in which an alleged victim of the alleged offense was under eleven years of age when the complaint or information was filed, whichever occurred earlier, upon motion of the prosecution, the testimony of the child victim at the preliminary hearing may be taken in a room other than the room in which the preliminary hearing is being conducted and be televised, by closed circuit equipment, into the room in which the preliminary hearing is being conducted, in accordance with division (C) of section 2907.41 of the Revised Code.

(C) In a case involving an alleged felony violation of section 2907.02, 2907.03, 2907.04, 2907.05, or 2907.12 of the Revised Code in which an alleged victim of the alleged offense was under eleven years of age when the complaint or information was filed, whichever occurred earlier, the court, on written motion of the prosecutor in the case filed at least three days prior to the hearing, shall order that all testimony of the child victim be recorded and preserved on videotape, in addition to being recorded for purposes of the transcript of the proceeding. If such an order is issued, it shall specifically identify the child victim concerning whose testimony it pertains, apply only during the testimony of the child victim it specifically identifies, and apply to all testimony of the child victim presented at the hearing, regardless of whether the child victim is called as a witness by the prosecution or by the defense.

(1986 H 108, eff. 10–14–86; 128 v 97)

2937.12 Motion for discharge; presentation on behalf of accused; finding of court

(A) At the conclusion of the presentation of the state's case accused may move for discharge for failure of proof or may offer evidence on his own behalf. Prior to the offering of evidence on behalf of the accused, unless accused is then represented by counsel, the court or magistrate shall advise accused:

(1) That any testimony of witnesses offered by him in the proceeding may, if unfavorable in any particular, be used against him at later trial;

(2) That accused himself may make a statement, not under oath, regarding the charge, for the purpose of explaining the facts in evidence;

(3) That he may refuse to make any statement and such refusal may not be used against him at trials;

(4) That any statement he makes may be used against him at trial.

(B) Upon conclusion of all the evidence and the statement, if any, of the accused, the court or magistrate shall either:

(1) Find that the crime alleged has been committed and that there is probable and reasonable cause to hold or recognize defendant to appear before the court of common pleas of the county or any other county in which venue appears, for trial pursuant to indictment by grand jury;

(2) Find that there is probable cause to hold or recognize defendant to appear before the court of common pleas for trial pursuant to indictment or information on such other charge, felony or misdemeanor, as the evidence indicates was committed by accused;

(3) Find that a misdemeanor was committed and there is probable cause to recognize accused to appear before himself or some other court inferior to the court of common pleas for trial upon such charge;

(4) Order the accused discharged from custody.

(128 v 97, eff. 1–1–60)

2937.13 Basis for finding; no appeal; further prosecution

In entering a finding, pursuant to section 2937.12 of the Revised Code, the court, while weighing credibility of witnesses, shall not be required to pass on the weight of the evidence and any finding requiring accused to stand trial on any charge shall be based solely on the presence of substantial credible evidence thereof. No appeal shall lie from such decision nor shall the discharge of defendant be a bar to further prosecution by indictment or otherwise.

(128 v 97, eff. 1–1–60)

2937.14 Entry of reason for change in charge

In any case in which accused is held or recognized to appear for trial on any charge other than the one on which he was arraigned the court or magistrate shall enter the reason for such charge on the journal of the court (if a court of record) or on the docket (if a court not of record) and shall file with the papers in the case the text of the charge found by him to be sustained by the evidence.

(128 v 97, eff. 1–1–60)

2937.15 Transcript of proceedings

Upon the conclusion of the hearing and finding, the magistrate, or if a court of record, the clerk of such court, shall complete all notations of appearance, motions, pleas, and findings on the criminal docket of the court, and shall transmit a transcript of the appearance docket entries, together with a copy of the original complaint and affidavits, if any, filed with the complaint, the journal or docket entry of reason for changes in the charge, if any, together with the order setting bail and the bail deposit, if any, filed, and together with the videotaped testimony, if any, prepared in accordance with division (C) of section 2937.11 of the Revised Code, to the clerk of the court in which the accused is to appear. Such transcript shall contain an itemized account of the costs accrued.

(1986 H 108, eff. 10–14–86; 128 v 97)

2937.16 When witnesses shall be recognized to appear

When an accused enters into a recognizance or is committed in default thereof, the judge or magistrate shall require such witnesses against the prisoner as he finds necessary, to enter into a recognizance to appear and testify before the proper court at a proper time, and not depart from such court without leave. If the judge or magistrate finds it necessary he may require such witnesses to give sufficient surety to appear at such court.

(1953 H 1, eff. 10–1–53; GC 13433–15)

2937.17 Recognizance for minor

A person may be liable in a recognizance for a minor to appear as a witness, or the judge or magistrate may take the minor's recognizance, in a sufficient sum, which is valid notwithstanding the disability of minority.

(1953 H 1, eff. 10–1–53; GC 13433–16)

2937.18 Detention of material witnesses

If a witness ordered to give recognizance fails to comply with such order, the judge or magistrate shall commit him to such custody or open or close detention as may be appropriate under the circumstances, until he complies with the order or is discharged. Commitment of the witness may be to the custody of any suitable person or public or private agency, or to an appropriate detention facility other than a jail, or to a jail, but the witness shall not be confined in association with prisoners charged with or convicted of crime. The witness, in lieu of the fee ordinarily allowed witnesses, shall be allowed twenty-five dollars for each day of custody or detention under such order, and shall be allowed mileage as provided for other witnesses, calculated on the distance from his home to the place of giving testimony and return. All proceedings in the case or cases in which the witness is held to appear shall be given priority over other cases and had with all due speed.

(1972 H 511, eff. 3–23–73; 1953 H 1; GC 13433–17)

2937.19 Subpoena of witnesses or documents

The magistrate or judge or clerk of the court in which proceedings are being had may issue subpoenas or other process to bring witnesses or documents before the magistrate or court in hearings pending before him either under Chapter 2937. or 2938. of the Revised Code.

In complaints to keep the peace a subpoena must be served within the county, or, in cases of misdemeanors and ordinance offenses, it may be served at any place in this state within one hundred miles of the place where the court or magistrate is scheduled to sit; in felony cases it may be served at any place within this state. In cases where such process is to be served outside the county, it may be issued to be served either by the bailiff or constable of the court or by a sheriff or police officer either by the county in which the court or magistrate sits or in which process is to be served.

(129 v 582, eff. 1–10–61; 128 v 97)

2937.20 Procedure in disqualification of inferior court judge

When a magistrate or a judge of a court inferior to the court of common pleas is interested in a cause pending before the magistrate or judge, is related to or has a bias or prejudice either for or against a party to a cause pending before the magistrate or judge or to a party's counsel, or is otherwise disqualified to sit in a cause pending before the magistrate or judge, on the filing of an affidavit of such party or counsel, setting forth the fact of that interest, relationship, bias, prejudice, or disqualification, the clerk or deputy clerk of the court, or the magistrate, shall enter the filing of the affidavit on the docket in that cause, and, forthwith notify the presiding judge of the court of common pleas or, if there is no presiding judge of the court, then a judge of the court of common pleas or if such judge is not available then a judge of the probate court of such county, who shall proceed without delay to examine into the affidavit, and, if the judge finds from all the evidence that the alleged interest, relationship, bias, prejudice, or disqualification exists, the judge shall designate another magistrate of the township or county, or another judge of the inferior court, or the court of common pleas to hear and determine that cause. The judge or magistrate so designated shall proceed to try the cause. The affidavit shall be filed not less than twenty-four hours before the time set for the hearing of the cause, unless such filing is unavoidably prevented. This section applies to criminal and civil proceedings.

(1995 H 151, eff. 12–4–95; 127 v 423, eff. 8–27–57; 1953 H 1; GC 13433–19)

2937.21 Continuance

No continuance at any stage of the proceeding, including that for determination of a motion, shall extend for more than ten days unless both the state and the accused consent thereto. Any continuance or delay in ruling contrary to the provisions of this section shall, unless procured by defendant or his counsel, be grounds for discharge of the defendant forthwith.

(128 v 97, eff. 1–1–60)

BAIL

2937.22 Forms of bail; receipts

Bail is security for the appearance of an accused to appear and answer to a specific criminal or quasi-criminal charge in any court or before any magistrate at a specific time or at any time to which a case may be continued, and not depart without leave. It may take any of the following forms:

(A) The deposit of cash by the accused or by some other person for him;

(B) The deposit by the accused or by some other person for him in form of bonds of the United States, this state, or any political subdivision thereof in a face amount equal to the sum set by the court or magistrate. In case of bonds not negotiable by delivery such bonds shall be properly endorsed for transfer.

(C) The written undertaking by one or more persons to forfeit the sum of money set by the court or magistrate, if the accused is in default for appearance, which shall be known as a recognizance.

All bail shall be received by the clerk of the court, deputy clerk of court, or by the magistrate, or by a special referee appointed by the supreme court pursuant to section 2937.46 of the Revised Code, and, except in cases of recognizances, receipt shall be given therefor by him.

(128 v 97, eff. 1–1–60)

2937.221 Use of driver's or commercial driver's license as bond in certain traffic violation arrests

(A) A person arrested without warrant for any violation listed in division (B) of this section, and having a current valid Ohio driver's or commercial driver's license,, if the person has been notified of the possible consequences of his actions as required by division (C) of this section, may post bond by depositing the license with the arresting officer if the officer and person so choose, or with the local court having jurisdiction if the court and person so choose. The license may be used as bond only during the period for which it is valid.

When an arresting officer accepts the driver's or commercial driver's license as bond, he shall note the date, time, and place of the court appearance on "the violator's notice to appear" and the notice shall serve as a valid Ohio driver's or commercial driver's license until the date and time appearing thereon. The arresting officer shall immediately forward the license to the appropriate court.

When a local court accepts the license as bond or continues the case to another date and time, it shall provide the person with a card in a form approved by the registrar of motor vehicles setting forth the license number, name, address, the date and time of the court appearance, and a statement that the license is being held as bond. The card shall serve as a valid license until the date and time contained in the card.

The court may accept other bond at any time and return the license to the person. The court shall return the license to the person when judgment is satisfied, including, but not limited to, compliance with any court orders, unless a suspension or revocation is part of the penalty imposed.

Neither "the violator's notice to appear" nor a court granted card shall continue driving privileges beyond the expiration date of the license.

If the person arrested fails to appear in court at the date and time set by the court or fails to satisfy the judgment of the court, including, but not limited to, compliance with all court orders within the time allowed by the court, the court may declare the forfeiture of the person's license. Thirty days after the declaration of forfeiture, the court shall forward the person's license to the registrar of motor vehicles. The registrar shall cancel the license and send written notification of the cancellation to the person at his last known address. No valid driver's or commercial driver's license shall be granted to the person for a period of one year after cancellation, unless the court having jurisdiction orders that the forfeiture be terminated.

(B) Division (A) of this section shall apply to persons arrested for violation of:

(1) Any of the provisions of Chapter 4511. or 4513. of the Revised Code, except sections 4511.19, 4511.20, 4511.251, and 4513.36 of the Revised Code;

(2) Any municipal ordinance substantially similar to a section included in division (B)(1) of this section;

(3) Any bylaw, rule, or regulation of the Ohio turnpike commission substantially similar to a section included in division (B)(1) of this section.

Division (A) of this section does not apply to those persons issued a citation for the commission of a minor misdemeanor under section 2935.26 of the Revised Code.

(C) No license shall be accepted as bond by an arresting officer or by a court under this section until the officer or court has notified the person that, if the person deposits the license with the officer or court and either does not appear on the date and at the time set by the officer or the court, if the court sets a time, or does not satisfy any judgment rendered, including, but not limited to, compliance with all court orders, the license will be canceled, the person will not be eligible for reissuance of the license or issuance of a new license for one year after cancellation, and the person is subject to any criminal penalties that may apply to the person.

(1994 H 687, eff. 10–12–94; 1989 S 49, eff. 11–3–89; 1989 H 381; 1986 S 356; 1978 S 351; 1975 H 1; 1973 H 234)

2937.23 Amount of bail; domestic violence offenders; anti–stalking violations

(A) In cases of felony, the amount of bail shall be fixed by the judge or magistrate. In cases of misdemeanor or violation of a municipal ordinance, it may be fixed by the judge, magistrate, or clerk of the court and may be in accordance with a schedule previously fixed by the judge or magistrate or, in cases when the judge, magistrate, or clerk of the court is not readily available, bail may be fixed by the sheriff, deputy sheriff, marshal, deputy marshal, police officer, or jailer having custody of the person charged, shall be in accordance with a schedule previously fixed by the judge or magistrate, and shall be taken only in the county courthouse, the municipal or township building, or the county or municipal jail. In all cases, it shall be fixed with consideration of the seriousness of the offense charged, the previous criminal record of the defendant, and the probability of his appearing at the trial of the case.

(B) In any case involving an alleged violation of section 2919.27 of the Revised Code or of a municipal ordinance that is substantially similar to that section, if the court determines that the violation of the temporary protection order or consent agreement allegedly involves conduct by the defendant that caused physical harm to the person or property of a family or household member covered by the order or agreement or conduct by that defendant that caused a family or household member to believe that the defendant would cause physical harm to that member or his property, the court shall determine whether it will order an evaluation of the mental condition of the defendant pursuant to division (A) of section 2919.271 of the Revised Code and, if it decides to so order, issue the order requiring that evaluation before it sets bail for the person charged with the violation.

(C) In any case involving an alleged violation of section 2903.214 of the Revised Code or of a municipal ordinance that is substantially similar to that section, if the court determines that the violation of the anti-stalking protection order allegedly involves conduct by the defendant that caused physical harm to the person or property of the person covered by the order or conduct by that defendant that caused the person covered by the order to believe that the defendant would cause physical harm to that person or his property, the court shall determine whether it will order an evaluation of the mental condition of the defendant pursuant to division (A) of section 2903.215 of the Revised Code and, if it decides to so order, issue the order requiring that evaluation before it sets bail for the person charged with the violation.

(1992 H 536, eff. 11–5–92; 1985 H 475; 129 v 557; 128 v 97)

2937.24   Oath to surety; form of affidavit

When a recognizance is offered under section 2937.22 of the Revised Code, the surety on which recognizance qualifies as a real property owner, the judge or magistrate shall require such surety to pledge to this state real property owned by the surety and located in this state. Whenever such pledge of real property has been given by any such proposed surety, he shall execute the usual form of recognizance, and in addition thereto there shall be filed his affidavit of justification of suretyship, to be attached to said recognizance as a part thereof. The surety may be required in such affidavit to depose as to whether he is, at the time of executing the same, surety upon any other recognizance and as to whether there are any unsatisfied judgments or executions against him. He may also be required to state any other fact which the court thinks relevant and material to a correct determination of the surety's sufficiency to act as bail. Such surety shall state in such affidavit where notices under section 2937.38 of the Revised Code may be served on himself, and service of notice of summons at such place is sufficient service for all purposes.

Such affidavit shall be executed by the proposed surety under an oath and may be in the following form:

"State of Ohio, County of ＿＿＿＿＿, ss:

＿＿＿＿＿ residing at ＿＿＿＿＿, who offers himself as surety for ＿＿＿＿＿ being first duly sworn, says that he owns in his own legal right, real property subject to execution, located in the county of ＿＿＿＿＿, State of Ohio, consisting of ＿＿＿＿＿ and described as follows to wit: ＿＿＿＿＿; that the title to the same is in his own name; that the value of the same is not less than ＿＿＿ dollars, and is subject to no encumbrances whatever except ＿＿＿＿＿; that he is not surety upon any unpaid or forfeited recognizance, and that he is not party to any unsatisfied judgment upon any recognizance; that he is worth not less than ＿＿＿ dollars over and above all debts, liabilities, and lawful claims against him, and all liens, encumbrances, and lawful claims against his property."

(1953 H 1, eff. 10–1–53; GC 13435–4)

date certain, or from day to day, or in case of the common pleas court on the first day of the next term thereof, and not depart without leave.

(128 v 97, eff. 1–1–60; 1953 H 1; GC 13435–11)

2937.32   Confinement for unbailable offenses and lack of sufficient bail

If an offense is not bailable or sufficient bail is not offered, the accused shall be committed to the jail of the county in which he is to be tried or, in the case of offense against a municipality, in the jail of said municipality if such there be.

(128 v 97, eff. 1–1–60; 1953 H 1; GC 13435–12)

2937.33   Receipt of recognizance

When a transcript or recognizance is received by the clerk of the court of common pleas, or of any court of record to which proceedings are transferred, he shall enter the same upon the appearance docket of the court, with the date of the filing of such transcript or recognizance, the date and amount of the recognizance, the names of the sureties, and the costs. Such recognizance is then of record in such court, and is proceeded on by process issuing therefrom, in a like manner as if it had been entered into before such court. When a court having recognizance of an offense takes a recognizance, it is a sufficient record thereof to enter upon the journal of such court the title of the case, the crime charged, the names of the sureties, the amount of the recognizance, and the time therein required for the appearance of the accused. In making the complete record, when required to be made, recognizances whether returned to or taken in such court shall be recorded in full, if required by the prosecutor or the accused.

(128 v 97, eff. 1–1–60; 1953 H 1; GC 13435–13)

2937.34   Accused unlawfully detained; examining court to be held

When a person is committed to jail, charged with an offense for which he has not been indicted, and claims to be unlawfully detained, the sheriff on demand of the accused or his counsel shall forthwith notify the court of common pleas, and the prosecuting attorney, to attend an examining court, the time of which shall be fixed by the judge. The judge shall hear said cause or complaint, examine the witnesses, and make such order as the justice of the case requires, and for such purpose the court may admit to bail, release without bond, or recommit to jail in accordance with the commitment. In the absence of the judge of the court of common pleas, the probate judge shall hold such examining court.

(1953 H 1, eff. 10–1–53; GC 13435–14)

2937.35   Forfeit of bail

Upon the failure of the accused or witness to appear in accordance with its terms the bail may in open court be adjudged forfeit, in whole or in part by the court or magistrate before whom he is to appear. But such court or magistrate may, in its discretion, continue the cause to a later date certain, giving notice of such date to him and the bail depositor or sureties, and adjudge the bail forfeit upon failure to appear at such later date.

(128 v 97, eff. 1–1–60)

2937.36   Forfeiture proceedings

Upon declaration of forfeiture, the magistrate or clerk of the court adjudging forfeiture shall proceed as follows:

(A) As to each bail, he shall proceed forthwith to deal with the sum deposited as if the same were imposed as a fine for the offense charged and distribute and account for the same accordingly provided that prior to so doing, he may satisfy accrued costs in the case out of the fund.

(B) As to any securities deposited, he shall proceed to sell the same, either at public sale advertised in the same manner as sale on chattel execution, or through any state or national bank performing such service upon the over the counter securities market and shall apply proceeds of sale, less costs or brokerage thereof as in cases of forfeited cash bail. Prior to such sale, the clerk shall give notices by ordinary mail to the depositor, at his address listed of record, if any, of his intention so to do, and such sale shall not proceed if the depositor, within ten days of mailing of such notice appears, and redeems said securities by either producing the body of the defendant in open court or posting the amount set in the recognizance in cash, to be dealt with as forfeited cash bail.

(C) As to recognizances he shall notify accused and each surety by ordinary mail at the address shown by them in their affidavits of qualification or on the record of the case, of the default of the accused and the adjudication of forfeiture and require each of them to show cause on or before a date certain to be stated in the notice, and which shall be not less than twenty nor more than thirty days from date of mailing notice, why judgment should not be entered against each of them for the penalty stated in the recognizance. If good cause by production of the body of the accused or otherwise is not shown, the court or magistrate shall thereupon enter judgment against the sureties or either of them, so notified, in such amount, not exceeding the penalty of the bond, as has been set in the adjudication of forfeiture, and shall award execution therefor as in civil cases. The proceeds of sale shall be received by the clerk or magistrate and distributed as on forfeiture of cash bail.

(128 v 97, eff. 1–1–60)

2937.37   Levy on property in judgment against surety

A magistrate or court of record inferior to the court of common pleas may proceed to judgment against a surety on a recognizance, and levy on his personal property, notwithstanding that the bond may exceed the monetary limitations on the jurisdiction of such court in civil cases, and jurisdiction over the person of surety shall attach from the mailing of the notice specified in section 2937.36 of the Revised Code, notwithstanding that such surety may not be within the territorial jurisdiction of the court; but levy on real property shall be made only through issuance, return, and levy made under certificate of judgment issued to the clerk of the court of common pleas pursuant to section 2329.02 of the Revised Code.

(128 v 97, eff. 1–1–60)

2937.38   Minority no defense in forfeiture proceedings

In any matter in which a minor is admitted to bail pursuant to Chapter 2937. of the Revised Code, the minority of the accused shall not be available as a defense to judgment against principal or surety, or against the sale of securities or transfer of cash bail, upon forfeiture.

(128 v 97, eff. 1–1–60)

2937.39   Remission of penalty

After judgment has been rendered against surety or after securities sold or cash bail applied, the court or magistrate, on the appearance, surrender, or re-arrest of the accused on the charge, may remit all or such portion of the penalty as it deems just and in the case of previous application and transfer of cash or proceeds, the magistrate or clerk may deduct an amount equal to the amount so transferred from subsequent payments to the agencies receiving such proceeds of forfeiture until the amount is recouped for the benefit of the person or persons entitled thereto under order or remission.

(128 v 97, eff. 1–1–60)

2937.40   Release of bail and sureties;   use to satisfy fine or costs only when deposited by accused

(A) Bail of any type that is deposited under sections 2937.22 to 2937.45 of the Revised Code or Criminal Rule 46 by a person other than the accused shall be discharged and released, and sureties on recognizances shall be released, in any of the following ways:

(1) When a surety on a recognizance or the depositor of cash or securities as bail for an accused desires to surrender the accused before the appearance date, the surety is discharged from further responsibility or the deposit is redeemed in either of the following ways:

(a) By delivery of the accused into open court;

(b) When, on the written request of the surety or depositor, the clerk of the court to which recognizance is returnable or in which deposit is made issues to the sheriff a warrant for the arrest of the accused and the sheriff indicates on the return that he holds the accused in his jail.

(2) By appearance of the accused in accordance with the terms of the recognizance or deposit and the entry of judgment by the court or magistrate;

(3) By payment into court, after default, of the sum fixed in the recognizance or the sum fixed in the order of forfeiture, if it is less.

(B) When cash or securities have been deposited as bail by a person other than the accused and the bail is discharged and released pursuant to division (A) of this section, or when property has been pledged by a surety on recognizance and the surety on recognizance has been released pursuant to division (A) of this section, the court shall not deduct any amount from the cash or securities or declare forfeited and levy or execute against pledged property. The court shall not apply any of the deposited cash or securities toward, or declare forfeited and levy or execute against property pledged for a recognizance for, the satisfaction of any penalty or fine, and court costs, assessed against the accused upon his conviction or guilty plea, except upon express approval of the person who deposited the cash or securities or the surety.

(C) Bail of any type that is deposited under sections 2937.22 to 2937.45 of the Revised Code or Criminal Rule 46 by an accused shall be discharged and released to the accused, and property pledged by an accused for a recognizance shall be discharged, upon the appearance of the accused in accordance with the terms of the recognizance or deposit and the entry of judgment by the court or magistrate, except that, if the defendant is not indigent, the court may apply deposited bail toward the satisfaction of a penalty or fine, and court costs, assessed against the accused upon his conviction or guilty plea, and may declare forfeited and levy or execute against pledged property for the satisfaction of a penalty or fine, and court costs, assessed against the accused upon his conviction or guilty plea.

(D) Notwithstanding any other provision of this section, an Ohio driver's or commercial driver's license that is deposited as bond may be forfeited and otherwise handled as provided in section 2937.221 of the Revised Code.

(1990 S 338, eff. 11–28–90; 1989 H 381; 1986 S 356; 1980 H 402; 128 v 97)

2937.41   Return of bail; notice of discharge of recognizance

On the discharge of bail, the magistrate or clerk of the court shall return, subject to division (B) or (C) of section 2937.40 of the Revised Code, deposited cash or securities to the depositor, but the magistrate or clerk of the court may require presentation of an issued original receipt as a condition to the return. In the case of discharged recognizances, subject to division (B) or (C) of section 2937.40 of the Revised Code, the magistrate or clerk of the court shall endorse the satisfaction on the recognizance and shall forthwith transmit to the county recorder the notice of discharge provided for in section 2937.26 of the Revised Code.

(1980 H 402, eff. 5–13–80; 128 v 97)

2937.42   Defect in form of recognizance

Forfeiture of a recognizance shall not be barred or defeated or a judgment thereon reversed by the neglect or omission to note or record the default, or by a defect in the form of such recognizance, if it appears from the tenor thereof at what court the party or witness was bound to appear and that the court or officer before whom it was taken was authorized to require and take such recognizance.

(128 v 97, eff. 1–1–60; 1953 H 1; GC 13435–22)

2937.43   Arrest for failure to appear; issuance of warrant

Should the accused fail to appear as required, after having been released pursuant to section 2937.29 of the Revised Code, the court having jurisdiction at the time of such failure may, in addition to any other action provided by law, issue a warrant for the arrest of such accused.

(131 v H 47, eff. 8–10–65)

2937.44 Form of recognizance

Recognizances substantially in the forms following are sufficient:

RECOGNIZANCE OF THE ACCUSED

The State of Ohio, _____ County, ss:

Be it remembered, that on the _____ day of _____, in the year _____ E.F. and G.H. personally appeared before me, and jointly and severally acknowledged themselves to owe the state of Ohio, the sum of _____ dollars, to be levied on their goods, chattels, lands, and tenements, if default is made in the condition following, to wit:

The condition of this recognizance is such that if the above bound E.F. personally appears before the court of common pleas on the first day of the next term thereof, then and there to answer a charge of (here name the offense with which the accused is charged) and abide the judgment of the court and not depart without leave, then this recognizance shall be void; otherwise it shall be and remain in full force and virtue in law.

Taken and acknowledged before me, on the day and year above written.

A.B., Judge

RECOGNIZANCE OF WITNESS

The State of Ohio, _____ County, ss:

Be it remembered, that on the _____ day of _____, in the year _____ E.F. and G.H. personally appeared before me and jointly and severally acknowledged themselves to owe the state of Ohio, the sum of _____ dollars, to be levied on their goods, chattels, lands, and tenements, if default is made in the condition following, to wit:

The condition of this recognizance is such that if the above bound E.F. personally appears before the court of common pleas on the first day of the next term thereof then and there to give evidence on behalf of the state, touching such matters as shall then and there be required of him, and not depart the court without leave, then this recognizance shall be void, otherwise it shall remain in full force and virtue in law.

Taken and acknowledged before me, on the day and year above written.

A.B., Judge

TO KEEP THE PEACE

The State of Ohio, _____ County, ss:

Be it remembered, that on the _____ day of _____, in the year of _____ E.F., and G.H. personally appeared before me, and jointly and severally acknowledged themselves to owe the state of Ohio, the sum of _____ dollars, to be levied on their goods, chattels, lands, and tenements, if default is made in the condition following, to wit:

The condition of this recognizance is such that if the above bound E.F. personally appears before the court of common pleas, on the first day of the next term thereof, then and there to answer unto a complaint of C.D. that he has reason to fear, and does fear, that the said E.F. will (here state the charge in the complaint), and abide the order of the court thereon, and in the meantime to keep the peace and be of good behavior toward the citizens of the state generally, and especially toward the said C.D., then this recognizance shall be void; otherwise it shall be and remain in full force and virtue in law.

Taken and acknowledged before me, on the day and year above written.

A.B., Judge

(127 v 1039, eff. 1–1–58; 1953 H 1; GC 13435–24)

2937.45 Forms of commitments

Commitments substantially in the forms following are sufficient:

COMMITMENT AFTER

EXAMINATION

The State of Ohio, _____ County, ss:

To the Keeper of the Jail of the County aforesaid, greeting:

Whereas, E.F. has been arrested, on the oath of C.D., for (here describe the offense), and has been examined by me on such charge, and required to give bail in the sum of _____ dollars for his appearance before the court of common pleas with which requisition he has failed to comply. Therefore, in the name of the state of Ohio, I command you to receive the said E.F. into your custody, in the jail of the county aforesaid, there to remain until discharged by due course of law.

Given under my hand, this _____ day of _____

A.B., Judge

COMMITMENT PENDING

EXAMINATION

The State of Ohio, _____ County, ss:

To the Keeper of the Jail of the County aforesaid, greeting:

Whereas, E.F. has been arrested on the oath of C.D., for (here describe the offense) and has been brought before me for examination and the same has been necessarily postponed by reason of (here state the cause of delay). Therefore, I command you, in the name of the state of Ohio, to receive the said E.F. into your custody in the jail of the county aforesaid (or in such other place as the justice shall name) there to remain until discharged by due course of law.

Given under my hand, this _____ day of _____

A.B., Judge

(127 v 1039, eff. 1–1–58; 1953 H 1; GC 13435–25)

UNIFORM PROCEDURES IN TRAFFIC CASES

2937.46   Supreme court authorized to set uniform procedures in traffic cases

The supreme court of Ohio may, in the interest of uniformity of procedure in the various courts, and for the purpose of promoting prompt and efficient disposition of cases arising under the traffic laws of this state and related ordinances, makes [1] uniform rules for practice and procedure in courts inferior to the court of common pleas not inconsistent with the provisions of Chapter 2937. of the Revised Code, including, but not limited to:

(A) Separation of arraignment and trial of traffic and other types of cases;

(B) Consolidation of cases for trial;

(C) Transfer of cases within the same county for the purpose of trial;

(D) Designation of special referees for hearings or for receiving pleas or bail at times when courts are not in session;

(E) Fixing of reasonable bonds, and disposition of cases in which bonds have been forfeited.

All of said rules, when promulgated by the supreme court, shall be fully binding on all courts inferior to the court of common pleas and shall effect a cancellation of any local court rules inconsistent therewith.

(129 v 582, eff. 1–10–61; 128 v 97)

[1] Prior and current versions differ; although no amendment to this language was indicated in 129 v 582, "makes" appeared as "make" in 128 v 97.

PENALTY

2937.99   Penalties

Whoever fails to appear as required, after having been released pursuant to section 2937.29 of the Revised Code, shall be sentenced as follows:

(A) If the release was in connection with a charge of the commission of a felony or pending appeal after conviction of a felony, he shall be fined not more than five thousand dollars or imprisoned in a state correctional institution for not less than one nor more than five years, or both.

(B) If the release was in connection with a charge of the commission of a misdemeanor or for appearance as a witness, he shall be fined not more than one thousand dollars or imprisoned not more than one year, or both.

This section does not apply to misdemeanors and related ordinance offenses arising under Chapters 4501., 4503., 4505., 4507., 4509., 4511., 4513., 4517., 4549., and 5577. of the Revised Code, except that this section does apply to violations of sections 4511.19, 4549.02, and 4549.021 of the Revised Code and ordinance offenses related to such sections.

(1994 H 571, eff. 10–6–94; 131 v H 47, eff. 8–10–65)

TRIAL—MAGISTRATE COURTS

PRELIMINARY PROVISIONS

PRELIMINARY PROVISIONS

2938.01 Definitions

The definition of "magistrate" set forth in section 2931.01 of the Revised Code, and the definition of "peace officer," "prosecutor," and "offense" set forth in section 2935.01 of the Revised Code applies to Chapter 2938 of the Revised Code.

(128 v 97, eff. 1–1–60)

2938.02 Applicability of provisions

The provisions of Chapter 2938. of the Revised Code shall apply to trial on the merits of any misdemeanor, ordinance offense, prosecution for the violation of any rule or regulation of any governmental body authorized to adopt penal regulations, or to complaints to keep the peace, which may be instituted in and retained for trial on the merits in any court or before any magistrate inferior to the court of common pleas; provided that in juvenile courts, where the conduct of any person under the age of eighteen years is made the subject of inquiry and for which special provision is made by Chapter 2151. of the Revised Code, such matters shall be tried, adjusted, or disposed of pursuant to Chapter 2151. of the Revised Code.

(128 v 97, eff. 1–1–60)

2938.03 Setting and continuing cases; assignment of additional judges

The magistrate, or judge or clerk of court of record, shall set all criminal cases for a trial at a date not later than thirty days after plea is received, or in those cases in which the charge has been reduced on preliminary hearing or has been certified by another magistrate, then at a date not later than thirty days from fixing of charge or receipt of transcript as the case may be. Continuances beyond such date shall be granted only upon notice to the opposing party and for good cause shown.

Criminal cases shall be given precedence over civil matters in all assignments for trial and if the volume of contested criminal matters in courts of more than one judge is such as to require it, the chief justice or presiding judge of such court shall assign additional judges from other divisions of the court to assist in the trial of such criminal matters; in the case of county courts, the presiding judge of the court of common pleas shall assign county judges from other areas of jurisdiction within the county to assist those county judges whose volume of criminal cases requires assistance.

(128 v 97, eff. 1–1–60)

JURIES

2938.04   Jury trial

In courts of record right to trial by jury as defined in section 2945.17 of the Revised Code shall be claimed by making demand in writing therefor and filing the same with the clerk of the court not less than three days prior to the date set for trial or on the day following receipt of notice whichever is the later.   Failure to claim jury trial as provided in this section is a complete waiver of right thereto.   In courts not of record jury trial may not be had, but failure to waive jury in writing where right to jury trial may be asserted shall require the magistrate to certify such case to a court of record as provided in section 2937.08 of the Revised Code.

(129 v 582, eff. 1–10–61; 128 v 97)

2938.05   Withdrawal of claim of jury

Claim of jury, once made, may be withdrawn by written waiver of jury but in such case the court may, if a jury has been summoned, require accused to pay all costs of mileage and fees of members of the venire for one day's service, notwithstanding the outcome of the case.   No withdrawal of claim for jury shall effect any re-transfer of a case, once it has been certified to a court of record.

(128 v 97, eff. 1–1–60)

2938.06   Number of jurors; challenges

If the number of jurors to be sworn in a case is not stated in the claim, the number to be sworn shall be twelve, but the accused may stipulate for a jury of six, provided in such case the number of pre-emptory [1] challenges shall be limited to two on each side.

(128 v 97, eff. 1–1–60)

[1] So in original.

PRACTICE AND PROCEDURE

2938.07   Authority of magistrate or judge

The magistrate or judge of the trial court shall control all proceedings during a criminal trial and shall limit the introduction of evidence and argument of counsel to relevant and material matters with a view to expeditious and effective ascertainment of truth regarding the matters in issue.

(128 v 97, eff. 1–1–60)

2938.08   Presumption of innocence

A defendant in a criminal action is presumed to be innocent until he is proved guilty of the offense charged, and in case of a reasonable doubt whether his guilt is satisfactorily shown, he shall be acquitted.   The presumption of innocence places upon the state (or the municipality) the burden of proving him guilty beyond a reasonable doubt.

In charging a jury the trial court shall state the meaning of the presumption of innocence and of reasonable doubt in each case.

(128 v 97, eff. 1–1–60)

2938.09   Grounds of objection to be stated

In the trial of any criminal case, the grounds of an objection to any ruling or action of the judge or magistrate shall be stated if required by him.

(1986 H 412, eff. 3–17–87; 128 v 97)

2938.10   Territorial jurisdiction

The state or municipality in all cases must prove the offense committed within the territorial jurisdiction of the court, and in ordinance cases within the municipality, except as to those offenses in which the court has county wide jurisdiction created by statute and as to those cases in which certification has been made pursuant to section 2937.08 of the Revised Code.
(128 v 97, eff. 1–1–60)

2938.11   Order of proceedings of trial

The trial of an issue shall proceed before the trial court or jury as follows:

(A) Counsel may state the case for the prosecution, including the evidence by which he expects to sustain it.

(B) Counsel for the defendant may state his defense, including the evidence which he expects to offer.

(C) The prosecution then shall produce all its evidence, and the defendant may follow with his evidence, but the court or magistrate, in the furtherance of justice and for good cause shown, may permit evidence to be offered by either side out of its order and may permit rebuttal evidence to be offered by the prosecution.

(D) When the evidence is concluded, unless the case is submitted without argument, counsel for the prosecution shall commence, defendant or his counsel follow, and counsel for the prosecution conclude his argument either to the court or jury. The judge or magistrate may impose a reasonable time limit on argument.

(E) The judge, after argument is concluded in a jury case, forthwith shall charge the jury on the law pertaining to the case and controlling their deliberations, which charge shall not be reduced to writing and taken into the jury room unless the trial judge in his discretion shall so order.

(F) Any verdict arrived at by the jury, or finding determined by the judge or magistrate in trial to the court, shall be announced and received only in open court as soon as it is determined. Any finding by the judge or magistrate shall be announced in open court not more than forty-eight hours after submission of the case to him.
(1986 H 412, eff. 3–17–87; 128 v 97)

2938.12   When accused may be tried in his absence

A person being tried for a misdemeanor, either to the court, or to a jury, upon request in writing, subscribed by him, may, with the consent of the judge or magistrate, be tried in his absence, but no right shall exist in the defendant to be so tried. If after trial commences a person being tried escapes or departs without leave, the trial shall proceed and verdict or finding be received and sentence passed as if he were personally present.
(128 v 97, eff. 1–1–60)

2938.13   Responsibility for prosecution

In any case prosecuted for violation of a municipal ordinance the village solicitor or city director of law, and for a statute, he or the prosecuting attorney, shall present the case for the municipal corporation and the state respectively, but either may delegate the responsibility to some other attorney in a proper case, or, if the defendant be unrepresented by counsel may with leave of court, withdraw from the case. But the magistrate or judge shall not permit prosecution of any criminal case by private attorney employed or retained by a complaining witness.
(1977 H 219, eff. 11–1–77; 128 v 97)

2938.14   Venires for juries

Venires for juries in courts of record inferior to the court of common pleas shall be drawn and summoned in the manner provided in the various acts creating such courts. But no challenge to the array shall be sustained in any case for the reason that some of the venire are not residents of the territory of the court, if it appears that the venire was regularly drawn and certified by the jury commissioners of county or municipality as the case may be.

(129 v 582, eff. 1–10–61; 128 v 97)

2938.15 Rules of evidence and procedure

The rules of evidence and procedure, including those governing notices, proof of special matters, depositions, and joinder of defendants and offenses set forth in Chapter 2945. of the Revised Code, which are not, by their nature, inapplicable to the trial of misdemeanors, shall prevail in trials under Chapter 2938. of the Revised Code where no special provision is made in such chapter, or where no provision is made by rule of the supreme court adopted pursuant to section 2937.46 of the Revised Code.

(129 v 582, eff. 1–10–61; 128 v 97)

GRAND JURORS

GRAND JURORS

2939.01   Definition of magistrate

The definition of "magistrate" set forth in section 2931.01 of the Revised Code applies to Chapter 2939. of the Revised Code.

(1953 H 1, eff. 10–1–53)

2939.02   Selection of grand jury

Grand juries shall consist of fifteen persons who satisfy the qualifications of a juror specified in section 2313.42 of the Revised Code. Persons to serve as grand jurors in the court of common pleas of each county shall be selected from the persons whose names are contained in the annual jury list and from the ballots deposited in the jury wheel, or in the automation data processing storage drawer, or from the names contained in an automated data processing information storage device as prescribed by sections 2313.07, 2313.08, and 2313.35 of the Revised Code.

At the time of the selection of the persons who are to constitute the grand jury, the commissioners of jurors shall draw from the jury wheel, or draw by utilizing the automation data processing equipment and procedures described in section 2313.07 of the Revised Code, ballots containing the names of not less than twenty-five persons. The first fifteen persons whose names are drawn shall constitute the grand jury, if they can be located and served by the sheriff, and if they are not excused by the court or a judge of the court. If any of the first fifteen persons whose names are so drawn are not located or are unable to serve and are for that reason excused by the court or by a judge of the court, whose duty it is to supervise the impaneling of the grand jury, the judge shall then designate the person whose name next appears on the list of persons drawn, to serve in the place of the person not found or excused and shall so continue to substitute the names of the persons drawn in the order in which they were drawn, to fill all vacancies resulting from persons not being found or having been excused by the court or the judge of the court, until the necessary fifteen persons are selected to make up the grand jury. If all of the names appearing on the list of persons drawn are exhausted before the grand jury is complete, the judge shall order the commissioners of jurors to draw such additional names as the judge determines, and shall proceed to fill the vacancies from those names in the order in which they are drawn.

The judge of the court of common pleas may select any person who satisfies the qualifications of a juror and whose name is not included in the annual jury list or on a ballot deposited in the jury wheel or automation data processing storage drawer, or whose name is not contained in an automated data processing information storage device, to preside as foreman of the grand jury, in which event the grand jury shall consist of the foreman so selected and fourteen additional grand jurors selected from the jury wheel or by use of the automation data processing equipment and procedures in the manner provided in this section.

(1984 H 183, eff. 10–1–84; 1969 H 424; 131 v S 20; 130 v S 103; 1953 H 1; GC 11419–34)

2939.03   Grand jurors subject to same provisions and regulations as other jurors

A grand jury is drawn and notified by the same persons, from the same jury wheel, automation data processing storage drawer, or automated data processing information storage device and in the same manner as other jurors are drawn and notified under sections 2939.02 to 2939.04, inclusive, and 2313.01 to 2313.46, inclusive, of the Revised Code. Grand jurors so drawn and notified may be excused from service for the same reasons and in the same manner as other jurors under such sections, and not otherwise. They are subject to the same fines and penalties for nonattendance and otherwise as are other jurors under such sections. The duties and the powers of courts of common pleas and clerks of courts of common pleas, and of the commissioners of jurors in regard to grand jurors, in all respects are the same as in regard to other jurors.

(1969 H 424, eff. 11–25–69; 131 v S 20; 1953 H 1; GC 11419–35)

2939.031   Alternate juror for grand jury; selection of

When it appears to the judge impaneling a grand jury that the inquiry is likely to be protracted, or upon direction of the judge, an additional or alternate juror shall be selected in the same manner as the regular jurors in the inquiry are selected. The additional or alternate juror shall be sworn and seated near the jury, with equal opportunity for seeing and hearing the proceedings, shall attend the inquiry at all times and shall obey all orders and admonitions of the court or foreman. When the jurors are ordered kept together, the alternate juror shall be kept with them. The additional or alternate juror shall be liable as a regular juror for failure to attend the inquiry or to obey any order or admonition of the court or foreman. He shall receive the same compensation as other jurors, and except as provided in this section shall be discharged upon the final submission of the bill to the foreman.

If before the final submission of the bill to the jury, a juror dies or is discharged by the judge or foreman due to incapacity, absence, or disqualification of such juror, the additional or alternate juror, upon order of the judge or foreman, shall become one of the jury and serve in all respects as though selected as an original juror during the absence or incapacity of an original juror.

(125 v 345, eff. 10–14–53)

2939.04 Grand jurors; compensation

The compensation of grand jurors shall be fixed by resolution of the board of county commissioners, not to exceed ten dollars for each day's attendance, payable out of the county treasury. Except in counties of less than one hundred thousand population according to the last federal census, in which counties the judge of the court of common pleas shall make rules and regulations in his own county applicable thereto, a person who has served as a grand juror at a term of court is prohibited from serving again, either as a grand juror or petit juror, in that jury year in which the service is rendered, or in the next jury year. He is entitled to a certificate of exemption in like manner as a petit juror. The court of common pleas may order the drawing of a special jury to sit at any time public business requires it.

(1974 S 465, eff. 3–4–75; 1953 H 1; GC 11419–36)

2939.05 Clerk to make list of persons required to appear—Repealed

(129 v 1201, eff. 9–11–61; 1953 H 1; GC 13436–1)

2939.06 Oath to grand jurors

When a grand jury is impaneled the court of common pleas shall appoint one of the members thereof as foreman, and shall administer, or cause to be administered, to said jurors an oath in the following words:

"You and each of you do solemnly swear that you will diligently inquire, and true presentment make of all such matters and things as shall be given you in charge of [1] otherwise come to your knowledge, touching the present service; the counsel of the state, your own, and your fellows, you shall keep secret unless called on in a court of justice to make disclosures; and you shall present no person through malice, hatred, or ill will, nor shall you leave any person unpresented through fear, favor, or affection, or for any reward or hope thereof, but in all your presentments you shall present the truth, the whole truth, and nothing but the truth, according to the best of your skill and understanding.

(1953 H 1, eff. 10–1–53; GC 13436–3)

[1] So in original; should this read: "or"?

2939.07 Charge of the court

The grand jurors, after being sworn, shall be charged as to their duty by the judge of the court of common pleas, who shall call their attention particularly to the obligation of secrecy which their oaths impose, and explain to them the law applicable to such matters as may be brought before them.

(1953 H 1, eff. 10–1–53; GC 13436–4)

2939.08 Duty of grand jury

After the charge of the court of common pleas, the grand jury shall retire with the officer appointed to attend it, and proceed to inquire of and present all offenses committed within the county.

(1953 H 1, eff. 10–1–53; GC 13436–5)

2939.09 Clerk of grand jury

The grand jury may appoint one of its members to be its clerk to preserve the minutes of its proceedings and actions in all cases pending before it. Such minutes shall be delivered to the prosecuting attorney before the jury is discharged.

(1953 H 1, eff. 10–1–53; GC 13436–6)

OFFICIALS

2939.10 Who shall have access to grand jury

The prosecuting attorney or assistant prosecuting attorney may at all times appear before the grand jury to give information relative to a matter cognizable by it, or advice upon a legal matter when required. The prosecuting attorney may interrogate witnesses before the grand jury when the grand jury or the prosecuting attorney finds it necessary, but no person other than the grand jurors shall be permitted to remain in the room with the jurors while the jurors are expressing their views or giving their votes on a matter before them. In all matters or cases which the attorney general is required to investigate or prosecute by the governor or general assembly, or which a special prosecutor is required by section 177.03 of the Revised Code to investigate and prosecute, the attorney general or the special prosecutor, respectively, shall have and exercise any or all rights, privileges, and powers of prosecuting attorneys, and any assistant or special counsel designated by the attorney general or special prosecutor for that purpose, has the same authority. Proceedings in relation to such matters or cases are under the exclusive supervision and control of the attorney general or the special prosecutor.

(1986 S 74, eff. 9–3–86; 1953 H 1; GC 13436–7)

2939.11 Official reporters

The official shorthand reporter of the county, or any shorthand reporter designated by the court of common pleas, at the request of the prosecuting attorney, or any such reporter designated by the attorney general in investigations conducted by him, may take shorthand notes of testimony before the grand jury, and furnish a transcript to the prosecuting attorney or the attorney general, and to no other person. The shorthand reporter shall withdraw from the jury room before the jurors begin to express their views or take their vote on the matter before them. Such reporter shall take an oath to be administered by the judge after the grand jury is sworn, imposing an obligation of secrecy to not disclose any testimony taken or heard except to the grand jury, prosecuting attorney, or attorney general, unless called upon in court to make disclosures.

(1953 H 1, eff. 10–1–53; GC 13436–8)

2939.12 Clerk to issue subpoenas for witnesses

When required by the grand jury, prosecuting attorney, or judge of the court of common pleas, the clerk of the court of common pleas shall issue subpoenas and other process to any county to bring witnesses to testify before such jury.

(1953 H 1, eff. 10–1–53; GC 13436–9)

WITNESSES

2939.121 Employee's attendance before grand jury under subpoena; employer may not penalize

No employer shall discharge or terminate from employment, threaten to discharge or terminate from employment, or otherwise punish or penalize any employee because of time lost from regular employment as a result of the employee's attendance at any proceeding before a grand jury pursuant to a subpoena. This section generally does not require and shall not be construed to require an employer to pay an employee for time lost resulting from attendance at any grand jury proceeding. However, if an employee is subpoenaed to appear at a grand jury proceeding and the proceeding pertains to an offense against the employer or an offense involving the employee during the course of his employment, the employer shall not decrease or withhold the employee's pay for any time lost as a result of compliance with the subpoena. Any employer who knowingly violates this section is in contempt of court.

(1984 S 172, eff. 9–26–84)

2939.13 Oath to witnesses

Before a witness is examined by the grand jury, an oath shall be administered to him by the foreman of the grand jury or by the judge of the court of common pleas or the clerk of the court of common pleas, truly to testify of such matters and things as may lawfully be inquired of before such jury. A certificate that the oath has been administered shall be indorsed on the subpoena of the witness or otherwise made by the foreman of the grand jury, judge, or clerk certifying the attendance of said witness to the clerk of the court.

(1953 H 1, eff. 10–1–53; GC 13436–10)

2939.14   Proceedings when witness refuses to testify

If a witness before a grand jury refuses to answer an interrogatory, the court of common pleas shall be informed in writing, in which such interrogatory shall be stated, with the excuse for the refusal given by the witness. The court shall determine whether the witness is required to answer, and the grand jury shall be forthwith informed of such decision.

(1953 H 1, eff. 10–1–53; GC 13436–11)

2939.15   Court may proceed against witness for contempt

If the court of common pleas determines that a witness before a grand jury is required to answer an interrogatory and such witness persists in his refusal, he shall be brought before the court, which shall proceed in a like manner as if such witness had been interrogated and refused to answer in open court.

(1953 H 1, eff. 10–1–53; GC 13436–12)

GENERAL PROVISIONS

2939.16   Court may appoint grand juror in case of death

In case of sickness, death, discharge, or nonattendance of a grand juror after the grand jury is sworn, the court may cause another to be sworn in his stead. The court shall charge such juror as required by section 2939.07 of the Revised Code.

(1953 H 1, eff. 10–1–53; GC 13436–13)

2939.17   New grand jury may be summoned

After the grand jury is discharged, the court of common pleas, when necessary, may order the drawing and impaneling of a new grand jury, which shall be summoned and returned as provided by section 2939.03 of the Revised Code and shall be sworn and proceed in the manner provided by sections 2939.06 to 2939.24, inclusive, of the Revised Code. Whenever the governor or general assembly directs the attorney general to conduct any investigation or prosecution, the court of common pleas or any judge thereof, on written request of the attorney general, shall order a special grand jury to be summoned, and such special grand jury may be called and discharge its duties either before, during, or after any session of the regular grand jury, and its proceedings shall be independent of the proceedings of the regular grand jury but of the same force and effect.

Whenever a witness is necessary to a full investigation by the attorney general under this section, or to secure or successfully maintain and conclude a prosecution arising out of any such investigation, the judge of the court of common pleas may grant to such witness immunity from any prosecution based on the testimony or other evidence given by the witness in the course of the investigation or prosecution, other than a prosecution for perjury in giving such testimony or evidence.

(1970 H 956, eff. 9–16–70; 129 v 1201; 1953 H 1; GC 13436–14)

2939.18   Fact of indictment shall be kept secret

No grand juror, officer of the court, or other person shall disclose that an indictment has been found against a person not in custody or under bail, before such indictment is filed and the case docketed, except by the issue of process.

(1953 H 1, eff. 10–1–53; GC 13436–15)

2939.19   Testimony of grand jurors

No grand juror may state or testify in court in what manner any member of the grand jury voted or what opinion was expressed by any juror on any question before the grand jury.

(1953 H 1, eff. 10–1–53; GC 13436–16)

2939.20   Indictment by twelve jurors

At least twelve of the grand jurors must concur in the finding of an indictment.   When so found, the foreman shall indorse on such indictment the words "A true bill" and subscribe his name as foreman.

(1953 H 1, eff. 10–1–53; GC 13436–17)

2939.21   Grand jury to visit county jail

Once every three months, the grand jurors shall visit the county jail, examine its condition, and inquire into the discipline and treatment of the prisoners, their habits, diet, and accommodations.   They shall report on these matters to the court of common pleas in writing. The clerk of the court of common pleas shall forward a copy of the report to the department of rehabilitation and correction.

(1982 S 23, eff. 7–6–82; 1976 H 390; 1953 H 1; GC 13436–20)

2939.22   Proceedings when indictments are returned

Indictments found by a grand jury shall by presented by the foreman to the court of common pleas, and filed with the clerk of the court of common pleas, who shall indorse thereon the date of such filing and enter each case upon the appearance docket and the trial docket of the term when the persons indicted have been arrested.   The court shall assign such indictments for trial under section 2945.02 of the Revised Code, and recognizances of defendants and witnesses shall be taken for their appearance in court.   When a case is continued to the next term of court, such recognizance shall require the appearance of the defendants and witnesses at a time designated by the court.   Secret indictments shall not be docketed by name until after the apprehension of the accused.

(1953 H 1, eff. 10–1–53; GC 13436–21)

2939.23   Report to court when indictment not found

If an indictment is not found by the grand jury, against an accused who has been held to answer, such fact shall be reported by the foreman to the court of common pleas.

(1953 H 1, eff. 10–1–53; GC 13436–22)

2939.24   Disposition of person in jail and not indicted

If a person held in jail charged with an indictable offense is not indicted at the term of court at which he is held to answer, he shall be discharged unless:

(A) He was committed on such charge after the discharge of the grand jury.

(B) The transcript has not been filed.

(C) There is not sufficient time at such term of court to investigate said cause.

(D) The grand jury, for good cause, continues the hearing of said charge until the next term of court.

(E) It appears to the court of common pleas that a witness for the state has been enticed or kept away, detained, or prevented from attending court by sickness or unavoidable accident.

(1953 H 1, eff. 10–1–53; GC 13436–23)

OUT–OF–STATE WITNESS

2939.25   Definition of witness, state, and summons

As used in sections 2939.25 to 2939.29, inclusive, of the Revised Code:

(A) "Witness" includes a person whose testimony is desired in any proceeding or investigation by a grand jury or in a criminal action, prosecution, or proceeding.

(B) "State" includes any territory of the United States and District of Columbia.

(C) "Summons" includes a subpoena, order, or other notice requiring the appearance of a witness.

(1953 H 1, eff. 10–1–53; GC 13436–24)

2939.26 Foreign court may compel witnesses

If a judge of a court of record in any state which by its laws has made provision for commanding persons within that state to attend and testify in this state, certifies under the seal of such court that there is a criminal prosecution pending in such court, or that a grand jury investigation has commenced or is about to commence, that a person being within this state is a material witness in such prosecution or grand jury investigation, and that his presence will be required for a specified number of days, upon presentation of such certificate to any judge of a court of record in the county in this state in which such person is, such judge shall fix a time and place for a hearing and shall make an order directing the witness to appear at a time and place certain for the hearing.

If at a hearing such judge determines that the witness is material and necessary, that it will not cause undue hardship to the witness to be compelled to attend and testify in the prosecution or grand jury investigation in the other state, and that the laws of the state in which the prosecution is pending, or grand jury investigation has commenced or is about to commence, and of any other state through which the witness may be required to pass by ordinary course of travel, will give to him protection from arrest and the service of civil and criminal process, he shall issue a summons, with a copy of the certificate attached, directing the witness to attend and testify in the court where the prosecution is pending, or where a grand jury investigation has commenced or is about to commence, at a time and place specified in the summons. In any such hearing the certificate is prima-facie evidence of all the facts stated therein.

If said certificate recommends that the witness be taken into immediate custody and delivered to an officer of the requesting state to assure his attendance in the requesting state, such judge may, in lieu of notification of the hearing, direct that such witness be forthwith brought before him for said hearing. If the judge at the hearing is satisfied of the desirability of such custody and delivery, for which determination the certificate is prima-facie proof of such desirability, he may, in lieu of issuing subpoena or summons, order that said witness be forthwith taken into custody and delivered to an officer of the requesting state.

If the witness, who is summoned as provided in this section, after being paid or tendered by some properly authorized person the sum of ten cents a mile for each mile by the ordinary traveled route to and from the court where the prosecution is pending and five dollars for each day, that he is required to travel and attend as a witness, fails without good cause to attend and testify as directed in the summons, he shall be punished in the manner provided for the punishment of any witness who disobeys a summons issued from a court of record in this state.

(1953 H 1, eff. 10–1–53; GC 13436–25)

2939.27 Certificate to specify time witness will be required; mileage and fees

If a person in any state, which by its laws has made provision for commanding persons within its borders to attend and testify in criminal prosecutions or grand jury investigations commenced or about to commence, in this state, is a material witness in a prosecution pending in a court of record in this state, or in a grand jury investigation which has commenced or is about to commence, a judge of such court may issue a certificate under the seal of the court stating these facts and specifying the number of days the witness will be required. Said certificate may include a recommendation that the witness be taken into immediate custody and delivered to an officer of this state to assure his attendance in this state. This certificate shall be presented to a judge of a court of record in the county in which the witness is found.

If the witness is summoned to attend and testify in this state he shall be tendered the sum of ten cents a mile for each mile by the ordinary traveled route to and from the court where the prosecution is pending, and five dollars for each day that he is required to travel and attend as a witness. A witness who has appeared in accordance with the summons shall not be required to remain within this state a longer period of time than the period mentioned in the certificate, unless otherwise ordered by the court. If such witness, after coming into this state, fails without good cause to attend and testify as directed in the summons, he shall be punished in the manner provided for the punishment of any witness who disobeys a summons issued from a court of record in this state.

(1953 H 1, eff. 10–1–53; GC 13436–26)

2939.28 Exemption from arrest

If a person comes into this state in obedience to a summons directing him to attend and testify in this state, while in this state pursuant to such summons he is not subject to arrest or the service of process, civil or criminal, in connection with matters which arose before his entrance into this state under the summons.

If a person passes through this state while going to another state in obedience to a summons to attend and testify in that state or while returning therefrom, while so passing through this state he is not subject to arrest or the service of process, civil or criminal, in connection with matters which arose before his entrance into this state under the summons.

(1953 H 1, eff. 10–1–53; GC 13436–27)

2939.29 Construction

Sections 2939.25 to 2939.28, inclusive, of the Revised Code shall be so interpreted and construed as to effectuate their general purpose, to make the law of this state uniform with the law of other states which enact similar uniform legislation.

(1953 H 1, eff. 10–1–53; GC 13436–28)

CHAPTER 2941

INDICTMENT

MAGISTRATE DEFINED

MAGISTRATE DEFINED

2941.01   Definition of magistrate

The definition of "magistrate" set forth in section 2931.01 of the Revised Code applies to Chapter 2941. of the Revised Code.

(1953 H 1, eff. 10–1–53)

INDICTMENTS AND INFORMATIONS

2941.02   Informations

All sections of the Revised Code which apply to prosecutions upon indictments, the process thereon, and the issuing and service thereof, to commitments, bails, motions, pleadings, trials, appeals, and punishments, to the execution of any sentence, and all other proceedings in cases of indictments whether in the court of original or appellate jurisdiction, apply to informations, and all prosecutions and proceedings thereon.

(1953 H 1, eff. 10–1–53; GC 13437–1)

2941.021   Prosecution by information

Any criminal offense which is not punishable by death or life imprisonment may be prosecuted by information filed in the common pleas court by the prosecuting attorney if the defendant, after he has been advised by the court of the nature of the charge against him and of his rights under the constitution, is represented by counsel or has affirmatively waived counsel by waiver in writing and in open court, waives in writing and in open court prosecution by indictment.

(128 v 53, eff. 11–9–59)

2941.03   Sufficiency of indictments or informations

An indictment or information is sufficient if it can be understood therefrom:

(A) That it is entitled in a court having authority to receive it, though the name of the court is not stated;

(B) If it is an indictment, that it was found by a grand jury of the county in which the court was held, of [*sic*] if it is an information, that it was subscribed and presented to the court by the prosecuting attorney of the county in which the court was held;

(C) That the defendant is named, or, if his name cannot be discovered, that he is described by a fictitious name, with a statement that his true name is unknown to the jury or prosecuting attorney, but no name shall be stated in addition to one necessary to identify the accused;

(D) That an offense was committed at some place within the jurisdiction of the court, except where the act, though done without the local jurisdiction of the county, is triable therein;

(E) That the offense was committed at some time prior to the time of finding of the indictment or filing of the information.

(1953 H 1, eff. 10–1–53; GC 13437–2)

2941.04   Two or more offenses in one indictment

An indictment or information may charge two or more different offenses connected together in their commission, or different statements of the same offense, or two or more different offenses of the same class of crimes or offenses, under separate counts, and if two or more indictments or informations are filed in such cases the court may order them to be consolidated.

The prosecution is not required to elect between the different offenses or counts set forth in the indictment or information, but the defendant may be convicted of any number of the offenses charged, and each offense upon which the defendant is convicted must be stated in the verdict.   The court in the interest of justice and for good cause shown, may order different offenses or counts set forth in the indictment or information tried separately or divided into two or more groups and each of said groups tried separately.   A verdict of acquittal of one or more counts is not an acquittal of any other count.

(1953 H 1, eff. 10–1–53; GC 13437–3)

2941.05   Statement charging an offense

In an indictment or information charging an offense, each count shall contain, and is sufficient if it contains in substance, a statement that the accused has committed some public offense therein specified.   Such statement may be made in ordinary and concise language without any technical averments or any allegations not essential to be proved.   It may be in the words of the section of the Revised Code describing the offense or declaring the matter charged to be a public offense, or in any words sufficient to give the accused notice of the offense of which he is charged.

(126 v 392, eff. 3–17–55; 1953 H 1; GC 13437–4)

2941.06   Form of indictment or information

An indictment may be substantially in the following form:

The State of Ohio,)

ss.

———— County)

In the Year of our Lord one thousand nine hundred and ——.

The jurors of the Grand Jury of the State of Ohio, within and for the body of the County aforesaid, on their oaths, in the name and by the authority of the State of Ohio, do find and present that A.B., on the ———— day of ———— 19 —— at the county of ———— aforesaid, did ———— (here insert the name of the offense if it has one, such as murder, arson, or the like, or if a misdemeanor having no general name, insert a brief description of it as given by law) contrary to the form of the statute in such case made and provided, and against the peace and dignity of the State of Ohio.

———— C.D. ————

Prosecuting Attorney

(Indorsed) A true bill.

E.F., Foreman of the Grand Jury.

(1976 H 390, eff. 8–6–76; 1953 H 1; GC 13437–5)

2941.07 Bill of particulars

Upon written request of the defendant made not later than five days prior to the date set for trial, or upon order of the court, the prosecuting attorney shall furnish a bill of particulars setting up specifically the nature of the offense charged and the conduct of the defendant which is alleged to constitute the offense.

(1972 H 511, eff. 1–1–74; 1953 H 1; GC 13437–6)

2941.08 Certain defects do not render indictment invalid

An indictment or information is not made invalid, and the trial, judgment, or other proceedings stayed, arrested, or affected:

(A) By the omission of "with force and arms," or words of similar import, or "as appears by the record";

(B) For omitting to state the time at which the offense was committed, in a case in which time is not of the essence of the offense;

(C) For stating the time imperfectly;

(D) For stating imperfectly the means by which the offense was committed except insofar as means is an element of the offense;

(E) For want of a statement of the value or price of a matter or thing, or the amount of damages or injury, where the value or price or the amount of damages or injury is not of the essence of the offense, and in such case it is sufficient to aver that the value or price of the property is less than, equals, or exceeds the certain value or price which determines the offense or grade thereof;

(F) For the want of an allegation of the time or place of a material fact when the time and place have been once stated therein;

(G) Because dates and numbers are represented by figures;

(H) For an omission to allege that the grand jurors were impaneled, sworn, or charged;

(I) For surplusage or repugnant allegations when there is sufficient matter alleged to indicate the crime and person charged;

(J) For want of averment of matter not necessary to be proved;

(K) For other defects or imperfections which do not tend to prejudice the substantial rights of the defendant upon the merits.

(1953 H 1, eff. 10–1–53; GC 13437–7)

2941.09 Identification of corporation

In any indictment or information it is sufficient for the purpose of identifying any group or association of persons, not incorporated, to state the proper name of such group or association, to state any name or designation by which the group or association has been or is known, to state the names of all persons in such group or association or of one or more of them, or to state the name of one or more persons in such group or association referring to the others as "another" or "others." It is sufficient for the purpose of identifying a corporation to state the corporate name of such corporation, or any name or designation by which such corporation has been or is known.

(1953 H 1, eff. 10–1–53; GC 13437–8)

2941.10 Indictment complete

No indictment or information for any offense created or defined by statute is objectionable for the reason that it fails to negative any exception, excuse, or proviso contained in the statute creating or defining the offense. The fact that the charge is made is an allegation that no legal excuse for the doing of the act exists in the particular case.

(1953 H 1, eff. 10–1–53; GC 13437–9)

PLEADING, AVERMENTS, AND ALLEGATIONS

2941.11   Pleading prior conviction

Whenever it is necessary to allege a prior conviction of the accused in an indictment or information, it is sufficient to allege that the accused was, at a certain stated time, in a certain stated court, convicted of a certain stated offense, giving the name of the offense, or stating the substantial elements thereof.

(1953 H 1, eff. 10–1–53; GC 13437–10)

2941.12   Pleading a statute

In pleading a statute or right derived therefrom it is sufficient to refer to the statute by its title, or in any other manner which identifies the statute. The court must thereupon take judicial notice of such statute.

(1953 H 1, eff. 10–1–53; GC 13437–11)

2941.13   Pleading a judgment

In pleading a judgment or other determination of, or a proceeding before, any court or officer, civil or military, it is not necessary to allege the fact conferring jurisdiction on such court or officer. It is sufficient to allege generally that such judgment or determination was given or made or such proceedings had.

(1953 H 1, eff. 10–1–53; GC 13437–12)

2941.14   Allegations in homicide indictment

(A) In an indictment for aggravated murder, murder, or voluntary or involuntary manslaughter, the manner in which, or the means by which the death was caused need not be set forth.

(B) Imposition of the death penalty for aggravated murder is precluded unless the indictment or count in the indictment charging the offense specifies one or more of the aggravating circumstances listed in division (A) of section 2929.04 of the Revised Code. If more than one aggravating circumstance is specified to an indictment or count, each shall be in a separately numbered specification, and if an aggravating circumstance is specified to a count in an indictment containing more than one count, such specification shall be identified as to the count to which it applies.

(C) A specification to an indictment or count in an indictment charging aggravated murder shall be stated at the end of the body of the indictment or count, and may be in substantially the following form:

Specification (or, *Specification 1*, or *Specification to the First Count*, or, *Specification 1 to the First Count*). The Grand Jurors further find and specify that (set forth the applicable aggravating circumstance listed in divisions (A)(1) to (8) of section 2929.04 of the Revised Code. The aggravating circumstance may be stated in the words of the subdivision in which it appears, or in words sufficient to give the accused notice of the same).

(1981 S 1, eff. 10–19–81; 1973 H 716; 1972 H 511; 1953 H 1; GC 13437–13)

2941.141   Specification concerning possession of firearm essential to affect sentence

(A) Imposition of a term of actual incarceration upon an offender under division (A) of section 2929.71 of the Revised Code for having a firearm on or about his person or under his control while committing a felony is precluded unless the indictment, count in the indictment, or information charging the offense specifies that the offender had a firearm on or about his person or under his control while committing the offense. A specification to an indictment, count in the indictment, or information charging the offender with having a firearm on or about his person or under his control while committing a felony shall be stated at the end of the body of the indictment, count, or information, and shall be in substantially the following form:

"SPECIFICATION (or, SPECIFICATION TO THE FIRST COUNT), The Grand Jurors (or insert the person's or the prosecuting attorney's name when appropriate) further find and specify that (set forth that the offender had a firearm on or about his person or under his control while committing the offense)."

(B) As used in this section, "firearm" has the same meaning as in section 2923.11 of the Revised Code.

(1990 H 669, eff. 1–10–91; 1990 S 258; 1982 H 269, § 4, S 199)

2941.142   Specifications to support term of actual incarceration

Imposition of a term of actual incarceration upon an offender pursuant to division (B)(1)(b), (2)(b), or (3)(b) of section 2929.11 of the Revised Code because the offender has previously been convicted of or pleaded guilty to any aggravated felony of the first, second, or third degree, aggravated murder or murder, or any offense set forth in any existing or former law of this state, any other state, or the United States that is substantially equivalent to any aggravated felony of the first, second, or third degree or to aggravated murder or murder is precluded unless the indictment, count in the indictment, or information charging the offense specifies that the offender has previously been convicted of or pleaded guilty to such an offense. Such a specification shall be stated at the end of the body of the indictment, count, or information and shall be in substantially the following form:

"SPECIFICATION (or, SPECIFICATION TO THE FIRST COUNT). The grand jurors (or insert the person's or the prosecuting attorney's name when appropriate) further find and specify that (set forth that the offender has previously been convicted and name the offense)."

A certified copy of the entry of judgment in such prior conviction together with evidence sufficient to identify the defendant named in the entry as the offender in the case at bar is sufficient to prove the prior conviction. If an indictment, count in an indictment, or information that charges a defendant with an aggravated felony contains such a specification, the defendant may request that the trial judge, in a case tried by a jury, determine the existence of the specification at the sentencing hearing.

(1983 S 210, eff. 7–1–83)

2941.143   Specifications to support indefinite term

Imposition of an indefinite term pursuant to division (B)(6) or (7) of section 2929.11 of the Revised Code is precluded unless the indictment, count in the indictment, or information charging the offense specifies either that, during the commission of the offense, the offender caused physical harm to any person or made an actual threat of physical harm to any person with a deadly weapon, as defined in section 2923.11 of the Revised Code, or that the offender has previously been convicted of or pleaded guilty to an offense of violence. Such a specification shall be stated at the end of the body of the indictment, count, or information and shall be in substantially the following form:

"SPECIFICATION (or, SPECIFICATION TO THE FIRST COUNT). The grand jurors (or insert the person's or the prosecuting attorney's name when appropriate) further find and specify that (set forth the allegation either that, during the commission of the offense, the offender caused physical harm to any person, or made an actual threat of physical harm to any person with a deadly weapon, or that the offender has previously been convicted of or pleaded guilty to an offense of violence)."

A certified copy of the entry of judgment in such prior conviction together with evidence sufficient to identify the defendant named in the entry as the offender in the case at bar is sufficient to prove the prior conviction. If an indictment, count in an indictment, or information that charges a defendant with a third or fourth degree felony contains such a specification, the defendant may request that the trial judge, in a case tried by a jury, determine the existence of the specification at the sentencing hearing.

(1983 S 210, eff. 7–1–83)

2941.144 Specification concerning possession of automatic firearm or firearm with silencer

(A) Imposition of a term of actual incarceration upon an offender under division (A) of section 2929.72 of the Revised Code for having a firearm that is an automatic firearm or that was equipped with a firearm muffler or silencer on or about his person or under his control while committing a felony is precluded unless the indictment, count in the indictment, or information charging the offense specifies that the offender did have such a firearm on or about his person or under his control while committing the offense. A specification to an indictment, count in an indictment, or information charging the offender with having a firearm that is an automatic firearm or that was equipped with a firearm muffler or silencer on or about his person or under his control while committing a felony shall be stated at the end of the body of the indictment, count, or information, and shall be stated in substantially the following form:

"SPECIFICATION (or, SPECIFICATION TO THE FIRST COUNT). The Grand Jurors (or insert the person's or the prosecuting attorney's name when appropriate) further find and specify that (set forth that the offender had a firearm that is an automatic firearm or that was equipped with a firearm muffler or silencer on or about his person or under his control while committing the offense)."

(B) As used in this section, "firearm" and "automatic firearm" have the same meanings as in section 2923.11 of the Revised Code.

(1990 S 258, eff. 11–20–90)

2941.15 Sufficiency of indictment for forgery

In an indictment or information for falsely making, altering, forging, printing, photographing, uttering, disposing of, or putting off an instrument, it is sufficient to set forth the purport and value thereof. Where the instrument is a promise to pay money conditionally, it is not necessary to allege that the condition has been performed.

(1953 H 1, eff. 10–1–53; GC 13437–14)

2941.16 Sufficient description for forgery

In an indictment or information for engraving or making the whole or part of an instrument, matter, or thing, or for using or having the unlawful custody or possession of a plate or other material upon which the whole or part of an instrument, matter, or thing was engraved or made, or for having the unlawful custody or possession of a paper upon which the whole or part of an instrument, matter, or thing was made or printed, it is sufficient to describe such instrument, matter, or thing by any name or designation by which it is usually known.

(1953 H 1, eff. 10–1–53; GC 13437–15)

2941.17 Description by usual name or purport

In all cases when it is necessary to make an averment in an indictment or information as to a writing, instrument, tool, or thing, it is sufficient to describe it by any name or designation by which it is usually known, or by the purport thereof.

(1972 H 511, eff. 1–1–74; 1953 H 1; GC 13437–16)

2941.18 Allegations in perjury indictment

In an indictment or information for perjury or falsification, it is not necessary to set forth any part of a record or proceeding, or the commission or authority of the court or other authority before which perjury or falsification was committed.

(1972 H 511, eff. 1–1–74; 1953 H 1; GC 13437–17)

2941.19 Alleging intent to defraud

It is sufficient in an indictment or information where it is necessary to allege an intent to defraud, to allege that the accused did the act with intent to defraud, without alleging an intent to defraud a particular person or corporation. On the trial of such an indictment or information, an intent to defraud a particular person need not be proved. It is sufficient to prove that the accused did the act charged with intent to defraud.

(1953 H 1, eff. 10–1–53; GC 13437–18)

2941.20   Allegations sufficient for unlawfully selling liquor

An indictment, information, or affidavit charging a violation of law relative to the sale, possession, transportation, buying, or giving intoxicating liquor to any person, need not allege the kind of liquor sold, nor the person by whom bought except that such charge must be sufficient to inform the accused of the particular offense with which he is charged.

(1953 H 1, eff. 10–1–53; GC 13437–19)

2941.21   Averments as to joint ownership

In an indictment or information for an offense committed upon, or in relation to, property belonging to partners or joint owners, it is sufficient to allege the ownership of such property to be in such partnership by its firm name, or in one or more of such partners or owners without naming all of them.

(1953 H 1, eff. 10–1–53; GC 13437–20)

2941.22   Averments as to will or codicil

In an indictment or information for stealing a will, codicil, or other testamentary instrument, or for forgery thereof, or, for a fraudulent purpose, keeping, destroying, or secreting it, whether in relation to real or personal property, or during the life of a testator or after his death, it is not necessary to allege the ownership or value thereof.

(1953 H 1, eff. 10–1–53; GC 13437–21)

2941.23   Averments as to election

In an indictment or information for an offense committed in relation to an election, it is sufficient to allege that such election was authorized by law, without stating the names of the officers holding it or the person voted for or the offices to be filled at the election.

(1953 H 1, eff. 10–1–53; GC 13437–22)

2941.24   Counts for embezzlement and larceny—Repealed

(1973 H 716, eff. 1–1–74; 1953 H 1; GC 13437–23)

2941.25   Multiple counts

(A) Where the same conduct by defendant can be construed to constitute two or more allied offenses of similar import, the indictment or information may contain counts for all such offenses, but the defendant may be convicted of only one.

(B) Where the defendant's conduct constitutes two or more offenses of dissimilar import, or where his conduct results in two or more offenses of the same or similar kind committed separately or with a separate animus as to each, the indictment or information may contain counts for all such offenses, and the defendant may be convicted of all of them.

(1972 H 511, eff. 1–1–74)

PROCEDURE

2941.26   Variance

When, on the trial of an indictment or information, there appears to be a variance between the statement in such indictment or information and the evidence offered in proof thereof, in the Christian name or surname, or other description of a person therein named or described, or in the name or description of a matter or thing therein named or described, such variance is not ground for an acquittal of the defendant unless the court before which the trial is had finds that such variance is material to the merits of the case or may be prejudicial to the defendant.

(1953 H 1, eff. 10–1–53; GC 13437–25)

2941.27 Proof of dilatory plea

No plea in abatement, or other dilatory plea to the indictment or information, shall be received by any court unless the party offering such plan proves the truth thereof by affidavit, or by some other sworn evidence.

(1953 H 1, eff. 10–1–53; GC 13437–26)

2941.28 Misjoinder of parties or offenses

No indictment or information shall be quashed, set aside, or dismissed for any of the following defects:

(A) That there is a misjoinder of the parties accused;

(B) That there is a misjoinder of the offenses charged in the indictment or information, or duplicity therein;

(C) That any uncertainty exists therein.

If the court is of the opinion that either defect referred to in division (A) or (B) of this section exists in any indictment or information, it may sever such indictment or information into separate indictments or informations or into separate counts.

If the court is of the opinion that the defect referred to in division (C) of this section exists in the indictment or information, it may order the indictment or information amended to cure such defect, provided no change is made in the name or identity of the crime charged.

(1953 H 1, eff. 10–1–53; GC 13437–27)

2941.29 Time for objecting to defect in indictment

No indictment or information shall be quashed, set aside, or dismissed, or motion to quash be sustained, or any motion for delay of sentence for the purpose of review be granted, nor shall any conviction be set aside or reversed on account of any defect in form or substance of the indictment or information, unless the objection to such indictment or information, specifically stating the defect claimed, is made prior to the commencement of the trial, or at such time thereafter as the court permits.

(1953 H 1, eff. 10–1–53; GC 13437–28)

2941.30 Amending an indictment

The court may at any time before, during, or after a trial amend the indictment, information, or bill of particulars, in respect to any defect, imperfection, or omission in form or substance, or of any variance with the evidence, provided no change is made in the name or identity of the crime charged. If any amendment is made to the substance of the indictment or information or to cure a variance between the indictment or information and the proof, the accused is entitled to a discharge of the jury on his motion, if a jury has been impaneled, and to a reasonable continuance of the cause, unless it clearly appears from the whole proceedings that he has not been misled or prejudiced by the defect or variance in respect to which the amendment is made, or that his rights will be fully protected by proceeding with the trial, or by a postponement thereof to a later day with the same or another jury. In case a jury is discharged from further consideration of a case under this section, the accused was not in jeopardy. No action of the court in refusing a continuance or postponement under this section is reviewable except after motion to and refusal by the trial court to grant a new trial therefor, and no appeal based upon such action of the court shall be sustained, nor reversal had, unless from consideration of the whole proceedings, the reviewing court finds that the accused was prejudiced in his defense or that a failure of justice resulted.

(1953 H 1, eff. 10–1–53; GC 13437–29)

2941.31 Record of quashed indictment

In criminal prosecutions, when the indictment or information has been quashed or the prosecuting attorney has entered a nolle prosequi thereon, or the cause or indictment is disposed of otherwise than upon trial, a complete record shall not be made by the clerk of the court of common pleas unless ordered to do so by the court of common pleas.

(1953 H 1, eff. 10–1–53; GC 13437–30)

2941.32   Proceedings when two indictments pending

If two or more indictments or informations are pending against the same defendant for the same criminal act, the prosecuting attorney must elect upon which he will proceed, and upon trial being had upon one of them, the remaining indictments or information shall be quashed.

(1953 H 1, eff. 10–1–53; GC 13437–31)

2941.33   Nolle prosequi

The prosecuting attorney shall not enter a nolle prosequi in any cause without leave of the court, on good cause shown, in open court. A nolle prosequi entered contrary to this section is invalid.

(1953 H 1, eff. 10–1–53; GC 13437–32)

2941.34   Lost or destroyed indictment

If an indictment or information is mutilated, obliterated, lost, mislaid, destroyed, or stolen, or for any other reason cannot be produced at the arraignment or trial of the defendant, the court may substitute a copy.

(127 v 847, eff. 9–16–57; 1953 H 1; GC 13437–33)

MISDEMEANOR

2941.35   Prosecutions for misdemeanor

Prosecutions for misdemeanors may be instituted by a prosecuting attorney by affidavit or such other method as is provided by law in such courts as have original jurisdiction in misdemeanors. Laws as to form, sufficiency, amendments, objections, and exceptions to indictments and as to the service thereof apply to such affidavits and warrants issued thereon.

(1953 H 1, eff. 10–1–53; GC 13437–34)

WARRANTS

2941.36   Warrant for arrest of accused

A warrant may be issued at any time by an order of a court, or on motion of a prosecuting attorney after the indictment, information, or affidavit is filed. When directed to the sheriff of the county where such indictment was found or information or affidavit filed, he may pursue and arrest the accused in any county and commit him to jail or present him in open court, if court is in session.

(1953 H 1, eff. 10–1–53; GC 13438–1)

2941.37   Warrant when accused is nonresident

When an accused resides out of the county in which the indictment was found or information filed, a warrant may issue thereon, directed to the sheriff of the county where such accused resides or is found. Such sheriff shall arrest the accused and convey him to the county from which such warrant was issued, and there commit him to jail or present him in open court, if court is in session.

(1953 H 1, eff. 10–1–53; GC 13438–2)

2941.38   Warrant when accused escapes

When an accused escapes and forfeits his recognizance after the jury is sworn, a warrant reciting the facts may issue at the request of the prosecuting attorney, to the sheriff of any county, who shall pursue, arrest, and commit the accused to the jail of the county from which such warrant issued, until he is discharged.

(1953 H 1, eff. 10–1–53;　GC 13438–3)

CONVICTS

2941.39　Indictment of convicts

When a convict in a state correctional institution is indicted for a felony committed while confined in the correctional institution, he shall remain in the custody of the warden or superintendent of the institution subject to the order of the court of common pleas of the county in which the institution is located.

(1994 H 571, eff. 10–6–94;　1953 H 1, eff. 10–1–53;　GC 13438–4)

2941.40　Convicts removed for sentence or trial

A convict in a state correctional institution, who escaped, forfeited his recognizance before receiving sentence for a felony, or against whom an indictment or information for felony is pending, may be removed to the county in which the conviction was had or the indictment or information was pending for sentence or trial, upon the warrant of the court of common pleas of the county.

(1994 H 571, eff. 10–6–94;　1969 H 508, eff. 10–24–69;　1953 H 1;　GC 13438–5)

2941.401　Request by a prisoner for trial on pending charges

When a person has entered upon a term of imprisonment in a correctional institution of this state, and when during the continuance of the term of imprisonment there is pending in this state any untried indictment, information, or complaint against the prisoner, he shall be brought to trial within one hundred eighty days after he causes to be delivered to the prosecuting attorney and the appropriate court in which the matter is pending, written notice of the place of his imprisonment and a request for a final disposition to be made of the matter, except that for good cause shown in open court, with the prisoner or his counsel present, the court may grant any necessary or reasonable continuance.　The request of the prisoner shall be accompanied by a certificate of the warden or superintendent having custody of the prisoner, stating the term of commitment under which the prisoner is being held, the time served and remaining to be served on the sentence, the amount of good time earned, the time of parole eligibility of the prisoner, and any decisions of the adult parole authority relating to the prisoner.

The written notice and request for final disposition shall be given or sent by the prisoner to the warden or superintendent having custody of him, who shall promptly forward it with the certificate to the appropriate prosecuting attorney and court by registered or certified mail, return receipt requested.

The warden or superintendent having custody of the prisoner shall promptly inform him in writing of the source and contents of any untried indictment, information, or complaint against him, concerning which the warden or superintendent has knowledge, and of his right to make a request for final disposition thereof.

Escape from custody by the prisoner, subsequent to his execution of the request for final disposition, voids the request.

If the action is not brought to trial within the time provided, subject to continuance allowed pursuant to this section, no court any longer has jurisdiction thereof, the indictment, information, or complaint is void, and the court shall enter an order dismissing the action with prejudice.

This section does not apply to any person adjudged to be mentally ill or who is under sentence of life imprisonment or death, or to any prisoner under sentence of death.

(1994 H 571, eff. 10–6–94;　1969 S 355, eff. 11–18–69)

2941.41 Warrant for removal

A warrant for removal specified in section 2941.40 of the Revised Code shall be in the usual form, except that it shall set forth that the accused is in a state correctional institution. The warrant shall be directed to the sheriff of the county in which the conviction was had or the indictment or information is pending. When a copy of the warrant is presented to the warden or the superintendent of a state correctional institution, he shall deliver the convict to the sheriff who shall convey him to the county and commit him to the county jail. For removing and returning the convict, the sheriff shall receive the fees allowed for conveying convicts to a state correctional institution.

(1994 H 571, eff. 10–6–94; 1981 H 145, eff. 5–28–81; 1953 H 1; GC 13438–6)

2941.42 Convict to be confined

A convict removed as provided by section 2941.41 of the Revised Code shall be kept in jail subject to be taken into court for sentence or trial. If the case is continued or the execution of the sentence is suspended, the court may order him to be returned to the state correctional institution by the sheriff, who shall deliver him, with a certified copy of the order, to the warden, who shall again deliver the convict to the sheriff upon another certified order of the court.

(1994 H 571, eff. 10–6–94; 1953 H 1, eff. 10–1–53; GC 13438–7)

2941.43 Disposition of prisoner following trial for another offense

If the convict referred to in section 2941.40 of the Revised Code is acquitted, he shall forthwith returned [1] by the sheriff to the state correctional institution to serve out the remainder of his sentence. If he is sentenced to imprisonment in a state correctional institution, he shall be returned to the state correctional institution by the sheriff to serve his new term. If he is sentenced to death, the death sentence shall be executed as if he were not under sentence of imprisonment in a state correctional institution.

(1994 H 571, eff. 10–6–94; 1972 H 511, eff. 1–1–74; 131 v H 700; 1953 H 1; GC 13438–8)

[1] So in original; should this read "be returned"?

2941.44 Arrests and return of escaped convicts; expenses

Sheriffs, deputy sheriffs, marshals, deputy marshals, watchmen, police officers, and coroners may arrest a convict escaping from a state correctional institution and forthwith convey him to the institution and deliver him to the warden of the institution. They shall be allowed ten cents per mile going to and returning from the institution and additional compensation that the warden finds reasonable for the necessary expense incurred.

(1994 H 571, eff. 10–6–94; 128 v 542, eff. 7–17–59; 1953 H 1; GC 13438–9)

2941.45 Trial of persons serving sentence

Any person serving a sentence in jail or the workhouse, who is indicted or informed against for another offense, may be brought before the court of common pleas upon warrant for that purpose, for arraignment and trial. Such person shall remain in the custody of the jailer or keeper of the workhouse, but may be temporarily confined in the jail, if a prisoner in the workhouse.

If such prisoner is convicted and sentenced upon trial, he shall be returned to the jail or workhouse to serve out the former sentence before the subsequent sentence is executed.

(1953 H 1, eff. 10–1–53; GC 13438–10)

2941.46 Arrest of convict or prisoner violating pardon or parole

(A) If a convict has been conditionally pardoned or a prisoner has been paroled from any state correctional institution, any peace officer may arrest the convict or prisoner without a warrant if the peace officer has reasonable ground to believe that the convict or prisoner has violated or is violating any rule governing the conduct of paroled prisoners prescribed by the adult parole authority or any of the following that is a condition of his pardon or parole:

(1) A condition that prohibits his ownership, posession, or use of a firearm, deadly weapon, ammunition, or dangerous ordnance;

(2) A condition that prohibits him from being within a specified structure or geographic area;

(3) A condition that confines him to a residence, facility, or other structure;

(4) A condition that prohibits him from contacting or communicating with any specified individual;

(5) A condition that prohibits him from associating with a specified individual.

(B) Upon making an arrest under this section, the arresting peace officer or his department or agency promptly shall notify the authority that the convict or prisoner has been arrested.

(C) Nothing in this section limits, or shall be construed to limit, the powers of arrest granted to certain law enforcement officers and citizens under sections 2935.03 and 2935.04 of the Revised Code.

(D) As used in this section:

(1) "State correctional institution," "pardon," "parole," "convict," and "prisoner" have the same meanings as in section 2967.01 of the Revised Code.

(2) "Peace officer" has the same meaning as in section 2935.01 of the Revised Code.

(3) "Firearm," "deadly weapon," and "dangerous ordnance" have the same meanings as in section 2923.11 of the Revised Code.

(1994 H 571, eff. 10–6–94; 1992 S 49, eff. 7–21–92; 130 v Pt 2, H 28; 1953 H 1; GC 13438–11)

MISCELLANEOUS PROVISIONS

2941.47 Summons on indictments against corporations

When an indictment is returned or information filed against a corporation, a summons commanding the sheriff to notify the accused thereof, returnable on the seventh day after its date, shall issue on praecipe of the prosecuting attorney. Such summons with a copy of the indictment shall be served and returned in the manner provided for service of summons upon corporations in civil actions. If the service cannot be made in the county where the prosecution began, the sheriff may make service in any other county of the state, upon the president, secretary, superintendent, clerk, treasurer, cashier, managing agent, or other chief officer thereof, or by leaving a copy at a general or branch office or usual place of doing business of such corporation, with the person having charge thereof. Such corporation shall appear by one of its officers or by counsel on or before the return day of the summons served and answer to the indictment or information by motion, demurrer, or plea, and upon failure to make such appearance and answer, the clerk of the court of common pleas shall enter a plea of "not guilty." Upon such appearance being made or plea entered, the corporation is before the court until the case is finally disposed of. On said indictment or information no warrant of arrest may issue except for individuals who may be included in such indictment or information.

(1953 H 1, eff. 10–1–53; GC 13438–12)

2941.48 Recognizance of witnesses

In any case pending in the court of common pleas, the court, either before or after indictment, may require any witness designated by the prosecuting attorney to enter into a recognizance, with or without surety, in such sum as the court thinks proper for his appearance to testify in such cause. A witness failing or refusing to comply with such order shall be committed to the county jail until he gives his testimony in such case or is ordered discharged by the court. If a witness is committed to jail upon order of court for want of such recognizance, he shall be paid while so confined like fees as are allowed witnesses by section 2335.08 of the Revised Code. The trial of such case has precedence over other cases and the court shall designate any early day for such trial.

(1953 H 1, eff. 10–1–53; GC 13438–13)

2941.49   Indictment to be served on accused

Within three days after the filing of an indictment for felony and in every other case when requested, the clerk of the court of common pleas shall make and deliver to the sheriff, defendant, or the defendant's counsel, a copy of such indictment. The sheriff, on receiving such copy, shall serve it on the defendant. A defendant, without his assent, shall not be arraigned or called on to answer to an indictment until one day has elapsed after receiving or having an opportunity to receive in person or by counsel, a copy of such indictment. (1953 H 1, eff. 10–1–53; GC 13439–1)

2941.50   Assignment of counsel to represent indigents—Repealed

(1975 H 164, eff. 1–13–76; 132 v S 486; 131 v H 362; 130 v H 511; 1953 H 1; GC 13439–2)

2941.51   Person represented shall reimburse for part of costs if able

(A) Counsel appointed to a case or selected by an indigent person under division (E) of section 120.16 or division (E) of section 120.26 of the Revised Code, or otherwise appointed by the court, except for counsel appointed by the court to provide legal representation for a person charged with a violation of an ordinance of a municipal corporation, shall be paid for their services by the county the compensation and expenses that the trial court approves. Each request for payment shall be accompanied by an affidavit of indigency completed by the indigent person on forms prescribed by the state public defender. Compensation and expenses shall not exceed the amounts fixed by the board of county commissioners pursuant to division (B) of this section.

(B) The board of county commissioners shall establish a schedule of fees by case or on an hourly basis to be paid by the county for legal services provided by appointed counsel. Prior to establishing such schedule, the board shall request the bar association or associations of the county to submit a proposed schedule. The schedule submitted shall be subject to the review, amendment, and approval of the board of county commissioners.

(C) In a case where counsel have been appointed to conduct an appeal under Chapter 120. of the Revised Code, such compensation shall be fixed by the court of appeals or the supreme court, as provided in divisions (A) and (B) of this section.

(D) The fees and expenses approved by the court under this section shall not be taxed as part of the costs and shall be paid by the county. However, if the person represented has, or reasonably may be expected to have, the means to meet some part of the cost of the services rendered to him, he shall reimburse the county in an amount that he reasonably can be expected to pay. The county shall pay to the state public defender a percentage of the reimbursement received from such person in an amount proportionate to the percentage of the costs of the person's case that were paid to the county by the state public defender pursuant to this section. The money paid to the state public defender shall be credited to the public defender reimbursement fund created pursuant to division (B)(5) of section 120.04 of the Revised Code.

(E) The county auditor shall draw his warrant on the county treasurer for the payment of such counsel in the amount fixed by the court, plus the expenses that the court fixes and certifies to the auditor. The county auditor shall report periodically, but not less than annually, to the board and to the Ohio public defender commission the amounts paid out pursuant to the approval of the court under this section, separately stating costs and expenses that are reimbursable under section 120.35 of the Revised Code. The board, after review and approval of the auditor's report, may then certify it to the state public defender for reimbursement. The state public defender shall review the report and, in accordance with the standards, guidelines, and maximums established pursuant to divisions (B)(7) and (8) of section 120.04 of the Revised Code, pay fifty per cent of the total cost, other than costs and expenses that are reimbursable under section 120.35 of the Revised Code, if any, of paying appointed counsel in each county and pay fifty per cent of costs and expenses that are reimbursable under section 120.35 of the Revised Code, if any, to the board.

(F) If any county system for paying appointed counsel fails to maintain the standards for the conduct of the system established by the rules of the Ohio public defender commission pursuant to divisions (B) and (C) of section 120.03 of the Revised Code or the standards established by the state public defender pursuant to division (B)(7) of section 102.04 of the Revised Code, the commission shall notify the board of county commissioners of the county that the county system for paying appointed counsel has failed to comply with its rules. Unless the board corrects the conduct of its appointed counsel system to comply with the rules within ninety days after the date of the notice, the state public defender may deny all or part of the county's reimbursement from the state provided for in this section.

(1995 H 117, eff. 6–30–95; 1985 H 201, eff. 7–1–85; 1984 S 271; 1983 H 291; 1975 H 164; 132 v H 1; 131 v H 362; 128 v 54; 1953 H 1; GC 13439–3)

2941.52 Reasonable time to except—Repealed

(1975 H 164, eff. 1–13–76; 1953 H 1; GC 13439–4)

2941.53 Exceptions to an indictment

An accused may except to an indictment by:

(A) A motion to quash;

(B) A plea in abatement;

(C) A demurrer.

(1953 H 1, eff. 10–1–53; GC 13439–5)

DEMURRERS AND MOTIONS

2941.54 Motion to quash

A motion to quash may be made when there is a defect apparent upon the face of the record, within the meaning of sections 2941.02 to 2941.35, inclusive, of the Revised Code, including defects in the form of indictment and in the manner in which an offense is charged.

(1953 H 1, eff. 10–1–53; GC 13439–6)

2941.55 Plea in abatement

Plea in abatement may be made when there is a defect in the record shown by facts extrinsic thereto.

(1953 H 1, eff. 10–1–53; GC 13439–7)

2941.56 Misnomer

If the accused pleads in abatement that he is not indicted by his true name, he must plead his true name which shall be entered on the minutes of the court. After such entry, the trial and proceedings on the indictment shall be had against him by that name, referring also to the name by which he is indicted, as if he had been indicted by his true name.

(1953 H 1, eff. 10–1–53; GC 13439–8)

2941.57 Demurrer

The accused may demur:

(A) When the facts stated in the indictment do not constitute an offense punishable by the laws of this state;

(B) When the intent is not alleged and proof thereof is necessary to make out the offense charged;

(C) When it appears on the face of the indictment that the offense charged is not within the jurisdiction of the court.

(1953 H 1, eff. 10–1–53; GC 13439–9)

2941.58 Accused not discharged when indictment quashed

When a motion to quash or a plea in abatement is adjudged in favor of the accused, the trial court may order the case to be resubmitted to the grand jury, if then pending, or to the next

succeeding grand jury. The accused then may be committed to jail or held to bail in such sum as the trial court requires for his appearance to answer at a time to be fixed by the court.
(1953 H 1, eff. 10–1–53; GC 13439–10)

2941.59   Waiver of defects

The accused waives all defects which may be excepted to by a motion to quash or a plea in abatement, by demurring to an indictment, or by pleading in bar or the general issue.
(1953 H 1, eff. 10–1–53; GC 13439–11)

2941.60   Answer to plea in abatement

The prosecuting attorney may demur to a plea in abatement if it is not sufficient in substance, or he may reply, setting forth any facts which may show there is no defect in the record as charged in the plea.
(1953 H 1, eff. 10–1–53; GC 13439–12)

2941.61   After demurrer accused may plead

After a demurrer to an indictment is overruled, the accused may plead under section 2943.03 of the Revised Code.
(1953 H 1, eff. 10–1–53; GC 13439–13)

2941.62   Hearing on motions and demurrers

Motions to quash, pleas in abatement, and demurrers shall be heard immediately upon their filing, unless the trial court, for good cause shown, sets another time for such hearing.
(1953 H 1, eff. 10–1–53; GC 13439–14)

2941.63   Counsel to assist prosecutor

The court of common pleas, or the court of appeals, whenever it is of the opinion that the public interest requires it, may appoint an attorney to assist the prosecuting attorney in the trial of a case pending in such court. The board of county commissioners shall pay said assistant to the prosecuting attorney such compensation for his services as the court approves.
(1953 H 1, eff. 10–1–53; GC 13439–15)

MAGISTRATE DEFINED

MAGISTRATE DEFINED

2943.01   Definition of magistrate

The definition of "magistrate" set forth in section 2931.01 of the Revised Code applies to Chapter 2943. of the Revised Code.

(1953 H 1, eff. 10–1–53)

ARRAIGNMENT

2943.02   Arraignment

An accused person shall be arraigned by the clerk of the court of common pleas, or his deputy, reading the indictment or information to the accused, unless the accused or his attorney waives the reading thereof. He shall then be asked to plead thereto. Arraignment shall be made immediately after the disposition of exceptions to the indictment, if any are filed, or, if no exceptions are filed, after reasonable opportunity has been given the accused to file such exceptions.

(1953 H 1, eff. 10–1–53; GC 13440–1)

PLEAS

2943.03   Pleas to indictment

Pleas to an indictment or information are:

(A) Guilty;

(B) Not guilty;

(C) A former judgment of conviction or acquittal of the offense;

(D) Once in jeopardy;

(E) Not guilty by reason of insanity.

A defendant who does not plead guilty may enter one or more of the other pleas. A defendant who does not plead not guilty by reason of insanity is conclusively presumed to have been sane at the time of the commission of the offense charged. The court may, for good cause shown, allow a change of plea at any time before the commencement of the trial.

(1953 H 1, eff. 10–1–53; GC 13440–2)

2943.031 Court advising defendants on possibility of deportation, exclusion, or denial of naturalization prior to accepting pleas

(A) Except as provided in division (B) of this section, prior to accepting a plea of guilty or a plea of no contest to an indictment, information, or complaint charging a felony or a misdemeanor other than a minor misdemeanor if the defendant previously has not been convicted of or pleaded guilty to a minor misdemeanor, the court shall address the defendant personally, provide the following advisement to the defendant that shall be entered in the record of the court, and determine that the defendant understands the advisement:

"If you are not a citizen of the United States, you are hereby advised that conviction of the offense to which you are pleading guilty (or no contest, when applicable) may have the consequences of deportation, exclusion from admission to the United States, or denial of naturalization pursuant to the laws of the United States."

Upon request of the defendant, the court shall allow him additional time to consider the appropriateness of the plea in light of the advisement described in this division.

(B) The court is not required to give the advisement described in division (A) of this section if either of the following applies:

(1) The defendant enters a plea of guilty on a written form, the form includes a question asking whether the defendant is a citizen of the United States, and the defendant answers that question in the affirmative;

(2) The defendant states orally on the record that he is a citizen of the United States.

(C) Except as provided in division (B) of this section, the defendant shall not be required at the time of entering a plea to disclose to the court his legal status in the United States.

(D) Upon motion of the defendant, the court shall set aside the judgment and permit the defendant to withdraw a plea of guilty or no contest and enter a plea of not guilty or not guilty by reason of insanity, if, after the effective date of this section, the court fails to provide the defendant the advisement described in division (A) of this section, the advisement is required by that division, and the defendant shows that he is not a citizen of the United States and that the conviction of the offense to which he pleaded guilty or no contest may result in his being subject to deportation, exclusion from admission to the United States, or denial of naturalization pursuant to the laws of the United States.

(E) In the absence of a record that the court provided the advisement described in division (A) of this section and if the advisement is required by that division, the defendant shall be presumed not to have received the advisement.

(F) Nothing in this section shall be construed as preventing a court, in the sound exercise of its discretion pursuant to Criminal Rule 32.1, from setting aside the judgment of conviction and permitting a defendant to withdraw his plea.

(1989 S 95, eff. 10–2–89)

2943.04 Form of plea

Pleas of guilty or not guilty may be oral. Pleas in all other cases shall be in writing, subscribed by the defendant or his counsel, and shall immediately be entered upon the minutes of the court.

(1953 H 1, eff. 10–1–53; GC 13440–3)

RIGHTS OF CRIME VICTIM

2943.041 Rights of crime victim in regard to prosecution of defendant—Repealed

(1994 S 186, eff. 10–12–94; 1994 H 571, eff. 10–6–94; 1987 S 6, § 1, eff. 6–10–87; 1987 S 6, § 3; 1984 S 172, § 1, 4)

DOUBLE JEOPARDY

2943.05 Form of plea of former conviction

If a defendant pleads that he has had former judgment of conviction or acquittal, or has been once in jeopardy, he must set forth in his plea the court, time, and place of such conviction, acquittal, or jeopardy. No claim of former judgment of conviction or acquittal, or jeopardy may be given in evidence under the plea of not guilty.

(1953 H 1, eff. 10–1–53; GC 13440–4)

2943.06 Trial of issue on plea of former conviction

If a defendant pleads a judgment of conviction, acquittal, or former jeopardy, the prosecuting attorney may reply that there is no such conviction, acquittal, or jeopardy. The issue thus made shall be tried to a jury, and on such trial the defendant must produce the record of such conviction, acquittal, or jeopardy, and prove that he is the person charged in such record, and he may also introduce other evidence to establish the identity of such offense. If the prosecuting attorney demurs to said plea and said demurrer is overruled, the prosecuting attorney may then reply to said plea.

(1953 H 1, eff. 10–1–53; GC 13440–5)

2943.07 What is not former acquittal

If a defendant was formerly acquitted on the ground of variance between the indictment or information and the proof, or if the indictment or information was dismissed, without a judgment of acquittal, upon an objection to its form or substance, or in order to hold the defendant for a higher offense, it is not an acquittal of the same offense.

(1953 H 1, eff. 10–1–53; GC 13440–6)

2943.08 What is former acquittal

Whenever a defendant is acquitted on the merits, he is acquitted of the same offense, notwithstanding any defect in form or substance in the indictment or information on which the trial was had.

(1953 H 1, eff. 10–1–53; GC 13440–7)

2943.09 Conviction or acquittal of a higher offense

When a defendant has been convicted or acquitted, or has been once in jeopardy upon an indictment or information, the conviction, acquittal, or jeopardy is a bar to another indictment or information for the offense charged in the former indictment or information, or for an attempt to commit the same offense, or for an offense necessarily included therein, of which he might have been convicted under the former indictment or information.

(1953 H 1, eff. 10–1–53; GC 13440–8)

2943.10 Proceedings after verdict on plea in bar

If the issue on the plea in bar under section 2943.06 of the Revised Code is found for the defendant he shall be discharged. If the issue is found against the defendant the case shall proceed and be disposed of upon his other pleas.

(1953 H 1, eff. 10–1–53; GC 13440–9)

CHAPTER 2945

TRIAL

PRELIMINARY PROVISIONS

TRIAL BY COURT

TRIAL PROCEDURE

TRIAL BY JURY

INSANITY

WITNESSES

PRELIMINARY PROVISIONS

2945.01   Definition of magistrate

The definition of "magistrate" set forth in section 2931.01 of the Revised Code applies to Chapter 2945. of the Revised Code.

(1953 H 1, eff. 10–1–53)

2945.02   Setting and continuing cases

The court of common pleas shall set all criminal cases for trial for a day not later than thirty days after the date of entry of the plea of the defendant.   No continuance of the trial shall be granted except upon affirmative proof in open court, upon reasonable notice, that the ends of justice require a continuance.

No continuance shall be granted for any other time than it is affirmatively proved the ends of justice require.

Whenever any continuance is granted, the court shall enter on the journal the reason for the same.

Criminal cases shall be given precedence over civil matters and proceedings.   The failure of the court to set such criminal cases for trial, as required by this section, does not operate as an acquittal, but upon notice of such failure or upon motion of the prosecuting attorney or a defendant, such case shall forthwith be set for trial within a reasonable time, not exceeding thirty days thereafter.

(1953 H 1, eff. 10–1–53; GC 13442–1)

2945.03   Control of trial

The judge of the trial court shall control all proceedings during a criminal trial, and shall limit the introduction of evidence and the argument of counsel to relevant and material matters with a view to expeditious and effective ascertainment of the truth regarding the matters in issue.

(1953 H 1, eff. 10–1–53; GC 13442–2)

2945.04   Protective orders available if it is found likely that intimidation of crime victim or witness or domestic violence will occur; procedures; contempt of court

(A) If a motion is filed with a court before which a criminal case is pending alleging that a person has committed or is reasonably likely to commit any act prohibited by section 2921.04 of the Revised Code in relation to the case, if the court holds a hearing on the motion, and if the court determines that the allegations made in the motion are true, the court may issue an order doing any or any combination of the following, subject to division (C) of this section:

(1) Directing the defendant in the case not to violate or to cease a violation of section 2921.04 of the Revised Code;

(2) Directing a person other than a defendant who is before the court, including, but not limited to, a subpoenaed witness or other person entering the courtroom of the court, not to violate or to cease a violation of section 2921.04 of the Revised Code;

(3) Directing the defendant or a person described in division (A)(2) of this section to maintain a prescribed geographic distance from any specified person who is before the court, including, but not limited to, the victim of the offense that is the basis of the case or a subpoenaed witness in the case;

(4) Directing the defendant or a person described in division (A)(2) of this section not to communicate with any specified person who is before the court, including, but not limited to, the victim of the offense or a subpoenaed witness in the case;

(5) Directing a specified law enforcement agency that serves a political subdivision within the territorial jurisdiction of the court to provide protection for any specified person who is before the court, including, but not limited to, the victim of the offense or a subpoenaed witness in the case;

(6) Any other reasonable order that would assist in preventing or causing the cessation of a violation of section 2921.04 of the Revised Code.

(B) If a motion is filed with a court in which a criminal complaint has been filed alleging that the offender or another person acting in concert with the offender has committed or is reasonably likely to commit any act that would constitute an offense against the person or property of the complainant, his ward, or his child, if the court holds a hearing on the motion, and if the court determines that the allegations made in the motion are true, the court may issue an order doing one or more of the following, subject to division (C) of this section:

(1) Directing the defendant in the case not to commit an act or to cease committing an act that constitutes an offense against the person or property of the complainant, his ward, or child;

(2) Directing a person other than the defendant who is before the court, including, but not limited to, a subpoenaed witness or other person entering the courtroom, not to commit an act or to cease committing an act that constitutes an offense against the person or property of the complainant, his ward, or child;

(3) Directing the defendant or a person described in division (B)(2) of this section to maintain a prescribed geographic distance from any specified person who is before the court, including, but not limited to, the complainant or the victim of the offense, or a subpoenaed witness in the case;

(4) Directing the defendant or a person described in division (B)(2) of this section not to communicate with any specified person who is before the court, including, but not limited to, the complainant, the victim of the offense, or a subpoenaed witness in the case;

(5) Directing a specified law enforcement agency that serves a political subdivision within the territorial jurisdiction of the court to provide protection for any specified person who is before the court, including, but not limited to, the complainant, the victim of the offense, or a subpoenaed witness in the case;

(6) When the complainant and the defendant cohabit with one another but the complainant is not a family or household member, as defined in section 2919.25 of the Revised Code, granting possession of the residence or household to the complainant to the exclusion of the defendant by evicting the defendant when the residence or household is owned or leased solely by the complainant or by ordering the defendant to vacate the premises when the residence or household is jointly owned or leased by the complainant and the defendant;

(7) Any other reasonable order that would assist in preventing or causing the cessation of an act that constitutes an offense against the person or property of the complainant, his ward, or child.

(C) No order issued under authority of division (A) or (B) of this section shall prohibit or be construed as prohibiting any attorney for the defendant in the case or for a person described in division (A)(2) or (B)(2) of this section from conducting any investigation of the pending criminal case, from preparing or conducting any defense of the pending criminal case, or from attempting to zealously represent his client in the pending criminal case within the bounds of the law. However, this division does not exempt any person from the prohibitions contained in section 2921.04 or any section of the Revised Code that constitutes an offense against the person or property of the complainant, his ward, or his child, or provide a defense to a charge of any violation of that section or of an offense of that nature.

(D)(1) A person who violates an order issued pursuant to division (A) of this section is subject to the following sanctions:

(a) Criminal prosecution for a violation of section 2921.04 of the Revised Code, if the violation of the court order constitutes a violation of that section;

(b) Punishment for contempt of court.

(2) A person who violates an order issued pursuant to division (B) of this section is subject to the following sanctions:

(a) Criminal prosecution for a violation of a section of the Revised Code that constitutes an offense against the person or property of the complainant, his ward, or child;

(b) Punishment for contempt of court.

(E)(1) The punishment of a person for contempt of court for violation of an order issued pursuant to division (A) of this section does not bar criminal prosecution of the person for a violation of section 2921.04 of the Revised Code.

(2) The punishment of a person for contempt of court for a violation of an order issued pursuant to division (B) of this section does not bar criminal prosecution of the person for an offense against the person or property of the complainant, his ward, or child.

(3) A person punished for contempt of court under this section is entitled to credit for the punishment imposed upon conviction of a violation of the offense arising out of the same activity, and a person convicted of such a violation shall not subsequently be punished for contempt of court arising out of the same activity.

(1994 H 335, eff. 12–9–94; 1984 S 172, eff. 9–26–84)

TRIAL BY COURT

2945.05 Defendant may waive jury trial

In all criminal cases pending in courts of record in this state, the defendant may waive a trial by jury and be tried by the court without a jury. Such waiver by a defendant, shall be in writing, signed by the defendant, and filed in said cause and made a part of the record thereof. It shall be entitled in the court and cause, and in substance as follows: "I _____, defendant in the above cause, hereby voluntarily waive and relinquish my right to a trial by jury, and elect to be tried by a Judge of the Court in which the said cause may be pending. I fully understand that under the laws of this state, I have a constitutional right to a trial by jury."

Such waiver of trial by jury must be made in open court after the defendant has been arraigned and has had opportunity to consult with counsel. Such waiver may be withdrawn by the defendant at any time before the commencement of the trial.

(1953 H 1, eff. 10–1–53; GC 13442–4)

2945.06 Jurisdiction of judge when jury trial is waived; three–judge court

In any case in which a defendant waives his right to trial by jury and elects to be tried by the court under section 2945.05 of the Revised Code, any judge of the court in which the cause is pending shall proceed to hear, try, and determine the cause in accordance with the rules and in like manner as if the cause were being tried before a jury. If the accused is charged with an offense punishable with death, he shall be tried by a court to be composed of three judges, consisting of the judge presiding at the time in the trial of criminal cases and two other judges to be designated by the presiding judge or chief justice of that court, and in case there is neither a presiding judge nor a chief justice, by the chief justice of the supreme court. The judges or a majority of them may decide all questions of fact and law arising upon the trial; however the accused shall not be found guilty or not guilty of any offense unless the judges unanimously find the accused guilty or not guilty. If the accused pleads guilty of aggravated murder, a court composed of three judges shall examine the witnesses, determine whether the accused is guilty of aggravated murder or any other offense, and pronounce sentence accordingly. The court shall follow the procedures contained in sections 2929.03 and 2929.04 of the Revised Code in all cases in which the accused is charged with an offense punishable by death. If in the composition of the court it is necessary that a judge from another county be assigned by the chief justice, the judge from another county shall be compensated for his services as provided by section 141.07 of the Revised Code.

(1981 S 1, eff. 10–19–81; 1953 H 1; GC 13442–5)

TRIAL PROCEDURE

2945.07 Recording presence of crime victim or member of family at trial; notices to be given—Repealed

(1994 S 186, eff. 10–12–94; 1994 H 571, eff. 10–6–94; 1987 S 6, § 1, eff. 6–10–87; 1987 S 6, § 3; 1984 S 172, § 1, 4)

2945.08 Prosecution in wrong county; proceeding

If it appears, on the trial of a criminal cause, that the offense was committed within the exclusive jurisdiction of another county of this state, the court must direct the defendant to be committed to await a warrant from the proper county for his arrest, but if the offense is a bailable offense the court may admit the defendant to bail with sufficient sureties conditioned, that he will, within such time as the court appoints, render himself amenable to a warrant for his arrest from the proper county, and if not sooner arrested thereon, will appear in court at the time fixed to surrender himself upon the warrant.

The clerk of the court of common pleas shall forthwith notify the prosecuting attorney of the county in which such offense was committed, in order that proper proceedings may be had in the case. A defendant in such case shall not be committed nor held under bond for a period of more than ten days.

(1953 H 1, eff. 10–1–53; GC 13442–6)

2945.09   Grounds of objection to be stated

In the trial of any criminal case, the grounds of an objection to any ruling or action of the court shall be stated if required by the court.

(1986 H 412, eff. 3–17–87; 1953 H 1; GC 13442–7)

2945.10   Order of proceedings of trial

The trial of an issue upon an indictment or information shall proceed before the trial court or jury as follows:

(A) Counsel for the state must first state the case for the prosecution, and may briefly state the evidence by which he expects to sustain it.

(B) The defendant or his counsel must then state his defense, and may briefly state the evidence which he expects to offer in support of it.

(C) The state must first produce its evidence and the defendant shall then produce his evidence.

(D) The state will then be confined to rebutting evidence, but the court, for good reason, in furtherance of justice, may permit evidence to be offered by either side out of its order.

(E) When the evidence is concluded, either party may request instructions to the jury on the points of law, which instructions shall be reduced to writing if either party requests it.

(F) When the evidence is concluded, unless the case is submitted without argument, the counsel for the state shall commence, the defendant or his counsel follow, and the counsel for the state conclude the argument to the jury.

(G) The court, after the argument is concluded and before proceeding with other business, shall forthwith charge the jury. Such charge shall be reduced to writing by the court if either party requests it before the argument to the jury is commenced. Such charge, or other charge or instruction provided for in this section, when so written and given, shall not be orally qualified, modified, or explained to the jury by the court. Written charges and instructions shall be taken by the jury in their retirement and returned with their verdict into court and remain on file with the papers of the case.

The court may deviate from the order of proceedings listed in this section.

(1953 H 1, eff. 10–1–53; GC 13442–8)

2945.11   Charge to the jury as to law and fact

In charging the jury, the court must state to it all matters of law necessary for the information of the jury in giving its verdict. The court must also inform the jury that the jury is the exclusive judge of all questions of fact. The court must state to the jury that in determining the question of guilt, it must not consider the punishment but that punishment rests with the judge except in cases of murder in the first degree or burglary of an inhabited dwelling.

(1953 H 1, eff. 10–1–53; GC 13442–9)

2945.12 When accused may be tried in his absence

A person indicted for a misdemeanor, upon request in writing subscribed by him and entered in the journal, may be tried in his absence by a jury or by the court. No other person shall be tried unless personally present, but if a person indicted escapes or forfeits his recognizance after the jury is sworn, the trial shall proceed and the verdict be received and recorded. If the offense charged is a misdemeanor, judgment and sentence shall be pronounced as if he were personally present. If the offense charged is a felony, the case shall be continued until the accused appears in court, or is retaken.

(1953 H 1, eff. 10–1–53; GC 13442–10)

2945.13 Joint trials in felony cases

When two or more persons are jointly indicted for a felony, except a capital offense, they shall be tried jointly unless the court, for good cause shown on application therefor by the prosecuting attorney or one or more of said defendants, orders one or more of said defendants to be tried separately.

(1953 H 1, eff. 10–1–53; GC 13442–11)

2945.14 Mistake in charging offense

If it appears during the trial and before submission to the jury or court, that a mistake has been made in charging the proper offense in the indictment or information, the court may order a discontinuance of trial without prejudice to the prosecution. The accused, if there is good cause to detain him, may be recognized to appear at the same or next succeeding term of court, or in default thereof committed to jail. In such case the court shall recognize the witnesses for the state to appear at the same time and testify.

(1953 H 1, eff. 10–1–53; GC 13442–12)

2945.15 Discharge of defendant

When two or more persons are tried jointly, before any of the accused has gone into his defense the trial court may direct one or more of such accused to be discharged that he may be a witness for the state.

An accused person, when there is not sufficient evidence to put him upon his defense, may be discharged by the court, but if not so discharged, shall be entitled to the immediate verdict of the jury in his favor. Such order of discharge, in either case, is a bar to another prosecution for the same offense.

(1953 H 1, eff. 10–1–53; GC 13442–13)

2945.16 View of the premises

When it is proper for the jurors to have a view of the place at which a material fact occurred, the trial court may order them to be conducted in a body, under the charge of the sheriff or other officer, to such place, which shall be shown to them by a person designated by the court. While the jurors are absent on such view no person other than such officer and such person so appointed, shall speak to them on any subject connected with the trial. The accused has the right to attend such view by the jury, but may waive this right.

The expense of such view as approved by the court shall be taxed as other costs in the case.

(129 v 1201, eff. 9–11–61; 1953 H 1; GC 13442–14)

TRIAL BY JURY

2945.17 Right of trial by jury

At any trial, in any court, for the violation of any statute of this state, or of any ordinance of any municipal corporation, except in cases in which the penalty involved does not exceed a fine of one hundred dollars, the accused has the right to be tried by a jury.

(1972 H 511, eff. 1–1–74; 1953 H 1; GC 13443)

2945.171   Verdict in writing

In all criminal cases the verdict of the jury shall be in writing and signed by each of the jurors concurring therein.

(129 v 336, eff. 9–28–61)

2945.18   Drawing jury in capital cases—Repealed

(1993 H 41, eff. 9–27–93; 1981 S 1)

2945.19   Obtaining a panel; procedures; conditions—Repealed

(1993 H 41, eff. 9–27–93; 1981 S 1)

2945.20   Separate trial for capital offense

When two or more persons are jointly indicted for a capital offense, each of such persons shall be tried separately. The court, for good cause shown on application therefor by the prosecuting attorney or one or more of the defendants, may order said defendants to be tried jointly.

(1953 H 1, eff. 10–1–53; GC 13443–3)

2945.21   Peremptory challenges in capital cases

(A)(1) In criminal cases in which there is only one defendant, each party, in addition to the challenges for cause authorized by law, may peremptorily challenge three of the jurors in misdemeanor cases and four of the jurors in felony cases other than capital cases. If there is more than one defendant, each defendant may peremptorily challenge the same number of jurors as if he were the sole defendant.

(2) Notwithstanding Criminal Rule 24, in capital cases in which there is only one defendant, each party, in addition to the challenges for cause authorized by law, may peremptorily challenge twelve of the jurors. If there is more than one defendant, each defendant may peremptorily challenge the same number of jurors as if he were the sole defendant.

(3) In any case in which there are multiple defendants, the prosecuting attorney may peremptorily challenge a number of jurors equal to the total number of peremptory challenges allowed to all of the defendants.

(B) If any indictments, informations, or complaints are consolidated for trial, the consolidated cases shall be considered, for purposes of exercising peremptory challenges, as though the defendants or offenses had been joined in the same indictment, information, or complaint.

(C) The exercise of peremptory challenges authorized by this section shall be in accordance with the procedures of Criminal Rule 24.

(1981 S 1, eff. 10–19–81; 1953 H 1; GC 13443–4)

2945.22   Peremptory challenges—Repealed

(1981 S 1, eff. 10–19–81; 1953 H 1; GC 13443–6)

2945.23   When peremptory challenges required

Except by agreement, neither the state nor the defendant shall be required to exercise any peremptory challenge until twelve jurors have been passed for cause and are in the panel.

(1953 H 1, eff. 10–1–53; GC 13443–7)

2945.24   Selecting juries for criminal cases

In all criminal cases, a jury summoned and impaneled under sections 2313.01 to 2313.47 of the Revised Code shall try the accused.

(1993 H 41, eff. 9–27–93; 1981 S 1; 1976 H 133; 1953 H 1; GC 13443–5)

2945.25   Causes of challenging of jurors

A person called as a juror in a criminal case may be challenged for the following causes:

(A) That he was a member of the grand jury that found the indictment in the case;

(B) That he is possessed of a state of mind evincing enmity or bias toward the defendant or the state; but no person summoned as a juror shall be disqualified by reason of a previously formed or expressed opinion with reference to the guilt or innocence of the accused, if the court is satisfied, from examination of the juror or from other evidence, that he will render an impartial verdict according to the law and the evidence submitted to the jury at the trial;

(C) In the trial of a capital offense, that he unequivocally states that under no circumstances will he follow the instructions of a trial judge and consider fairly the imposition of a sentence of death in a particular case. A prospective juror's conscientious or religious opposition to the death penalty in and of itself is not grounds for a challenge for cause. All parties shall be given wide latitude in voir dire questioning in this regard.

(D) That he is related by consanguinity or affinity within the fifth degree to the person alleged to be injured or attempted to be injured by the offense charged, or to the person on whose complaint the prosecution was instituted, or to the defendant;

(E) That he served on a petit jury drawn in the same cause against the same defendant, and that jury was discharged after hearing the evidence or rendering a verdict on the evidence that was set aside;

(F) That he served as a juror in a civil case brought against the defendant for the same act;

(G) That he has been subpoenaed in good faith as a witness in the case;

(H) That he is a chronic alcoholic, or drug dependent person;

(I) That he has been convicted of a crime that by law disqualifies him from serving on a jury;

(J) That he has an action pending between him and the state or the defendant;

(K) That he or his spouse is a party to another action then pending in any court in which an attorney in the cause then on trial is an attorney, either for or against him;

(L) That he is the person alleged to be injured or attempted to be injured by the offense charged, or is the person on whose complaint the prosecution was instituted, or the defendant;

(M) That he is the employer or employee, or the spouse, parent, son, or daughter of the employer or employee, or the counselor, agent, or attorney of any person included in division (L) of this section;

(N) That English is not his native language, and his knowledge of English is insufficient to permit him to understand the facts and law in the case;

(O) That he otherwise is unsuitable for any other cause to serve as a juror.

The validity of each challenge listed in this section shall be determined by the court.

(1981 S 1, eff. 10–19–81; 1980 H 965; 1953 H 1; GC 13443–8)

2945.26   Challenge for cause

Challenges for cause shall be tried by the court on the oath of the person challenged, or other evidence, and shall be made before the jury is sworn.

(1953 H 1, eff, 10–1–53; GC 13443–9)

2945.27   Examination of jurors by the court

The judge of the trial court shall examine the prospective jurors under oath or upon affirmation as to their qualifications to serve as fair and impartial jurors, but he shall permit reasonable examination of such jurors by the prosecuting attorney and by the defendant or his counsel.

(127 v 419, eff. 9–9–57; 1953 H 1; GC 13443–10)

2945.28   Form of oath to jury

In criminal cases jurors and the jury shall take the following oath to be administered by the trial court or the clerk of the court of common pleas: "You shall well and truly try, and true deliverance make between the State of Ohio and the defendant (giving his name). So help you God."

A juror shall be allowed to make affirmation and the words "this you do as you shall answer under the pains and penalties of perjury" shall be substituted for the words, "So help you God."

(1953 H 1, eff. 10–1–53; GC 13443–11, 13443–12)

2945.29   Jurors becoming unable to perform duties

If, before the conclusion of the trial, a juror becomes sick, or for other reason is unable to perform his duty, the court may order him to be discharged. In that case, if alternate jurors have been selected, one of them shall be designated to take the place of the juror so discharged. If, after all alternate jurors have been made regular jurors, a juror becomes too incapacitated to perform his duty, and has been discharged by the court, a new juror may be sworn and the trial begin anew, or the jury may be discharged and a new jury then or thereafter impaneled.

(1953 H 1, eff. 10–1–53; GC 13443–13)

2945.30   Medical attendance of juror

In case of sickness of any juror before the conclusion of the trial, the court may order that such juror receive medical attendance and shall order the payment of a reasonable charge for such medical attendance out of the judiciary fund.

(1953 H 1, eff. 10–1–53; GC 13443–14)

2945.31   Separation of jurors

After the trial has commenced, before or after the jury is sworn, the court may order the jurors to be kept in charge of proper officers, or they may be permitted to separate during the trial. If the jurors are kept in charge of officers of the court, proper arrangements shall be made for their care, maintenance, and comfort, under the orders and direction of the court. In case of necessity the court may permit temporary separation of the jurors.

(1953 H 1, eff. 10–1–53; GC 13443–15)

2945.32   Oath to officers if jury sequestered

When an order has been entered by the court of common pleas in any criminal cause, directing the jurors to be kept in charge of the officers of the court, the following oath shall be administered by the clerk of the court of common pleas to said officers: "You do solemnly swear that you will, to the best of your ability, keep the persons sworn as jurors on this trial, from separating from each other; that you will not suffer any communications to be made to them, or any of them, orally or otherwise; that you will not communicate with them, or any of them, orally or otherwise, except by the order of this court, or to ask them if they have agreed on their verdict, until they shall be discharged, and that you will not, before they render their verdict communicate to any person the state of their deliberations or the verdict they have agreed upon, so help you God." Any officer having taken such oath who willfully violates the same, or permits the same to be violated, is guilty of perjury and shall be imprisoned not less than one nor more than ten years.

(1953 H 1, eff. 10–1–53; GC 13443–16; Source—GC 12842)

2945.33   Keeping and conduct of jury after case submitted

When a cause is finally submitted the jurors must be kept together in a convenient place under the charge of an officer until they agree upon a verdict, or are discharged by the court. The court, except in cases where the offense charged may be punishable by death, may permit the jurors to separate during the adjournment of court overnight, under proper cautions, or under supervision of an officer. Such officer shall not permit a communication to be made to them, nor make any himself except to ask if they have agreed upon a verdict, unless he does so by order of the court. Such officer shall not communicate to any person, before the verdict is delivered, any matter in relation to their deliberation. Upon the trial of any prosecution for misdemeanor, the court may permit the jury to separate during their deliberation, or upon adjournment of the court overnight.

In cases where the offense charged may be punished by death, after the case is finally submitted to the jury, the jurors shall be kept in charge of the proper officer and proper arrangements for their care and maintenance shall be made as under section 2945.31 of the Revised Code.

(131 v H 708, eff. 11–9–65; 1953 H 1; GC 13448–1)

2945.34   Admonition if jurors separate during trial

If the jurors are permitted to separate during a trial, they shall be admonished by the court not to converse with, nor permit themselves to be addressed by any person, nor to listen to any conversation on the subject of the trial, nor form or express any opinion thereon, until the case is finally submitted to them.

(1953 H 1, eff. 10–1–53; GC 13443–17)

2945.35   Papers the jury may take

Upon retiring for deliberation, the jury, at the discretion of the court, may take with it all papers except depositions, and all articles, photographs, and maps which have been offered in evidence. No article or paper identified but not admitted in evidence shall be taken by the jury upon its retirement.

(1953 H 1, eff. 10–1–53; GC 13444–26)

2945.36   For what cause jury may be discharged

The trial court may discharge a jury without prejudice to the prosecution:

(A) For the sickness or corruption of a juror or other accident or calamity;

(B) Because there is no probability of such jurors agreeing;

(C) If it appears after the jury has been sworn that one of the jurors is a witness in the case;

(D) By the consent of the prosecuting attorney and the defendant.

The reason for such discharge shall be entered on the journal.

(1953 H 1, eff. 10–1–53; GC 13443–18)

INSANITY

2945.37   Competence to stand trial; raising of issue; procedures; municipal courts

(A) In a criminal action in a court of common pleas or municipal court, the court, prosecutor, or defense may raise the issue of the defendant's competence to stand trial. If the issue is raised before trial, the court shall hold a hearing on the issue as provided in this section. If the issue is raised after trial has begun, the court shall hold a hearing on the issue only for good cause shown.

A defendant is presumed competent to stand trial, unless it is proved by a preponderance of the evidence in a hearing under this section that because of his present mental condition he is incapable of understanding the nature and objective of the proceedings against him or of presently assisting in his defense.

The court shall not find a defendant incompetent to stand trial solely because he is receiving or has received treatment as a voluntary or involuntary mentally ill patient or mentally retarded resident under Chapter 5122. or 5123. of the Revised Code or because he is receiving or has received psychotropic drugs or other medication under medical supervision, even though without the drugs or medication the defendant might become incompetent to stand trial.

The court shall conduct the hearing within thirty days after the issue is raised, unless the defendant has been referred for examination under section 2945.371 of the Revised Code, in which case the court shall conduct the hearing within ten days after the filing of the report required by that section. A hearing may be continued for good cause shown.

The defendant shall be represented by counsel at the hearing. If the defendant is unable to obtain counsel, the court shall appoint counsel under Chapter 120. of the Revised Code before proceeding with the hearing.

The prosecutor and defense counsel may submit evidence on the issue of the defendant's competence to stand trial. A written report made under section 2945.371 of the Revised Code may be admitted into evidence at the hearing by stipulation of the prosecution and defense counsel, but if either objects to its admission, the report may be admitted under sections 2317.36 to 2317.38 of the Revised Code or other applicable statute or rule. A report made under section 2945.37 of the Revised Code is inadmissible into evidence in the criminal action against the defendant, but in such an action the prosecutor or defense counsel may call as witnesses any persons who examined the defendant or prepared a report pursuant to a referral under section 2945.371 of the Revised Code.

Upon the evidence submitted, the court shall determine the defendant's competence to stand trial and shall make an order under section 2945.38 of the Revised Code.

(B) As used in sections 2945.37 to 2945.40 of the Revised Code, "prosecutor" means the prosecuting attorney, village solicitor, city director of law, or similar officer who has the authority to prosecute a criminal case that is before the court or a criminal case in which the person was found incompetent to stand trial or found not guilty by reason of insanity.

(C) Municipal courts shall follow the procedures set forth in sections 2945.37 to 2945.40 of the Revised Code, except as provided in this division. Notwithstanding sections 2945.371 and 2945.39 of the Revised Code, a municipal court shall not order an evaluation of the defendant's competence to stand trial or the defendant's mental condition at the time of the commission of the offense to be conducted at any hospital operated by the department of mental health. Such evaluations shall be performed through community resources including, but not limited to, certified forensic centers, court probation departments, and community mental health agencies, and all expenses of such evaluations shall be borne by the court and taxed as costs in the case. If a defendant is found incompetent to stand trial or not guilty by reason of insanity, a municipal court may commit him as provided in section 2945.38 or 2945.40 of the Revised Code, whichever is applicable, except that the court shall make no commitment to the Oakwood forensic center.

(1988 S 156, eff. 7–1–89; 1981 H 694; 1980 S 297; 1978 H 565)

2945.371 Evaluations of mental condition

(A) If the issue of a defendant's competence to stand trial is raised under section 2945.37 of the Revised Code, the court may order one or more, but not more than three evaluations of the defendant's mental condition. The court shall do either of the following:

(1) Order that each evaluation be conducted through examination of the defendant by a forensic center designated by the department of mental health to conduct such examinations and make such evaluations in the area in which the court is located or by any other program or facility that is designated by the department of mental health or the department of mental retardation and developmental disabilities to conduct such examinations and make such evaluations provided the center, program, or facility is operated by the appropriate department or is certified by such department as being in compliance with the standards established under division (J) of section 5119.01 or division (C) of section 5123.04 of the Revised Code;

(2) Designate a center, program, or facility other than one designated by the department to conduct the examination.

In any case, the court may designate examiners other than the personnel of the center, program, facility, or department to make the examination. If more than one examination is ordered, the prosecutor and the defendant may recommend to the court an examiner whom each prefers to perform one of the examinations.

(B) If an evaluation is ordered, the defendant shall be available at the times and places established by the center, program, facility, or examiners. The court may order a defendant who has been released on bail or recognizance to submit to an examination under this section. If a defendant who has been released on bail or recognizance refuses to submit to a complete examination, the court may amend the conditions of bail or recognizance and order the sheriff to take the defendant into custody and deliver him to a center, program, or facility operated or certified by the department where he may be held for examination for a reasonable period of time not to exceed twenty days.

(C) A defendant who has not been released on bail or recognizance may be examined at his place of detention. The court at the request of the examiner may order the sheriff to transport the defendant to a program or facility operated by the department of mental health or the department of mental retardation and developmental disabilities, where he may be held for examination for a reasonable period of time not to exceed twenty days, and to return the defendant to the place of detention after the examination. Such an order may be made by a municipal court only upon the request of a certified forensic center examiner.

(D) The examiner shall file a written report with the court within thirty days after entry of an order for examination. The court shall provide copies of the report to the prosecutor and defense counsel. The report shall contain the findings of the examiner, the facts in reasonable detail on which the findings are based, and the opinion of the examiner as to the defendant's competence to stand trial. If the examiner reports that in his opinion the defendant is incompetent to stand trial, he shall also state his opinion on the likelihood of the defendant's becoming competent to stand trial within one year and if, in his opinion, the defendant is mentally ill or mentally retarded.

(E) An examiner appointed under this section may also be appointed under section 2945.39 of the Revised Code to examine a defendant who has entered a plea of not guilty by reason of insanity, but such an examiner shall prepare separate reports on the issue of competence to stand trial and the defense of not guilty by reason of insanity.

(F) As used in this chapter, "examiner" means a psychiatrist or licensed clinical psychologist, as defined in section 5122.01 of the Revised Code; provided that a licensed clinical psychologist shall meet the criteria of division (I)(1) of section 5122.01 of the Revised Code or be employed by a certified forensic center designated by the department of mental health to conduct examinations.

(1980 H 965, eff. 4–9–81; 1980 H 900, S 297; 1978 H 565)

2945.38 Effect of findings; medication; disposition of defendant; treatment; additional hearings; prosecutor to be notified before discharge

(A) If the court finds, upon the hearing provided for in section 2945.37 of the Revised Code, that the defendant is competent to stand trial, he shall be proceeded against as provided by law. If the defendant is found competent to stand trial and is receiving psychotropic drugs or other medication, the court shall authorize the continued administration of the drugs or medication or other appropriate treatment in order to maintain the defendant's competence to stand trial, unless the defendant's attending physician advises the court against continuation of the drugs, other medication, or treatment.

(B) If the court finds that the defendant is incompetent to stand trial, it shall also make a finding based on the evidence as to whether there is a substantial probability that the defendant will become competent to stand trial within one year, if the defendant is provided with a course of treatment.

(C) If the court finds that the defendant is incompetent to stand trial and that, even if he is provided with a course of treatment, there is not a substantial probability that he will become competent to stand trial within one year, and it appears to the court, through a review of the report of an examiner under section 2945.371 of the Revised Code or otherwise, that the defendant is mentally ill or mentally retarded, the court may cause an affidavit to be filed in the probate court under section 5122.11 or 5123.71 of the Revised Code alleging that the defendant is a mentally ill person subject to hospitalization by court order or a mentally retarded person subject to institutionalization by court order, as defined in sections 5122.01 and 5123.01 of the Revised Code. When the affidavit is filed, the trial court shall send to the probate court a copy of all written reports of the defendant's mental condition that were prepared pursuant to section 2945.371 of the Revised Code.

The court may issue the temporary order of detention that a probate court may issue under section 5122.11 or 5123.71 of the Revised Code, to remain in effect until the probable cause or initial hearing in the probate court. Further proceedings in the probate court are then civil proceedings governed by Chapter 5122. or 5123. of the Revised Code.

The chief clinical officer of the hospital or facility, or the managing officer of the institution, or director of the program, or the person to which the defendant is committed or admitted shall, at least ten days prior to the discharge or immediately upon learning of a change to voluntary status, send written notice to the prosecutor of the date on which the defendant will be discharged or has been admitted on voluntary status.

(D) If the court finds that the defendant is incompetent to stand trial and it appears to the court, through a review of the report of an examiner or otherwise, that the defendant is mentally ill or mentally retarded, but that there is a substantial probability he will become competent to stand trial within one year if provided a course of treatment, and the offense is one for which the defendant could be incarcerated, if convicted, it shall order the defendant to undergo treatment at a facility operated by the department of mental health or the department of mental retardation and developmental disabilities, at a facility certified by the department as qualified to treat mental illness or mental retardation, at a public or private community mental health or mental retardation facility, or it may order private treatment by a psychiatrist or other mental health or mental retardation professional. The order may restrict the defendant's freedom of movement, as the court considers necessary. In determining placement alternatives, the court shall consider the dangerousness of the person to himself and others, the need for security, the type of crime involved, and shall order the least restrictive alternative available that is consistent with public safety and treatment goals.

No defendant shall be required to undergo treatment under this division for longer than the lesser of fifteen months or one-third of the longest minimum sentence that might be imposed for conviction of a felony or one-third of the longest maximum sentence that might be imposed for conviction of a misdemeanor if the defendant is found guilty of the most serious crime with which he was charged at the time of the hearing. No order issued under this division shall remain in effect after the indictment, information, or complaint is dismissed. The court shall notify the prosecutor, defense counsel, and the chief clinical officer of the facility or the managing officer of the institution or facility at which, or person with whom, the defendant was ordered to undergo treatment pursuant to this division whenever an indictment, information, or complaint against a defendant is dismissed and whenever the court revokes an order made under this division. If the maximum time during which an order of the court may be in effect expires, the court shall, within three days, conduct another hearing under section 2945.37 of the Revised Code to determine if the defendant is competent to stand trial, but at the close of such a hearing, a disposition shall be made under division (A) of this section or if the defendant is found incompetent to stand trial, disposition shall be made as under division (C) of this section.

Any person committed pursuant to this division shall not voluntarily admit himself or be voluntarily admitted to a hospital pursuant to section 5122.02 of the Revised Code or to an institution pursuant to section 5123.69 of the Revised Code.

(E) The person who supervises the treatment of a defendant ordered to undergo treatment under division (D) of this section shall file a written report with the court and send copies to the prosecutor and defense counsel at the following times:

(1) After the first ninety days of treatment and after each one hundred eighty days of treatment thereafter;

(2) Whenever the person believes the defendant is competent to stand trial;

(3) Whenever the person believes that there is not a substantial probability that the defendant will become competent to stand trial;

(4) Fourteen days before expiration of the maximum time an order issued under division (D) of this section may be in effect, as specified in that division.

A report shall contain the findings of the examiner, the facts in reasonable detail on which the findings are based, and the opinion of the examiner as to the defendant's competence to stand trial. If the examiner finds that the defendant is incompetent to stand trial, he shall state an opinion in the report on the likelihood of the defendant's becoming competent to stand trial within one year.

(F) Within ten days after receipt of a report required by division (E) of this section, the court shall hold a hearing on the issue of the competence of the defendant to stand trial, as provided in section 2945.37 of the Revised Code. If at the conclusion of the hearing the court finds the defendant is competent to stand trial, the defendant shall be proceeded against as provided by law. If the court finds that the defendant is incompetent to stand trial, but that there is a substantial probability he will become competent to stand trial before expiration of the time limit specified for treatment under division (D) of this section, it may modify or continue in effect orders made at a previous hearing, still subject to the maximum time orders may be in effect, as originally established under division (D) of this section. If the court finds the defendant is incompetent to stand trial and that there is not a substantial probability that he will become competent to stand trial within the maximum time orders may be in effect, as originally established under division (D) of this section, the court shall make a disposition as under division (C) of this section.

(G) The court shall dismiss the indictment, information, or complaint against a defendant finally found incompetent to stand trial under division (C), (D), or (F) of this section or whenever the prosecutor notifies the court he does not intend to prosecute the charges specified in the indictment, information, or complaint.

(H) A dismissal under division (G) of this section is a bar to further criminal proceedings based on the same conduct unless all of the following conditions are present:

(1) After a finding under division (C), (D), or (F) of this section that the defendant was incompetent to stand trial, an affidavit alleging that the defendant was mentally ill and subject to hospitalization by court order or mentally retarded and subject to institutionalization by court order was filed and the defendant was either found mentally ill or mentally retarded and subject to hospitalization or institutionalization by court order, but was later released, or was not so found. Whenever the issue of competence to stand trial is raised, but no finding under division (C), (D), or (F) of this section occurs because before such a finding the court dismisses the indictment, information, or complaint upon notice from the prosecutor that the prosecutor does not intend to prosecute the charges, this division does not bar further criminal proceedings based on the same conduct, but divisions (H)(2), (3), and (4) of this section may bar further proceedings, if the conditions they specify are not present.

(2) The time the defendant has been involuntarily detained for examination or treatment under Chapter 5122. or 5123. of the Revised Code pursuant to the filing of an affidavit under division (C), (D), or (F) of this section and under this section and sections 2945.37 and 2945.371 of the Revised Code does not exceed one-third of the maximum sentence the defendant might have received if convicted of the most serious charge that was dismissed.

(3) Further criminal proceedings are not barred under sections 2945.71 to 2945.73 of the Revised Code.

(4) The period of limitation for the offense committed has not expired under section 2901.13 of the Revised Code, computed without regard to division (H) of that section.

(I) A defendant convicted of a crime and sentenced to a jail or workhouse shall have his sentence reduced by the total number of days he is confined for examination to determine his competence to stand trial or treatment under this section and sections 2945.37 and 2945.371 of the Revised Code.

(J) No statement made by a defendant in an examination or hearing relating to his competence to stand trial shall be used in evidence against him on the issue of guilt in any criminal action.

(K) Each court of common pleas and municipal court shall designate a permanent court officer or employee to file affidavits under division (C) of this section and section 2945.40 of the Revised Code.

(1988 S 156, eff. 7–1–89; 1980 H 965, H 900, S 297; 1978 H 565; 1975 S 185; 1953 H 1; GC 13441–2)

2945.381 Disposition of mentally incompetent persons; hearing—Repealed

(1978 H 565, eff. 11–1–78; 1975 S 185)

2945.39 Plea of not guilty by reason of insanity; procedures; admissions not available in criminal case

(A) If a defendant enters a plea of not guilty by reason of insanity, the court may order one or more, but not more than three, evaluations of the defendant's mental condition at the time of the commission of the offense. The court shall order that each evaluation be conducted through examination of the defendant by any of the following:

(1) A forensic center designated by the department of mental health to conduct such examinations and make such evaluations in the area in which the court is located;

(2) Any other program or facility that is designated by the department of mental health or the department of mental retardation and developmental disabilities to conduct such examinations and make such evaluations, provided the center, program, or facility is operated by the appropriate department or is certified by such department as being in compliance with the standards established under division (J) of section 5119.01 or division (C) of section 5123.04 of the Revised Code;

(3) A center, program, or facility designated by the court other than one designated by the appropriate department.

In any case, the court may designate examiners other than the personnel of the center, program, facility, or department to make the examination. If more than one examination is ordered, the prosecutor and the defendant may recommend to the court an examiner whom each prefers to have perform one of the examinations.

In conducting an evaluation pursuant to this section of a defendant's mental condition at the time of the commission of the offense, the examiner shall consider all relevant evidence. If the offense charged involves the use of force against another, the relevant evidence to be considered includes, but is not limited to, any evidence that the defendant suffered, at the time of the commission of the offense, from the "battered woman syndrome."

(B) If an evaluation is ordered, the defendant shall be available at the times and places established by the center, program, facility, or examiners. The court may order a defendant who has been released on bail or recognizance to submit to an examination under this section. If a defendant who has been released on bail or recognizance refuses to submit to a complete examination, the court may amend the conditions of bail or recognizance and order the sheriff to take the defendant into custody and deliver him to a program or facility operated by the department where he may be held for a reasonable time not to exceed twenty days.

(C) A defendant who has not been released on bail or recognizance may be examined at his place of detention, or the court at the request of the examiner may order the sheriff to transport the defendant to a program or facility operated by the department of mental health or the department of mental retardation and developmental disabilities, where he may be held for examination for a reasonable time not to exceed thirty days, and to return the defendant to the place of detention after the examination.

The court shall inform any examiner it appoints of the offense of which the defendant is charged.

The court shall notify the prosecutor and defense counsel immediately upon the appointment of an examiner under this section, and specify the name and address of the examiner. An examiner appointed under this section may be called as a witness by the court or any party and shall be subject to direct and cross-examination by the prosecutor and defense counsel. Neither the appointment nor the testimony of an examiner appointed under this section precludes the prosecutor or defense counsel from calling other witnesses to testify on the insanity issue.

The examiner shall complete the examination within thirty days after the court's order for the evaluation and shall prepare and provide to the court, prosecutor, and defense counsel a written report concerning the mental condition of the defendant.

If the court does not designate an examiner recommended by the defendant pursuant to division (A) of this section, the court shall inform the defendant that he may have independent expert evaluation and that if he is unable to obtain independent expert evaluation, it will be obtained for him, at public expense if he is indigent.

Persons appointed as examiners under this section shall be paid a reasonable amount for their services and expenses, as certified by the court and paid by the county in the case of county courts and courts of common pleas and by the legislative authority, as defined in section 1901.03 of the Revised Code, in the case of municipal courts.

(D) No statement made by a defendant in an examination or hearing relating to his mental condition at the time of the commission of an offense shall be used in evidence against him on the issue of guilt in any criminal action.

(1990 H 484, eff. 11–5–90; 1981 H 1; 1980 H 965, H 736, S 297, H 900; 1978 H 565)

2945.391 Applicability of not guilty by reason of insanity plea; impairment of reason not defense

For purposes of section 2945.40 and Chapters 5122. and 5123. of the Revised Code, a person is "not guilty by reason of insanity" relative to a charge of an offense only as described in division (N) of section 2901.01 of the Revised Code. Proof that a person's reason, at the time of the commission of an offense, was so impaired that he did not have the ability to refrain from doing his act or acts, does not constitute a defense.

(1990 S 24, eff. 7–24–90)

2945.392 Battered woman syndrome

(A) The declarations set forth in division (A) of section 2901.06 of the Revised Code apply in relation to this section.

(B) If a defendant is charged with an offense involving the use of force against another and the defendant enters a plea to the charge of not guilty by reason of insanity, the person may introduce expert testimony of the "battered woman syndrome" and expert testimony that the defendant suffered from that syndrome as evidence to establish the requisite impairment of the defendant's reason, at the time of the commission of the offense, that is necessary for a finding that the defendant is not guilty by reason of insanity. The introduction of any expert testimony under this division shall be in accordance with the Ohio Rules of Evidence.

(1990 H 484, eff. 11–5–90)

2945.40 Verdict of not guilty by reason of insanity; effects; procedures; commitment; conditional release; monitors; notice

(A) If a person is found not guilty by reason of insanity, the verdict shall state that finding, and the trial court shall conduct a full hearing to determine whether the person is a mentally ill person subject to hospitalization by court order or a mentally retarded person subject to institutionalization by court order, as defined in sections 5122.01 and 5123.01 of the Revised Code. Prior to the hearing, if the trial judge believes that there is probable cause that the person found not guilty by reason of insanity is such a mentally ill or mentally retarded person, he may issue a temporary order of detention for that person to remain in effect for seven court days or until the hearing, whichever occurs first.

Any person detained pursuant to such an order shall be held in a suitable facility taking into consideration the place and type of confinement prior to and during trial.

The hearing shall be held in the trial court within seven court days after the finding of not guilty by reason of insanity. Failure to conduct the hearing within the seven-day period shall cause the immediate discharge of the respondent, unless a continuance is granted by the judge for not longer than seven court days for good cause shown.

Except as otherwise provided in this section, the hearing shall be conducted pursuant to divisions (A)(1) to (5) and (A)(8) to (15) of section 5122.15 or divisions (A)(1) to (5) and (A)(8) to (14) of section 5123.76 of the Revised Code. The hearings shall be open to the public.

(B) Upon completion of the hearing, if the court finds there is not clear and convincing evidence that the person is a mentally ill or mentally retarded person subject to hospitalization or institutionalization by court order, the court immediately shall discharge the person, unless a detainer has been placed upon the person by the department of rehabilitation and correction, in which case the person shall be returned to that department.

(C) If the court finds by clear and convincing evidence that the person is a mentally ill or mentally retarded person subject to hospitalization or institutionalization by court order, it shall make a commitment authorized by divisions (C) to (E) of section 5122.15 or divisions (C) to (E) of section 5123.76 of the Revised Code, and shall send to the place of commitment all reports of the person's mental condition at the time of the offense and at the time of commitment that were prepared pursuant to section 2945.39 or Chapter 5122. or 5123. of the Revised Code and any other information the court considers relevant, including any part of the trial transcript. The commitment shall be pursuant to divisions (H) and (I) of section 5122.15 and divisions (H), (I), and (J) of section 5123.76 of the Revised Code, except as provided in this section.

(D)(1) In deciding the nature of commitment pursuant to division (C) of this section, the court shall order the implementation of the least restrictive commitment alternative available consistent with the public safety and the welfare of the person. As part of the least restrictive commitment alternative, the court may grant conditional release to a person found not guilty by reason of insanity. In determining whether to grant conditional release, the court shall evaluate the potential risks to public safety and the welfare of the person. In evaluating the potential risks to public safety, the court shall consider the current quantity of psychotropic drugs and other treatment the person is receiving and the likelihood the person will continue to take the drugs and continue the other treatment while on conditional release.

If the court makes a determination to grant a conditional release, it may set any conditions on the release with respect to treatment, evaluation, counseling, or control of the respondent that ensure the protection of the public safety and the welfare of the person.

(2) A conditional release granted pursuant to this section is a commitment. Any person granted a conditional release is entitled to the hearings on continued commitment pursuant to division (H) of section 5122.15 and division (H) of section 5123.76 of the Revised Code.

(3) If a person, agency, or facility is assigned to monitor a person on conditional release, it shall notify the court of any violation of the terms of the conditional release by the person being monitored immediately upon learning of the violation. Upon learning of the violation, the court may issue a temporary order of detention pursuant to division (A) of this section to remain in effect for seven days and shall, at the request of the prosecutor, or may on its own motion conduct a hearing, within seven days, in which the person has the same rights as at a full hearing pursuant to division (A) of this section on whether the conditional release shall be modified or terminated.

Before any hearing held pursuant to this division, the trial court shall give the prosecutor reasonable notice of the hearing. At any such hearing, the prosecutor shall present the case demonstrating that the person violated the terms of the conditional release.

(4) At any time after commitment pursuant to this section, if, after evaluating the potential risks to public safety and the welfare of the person, the chief clinical officer of the hospital or facility, or the managing officer of the institution, or director of the program, or the person to which a person found not guilty by reason of insanity is committed recommends the conditional release of the committed person, the chief clinical officer, managing officer, director, or person shall send written notice of the proposed conditional release by certified mail to the trial court in which the person was found not guilty by reason of insanity, the attorney general, and the prosecutor. No later than thirty days after receiving the notice, the trial court shall hold a full hearing on whether the conditional release should be granted and shall give the prosecutor and attorney general written notice of the time and place of the hearing at least fifteen days before it is held. At the conclusion of the hearing, the court may grant conditional release pursuant to this section.

(5) At any hearing in which the discharge of a person found not guilty by reason of insanity is at issue, the court, in determining whether to grant a conditional release in lieu of discharge, shall evaluate the potential risks to public safety and the welfare of the person in the same manner as under division (D)(1) of this section. The court may grant a conditional release of such a person pursuant to this section.

(6) Conditional release shall terminate no later than on the expiration of the maximum sentence the person could have served in a correctional institution if he had been convicted of the most serious offense for which he was found not guilty by reason of insanity. In case of such a termination of conditional release, the trial court judge shall notify the prosecutor of the termination at least ten days before it is scheduled to occur. The prosecutor may file an affidavit pursuant to section 5122.11 or 5123.71 of the Revised Code, for the hospitalization or institutionalization of the person whose conditional release was so terminated.

(E) A person committed under this section is entitled to all hearings on continued commitment applicable to him under either division (H) of section 5122.15 or division (H) of section 5123.76 of the Revised Code. At least fifteen days before such a hearing, the trial court judge shall send written notice of the hearing by certified mail, return receipt requested, to the attorney general and to the prosecutor in the case in which the person was found not guilty by reason of insanity. The hearings shall be held in accordance with division (G) of this section.

(F) Before discharging, releasing, authorizing a trial visit for, or transferring a person committed under this section, the chief clinical officer of the hospital or facility, or the managing officer of the institution, or director of the program, chief of the division of mental retardation and developmental disabilities programs or his designee, or person to which the person is committed shall send written notice by certified mail, return receipt requested, to the trial court in which the person was found not guilty by reason of insanity, the attorney general, and the prosecutor advising the trial court, the attorney general, and the prosecutor of the proposed discharge, release, trial visit, or transfer. The notice shall include the hospital's or facility's report on the current status of the person and its recommendations concerning the pending action.

No later than thirty days after receiving the notice, the trial court shall hold a full hearing on the person's commitment and shall give the prosecutor and the attorney general written notice of the time and place of that hearing at least fifteen days before it is held. At the conclusion of the hearing, the trial court may discharge, release, authorize a trial visit for, or transfer the person or continue commitment pursuant to division (C) of this section.

(G) At any hearing held pursuant to this section and Chapter 5122. or 5123. of the Revised Code to determine if a person found not guilty by reason of insanity will be committed, released, granted a trial visit, transferred, or discharged, the prosecutor shall present the case demonstrating that the person is a mentally ill or mentally retarded person subject to hospitalization or institutionalization by court order or the position of the county prosecutor on questions of the transfer, trial visit, or discharge. An attorney designated by the attorney general shall represent the hospital, facility, program, or institution to which the person was committed, if the person has been committed.

(H) A person who is found not guilty by reason of insanity cannot voluntarily commit himself to a hospital or institution pursuant to sections 5122.02, 5123.69, division (G) of section 5122.15, or division (G) of section 5123.76 of the Revised Code, unless the person, at a hearing held pursuant to division (A) of this section, was found:

(1) Not to be a mentally ill or mentally retarded person subject to hospitalization or institutionalization by court order; or

(2) To be a mentally ill or mentally retarded person subject to hospitalization or institutionalization by court order, was involuntarily committed pursuant to division (A) of this section, or section 5122.15 or 5123.76 of the Revised Code, and was finally discharged.

(I) In all hearings pursuant to this section, the person found not guilty by reason of insanity may retain counsel of his choice. If the person is indigent, the court shall appoint a public defender or other counsel to provide legal representation to such persons.

(J) The hearings held pursuant to divisions (D)(4), (E), and (F) of this section shall be held by the trial court judge, or if he is not available, by another judge of the court with jurisdiction over the matter. In the hearing judge's discretion, the hearing may be held in the county in which the trial court is located or in the county in which the hospital or facility is located.

(1994 H 571, eff. 10-6-94; 1990 S 24, eff. 7-24-90; 1988 S 156; 1981 H 1; 1980 H 965, S 297; 1978 H 565)

WITNESSES

2945.41   Rules applicable in criminal cases

The rules of evidence in civil causes, where applicable, govern in all criminal causes.
(1953 H 1, eff. 10–1–53;   GC 13444–1)

2945.42   Competency of witnesses

No person is disqualified as a witness in a criminal prosecution by reason of his interest in the prosecution as a party or otherwise, or by reason of his conviction of crime.   Husband and wife are competent witnesses to testify in behalf of each other in all criminal prosecutions, and to testify against each other in all actions, prosecutions, and proceedings for personal injury of either by the other, bigamy, or failure to provide for, neglect of, or cruelty to their children under eighteen years of age or their physically or mentally handicapped child under twenty-one years of age.   A spouse may testify against his spouse in a prosecution under sections 2903.11 to 2903.13, 2919.21, 2919.22, or 2919.25 of the Revised Code for cruelty to, neglect of, or abandonment of such spouse, in a prosecution against his spouse under section 2903.211, 2911.211, or 2919.27 of the Revised Code for the commission of the offense against the spouse who is testifying, or in a prosecution under section 2907.02 or 2907.12 of the Revised Code for the commission of rape or felonious sexual penetration against such spouse in a case in which the offense can be committed against a spouse.   Such interest, conviction, or relationship may be shown for the purpose of affecting the credibility of such witness.   Husband or wife shall not testify concerning a communication made by one to the other, or act done by either in the presence of the other, during coverture, unless the communication was made or act done in the known presence or hearing of a third person competent to be a witness, or in case of personal injury by either the husband or wife to the other, or rape or felonious sexual penetration in a case in which the offense can be committed against a spouse, or bigamy, or failure to provide for, or neglect or cruelty of either to their children under eighteen years of age or their physically or mentally handicapped child under twenty-one years of age, violation of a protection order or consent agreement, or neglect or abandonment of such spouse under such sections.   The presence or whereabouts of the husband or wife is not an act under this section. The rule is the same if the marital relation has ceased to exist.
(1992 H 536, eff. 11–5–92;   1985 H 475;   1980 H 920;   1975 H 1;   1971 S 312;   1953 H 1;   GC 13444–2)

2945.43   Defendant may testify

On the trial of a criminal cause, a person charged with an offense may, at his own request, be a witness, but not otherwise.   The failure of such person to testify may be considered by the court and jury and may be made the subject of comment by counsel.
(1953 H 1, eff. 10–1–53;   GC 13444–3)

2945.44   Court of common pleas to grant transactional immunity;   procedure;   exceptions

(A) In any criminal proceeding in this state or in any criminal or civil proceeding brought pursuant to sections 2923.31 to 2923.36 of the Revised Code, if a witness refuses to answer or produce information on the basis of his privilege against self-incrimination, the court of common pleas of the county in which the proceeding is being held, unless it finds that to do so would not further the administration of justice, shall compel the witness to answer or produce the information, if both of the following apply:

(1) The prosecuting attorney of the county in which the proceedings are being held makes a written request to the court of common pleas to order the witness to answer or produce the information, notwithstanding his claim of privilege;

(2) The court of common pleas informs the witness that by answering, or producing the information he will receive immunity under division (B) of this section.

(B) If, but for this section, the witness would have been privileged to withhold an answer or any information given in any criminal proceeding, and he complies with an order under division (A) of this section compelling him to give an answer or produce any information, he shall not be prosecuted or subjected to any criminal penalty in the courts of this state for or on account of any transaction or matter concerning which, in compliance with the order, he gave an answer or produced any information.

(C) A witness granted immunity under this section may be subjected to a criminal penalty for any violation of section 2921.11, 2921.12, or 2921.13 of the Revised Code, or for contempt committed in answering, failing to answer, or failing to produce information in compliance with the order.

(1985 H 5, eff. 1–1–86; 1978 H 491)

2945.45   Subpoenas to issue to any county

In all criminal cases, the clerk of the court of common pleas, upon a praecipe being filed, shall issue writs of subpoena for the witnesses named therein, directed to the sheriff of such county, or the county where such witnesses reside or are found, which shall be served and returned as in other cases.   Such sheriff, by writing indorsed on the writs, may depute a disinterested person to serve and return them.   The person so deputed to serve such subpoenas shall make a return of the service made, and make oath thereto before a person competent to administer oaths, which shall be indorsed on the writ.   The return may be forwarded through the post office, or otherwise.

(1953 H 1, eff. 10–1–53; GC 13444–5)

2945.451   Employee's attendance at proceeding in criminal case under subpoena; employer may not penalize

No employer shall discharge or terminate from employment, threaten to discharge or terminate from employment, or otherwise punish or penalize any employee because of time lost from regular employment as a result of the employee's attendance at any proceeding in a criminal case pursuant to a subpoena.   This section generally does not require and shall not be construed to require an employer to pay an employee for time lost as a result of attendance at any criminal proceeding.   However, if an employee is subpoenaed to appear at a criminal proceeding and the proceeding pertains to an offense against the employer or an offense involving the employee during the course of his employment, the employer shall not decrease or withhold the employee's pay for any time lost as a result of compliance with the subpoena. Any employer who knowingly violates this section is in contempt of court.

(1984 S 172, eff. 9–26–84)

2945.46   Attendance of witness enforced

Civil procedure relative to compelling the attendance and testimony of witnesses, their examination, the administering of oaths and affirmations, and proceedings for contempt to enforce the remedies and protect the rights of parties, extend to criminal cases as far as applicable.

(1953 H 1, eff. 10–1–53; GC 13444–6)

2945.47   Testimony of prisoners in criminal proceedings

(A) If it is necessary in a criminal proceeding before the court to procure the testimony of a person who is imprisoned in a workhouse, juvenile detention facility, jail, or state correctional institution within this state, or who is in the custody of the department of youth services, the court may require that the person's testimony be taken by deposition pursuant to Criminal Rule 15 at the place of the person's confinement, if the person is not a defendant in the case and if the court determines that the interests of justice do not demand that the person be brought before the court for the presentation of his testimony.   All witnesses for the prosecution shall be brought before the court.   The defendant may waive any right to compel the appearance of a person brought before the court pursuant to this division.

(B) If it is necessary in a criminal proceeding before the court to procure the testimony of a person who is imprisoned in a workhouse, a juvenile detention facility, or a jail within this state, the court may order a subpoena to be issued, directed to the keeper of the institution, commanding him to bring the prisoner named in the subpoena before the court.

The keeper, upon receiving the subpoena, shall take the witness before the court at the time and place named in the subpoena, and hold him until he is discharged by the court. When discharged, he shall be returned in the custody of such officer to the place of imprisonment from which he was taken, and the officer may command any assistance that he considers proper for the transportation of the witness.

(C) If it is necessary in a criminal proceeding before the court to procure the testimony of a person who is imprisoned in a state correctional institution within this state, or who is in the custody of the department of youth services, the court may order a subpoena to be issued directed to the sheriff of the county in which the indictment or grand jury proceeding is pending. When a copy of the subpoena is presented by the sheriff to the warden or superintendent of a state correctional institution, or to the person in charge of the facility in which a juvenile is confined, he shall deliver the witness at the institution or facility to the sheriff who shall take him before the court at the time and place named in the subpoena and hold him until he is discharged by the court. When discharged, he shall be returned in the custody of the sheriff to the place of imprisonment from which he was taken.

(D) The court shall, in the manner provided in Chapter 120. of the Revised Code, either assign counsel or designate a public defender to represent a juvenile subpoenaed as a witness under this section. Compensation for assigned counsel shall be made pursuant to section 2941.51 of the Revised Code.

(E) When a person's testimony is taken by deposition pursuant to division (A) of this section, the deposition shall be upon oral examination if either the prosecuting authority or the defendant who is taking the deposition requests that the deposition be upon oral examination, and may be videotaped if either the prosecuting authority or the defendant who is taking the deposition requests that it be recorded by means of videotape.

The person requesting the testimony of the person whose deposition is taken pursuant to division (A) of this section shall pay the expense of taking the deposition, except that the court may tax the expense as court costs in appropriate cases.

(1994 H 571, eff. 10–6–94; 1981 H 440, eff. 11–23–81; 1981 H 145; 1976 S 393; 129 v 322; 1953 H 1; GC 13444–7, 13444–8)

2945.48 Witness may be placed in jail

When a witness mentioned in section 2945.47 of the Revised Code is in attendance upon a court he may be placed in the jail of the county. The expenses of the officer in transporting him to and from such court, including compensation for the guard or attendant of such prisoner not exceeding the per diem salary of such guard for the time he is away from said institution, shall be allowed by the court and taxed and paid as other costs against the state.

(1953 H 1, eff. 10–1–53; GC 13444–9)

2945.49 Testimony of deceased or absent witness; videotaped testimony of child victim

(A) Testimony taken at an examination or a preliminary hearing at which the defendant is present, or at a former trial of the cause, or taken by deposition at the instance of the defendant or the state, may be used whenever the witness giving such testimony dies, or cannot for any reason be produced at the trial, or whenever the witness has, since giving such testimony, become incapacitated to testify. If such former testimony is contained within an authenticated transcript of such testimony, it shall be proven by the transcript, otherwise by other testimony.

(B)(1) At any trial on a charge of a felony violation of section 2907.02, 2907.03, 2907.04, 2907.05, or 2907.12 of the Revised Code in which the alleged victim of the alleged offense was under eleven years of age when the complaint or information was filed, whichever occurred earlier, the court, upon motion of the prosecutor in the case, may admit videotaped preliminary hearing testimony of the child victim as evidence at the trial, in lieu of the child victim appearing as a witness and testifying at the trial, if all of the following apply:

(a) The videotape of the testimony was made at the preliminary hearing at which probable cause of the violation charged was found;

(b) The videotape of the testimony was made in accordance with division (C) of section 2937.11 of the Revised Code;

(c) The testimony in the videotape is not excluded by the hearsay rule and otherwise is admissible under the Rules of Evidence. For purposes of this division, testimony is not excluded by the hearsay rule if the testimony is not hearsay under Evidence Rule 801, if the testimony is within an exception to the hearsay rule set forth in Evidence Rule 803, if the child victim who gave the testimony is unavailable as a witness, as defined in Evidence Rule 804, and the testimony is admissible under that rule, or if both of the following apply:

(i) The accused had an opportunity and similar motive at the preliminary hearing to develop the testimony of the child victim by direct, cross, or redirect examination;

(ii) The court determines that there is reasonable cause to believe that if the child victim who gave the testimony at the preliminary hearing were to testify in person at the trial, the child victim would experience serious emotional trauma as a result of his participation at the trial.

(2) If a child victim of an alleged felony violation of section 2907.02, 2907.03, 2907.04, 2907.05, 2907.06, 2907.12, 2907.21, 2907.31, 2907.32, 2907.321, 2907.322, or 2907.323, or division (B)(5) of section 2919.22 of the Revised Code testifies at the preliminary hearing in the case, the testimony of the child victim at the preliminary hearing was videotaped pursuant to division (C) of section 2937.11 of the Revised Code, and the defendant in the case files a written objection to the use, pursuant to division (B)(1) of this section, of the videotaped testimony at the trial, the court, immediately after the filing of the objection, shall hold a hearing to determine whether the videotaped testimony of the child victim should be admissible at trial under division (B)(1) of this section, and if it is admissible, whether the child victim should be required to provide limited additional testimony of the type described in this division. At the hearing held pursuant to this division, the defendant and the prosecutor in the case may present any evidence that is relevant to the issues to be determined at the hearing, but the child victim shall not be required to testify at the hearing.

After the hearing, the court shall not require the child victim to testify at the trial, unless it determines that both of the following apply:

(a) That the testimony of the child victim at trial is necessary for one or more of the following reasons:

(i) Evidence that was not available at the time of the testimony of the child victim at the preliminary hearing has been discovered;

(ii) The circumstances surrounding the case have changed sufficiently to necessitate that the child victim testify at the trial.

(b) That the testimony of the child victim at the trial is necessary to protect the right of the defendant to a fair trial.

The court shall enter its finding and the reasons for it in the journal. If the court requires the child victim to testify at the trial, the testimony of the victim shall be limited to the new evidence and changed circumstances and the child victim shall not otherwise be required to testify at the trial. The required testimony of the child victim may be given in person, or upon motion of the prosecution, may be taken by deposition in accordance with division (A) of section 2907.41 of the Revised Code provided the deposition is admitted as evidence under division (B) of that section, may be taken outside of the courtroom and televised into the courtroom in accordance with division (C) of that section, or may be taken outside of the courtroom and recorded for showing in the courtroom in accordance with division (D) of that section.

(3) If videotaped testimony of a child victim is admitted at trial in accordance with division (B)(1) of this section, the child victim shall not be compelled in any way to appear as a witness at the trial, except as provided in division (B)(2) of this section.

(C) An order issued pursuant to division (B) of this section shall specifically identify the child victim concerning whose testimony it pertains. The order shall apply only during the testimony of the child victim it specifically identifies.

(D) As used in this section, "prosecutor" has the same meaning as in section 2935.01 of the Revised Code.

(1986 H 108, eff. 10–14–86; 1953 H 1; GC 13444–10)

2945.50 Deposition in criminal cases

At any time after an issue of fact is joined upon an indictment, information, or an affidavit, the prosecution or the defendant may apply in writing to the court in which such indictment, information, or affidavit is pending for a commission to take the depositions of any witness. The court or a judge thereof may grant such commission and make an order stating in what manner and for what length of time notice shall be given to the prosecution or to the defendant, before such witness shall be examined.

(131 v H 153, eff. 10–13–65; 1953 H 1; GC 13444–11)

2945.51 When deposition may be taken; expenses

When a deposition is to be taken in this state, and a commission is granted under section 2945.50 of the Revised Code while the defendant is confined in jail, the sheriff or deputy or other person having custody of the defendant shall be ordered by the court to take the defendant to the place of the taking of the deposition, and have him before the officer at the time of taking such deposition. Such sheriff or deputy or other person having custody of the defendant shall be reimbursed for actual reasonable traveling expenses for himself and the defendant, the bills for the same, upon the approval of the board of county commissioners, to be paid from the county treasury on the warrant of the county auditor. Such sheriff shall receive as fees therefor, one dollar for each day in attendance thereat. Such fees and traveling expenses shall be taxed and collected as other fees and costs in the case.

(131 v H 153, eff. 10–13–65; 1953 H 1; GC 13444–12)

2945.52 Counsel appointed shall represent the defendant

Counsel assigned by the court to represent the defendant may attend upon and represent the defendant at the taking of a deposition under section 2945.50 of the Revised Code, and said counsel shall be paid a reasonable fee for his services in taking such deposition, in addition to the compensation allowed for defending such defendant, to be fixed by the court. He shall also be allowed his actual expenses incurred in going to and from the place of taking the deposition.

(1953 H 1, eff. 10–1–53; GC 13444–13)

2945.53 Right of accused to examine witness

In all cases in which depositions are taken by the state or the accused, to be used by or against the accused, as provided in sections 2945.50 to 2945.52, inclusive, of the Revised Code, the court shall by proper order provide and secure to the accused the means and opportunity to be present in person and with counsel at the taking of such deposition, and to examine the witness face to face, as fully and in the same manner as if in court. All expenses necessarily incurred in the securing of such means and opportunity, and the expenses of the prosecuting attorney in attending the taking of such deposition, shall be paid out of the county treasury upon the certificate of the court making such order.

(1953 H 1, eff. 10–1–53; GC 13444–14)

2945.54 Conduct of examination

The examination of witnesses by deposition in criminal cases shall be taken and certified, and the return thereof to the court made as for taking depositions under sections 2319.05 to 2319.31, inclusive, of the Revised Code. The commissioners appointed under section 2945.50 of the Revised Code to take depositions shall receive such compensation as the court directs, to be paid out of the county treasury and taxed as part of the costs in the case.

(1953 H 1, eff. 10–1–53; GC 13444–15)

2945.55   Testimony of previous identification

When identification of the defendant is an issue, a witness who has on previous occasion identified such person may testify to such previous identification. Such identification may be proved by other witnesses.

(1953 H 1, eff. 10–1–53; GC 13444–16)

2945.56   Rebuttal of defendant's character evidence

When the defendant offers evidence of his character or reputation, the prosecution may offer, in rebuttal thereof, proof of his previous conviction of a crime involving moral turpitude, in addition to other competent evidence.

(1953 H 1, eff. 10–1–53; GC 13444–17)

2945.57   Number of witnesses to character

The number of witnesses who are expected to testify upon the subject of character or reputation, for whom subpoenas are issued, shall be designated upon the praecipe and, except in cases of murder in the first and second degree, manslaughter, rape, assault with intent to commit rape, or selling intoxicating liquor to a person in the habit of becoming intoxicated, shall not exceed ten upon each side, unless a deposit of at least one per diem and mileage fee for each of such additional witnesses is first made with the clerk of the court of common pleas. Not more than ten witnesses upon each side shall be permitted to testify upon the question of character or reputation in a criminal cause unless their full per diem and mileage fees have been deposited or paid by the party in whose behalf they are sworn, and the clerk shall not issue a certificate for compensation to be paid out of the county treasury to a witness who has testified upon the subject of character or reputation, except as provided in this section.

(1953 H 1, eff. 10–1–53; GC 13444–18)

ALIBI

2945.58   Alibi

Whenever a defendant in a criminal cause proposes to offer in his defense, testimony to establish an alibi on his behalf, such defendant shall, not less than three days before the trial of such cause, file and serve upon the prosecuting attorney a notice in writing of his intention to claim such alibi. Notice shall include specific information as to the place at which the defendant claims to have been at the time of the alleged offense. If the defendant fails to file such written notice, the court may exclude evidence offered by the defendant for the purpose of proving such alibi.

(1953 H 1, eff. 10–1–53; GC 13444–20)

PROOF

2945.59   Proof of defendant's motive

In any criminal case in which the defendant's motive or intent, the absence of mistake or accident on his part, or the defendant's scheme, plan, or system in doing an act is material, any acts of the defendant which tend to show his motive or intent, the absence of mistake or accident on his part, or the defendant's scheme, plan, or system in doing the act in question may be proved, whether they are contemporaneous with or prior or subsequent thereto, notwithstanding that such proof may show or tend to show the commission of another crime by the defendant.

(1953 H 1, eff. 10–1–53; GC 13444–19)

2945.60   Proof in case of treason—Repealed

(1972 H 511, eff. 1–1–74; 1953 H 1; GC 13444–21)

2945.61   Proof in case of unauthorized military expedition—Repealed

(1972 H 511, eff. 1–1–74; 1953 H 1; GC 13444–21)

2945.62 Proof in case of perjury—Repealed

(1972 H 511, eff. 1–1–74; 1953 H 1; GC 13444–22)

2945.63 Proof of seduction of female—Repealed

(1972 H 511, eff. 1–1–74; 1953 H 1; GC 13444–23)

2945.64 Prima–facie evidence of embezzlement

Failure or refusal to pay over or produce public money by a person charged with the collection, receipt, transfer, disbursement, or safekeeping of such money, whether belonging to this state, a county, township, municipal corporation, or board of education, or other public money, or to account to or make settlement with a legal authority of the official accounts of such person, is prima-facie evidence of the embezzlement thereof. Upon the trial of such person for the embezzlement of public money, it is sufficient evidence for the purpose of showing a balance against him, to produce a transcript from the records of the auditor of state, director of budget and management, county auditor, or board of county commissioners. The refusal of such person, whether in or out of office, to pay a draft, order, or warrant drawn upon him by an authorized officer, for public money in his hands, or a refusal by a person promptly to pay over to his successor public money or securities on the legal requirement of an authorized officer of the state or county, on the trial of an indictment against him for embezzlement, is prima-facie evidence thereof.

(1985 H 201, eff. 7–1–85; 1953 H 1; GC 13444–25)

BILL OF EXCEPTIONS

2945.65 Bill of exceptions—Repealed

(1986 H 412, eff. 3–17–87; 129 v 1398; 128 v 141; 125 v 39; 1953 H 1; GC 13445–1)

2945.66 Proceedings on filing of bill of exceptions—Repealed

(1986 H 412, eff. 3–17–87; 1977 H 219; 131 v H 231; 1953 H 1; GC 13445–2)

2945.67 When prosecutor may appeal; when public defender to oppose

(A) A prosecuting attorney, village solicitor, city director of law, or the attorney general may appeal as a matter or [1] right any decision of a trial court in a criminal case, or any decision of a juvenile court in a delinquency case, which decision grants a motion to dismiss all or any part of an indictment, complaint, or information, a motion to suppress evidence, or a motion for the return of seized property or grants post conviction relief pursuant to sections 2953.21 to 2953.24 of the Revised Code, and may appeal by leave of the court to which the appeal is taken any other decision, except the final verdict, of the trial court in a criminal case or of the juvenile court in a delinquency case.

(B) In any proceeding brought pursuant to division (A) of this section, the court shall, in accordance with Chapter 120. of the Revised Code, appoint the county public defender, joint county public defender, or other counsel to represent any person who is indigent, is not represented by counsel, and does not waive his right to counsel.

(1978 H 1168, eff. 11–1–78)

[1] So in original; should this read "of"?

2945.68 Application by prosecutor, solicitor, or attorney general to file bill of exceptions—Repealed

(1995 S 2, eff. 7–1–96; 1978 H 1168, eff. 11–1–78; 1977 H 219; 131 v H 231; 1953 H 1; GC 13446–2)

2945.69 Appointment of attorney by trial judge—Repealed

(1978 H 1168, eff. 11–1–78; 1977 H 219; 131 v H 231; 1953 H 1; GC 13446–3)

2945.70 Decision of the court; appeal by the state—Repealed

(1978 H 1168, eff. 11–1–78; 1972 H 511; 131 v H 231; 1953 H 1; GC 13446–4)

SCHEDULE OF TRIAL AND HEARINGS

2945.71 Time within which hearing or trial must be held

(A) A person against whom a charge is pending in a court not of record, or against whom a charge of minor misdemeanor is pending in a court of record, shall be brought to trial within thirty days after his arrest or the service of summons.

(B) A person against whom a charge of misdemeanor, other than a minor misdemeanor, is pending in a court of record, shall be brought to trial:

(1) Within forty-five days after his arrest or the service of summons, if the offense charged is a misdemeanor of the third or fourth degree, or other misdemeanor for which the maximum penalty is imprisonment for not more than sixty days;

(2) Within ninety days after his arrest or the service of summons, if the offense charged is a misdemeanor of the first or second degree, or other misdemeanor for which the maximum penalty is imprisonment for more than sixty days.

(C) A person against whom a charge of felony is pending:

(1) Notwithstanding any provisions to the contrary in Criminal Rule 5(B), shall be accorded a preliminary hearing within fifteen consecutive days after his arrest if the accused is not held in jail in lieu of bail on the pending charge or within ten consecutive days after his arrest if the accused is held in jail in lieu of bail on the pending charge;

(2) Shall be brought to trial within two hundred seventy days after his arrest.

(D) A person against whom one or more charges of minor misdemeanor and one or more charges of misdemeanor other than minor misdemeanor, all of which arose out of the same act or transaction, are pending, or against whom charges of misdemeanors of different degrees, other than minor misdemeanors, all of which arose out of the same act or transaction, are pending shall be brought to trial within the time period required for the highest degree of misdemeanor charged, as determined under division (B) of this section.

(E) For purposes of computing time under divisions (A), (B), (C)(2), and (D) of this section, each day during which the accused is held in jail in lieu of bail on the pending charge shall be counted as three days. This division does not apply for purposes of computing time under division (C)(1) of this section.

(F) This section shall not be construed to modify in any way section 2941.401, or sections 2963.30 to 2963.35 of the Revised Code.

(1981 S 119, eff. 3–17–82; 1980 S 288; 1975 S 83; 1973 H 716; 1972 H 511)

2945.72 Extension of time for hearing or trial

The time within which an accused must be brought to trial, or, in the case of felony, to preliminary hearing and trial, may be extended only by the following:

(A) Any period during which the accused is unavailable for hearing or trial, by reason of other criminal proceedings against him, within or outside the state, by reason of his confinement in another state, or by reason of the pendency of extradition proceedings, provided that the prosecution exercises reasonable diligence to secure his availability;

(B) Any period during which the accused is mentally incompetent to stand trial or during which his mental competence to stand trial is being determined, or any period during which the accused is physically incapable of standing trial;

(C) Any period of delay necessitated by the accused's lack of counsel, provided that such delay is not occasioned by any lack of diligence in providing counsel to an indigent accused upon his request as required by law;

(D) Any period of delay occasioned by the neglect or improper act of the accused;

(E) Any period of delay necessitated by reason of a plea in bar or abatement, motion, proceeding, or action made or instituted by the accused;

(F) Any period of delay necessitated by a removal or change of venue pursuant to law;

(G) Any period during which trial is stayed pursuant to an express statutory requirement, or pursuant to an order of another court competent to issue such order;

(H) The period of any continuance granted on the accused's own motion, and the period of any reasonable continuance granted other than upon the accused's own motion;

(I) Any period during which an appeal filed pursuant to section 2945.67 of the Revised Code is pending.

(1978 H 1168, eff. 11–1–78; 1976 S 368; 1975 H 164; 1972 H 511)

2945.73 Discharge for delay in trial

(A) A charge of felony shall be dismissed if the accused is not accorded a preliminary hearing within the time required by sections 2945.71 and 2945.72 of the Revised Code.

(B) Upon motion made at or prior to the commencement of trial, a person charged with an offense shall be discharged if he is not brought to trial within the time required by sections 2945.71 and 2945.72 of the Revised Code.

(C) Regardless of whether a longer time limit may be provided by sections 2945.71 and 2945.72 of the Revised Code, a person charged with misdemeanor shall be discharged if he is held in jail in lieu of bond awaiting trial on the pending charge:

(1) For a total period equal to the maximum term of imprisonment which may be imposed for the most serious misdemeanor charged;

(2) For a total period equal to the term of imprisonment allowed in lieu of payment of the maximum fine which may be imposed for the most serious misdemeanor charged, when the offense or offenses charged constitute minor misdemeanors.

(D) When a charge of felony is dismissed pursuant to division (A) of this section, such dismissal has the same effect as a nolle prosequi. When an accused is discharged pursuant to division (B) or (C) of this section, such discharge is a bar to any further criminal proceedings against him based on the same conduct.

(1972 H 511, eff. 1–1–74)

DEGREE OF OFFENSE

2945.74 Defendant may be convicted of lesser offense

The jury may find the defendant not guilty of the offense charged, but guilty of an attempt to commit it if such attempt is an offense at law. When the indictment or information charges an offense, including different degrees, or if other offenses are included within the offense charged, the jury may find the defendant not guilty of the degree charged but guilty of an inferior degree thereof or lesser included offense.

If the offense charged is murder and the accused is convicted by confession in open court, the court shall examine the witnesses, determine the degree of the crime, and pronounce sentence accordingly.

(1953 H 1, eff. 10–1–53; GC 13448–2)

2945.75 Degree of offense; charge and verdict; prior convictions

(A) When the presence of one or more additional elements makes an offense one of more serious degree:

(1) The affidavit, complaint, indictment, or information either shall state the degree of the offense which the accused is alleged to have committed, or shall allege such additional element or elements. Otherwise, such affidavit, complaint, indictment, or information is effective to charge only the least degree of the offense.

(2) A guilty verdict shall state either the degree of the offense of which the offender is found guilty, or that such additional element or elements are present. Otherwise, a guilty verdict constitutes a finding of guilty of the least degree of the offense charged.

(B) Whenever in any case it is necessary to prove a prior conviction, a certified copy of the entry of judgment in such prior conviction together with evidence sufficient to identify the defendant named in the entry as the offender in the case at bar, is sufficient to prove such prior conviction.

(1972 H 511, eff. 1–1–74)

2945.76 Circumstances for acquittal for carrying concealed weapon—Repealed

(1972 H 511, eff. 1–1–74; 1969 H 288; 1953 H 1; GC 13448–4)

POST TRIAL PROCEDURE

2945.77 Polling jury

When the jurors agree upon their verdict, they must be conducted into court by the officer having them in charge.

Before the verdict is accepted, the jury may be polled at the request of either the prosecuting attorney or the defendant. If one of the jurors upon being polled declares that said verdict is not his verdict, the jury must further deliberate upon the case.

(1953 H 1, eff. 10–1–53; GC 13448–5)

2945.78 Recording the verdict

When the verdict given is such as the court may receive, it must be immediately entered in full upon the minutes.

(1953 H 1, eff. 10–1–53; GC 13448–6)

2945.79 Causes for new trial

A new trial, after a verdict of conviction, may be granted on the application of the defendant for any of the following causes affecting materially his substantial rights:

(A) Irregularity in the proceedings of the court, jury, prosecuting attorney, or the witnesses for the state, or for any order of the court, or abuse of discretion by which the defendant was prevented from having a fair trial;

(B) Misconduct of the jury, prosecuting attorney, or the witnesses for the state;

(C) Accident or surprise which ordinary prudence could not have guarded against;

(D) That the verdict is not sustained by sufficient evidence or is contrary to law; but if the evidence shows the defendant is not guilty of the degree of crime for which he was convicted, but guilty of a lesser degree thereof, or of a lesser crime included therein, the court may modify the verdict or finding accordingly, without granting or ordering a new trial, and pass sentence on such verdict or finding as modified, provided that this power extends to any court to which the cause may be taken on appeal;

(E) Error of law occurring at the trial;

(F) When new evidence is discovered material to the defendant, which he could not with reasonable diligence have discovered and produced at the trial. When a motion for a new trial is made upon the ground of newly discovered evidence, the defendant must produce at the hearing of said motion, in support thereof, the affidavits of the witnesses by whom such evidence is expected to be given, and if time is required by the defendant to procure such affidavits, the court may postpone the hearing of the motion for such length of time as under all the circumstances of the case is reasonable. The prosecuting attorney may produce affidavits or other evidence to impeach the affidavits of such witnesses.

(1953 H 1, eff. 10–1–53; GC 13449–1)

2945.80 Application for new trial

Application for a new trial shall be made by motion upon written grounds, and except for the cause of newly discovered evidence material for the person applying, which he could not with reasonable diligence have discovered and produced at the trial, shall be filed within three days after the verdict was rendered, or the decision of the court where a trial by jury has been waived, unless it is made to appear by clear and convincing proof that the defendant was unavoidably prevented from filing his motion for new trial in which case it shall be filed within three days from the order of the court finding that he was unavoidably prevented from filing such motion within the time provided herein.

Motions for new trial on account of newly discovered evidence shall be filed within one hundred twenty days following the day upon which the verdict was rendered, or the decision of the court where trial by jury has been waived. If it is made to appear by clear and convincing proof that the defendant was unavoidably prevented from the discovery of the evidence upon which he must rely, such motion shall be filed within three days from an order of the court finding that he was unavoidably prevented from discovering the evidence within the one hundred twenty day period.

(131 v S 389, eff. 11–1–65; 128 v 141; 1953 H 1; GC 13449–2)

2945.81   Causes to be sustained by affidavits

The causes enumerated in divisions (B) and (C) of section 2945.79 of the Revised Code must be sustained by affidavit showing their truth, and may be controverted by affidavits.

(1953 H 1, eff. 10–1–53; GC 13449–3)

2945.82   New trial

When a new trial is granted by the trial court, or when a new trial is awarded on appeal, the accused shall stand for trial upon the indictment or information as though there had been no previous trial thereof.

(1953 H 1, eff. 10–1–53; GC 13449–4)

2945.83   When new trial shall not be granted

No motion for a new trial shall be granted or verdict set aside, nor shall any judgment of conviction be reversed in any court because of:

(A) An inaccuracy or imperfection in the indictment, information, or warrant, provided that the charge is sufficient to fairly and reasonably inform the accused of the nature and cause of the accusation against him;

(B) A variance between the allegations and the proof thereof unless the accused is misled or prejudiced thereby;

(C) The admission or rejection of any evidence offered against or for the accused unless it affirmatively appears on the record that the accused was or may have been prejudiced thereby;

(D) A misdirection of the jury unless the accused was or may have been prejudiced thereby;

(E) Any other cause unless it appears affirmatively from the record that the accused was prejudiced thereby or was prevented from having a fair trial.

(1953 H 1, eff. 10–1–53; GC 13449–5)

2945.831   Motion not necessary for appellate review

A motion for a new trial is not a necessary prerequisite to obtain appellate review of the sufficiency or weight of the evidence in the trial of a criminal case.

(128 v 141, eff. 1–1–60)

2945.832   Taking and recording exceptions—Repealed

(1986 H 412, eff. 3–17–87; 128 v 141)

CHAPTER 2947

JUDGMENT; SENTENCE

MAGISTRATE DEFINED

MAGISTRATE DEFINED

2947.01   Definition of magistrate

The definition of "magistrate" set forth in section 2931.01 of the Revised Code applies to Chapter 2947. of the Revised Code.

(1953 H 1, eff. 10–1–53)

437

ARREST OF JUDGMENT

2947.02 Motion in arrest

A judgment may be arrested by the court upon motion of the defendant, or upon the court's own motion, for either of the following causes:

(A) The offense charged is not within the jurisdiction of the court;

(B) The facts stated in the indictment or information do not constitute an offense.

(1953 H 1, eff. 10–1–53; GC 13450–1)

2947.03 When judgment not arrested

A judgment shall not be arrested for a defect in form. Motions in arrest of judgment shall be made within three days after the verdict is rendered.

(1953 H 1, eff. 10–1–53; GC 13450–2)

2947.04 Effect of arrest of judgment

When a judgment is arrested, it places the defendant in a like position with respect to the prosecution as before the indictment or information was found. If, from the evidence at the trial, there is reason to believe that the defendant is guilty of an offense, the trial court shall order him to enter into a recognizance with sufficient surety for his appearance at the first day of the next term of such court, or the court having jurisdiction of the offense if within this state, otherwise the defendant shall be discharged.

(1953 H 1, eff. 10–1–53; GC 13450–3)

SENTENCING

2947.05 Defendant's and victim's rights before sentence

Before sentence is pronounced, the court shall inform the defendant of the verdict of the jury or of the finding of the court and shall ask the defendant whether he has anything to say as to why judgment should not be pronounced against him. The court shall give the prosecuting attorney an opportunity to give a statement with respect to the sentence in the case before sentence is pronounced and also shall permit the victim, or the victim's representative designated pursuant to section 2930.02 of the Revised Code, to give a statement with respect to the sentence in the case.

(1994 S 186, eff. 10–12–94; 1953 H 1, eff. 10–1–53; GC 13451–1)

2947.051 Victim impact statement for use in sentencing

(A) In all criminal cases in which a person is convicted of, pleads guilty to and the plea is accepted to, or pleads no contest to and is found guilty of a felony, the court, prior to sentencing the offender, shall order the preparation of a victim impact statement by the department of probation of the county in which the victim of the offense resides, by the court's own regular probation officer, or by a victim assistance program that is operated by the state, any county or municipal corporation, or any other governmental entity if the offender caused, attempted to cause, threatened to cause, or created the risk of physical harm to the victim of the offense. The court, in accordance with sections 2929.12 and 2929.14 of the Revised Code, shall consider the victim impact statement in determining the sentence to be imposed upon the offender.

(B) Each victim impact statement shall identify the victim of the offense, itemize any economic loss suffered by the victim as a result of the offense, identify any physical injury suffered by the victim as a result of the offense and the seriousness and permanence of the injury, identify any change in the victim's personal welfare or familial relationships as a result of the offense and any psychological impact experienced by the victim or the victim's family as a result of the offense, and contain any other information related to the impact of the offense upon the victim that the court requires. Each victim impact statement prepared under this section shall include any statement made by the victim pursuant to section 2930.13 of the Revised Code.

(C) A victim impact statement shall be kept confidential and is not a public record as defined in section 149.43 of the Revised Code. However, the court may furnish copies of the statement to both the defendant or his counsel and the prosecuting attorney. Any copies of a victim impact statement that are made available to the defendant or his counsel or to the prosecuting attorney shall be returned by the person to whom they were made available to the court immediately following the imposition of sentence upon the defendant.

(1994 S 186, eff. 10–12–94; 1982 H 269, § 4, eff. 7–1–83; 1982 S 199; 1980 S 384)

2947.052 Victim or family member to be notified of electronically monitored early release—Repealed

(1994 S 186, eff. 10–12–94; 1992 H 725, eff. 4–16–93)

2947.06 Testimony after verdict to mitigate penalty; reports confidential

The trial court may hear testimony in mitigation of a sentence at the term of conviction or plea, or at the next term. The prosecuting attorney may offer testimony on behalf of the state, to give the court a true understanding of the case. The court shall determine whether sentence ought immediately to be imposed or the defendant placed on probation. The court on its own motion may direct the department of probation of the county in which the defendant resides, or its own regular probation officer, to make any inquiries and presentence investigation reports that the court requires concerning the defendant. The presentence investigation reports shall be confidential and do not have to be furnished to the defendant or his counsel or to the prosecuting attorney unless the court in its discretion so orders.

The court may appoint not more than two psychologists or psychiatrists who shall make any reports concerning the defendant that the court requires for the purpose of determining the disposition of the case. Each psychologist or psychiatrist shall receive a fee to be fixed by the court and taxed in the costs of the case. The psychologist's or psychiatrist's reports shall be made in writing, in open court, and in the presence of the defendant, except in misdemeanor cases in which sentence may be pronounced in the absence of the defendant. A copy of each report of a psychologist or psychiatrist may be furnished to the defendant, if present, who may examine the persons making the same, under oath, as to any matter or thing contained in the report.

(1987 H 73, § 5, eff. 10–1–89; 1987 H 73, § 1; 1982 H 269, § 4, S 199; 130 v H 686; 1953 H 1; GC 13451–2)

2947.061 Probation after serving thirty days of sentence; hearing; exception; limitations

(A) Subject to sections 2951.02 to 2951.09 of the Revised Code, the trial court, upon motion of the defendant made not earlier than thirty days nor later than sixty days after the defendant, having been sentenced, is delivered into the custody of the keeper of the institution in which the defendant is to begin serving the defendant's sentence or upon the court's own motion during the same thirty-day period, may suspend the further execution of the defendant's sentence and place the defendant on probation upon the terms that, consistent with all required conditions of probation prescribed by division (C) of section 2951.02 of the Revised Code, the court determines, notwithstanding the expiration of the term of court during which the defendant was sentenced.

The court shall hear any motion filed under this division within sixty days after the filing date of the motion and shall enter its ruling on the motion within ten days after the hearing on the motion.

This division does not apply to a defendant who is sentenced for the commission of an aggravated felony of the first, second, or third degree.

(B) Subject to sections 2951.02 to 2951.09 of the Revised Code and notwithstanding the expiration of the term of court during which the defendant was sentenced, the trial court, upon the motion of the defendant, may suspend the further execution of the defendant's sentence and place the defendant on probation upon the terms that, consistent with all required conditions of probation prescribed by division (C) of section 2951.02 of the Revised Code, the court determines, if the defendant was sentenced for an aggravated felony of the first, second, or third degree, is not serving a term of actual incarceration, is confined in a state correctional institution, and files the motion at any time after serving six months in the custody of the department of rehabilitation and correction.

A defendant shall not file more than one motion pursuant to this division for each sentence imposed upon the defendant, and the court shall deny, without hearing, any motion not authorized by this division or prohibited by this division. The court shall hear any motion authorized by this division within sixty days after it is filed and shall enter its ruling on the motion within ten days after the hearing. In ruling on the motion, the court shall consider any statement made pursuant to section 2930.17 of the Revised Code by the victim of the offense for which sentence was imposed.

(C) The authority granted by this section shall be exercised by the judge who imposed the sentence for which the suspension is being considered, unless the judge is unable to act on the authority granted by this section and it appears that the judge's inability reasonably may be expected to continue beyond the time limit for exercising the authority granted by this section. In that case, a judge of the court in which the sentence was imposed or a judge assigned to that court may dispose of a motion filed under this section in accordance with an assignment of the presiding judge or as prescribed by the rules or practices concerning responsibility for disposition of criminal matters.

(1995 H 4, eff. 11–9–95; 1994 S 186, eff. 10–12–94; 1994 H 571, eff. 10–6–94; 1982 H 269, eff. 7–1–83; 1982 S 199; 1976 H 837; 1969 H 686; 131 v H 781)

2947.062 Attendance of prisoner at probation hearing; transportation

If a hearing is granted pursuant to section 2947.061 of the Revised Code, the prisoner shall attend the hearing if so ordered by the court. When a copy of the journal entry containing the order is presented to the warden or other head of a state correctional institution, he shall deliver the prisoner to the sheriff, who shall convey him to the county in which the hearing is to be held. The approval of the governor on the journal entry shall not be required.

(1994 H 571, eff. 10–6–94; 1983 H 291, eff. 7–1–83; 1970 H 1136)

2947.07 When court to pronounce judgment

If a convicted defendant does not show sufficient cause as to why judgment should not be pronounced, the court shall pronounce the judgment.

(1953 H 1, eff. 10–1–53; GC 13451–4)

2947.08 Time of execution in capital cases

In cases where the death sentence is imposed, at least one hundred twenty days shall intervene between the day of sentence and the day appointed for the execution thereof.

(131 v H 24, eff. 8–10–65; 1953 H 1; GC 13451–5)

2947.09 Sentence to hard labor—Repealed

(1972 H 511, eff. 1–1–74; 1970 S 460; 1953 H 1; GC 13451–6)

2947.10 Punishment by fine and imprisonment—Repealed

(1972 H 511, eff. 1–1–74; 1953 H 1; GC 13451–7)

2947.11 Conditional sentence for misdemeanor—Repealed

(1972 H 511, eff. 1–1–74; 1970 S 460; 1953 H 1; GC 13451–8)

2947.12 Time and manner of payment of fine—Repealed

(1972 H 511, eff. 1–1–74; 1953 H 1; GC 13451–8a)

2947.13 Remission or suspension of sentence—Repealed

(1972 H 511, eff. 1–1–74; 1971 H 139; 1953 H 1; GC 13451–8b)

2947.14   Satisfaction of fine and costs; determination of ability to pay must precede commitment; hearing on change of circumstances

(A) If a fine is imposed as a sentence or a part of a sentence, the court or magistrate that imposed the fine may order that the offender be committed to the jail or workhouse until the fine is paid or secured to be paid, or he is otherwise legally discharged, if the court or magistrate determines at a hearing that the offender is able, at that time, to pay the fine but refuses to do so. The hearing required by this section shall be conducted at the time of sentencing.

(B) At the hearing, the offender has the right to be represented by counsel and to testify and present evidence as to his ability to pay the fine. If a court or magistrate determines after considering the evidence presented by an offender, that the offender is able to pay a fine, the determination shall be supported by findings of fact set forth in a judgment entry that indicate the offender's income, assets, and debts, as presented by the offender, and his ability to pay.

(C) If the court or magistrate has found the offender able to pay a fine at a hearing conducted in compliance with divisions (A) and (B) of this section, and the offender fails to pay the fine, a warrant may be issued for the arrest of the offender. Any offender held in custody pursuant to such an arrest shall be entitled to a hearing on the first regularly scheduled court day following the date of arrest in order to inform the court or magistrate of any change of circumstances that has occurred since the time of sentencing and that affects his ability to pay the fine. The right to the hearing on any change of circumstances may be waived by the offender.

At the hearing to determine any change of circumstances, the offender has the right to testify and present evidence as to any portion of his income, assets, or debts that has changed in such a manner as to affect his ability to pay the fine. If a court or magistrate determines, after considering any evidence presented by the offender, that the offender remains able to pay the fine, that determination shall be supported by a judgment entry that includes findings of fact upon which such a determination is based.

(D) No person shall be ordered to be committed to a jail or workhouse or otherwise be held in custody in satisfaction of a fine imposed as the whole or a part of a sentence except as provided in this section. Any person imprisoned pursuant to this section shall receive credit upon the fine at the rate of thirty dollars per day or fraction of a day. If the unpaid fine is less than thirty dollars, the person shall be imprisoned one day.

(E) No commitment pursuant to this section shall exceed six months.
(1984 H 113, eff. 1–8–85; 1984 H 277; 1970 S 460; 1953 H 1; GC 13451–9)

MISCELLANEOUS PROVISIONS

2947.15   Jail limits and proceeds of convict labor; rehabilitation of prisoners

Persons committed to jail by a judge or magistrate for nonpayment of fine, or convicts sentenced to hard labor in the county jail, shall perform labor under the direction of the board of county commissioners within or outside the jail, within the county, and the board shall adopt orders and rules in relation to the performance of labor and the sheriff or other officer having the custody of the persons or convicts shall be governed by the orders and rules. The sheriff of the county shall collect the proceeds of the labor of the persons or convicts, pay it into the county treasury, take the county treasurer's duplicate receipts for the amount paid, and forthwith deposit one of them with the county auditor. The sheriff, with the approval of the board, may provide for the vocational training and rehabilitation of prisoners confined in the county jail.

This section does not apply to prisoners participating in a county jail industry program established under section 5147.30 of the Revised Code.
(1990 H 51, eff. 11–8–90; 1990 H 588; 1970 S 460; 125 v 385; 1953 H 1; GC 13451–10)

2947.151   Reduction of jail sentence

The sheriff in charge of a county jail may, upon a consideration of the quality and amount of work done in the kitchen, in the jail offices, on the jail premises, or elsewhere, allow reductions of inmates' sentences as follows:

(A) On sentences of ninety days or less, up to three days for each thirty days of sentence;

(B) On sentences longer than ninety days but not longer than six months, up to four days for each thirty days of sentence;

(C) On sentences longer than six months, up to five days for each thirty days of sentence.

The reduction of the inmate's sentence, shall become effective only upon the written concurrence of the presiding or sentencing judge or magistrate of the court where the sentence was imposed.

This section shall in no way restrict any other powers vested in the presiding or sentencing judge or magistrate of the court where the sentence was imposed.

(128 v 595, eff. 10–1–59)

2947.16   Recognizance

A person convicted of a misdemeanor may be required by the judge or magistrate to enter into a recognizance, with sufficient surety, in such sum as the judge or magistrate finds proper, to keep the peace and be of good behavior for such time, not exceeding two years, as the court directs.   The court may order such person to stand committed until such order is complied with or he is discharged by law, but the court may discharge such person at any time of [1] his own recognizance, or cancel such recognizance.

(1953 H 1, eff. 10–1–53; GC 13451–11)

[1] So in original; should this read "on"?

2947.17   Breach of a condition of a recognizance

In case of a breach of the condition of any recognizance given under section 2947.16 of the Revised Code, the same proceedings shall be had as are prescribed in relation to forfeiture of other recognizances.

(1980 H 736, eff. 10–16–80; 1969 H 228; 1953 H 1; GC 13451–12)

2947.18   Sentence to workhouse for jail offense

Where the board of county commissioners of a county, or legislative authority of a municipal corporation having no workhouse, has made provisions for receiving prisoners into the workhouse of a city in any other county or district in the state, a court or magistrate, where imprisonment in jail may lawfully be imposed in such case, may sentence persons convicted of a misdemeanor, including a violation of a municipal ordinance, to such workhouse.

(1970 S 460, eff. 9–3–70; 1953 H 1; GC 13451–13)

2947.19   Maintenance of prisoners; reimbursement by prisoner

(A) In any county that has no workhouse, but which contains a city that has a workhouse maintained by the city, the board of county commissioners may agree with the proper authorities of such city upon terms under which persons convicted of misdemeanors shall be maintained in the city workhouse at the expense of the county.   In the case of persons committed to the city workhouse for the violation of a law of this state, whether the commitment is from the court of common pleas, magistrate's court, or other court, the cost of maintaining those persons committed shall be paid out of the general fund of the county, on the allowance of the board of county commissioners, provided that all persons committed to the city workhouse for the violation of ordinances of the city shall be maintained in such workhouse at the sole cost of the city.

(B) The board of county commissioners or the legislative authority of the city may require a person who was convicted of an offense other than a minor misdemeanor and who is confined in the city workhouse as provided in division (A) of this section, to reimburse the county or the city, as the case may be, for its expenses incurred by reason of his confinement, including, but not limited to, the expenses relating to the provision of food, clothing, and shelter.   The amount of reimbursement shall be determined by a court at a hearing held pursuant to section 2929.15 of the Revised Code.

Upon the authorization of the board of county commissioners or of the legislative authority of the city, the prosecuting attorney of the county or the city director of law may institute an appropriate civil action in the name of the state if instituted by the county or in the name of the city, in the court of common pleas of the county in which the workhouse is located, to recover from the convict the reimbursement for the expenses of his confinement in the city workhouse, as determined by a court pursuant to section 2929.15 of the Revised Code. The action shall be brought within one year after the person is released from incarceration. The amount recovered shall be paid into the treasury of the county or city that incurred the expenses.

(1984 H 363, eff. 9–26–84; 1975 H 205; 1953 H 1; GC 13451–14)

2947.20 Commitment in lieu of fine; credit for time served; determination of ability to pay must precede commitment—Repealed

(1984 H 113, eff. 1–8–85; 1984 H 277; 1972 H 511; 1970 S 460; 1953 H 1; GC 13451–15)

2947.21 Commitment to workhouse

When a person is sentenced to a workhouse by the court of common pleas, the clerk of the court of common pleas shall make and deliver to the sheriff a certified copy of the judgment, which shall describe the crime charged and the sentence of the court. Such copy shall be delivered by the sheriff to the officer in charge of the workhouse and shall be his warrant for detaining such person in custody. In case of such conviction by any other court or magistrate, the court or magistrate shall make a certified transcript of the docket in the case, which, in like manner, shall be delivered to the marshal, constable, or sheriff to be delivered by him to the proper officer in charge of the workhouse and be such officer's warrant for detaining such person in custody.

When a person is sentenced to a jail or workhouse under division (C)(2) of section 2929.51 of the Revised Code, the court shall certify a transcript of the docket in the case, which shall be delivered by him to the proper officer in charge of the workhouse or jail and be such officer's warrant for detaining such person in custody during the prescribed period or periods.

(1980 H 736, eff. 10–16–80; 1969 H 228; 1953 H 1; GC 13451–16)

2947.22 Person may be confined in jail temporarily

A person sentenced to a workhouse may be confined in the jail of the county in which he was convicted, for such period as is necessary to procure the papers and make arrangements to transport him to the workhouse.

(1953 H 1, eff. 10–1–53; GC 13451–17)

2947.23 Judgment for costs and jury fees

In all criminal cases, including violations of ordinances, the judge or magistrate shall include in the sentence the costs of prosecution and render a judgment against the defendant for such costs. If a jury has been sworn at the trial of a case, the fees of the jurors shall be included in the costs, which shall be paid to the public treasury from which the jurors were paid.

(1953 H 1, eff. 10–1–53; GC 13451–18)

MENTALLY DEFICIENT AND PSYCHOPATHIC OFFENDERS

2947.24 Definitions—Repealed

(1978 H 565, eff. 11–1–78; 1977 H 1; 1972 H 494; 1969 H 688; 130 v H 430; 125 v 823; 1953 H 1; GC 13451–19)

2947.25 Psychiatric examination before sentence; hearing on report of examination—Repealed

(1978 H 565, eff. 11–1–78; 1977 H 1; 1976 H 244; 1972 H 494, H 511; 1969 H 688; 132 v S 316; 129 v 1448; 126 v 392; 125 v 823; 1953 H 1; GC 13451–20)

2947.26 Postponement of commitment; release—Repealed

(1978 H 565, eff. 11–1–78; 1969 H 688; 1953 H 1; GC 13451–21)

2947.27 Recovery or improvement of inmate—Repealed

(1978 H 565, eff. 11–1–78; 1977 H 1; 1975 H 1; 1972 H 494; 1970 S 272; 132 v S 316, H 1; 125 v 823; 1953 H 1; GC 13451–22)

2947.271 Right to periodic review of case—Repealed

(1978 H 565, eff. 11–1–78; 1975 H 1; 1972 H 511)

2947.28 Application for release—Repealed

(1978 H 565, eff. 11–1–78; 1972 H 494; 1969 H 688; 125 v 823; 1953 H 1; GC 13451–22a)

2947.29 Existing statutes not affected—Repealed

(1978 H 565, eff. 11–1–78; 1953 H 1; GC 13451–23)

2947.30 Possession of firearm while committing certain crimes, additional sentence—Repealed

(1972 H 511, eff. 1–1–74; 1972 H 143; 132 v H 996)

2947.31 Court may permit sentence to be served at other times; may suspend remainder—Repealed

(1972 H 511, eff. 1–1–74; 1969 H 228)

MAGISTRATE DEFINED

2949.01 Definition of magistrate

The definition of "magistrate" set forth in section 2931.01 of the Revised Code applies to Chapter 2949. of the Revised Code.

(1953 H 1, eff. 10–1–53)

SUSPENSION OF SENTENCE

2949.02 Suspension of execution of sentence or judgment pending appeal to court of appeals; bail; exceptions

(A)(1) If a person is convicted of any bailable offense, including, but not limited to, a violation of an ordinance of a municipal corporation, in a municipal or county court or in a court of common pleas and if the person gives to the trial judge or magistrate a written notice of his intention to file or apply for leave to file an appeal to the court of appeals, the trial judge or magistrate may suspend, subject to division (A)(2)(b) of section 2953.09 of the Revised Code, execution of the sentence or judgment imposed for any fixed time that will give the person time either to prepare and file, or to apply for leave to file, the appeal. In all bailable cases, except as provided in division (B) of this section, the trial judge or magistrate may release the person on bail in accordance with Criminal Rule 46, which bail shall at least be conditioned that the person will appeal without delay and abide by the judgment and sentence of the court.

(B) Notwithstanding any provision of Criminal Rule 46 to the contrary, a trial judge of a court of common pleas shall not release on bail pursuant to division (A) of this section a person who is convicted of a bailable offense if he is sentenced to imprisonment for life or if that offense is a violation of section 2903.01, 2903.02, 2903.03, 2903.04, 2903.11, 2905.01, 2905.02, 2905.11, 2907.02, 2907.12, 2909.02, 2911.01, 2911.02, or 2911.11 of the Revised Code.

(C) If a trial judge of a court of common pleas is prohibited by division (B) of this section from releasing on bail pursuant to division (A) of this section a person who is convicted of a bailable offense and not sentenced to imprisonment for life, the appropriate court of appeals or two judges of it, upon motion of such a person and for good cause shown, may release the person on bail in accordance with Appellate Rule 8 and Criminal Rule 46, which bail shall at least be conditioned as described in division (A) of this section.

(1986 H 412, eff. 3–17–87; 1982 H 269, § 4, S 199; 1953 H 1; GC 13453–1)

2949.03 Suspension of execution of sentence or judgment pending appeal to supreme court

If a judgment of conviction by a court of common pleas, municipal court, or county court is affirmed by a court of appeals and remanded to the trial court for execution of the sentence or judgment imposed, and the person so convicted gives notice of his intention to file a notice of appeal to the supreme court, the trial court, on the filing of a motion by such person within three days after the rendition by the court of appeals of the judgment of affirmation, may further suspend, subject to division (A)(2)(b) of section 2953.09 of the Revised Code, the execution of the sentence or judgment imposed for a time sufficient to give such person an opportunity to file a notice of appeal to the supreme court, but the sentence or judgment imposed shall not be suspended more than thirty days for that purpose.

(1986 H 412, eff. 3–17–87; 1953 H 1; GC 13453–2)

2949.04 Increase or decrease of bail

When bail is fixed pursuant to division (B) of section 2953.03 or section 2949.02 or 2953.09 of the Revised Code in connection with an appeal, a reduction or increase in the amount of that bail or other change in that bail shall not be required of the accused during the pendency of the appeal unless the trial judge or magistrate, or the court in which the appeal is being prosecuted, finds that there is good cause to reduce or increase the amount of that bail or good cause for any other change in that bail. If the court in which the appeal is being prosecuted finds there is good cause to reduce or increase the amount of that bail or good cause for any other change in that bail, it shall order the reduction, increase, or other change in accordance with Criminal Rule 46, and the new bail shall be in the amount and form so ordered and otherwise be to the approval of and filed with the clerk of the court in which the appeal is being prosecuted.

(1986 H 412, eff. 3–17–87; 129 v 423; 1953 H 1; GC 13453–3)

EXECUTION OF SENTENCE GENERALLY

2949.05 Execution of sentence or judgment

If no appeal is filed, if leave to file an appeal or certification of a case is denied, if the judgment of the trial court is affirmed on appeal, or if post-conviction relief under section 2953.21 of the Revised Code is denied, the trial court or magistrate shall carry into execution the sentence or judgment which had been pronounced against the defendant.

(1986 H 412, eff. 3–17–87; 1969 S 354; 129 v 423; 1953 H 1; GC 13453–4)

2949.06 Recapture after escape

If a person escapes after sentence and before confinement in a state correctional institution or jail, the clerk of the trial court, upon application of the prosecuting attorney or by order of the court, shall issue a warrant stating the conviction and sentence and commanding the sheriff to pursue the person into any county of this state. The sheriff shall take into custody the person so escaping and shall make return of the warrant to the court if it is in session, and if it is not in session he shall commit the accused to the jail of the county and bring him before the court at the next session of the court. The court shall set aside the former sentence and again pronounce judgment upon the verdict.

(1994 H 571, eff. 10–6–94; 1953 H 1, eff. 10–1–53; GC 13453–5)

2949.07 Computing time served

If a convict escapes from a state correctional institution, the time the convict is absent from the institution because of his escape shall not be credited as a part of the time for which he was sentenced.

(1994 H 571, eff. 10–6–94; 1953 H 1, eff. 10–1–53; GC 13453–6)

2949.08 Confinement of convicts; reduction of sentence for confinement prior to conviction

(A) When a person convicted of a misdemeanor is sentenced to imprisonment in jail or the workhouse, the judge or magistrate shall order him into the custody of the sheriff or constable, who shall deliver him with the record of his conviction, to the jailer or keeper, in whose custody he shall remain until the term of his imprisonment expires or he is otherwise legally discharged.

(B) The record of the person's conviction shall specify the total number of days, if any, that the person was confined for any reason arising out of the offense for which he was convicted and sentenced prior to delivery to the jailer or keeper under this section. The record shall be used to determine any reduction of sentence under division (C) of this section.

(C) The jailer, administrator, or keeper in charge of a jail or workhouse shall reduce the sentence of a person delivered into his custody pursuant to division (A) of this section by the total number of days the prisoner was confined for any reason arising out of the offense for which the prisoner was convicted and sentenced, including confinement in lieu of bail while awaiting trial, confinement for examination to determine his competence to stand trial or to determine sanity, and confinement while awaiting transportation to the place where he is to serve his sentence.

(D) For purposes of divisions (B) and (C) of this section, a person shall be considered to have been confined for a day if the person was confined for any period or periods of time totaling more than eight hours during that day.

(1979 S 23, eff. 3–27–80; 1953 H 1; GC 13454–1)

2949.09 Execution for fine

When a judge or magistrate renders judgment for a fine, an execution may issue for such judgment and costs of prosecution, to be levied on the property, or in default thereof, upon the body of the defendant for nonpayment of the fine. The officer holding such writ may arrest such defendant in any county and commit him to the jail of the county in which such writ issued, until such fine is paid or secured to be paid or he is otherwise legally discharged. (1970 S 460, eff. 9–3–70; 1953 H 1; GC 13454–2)

2949.091 Fees and costs

(A)(1) The court, in which any person is convicted of or pleads guilty to any offense other than a traffic offense that is not a moving violation, shall impose the sum of eleven dollars as costs in the case in addition to any other court costs that the court is required by law to impose upon the offender. All such moneys shall be transmitted on the first business day of each month by the clerk of the court to the treasurer of state and deposited by the treasurer of state into the general revenue fund. The court shall not waive the payment of the additional eleven dollars court costs, unless the court determines that the offender is indigent and waives the payment of all court costs imposed upon the indigent offender.

(2) The juvenile court, in which a child is found to be a delinquent child or a juvenile traffic offender for an act which, if committed by an adult, would be an offense other than a traffic offense that is not a moving violation, shall impose the sum of eleven dollars as costs in the case in addition to any other court costs that the court is required or permitted by law to impose upon the delinquent child or juvenile traffic offender. All such moneys shall be transmitted on the first business day of each month by the clerk of the court to the treasurer of state and deposited by the treasurer of state into the general revenue fund. The eleven dollars court costs shall be collected in all cases unless the court determines the juvenile is indigent and waives the payment of all court costs, or enters an order on its journal stating that it has determined that the juvenile is indigent, that no other court costs are to be taxed in the case, and that the payment of the eleven dollars court costs is waived.

(B) Whenever a person is charged with any offense other than a traffic offense that is not a moving violation and posts bail, the court shall add to the amount of the bail the eleven dollars required to be paid by division (A)(1) of this section. The eleven dollars shall be retained by the clerk of the court until the person is convicted, pleads guilty, forfeits bail, is found not guilty, or has the charges against him dismissed. If the person is convicted, pleads guilty, or forfeits bail, the clerk shall transmit the eleven dollars to the treasurer of state, who shall deposit it into the general revenue fund. If the person is found not guilty or the charges against him are dismissed, the clerk shall return the eleven dollars to the person.

(C) No person shall be placed or held in a detention facility for failing to pay the additional eleven dollars court costs or bail that are required to be paid by this section.

(D) As used in this section:

(1) "Moving violation" and "bail" have the same meanings as in section 2743.70 of the Revised Code.

(2) "Detention facility" has the same meaning as in section 2921.01 of the Revised Code. (1991 H 298, eff. 7–26–91; 1990 S 131; 1989 H 111; 1987 H 171; 1983 H 291)

2949.092 Waiver of additional court costs

If a person is convicted of or pleads guilty to an offense and the court specifically is required, pursuant to section 2743.70 or 2949.091 of the Revised Code or pursuant to any other section of the Revised Code, to impose a specified sum of money as costs in the case in addition to any other costs that the court is required or permitted by law to impose in the case, the court shall not waive the payment of the specified additional court costs that the section of the Revised Code specifically requires the court to impose unless the court determines that the offender is indigent and the court waives the payment of all court costs imposed upon the offender. (1990 S 131, eff. 7–25–90)

2949.10 Execution for fine to issue to other county

An execution under section 2949.09 of the Revised Code may issue to the sheriff of any county in which the defendant resides, is found, or has property, and the sheriff shall execute the writ. If the defendant is taken, the sheriff shall commit him to the jail of the county in which the writ issued and deliver a certified copy of the writ to the sheriff of such county, who shall detain the offender until he is discharged as provided in such section.

(1953 H 1, eff. 10–1–53; GC 13454–3)

2949.11   Fines paid into county treasury

Unless otherwise required in the Revised Code, an officer who collects a fine shall pay it into the treasury of the county in which such fine was assessed, within twenty days after the receipt of the fine, to the credit of the county general fund. The county treasurer shall issue duplicate receipts for the fine, and the officer making the collection shall deposit one of these receipts with the county auditor.

(1986 S 54, eff. 5–6–86; 125 v 903; 1953 H 1; GC 13454–4)

2949.111   Priority of assignment of payments to satisfaction of costs, restitution, fines, and probation fees

(A) As used in this section:

(1) "Costs" means any court costs that the court requires an offender to pay, any reimbursement for the costs of confinement that the court orders an offender to pay pursuant to section 2929.15 of the Revised Code, any fee for the costs of electronically monitored house arrest that an offender agrees to pay pursuant to section 2929.23 of the Revised Code, any reimbursement for the costs of an investigation or prosecution that the court orders an offender to pay pursuant to section 2929.28 of the Revised Code, or any other costs that the court orders an offender to pay.

(2) "Probation fees" means any fees that a court, pursuant to section 2951.021 of the Revised Code and as a condition of probation, requires an offender who is placed on probation to pay for probation services.

(B) Unless the court, in accordance with division (C) of this section, enters in the record of the case a different method of assigning a payment toward the satisfaction of costs, restitution, a fine, or probation fees, if a person who is charged with a criminal offense is convicted of or pleads guilty to the offense, if the court orders the offender to pay any combination of costs, restitution, a fine, or probation fees, and if the offender makes any payment to a clerk of court toward the satisfaction of the costs, restitution, fine, or probation fees, the clerk of the court shall assign the offender's payment so made toward the satisfaction of the costs, restitution, fine, or probation fees in the following manner:

(1) If the court ordered the offender to pay any costs, the offender's payment shall be assigned toward the satisfaction of the costs until the court costs have been entirely paid.

(2) If the court ordered the offender to pay any restitution and if all of the costs that the court ordered the offender to pay, if any, have been paid, the remainder of the offender's payment after any assignment required under division (B)(1) of this section shall be assigned toward the satisfaction of the restitution until the restitution has been entirely paid.

(3) If the court ordered the offender to pay any fine and if all of the costs and restitution that the court ordered the offender to pay, if any, have been paid, the remainder of the offender's payment after any assignments required under divisions (B)(1) and (2) of this section shall be assigned toward the satisfaction of the fine until the fine has been entirely paid.

(4) If the court ordered the offender to pay any probation fees and if all of the costs, restitution, and fine that the court ordered the offender to pay, if any, have been paid, the remainder of the offender's payment after any assignments required under divisions (B)(1), (2), and (3) of this section shall be assigned toward the satisfaction of the probation fees until the probation fees have been entirely paid.

(C) If a person who is charged with a criminal offense is convicted of or pleads guilty to the offense and if the court orders the offender to pay any combination of costs, restitution, a fine, or probation fees, the court, at the time it orders the offender to pay the combination of costs, restitution, a fine, or probation fees, may prescribe a method of assigning payments that the person makes toward the satisfaction of the costs, restitution, fine, or probation fees that differs from the method set forth in division (B) of this section. If the court prescribes a method of assigning payments under this division, the court shall enter in the record of the case the method so prescribed. Upon the entry in the record of the case of the method of assigning payments prescribed pursuant to this division, if the offender makes any payment to a clerk of court for the costs, restitution, fine, or probation fees, the clerk of the court shall assign the payment so made toward the satisfaction of the costs, restitution, fine, or probation fees in the manner prescribed by the court and entered in the record of the case instead of in the manner set forth in division (B) of this section.

(1994 H 406, eff. 11–11–94)

COSTS AND TRANSPORTATION OF CONVICTS

2949.12 Conveying convicted felon to reception facility

Unless the execution of sentence is suspended, a convicted felon who is sentenced to serve a term of imprisonment in a state correctional institution shall be conveyed, within five days after sentencing, excluding Saturdays, Sundays, and legal holidays, by the sheriff of the county in which the conviction was had to the facility that is designated by the department of rehabilitation and correction for the reception of convicted felons. The sheriff shall deliver the convicted felon into the custody of the managing officer of the reception facility, and, at that time, shall present the managing officer with a copy of the convicted felon's sentence that clearly describes each offense for which the felon was sentenced to a correctional institution, designates each section of the Revised Code that the felon violated and that resulted in his conviction and sentence to a correctional institution, designates the sentence imposed for each offense for which the felon was sentenced to a correctional institution, and pursuant to section 2967.191 of the Revised Code, specifies the total number of days, if any, that the felon was confined, for any reason, prior to conviction and sentence. The sheriff, at that time, also shall present the managing officer with a copy of the indictment. If the record in the convicted felon's case includes a notation entered pursuant to division (A) of section 2943.041 or division (A) of section 2945.07 of the Revised Code that indicates that a victim or a representative member of a victim's family was present at a proceeding of a type described in that division and that identifies the victim or the representative member by name, a copy of the notation also shall be attached to the copy of the sentence. The clerk of the court of common pleas shall furnish the copies of the sentence and indictment, and of the notation of appearance by the victim or a representative member of the victim's family. In the case of a person under the age of eighteen years who is certified to the court of common pleas by the juvenile court, a copy of the certification also shall be attached to the copy of the indictment.

The convicted felon shall be assigned to an institution or designated to be housed in a county, multicounty, municipal, municipal-county, or multicounty-municipal jail or workhouse, if authorized pursuant to section 5120.161 of the Revised Code, shall be conveyed to the institution, jail, or workhouse, and shall be kept within such institution, jail, or workhouse until the term of his imprisonment expires, he is pardoned or paroled, or he is transferred under laws permitting the transfer of prisoners. If the execution of his sentence is suspended, and the judgment thereafter affirmed, he shall be conveyed, in the same manner as if the execution of his sentence had not been suspended, to the reception facility as soon as practicable after the judge directs the execution of sentence. The trial judge or other judge of the court may, in his discretion and for good cause shown, extend the time of such conveyance.

(1994 H 571, eff. 10–6–94; 1988 H 708, eff. 4–19–88; 1987 H 261, H 455, S 6, § 3; 1984 S 172, § 1, 3; 1983 S 210; 1982 H 269, § 4, S 199; 1976 H 685; 1973 S 254; 1953 H 1; GC 13455–1)

2949.13 Sheriff may require assistance

During the time the sheriff is conveying a convicted felon to an institution for imprisonment therein, he may secure him in a jail and demand the assistance of a sheriff, jailer, or other person in keeping such prisoner, as if he were in his own county. Such sheriff, jailer, or other person is liable, on refusal, to like penalties as if the sheriff making the demand were in his own county.

(1953 H 1, eff. 10–1–53; GC 13455–2)

2949.14   Cost bill in case of felony

Upon conviction of a nonindigent person for a felony, the clerk of the court of common pleas shall make and certify under his hand and seal of the court, a complete itemized bill of the costs made in such prosecution, including the sum paid by the board of county commissioners, certified by the county auditor, for the arrest and return of the person on the requisition of the governor, or on the request of the governor to the president of the United States, or on the return of the fugitive by a designated agent pursuant to a waiver of extradition except in cases of parole violation.   Such bill of costs shall be presented by such clerk to the prosecuting attorney, who shall examine each item therein charged and certify to it if correct and legal. Upon certification by the prosecuting attorney, the clerk shall attempt to collect the costs from the person convicted.

(1983 H 291, eff. 7–1–83; 132 v S 447; 1953 H 1; GC 13455–3)

2949.15   Writs of execution to issue

If a nonindigent person convicted of a felony fails to pay the costs of prosecution pursuant to section 2949.14 of the Revised Code, the clerk of the court of common pleas shall forthwith issue to the sheriff of the county in which the indictment was found, and to the sheriff of any other county in which the person has property, executions against his property for fines and the costs of prosecution, which shall be served and returned within ten days, with the proceedings of such sheriff or the certification that there is no property upon which to levy, indorsed thereon.

When a levy is made upon property under such execution, a writ shall forthwith be issued by the clerk for the sale thereof, and such sheriff shall sell the property and make return thereof, and after paying the costs of conviction, execution, and sale, pay the balance to the person authorized to receive it.

(1983 H 291, eff. 7–1–83; 1953 H 1; GC 13455–4)

2949.16   Costs on execution for felony—Repealed

(1983 H 291, eff. 7–1–83; 1953 H 1; GC 13455–5)

2949.17   Transportation of prisoners; expenses

The sheriff may take one guard for every two convicted felons to be transported to a correctional institution.   The trial judge may authorize a larger number of guards upon written application of the sheriff, in which case a transcript of the order of the judge shall be certified by the clerk of the court of common pleas under the seal of the court, and the sheriff shall deliver the order with the convict to the person in charge of the correctional institution.   In order to obtain reimbursement for the county for the expenses of transportation for indigent convicted felons, the clerk of the court of common pleas shall prepare a transportation cost bill for each indigent convicted felon transported pursuant to this section for an amount equal to ten cents a mile from the county seat to the state correctional institution and return for the sheriff and each of the guards and five cents a mile from the county seat to the state correctional institution for each prisoner.   The number of miles shall be computed by the usual route of travel.

(1994 H 571, eff. 10–6–94; 1983 H 291, eff. 7–1–83; 1981 H 694; 1979 H 204; 128 v 542; 1953 H 1; GC 13455–6)

2949.18   Certification and payment of cost bill—Repealed

(1983 H 291, eff. 7–1–83; 1981 H 694; 1979 H 204; 1953 H 1; GC 13455–7)

2949.19   Subsidy by state for certain costs

The clerk of the court of common pleas shall report to the state public defender all cases in which an indigent person was convicted of a felony, all cases in which reimbursement is required by section 2949.20 of the Revised Code, and all cost bills for transportation that are prepared pursuant to section 2949.17 of the Revised Code.   The reports shall be filed for each fiscal quarter within thirty days after the end of the quarter on a form prescribed by the state public defender and shall be accompanied by a certification of a judge of the court that in all cases listed in the report the defendant was determined to be indigent and convicted of a felony or that the case is reported pursuant to section 2949.20 of the Revised Code and that for each transportation cost bill submitted pursuant to section 2949.17 of the Revised Code that the convicted felon was determined to be indigent. The state public defender shall review the reports and prepare a transportation cost voucher and a quarterly subsidy voucher for each county for the amounts he finds to be correct. To compute the quarterly subsidy, the state public defender first shall subtract the total of all transportation cost vouchers that he approves for payment for the quarter from one-fourth of his total appropriation for criminal costs subsidy for the fiscal year of which the quarter is part. He then shall compute a base subsidy amount per case by dividing the remainder by the total number of cases from all counties he approves for subsidy for the quarter. The quarterly subsidy voucher for each county shall then be the product of the base subsidy amount times the number of cases submitted by the county and approved for subsidy for the quarter. Payment shall be made to the clerk.

The clerk shall keep a record of all cases submitted for the subsidy in which the defendant was bound over to the court of common pleas from the municipal court. Upon receipt of the quarterly subsidy, the clerk shall pay to the clerk of the municipal court, for municipal court costs in such cases, an amount that does not exceed fifteen dollars per case, shall pay foreign sheriffs for their services, and shall deposit the remainder of the subsidy to the credit of the general fund of the county. The clerk of the court of common pleas then shall stamp his records "subsidy costs satisfied."

(1987 H 171, eff. 7–1–87; 1985 H 201; 1984 H 462; 1983 H 291; 1981 H 694; 1979 H 204; 130 v S 342; 1953 H 1; GC 13455–8)

2949.20 Reimbursement in case of reversal

In any case of final judgment of reversal as provided in section 2953.07 of the Revised Code, whenever the state of Ohio is the appellee, the clerk of the court of common pleas of the county in which sentence was imposed shall certify the case to the state public defender for reimbursement in the report required by section 2949.19 of the Revised Code.

(1983 H 291, eff. 7–1–83; 1981 H 694; 1979 H 204; 1953 H 1; GC 13455–9)

2949.201 State public defender to estimate reimbursements

On or before the first day of February of even-numbered years, the state public defender shall report to the speaker and minority leader of the house of representatives, the president and minority leader of the senate, the office of budget and management, and the legislative budget office of the legislative service commission an estimate of the amount of money that will be required for the next fiscal biennium to make the payments required by section 2949.19 of the Revised Code.

(1983 H 291, eff. 7–1–83; 1981 H 694)

2949.21 Conveyance to correctional institution

A writ for the execution of the death penalty shall be directed to the sheriff by the court issuing it, and the sheriff, within thirty days and in a private manner, shall convey the prisoner to the facility designated by the director of rehabilitation and correction for the reception of the prisoner. For conducting the prisoner to the facility, the sheriff shall receive like fees and mileage as in other cases, when approved by the warden of the facility. After the procedures performed at the reception facility are completed, the prisoner shall be assigned to an appropriate correctional institution, conveyed to the institution, and kept within the institution until the execution of his sentence.

(1994 H 571, eff. 10–6–94; 1992 S 359, eff. 12–22–92; 1953 H 1; GC 13456–1)

DEATH SENTENCE

2949.22 Execution of death sentence

(A) Except as provided in division (B)(1) of this section, a death sentence shall be executed by causing a current of electricity, of sufficient intensity to cause death, to pass through the body of the person upon whom the sentence was imposed. The application of the current shall be continued until the person upon whom the sentence was imposed is dead. The warden of the correctional institution in which the sentence is to be executed or another person selected by the director of rehabilitation and correction shall ensure that the death sentence is executed.

(B)(1) Any person sentenced to death may elect to be executed by lethal injection instead of by electrocution as described in division (A) of this section. The election shall be made no later than one week prior to the scheduled date of execution of the person by filing a written notice of the election with the department of rehabilitation and correction. If a person sentenced to death timely files with the department a written notice of an election to be executed by lethal injection, the person's death sentence shall be executed by causing the application to the person of a lethal injection of a drug or combination of drugs of sufficient dosage to quickly and painlessly cause death instead of by electrocution as described in division (A) of this section. The application of the drug or combination of drugs shall be continued until the person is dead. The warden of the correctional institution in which the sentence is to be executed or another person selected by the director of rehabilitation and correction shall ensure that the death sentence is executed.

If a person sentenced to death does not timely file with the department a written notice of election to be executed by lethal injection, his death sentence shall be executed by electrocution in accordance with division (A) of this section.

(2) Neither a person's timely filing of a written notice of election under division (B)(1) of this section nor a person's failure to file or timely file a written notice of election under that division shall affect or waive any right of appeal or postconviction relief that may be available under the laws of this state or the United States relative to the conviction for which the sentence of death was imposed upon the person or relative to the imposition or execution of that sentence of death.

(C) A death sentence shall be executed within the walls of the state correctional institution designated by the director of rehabilitation and correction as the location for executions, within an enclosure to be prepared for that purpose, under the direction of the warden of the institution or, in his absence, a deputy warden, and on the day designated by the judge passing sentence or otherwise designated by a court in the course of any appellate or postconviction proceedings. The enclosure shall exclude public view.

(D) If a death sentence is required to be executed by lethal injection because the person sentenced to death elected to be executed by lethal injection pursuant to division (B)(1) of this section and if the execution of a death sentence by lethal injection is determined to be unconstitutional, the death sentence shall be executed by causing a current of electricity, of sufficient intensity to cause death, to pass through the body of the person upon whom the sentence was imposed. The application of the current shall be continued until the person is dead. The warden of the state correctional institution in which the sentence is to be executed or another person selected by the director of rehabilitation and correction shall ensure that the death sentence is executed.

(E) No change in the law made by this amendment constitutes a declaration by or belief of the general assembly that execution of a death sentence by electrocution is a cruel and unusual punishment proscribed by the Ohio Constitution or the United States Constitution.

(1994 H 571, eff. 10–6–94; 1993 H 11, eff. 10–1–93; 1992 S 359; 1953 H 1; GC 13456–2)

2949.23   Time of execution—Repealed

(1992 S 359, eff. 12–22–92; 1953 H 1; GC 13456–3)

2949.24   Execution and return of warrant

Unless a suspension of execution is ordered by the court of appeals in which the cause is pending on appeal or the supreme court for a case in which a sentence of death is imposed for an offense committed before January 1, 1995, or by the supreme court for a case in which a sentence of death is imposed for an offense committed on or after January 1, 1995, or is ordered by two judges or four justices of that court, the warden or another person selected by the director of rehabilitation and correction shall proceed at the time and place named in the warrant to ensure that the death sentence of the prisoner under death sentence is executed in accordance with section 2949.22 of the Revised Code. The warden shall make the return to the clerk of the court of common pleas of the county immediately from which the prisoner was sentenced of the manner of the execution of the warrant. The clerk shall record the warrant and the return in the records of the case.

(1995 S 4, eff. 9–21–95; 1992 S 359, eff. 12–22–92; 1953 H 1; GC 13456–4)

2949.25 Attendance at execution

(A) At the execution of a death sentence, only the following persons may be present:

(1) The warden of the state correctional institution in which the sentence is executed or a deputy warden, any other person selected by the director of rehabilitation and correction to ensure that the death sentence is executed, any persons necessary to execute the death sentence by electrocution or lethal injection, and the number of correction officers that the warden thinks necessary;

(2) The sheriff of the county in which the prisoner was tried and convicted;

(3) The director of rehabilitation and correction, or his agent;

(4) Physicians of the state correctional institution in which the sentence is executed;

(5) The clergyman in attendance upon the prisoner, and not more than three other persons, to be designated by the prisoner, who are not confined in any state institution;

(6) Not more than three persons to be designated by the immediate family of the victim;

(7) Representatives of the news media as authorized by the director of rehabilitation and correction.

(B) The director shall authorize at least one representative of a newspaper, at least one representative of a television station, and at least one representative of a radio station to be present at the execution of the sentence under division (A)(7) of this section.

(1994 H 571, eff. 10–6–94; 1993 H 11, eff. 10–1–93; 1992 S 359; 1972 H 494; 125 v 823; 1953 H 1; GC 13456–5)

2949.26 Disposition of body of executed convict

The body of an executed convict shall be returned for burial in any county of the state, to friends who made written request therefor, if made to the warden the day before or on the morning of the execution. The warden may pay the transportation and other funeral expenses, not to exceed fifty dollars.

If no request is made by such friends therefor, such body shall be disposed of as provided by section 1713.34 of the Revised Code and the rules of the department of human services.

(1985 H 201, eff. 7–1–85; 1953 H 1; GC 13456–6)

2949.27 Escape, rearrest, and execution

If a convicted felon escapes after sentence of death, and is not retaken before the time fixed for his execution, any sheriff may rearrest and commit him to the county jail, and make return thereof to the court in which the sentence was passed. Such court shall again fix the time for execution, which shall be carried into effect as provided in sections 2949.21 to 2949.26, inclusive, of the Revised Code.

(1953 H 1, eff. 10–1–53; GC 13456–7)

2949.28 Inquiry on sanity of convict

If a convict sentenced to death appears to be insane, the warden or the sheriff having custody of such convict shall give notice thereof to a judge of the court of common pleas of the county in which the prisoner is confined. Said judge shall inquire into such insanity at a time and place to be fixed by said judge, or impanel a jury for that purpose and shall give immediate notice thereof to the prosecuting attorney of the county in which the prisoner was convicted. Execution of the sentence shall be suspended pending completion of the inquiry.

(1969 S 354, eff. 11–18–69; 1953 H 1; GC 13456–8)

2949.29 Proceedings on the insanity inquiry

In addition to the warden or sheriff, the judge of the court of common pleas, clerk of the court of common pleas, and prosecuting attorney shall attend the inquiry commenced as provided in section 2949.28 of the Revised Code. Witnesses may be produced and examined before the judge or jury, and all findings shall be in writing signed by the judge or jury. If it is found that the convict is not insane, the sentence shall be executed at the time previously appointed, unless such time has passed pending completion of the inquiry, in which case the judge conducting the inquiry shall appoint a time for execution. If it is found that the convict is insane, the judge shall suspend the execution until the warden or sheriff receives a warrant from the governor directing such execution as provided in section 2949.30 of the Revised Code. The finding, and the order of such judge, certified by him, shall be entered on the journal of the court by the clerk.

(1969 S 354, eff. 11–18–69; 1953 H 1; GC 13456–9)

2949.30 When convict restored, governor to order execution

If a convict under sentence of death is found insane under section 2949.29 of the Revised Code, and if he is subsequently restored, the warden or sheriff having custody of such convict shall forthwith transmit a copy of the finding of restoration to the governor, who, when convinced that the convict is of sound mind, shall issue a warrant appointing a time for his execution.

(130 v H 428, eff. 9–27–63; 1953 H 1; GC 13456–10)

2949.31 Pregnant prisoners

If a female convict sentenced to death appears to be pregnant, the warden or sheriff having custody of such convict shall give notice thereof to a judge of the court of common pleas of the county in which the prisoner is confined, and like proceedings shall be had as are provided under sections 2949.28 and 2949.29 of the Revised Code in case of an insane convict sentenced to death.

(1953 H 1, eff. 10–1–53; GC 13456–11)

2949.32 When execution to be ordered

If a jury, impaneled as provided in section 2949.28 of the Revised Code in the case of a convict who appears to be insane, finds that a female convict under sentence of death is not with child, the sentence shall be executed at the time previously appointed, unless such time has passed pending completion of the inquiry, in which case the judge conducting the inquiry shall appoint a time for execution. If the jury finds that such female convict is with child, the judge conducting the inquiry shall suspend the execution of her sentence and transmit such finding to the governor, who, when satisfied that such convict is no longer pregnant, shall issue a warrant appointing a time for her execution.

(1969 S 354, eff. 11–18–69; 1953 H 1; GC 13456–12)

2949.33 When cumulative sentence may be imposed—Repealed

(1973 H 716, eff. 1–1–74; 1972 H 511; 1953 H 1; GC 13457–1)

2949.34 Sentence of habitual offender—Repealed

(1973 H 716, eff. 1–1–74; 1972 H 511; 1970 S 460; 1953 H 1; GC 13457–2)

2949.35 Exceptions—Repealed

(1973 H 716, eff. 1–1–74; 1972 H 511; 1953 H 1; GC 13457–3)

2949.36 Parole from workhouse—Repealed

(1973 H 716, eff. 1–1–74; 1972 H 511; 1953 H 1; GC 13457–4)

2950.01   Definitions

As used in sections 2950.01 to 2950.08 of the Revised Code:

(A) "Habitual sex offender" includes any person who is convicted two or more times, in separate criminal actions, for commission of any of the sex offenses set forth in division (B) of this section.   Convictions which result from or are connected with the same act, or result from offenses committed at the same time, shall be counted for the purpose of this section as one conviction.   Any conviction set aside pursuant to law, is not a conviction for purposes of this section.

(B) As used in this section, "sex offense" means:

(1) A violation of section 2907.02, 2907.03, 2907.05, 2907.08, or 2907.09, of the Revised Code, a felony violation under section 2907.04 of the Revised Code, a violation of division (A)(4) of section 2907.06 of the Revised Code, and a violation of division (A) or (B) of section 2907.07 of the Revised Code;

(2) A violation of any former law of this state, substantially equivalent to any offense listed in division (B)(1) of this section;

(3) An offense under an existing or former municipal ordinance or law of another state or the federal government, substantially equivalent to any offense listed in division (B)(1) of this section;

(4) Violation of any prohibition against conspiracy or attempt to commit, or complicity in committing, any offense listed in division (B)(1), (2), or (3) of this section.

(1972 H 511, eff. 1–1–74; 130 v S 160)

2950.02   Registration with chief of police or sheriff

Any habitual sex offender shall, within thirty days of his coming into any county in which he resides or is temporarily domiciled for more than thirty days, register with the chief of police of the city in which he resides or the sheriff of the county if he resides in an area other than a city.

(130 v S 160, eff. 10–4–63)

2950.03   Discharge of habitual sex offender from correctional institution; duties of official in charge

Any habitual sex offender who is discharged or paroled from the jail, workhouse, state correctional institution, or other institution in which he was confined because of the commission or attempt to commit one of the offenses defined in division (B) of section 2950.01 of the Revised Code, prior to discharge, parole, or release, shall be informed of his duty to register under sections 2950.01 to 2950.08 of the Revised Code by the official in charge of the place of confinement or hospital, and the official shall require the person to read and sign a form, as may be required by the bureau of criminal identification and investigation, stating that the duty of the person to register under sections 2950.01 to 2950.08 of the Revised Code has been explained to him. The official in charge of the place of confinement or hospital shall obtain the address where the person expects to reside upon his discharge, parole, or release and shall report the address to the bureau. The official in charge of the place of confinement or hospital shall give one copy of the form to the person and shall send two copies to the bureau, and the bureau shall forward one copy to the appropriate law enforcement agency having local jurisdiction where the person expects to reside upon his discharge, parole, or release.

(1994 H 571, eff. 10–6–94; 130 v S 160, eff. 10–4–63)

2950.04 Release of habitual sex offender; duties of court

Any habitual sex offender as defined by section 2950.01 of the Revised Code who is released on probation, or discharged upon payment of a fine, or given a suspended sentence, shall prior to such release, discharge, or suspension be informed of his duty to register under sections 2950.01 to 2950.08, inclusive, of the Revised Code, by the court in which he has been convicted, and the court shall require the person to read and sign such form as may be required by the bureau of criminal identification and investigation, stating that the duty of the person to register under sections 2950.01 to 2950.08, inclusive, of the Revised Code, has been explained to him. The court shall obtain the address where the person expects to reside upon his release or discharge, and shall report within three days such address to the bureau. The court shall give one copy of the form to the person, and shall send two copies to the bureau, which bureau shall forward one copy to the appropriate law enforcement agency having local jurisdiction where the person expects to reside upon his discharge, parole, or release.

(130 v S 160, eff. 10–4–63)

2950.05 Change of address; duty to inform

If any person required to register under sections 2950.01 to 2950.08, inclusive, of the Revised Code, changes his residence address, he shall inform the law enforcement agency with whom he last registered of his new address, in writing, within ten days. The law enforcement agency shall, within three days after receipt of such information, forward it to the bureau of criminal identification and investigation. The bureau shall forward appropriate registration data to the law enforcement agency having local jurisdiction of the new place of residence.

(130 v S 160, eff. 10–4–63)

2950.06 Registration period; termination

Any person required to register under sections 2950.01 to 2950.08, inclusive, of the Revised Code, shall be required to register for a period of ten years after conviction if not imprisoned, and if imprisoned, for a period of ten years after release from prison by discharge or parole. Liability for registration terminates at the expiration of ten years from date of initial registration, providing such convicted habitual sex offender does not, during said period, become again liable to registration under sections. 2950.01 to 2950.08, inclusive, of the Revised Code.

(130 v S 160, eff. 10–4–63)

2950.07 Registration requirements

Registration as required by sections 2950.01 to 2950.08, inclusive, of the Revised Code, shall consist of a statement in writing signed by such person giving such information as may be required by the bureau of criminal identification and investigation and the fingerprints and photograph of such person. Within three days thereafter the registering law enforcement agency shall forward such statement, fingerprints, and photograph to the bureau.

(130 v S 160, eff. 10–4–63)

2950.08 Public inspection of registration data prohibited

The statements, photographs, and fingerprints required by section 2950.07 of the Revised Code, shall not be open to inspection by the public or by any person other than the following:

(A) A regularly employed peace or other law enforcement officer;

(B) An authorized employee of the bureau of criminal identification and investigation for the purpose of providing information to a board or person pursuant to division (F) of section 109.57 of the Revised Code.

(1989 S 140, eff. 10–2–89; 130 v S 160)

2950.99   Penalties

Whoever violates sections 2950.01 to 2950.08 of the Revised Code, is guilty of a misdemeanor of the first degree, on a first offense; on each subsequent offense such person is guilty of a felony of the fourth degree.

(1972 H 511, eff. 1–1–74; 130 v S 160)

CHAPTER 2951

PROBATION

2951.01   Definition of magistrate

The definition of "magistrate" set forth in section 2931.01 of the Revised Code applies to Chapter 2951. of the Revised Code.

(1953 H 1, eff. 10–1–53)

2951.02   Criteria for probation; conditions of probation; community service work; suspension of sentence; effect of use of firearm; ignition interlock devices

(A) In determining whether to suspend sentence of imprisonment and place an offender on probation or whether to otherwise suspend an offender's sentence of imprisonment pursuant to division (D)(2) or (4) of section 2929.51 of the Revised Code, the court shall consider the risk that the offender will commit another offense and the need for protecting the public from the risk, the nature and circumstances of the offense, and the history, character, and condition of the offender.

(B) The following do not control the court's discretion but shall be considered in favor of placing an offender on probation or in favor of otherwise suspending an offender's sentence of imprisonment pursuant to division (D)(2) or (4) of section 2929.51 of the Revised Code:

(1) The offense neither caused nor threatened serious harm to persons or property, or the offender did not contemplate that it would do so.

(2) The offense was the result of circumstances unlikely to recur.

(3) The victim of the offense induced or facilitated it.

(4) There are substantial grounds tending to excuse or justify the offense, though failing to establish a defense.

(5) The offender acted under strong provocation.

(6) The offender has no history of prior delinquency or criminal activity, or has led a law-abiding life for a substantial period before commission of the present offense.

(7) The offender is likely to respond affirmatively to probationary or other court-imposed treatment.

(8) The character and attitudes of the offender indicate that the offender is unlikely to commit another offense.

(9) The offender has made or will make restitution or reparation to the victim of the offense for the injury, damage, or loss sustained.

(10) Imprisonment of the offender will entail undue hardship to the offender or the offender's dependents.

(C) When an offender is placed on probation or when an the [1] offender's sentence otherwise is suspended pursuant to division (D)(2) or (4) of section 2929.51 of the Revised Code, the probation or other suspension shall be at least on condition that, during the period of probation or other suspension, the offender shall abide by the law, including, but not limited to, complying with the provisions of Chapter 2923. of the Revised Code relating to the possession, sale, furnishing, transfer, disposition, purchase, acquisition, carrying, conveying, or use of, or other conduct involving, a firearm or dangerous ordnance, as defined in section 2923.11 of the Revised Code, and shall not leave the state without the permission of the court or the offender's probation officer. In the interests of doing justice, rehabilitating the offender, and ensuring the offender's good behavior, the court may impose additional requirements on the offender, including, but not limited to, requiring the offender to make restitution for all or part of the property damage that is caused by the offender's offense and for all or part of the value of the property that is the subject of any theft offense, as defined in division (K) of section 2913.01 of the Revised Code, that the offender committed. Compliance with the additional requirements also shall be a condition of the offender's probation or other suspension.

During the period of an offender's probation or other suspension, authorized probation officers who are engaged within the scope of their supervisory duties or responsibilities may search, with or without a warrant, the person of the offender, the place of residence of the offender, and a motor vehicle, another item of tangible or intangible personal property, or other real property in which the offender has a right, title, or interest or for which the offender has the express or implied permission of a person with a right, title, or interest to use, occupy, or possess if the probation officers have reasonable grounds to believe that the offender is not abiding by the law or otherwise is not complying with the conditions of the offender's probation or other suspension. The court that places the offender on probation or that suspends the offender's sentence of imprisonment pursuant to division (D)(2) or (4) of section 2929.51 of the Revised Code shall provide the offender with a written notice that informs the offender that authorized probation officers who are engaged within the scope of their supervisory duties or responsibilities may conduct those types of searches during the period of probation or other suspension if they have reasonable grounds to believe that the offender is not abiding by the law or otherwise is not complying with the conditions of the offender's probation or other suspension.

(D) The following do not control the court's discretion but shall be considered against placing an offender on probation and against otherwise suspending an offender's sentence of imprisonment pursuant to division (D)(2) or (4) of section 2929.51 of the Revised Code:

(1) The offender recently has violated the conditions of any probation, parole, or pardon, or any suspension pursuant to division (D)(2) or (4) of section 2929.51 of the Revised Code, previously granted the offender.

(2) There is a substantial risk that, while at liberty during the period of probation or other suspension, the offender will commit another offense.

(3) The offender is in need of correctional or rehabilitative treatment that can be provided best by the offender's commitment to a state correctional institution.

(4) Regardless of whether the offender knew the age of the victim, the victim of the offense was sixty-five years of age or older or permanently and totally disabled at the time of the commission of the offense.

(E) The criteria listed in divisions (B) and (D) of this section shall not be construed to limit the matters that may be considered in determining whether to suspend sentence of imprisonment and place an offender on probation or whether to otherwise suspend an offender's sentence of imprisonment pursuant to division (D)(2) or (4) of section 2929.51 of the Revised Code.

(F) An offender shall not be placed on probation and shall not otherwise have the offender's a [2] sentence of imprisonment suspended pursuant to division (D)(2) or (4) of section 2929.51 of the Revised Code when any of the following applies:

(1) The offense involved is aggravated murder or murder.

(2) The offender is a repeat offender or a dangerous offender, as defined in section 2929.01 of the Revised Code.

(3) The offense involved was not a violation of section 2923.12 of the Revised Code and was committed while the offender was armed with a firearm or dangerous ordnance, as defined in section 2923.11 of the Revised Code.

(4) The offense involved is a violation of section 2907.02 or 2907.12 of the Revised Code.

(5) The offender is not eligible for probation or shock probation pursuant to division (C) of section 2903.06 or 2903.07 of the Revised Code or is sentenced to a term of actual incarceration.

(6) The offense involved was a violation of section 2923.12 of the Revised Code, the weapon involved in the offense was a firearm or dangerous ordnance, as defined in section 2923.11 of the Revised Code, and the offense involved was committed aboard an aircraft or with purpose to carry a concealed firearm or dangerous ordnance, as defined in section 2923.11 of the Revised Code, aboard an aircraft.

(G) An offender who is convicted of or pleads guilty to a violation of section 2923.12 of the Revised Code in which the weapon involved was a firearm or dangerous ordnance, as defined in section 2923.11 of the Revised Code, and who previously has been convicted of or pleaded guilty to a violation of section 2923.12 of the Revised Code in which the weapon involved was a firearm or dangerous ordnance, as defined in section 2923.11 of the Revised Code, shall not be placed on probation and shall not otherwise have the offender's a [3] sentence of imprisonment suspended pursuant to division (D)(2) or (4) of section 2929.51 of the Revised Code, except that the offender may be placed on probation pursuant to section 2947.061 of the Revised Code.

(H)(1) When an offender is convicted of a misdemeanor, the court may require the offender, as a condition of probation or as a condition of otherwise suspending the offender's sentence pursuant to division (D)(2) or (4) of section 2929.51 of the Revised Code, in addition to the conditions of probation or other suspension imposed pursuant to division (C) of this section, to perform supervised community service work under the authority of health districts, park districts, counties, municipal corporations, townships, other political subdivisions of the state, or agencies of the state or any of its political subdivisions, or under the authority of charitable organizations that render services to the community or its citizens, in accordance with this division. Supervised community service work shall not be required as a condition of probation or other suspension under this division unless the offender agrees to perform the work offered as a condition of probation or other suspension by the court. The court may require an offender who agrees to perform the work to pay to it a reasonable fee to cover the costs of the offender's participation in the work, including, but not limited to, the costs of procuring a policy or policies of liability insurance to cover the period during which the offender will perform the work.

A court may permit any offender convicted of a misdemeanor to satisfy the payment of a fine imposed for the offense by performing supervised community service work as described in this division if the offender requests an opportunity to satisfy the payment by this means and if the court determines the offender is financially unable to pay the fine.

The supervised community service work that may be imposed under this division shall be subject to the following limitations:

(a) The court shall fix the period of the work and, if necessary, shall distribute it over weekends or over other appropriate times that will allow the offender to continue at the offender's occupation or to care for the offender's family. The period of the work as fixed by the court shall not exceed an aggregate of two hundred hours.

(b) An agency, political subdivision, or charitable organization must agree to accept the offender for the work before the court requires the offender to perform the work for it. A court shall not require an offender to perform supervised community service work for an agency, political subdivision, or charitable organization at a location that is an unreasonable distance from the offender's residence or domicile, unless the offender is provided with transportation to the location where the work is to be performed.

(c) A court may enter into an agreement with a county department of human services for the management, placement, and supervision of offenders eligible for community service work in department of human services programs established pursuant to sections 5101.80 to 5101.94 or section 5101.21 or 5107.30 of the Revised Code. If a court and a county department of human services have entered into an agreement of that nature, the clerk of that court is authorized to pay directly to the department of human services all or a portion of the fees collected by the court pursuant to this division in accordance with the terms of its agreement.

(d) Community service work that a court requires under this division shall be supervised by an official of the agency, political subdivision, or charitable organization for which the work is performed or by a person designated by the agency, political subdivision, or charitable organization. The official or designated person shall be qualified for the supervision by education, training, or experience, and periodically shall report, in writing, to the court and to the offender's probation officer concerning the conduct of the offender in performing the work.

(2) When an offender is convicted of a felony, the court may require the offender, as a condition of probation, in addition to the conditions of probation imposed pursuant to division (C) of this section, to perform supervised community service work in accordance with this division and under the authority of any agency, political subdivision, or charitable organization as described in division (H)(1) of this section. Supervised community service work shall not be required as a condition of probation under this division unless the offender agrees to perform the work offered as a condition of probation by the court. The court may require an offender who agrees to perform the work to pay to it a reasonable fee to cover the costs of the offender's participation in the work, including, but not limited to, the costs of procuring a policy or policies of liability insurance to cover the period during which the offender will perform the work.

A court may permit an offender convicted of a felony to satisfy the payment of a fine imposed for the offense by performing supervised community service work as described in this division if the offender requests an opportunity to satisfy the payment by this means and if the court determines the offender is financially unable to pay the fine.

The supervised community service work that may be imposed under this division shall be subject to the limitations specified in divisions (H)(1)(a) to (d) of this section.

(I)(1) When an offender is convicted of a violation of section 4511.19 of the Revised Code, a municipal ordinance relating to operating a vehicle while under the influence of alcohol, a drug of abuse, or alcohol and a drug of abuse, a municipal ordinance relating to operating a vehicle with a prohibited concentration of alcohol in the blood, breath, or urine, or section 2903.06 or 2903.07 of the Revised Code or a municipal ordinance that is substantially similar to section 2903.07 of the Revised Code and that provides for that type of finding by a jury or judge in a case in which the jury or judge found that the offender was under the influence of alcohol at the time of the commission of the offense, the court may require, as a condition of probation in addition to the required conditions of probation and the discretionary conditions of probation that may be imposed pursuant to division (C) of this section, any suspension or revocation of a driver's or commercial driver's license or permit or nonresident operating privilege, and all other penalties provided by law or by ordinance, that the offender operate only a motor vehicle equipped with an ignition interlock device that is certified pursuant to section 4511.83 of the Revised Code.

(2) When a court requires an offender, as a condition of probation pursuant to division (I)(1) of this section, to operate only a motor vehicle equipped with an ignition interlock device that is certified pursuant to section 4511.83 of the Revised Code, the offender immediately shall surrender the offender's driver's or commercial driver's license or permit to the court. Upon the receipt of the offender's license or permit, the court shall issue an order authorizing the offender to operate a motor vehicle equipped with a certified ignition interlock device, deliver the offender's license or permit to the bureau of motor vehicles, and include in the abstract of the case forwarded to the bureau pursuant to section 4507.021 of the Revised Code

the conditions of probation imposed pursuant to division (I)(1) of this section. The court shall give the offender a copy of its order, and that copy shall be used by the offender in lieu of a driver's or commercial driver's license or permit until the bureau issues a restricted license to the offender.

(3) Upon receipt of an offender's driver's or commercial driver's license or permit pursuant to division (I)(2) of this section, the bureau of motor vehicles shall issue a restricted license to the offender. The restricted license shall be identical to the surrendered license, except that it shall have printed on its face a statement that the offender is prohibited from operating a motor vehicle that is not equipped with an ignition interlock device that is certified pursuant to section 4511.83 of the Revised Code. The bureau shall deliver the offender's surrendered license or permit to the court upon receipt of a court order requiring it to do so, or reissue the offender's license or permit under section 4507.54 of the Revised Code if the registrar destroyed the offender's license or permit under that section. The offender shall surrender the restricted license to the court upon receipt of his surrendered license or permit.

(4) If an offender violates a requirement of the court imposed under division (I)(1) of this section, the offender's driver's or commercial driver's license or permit or nonresident operating privilege may be suspended as provided in section 4507.16 of the Revised Code.

(5) As used in this division, "ignition interlock device" has the same meaning as in section 4511.83 of the Revised Code.

(1995 H 167, eff. 11–15–95; 1995 H 4, eff. 11–9–95; 1994 H 687, eff. 10–12–94; 1994 H 571, eff. 10–6–94; 1993 H 152, eff. 7–1–93; 1990 S 258; 1989 H 381; 1988 H 322, H 429; 1983 S 210; 1982 S 432; 1981 H 1; 1980 H 682, H 892; 1978 S 119; 1975 S 144; 1972 H 511)

[1] Language appears as the result of the harmonization of 1995 H 167 and 1995 H 4.
[2] Language appears as the result of the harmonization of 1995 H 167 and 1995 H 4.
[3] Language appears as the result of the harmonization of 1995 H 167 and 1995 H 4.

Historical and Statutory Notes

Ed. Note: Comparison of these amendments [1995 H 167, eff. 11–15–95 and 1995 H 4, eff. 11–9–95] in pursuance of section 1.52 of the Revised Code discloses that they are not irreconcilable, so that they are required by that section to be harmonized to give effect to each amendment. In recognition of this rule of construction, changes made by 1995 H 167, eff. 11–15–95, and 1995 H 4, eff. 11–9–95, have been incorporated in the above amendment. See *Baldwin's Ohio Legislative Service*, 1995, pages 8/L–3027 and 7/L–1485, for original versions of these Acts.

2951.021 Probation fees

(A) As used in this section:

(1) "Multicounty department of probation" means a probation department established under section 2301.27 of the Revised Code to serve more than one county.

(2) "Probation agency" means a county department of probation, a multicounty department of probation, a municipal court department of probation established under section 1901.33 of the Revised Code, or the adult parole authority.

(3) "County–operated municipal court" and "legislative authority" have the same meanings as in section 1901.03 of the Revised Code.

(4) "Detention facility" has the same meaning as in section 2921.01 of the Revised Code.

(B)(1) If a court places an offender on probation under the control and supervision of a probation agency, the court may require the offender, as a condition of probation, to pay a monthly probation fee of not more than fifty dollars for probation services. If the court requires an offender to pay a monthly probation fee and the offender will be under the control of a county department of probation, a multicounty department of probation, or a municipal court department of probation established under section 1901.33 of the Revised Code, the court shall specify whether the offender is to pay the fee to the probation agency that will have control over him or to the clerk of the court for which the probation agency is established. If the court requires an offender to pay a monthly probation fee and the offender will be under the control of the adult parole authority, the court shall specify that the offender is to pay the fee to the clerk of the court of common pleas.

(2) No person shall be assessed, in any month, more than fifty dollars in probation fees.

(3) The prosecuting attorney of the county or the chief legal officer of a municipal corporation in which is located the court that imposed sentence upon an offender may bring a civil action to recover unpaid monthly probation fees that the offender was required to pay. Any amount recovered in the civil action shall be paid into the appropriate county or municipal probation services fund in accordance with division (C) of this section.

(4) The failure of an offender to comply with a condition of probation that he pay a monthly probation fee imposed under division (B)(1) of this section shall not constitute the basis for a revocation of his probation and the imposition of his sentence under section 2951.09 of the Revised Code but may be considered with any other factors that form the basis of a revocation of probation. If the court determines at a hearing held pursuant to section 2951.09 of the Revised Code that the offender failed to pay a monthly probation fee imposed under division (B)(1) of this section and that no other factors warranting revocation of probation are present, the court shall not revoke the offender's probation, shall remand the offender to the custody of the probation agency, and may impose any additional conditions of probation upon the offender, including a requirement that the offender perform community service, as the ends of justice require. Any requirement imposed pursuant to division (B)(4) of this section that the offender perform community service shall be in addition to and shall not limit or otherwise affect any order that the offender perform community service pursuant to division (H)(1)(a) of section 2951.02 of the Revised Code.

(C) Prior to the last day of the month in each month during the period of probation, an offender who is ordered to pay a monthly probation fee under this section shall pay the fee to the probation agency that has control and supervision over him or to the clerk of the court for which the probation agency is established, as specified by the court, except that, if the probation agency is the adult parole authority, the offender shall pay the fee to the clerk of the court of common pleas. Each probation agency or clerk of a court that receives any monthly probation fees shall keep a record of the monthly probation fees that are paid to the agency or the clerk and shall give a written receipt to each person who pays a probation fee to the agency or clerk.

(D) Subject to division (F) of this section, all monthly probation fees collected under this section by a probation agency or the clerk of a court shall be disposed of in the following manner:

(1) For offenders who are under the control and supervision of a county department of probation or a municipal court department of probation in a county-operated municipal court, on or before the fifth business day of each month, the chief probation officer or his designee or the clerk of the court shall pay all monthly probation fees collected in the previous month to the county treasurer of the county in which the county department of probation or municipal court department of probation is established for deposit into the county probation services fund established in the county treasury of that county pursuant to division (A)(1) section 321.44 of the Revised Code.

(2) For offenders who are under the control and supervision of a multicounty department of probation, on or before the fifth business day of each month, the chief probation officer or his designee or the clerk of the court shall pay all monthly probation fees collected in the previous month to the county treasurer of the county in which is located the court of common pleas that placed the offender on probation under the control of the department for deposit into the county probation services fund established in the county treasury of that county pursuant to division (A)(1) of section 321.44 of the Revised Code and for subsequent appropriation and transfer in accordance with division (A)(2) of that section to the appropriate multicounty probation services fund established pursuant to division (B) of that section.

(3) For offenders who are under the control and supervision of a municipal court department of probation in a municipal court that is not a county-operated municipal court, on or before the fifth business day of each month, the chief probation officer or his designee or the clerk of the court shall pay all monthly probation fees collected in the previous month to the treasurer of the municipal corporation for deposit into the municipal probation services fund established pursuant to section 737.41 of the Revised Code.

(4) For offenders who are under the control and supervision of the adult parole authority, the clerk of the court of common pleas, on or before the fifth business day of January, April, July, and October, shall pay all monthly probation fees collected by the clerk in the previous three months to the treasurer of the county in which is located the court of common pleas that placed the offender on probation under the control of the authority for deposit into the county probation services fund established in the county treasury of that county pursuant to division (A)(1) of section 321.44 of the Revised Code and for subsequent appropriation and transfer in accordance with division (A)(2) of that section to the adult parole authority probation services fund established pursuant to section 5149.06 of the Revised Code.

(E) Not later than the first day of December of each year, each probation agency shall prepare a report regarding its use of money from a county probation services fund, a multicounty probation services fund, a municipal probation services fund, or the adult parole authority probation services fund, whichever is applicable. The report shall specify the amount appropriated from the fund to the probation agency during the current calendar year, an estimate of the amount that the probation agency will expend by the end of the year, a summary of how the amount appropriated has been expended for probation services, and an estimate of the amount of probation fees that the probation agency will collect and pay to the appropriate treasurer for deposit in the appropriate fund in the next calendar year. The report shall be filed with one of the following:

(1) If the probation agency is a county department of probation or a municipal court department of probation in a county-operated municipal court, with the board of county commissioners of that county;

(2) If the probation agency is a multicounty department of probation, with the board of county commissioners of the county whose treasurer, in accordance with section 2301.27 of the Revised code, is designated as the treasurer to whom probation fees collected under this section are to be appropriated and transferred under division (A)(2) of section 321.44 of the Revised Code;

(3) If the probation agency is a department of probation of a municipal court that is not a county-operated municipal court, with the legislative authority of the municipal corporation that operates the court;

(4) If the probation agency is the adult parole authority, with the chairmen of the finance committees of the senate and the house of representatives, the directors of the office of budget and management and the legislative budget office, and the board of county commissioners in each county for which the adult parole authority provides probation services.

(F) If the clerk of a court of common pleas or the clerk of a municipal court collects any monthly probation fees under this section, the clerk may retain up to two per cent of the fees so collected to cover any administrative costs experienced in complying with his duties under this section.

(1994 H 406, eff. 11–11–94)

2951.03 Presentence investigation reports; confidentiality

(A) No person who has pleaded guilty to or has been convicted of a felony shall be placed on probation until a written presentence investigation report by a probation officer has been considered by the court. The probation officer shall inquire into the circumstances of the offense and the criminal record, social history, and present condition of the defendant. Whenever the probation officer considers it advisable, his investigation may include a physical and mental examination of the defendant. If a defendant is committed to any institution, the presentence investigation report shall be sent to the institution with the entry of commitment. If a defendant is committed to any institution and a presentence investigation report is not prepared regarding that defendant pursuant to this section, section 2947.06 of the Revised Code, or Criminal Rule 32.2, the director of the department of rehabilitation and correction or his designee may order that an offender background investigation and report be conducted and prepared regarding the person pursuant to section 5120.16 of the Revised Code. If, pursuant to section 2930.13 of the Revised Code, the victim of the offense of which the defendant has been convicted wishes to make a statement regarding the impact of the offense for the probation officer's use in preparing the presentence investigation report, the probation officer shall comply with the requirements of that section.

(B)(1) If a presentence investigation report is prepared pursuant to this section or section 2947.06 of the Revised Code, or Criminal Rule 32.2, the court, at a reasonable time before imposing sentence, shall permit the defendant or his counsel to read the report, except that the court shall not permit the defendant or his counsel to read any of the following:

(a) Any recommendation as to sentence;

(b) Any diagnostic opinions that, if disclosed, the court believes might seriously disrupt a program of rehabilitation for the defendant;

(c) Any sources of information obtained upon a promise of confidentiality;

(d) Any other information that, if disclosed, the court believes might result in physical harm or some other type of harm to the defendant or to any other person.

(2) Prior to sentencing, the court shall permit the defendant and his counsel to comment on the presentence investigation report and, in its discretion, may permit the defendant and his counsel to introduce testimony or other information that relates to any alleged factual inaccuracy contained in the report.

(3) If the court believes that any information in the presentence investigation report should not be disclosed pursuant to division (B)(1) of this section, the court, in lieu of making the report or any part of the report available, shall state orally or in writing a summary of the factual information contained in the report that will be relied upon in determining the defendant's sentence. The court shall permit the defendant and his counsel to comment upon the oral or written summary of the report.

(4) Any material that is disclosed to the defendant or his counsel pursuant to this section shall be disclosed to the prosecutor who is handling the prosecution of the case against the defendant.

(5) If the comments of the defendant or his counsel, the testimony they introduce, or any of the other information they introduce alleges any factual inaccuracy in the presentence investigation report or the summary of the report, the court shall do either of the following with respect to each alleged factual inaccuracy:

(a) Make a finding as to the allegation;

(b) Make a determination that no finding is necessary with respect to the allegation, because the factual matter will not be taken into account in the sentencing of the defendant.

(6) Any copies of the presentence investigation report that are made available pursuant to this section to the defendant or his counsel or to the prosecutor shall be returned to the court, probation officer, or investigator immediately after the imposition of sentence or the granting of probation, unless the court, in its discretion, directs otherwise.

(C) A court's decision as to the content of a summary under division (B)(3) of this section or as to the withholding of information under division (B)(1)(a), (b), (c), or (d) of this section shall be considered to be within the discretion of the court. No appeal can be taken from either such decision, and neither such decision shall be the basis for a reversal of the sentence imposed.

(D) As used in this section, "prosecutor" has the same meaning as in section 2935.01 of the Revised Code.

(1994 S 186, eff. 10–12–94; 1994 H 571, eff. 10–6–94; 1990 S 258, eff. 11–20–90; 1987 H 73, § 1, 5; 130 v H 686; 1953 H 1; GC 13452–1a)

Historical and Statutory Notes

Ed. Note: A special endorsement by the Legislative Service Commission states, "Comparison of these amendments [1994 S 186, eff. 10–12–94 and 1994 H 571, eff. 10–6–94] in pursuance of section 1.52 of the Revised Code discloses that they are not irreconcilable, so that they are required by that section to be harmonized to give effect to each amendment." In recognition of this rule of construction, changes made by 1994 S 186, eff. 10–12–94, and 1994 H 571, eff. 10–6–94, have been incorporated in the above amendment. See *Baldwin's Ohio Legislative Service*, 1994 Laws of Ohio,

pages 5–927 and 5–1162 for original versions of
these Acts.

2951.04 Conditional probation for drug treatment

(A) If the court has reason to believe that an offender convicted of a felony or misdemeanor is a drug dependent person or is in danger of becoming a drug dependent person, the court may, and when the offender has been convicted the court shall, advise the offender that he has a right to request conditional probation for purposes of treatment and rehabilitation.

(B) Within a reasonable time after receipt of the request for conditional probation, the court shall hold a hearing to determine if the offender is eligible for conditional probation. The offender is eligible for conditional probation if the court finds that:

(1) The offender is drug dependent or is in danger of becoming drug dependent, and he may benefit from rehabilitation or treatment;

(2) The offender has been accepted into an appropriate drug treatment facility or program for rehabilitation or treatment. Such a facility or program includes a program licensed by the department of alcohol and drug addiction services pursuant to section 3793.11 of the Revised Code, a program certified by the department pursuant to section 3793.06 of the Revised Code, a public or private hospital, the veterans administration or other agencies of the federal government, or private care or treatment rendered by a physician or a psychologist licensed in the state.

(3) The offender has committed an offense for which probation may be granted in accordance with section 2951.02 of the Revised Code. For purposes of this section, the fact that an offender is a repeat offender as defined in section 2929.01 of the Revised Code shall not conclusively bar him from the conditional probation authorized by this section if the offenses for which he has been convicted and for which he previously had been imprisoned involved violations of section 2925.11 or 2925.12 of the Revised Code or would have been violations of either section if they had been in effect at the time of the violations.

(C) If the court finds that an offender is eligible for conditional probation, the court may suspend execution of the sentence imposed after completion of any period of actual incarceration required by Chapter 2925. of the Revised Code, and place the offender on probation subject to this chapter and under the control and supervision of the county probation department or the adult parole authority.

Probation under this section shall be conditioned upon the offender's voluntary entrance into an appropriate drug treatment facility or program, his faithful submission to the rehabilitation or treatment prescribed for his drug dependence or danger of drug dependence, and other conditions as the court orders.

The court shall not suspend execution of a sentence and place the offender on conditional probation, until the court affirmatively finds that the offender is not, or there is no substantial risk of his becoming, a dangerous offender as defined in section 2929.01 of the Revised Code, and such finding is entered into the record.

Probation granted under this section shall continue for any period that the court determines. The period of probation may be extended, but the total period of probation, whether for rehabilitation or treatment or otherwise, shall not exceed five years.

(D) At the hearing provided for in division (B) of this section, the offender and the prosecuting attorney shall be afforded the opportunity to present evidence to establish his eligibility or ineligibility for probation under this section.

Upon the request of the offender, and to aid the offender in establishing his eligibility for probation, the court may refer the offender for medical and psychiatric examination to the department of mental health, to a state facility designated by the department, to a psychiatric clinic approved by the department, or to a facility or program described in division (B)(2) of this section. However, the psychiatric portion of a referral pursuant to this division shall be performed only by a court-appointed individual who has not previously treated the offender or any member of his immediate family.

(E) Treatment of a drug dependent person, or a person in danger of becoming a drug dependent person, who has been placed on conditional probation under this section may include hospitalization under close supervision or otherwise, release on an outpatient status under supervision, and such other treatment or after-care as the appropriate drug treatment facility or program considers necessary or desirable to rehabilitate or treat the person, including the continued maintenance of an existing drug dependence through the administration of methadone pursuant to section 3719.61 of the Revised Code. An offender released from hospitalization or rehabilitation or treatment, but still subject to a term of probation, may be rehospitalized or returned to rehabilitation or treatment at any time it becomes necessary.

(F) If, at any time after rehabilitation or treatment has commenced, the appropriate drug treatment facility or program reports to the probation officer that the offender is rehabilitated and further rehabilitation or treatment is unnecessary, or that maximum benefit of rehabilitation or treatment has been achieved, the offender shall be relieved of the condition of rehabilitation or treatment, and the court may discharge him or place him on an additional period of probation, upon any conditions that the court considers necessary. If, at any time after rehabilitation or treatment has commenced, the facility or program reports to the probation officer that the offender fails to submit to or follow the prescribed rehabilitation or treatment, or has become a discipline problem, the offender shall be arrested as provided in section 2951.08 of the Revised Code and be removed from the treatment facility or program, and the court immediately shall hold a hearing to determine if the offender failed to submit to or follow the prescribed rehabilitation or treatment or is a discipline problem. If the court determines that the offender failed to submit to or follow the prescribed rehabilitation or treatment or is a discipline problem, it immediately shall revoke the offender's conditional probation and any suspension of the offender's sentence of imprisonment, and impose upon the offender any term of imprisonment that might have been imposed upon the offender at the time of sentencing.

At any time and for any appropriate reason, the offender, his probation officer, the authority or department that has the duty to control and supervise the offender as provided for in section 2951.05 of the Revised Code, or the facility or program may petition the court to reconsider, suspend, or modify its order for rehabilitation or treatment concerning that person.

(G) The appropriate drug treatment facility or program shall report to the authority or department that has the duty to control and supervise the offender as provided for in section 2951.05 of the Revised Code, at any periodic reporting period the court requires and whenever the offender is changed from an inpatient to an outpatient, is transferred to another treatment facility or program, fails to submit to or follow the prescribed rehabilitation or treatment, becomes a discipline problem, is rehabilitated, or obtains the maximum benefit of rehabilitation or treatment.

(H) Any offender placed on conditional probation by the terms of this section shall be liable for expenses incurred during the course of rehabilitation or treatment, and if the offender is rehabilitated or treated in a benevolent institution under the jurisdiction of the department of mental health, he is subject to Chapter 5121. of the Revised Code.

(I) The provisions of this section do not affect or limit, and are not affected or limited by, the provisions of division (E) of section 2929.51 of the Revised Code.

(1994 H 385, eff. 7–19–94; 1990 S 258, eff. 11–20–90; 1989 H 317; 1985 H 475; 1980 H 900; 1975 H 300)

2951.041 Drug treatment in lieu of conviction

(A) If the court has reason to believe that an offender charged with a felony or misdemeanor is a drug dependent person or is in danger of becoming a drug dependent person, the court shall accept, prior to the entry of a plea, that offender's request for treatment in lieu of conviction. If the offender requests treatment in lieu of conviction, the court shall stay all criminal proceedings pending the outcome of the hearing to determine whether the offender is a person eligible for treatment in lieu of conviction. At the conclusion of the hearing, the court shall enter its findings and accept the offender's plea.

(B) The offender is eligible for treatment in lieu of conviction if the court finds that:

(1) The offender's drug dependence or danger of drug dependence was a factor leading to the criminal activity with which he is charged, and rehabilitation through treatment would substantially reduce the likelihood of additional criminal activity;

(2) The offender has been accepted into an appropriate drug treatment facility or program. Such a facility or program includes a program licensed by the department of alcohol and drug addiction services pursuant to section 3793.11 of the Revised Code, a program certified by the department pursuant to section 3793.06 of the Revised Code, a public or private hospital, the veterans administration or other agency of the federal government, or private care or treatment rendered by a physician or a psychologist licensed in the state.

(3) If the offender were convicted he would be eligible for probation under section 2951.02 of the Revised Code, except that a finding of any of the criteria listed in divisions (D) and (F) of that section shall cause the offender to be conclusively ineligible for treatment in lieu of conviction;

(4) The offender is not a repeat offender or dangerous offender as defined in section 2929.01 of the Revised Code;

(5) The offender is not charged with any offense defined in section 2925.02, 2925.03, or 2925.21 of the Revised Code.

Upon such a finding and if the offender enters a plea of guilty or no contest, the court may stay all criminal proceedings and order the offender to a period of rehabilitation. If a plea of not guilty is entered, a trial shall precede further consideration of the offender's request for treatment in lieu of conviction.

(C) The offender and the prosecuting attorney shall be afforded the opportunity to present evidence to establish eligibility or ineligibility for treatment in lieu of conviction, and the prosecuting attorney may make a recommendation to the court concerning whether the offender should receive treatment in lieu of conviction. Upon the request of the offender and to aid the offender in establishing his eligibility for treatment in lieu of conviction, the court may refer the offender for medical and psychiatric examination to the department of mental health, to a state facility designated by the department, to a psychiatric clinic approved by the department, or to a facility or program described in division (B)(2) of this section. However, the psychiatric portion of an examination pursuant to a referral under this division shall be performed only by a court-appointed individual who has not previously treated the offender or a member of his immediate family.

(D) An offender found to be eligible for treatment in lieu of conviction and ordered to a period of rehabilitation shall be placed under the control and supervision of the county probation department or the adult parole authority as provided in this chapter as if he were on probation. The court shall order a period of rehabilitation to continue for any period that the judge or magistrate determines. The period of rehabilitation may be extended, but the total period shall not exceed three years. The period of rehabilitation shall be conditioned upon the offender's voluntary entrance into an appropriate drug treatment facility or program, faithful submission to prescribed treatment, and upon any other conditions that the court orders.

(E) Treatment of a person ordered to a period of rehabilitation under this section may include hospitalization under close supervision or otherwise, release on an outpatient status under supervision, and such other treatment or after-care as the appropriate drug treatment facility or program considers necessary or desirable to rehabilitate such person. Persons released from hospitalization or treatment but still subject to the ordered period of rehabilitation may be rehospitalized or returned to treatment at any time it becomes necessary for their treatment and rehabilitation.

(F) If the appropriate drug treatment facility or program reports to the probation officer that the offender has successfully completed treatment and is rehabilitated, the court may dismiss the charges pending against the offender. If the facility or program reports to the probation officer that the offender has successfully completed treatment and is rehabilitated or has obtained maximum benefits from treatment, and that the offender has completed the period of rehabilitation and other conditions ordered by the court, the court shall dismiss the charges pending against the offender. If the facility or program reports to the probation officer that the offender has failed treatment, has failed to submit to or follow the prescribed treatment, or has become a discipline problem, if the offender does not satisfactorily complete the period of rehabilitation or the other conditions ordered by the court, or if the offender violates the conditions of the period of rehabilitation, the offender shall be arrested as provided in section 2951.08 of the Revised Code and removed from the facility or program, and the court immediately shall hold a hearing to determine if the offender failed treatment, failed to submit to or follow the prescribed treatment, did not satisfactorily complete the period of rehabilitation or any other condition ordered by the court, or violated any condition of the period of rehabilitation. If the court so determines, it immediately shall enter an adjudication of guilt and shall impose upon the offender a term of imprisonment.

At any time and for any appropriate reason, the offender, his probation officer, the authority or department that has the duty to control and supervise the offender as provided for in section 2951.05 of the Revised Code, or the facility or program may petition the court to reconsider, suspend, or modify its order for treatment concerning that person.

(G) The appropriate drug treatment facility or program shall report to the authority or department that has the duty to control and supervise the offender as provided for in section 2951.05 of the Revised Code, at any periodic reporting period the court requires and whenever the offender is changed from an inpatient to an outpatient, is transferred to another treatment facility or program, fails treatment, fails to submit to or follow the prescribed treatment, becomes a discipline problem, does not satisfactorily complete the period of rehabilitation or other conditions ordered by the court, has violated the conditions of the period of rehabilitation, is rehabilitated, or obtains the maximum benefit of treatment.

(H) If, on the offender's motion, the court finds that the offender has successfully completed the period of rehabilitation ordered by the court, is rehabilitated, is no longer drug dependent or in danger of becoming drug dependent, and has completed all other conditions, the court shall dismiss the proceeding against him. Successful completion of a period of rehabilitation under this section shall be without adjudication of guilt and is not a criminal conviction for purposes of disqualifications or disabilities imposed by law and upon conviction of a crime, and the court may order the sealing of records in the manner provided in sections 2953.31 to 2953.36 of the Revised Code.

(I) An order denying treatment in lieu of conviction under this section shall not be construed to prevent conditional probation under section 2951.04 of the Revised Code.

(J) Any person ordered to treatment by the terms of this section shall be liable for expenses incurred during the course of treatment, and if he is treated in a benevolent institution under the jurisdiction of the department of mental health, he is subject to Chapter 5121. of the Revised Code.

(K) An offender charged with a drug abuse offense, other than a minor misdemeanor involving marihuana, and otherwise eligible for treatment in lieu of conviction may request and may be ordered to a period of rehabilitation even though the findings required by divisions (B)(1) and (2) of this section are not made. An order to rehabilitation under this division shall be subject to such conditions as the court requires but shall not be conditioned upon entry into an appropriate drug treatment facility or program.

(1994 H 385, eff. 7–19–94; 1990 S 258, eff. 11–20–90; 1989 H 317; 1980 H 900; 1975 H 300)

2951.05   Control and supervision of offender on probation

If an offender mentioned in section 2951.02 of the Revised Code resides in the county in which the trial was conducted, the court that issues an order of probation shall place the offender under the control and supervision of a department of probation in the county that serves the court. If there is no department of probation in the county that serves the court, the probation order, under section 2301.32 of the Revised Code, may place the offender on probation in charge of the adult parole authority created by section 5149.02 of the Revised Code that then shall have the powers and duties of a county department of probation. If the offender resides in a county other than the county in which the court granting probation is located and a county department of probation has been established in the county of residence or the county of residence is served by a multicounty probation department, the order of probation may request the court of common pleas of the county in which the offender resides to receive him into the control and supervision of that county or multicounty department of probation, subject to the jurisdiction of the trial judge over and with respect to the person of the offender, and to the rules governing that department of probation. If the offender's county of residence has no county or multicounty department of probation, the judge may place him on probation in charge of the adult parole authority created by section 5149.02 of the Revised Code.

As used in this section, "multicounty department of probation" means a probation department established under section 2301.27 of the Revised Code to serve more than one county. (1994 H 406, eff. 11–11–94; 130 v Pt 2, H 28, eff. 3–18–65; 129 v 481; 128 v 959; 125 v 823; 1953 H 1; GC 13452–3)

2951.06 Release from custody

Upon entry in the records of the judge or magistrate, of the order for probation provided for in section 2951.02 of the Revised Code, the defendant shall be released from custody as soon as the requirements and conditions required by the judge supervising the probation, have been met. The defendant shall continue under the control and supervision of the adult parole authority created by section 5149.02 of the Revised Code or the county department of probation, to the extent required by law, the conditions of the order of probation, and the rules and regulations governing said agency of probation. (130 v Pt 2, H 28, eff. 3–18–65; 129 v 481; 125 v 823; 1953 H 1; GC 13452–4)

2951.07 Probation period

Probation under section 2951.02 of the Revised Code continues for the period that the judge or magistrate determines and, subject to divisions (H)(1)(a) and (2) of that section, may be extended. Except as provided in divisions (H)(1)(a) and (2) of that section, the total period of probation shall not exceed five years. If the probationer absconds or otherwise absents himself from the jurisdiction of the court without permission from the county department of probation or the court to do so, or if he is confined in any institution for the commission of any offense whatever, the probation period ceases to run until such time as he is brought before the court for its further action. (1990 S 258, eff. 11–20–90; 1953 H 1; GC 13452–5)

2951.08 Arrest of person violating probation

(A) During a period of probation, any field officer or probation officer may arrest the person on probation without a warrant and bring him before the judge or magistrate before whom the cause was pending. During a period of probation, any peace officer may arrest the person on probation without a warrant upon the written order of the chief county probation officer if the person on probation is under the supervision of that county department of probation or on the order of an officer of the adult parole authority created pursuant to section 5149.02 of the Revised Code if the person on probation is under the supervision of the authority. During a period of probation, any peace officer may arrest the person on probation on the warrant of the judge or magistrate before whom the cause was pending.

During a period of probation, any peace officer may arrest the person on probation without a warrant if the peace officer has reasonable ground to believe the person on probation has violated or is violating any of the following that is a condition of his probation:

(1) A condition that prohibits his ownership, possession, or use of a firearm, deadly weapon, ammunition, or dangerous ordnance;

(2) A condition that prohibits him from being within a specified structure or geographic area;

(3) A condition that confines him to a residence, facility, or other structure;

(4) A condition that prohibits him from contacting or communicating with any specified individual;

(5) A condition that prohibits him from associating with a specified individual.

(B) Upon making an arrest under this section, the arresting field officer, probation officer, or peace officer or his department or agency promptly shall notify the chief probation officer or the chief probation officer's designee that the person has been arrested. Upon being notified that a peace officer has made an arrest under this section, the chief probation officer or designee, or another probation officer designated by the chief probation officer, promptly shall bring the person who was arrested before the judge or magistrate before whom the cause was pending.

(C) Nothing in this section limits, or shall be construed to limit, the powers of arrest granted to certain law enforcement officers and citizens under sections 2935.03 and 2935.04 of the Revised Code.

(D) As used in this section:

(1) "Peace officer" has the same meaning as in section 2935.01 of the Revised Code.

(2) "Firearm," "deadly weapon," and "dangerous ordnance" have the same meanings as in section 2923.11 of the Revised Code.

(1994 H 406, eff. 11–11–94; 1992 S 49, eff. 7–21–92; 130 v Pt 2, H 28; 129 v 481; 125 v 823; 1953 H 1; GC 13452–6)

2951.09   Procedure against defendant; rights of citizenship restored; journal entry

When a defendant on probation is brought before the judge or magistrate under section 2951.08 of the Revised Code, the judge or magistrate immediately shall inquire into the conduct of the defendant, and may terminate the probation and impose any sentence that originally could have been imposed or continue the probation and remand the defendant to the custody of the probation authority, at any time during the probationary period. When the ends of justice will be served and the good conduct of the person so held warrants it, the judge or magistrate may terminate the period of probation. At the end or termination of the period of probation, the jurisdiction of the judge or magistrate to impose sentence ceases and the defendant shall be discharged. If the defendant was convicted of or pleaded guilty to a felony, the judge of the court of common pleas may restore his rights of citizenship, of which he may or shall have been deprived by reason of his conviction under section 2961.01 of the Revised Code, and, if the court restores his citizenship, an entry to that effect shall be made on the journal of the court in the action in which the conviction or plea of guilty was entered.

A probation officer shall receive necessary expenses in the performance of his duties.

(1990 S 258, eff. 11–20–90; 1953 H 1; GC 13452–7)

2951.10   Final order

An order suspending the imposition of sentence and placing the defendant on probation is a final order from which appeal may be prosecuted.

(1953 H 1, eff. 10–1–53; GC 13452–9)

2951.11   Parole by board of county commissioners—Repealed

(1972 H 511, eff. 1–1–74; 1970 S 460; 1953 H 1; GC 13452–10)

2951.12   Recommitment of such persons—Repealed

(1975 H 1, eff. 6–13–75; 1970 S 460; 1953 H 1; GC 13452–11)

2951.13   Attendance of prisoner at probation revocation hearing; transportation

A convict confined in a state correctional institution while on probation granted after a former conviction may be removed from the institution for the purpose of attending a hearing on revocation of the probation. When a copy of the journal entry ordering the probation revocation hearing is presented to the warden or superintendent of the institution where the convict is confined, he shall deliver the convict to the sheriff of the county where the hearing is to be held, who shall convey the convict to and from the hearing. The approval of the governor on the journal entry is not required.

(1994 H 571, eff. 10–6–94; 1983 H 291, eff. 7–1–83; 1970 H 1136)

APPEALS; OTHER POSTCONVICTION REMEDIES

GENERAL PROVISIONS

GENERAL PROVISIONS

2953.01   Definition of magistrate

The definition of "magistrate" set forth in section 2931.01 of the Revised Code applies to Chapter 2953. of the Revised Code.

(1953 H 1, eff. 10–1–53)

2953.02 Review of judgments and final orders

In a capital case in which a sentence of death is imposed for an offense committed before January 1, 1995, and in any other criminal case, including a conviction for the violation of an ordinance of a municipal corporation, the judgment or final order of a court of record inferior to the court of appeals may be reviewed in the court of appeals. A final order of an administrative officer or agency may be reviewed in the court of common pleas. A judgment or final order of the court of appeals involving a question arising under the Constitution of the United States or of this state may be appealed to the supreme court as a matter of right. This right of appeal from judgments and final orders of the court of appeals shall extend to cases in which a sentence of death is imposed for an offense committed before January 1, 1995, and in which the death penalty has been affirmed, felony cases in which the supreme court has directed the court of appeals to certify its record, and in all other criminal cases of public or general interest wherein the supreme court has granted a motion to certify the record of the court of appeals. In a capital case in which a sentence of death is imposed for an offense committed on or after January 1, 1995, the judgment or final order may be appealed from the trial court directly to the supreme court as a matter of right. The supreme court in criminal cases shall not be required to determine as to the weight of the evidence, except that, in cases in which a sentence of death is imposed for an offense committed on or after January 1, 1995, and in which the question of the weight of the evidence to support the judgment has been raised on appeal, the supreme court shall determine as to the weight of the evidence to support the judgment and shall determine as to the weight of the evidence to support the sentence of death as provided in section 2929.05 of the Revised Code.

(1995 S 4, eff. 9–21–95; 1981 S 1, eff. 10–19–81; 1970 S 530; 128 v 141; 1953 H 1; GC 13459–1)

2953.03 Suspension of execution of sentence or judgment when new trial motion filed; bail

(A) If a motion for a new trial is filed pursuant to Criminal Rule 33 by a defendant who is convicted of a misdemeanor under the Revised Code or an ordinance of a municipal corporation, and if that defendant was on bail at the time of the conviction of that offense, the trial judge or magistrate shall suspend execution of the sentence or judgment imposed pending the determination on the motion for a new trial and shall determine the amount and nature of any bail that is required of the defendant in accordance with Criminal Rule 46.

(B) If a notice of appeal is filed pursuant to the Rules of Appellate Procedure or Chapter 1905. of the Revised Code by a defendant who is convicted in a municipal, county, or mayor's court or a court of common pleas of a misdemeanor under the Revised Code or an ordinance of a municipal corporation, if that defendant was on bail at the time of the conviction of that offense, and if execution of the sentence or judgment imposed is suspended, the trial court or magistrate or the court in which the appeal is being prosecuted shall determine the amount and nature of any bail that is required of the defendant as follows:

(1) In the case of an appeal to a court of appeals by a defendant who is convicted in a municipal or county court or a court of common pleas, in accordance with Appellate Rule 8 and Criminal Rule 46;

(2) In the case of an appeal to a municipal or county court by a defendant who is convicted in a mayor's court, in accordance with Criminal Rule 46.

(1986 H 412, eff. 3–17–87)

2953.04 Proceedings to review—Repealed

(1986 H 412, eff. 3–17–87; 1953 H 1; GC 13459–3)

2953.05 Appeals—Repealed

(1986 H 412, eff. 3–17–87; 128 v 141; 1953 H 1; GC 13459–4)

2953.051 Suspension of sentence; continuance of bail—Repealed

(1986 H 412, eff. 3–17–87; 128 v 141)

2953.06 Notice of appeal served upon prosecuting attorney—Repealed

(1986 H 412, eff. 3–17–87; 1953 H 1; GC 13459–5)

2953.07 Judgments on appeal; capital cases

(A) Upon the hearing of an appeal other than an appeal from a mayor's court, the appellate court may affirm the judgment or reverse it, in whole or in part, or modify it, and order the accused to be discharged or grant a new trial. The appellate court may remand the accused for the sole purpose of correcting a sentence imposed contrary to law. If the judgment is reversed, the appellant shall recover from the appellee all court costs incurred to secure the reversal, including the cost of transcripts. In capital cases, when the judgment is affirmed and the day fixed for the execution is passed, the appellate court shall appoint a day for it, and the clerk of the appellate court shall issue a warrant under the seal of the appellate court, to the sheriff of the proper county, or the warden of the appropriate state correctional institution, commanding the sheriff or warden to carry the sentence into execution on the day so appointed. The sheriff or warden shall execute and return the warrant as in other cases, and the clerk shall record the warrant and return.

(B) As used in this section, "appellate court" means, for a case in which a sentence of death is imposed for an offense committed before January 1, 1995, both the court of appeals and the supreme court, and for a case in which a sentence of death is imposed for an offense committed on or after January 1, 1995, the supreme court.

(1995 S 4, eff. 9–21–95; 1994 H 571, eff. 10–6–94; 1986 H 412, eff. 3–17–87; 1953 H 1; GC 13459–6)

SUPREME COURT

2953.08 Appeal filed in supreme court—Repealed

(1986 H 412, eff. 3–17–87; 1953 H 1; GC 13459–7)

SUSPENSION OF SENTENCE

2953.09 Suspension of execution of sentence or judgment when appeal to supreme court filed; bail; exceptions

(A)(1) Upon filing an appeal in the supreme court, the execution of the sentence or judgment imposed in cases of felony is suspended.

(2)(a) If a notice of appeal is filed pursuant to the Rules of Appellate Procedure by a defendant who is convicted in a municipal or county court or a court of common pleas of a felony or misdemeanor under the Revised Code or an ordinance of a municipal corporation, the filing of the notice of appeal does not suspend execution of the sentence or judgment imposed. However, consistent with divisions (A)(2)(b), (B), and (C) of this section, Appellate Rule 8, and Criminal Rule 46, the municipal or county court, court of common pleas, or court of appeals may suspend execution of the sentence or judgment imposed during the pendency of the appeal, and shall determine whether that defendant is entitled to bail and the amount and nature of any bail that is required. Such bail shall at least be conditioned that the defendant will prosecute the appeal without delay and abide by the judgment and sentence of the court.

(b)(i) A court of common pleas or court of appeals may suspend the execution of a sentence of death imposed for an offense committed before January 1, 1995, only if no date for execution has been set by the supreme court, good cause is shown for the suspension, the defendant files a motion requesting the suspension, and notice has been given to the prosecuting attorney of the appropriate county.

(ii) A court of common pleas may suspend the execution of a sentence of death imposed for an offense committed on or after January 1, 1995, only if no date for execution has been set by the supreme court, good cause is shown, the defendant files a motion requesting the suspension, and notice has been given to the prosecuting attorney of the appropriate county.

(iii) A court of common pleas or court of appeals may suspend the execution of the sentence or judgment imposed for a felony in a capital case in which a sentence of death is not imposed only if no date for execution of the sentence has been set by the supreme court, good cause is shown for the suspension, the defendant files a motion requesting the suspension, and only after notice has been given to the prosecuting attorney of the appropriate county.

(B) Notwithstanding any provision of Criminal Rule 46 to the contrary, a trial judge of a court of common pleas shall not release on bail pursuant to division (A)(2)(a) of this section a defendant who is convicted of a bailable offense if the defendant is sentenced to imprisonment for life or if that offense is a violation of section 2903.01, 2903.02, 2903.03, 2903.04, 2903.11, 2905.01, 2905.02, 2905.11, 2907.02, 2907.12, 2909.02, 2911.01, 2911.02, or 2911.11 of the Revised Code.

(C) If a trial judge of a court of common pleas is prohibited by division (B) of this section from releasing on bail pursuant to division (A)(2)(a) of this section a defendant who is convicted of a bailable offense and not sentenced to imprisonment for life, the appropriate court of appeals or two judges of it, upon motion of such a defendant and for good cause shown, may release the defendant on bail in accordance with division (A)(2) of this section.

(1995 S 4, eff. 9–21–95; 1986 H 412, eff. 3–17–87; 1982 H 269, § 4, S 199; 129 v 423; 1953 H 1; GC 13459–8)

2953.10   Supreme court's power to suspend sentence

When an appeal is taken from a court of appeals to the supreme court, the supreme court has the same power and authority to suspend the execution of sentence during the pendency of the appeal and admit the defendant to bail as does the court of appeals unless another section of the Revised Code or the Rules of Practice of the Supreme Court specify a distinct bail or suspension of sentence authority.

When an appeal in a case in which a sentence of death is imposed for an offense committed on or after January 1, 1995, is taken directly from the trial court to the supreme court, the supreme court has the same power and authority to suspend the execution of the sentence during the pendency of the appeal and admit the defendant to bail as does the court of appeals for cases in which a sentence of death is imposed for an offense committed before January 1, 1995, unless another section of the Revised Code or the Rules of Practice of the Supreme Court specify a distinct bail or suspension of sentence authority.

(1995 S 4, eff. 9–21–95; 1986 H 412, eff. 3–17–87; 1953 H 1; GC 13459–8a)

2953.11   Custody of defendant under suspended sentence

In cases of conviction of felony, except for aggravated murder, where the defendant has been committed to a state correctional institution and sentence is suspended, the clerk of the court in which the entry is made suspending the sentence under the seal of the court, shall forthwith certify the suspension to the warden of the state correctional institution, who shall deliver the defendant to the sheriff of the county in which the defendant was convicted. The sheriff shall thereupon convey the defendant to the jail of the county in which he was convicted and keep him in custody unless admitted to bail pending the decision on the appeal or the termination of the suspension of sentence. If the judgment is affirmed, or the suspension of sentence terminated, the defendant shall be conveyed by the sheriff to the state correctional institution to serve the balance of his term of sentence. The supreme court in the order allowing the filing of an appeal, may provide that the defendant shall remain in the custody of the warden of the state correctional institution pending the decision of the court in such case.

(1994 H 571, eff. 10–6–94; 129 v 322, eff. 7–14–61; 1953 H 1; GC 13459–9)

2953.12   No suspension in misdemeanors unless recognizance given—Repealed

(1986 H 412, eff. 3–17–87; 1953 H 1; GC 13459–10)

REVERSAL

2953.13   Certification when judgment reversed

When a defendant has been committed to a state correctional institution and the judgment, by virtue of which the commitment was made, is reversed on appeal, and the defendant is entitled to his discharge or a new trial, the clerk of the court reversing the judgment, under the seal thereof, shall forthwith certify said reversal to the warden of the state correctional institution.

The warden, on receipt of the certificate, if a discharge of the defendant is ordered, shall forthwith discharge him from the state correctional institution.

If a new trial is ordered, the warden shall forthwith cause the defendant to be conveyed to the jail of the county in which he was convicted, and committed to the custody of the sheriff thereof.

(1994 H 571, eff. 10–6–94; 1953 H 1, eff. 10–1–53; GC 13459–11 to 13459–13)

APPEAL BY STATE

2953.14 Appeal by prosecuting authority

Whenever a court superior to the trial court renders judgment adverse to the state in a criminal action or proceeding, the state, through either the prosecuting attorney or the attorney general, may institute an appeal to reverse such judgment in the next higher court. If the conviction was for a violation of a municipal ordinance, such appeal may be brought by the village solicitor, city director of law, or other chief legal officer of the municipal corporation. Like proceedings shall be had in the higher court at the hearing of the appeal as in the review of other criminal actions or proceedings. The clerk of the court rendering the judgment sought to be reversed, on application of the prosecuting attorney, attorney general, solicitor, director of law, or other chief legal officer shall make a transcript of the docket and journal entries in the action or proceeding, and transmit it with all papers and files in the action or proceeding to the higher court.

(1986 H 412, eff. 3–17–87; 1977 H 219; 1953 H 1; GC 13459–14)

POSTCONVICTION REMEDIES

2953.21 Petition for postconviction relief

(A)(1) Any person who has been convicted of a criminal offense or adjudicated a delinquent child and who claims that there was such a denial or infringement of his rights as to render the judgment void or voidable under the Ohio Constitution or the Constitution of the United States may file a petition in the court that imposed sentence, stating the grounds for relief relied upon, and asking the court to vacate or set aside the judgment or sentence or to grant other appropriate relief. The petitioner may file a supporting affidavit and other documentary evidence in support of the claim for relief.

(2) A petition under division (A)(1) of this section shall be filed no later than one hundred eighty days after the date on which the trial transcript is filed in the court of appeals in the direct appeal of the judgment of conviction or adjudication or the date on which the trial transcript is filed in the supreme court if the direct appeal involves a sentence of death. If no appeal is taken, the petition shall be filed no later than one hundred eighty days after the expiration of the time for filing the appeal.

(3) In a petition filed under division (A) of this section, a person upon whom a sentence of death has been imposed may ask the court to render void or voidable the judgment with respect to the conviction of aggravated murder or the specification of an aggravating circumstance.

(4) A petitioner shall state in the original or amended petition filed under division (A) of this section all grounds for relief claimed by the petitioner. Except as provided in section 2953.23 of the Revised Code, any ground for relief that is not so stated in the petition is waived.

(B) The clerk of the court in which the petition is filed shall docket the petition and bring it promptly to the attention of the court. The petitioner need not serve a copy of the petition on the prosecuting attorney. The clerk of the court in which the petition is filed immediately shall forward a copy of the petition to the prosecuting attorney of that county.

(C) The court shall consider a petition that is timely filed under division (A)(2) of this section even if a direct appeal of the judgment is pending. Before granting a hearing, the court shall determine whether there are substantive grounds for relief. In making such a determination, the court shall consider, in addition to the petition and supporting affidavits, all the files and records pertaining to the proceedings against the petitioner, including, but not limited to, the indictment, the court's journal entries, the journalized records of the clerk of the court, and the court reporter's transcript. The court reporter's transcript, if ordered and certified by the court, shall be taxed as court costs. If the court dismisses the petition, it shall make and file findings of fact and conclusions of law with respect to such dismissal.

(D) Within ten days after the docketing of the petition, or within any further time that the court may fix for good cause shown, the prosecuting attorney shall respond by answer or motion. Within twenty days from the date the issues are made up, either party may move for summary judgment. The right to summary judgment shall appear on the face of the record.

(E) Unless the petition and the files and records of the case show the petitioner is not entitled to relief, the court shall proceed to a prompt hearing on the issues even if a direct appeal of the case is pending. If the court notifies the parties that it has found grounds for granting relief, either party may request an appellate court in which a direct appeal of the judgment is pending to remand the pending case to the court.

(F) At any time before the answer or motion is filed, the petitioner may amend the petition with or without leave or prejudice to the proceedings. The petitioner may amend the petition with leave of court at any time thereafter.

(G) If the court does not find grounds for granting relief, it shall make and file findings of fact and conclusions of law and shall enter judgment denying relief on the petition. If no direct appeal of the case is pending and the court finds grounds for relief or if a pending direct appeal of the case has been remanded to the court pursuant to a request made pursuant to division (E) of this section and the court finds grounds for granting relief, it shall make and file findings of fact and conclusions of law and shall enter a judgment that vacates and sets aside the judgment in question, and, in the case of a prisoner in custody, shall discharge or resentence the prisoner or grant a new trial as may appear appropriate. The court also may make supplementary orders to the relief granted, concerning such matters as rearraignment, retrial, custody, and bail. If the trial court's order granting the petition is reversed on appeal and if the direct appeal of the case has been remanded from an appellate court pursuant to a request under division (E) of this section, the appellate court reversing the order granting the petition shall notify the appellate court in which the direct appeal of the case was pending at the time of the remand of the reversal and remand of the trial court's order. Upon the reversal and remand of the trial court's order granting the petition, regardless of whether notice is sent or received, the direct appeal of the case that was remanded is reinstated.

(H) Upon the filing of a petition pursuant to this section by a prisoner in a state correctional institution who has received the death penalty, the court may stay execution of the judgment challenged by the petition.

(I) The remedy set forth in this section is the exclusive remedy by which a person may bring a collateral challenge to the validity of a conviction or sentence in a criminal case or the validity of an adjudication of a child as a delinquent child for the commission of an act that would be a criminal offense if committed by an adult or a related order of disposition.

(1995 S 4, eff. 9–21–95; 1994 H 571, eff. 10–6–94; 1986 H 412, eff. 3–17–87; 132 v H 742; 131 v S 383)

2953.22   Hearing

If a hearing is granted pursuant to section 2953.21 of the Revised Code, the petitioner shall be permitted to attend the hearing. Testimony of the prisoner or other witnesses may be offered by deposition.

If the petitioner is in a state correctional institution, he may be returned for the hearing upon the warrant of the court of common pleas of the county where the hearing is to be held. The approval of the governor on the warrant shall not be required. The warrant shall be directed to the sheriff of the county in which the hearing is to be held. When a copy of the warrant is presented to the warden or other head of a state correctional institution, he shall deliver the convict to the sheriff, who shall convey him to the county. For removing and returning the convict, the sheriff shall receive the fees allowed for conveying convicts to the correctional institution.

(1994 H 571, eff. 10–6–94; 132 v H 742, eff. 12–9–67)

2953.23 Second or successive petitions; order; appeal

(A) Whether a hearing is or is not held on a petition filed pursuant to section 2953.21 of the Revised Code, a court may not entertain a petition filed after the expiration of the period prescribed in division (A) of that section or a second petition or successive petitions for similar relief on behalf of a petitioner unless both of the following apply:

(1) Either of the following applies:

(a) The petitioner shows that the petitioner was unavoidably prevented from discovery of the facts upon which the petitioner must rely to present the claim for relief.

(b) Subsequent to the period prescribed in division (A)(2) of section 2953.21 of the Revised Code or to the filing of an earlier petition, the United States Supreme Court recognized a new federal or state right that applies retroactively to persons in the petitioner's situation, and the petition asserts a claim based on that right.

(2) The petitioner shows by clear and convincing evidence that, but for constitutional error at trial, no reasonable factfinder would have found the petitioner guilty of the offense of which the petitioner was convicted or, if the claim challenges a sentence of death that, but for constitutional error at the sentencing hearing, no reasonable factfinder would have found the petitioner eligible for the death sentence.

(B) An order awarding or denying relief sought in a petition filed pursuant to section 2953.21 of the Revised Code is a final judgment and may be appealed pursuant to Chapter 2953. of the Revised Code.

(1995 S 4, eff. 9–21–95; 132 v H 742, eff. 12–9–67)

2953.24 Court appointed counsel; compensation—Repealed

(1975 H 164, eff. 1–13–76; 132 v H 742)

SEALING OF RECORDS

2953.31 Definitions

As used in sections 2953.31 to 2953.36 of the Revised Code:

(A) "First offender" means anyone who has been convicted of an offense in this state or any other jurisdiction, and who previously or subsequently has not been convicted of the same or a different offense in this state or any other jurisdiction. When two or more convictions result from or are connected with the same act, or result from offenses committed at the same time, they shall be counted as one conviction.

For purposes of, and except as otherwise provided in, this division, a conviction for a minor misdemeanor, a conviction for a violation of any section in Chapter 4511., 4513., or 4549. of the Revised Code, or a conviction for a violation of a municipal ordinance that is substantially similar to any section in those chapters, is not a previous or subsequent conviction. A conviction for a violation of section 4511.19, 4511.192, 4511.251, 4549.02, 4549.021, 4549.03, 4549.042, or 4549.07, or sections 4549.41 to 4549.46 of the Revised Code, or a conviction for a violation of a municipal ordinance that is substantially similar to any of those sections, shall be considered a previous or subsequent conviction.

(B) "Prosecutor" means the county prosecuting attorney, city director of law, village solicitor, or similar chief legal officer, who has the authority to prosecute a criminal case in the court in which the case is filed.

(C) "Bail forfeiture" means the forfeiture of bail by a defendant who is arrested for the commission of a misdemeanor, other than a defendant in a traffic case as defined in Traffic Rule 2, if the forfeiture is pursuant to an agreement with the court and prosecutor in the case.

(1990 S 382, eff. 12–31–90; 1989 S 49; 1988 H 175; 1984 H 227; 1973 S 5)

2953.32 Sealing of record of first offense; application; hearing; fee; re–examination of sealed record

(A)(1) Except as provided in section 2953.61 of the Revised Code, a first offender may apply to the sentencing court if convicted in this state, or to a court of common pleas if convicted in another state or in a federal court, for the sealing of the record of his conviction, at the expiration of three years after his final discharge if convicted of a felony, or at the expiration of one year after his final discharge if convicted of a misdemeanor.

(2) Any person who has been arrested for any misdemeanor offense and who has effected a bail forfeiture may apply to the court in which the misdemeanor criminal case was pending when bail was forfeited for the sealing of his record in the case. Except as provided in section 2953.61 of the Revised Code, the application may be filed at any time after the expiration of one year from the date on which the bail forfeiture was entered upon the minutes of the court or the journal, whichever entry occurs first.

(B) Upon the filing of an application under this section, the court shall set a date for a hearing and shall notify the prosecutor for the case of the hearing on the application. The prosecutor may object to the granting of the application by filing an objection with the court prior to the date set for the hearing. The prosecutor shall specify in the objection the reasons he believes justify a denial of the application. The court shall direct its regular probation officer, a state probation officer, or the department of probation of the county in which the applicant resides to make inquiries and written reports as the court requires concerning the applicant.

(C)(1) The court shall do each of the following:

(a) Determine whether the applicant is a first offender or whether the forfeiture of bail was agreed to by the applicant and the prosecutor in the case;

(b) Determine whether criminal proceedings are pending against the applicant;

(c) If the applicant is a first offender who applies pursuant to division (A)(1) of this section, determine whether the applicant has been rehabilitated to the satisfaction of the court;

(d) If the prosecutor has filed an objection in accordance with division (B) of this section, consider the reasons against granting the application specified by the prosecutor in the objection;

(e) Weigh the interests of the applicant in having the records pertaining to his conviction sealed against the legitimate needs, if any, of the government to maintain those records.

(2) If the court determines, after complying with division (C)(1) of this section, that the applicant is a first offender or the subject of a bail forfeiture, that no criminal proceeding is pending against him, and that the interests of the applicant in having the records pertaining to his conviction or bail forfeiture sealed are not outweighed by any legitimate governmental needs to maintain such records, and that the rehabilitation of an applicant who is a first offender applying pursuant to division (A)(1) of this section has been attained to the satisfaction of the court, the court, except as provided in division (G) of this section, shall order all official records pertaining to the case sealed and, except as provided in division (F) of this section, all index references to the case deleted and, in the case of bail forfeitures, shall dismiss the charges in the case. The proceedings in the case shall be considered not to have occurred and the conviction or bail forfeiture of the person who is the subject of the proceedings shall be sealed, except that upon conviction of a subsequent offense, the sealed record of prior conviction or bail forfeiture may be considered by the court in determining the sentence or other appropriate disposition, including the relief provided for in sections 2953.31 to 2953.33 of the Revised Code.

(3) Upon the filing of an application under this section, the applicant, unless he is indigent, shall pay a fee of fifty dollars. The court shall pay thirty dollars of the fee into the state treasury. It shall pay twenty dollars of the fee into the county general revenue fund if the sealed conviction or bail forfeiture was pursuant to a state statute, or into the general revenue fund of the municipal corporation involved if the sealed conviction or bail forfeiture was pursuant to a municipal ordinance.

(D) Inspection of the sealed records included in the order may be made only by the following persons or for the following purposes:

(1) By any law enforcement officer or any prosecutor, or his assistants, to determine whether the nature and character of the offense with which a person is to be charged would be affected by virtue of the person's previously having been convicted of a crime;

(2) By the parole or probation officer of the person who is the subject of the records, for the exclusive use of the officer in supervising the person while he is on parole or probation and in making inquiries and written reports as requested by the court or adult parole authority;

(3) Upon application by the person who is the subject of the records, by the persons named in his application;

(4) By a law enforcement officer who was involved in the case, for use in the officer's defense of a civil action arising out of the officer's involvement in that case;

(5) By any prosecuting attorney or his assistants to determine a defendant's eligibility to enter a pre-trial diversion program established pursuant to section 2935.36 of the Revised Code;

(6) By any law enforcement agency or any authorized employee of a law enforcement agency or by the department of rehabilitation and correction as part of a background investigation of a person who applies for employment with the agency as a law enforcement officer or with the department as a corrections officer;

(7) By any law enforcement agency or any authorized employee of a law enforcement agency, for the purposes set forth in, and in the manner provided in, section 2953.321 of the Revised Code;

(8) By the bureau of criminal identification and investigation or any authorized employee of the bureau for the purpose of providing information to a board or person pursuant to division (F) of section 109.57 of the Revised Code.

When the nature and character of the offense with which a person is to be charged would be affected by the information, it may be used for the purpose of charging the person with an offense.

(E) In any criminal proceeding, proof of any otherwise admissible prior conviction may be introduced and proved, notwithstanding the fact that for any such prior conviction an order of sealing previously was issued pursuant to sections 2953.31 to 2953.36 of the Revised Code.

(F) The person or governmental agency, office, or department that maintains sealed records pertaining to convictions or bail forfeitures that have been sealed pursuant to this section may maintain a manual or computerized index to the sealed records. The index shall contain only the name of, and alphanumeric identifiers that relate to, the persons who are the subject of the sealed records, the word "sealed," and the name of the person, agency, office, or department that has custody of the sealed records, and shall not contain the name of the crime committed. The index shall be made available by the person who has custody of the sealed records only for the purposes set forth in divisions (C), (D), and (E) of this section.

(G) Notwithstanding any provision of this section or section 2953.33 of the Revised Code that requires otherwise, a board of education of a city, local, exempted village, or joint vocational school district that maintains records of an individual who has been permanently excluded under sections 3301.121 and 3313.662 of the Revised Code is permitted to maintain records regarding a conviction that was used as the basis for the individual's permanent exclusion, regardless of a court order to seal the record. An order issued under this section to seal the record of a conviction does not revoke the adjudication order of the superintendent of public instruction to permanently exclude the individual who is the subject of the sealing order. An order issued under this section to seal the record of a conviction of an individual may be presented to a district superintendent as evidence to support the contention that the superintendent should recommend that the permanent exclusion of the individual who is the subject of the sealing order be revoked. Except as otherwise authorized by this division and sections 3301.121 and 3313.662 of the Revised Code, any school employee in possession of or having access to the sealed conviction records of an individual that were the basis of a permanent exclusion of the individual is subject to section 2953.35 of the Revised Code.

(1994 H 571, eff. 10–6–94; 1992 H 154, eff. 7–31–92; 1989 S 140; 1988 H 175; 1987 H 8; 1984 H 227; 1979 H 105; 1977 H 219; 1973 S 5)

2953.321　Confidentiality of investigatory work product; violations; exceptions

(A) As used in this section, "investigatory work product" means any records or reports of a law enforcement officer or agency that are excepted from the definition of "official records" contained in section 2953.51 of the Revised Code and that pertain to a case the records of which have been ordered sealed pursuant to division (C)(2) of section 2953.32 of the Revised Code.

(B) Upon the issuance of an order by a court pursuant to division (C)(2) of section 2953.32 of the Revised Code directing that all official records pertaining to a case be sealed:

(1) Every law enforcement officer who possesses investigatory work product immediately shall deliver that work product to his employing law enforcement agency.

(2) Except as provided in division (B)(3) of this section, every law enforcement agency that possesses investigatory work product shall close that work product to all persons who are not directly employed by the law enforcement agency and shall treat that work product, in relation to all persons other than those who are directly employed by the law enforcement agency, as if it did not exist and never had existed.

(3) A law enforcement agency that possesses investigatory work product may permit another law enforcement agency to use that work product in the investigation of another offense if the facts incident to the offense being investigated by the other law enforcement agency and the facts incident to an offense that is the subject of the case are reasonably similar. The agency that permits the use of investigatory work product may provide the other agency with the name of the person who is the subject of the case if it believes that the name of the person is necessary to the conduct of the investigation by the other agency.

(C)(1) Except as provided in division (B)(3) of this section, no law enforcement officer or other person employed by a law enforcement agency shall knowingly release, disseminate, or otherwise make the investigatory work product or any information contained in that work product available to, or discuss any information contained in it with, any person not employed by the employing law enforcement agency.

(2) No law enforcement agency, or person employed by a law enforcement agency, that receives investigatory work product pursuant to division (B)(3) of this section shall use that work product for any purpose other than the investigation of the offense for which it was obtained from the other law enforcement agency, or disclose the name of the person who is the subject of the work product except when necessary for the conduct of the investigation of the offense, or the prosecution of the person for committing the offense, for which it was obtained from the other law enforcement agency.

(D) Whoever violates division (C)(1) or (2) of this section is guilty of divulging confidential investigatory work product, a misdemeanor of the fourth degree.

(1988 H 175, eff. 6–29–88)

2953.33　Restoration of rights upon sealing of record

(A) Except as provided in division (G) of section 2953.32 of the Revised Code, an order to seal the record of a person's conviction restores the person who is the subject of the order to all rights and privileges not otherwise restored by termination of sentence or probation or by final release on parole.

(B) In any application for employment, license, or other right or privilege, any appearance as a witness, or any other inquiry, except as provided in division (E) of section 2953.32 of the Revised Code, a person may be questioned only with respect to convictions not sealed, bail forfeitures not expunged under section 2953.42 of the Revised Code as it existed prior to June

29, 1988, and bail forfeitures not sealed, unless the question bears a direct and substantial relationship to the position for which the person is being considered.

(1992 H 154, eff. 7–31–92; 1988 H 175; 1979 H 105; 1973 S 5)

2953.34   Other remedies not precluded

Nothing in sections 2953.31 to 2953.33 of the Revised Code precludes a first offender from taking an appeal or seeking any relief from his conviction or from relying on it in lieu of any subsequent prosecution for the same offense.

(1973 S 5, eff. 1–1–74)

2953.35   Divulging sealed records prohibited

(A) Except as authorized by divisions (D), (E), and (F) of section 2953.32 of the Revised Code, any officer or employee of the state, or a political subdivision of the state, who releases or otherwise disseminates or makes available for any purpose involving employment, bonding, or licensing in connection with any business, trade, or profession to any person, or to any department, agency, or other instrumentality of the state, or any political subdivision of the state, any information or other data concerning any arrest, complaint, indictment, trial, hearing, adjudication, conviction, or correctional supervision the records with respect to which he had knowledge of were sealed by an existing order issued pursuant to sections 2953.31 to 2953.36 of the Revised Code, or were expunged by an order issued pursuant to section 2953.42 of the Revised Code as it existed prior to the effective date of this amendment, is guilty of divulging confidential information, a misdemeanor of the fourth degree.

(B) Any person who, in violation of section 2953.32 of the Revised Code, uses, disseminates, or otherwise makes available any index prepared pursuant to division (F) of section 2953.32 of the Revised Code is guilty of a misdemeanor of the fourth degree.

(1988 H 175, eff. 6–29–88; 1979 H 105; 1975 H 1; 1973 S 5)

2953.36   Convictions precluding sealing

Sections 2953.31 to 2953.35 of the Revised Code do not apply to convictions when the offender is not eligible for probation, convictions under section 2907.02, 2907.03, 2907.04, 2907.05, 2907.06, 2907.12, 2907.321, 2907.322, or 2907.323 or Chapter 4507., 4511., or 4549. of the Revised Code, or bail forfeitures in a traffic case as defined in Traffic Rule 2.

(1994 H 335, eff. 12–9–94; 1988 H 175, eff. 6–29–88; 1973 S 5)

EXPUNGEMENT OF RECORDS

2953.41   Definitions—Repealed

(1988 H 175, eff. 6–29–88; 1978 S 192)

2953.42   Expungement of record of agreed bail forfeiture—Repealed

(1988 H 175, eff. 6–29–88; 1978 S 192)

2953.43   Effects of expungement; release of information on offense—Repealed

(1988 H 175, eff. 6–29–88; 1978 S 192)

SEALING OF RECORDS—FURTHER PROVISIONS

2953.51   Definitions

As used in sections 2953.51 to 2953.55 of the Revised Code:

(A) "No bill" means a report by the foreman or deputy foreman of a grand jury that an indictment is not found by the grand jury against a person who has been held to answer before the grand jury for the commission of an offense.

(B) "Prosecutor" has the same meaning as in section 2953.31 of the Revised Code.

(C) "Court" means the court in which a case is pending at the time a finding of not guilty in the case or a dismissal of the complaint, indictment, or information in the case is entered on the minutes or journal of the court, or the court to which the foreman or deputy foreman of a grand jury reports, pursuant to section 2939.23 of the Revised Code, that the grand jury has returned a no bill.

(D) "Official records" means all records that are possessed by any public office or agency that relate to a criminal case, including, but not limited to: the notation to the case in the criminal docket; all subpoenaes [sic] issued in the case; all papers and documents filed by the defendant or the prosecutor in the case; all records of all testimony and evidence presented in all proceedings in the case; all court files, papers, documents, folders, entries, affidavits, or writs that pertain to the case; all computer, microfilm, microfiche, or microdot records, indices, or references to the case; all index references to the case; all fingerprints and photographs; all records and investigative reports pertaining to the case that are possessed by any law enforcement officer or agency, except that any records or reports that are the specific investigatory work product of a law enforcement officer or agency are not and shall not be considered to be official records when they are in the possession of that officer or agency; and all investigative records and reports other than those possessed by a law enforcement officer or agency pertaining to the case.

(1984 H 227, eff. 9–26–84)

2953.52 Application to have records sealed; grounds; order

(A)(1) Any person, who is found not guilty of an offense by a jury or a court or who is the defendant named in a dismissed complaint, indictment, or information, may apply to the court for an order to seal his official records in the case. Except as provided in section 2953.61 of the Revised Code, the application may be filed at any time after the finding of not guilty or the dismissal of the complaint, indictment, or information is entered upon the minutes of the court or the journal, whichever entry occurs first.

(2) Any person, against whom a no bill is entered by a grand jury, may apply to the court for an order to seal his official records in the case. Except as provided in section 2953.61 of the Revised Code, the application may be filed at any time after the expiration of two years after the date on which the foreman or deputy foreman of the grand jury reports to the court that the grand jury has reported a no bill.

(B)(1) Upon the filing of an application pursuant to division (A) of this section, the court shall set a date for a hearing and shall notify the prosecutor in the case of the hearing on the application. The prosecutor may object to the granting of the application by filing an objection with the court prior to the date set for the hearing. The prosecutor shall specify in the objection the reasons he believes justify a denial of the application.

(2) The court shall do each of the following:

(a) Determine whether the person was found not guilty in the case, or the complaint, indictment, or information in the case was dismissed, or a no bill was returned in the case and a period of two years or a longer period as required by section 2953.61 of the Revised Code has expired from the date of the report to the court of that no bill by the foreman or deputy foreman of the grand jury;

(b) Determine whether criminal proceedings are pending against the person;

(c) If the prosecutor has filed an objection in accordance with division (B)(1) of this section, consider the reasons against granting the application specified by the prosecutor in the objection;

(d) Weigh the interests of the person in having the official records pertaining to the case sealed against the legitimate needs, if any, of the government to maintain those records.

(3) If the court determines, after complying with division (B)(2) of this section, that the person was found not guilty in the case, that the complaint, indictment, or information in the case was dismissed, or that a no bill was returned in the case and that the appropriate period of time has expired from the date of the report to the court of the no bill by the foreman or deputy foreman of the grand jury; that no criminal proceedings are pending against the person; and the interests of the person in having the records pertaining to the case sealed are

not outweighed by any legitimate governmental needs to maintain such records, the court shall issue an order directing that all official records pertaining to the case be sealed and that, except as provided in section 2953.53 of the Revised Code, the proceedings in the case be deemed not to have occurred.

(1988 H 175, eff. 6–29–88; 1984 H 227)

2953.53 Notices of order to seal; offices and agencies affected; examination of sealed record

(A) The court shall send notice of any order to seal official records issued pursuant to section 2953.52 of the Revised Code to any public office or agency that the court knows or has reason to believe may have any record of the case, whether or not it is an official record, that is the subject of the order. The notice shall be sent by certified mail, return receipt requested.

(B) A person whose official records have been sealed pursuant to an order issued pursuant to section 2953.52 of the Revised Code may present a copy of that order and a written request to comply with it, to a public office or agency that has a record of the case that is the subject of the order.

(C) An order to seal official records issued pursuant to section 2953.52 of the Revised Code applies to every public office or agency that has a record of the case that is the subject of the order, regardless of whether it receives notice of the hearing on the application for the order to seal the official records or receives a copy of the order to seal the official records pursuant to division (A) or (B) of this section.

(D) Upon receiving a copy of an order to seal official records pursuant to division (A) or (B) of this section or upon otherwise becoming aware of an applicable order to seal official records issued pursuant to section 2953.52 of the Revised Code, a public office or agency shall comply with the order and, if applicable, with the provisions of section 2953.54 of the Revised Code, except that it may maintain a record of the case that is the subject of the order if the record is maintained for the purpose of compiling statistical data only and does not contain any reference to the person who is the subject of the case and the order.

A public office or agency also may maintain an index of sealed official records, in a form similar to that for sealed records of conviction as set forth in division (F) of section 2953.32 of the Revised Code, access to which may not be afforded to any person other than the person who has custody of the sealed official records. The sealed official records to which such an index pertains shall not be available to any person, except that the official records of a case that have been sealed may be made available to the following persons for the following purposes:

(1) To the person who is the subject of the records upon written application, and to any other person named in the application, for any purpose;

(2) To a law enforcement officer who was involved in the case, for use in the officer's defense of a civil action arising out of the officer's involvement in that case;

(3) To a prosecuting attorney or his assistants to determine a defendant's eligibility to enter a pre-trial diversion program established pursuant to section 2935.36 of the Revised Code.

(1988 H 175, eff. 6–29–88; 1987 H 8; 1984 H 227)

2953.54 Exceptions; offense of divulging confidential information

(A) Upon the issuance of an order by a court under division (B) of section 2953.52 of the Revised Code directing that all official records pertaining to a case be sealed and that the proceedings in the case be deemed not to have occurred:

(1) Every law enforcement officer possessing records or reports pertaining to the case that are his specific investigatory work product and that are excepted from the definition of "official records" contained in section 2953.51 of the Revised Code shall immediately deliver the records and reports to his employing law enforcement agency. Except as provided in division (A)(3) of this section, no such officer shall knowingly release, disseminate, or otherwise make the records and reports or any information contained in them available to, or discuss any information contained in them with, any person not employed by the officer's employing law enforcement agency.

(2) Every law enforcement agency that possesses records or reports pertaining to the case that are its specific investigatory work product and that are excepted from the definition of "official records" contained in section 2953.51 of the Revised Code, or that are the specific investigatory work product of a law enforcement officer it employs and that were delivered to it under division (A)(1) of this section shall, except as provided in division (A)(3) of this section, close the records and reports to all persons who are not directly employed by the law enforcement agency and shall, except as provided in division (A)(3) of this section, treat the records and reports, in relation to all persons other than those who are directly employed by the law enforcement agency, as if they did not exist and had never existed. Except as provided in division (A)(3) of this section, no person who is employed by the law enforcement agency shall knowingly release, disseminate, or otherwise make the records and reports in the possession of the employing law enforcement agency or any information contained in them available to, or discuss any information contained in them with, any person not employed by the employing law enforcement agency.

(3) A law enforcement agency that possesses records or reports pertaining to the case that are its specific investigatory work product and that are excepted from the definition of "official records" contained in division (D) of section 2953.51 of the Revised Code, or that are the specific investigatory work product of a law enforcement officer it employs and that were delivered to it under division (A)(1) of this section may permit another law enforcement agency to use the records or reports in the investigation of another offense, if the facts incident to the offense being investigated by the other law enforcement agency and the facts incident to an offense that is the subject of the case are reasonably similar. The agency that provides the records and reports may provide the other agency with the name of the person who is the subject of the case, if it believes that the name of the person is necessary to the conduct of the investigation by the other agency.

No law enforcement agency, or person employed by a law enforcement agency, that receives from another law enforcement agency records or reports pertaining to a case the records of which have been ordered sealed pursuant to division (B) of section 2953.52 of the Revised Code shall use the records and reports for any purpose other than the investigation of the offense for which they were obtained from the other law enforcement agency, or disclose the name of the person who is the subject of the records or reports except when necessary for the conduct of the investigation of the offense, or the prosecution of the person for committing the offense, for which they were obtained from the other law enforcement agency.

(B) Whoever violates division (A)(1), (2), or (3) of this section is guilty of divulging confidential information, a misdemeanor of the fourth degree.

(1984 H 227, eff. 9–26–84)

2953.55 Effects of order; offense

(A) In any application for employment, license, or any other right or privilege, any appearance as a witness, or any other inquiry, a person may not be questioned with respect to any record that has been sealed pursuant to section 2953.52 of the Revised Code. If an inquiry is made in violation of this section, the person whose official record was sealed may respond as if the arrest underlying the case to which the sealed official records pertain and all other proceedings in that case did not occur, and the person whose official record was sealed shall not be subject to any adverse action because of the arrest, the proceedings, or his response.

(B) An officer or employee of the state or any of its political subdivisions who knowingly releases, disseminates, or makes available for any purpose involving employment, bonding, licensing, or education to any person or to any department, agency, or other instrumentality of the state, or of any of its political subdivisions, any information or other data concerning any arrest, complaint, indictment, information, trial, adjudication, or correctional supervision, the records of which have been sealed pursuant to section 2953.52 of the Revised Code, is guilty of divulging confidential information, a misdemeanor of the fourth degree.

(1984 H 227, eff. 9–26–84)

2953.61   Effect of multiple offenses with different dispositions

When a person is charged with two or more offenses as a result of or in connection with the same act and at least one of the charges has a final disposition that is different than the final disposition of the other charges, the person may not apply to the court for the sealing of his record in any of the cases until such time as he would be able to apply to the court and have all of the records in all of the cases pertaining to those charges sealed pursuant to divisions (A)(1) and (2) of section 2953.32 and divisions (A)(1) and (2) of section 2953.52 of the Revised Code.

(1988 H 175, eff. 6–29–88)

CHAPTER 2961

DISFRANCHISED CONVICTS; HABITUAL CRIMINALS

2961.01 Civil rights of convicted felons

A person convicted of a felony under the laws of this or any other state or the United States, unless his conviction is reversed or annulled, is incompetent to be an elector or juror, or to hold an office of honor, trust, or profit. When any such person is granted probation, parole, or a conditional pardon, he is competent to be an elector during the period of probation or parole or until the conditions of his pardon have been performed or have transpired, and thereafter following his final discharge. The full pardon of a convict restores the rights and privileges so forfeited under this section, but a pardon shall not release a convict from the costs of his conviction in this state, unless so specified.

(1972 H 511, eff. 1–1–74; 1953 H 1; GC 13458–1)

2961.02 Convict of another state—Repealed

(1972 H 511, eff. 1–1–74; 1953 H 1; GC 13458–2)

2961.03 Revocation of license in certain cases

Whenever a person engaged in business as a secondhand dealer, junk dealer, transient dealer, peddler, itinerant vendor, or pawnbroker, under a license issued under any law of this state or under any ordinance of a municipal corporation, is convicted and sentenced for knowingly and fraudulently buying, receiving, or concealing goods or property which has been stolen, taken by robbers, embezzled, or obtained by false pretenses, such judgment of conviction, in addition to the other penalties provided by law for such offense, acts as a cancellation and revocation of such license to conduct such business, and the court in which such conviction was had shall forthwith certify to the authority which issued such license, the fact of such conviction. A person who has been so convicted and whose license has been canceled or revoked, shall not again be licensed to engage in such business, or any of the businesses enumerated in this section, unless such person is pardoned by the governor.

(1953 H 1, eff. 10–1–53; GC 13458–3)

2961.11 Habitual criminal—Repealed

(1972 H 511, eff. 1–1–74; 132 v S 86; 1953 H 1; GC 13744–1)

2961.12 Habitual criminal, life imprisonment—Repealed

(1972 H 511, eff. 1–1–74; 1953 H 1; GC 13744–2)

2961.13 Indictment; pleas; procedure—Repealed

(1972 H 511, eff. 1–1–74; 1953 H 1; GC 13744–3)

EXTRADITION

DEFINITIONS

DEFINITIONS

2963.01   Definitions

As used in sections 2963.01 to 2963.27, inclusive, of the Revised Code:

(A) "Governor" includes any person performing the functions of governor by authority of the law of this state.

(B) "Executive authority" includes the governor, and any person performing the functions of governor in a state other than this state.

(C) "State," referring to a state other than this state, includes any state or territory, organized or unorganized, of the United States.

(1953 H 1, eff. 10–1–53; GC 109–1)

FUGITIVES FROM OTHER STATES

2963.02   Governor to deliver fugitives from justice

Subject to sections 2963.01 to 2963.27, inclusive, of the Revised Code, the constitution of the United States and all acts of congress enacted in pursuance thereof, the governor shall have arrested and delivered to the executive authority of any other state of the United States, any person charged in that state with treason, felony, or other crime, who has fled from justice and is found in this state.

(1953 H 1, eff. 10–1–53; GC 109–2)

2963.03   Demand for extradition

No demand for the extradition of a person charged with crime in another state shall be recognized by the governor unless the demand is in writing alleging, except in cases arising under section 2963.06 of the Revised Code, that the accused was present in the demanding state at the time of the commission of the alleged crime, and that thereafter he fled from the state, and unless the demand is accompanied by:

(A) A copy of an indictment found or by information supported by affidavit in the state having jurisdiction of the crime, or by a copy of an affidavit made before a magistrate there, together with a copy of any warrant which was issued thereupon;

(B) A copy of a judgment of conviction or of a sentence imposed in execution thereof, together with a statement by the executive authority of the demanding state that the person claimed has escaped from confinement or has broken the terms of his bail, probation, or parole. The indictment, information, or affidavit made before the magistrate must substantially charge the person demanded with having committed a crime under the law of that state. The copy of indictment, information, affidavit, judgment of conviction, or sentence must be authenticated by the executive authority making the demand.

(1953 H 1, eff. 10–1–53; GC 109–3)

2963.04   Demand investigated by order of governor

When a demand is made upon the governor of this state by the executive authority of another state for the surrender of a person charged with crime, the governor may call upon the attorney general or any prosecuting officer in this state to investigate or assist in investigating the demand, and to report to him the situation and circumstances of the person so demanded, and whether such person ought to be surrendered.

(1953 H 1, eff. 10–1–53; GC 109–4)

2963.05   Extradition upon agreement to return prisoner

When it is desired to have returned to this state a person charged in this state with a crime, and such person is imprisoned or is held under criminal proceedings then pending against him in another state, the governor may agree with the executive authority of such other state for the extradition of such person before the conclusion of such proceedings or his term of sentence in such other state, upon condition that such person be returned to such other state at the expense of this state as soon as the prosecution in this state is terminated.

The governor may also surrender, on demand of the executive authority of any other state, any person in this state who is charged under section 2963.21 of the Revised Code with having violated the laws of the state whose executive authority is making the demand, even though such person left the demanding state involuntarily. This section shall be carried out by conforming to the procedure outlined in sections 2963.01 to 2963.27, inclusive, of the Revised Code.

(1953 H 1, eff. 10–1–53; GC 109–5)

2963.06   Governor may surrender anyone charged with crime against another state

The governor may surrender, on demand of the executive authority of any other state, any person in this state charged in such other state in the manner provided in section 2963.03 of the Revised Code with committing an act in this state, or in a third state, intentionally resulting in a crime in the state whose executive authority is making the demand, and sections 2963.01 to 2963.27, inclusive, of the Revised Code, apply to such cases, even though the accused was not in that state at the time of the commission of the crime, and has not fled therefrom.

(1953 H 1, eff. 10–1–53; GC 109–6)

2963.07   Warrant for arrest

If the governor decides that a demand for extradition should be complied with, he shall sign a warrant of arrest, which shall be sealed with the state seal and be directed to any peace officer or other person whom the governor finds fit to entrust with the execution thereof.   The warrant must substantially recite the facts necessary to the validity of its issuance.

Such warrant shall authorize the peace officer or other person to whom directed to arrest the accused at any time and any place where he may be found within the state and to command the aid of all peace officers or other persons in the execution of the warrant, and to deliver the accused, subject to sections 2963.01 to 2963.27, inclusive, of the Revised Code, to the authorized agent of the demanding state.

(1953 H 1, eff. 10–1–53; GC 109–7, 109–8)

2963.08   Authority to arrest accused

Every peace officer or other person empowered to make an arrest under section 2963.07 of the Revised Code has the same authority, in arresting the accused, to command assistance therein as peace officers have in the execution of any criminal process directed to them, with like penalties against those who refuse their assistance.

(1953 H 1, eff. 10–1–53; GC 109–9)

2963.09   Mandatory hearing

No person arrested upon a warrant under section 2963.07 of the Revised Code shall be delivered to the agent whom the executive authority demanding him appointed to receive him unless such person is first taken forthwith before a judge of a court of record in this state, who shall inform him of the demand made for his surrender and of the crime with which he is charged, and that he has the right to demand and procure legal counsel.   If the prisoner or his counsel desires to test the legality of his arrest, the judge shall fix a reasonable time to be allowed him within which to apply for a writ of habeas corpus.   When such writ is applied for, notice thereof and of the time and place of hearing thereon, shall be given to the prosecuting officer of the county in which the arrest is made and in which the accused is in custody, and to the said agent of the demanding state.

Whoever violates this section by willfully delivering a person arrested upon the governor's warrant to an agent for extradition of the demanding state before a hearing, shall be fined not more than one thousand dollars or imprisoned not more than six months, or both.

(1953 H 1, eff. 10–1–53; GC 109–10)

2963.10   Prisoner may be confined while enroute

A peace officer or other person executing a warrant of arrest issued by the governor, or an agent of the demanding state to whom the prisoner has been delivered, may, when necessary, confine the prisoner in the jail of any county or city through which he may pass.

The officer or agent of a demanding state to whom a prisoner has been delivered following extradition proceedings in another state, or to whom a prisoner has been delivered after waiving extradition in such other state, and who is passing through this state with such a prisoner for the purpose of immediately returning such prisoner to the demanding state may, when necessary, confine the prisoner in the jail of any county or city through which he may pass.   Such officer or agent shall produce and show to the keeper of such jail his warrant and other written evidence of the fact that he is actually transporting such prisoner to the demanding state after a requisition by the executive authority of such demanding state.   Such prisoner may not demand a new requisition while in this state.

The keeper of such jail must receive and safely keep a prisoner delivered to him under this section, until the officer or agent having charge of him is ready to proceed on his route. Such officer or agent is chargeable with the expense of such keeping.

(1953 H 1, eff. 10–1–53; GC 109–12)

2963.11 Fugitive from justice

When, on the oath of a credible person before any judge or magistrate of this state, any person within this state is charged with the commission of any crime in any other state and with having fled from justice, or with having been convicted of a crime in that state and having escaped from confinement, or having broken the terms of his bail, probation, or parole, or whenever complaint has been made before any judge or magistrate in this state setting forth on the affidavit of any credible person in another state that a crime has been committed in such other state and that the accused has been charged in such state with the commission of the crime, and, has fled from justice, or with having been convicted of a crime in that state and having escaped from confinement, or having broken the terms of his bail, probation, or parole, and is believed to be in this state, the judge or magistrate shall issue a warrant directed to any peace officer, commanding him to apprehend the person named therein, wherever he may be found in this state, and to bring him before the same or any other judge, magistrate, or court which may be available in or convenient of access to the place where the arrest may be made, to answer the charge or complaint and affidavit, and a certified copy of the sworn charge or complaint and affidavit upon which the warrant is issued shall be attached to the warrant.

This section does not apply to cases arising under section 2963.06 of the Revised Code.

(1953 H 1, eff. 10–1–53; GC 109–13)

2963.12 Arrest without warrant

An arrest may be made by any peace officer or a private person without a warrant upon reasonable information that the accused stands charged in the courts of any state with a crime punishable by death or imprisonment for a term exceeding one year. When so arrested the accused must be taken before a judge or magistrate with all practicable speed and complaint must be made against him under oath setting forth the ground for the arrest, as provided in section 2963.11 of the Revised Code. Thereafter his answer shall be heard as if he had been arrested on a warrant.

(1953 H 1, eff. 10–1–53; GC 109–14)

2963.13 Fugitive to be confined pending requisition

If from the examination before the judge or magistrate it appears that the person held under section 2963.11 or 2963.12 of the Revised Code is the person charged with having committed the crime alleged and that he has fled from justice, the judge or magistrate must, by a warrant reciting the accusation, commit him to the county jail for such a time, not to exceed thirty days and specified in the warrant, as will enable the arrest of the accused to be made under a warrant of the governor on a requisition of the executive authority of the state having jurisdiction of the offense, unless the accused furnishes bail or until he is legally discharged.

(1953 H 1, eff. 10–1–53; GC 109–15)

2963.14 Bail

Unless the offense with which the prisoner is charged under sections 2963.11 and 2963.12 of the Revised Code is shown to be an offense punishable by death or life imprisonment under the laws of the state in which it was committed, a judge or magistrate in this state may admit the person arrested to bail by bond, with sufficient sureties and in such sum as he deems proper, conditioned for his appearance before said judge or magistrate at a time specified in such bond, and for his surrender, to be arrested upon the warrant of the governor of this state.

(1953 H 1, eff. 10–1–53; GC 109–16)

2963.15   Release of accused

If the accused mentioned in section 2963.14 of the Revised Code is not arrested under warrant of the governor by the expiration of the time specified in the warrant or bond, a judge or magistrate may discharge him or may recommit him for a further period not to exceed sixty days, or a judge or magistrate may again take bail for his appearance and surrender, under said section, but within a period not to exceed sixty days after the date of such new bond.

(1953 H 1, eff. 10–1–53; GC 109–17)

2963.16   Forfeited recognizance

If a prisoner admitted to bail under section 2963.14 of the Revised Code fails to appear and surrender himself according to the conditions of his bond, the judge or magistrate, by proper order, shall declare the bond forfeited and order his immediate arrest without warrant if he is within this state.   Recovery may be had on such bond in the name of the state as in the case of other bonds given by the accused in criminal proceedings.

(1953 H 1, eff. 10–1–53; GC 109–18)

2963.17   Governor may hold fugitive indicted in this state or surrender him

If a criminal prosecution has been instituted under the laws of this state against a person sought by another state under sections 2963.01 to 2963.27, inclusive, of the Revised Code, and is still pending, the governor may surrender him on demand of the executive authority of another state or hold him until he has been tried and discharged or convicted and punished in this state.

(1953 H 1, eff. 10–1–53; GC 109–19)

2963.18   Guilt not to be inquired into by governor or in extradition proceedings

The guilt or innocence of an accused as to the crime of which he is charged may not be inquired into by the governor or in any proceeding after a demand for extradition accompanied by a charge of crime under section 2963.03 of the Revised Code has been presented to the governor, except as it may be involved in identifying the person held as the person charged with the crime.

(1953 H 1, eff. 10–1–53; GC 109–20)

2963.19   Governor may recall warrant for arrest

The governor may recall his warrant of arrest issued under section 2963.07 of the Revised Code or may issue another warrant whenever he thinks is proper.

(1953 H 1, eff. 10–1–53; GC 109–21)

FUGITIVES FROM THIS STATE

2963.20   Governor to demand fugitive from this state

Whenever the governor demands a person charged with crime, or with escaping from confinement, or breaking the terms of his bail, probation, or parole in this state, from the executive authority of any other state, or from the chief justice or an associate justice of the supreme court of the District of Columbia authorized to receive such demand under the laws of the United States, he shall issue a warrant under the seal of this state, to some agent, commanding him to receive the person so charged and convey such person to the proper officer of the county in which the offense was committed.

(1953 H 1, eff. 10–1–53; GC 109–22)

2963.21   Application for requisition for return of fugitive

When the return to this state of a person charged with crime in this state is required, the prosecuting attorney shall present to the governor his written application for a requisition for the return of the person charged, in which application shall be stated the name of the person so charged, the crime charged against him, the approximate time, place, and circumstances of its commission, the state in which he is believed to be, including the location of the accused therein at the time the application is made. The prosecuting attorney shall certify that in his opinion the ends of justice require the arrest and return of the accused to this state for trial and that the proceeding is not instituted to enforce a private claim.

When the return to this state is required of a person who has been convicted of a crime in this state and has escaped from confinement or broken the terms of his bail, probation, or parole, the prosecuting attorney of the county in which the offense was committed, the pardon and parole commission, or the warden of the institution or sheriff of the county, from which escape was made, shall present to the governor a written application for a requisition for the return of such person, in which application shall be stated the name of the person, the crime of which he was convicted, the circumstances of his escape from confinement or of the breach of the terms of his bail, probation, or parole, the state in which he is believed to be, including the location of the person therein at the time application is made.

Such application shall be verified by affidavit, executed in duplicate, and accompanied by two certified copies of the indictment returned, or information and affidavit filed, or of the complaint made to the judge or magistrate, stating the offense with which the accused is charged, or of the judgment of conviction, or of the sentence. The prosecuting officer, commission, warden, or sheriff may also attach such further affidavits and other documents in duplicate as he finds proper to be submitted with such application. One copy of the application, with the action of the governor indicated by indorsement thereon, and one of the certified copies of the indictment, complaint, information, and affidavits, or of the judgment of conviction or of the sentence shall be filed in the office of the secretary of state to remain of record in that office. The other copies of all papers shall be forwarded with the governor's requisition.

(1953 H 1, eff. 10–1–53; GC 109–23)

2963.22   Reimbursement of fees

The director of budget and management shall provide for reimbursement of the fees to the officers of the state on whose governor the requisition is made under section 2963.21 of the Revised Code, and all necessary travel in returning the prisoner at the rates governing travel that have been adopted pursuant to section 126.31 of the Revised Code, on the certificate of the governor of such state.

(1990 S 336, eff. 4–10–90; 1985 H 201; 1953 H 1; GC 109–24)

2963.23   Accused immune from civil suits until conviction or return home

A person brought into this state by, or after waiver of, extradition based on a criminal charge is not subject to service of personal process in any civil action in this state until he has been convicted in the criminal proceeding, or, if acquitted, until he has had reasonable opportunity to return to the state from which he was extradited.

(1953 H 1, eff. 10–1–53; GC 109–25)

2963.24   Extradition hearing waived

Any person arrested in this state charged with having committed any crime in another state or alleged to have escaped from confinement, or broken the terms of his bail, probation, or parole may waive the issuance and service of the warrant provided for in section 2963.07 of the Revised Code and all other procedure incidental to extradition proceedings, by executing or subscribing in the presence of a judge of any court of record within this state, a writing which states that he consents to return to the demanding state. Before such waiver is executed or subscribed by such person the judge in open court shall inform such person of his rights to the issuance and service of a warrant of extradition and to obtain a writ of habeas corpus as provided for in section 2963.09 of the Revised Code.

When such consent has been executed it shall forthwith be forwarded to the office of the governor and filed therein. The judge shall direct the officer having such person in custody to deliver forthwith such person to the accredited agent of the demanding state, and shall deliver to such agent a copy of such consent. This section does not limit the rights of the accused person to return voluntarily and without formality to the demanding state before any such

demand has been made, nor is this waiver procedure an exclusive procedure or a limitation on the powers, rights, or duties of the officers of the demanding state or of this state.
(1953 H 1, eff. 10–1–53; GC 109–26)

2963.25 Right to punish or regain custody by this state not waived

Sections 2963.01 to 2963.27, inclusive, of the Revised Code do not constitute a waiver by this state of its right, power, or privilege to try such demanded person for crime committed within this state, or of its right, power, or privilege to regain custody of such person by extradition proceedings or otherwise for the purpose of trial, sentence, or punishment for any crime committed within this state, nor are any proceedings had under such sections, which result in, or fail to result in, extradition, a waiver by this state of any of its rights, privileges, or jurisdiction.
(1953 H 1, eff. 10–1–53; GC 109–27)

2963.26 Extradited fugitive may be tried for other crimes committed in this state

A person returned to this state by, or after waiver of, extradition proceedings, may be tried in this state for other crimes which he may be charged with having committed here, as well as that specified in the requisition for his extradition.
(1953 H 1, eff. 10–1–53; GC 109–28)

2963.27 Uniform interpretation

Sections 2963.01 to 2963.26, inclusive, of the Revised Code shall be so interpreted and construed as to make the law of this state uniform with the law of those states which enact similar legislation.
(1953 H 1, eff. 10–1–53; GC 109–29)

2963.28 Request by governor for extradition of criminal

If it appears to the governor by sworn evidence in writing that a person has committed a crime within this state for which such person may be delivered to the United States or its authorities by a foreign government or its authorities, because of laws of the United States, or of a treaty between the United States and a foreign government, and that such person is a fugitive from justice of this state, and may be found within the territory of such foreign government, the governor, under the great seal of Ohio, shall request the president of the United States, or the secretary of state of the United States, to take any steps necessary for the extradition of such person and his delivery to any agent of this state appointed by the governor, or to the proper officer of the county within which he is charged with the commission of such crime.
(1953 H 1, eff. 10–1–53; GC 116)

2963.29 Governor must be satisfied by evidence of good faith

The governor shall not request the extradition of a person under section 2963.28 of the Revised Code unless he is satisfied by sworn evidence that extradition is sought in good faith for the punishment of the crime named and not for the purpose of collecting a debt or pecuniary mulct or of bringing the alleged fugitive within this state to serve him with civil process, or with criminal process other than for the crime for which his extradition is sought.
(1953 H 1, eff. 10–1–53; GC 117)

INTERSTATE AGREEMENT ON DETAINERS

2963.30 Interstate agreement on detainers

The Interstate Agreement on Detainers is hereby enacted into law and entered into by this state with all other jurisdictions legally joining therein, in the form substantially as follows:

THE INTERSTATE AGREEMENT
ON DETAINERS

The contracting states solemnly agree that:

Article I

The party states find that charges outstanding against a prisoner, detainers based on untried indictments, informations or complaints, and difficulties in securing speedy trials of persons already incarcerated in other jurisdictions, produce uncertainties which obstruct programs of prisoner treatment and rehabilitation. Accordingly, it is the policy of the party states and the purpose of this agreement to encourage the expeditious and orderly disposition of such charges and determination of the proper status of any and all detainers based on untried indictments, informations or complaints. The party states also find that proceedings with reference to such charges and detainers, when emanating from another jurisdiction, cannot properly be had in the absence of cooperative procedures. It is the further purpose of this agreement to provide such cooperative procedures.

Article II

As used in this agreement:

(a) "State" shall mean a state of the United States: the United States of America: a territory or possession of the United States: the District of Columbia: the Commonwealth of Puerto Rico.

(b) "Sending state" shall mean a state in which a prisoner is incarcerated at the time that he initiates a request for final disposition pursuant to Article III hereof or at the time that a request for custody or availability is initiated pursuant to Article IV hereof.

(c) "Receiving state" shall mean the state in which trial is to be had on an indictment, information or complaint pursuant to Article III or Article IV hereof.

Article III

(a) Whenever a person has entered upon a term of imprisonment in a penal or correctional institution of a party state, and whenever during the continuance of the term of imprisonment there is pending in any other party state any untried indictment, information or complaint on the basis of which a detainer has been lodged against the prisoner, he shall be brought to trial within one hundred eighty days after he shall have caused to be delivered to the prosecuting officer and the appropriate court of the prosecuting officer's jurisdiction written notice of the place of his imprisonment and his request for a final disposition to be made of the indictment, information or complaint: provided that for good cause shown in open court, the prisoner or his counsel being present, the court having jurisdiction of the matter may grant any necessary or reasonable continuance. The request of the prisoner shall be accompanied by a certificate of the appropriate official having custody of the prisoner, stating the term of commitment under which the prisoner is being held, the time already served, the time remaining to be served on the sentence, the amount of good time earned, the time of parole eligibility of the prisoner, and any decisions of the state parole agency relating to the prisoner.

(b) The written notice and request for final disposition referred to in paragraph (a) hereof shall be given or sent by the prisoner to the warden, commissioner of corrections or other official having custody of him, who shall promptly forward it together with the certificate to the appropriate prosecuting official and court by registered or certified mail, return receipt requested.

(c) The warden, commissioner of corrections or other official having custody of the prisoner shall promptly inform him of the source and contents of any detainer lodged against him and shall also inform him of his right to make a request for final disposition of the indictment, information or complaint on which the detainer is based.

(d) Any request or final disposition made by a prisoner pursuant to paragraph (a) hereof shall operate as a request for final disposition of all untried indictments, informations or complaints on the basis of which detainers have been lodged against the prisoner from the state to whose prosecuting official the request for final disposition is specifically directed. The warden, commissioner of corrections or other officials having custody of the prisoner shall forthwith notify all appropriate prosecuting officers and courts in the several jurisdictions within the state to which the prisoner's request for final disposition is being sent of the proceeding being initiated by the prisoner. Any notification sent pursuant to this paragraph shall be accompanied by copies of the prisoner's written notice, request, and the certificate. If trial is not had on any indictment, information or complaint contemplated hereby prior to the return of the prisoner to the original place of imprisonment, such indictment, information or complaint shall not be of any further force or effect, and the court shall enter an order dismissing the same with prejudice.

(e) Any request for final disposition made by a prisoner pursuant to paragraph (a) hereof shall also be deemed to be a waiver of extradition with respect to any charge or proceeding contemplated thereby or included therein by reason of paragraph (d) hereof, and a waiver of extradition to the receiving state to serve any sentence there imposed upon him, after completion of his term of imprisonment in the sending state. The request for final disposition shall also constitute a consent by the prisoner to the production of his body in any court where his presence may be required in order to effectuate the purposes of this agreement and a further consent voluntarily to be returned to the original place of imprisonment in accordance with the provisions of this agreement. Nothing in this paragraph shall prevent the imposition of a concurrent sentence if otherwise permitted by law.

(f) Escape from custody by the prisoner subsequent to his execution of the request for final disposition referred to in paragraph (a) hereof shall void the request.

Article IV

(a) The appropriate officer of the jurisdiction in which an untried indictment, information or complaint is pending shall be entitled to have a prisoner against whom he has lodged a detainer and who is serving a term of imprisonment in any party state made available in accordance with Article V (a) hereof upon presentation of a written request for temporary custody or availability to the appropriate authorities of the state in which the prisoner is incarcerated: provided that the court having jurisdiction of such indictment, information or complaint shall have duly approved, recorded and transmitted the request: and provided further that there shall be a period of thirty days after receipt by the appropriate authorities before the request be honored, within which period the governor of the sending state may disapprove the request for temporary custody or availability, either upon his own motion or upon motion of the prisoner.

(b) Upon receipt of the officer's written request as provided in paragraph (a) hereof, the appropriate authorities having the prisoner in custody shall furnish the officer with a certificate stating the term of commitment under which the prisoner is being held, the time already served, the time remaining to be served on the sentence, the amount of good time earned, the time of parole eligibility of the prisoner, and any decisions of the state parole agency relating to the prisoner. Said authorities simultaneously shall furnish all other officers and appropriate courts in the receiving state who have lodged detainers against the prisoner with similar certificates and with notices informing them of the request for custody or availability and of the reasons therefor.

(c) In respect of any proceeding made possible by this Article, trial shall be commenced within one hundred twenty days of the arrival of the prisoner in the receiving state, but for good cause shown in open court, the prisoner or his counsel being present, the court having jurisdiction of the matter may grant any necessary or reasonable continuance.

(d) Nothing contained in this Article shall be construed to deprive any prisoner of any right which he may have to contest the legality of his delivery as provided in paragraph (a) hereof, but such delivery may not be opposed or denied on the ground that the executive authority of the sending state has not affirmatively consented to or ordered such delivery.

(e) If trial is not had on any indictment, information or complaint contemplated hereby prior to the prisoner's being returned to the original place of imprisonment pursuant to Article V (e) hereof, such indictment, information or complaint shall not be of any further force or effect, and the court shall enter an order dismissing the same with prejudice.

Article V

(a) In response to a request made under Article III or Article IV hereof, the appropriate authority in a sending state shall offer to deliver temporary custody of such prisoner to the appropriate authority in the state where such indictment, information or complaint is pending against such person in order that speedy and efficient prosecution may be had. If the request for final disposition is made by the prisoner, the offer of temporary custody shall accompany the written notice provided for in Article III of this agreement. In the case of a federal prisoner, the appropriate authority in the receiving state shall be entitled to temporary custody as provided by this agreement or to the prisoner's presence in federal custody at the place of trial, whichever custodial arrangement may be approved by the custodian.

(b) The officer or other representative of a state accepting an offer of temporary custody shall present the following upon demand:

(1) Proper identification and evidence of his authority to act for the state into whose temporary custody the prisoner is to be given.

(2) A duly certified copy of the indictment, information or complaint on the basis of which the detainer has been lodged and on the basis of which the request for temporary custody of the prisoner has been made.

(c) If the appropriate authority shall refuse or fail to accept temporary custody of said person, or in the event that an action on the indictment, information or complaint on the basis of which the detainer has been lodged is not brought to trial within the period provided in Article III or Article IV hereof, the appropriate court of the jurisdiction where the indictment, information or complaint has been pending shall enter an order dismissing the same with prejudice, and any detainer based thereon shall cease to be of any force or effect.

(d) The temporary custody referred to in this agreement shall be only for the purpose of permitting prosecution on the charge or charges contained in one or more untried indictments, informations or complaints which form the basis of the detainer or detainers or for prosecution on any other charge or charges arising out of the same transaction, except for his attendance at court and while being transported to or from any place at which his presence may be required, the prisoner shall be held in a suitable jail or other facility regularly used for persons awaiting prosecution.

(e) At the earliest practicable time consonant with the purposes of this agreement, the prisoner shall be returned to the sending state.

(f) During the continuance of temporary custody or while the prisoner is otherwise being made available for trial as required by this agreement, time being served on the sentence shall continue to run but good time shall be earned by the prisoner only if, and to the extent that, the law and practice of the jurisdiction which imposed the sentence may allow.

(g) For all purposes other than that for which temporary custody as provided in this agreement is exercised, the prisoner shall be deemed to remain in the custody of and subject to the jurisdiction of the sending state and any escape from temporary custody may be dealt with in the same manner as an escape from the original place of imprisonment or in any other manner permitted by law.

(h) From the time that a party state receives custody of a prisoner pursuant to this agreement until such prisoner is returned to the territory and custody of the sending state, the state in which the one or more untried indictments, informations or complaints are pending or in which trial is being had shall be responsible for the prisoner and shall also pay all costs of transporting, caring for, keeping and returning the prisoner, the provisions of this paragraph shall govern unless the states concerned shall have entered into a supplementary agreement providing for a different allocation of costs and responsibilities as between or among themselves. Nothing herein contained shall be construed to alter or affect any internal relationship among the departments, agencies and officers of and in the government of a party state, or between a party state and its subdivisions, as to the payment of costs, or responsibilities therefor.

Article VI

(a) In determining the duration and expiration dates of the time periods provided in Articles III and IV of this agreement, the running of said time periods shall be tolled whenever and for as long as the prisoner is unable to stand trial, as determined by the court having jurisdiction of the matter.

(b) No provision of this agreement, and no remedy made available by this agreement, shall apply to any person who is adjudged to be mentally ill, or who is under sentence of death.

Article VII

Each state party to this agreement shall designate an officer who, acting jointly with like officers of other party states, shall promulgate rules and regulations to carry out more effectively the terms and provisions of this agreement, and who shall provide, within and without the state, information necessary to the effective operation of this agreement.

Article VIII

This agreement shall enter into full force and effect as to a party state when such state has enacted the same into law. A state party to this agreement may withdraw herefrom by enacting a statute repealing the same. However, the withdrawal of any state shall not affect the status of any proceedings already initiated by inmates or by state officers at the time such withdrawal takes effect, nor shall it affect their rights in respect thereof.

Article IX

This agreement shall be liberally construed so as to effectuate its purposes. The provisions of this agreement shall be severable and if any phrase, clause, sentence or provision of this agreement is declared to be contrary to the constitution of any party state or of the United States or the applicability thereof to any government, agency, person or circumstance is held invalid, the validity of the remainder of this agreement and the applicability thereof to any agreement, agency, person or circumstance shall not be affected thereby. If this agreement shall be held contrary to the constitution of any state party hereto, the agreement shall remain in full force and effect as to the remaining states and in full force and effect as to the state affected as to all severable matters.

(1969 S 356, eff. 11–18–69)

2963.31   Definition of "appropriate court"

As used in section 2963.30 of the Revised Code, with reference to the courts of this state, "appropriate court" means the court of record having jurisdiction of the indictment, information, or complaint.

(1969 S 356, eff. 11–18–69)

2963.32   Duty to effectuate agreement

The courts, departments, agencies, and officers of this state and its political subdivisions shall do all things that are necessary to effectuate the agreement adopted pursuant to section 2963.30 of the Revised Code and that are appropriate within their respective jurisdictions and consistent with their duties and authority. The warden or other official in charge of a correctional institution in this state shall give over the person of any inmate of the institution when so required by the operation of the agreement.

(1994 H 571, eff. 10–6–94; 1969 S 356, eff. 11–18–69)

2963.33   Habitual offenders—Repealed

(1972 H 511, eff. 1–1–74; 1969 S 356)

2963.34   Escape and aiding escape

A person, while in another state pursuant to the agreement, adopted pursuant to section 2963.30 of the Revised Code, is subject to the prohibitions and penalties provided by sections 2921.34 and 2921.35 of the Revised Code.

(1972 H 511, eff. 1–1–74; 1969 S 356)

2963.35   Duty of warden

The chief of the adult parole authority is designated as the administrator as required by Article VII of the agreement adopted pursuant to section 2963.30 of the Revised Code. The administrator, acting jointly with like officers of other party states, shall, in accordance with Chapter 119. of the Revised Code, promulgate rules and regulations to carry out the terms of the agreement. The administrator is authorized and empowered to cooperate with all departments, agencies, and officers of this state and its political subdivisions, in facilitating the proper administration of the agreement or of any supplementary agreement or agreements entered into by this state thereunder.

(1969 S 356, eff. 11–18–69)

CHAPTER 2965

PARDON; PAROLE

2965.01   Definitions—Repealed

(130 v Pt 2, H 28, eff. 3–18–65; 129 v 1667; 128 v 959; 126 v 307; 125 v 823; 1953 H 1; GC 2209)

2965.02   Pardon and parole commission—Repealed

(130 v Pt 2, H 28, eff. 3–18–65; 128 v 959; 1953 H 1; GC 2209–1)

2965.03   Qualifications of members—Repealed

(130 v Pt 2, H 28, eff. 3–18–65; 128 v 959; 1953 H 1; GC 2209–2)

2965.04   Oath of office; bond—Repealed

(130 v Pt 2, H 28, eff. 3–18–65; 125 v 823; 1953 H 1; GC 2209–3)

2965.05   Meetings; rules and regulations—Repealed

(130 v Pt 2, H 28, eff. 3–18–65; 129 v 1667; 128 v 959; 1953 H 1; GC 2209–4)

2965.06   Legal advisor—Repealed

(130 v Pt 2, H 28, eff. 3–18–65; 1953 H 1; GC 2209–5)

2965.07   Salary and expenses—Repealed

(130 v Pt 2, H 28, eff. 3–18–65; 128 v 959; 127 v 7, 382; 126 v 640; 125 v 289, 823; 1953 H 1; GC 2209–6)

2965.08   Executive secretary; employees—Repealed

(130 v Pt 2, H 28, eff. 3–18–65; 129 v 481; 125 v 823; 1953 H 1; GC 2209–7)

2965.09   Pardons and reprieves—Repealed

(130 v Pt 2, H 28, eff. 3–18–65; 1953 H 1; GC 2209–8)

2965.10   Pardon or commutation—Repealed

(130 v Pt 2, H 28, eff. 3–18–65; 1953 H 1; GC 2209–9)

2965.11   Temporary release—Repealed

(130 v Pt 2, H 28, eff. 3–18–65; 1953 H 1; GC 2209–10)

2965.12   Warrants of pardon—Repealed

(130 v Pt 2, H 28, eff. 3–18–65; 1953 H 1; GC 2209–11)

2965.13   Application for executive pardon—Repealed

(130 v Pt 2, H 28, eff. 3–18–65; 1953 H 1; GC 2209–12)

2965.14   Reprieve—Repealed

(130 v Pt 2, H 28, eff. 3–18–65; 1953 H 1; GC 2209–13)

2965.15   Warrant of reprieve—Repealed

(130 v Pt 2, H 28, eff. 3–18–65; 1953 H 1; GC 2209–14)

2965.16   Confinement of prisoner during reprieve—Repealed

(130 v Pt 2, H 28, eff. 3–18–65; 1953 H 1; GC 2209–15)

2965.17   Final release—Repealed

(130 v Pt 2, H 28, eff. 3–18–65; 128 v 959; 1953 H 1; GC 2209–16)

2965.18   Notice of pendency of pardon—Repealed

(130 v Pt 2, H 28, eff. 3–18–65; 1953 H 1; GC 2209–17)

2965.19   Oaths; subpoenas; witnesses; fees—Repealed

(130 v Pt 2, H 28, eff. 3–18–65; 1953 H 1; GC 2209–18)

2965.20   Bureau of probation and parole; firearms for parole officers—Repealed

(130 v Pt 2, H 28, eff. 3–18–65; 130 v H 1; 129 v 481; 128 v 959; 127 v 118; 1953 H 1; GC 2209–19)

2965.201   Duties of pardon and parole commission—Repealed

(130 v Pt 2, H 28, eff. 3–18–65; 129 v 481)

2965.21   Violation of pardon or parole—Repealed

(130 v Pt 2, H 28, eff. 3–18–65; 128 v 959; 1953 H 1; GC 2209–20)

2965.211   Diagnosis and treatment of mentally ill parolees—Repealed

(130 v Pt 2, H 28, eff. 3–18–65; 129 v 1811)

2965.22   Biennial report to governor—Repealed

(130 v Pt 2, H 28, eff. 3–18–65; 1953 H 1; GC 2209–21)

2965.23   Prisoners eligible for parole; procedure for parole—Repealed

(130 v Pt 2, H 28, eff. 3–18–65; 1953 H 1; GC 2210–1)

2965.31   Diminution of minimum sentence for good behavior—Repealed

(130 v Pt 2, H 28, eff. 3–18–65; 1953 H 1; GC 2210)

2965.32   Transfer of prisoners—Repealed

(130 v Pt 2, H 28, eff. 3–18–65; 125 v 823; 1953 H 1; GC 2210–2)

2965.33 Transfer shall make no change in term of sentence—Repealed

(130 v Pt 2, H 28, eff. 3–18–65; 1953 H 1; GC 2210–3)

2965.34 Interstate compact as to parolees and probationers—Repealed

(130 v Pt 2, H 28, eff. 3–18–65; 127 v 115; 1953 H 1; GC 108–1)

2965.341 Definitions; state as party to compact—Repealed

(130 v Pt 2, H 28, eff. 3–18–65; 127 v 115)

2965.35 Eligibility when serving consecutive sentences—Repealed

(130 v Pt 2, H 28, eff. 3–18–65; 127 v 213)

2965.36 Persons employed by other states may be deputized—Repealed

(130 v Pt 2, H 28, eff. 3–18–65; 130 v H 1; 129 v 1667)

2965.37 Contracts for sharing cost of returning parole violators—Repealed

(130 v Pt 2, H 28, eff. 3–18–65; 130 v H 1; 129 v 1667)

CHAPTER 2967

PARDON; PAROLE; PROBATION

2967.01   Definitions

As used in this chapter:

(A) "State correctional institution" includes any institution or facility that is operated by the department of rehabilitation and correction and that is used for the custody, care, or treatment of criminal, delinquent, or psychologically or psychiatrically disturbed offenders.

(B) "Pardon" means the remission of penalty by the governor in accordance with the power vested in the governor by the constitution. Pardons may be granted after conviction and may be absolute and entire, or partial, and may be granted upon conditions precedent or subsequent.

(C) "Commutation" or "commutation of sentence" means the substitution by the governor of a lesser for a greater punishment. A sentence may be commuted without the consent of the convict, except when granted upon the acceptance and performance by the convict of conditions precedent. After commutation, the commuted sentence shall be the only one in existence. The commutation may be stated in terms of commuting from a named crime to a lesser included crime, in terms of commuting from a minimum and maximum sentence in months and years to a minimum and maximum sentence in months and years, or in terms of commuting from one definite sentence in months and years to a lesser definite sentence in months and years.

503

(D) "Reprieve" means the temporary suspension by the governor of the execution of a sentence. A reprieve may be granted without the consent of and against the will of the convict.

(E) "Parole" means a release from confinement in any state correctional institution by the adult parole authority created by section 5149.02 of the Revised Code that is subject to the eligibility criteria specified in this chapter and that is under the terms and conditions, and for the period of time, prescribed by the authority in its published rules and official minutes or required by division (A) of section 2967.131 of the Revised Code or another provision of this chapter. A parolee so released shall be supervised by the authority. Legal custody of a parolee shall remain in the department of rehabilitation and correction until a final release is granted by the authority pursuant to section 2967.16 of the Revised Code.

(F) "Head of a state correctional institution" or "head of the institution" means the resident head of the institution and the person immediately in charge of the institution, whether designated warden or superintendent, or by whatever name the head is known.

(G) "Convict" means a person who has been convicted of a felony under the laws of this state, whether or not actually confined in a state correctional institution, unless the person has been pardoned or has served the person's sentence.

(H) "Prisoner" means a person who is in actual confinement in a state correctional institution.

(I) "Parolee" means any inmate who has been released from confinement by order of the adult parole authority or conditionally pardoned, who is under supervision of the adult parole authority and has not been granted a final release, and who has not been declared in violation of his parole by the authority or is performing the prescribed conditions of a conditional pardon.

(J) "Final release" means a remission by the adult parole authority of the balance of the sentence of a parolee or prisoner that is recorded in the official minutes of the authority.

(K) "Parole violator" means any parolee who has been declared to be in violation of the condition of parole or shock parole specified in division (A) of section 2967.131 of the Revised Code or in violation of any other term, condition, or rule of parole, the determination of which has been made by the adult parole authority and recorded in its official minutes.

(L) "Administrative release" means a termination of jurisdiction over a particular sentence by the adult parole authority for administrative convenience.

(M) "Furloughee" means a prisoner who has been released to conditional confinement by the adult parole authority pursuant to section 2967.26 of the Revised Code or who has been released by the department of rehabilitation and correction pursuant to ection 2967.27 of the Revised Code.

(1995 H 4, eff. 11–9–95; 1994 H 571, eff. 10–6–94; 1982 H 269, § 4, eff. 7–1–83; 1982 S 199; 1980 S 52; 1972 H 494; 131 v H 333; 130 v Pt 2, H 28)

2967.02   Administration of pardon, probation, parole by adult parole authority

Sections 2967.01 to 2967.25, inclusive, of the Revised Code, and other sections of the Revised Code governing pardon, probation, and parole, shall be administered by the adult parole authority created by section 5149.02 of the Revised Code.

(130 v Pt 2, H 28, eff. 3–18–65)

2967.03   Pardon, commutation, or reprieve

The adult parole authority may exercise its functions and duties in relation to the pardon, commutation, or reprieve of a convict upon direction of the governor or upon its own initiative, and in relation to the parole of a prisoner eligible for parole, upon the initiative of the head of the institution wherein the prisoner is confined, or upon its own initiative. When a prisoner becomes eligible for parole, the head of the institution in which such prisoner is confined shall notify the authority in the manner prescribed by the authority. The authority may investigate and examine, or cause the investigation and examination of, prisoners confined in state correctional institutions concerning their conduct therein, their mental and moral qualities and characteristics, their knowledge of a trade or profession, their former means of livelihood, their family relationships, and any other matters affecting their fitness to be at liberty without being a threat to society.

The authority may recommend to the governor the pardon, commutation, or reprieve of sentence of any convict or prisoner, or grant a parole to any prisoner, if in its judgment there is reasonable ground to believe that, if the convict is granted a pardon, commutation, or reprieve, or the prisoner is paroled, such action would further the interests of justice and be consistent with the welfare and security of society. However, the authority shall not recommend a pardon or commutation of sentence of, or grant a parole to, any convict or prisoner until the authority has complied with the applicable notice requirements of section 2930.16 of the Revised Code and has considered any statement made by a victim or a victim's representative that is relevant to the convict's or prisoner's case and that was sent to the authority pursuant to section 2930.17 of the Revised Code and any other statement made by a victim or a victim's representative that is relevant to the convict's or prisoner's case and that was received by the authority after it provided notice of the pendency of the action under section 2967.12 of the Revised Code. The trial judge and prosecuting attorney of the trial court in which a person was convicted shall furnish, at the request of the authority, a summarized statement of the facts proved at the trial, and of all other facts having reference to the propriety of recommending a pardon or commutation, or granting a parole, together with a recommendation for or against a pardon, commutation, or parole, and the reasons for such recommendation. All state and local officials shall furnish information to the authority, when so requested by it in the performance of its duties.

(1994 S 186, eff. 10–12–94; 1994 H 571, eff. 10–6–94; 1987 S 6, § 1, eff. 6–10–87; 1987 S 6, § 3; 1984 S 172, § 1, 3; 130 v Pt 2, H 28)

Historical and Statutory Notes

Ed. Note: A special endorsement by the Legislative Service Commission states, "Comparison of these amendments [1994 S 186, eff. 10–12–94 and 1994 H 571, eff. 10–6–94] in pursuance of section 1.52 of the Revised Code discloses that they are not irreconcilable, so that they are required by that section to be harmonized to give effect to each amendment." In recognition of this rule of construction, changes made by 1994 S 186, eff. 10–12–94, and 1994 H 571, eff. 10–6–94, have been incorporated in the above amendment. See *Baldwin's Ohio Legislative Service*, 1994 Laws of Ohio, pages 5–928 and 5–1165, for original versions of these Acts.

2967.04 Pardons and commutations; conditions; effect

(A) A pardon or commutation may be granted upon such conditions precedent or subsequent as the governor may impose, which conditions shall be stated in the warrant. Such pardon or commutation shall not take effect until the conditions so imposed are accepted by the convict or prisoner so pardoned or having his sentence commuted, and his acceptance is indorsed upon the warrant, signed by him, and attested by one witness. Such witness shall go before the clerk of the court of common pleas in whose office the sentence is recorded and prove the signature of the convict. The clerk shall thereupon record the warrant, indorsement, and proof in the journal of the court, which record, or a duly certified transcript thereof, shall be evidence of such pardon or commutation, the conditions thereof, and the acceptance of the conditions.

(B) An unconditional pardon relieves the person to whom it is granted of all disabilities arising out of the conviction or convictions from which it is granted. For purposes of this section, "unconditional pardon" includes a conditional pardon with respect to which all conditions have been performed or have transpired.

(1972 H 511, eff. 1–1–74; 130 v Pt 2, H 28)

2967.05 Release of prisoner in imminent danger of death; return to institution from which released

Upon recommendation of the director of rehabilitation and correction, accompanied by a certificate of the attending physician that a prisoner or convict is in imminent danger of death, the governor may order his release as if on parole, reserving the right to return him to the institution pursuant to this section. If, subsequent to his release, his health improves so that he is no longer in imminent danger of death, he shall be returned, by order of the governor, to the institution from which he was released. If he violates any rules or conditions applicable to him, he may be returned to an institution under the control of the department of rehabilitation and correction.

(1994 H 571, eff. 10–6–94; 1982 H 269, § 4, eff. 7–1–83; 1982 S 199; 132 v S 394)

2967.06   Warrants of pardon and commutation

Warrants of pardon and commutation shall be issued in triplicate, one to be given to the convict, one to be filed with the clerk of the court of common pleas in whose office the sentence is recorded, and one to be filed with the head of the institution in which the convict was confined, in case he was confined.

All warrants of pardon, whether conditional or otherwise, shall be recorded by said clerk and the officer of the institution with whom such warrants and copies are filed, in a book provided for that purpose, which record shall include the indorsements on such warrants. A copy of such a warrant with all indorsements, certified by said clerk under seal, shall be received in evidence as proof of the facts set forth in such copy with indorsements.

(130 v Pt 2, H 28, eff. 3–18–65)

2967.07   Application for executive pardon, commutation, or reprieve

All applications for pardon, commutation of sentence, or reprieve shall be made in writing to the adult parole authority. Upon the filing of such application, or when directed by the governor in any case, a thorough investigation into the propriety of granting a pardon, commutation, or reprieve shall be made by the authority, which shall report in writing to the governor a brief statement of the facts in the case, together with the recommendation of the authority for or against the granting of a pardon, commutation, or reprieve, the grounds therefor and the records or minutes relating to the case.

(130 v Pt 2, H 28, eff. 3–18–65)

2967.08   Reprieve to a person under sentence of death

The governor may grant a reprieve for a definite time to a person under sentence of death, with or without notices or application.

(130 v Pt 2, H 28, eff. 3–18–65)

2967.09   Warrant of reprieve

On receiving a warrant of reprieve, the head of the institution, sheriff, or other officer having custody of the person reprieved, shall file it forthwith with the clerk of the court of common pleas in which the sentence is recorded, who shall thereupon record the warrant in the journal of the court.

(130 v Pt 2, H 28, eff. 3–18–65)

2967.10   Confinement of prisoner during reprieve

When the governor directs in a warrant of reprieve that the prisoner be confined in a state correctional institution for the time of the reprieve or any part thereof, the sheriff or other officer having the prisoner in custody shall convey him to the state correctional institution in the manner provided for the conveyance of convicts, and the warden shall receive the prisoner and warrant and proceed as the warrant directs. At the expiration of the time specified in the warrant for the confinement of the prisoner in the state correctional institution, the warden shall deal with him according to the sentence as originally imposed, or as modified by executive clemency as shown by a new warrant of pardon, commutation, or reprieve executed by the governor.

(1994 H 571, eff. 10–6–94; 130 v Pt 2, H 28, eff. 3–18–65)

2967.12 Notice of pendency of pardon, commutation, or parole; rights of crime victim or representative

(A) Except as provided in division (F) of this section, at least three weeks before the adult parole authority recommends any pardon or commutation of sentence, or grants any parole, notice of the pendency of the pardon, commutation, or parole, setting forth the name of the person on whose behalf it is made, the crime of which he was convicted, the time of conviction, and the term of sentence, shall be sent to the prosecuting attorney and the judge of the court of common pleas of the county in which the indictment against the convict was found. If there is more than one judge of that court of common pleas, the notice shall be sent to the presiding judge of the court.

(B) If a request for notification has been made pursuant to section 2930.16 of the Revised Code, the adult parole authority also shall send a notice to the victim or the victim's representative prior to recommending any pardon or commutation of sentence for, or granting any parole to, the person. The notice shall be provided at the same time as the notice required by division (A) of this section and shall contain the information required to be set forth in that notice. The notice also shall inform the victim or the victim's representative that he may send a written statement relative to the victimization and the pending action to the adult parole authority and that any statement received by the adult parole authority prior to recommending a pardon or commutation or granting a parole will be considered by the authority before a pardon or commutation is recommended or a parole is granted.

(C) When notice of the pendency of any pardon, commutation, or parole has been given as provided in division (A) of this section and a hearing on the pardon, commutation, or parole is continued to a date certain, notice of the further consideration of the pardon, commutation, or parole shall be given by mail to the proper judge and prosecuting attorney at least ten days before the further consideration. When notice of the pendency of any pardon, commutation, or parole has been given as provided in division (B) of this section and a hearing on it is continued to a date certain, notice of the further consideration shall be given to the victim or the victim's representative in accordance with section 2930.03 of the Revised Code.

(D) In case of an application for the pardon or commutation of sentence of a person sentenced to capital punishment, the governor may modify the requirements of notification and publication if there is not sufficient time for compliance therewith before the date fixed for the execution of sentence.

(E) The failure of the adult parole authority to comply with the notice provisions of division (A), (B), or (C) of this section does not give any rights or any grounds for appeal or post-conviction relief to the person serving the sentence.

(F) Divisions (A), (B), and (C) of this section do not apply to the parole of a person that is of the type described in division (B)(2)(c) of section 5120.031 of the Revised Code.

(1994 S 186, eff. 10–12–94; 1990 S 258, eff. 11–20–90; 1987 S 6, § 3; 1984 S 172, § 1, 3; 130 v Pt 2, H 28)

2967.121 Notice to prosecuting attorney of pending release of certain prisoners

(A) At least two weeks before any convict who is serving a sentence for committing an aggravated felony is released from confinement in any state correctional institution pursuant to a pardon, commutation, parole, or shock parole pursuant to section 2967.31 of the Revised Code, the adult parole authority shall send notice of the release to the prosecuting attorney of the county in which the indictment of the convict was found.

(B) The notice required by division (A) of this section may be contained in a weekly list of all aggravated felons who are scheduled for release. The notice shall contain all of the following:

(1) The name of the convict being released;

(2) The date of the convict's release;

(3) The offense for the violation of which the convict was convicted and incarcerated;

(4) The date of the convict's conviction pursuant to which he was incarcerated;

(5) The sentence to which the convict was sentenced for that conviction;

(6) The length of any supervision that the convict will be under;

(7) The name, business address, and business phone number of the convict's supervising officer;

(8) The address at which the convict will reside.

(1994 H 571, eff. 10–6–94; 1984 H 399, eff. 9–26–84)

2967.13   Parole eligibility

(A) A prisoner serving a sentence of imprisonment for a felony for which an indefinite term of imprisonment is imposed becomes eligible for parole at the expiration of his minimum term, diminished as provided in sections 2967.19, 2967.193, and 5145.11 of the Revised Code.

(B) A prisoner serving a sentence of imprisonment for life for the offense of first degree murder or aggravated murder, which sentence was imposed for an offense committed prior to October 19, 1981, becomes eligible for parole after serving a term of fifteen full years.

(C) A prisoner serving a sentence of imprisonment for life with parole eligibility after serving twenty years of imprisonment imposed pursuant to section 2929.022 or 2929.03 of the Revised Code becomes eligible for parole after serving a term of twenty years, diminished as provided in sections 2967.19, 2967.193, and 5145.11 of the Revised Code.

(D) A prisoner serving a sentence of imprisonment for life with parole eligibility after serving twenty full years of imprisonment imposed pursuant to section 2929.022 or 2929.03 of the Revised Code becomes eligible for parole after serving a term of twenty full years. A person serving such a sentence is not entitled to any diminution of the twenty full years that he is required to serve before parole eligibility under section 2967.19, 2967.193, or 5145.11 of the Revised Code.

(E) A prisoner serving a sentence of imprisonment for life with parole eligibility after serving thirty full years of imprisonment imposed pursuant to section 2929.022 or 2929.03 of the Revised Code becomes eligible for parole after serving a term of thirty full years. A person serving such a sentence is not entitled to any diminution of the thirty full years that he is required to serve before parole eligibility under section 2967.19, 2967.193, or 5145.11 of the Revised Code.

(F) A prisoner serving a sentence of imprisonment for life for an offense other than the offense of first degree murder or aggravated murder, which sentence was imposed prior to October 19, 1981, serving a term of imprisonment for life for rape or felonious sexual penetration or for the offense described in section 2927.03 of the Revised Code, or serving a minimum term or terms, whether consecutive or otherwise, of imprisonment longer than fifteen years, imposed under any former law of this state, becomes eligible for parole after serving a term of ten full years' imprisonment.

(G) A prisoner serving a sentence of imprisonment for life for the offense of first degree murder or aggravated murder, which sentence was imposed for an offense committed prior to October 19, 1981, consecutively to any other term of imprisonment becomes eligible for parole after serving fifteen full years as to each such sentence of life imprisonment, plus the minimum term or terms, diminished as provided in sections 2967.19, 2967.193, and 5145.11 of the Revised Code, or in the case of another type of life sentence, the number of years before parole eligibility, diminished as provided in sections 2967.19, 2967.193, and 5145.11 of the Revised Code, if applicable, of the other sentences consecutively imposed, except that in no case shall the total number of years that such a person is required to serve before becoming eligible for parole exceed twenty years of imprisonment.

(H) A prisoner serving a sentence of imprisonment for life with parole eligibility after serving twenty years of imprisonment imposed pursuant to section 2929.022 or 2929.03 of the Revised Code, consecutively to any other term of imprisonment becomes eligible for parole after serving twenty years as to each such sentence of life imprisonment, diminished as provided in sections 2967.19, 2967.193, and 5145.11 of the Revised Code, plus the minimum term or terms, diminished as provided in sections 2967.19, 2967.193, and 5145.11 of the Revised Code, or in the case of another type of life sentence, the number of years before parole eligibility, diminished as provided in sections 2967.19, 2967.193, and 5145.11 of the Revised Code, if applicable, of the other sentences consecutively imposed.

(I) A prisoner serving a sentence of imprisonment for life with parole eligibility after serving twenty full years of imprisonment imposed pursuant to section 2929.022 or 2929.03 of the Revised Code, consecutively to any other term of imprisonment becomes eligible for parole after serving twenty full years as to each such sentence of life imprisonment, plus the minimum term or terms, diminished as provided in sections 2967.19, 2967.193, and 5145.11 of the Revised Code, or in the case of another type of life sentence, the number of years before parole eligibility, diminished as provided in sections 2967.19, 2967.193, and 5145.11 of the Revised Code, if applicable, of the other sentences consecutively imposed.

(J) A prisoner serving a sentence of imprisonment for life with parole eligibility after serving thirty full years of imprisonment imposed pursuant to section 2929.022 or 2929.03 of the Revised Code, consecutively to any other term of imprisonment becomes eligible for parole after serving thirty full years as to each such sentence of life imprisonment, plus the minimum term or terms, diminished as provided in sections 2967.19, 2967.193, and 5145.11 of the Revised Code, or in the case of another type of life sentence, the number of years before parole eligibility, diminished as provided in sections 2967.19, 2967.193, and 5145.11 of the Revised Code, if applicable, of the other sentences consecutively imposed.

(K) A prisoner serving a definite term of imprisonment for a felony of the third or fourth degree shall be released from imprisonment when he has served the full term of his definite sentence, diminished as provided in sections 2967.19, 2967.193, and 5145.11 of the Revised Code, and may be released from imprisonment pursuant to section 2967.18, 2967.23, or 2967.31 of the Revised Code.

(L) The cumulative total of any diminution of sentence granted under section 2967.19 of the Revised Code, any days of credit awarded under section 2967.193 of the Revised Code, and any diminution of sentence granted under section 5145.11 of the Revised Code shall not exceed, for any prisoner, one-third of the minimum or definite sentence, or in the case of a sentence of life imprisonment, one-third of the number of years before parole eligibility, of the sentence imposed upon the prisoner. No prisoner shall be eligible for parole before serving two-thirds of the sentence imposed by the sentencing court, reduced as provided in section 2967.191 of the Revised Code.

(1994 H 571, eff. 10–6–94; 1992 S 331, eff. 11–13–92; 1988 H 708; 1987 H 261, H 5; 1983 S 210; 1982 H 269, S 199; 1981 S 1; 1972 H 511)

2967.131 Releasees to abide by firearms laws; searches authorized

(A) In addition to any other terms and conditions of a conditional pardon, parole, shock parole, furlough, or other form of authorized release from confinement in a state correctional institution that is granted to an individual and that involves the placement of the individual under the supervision of the adult parole authority, the authority or, in the case of a conditional pardon, the governor shall include in the terms and conditions of the conditional pardon, parole, shock parole, furlough, or other form of authorized release the condition that the releasee abide by the law, including, but not limited to, complying with the provisions of Chapter 2923. of the Revised Code relating to the possession, sale, furnishing, transfer, disposition, purchase, acquisition, carrying, conveying, or use of, or other conduct involving, a firearm or dangerous ordnance, as defined in section 2923.11 of the Revised Code, during the period of the releasee's conditional pardon, parole, shock parole, furlough, or other form of authorized release.

(B) During the period of a conditional pardon, parole, shock parole, furlough, or other form of authorized release from confinement in a state correctional institution that is granted to an individual and that involves the placement of the individual under the supervision of the adult parole authority, authorized field officers of the authority who are engaged within the scope of their supervisory duties or responsibilities may search, with or without a warrant, the person of the releasee, the place of residence of the releasee, and a motor vehicle, another item of tangible or intangible personal property, or other real property in which the releasee has a right, title, or interest or for which the releasee has the express or implied permission of a person with a right, title, or interest to use, occupy, or possess if the field officers have reasonable grounds to believe that the releasee is not abiding by the law or otherwise is not complying with the terms and conditions of the releasee's conditional pardon, parole, shock parole, furlough, or other form of authorized release. The authority shall provide each releasee with a written notice that informs the releasee that authorized field officers of the authority who are engaged within the scope of their supervisory duties or responsibilities may conduct those types of searches during the period of the conditional pardon, parole, shock parole, furlough, or other form of authorized release if they have reasonable grounds to believe that the releasee is not abiding by the law or otherwise is not complying with the terms and conditions of the releasee's conditional pardon, parole, shock parole, furlough, or other form of authorized release.

(1995 H 4, eff. 11–9–95)

2967.14 Halfway house; requirement of residence; funding; licensing

(A) The adult parole authority may require a parolee to reside in a halfway house or other suitable community residential center that has been licensed by the division of parole and community services pursuant to division (C) of this section during a part or for the entire period of the parolee's conditional release. The court of common pleas that placed an offender on probation may require him to reside in a halfway house or other suitable community residential center that is designated by the court and that has been licensed by the division pursuant to division (C) of this section during a part or for the entire period of the offender's probation.

(B) The division of parole and community services may enter into agreements with any agency, public or private, or a department or political subdivision of the state, that operates a halfway house or community residential center that has been licensed by the division pursuant to division (C) of this section. An agreement shall provide for housing, supervision, and other services that are required for parolees and probationers who have been assigned to a halfway house or community residential center. An agreement shall provide for per diem payments to the agency, department, or political subdivision on behalf of each parolee and probationer assigned to a halfway house or community residential center that is operated by the agency, department, or political subdivision and that has been licensed by the division. The per diem payments shall be equal to the halfway house's or community residential center's average daily per capita costs with its facility at full occupancy. The per diem payments shall not exceed the total operating costs of the halfway house or community residential center during the term of an agreement. The director of rehabilitation and correction shall adopt rules in accordance with Chapter 119. of the Revised Code for determining includable and excludable costs and income to be used in computing the agency's average daily per capita costs with its facility at full occupancy.

The department of rehabilitation and correction may use a portion of the amount appropriated to the department each fiscal year for the halfway house and community residential center program to pay for contracts for nonresidential services for offenders under the supervision of the adult parole authority. The nonresidential services may include, but are not limited to, treatment for substance abuse, mental health counseling, and counseling for sex offenders.

(C) The division of parole and community services may license a halfway house or community residential center as a suitable facility for the care and treatment of adult offenders only if the halfway house or community residential center complies with the standards that the division adopts in accordance with Chapter 119. of the Revised Code for the licensure of halfway houses and community residential centers. The division shall annually inspect each licensed halfway house and licensed community residential center to determine if it is in compliance with the licensure standards.

(1994 H 571, eff. 10–6–94; 1992 S 331, eff. 11–13–92; 1981 H 694; 1976 H 637)

2967.15 Violation of pardon or parole

Note: See also following version of this section, and Publisher's Note.

(A) Any adult parole authority field officer who has reasonable cause to believe that any parolee, furloughee, or other releasee under the supervision of the adult parole authority has violated or is violating any term or condition of his pardon, parole, furlough, or release may arrest the person without a warrant or order any peace officer to arrest the person without a warrant. A person so arrested shall be confined in the jail of the county in which he is arrested or in another facility designated by the chief of the adult parole authority until a determination is made regarding his release status. Upon making an arrest under this section, the arresting or supervising adult parole authority field officer promptly shall notify the superintendent of parole supervision or his designee, in writing, that the person has been arrested and is in custody and submit in detail an appropriate report of the reason for the arrest.

(B) Prior to the revocation of a person's pardon, parole, furlough, or other release by the adult parole authoritiy, the adult parole authority shall grant the person a hearing pursuant to rules adopted by the department of rehabilitation and correction in accordance with Chapter 119. of the Revised Code, except that the adult parole authority is not required to grant the person a hearing if the person is convicted of or pleads guilty to an offense that the person committed while the person was released on a pardon or was on parole, furlough, or other release and upon which the revocation of the person's pardon, parole, furlough, or release is based.

If a person is found to be a violator of the conditions of his pardon or commutation, the authority forthwith shall transmit to the governor its recommendation concerning the violation, and the violator shall be retained in custody until the governor issues an order concerning the violation.

If the authority fails to make a determination of the case of the parolee alleged to be a violator of the conditions of his pardon or parole within a reasonable time, the parolee shall be released from custody under the same terms and conditions of his original pardon or parole.

(C)(1) If a parolee, furloughee, or other releasee absconds from supervision, that fact shall be reported by the superintendent to the authority, in writing, and the authority shall enter an order upon its official minutes declaring that person to be a violator at large. The superintendent, upon being advised of the apprehension and availability for return of a violator at large, shall recommend to the authority that he be returned to the institution or restored to parole, furlough, or other release. If the violator is not restored to parole, furlough, or other release, he shall be returned to a state correctional institution.

The time between the date on which a parolee, furloughee, or other releasee is declared to be a violator or violator at large and the date on which that person is returned to custody in this state under the immediate control of the adult parole authority shall not be counted as time served under the sentence imposed on that person.

(2) A furloughee or any releasee other than a person who is released on parole or pardon is considered to be in custody while on furlough or other release, and, if he absconds from supervision, he may be prosecuted for the offense of escape.

(D) A parolee, furloughee, or other releasee who has violated any term or condition of pardon, parole, furlough, or other release shall be declared to be a violator if he is committed to a correctional institution outside the state to serve a sentence imposed upon him by a federal court or a court of another state or if he otherwise leaves the state.

(E) As used in this section, "peace officer" has the same meaning as in section 2935.01 of the Revised Code.

(1995 H 117, eff. 6–30–95; 1994 H 571, eff. 10–6–94; 1992 S 49, eff. 7–21–92; 130 v Pt 2, H 28)

Note: See also following version of this section, and Publisher's Note.

2967.15 Violation of pardon or parole

Note: See also preceding version of this section, and Publisher's Note.

(A) An adult parole authority field officer who has reasonable cause to believe that a parolee, furloughee, or other releasee under the supervision of the adult parole authority has violated or is violating the condition of a conditional pardon, parole, shock parole, furlough, or other form of authorized release specified in division (A) of section 2967.131 of the Revised Code or any other term or condition of the person's conditional pardon, parole, shock parole, furlough, or other form of authorized release may arrest the person without a warrant or order a peace officer to arrest the person without a warrant. A person so arrested shall be confined in the jail of the county in which the person is arrested or in another facility designated by the chief of the adult parole authority until a determination is made regarding the person's release status. Upon making an arrest under this section, the arresting or supervising adult parole authority field officer promptly shall notify the superintendent of parole supervision or the superintendent's designee, in writing, that the person has been arrested and is in custody and submit in detail an appropriate report of the reason for the arrest.

(B) Subsequent to the arrest of a parolee, furloughee, or other releasee pursuant to this section, the person shall be granted a hearing to determine whether the person has violated the condition of a conditional pardon, parole, shock parole, furlough, or other form of authorized release specified in division (A) of section 2967.131 of the Revised Code or any of the other terms and conditions of the person's conditional pardon, parole, shock parole, furlough, or other form of authorized release and whether the person should be returned to a state correctional institution, except that a parolee, furloughee, or other releasee who is convicted of or pleads guilty to an offense committed while on a conditional pardon, parole, shock parole, furlough, or other form of authorized release is not entitled to the hearing. A member of the parole board, a hearing officer, or another person designated by the chief of the authority shall conduct the hearing in accordance with rules adopted by the director of rehabilitation and correction.

If the person who conducts the hearing decides that the parolee, furloughee, or other releasee does not have to return to a state correctional institution, the parolee, furloughee, or releasee immediately shall be released, provided there are no unadjudicated criminal charges pending against the parolee, furloughee, or releasee in this state.

If the person who conducts the hearing decides that the parolee, furloughee, or other releasee should return to a state correctional institution, the superintendent, within a reasonable time, shall order the return of the parolee, furloughee, or releasee to an institution.

If a parolee is declared to be a violator of the conditions of the parolee's conditional pardon, the authority forthwith shall transmit to the governor its recommendation concerning that violation, and the violator shall be retained in custody until the governor issues an order concerning that violation.

If the authority fails to make a determination of the case of a parolee alleged to be a violator of the terms and conditions of the parolee's conditional pardon, parole, or shock parole within a reasonable time, the parolee shall be released from custody under the same terms and conditions of the parolee's original conditional pardon, parole, or shock parole.

(C)(1) If a parolee, furloughee, or other releasee absconds from supervision, that fact shall be reported by the superintendent to the authority, in writing, and the authority shall enter an order upon its official minutes declaring that person to be a violator at large. The superintendent, upon being advised of the apprehension and availability for return of a violator at large, shall recommend to the authority that the violator at large be returned to the institution or restored to parole, furlough, or other form of authorized release. If the violator is not restored to parole, furlough, or other form of authorized release, the violator shall be returned to a state correctional institution.

The time between the date on which a parolee, furloughee, or other releasee is declared to be a violator or violator at large and the date on which that person is returned to custody in this state under the immediate control of the adult parole authority shall not be counted as time served under the sentence imposed on that person.

(2) A furloughee or a releasee other than a person who is released on parole, shock parole, or conditional pardon is considered to be in custody while on furlough or other release, and, if the furloughee or releasee absconds from supervision, the furloughee or releasee may be prosecuted for the offense of escape.

(D) A person who is a parolee, furloughee, or other releasee and who has violated a term or condition of the person's conditional pardon, parole, shock parole, furlough, or other form of authorized release shall be declared to be a violator if the person is committed to a correctional institution outside the state to serve a sentence imposed upon the person by a federal court or a court of another state or if the person otherwise leaves the state.

(E) As used in this section, "peace officer" has the same meaning as in section 2935.01 of the Revised Code.

(1995 H 4, eff. 11–9–95; 1994 H 571, eff. 10–6–94; 1992 S 49, eff. 7–21–92; 130 v Pt 2, H 28)

Note: See also preceding version of this section, and Publisher's Note.

Historical and Statutory Notes

Publisher's Note: 2967.15 was amended by 1995 H 117, eff. 6–30–95 and 1995 H 4, eff. 11–9–95. Harmonization pursuant to section 1.52 of the Revised Code is in question. See *Baldwin's Ohio Legislative Service*, 1995, pages 6/L–671 and 7/L–1490 for original versions of these Acts.

2967.16 Final release of paroled prisoners

(A) Except as provided in division (C) of this section, when a paroled prisoner has faithfully performed the conditions and obligations of his parole and has obeyed the rules and regulations adopted by the adult parole authority that apply to him, the authority upon the recommendation of the superintendent of parole supervision may enter upon its minutes a final release and thereupon shall issue to the paroled prisoner a certificate of final release, but no final release shall be granted earlier than one year after the prisoner is released from the institution on parole unless his maximum sentence has expired prior thereto, and in the case of a prisoner whose minimum sentence is life imprisonment, no final release shall be granted earlier than five years after the prisoner is released from the institution on parole.

(B) A prisoner who has served the maximum term of his sentence or who has been granted his final release by the adult parole authority shall be restored to the rights and privileges forfeited by his conviction.

(C) Division (A) of this section does not apply to a prisoner in the shock incarceration program established pursuant to section 5120.031 of the Revised Code.

(1994 H 314, eff. 9–29–94; 131 v H 848, eff. 11–1–65; 130 v Pt 2, H 28)

2967.17 Administrative release of parole violator

The adult parole authority, in its discretion, may grant an administrative release to a parole violator serving another felony sentence in a correctional institution within or without this state for the purpose of consolidation of the records or if justice would best be served or to a parole violator at large whose case has been inactive for at least ten years following the date of declaration of parole violation;

(C) [1] To a parolee taken into custody by the immigration and naturalization service of the United States department of justice and deported from the United States.

An administrative release shall not be granted except upon the concurrence of a majority of the parole board and approval of the chief of the adult parole authority and shall not operate to restore the rights and privileges forfeited by conviction as provided in section 2961.01 of the Revised Code. Any person granted an administrative release under this section may subsequently apply for a commutation of sentence for the purpose of regaining the rights and privileges forfeited by conviction.

(1994 S 242, eff. 10–6–94; 1994 H 571, eff. 10–6–94; 131 v H 333, eff. 10–20–65)

[1] Paragraph designation is the result of the harmonization of 1994 S 242 and 1994 H 571.

Historical and Statutory Notes

Ed. Note: A special endorsement by the Legislative Service Commission states, "Comparison of these amendments [1994 S 242, eff. 10–6–94 and 1994 H 571, eff. 10–6–94] in pursuance of section 1.52 of the Revised Code discloses that they are not irreconcilable, so that they are required by that section to be harmonized to give effect to each amendment." In recognition of this rule of construction, changes made by 1994 S 242, eff. 10–6–94, and 1994 H 571, eff. 10–6–94, have been incorporated in the above amendment. See *Baldwin's Ohio Legislative Service*, 1994 Laws of Ohio, pages 5–1040 and 5–1168, for original versions of these Acts.

2967.18 Reduction of sentences or advance of release dates when overcrowding emergency exists; when sentence reduction or advance of release date prohibited

(A) Whenever the director of rehabilitation and correction determines that the total population of the state correctional institutions for males and females, the total population of the state correctional institutions for males, or the total population of the state correctional institutions for females exceeds the capacity of those institutions and that an overcrowding emergency exists, he shall notify the correctional institution inspection committee of the emergency and provide the committee with information in support of his determination. The director shall not notify the committee that an overcrowding emergency exists unless he determines that no other reasonable method is available to resolve the overcrowding emergency.

(B) On receipt of the notice given pursuant to division (A) of this section, the correctional institution inspection committee promptly shall review the determination of the director of rehabilitation and correction. Notwithstanding any other provision of the Revised Code or the Administrative Code that governs the lengths of criminal sentences or sets forth the time within which a prisoner is eligible for parole or that regulates the procedure for granting parole to prisoners confined in state correctional institutions, the committee may recommend either of the following to the governor:

(1) That the minimum sentences of eligible male, female, or all prisoners, as determined under division (E) of this section, be reduced by thirty, sixty, or ninety days, in the manner prescribed in that division;

(2) That the release dates of male, female, or all prisoners serving determinate sentences of longer than nine months for nonviolent offenses be advanced by thirty, sixty, or ninety days.

(C) If the correctional institution inspection committee disagrees with the determination of the director of rehabilitation and correction that an overcrowding emergency exists, if the committee finds that an overcrowding emergency exists but does not make a recommendation pursuant to division (B) of this section, or if the committee does not make a finding or a recommendation pursuant to that division within thirty days of receipt of the notice given pursuant to division (A) of this section, the director may recommend to the governor that either of the actions set forth in division (B)(1) or (2) of this section be taken.

(D) Upon receipt of a recommendation from the correctional institution inspection committee or the director of rehabilitation and correction made pursuant to this section, the governor may declare in writing that an overcrowding emergency exists in all of the institutions within the control of the department in which men are confined, in which women are confined, or both. The declaration shall state which of the actions set forth in division (B)(1) or (2) of this section the adult parole authority shall take. After the governor makes the declaration, the director shall file a copy of it with the secretary of state, which copy shall be a public record.

The department may begin to implement the declaration of the governor made pursuant to this section on the date that it is filed with the secretary of state. The department shall begin to implement the declaration within thirty days after the date of filing. If the declaration states that the action set forth in division (B)(1) of this section is to be taken, the declaration shall be implemented in accordance with division (E) of this section.

(E)(1) No reduction of sentence pursuant to division (B)(1) of this section shall be granted to any of the following:

(a) A person who is serving a term of imprisonment for aggravated murder, murder, voluntary manslaughter, involuntary manslaughter, felonious assault, kidnapping, rape, felonious sexual penetration, aggravated arson, aggravated robbery, or conspiracy in, complicity in, or attempt to commit any of those offenses;

(b) A person who is serving a term of imprisonment for any felony other than carrying a concealed weapon that was committed while the person had a firearm, as defined in section 2923.11 of the Revised Code, on or about his person or under his control;

(c) A person who is serving a term of imprisonment for a violation of division (A)(1), (5), or (7) of section 2925.03 of the Revised Code;

(d) A person who is serving a term of imprisonment for engaging in a pattern of corrupt activity;

(e) A person who is serving a term of imprisonment for gross patient abuse and who in addition to the offense for which he is serving the term of imprisonment, previously has been convicted of or pleaded guilty to the offense of gross patient abuse;

(f) A person who was denied parole during the term of imprisonment he is currently serving.

(2) A declaration of the governor that requires the adult parole authority to take the action set forth in division (B)(1) of this section shall be implemented only by reducing the minimum sentences of prisoners who are not in any of the categories set forth in division (E)(1) of this section, and only by granting reductions of minimum sentences in the following order:

(a) Under any such declaration, minimum sentences initially shall be reduced only for persons who are not in any of the categories set forth in division (E)(1) of this section and who are not serving a term of imprisonment for any of the following offenses:

(i) An offense of violence that is an aggravated felony of the first, second, or third degree or that is a felony of the first or second degree;

(ii) An offense set forth in Chapter 2925. of the Revised Code that is a felony of the first or second degree.

(b) If every person serving a term of imprisonment at the time of the implementation of any such declaration who is in the class of persons eligible for the initial reduction of minimum sentences, as described in division (E)(2)(a) of this section, has received a total of ninety days of sentence reduction for each three years of imprisonment actually served, then minimum sentences may be reduced for all other persons serving a term of imprisonment at that time who are not in any of the categories set forth in division (E)(1) of this section.

(F) An offender who is released from a state correctional institution pursuant to this section shall be deemed paroled and subject to supervision by the adult parole authority.

(G) If more than one overcrowding emergency is declared while a prisoner is serving a term of imprisonment, the total sentence reduction for that prisoner as the result of multiple declarations shall not exceed ninety days for each three years of imprisonment actually served.

(1994 H 571, eff. 10–6–94; 1993 H 152, eff. 7–1–93; 1991 H 298; 1987 H 262; 1982 H 269, S 199)

2967.19 Deduction from sentence for faithful observance of rules; procedures

(A) Except as provided in division (F) of this section, a person confined in a state correctional institution is entitled to a deduction from his minimum or definite sentence of thirty per cent of the sentence, prorated for each month of the sentence during which he faithfully has observed the rules of the institution. Any deduction earned under this division shall be credited to the person pursuant to division (E) of this section.

(B) Except as provided in division (F) of this section, a person confined in a state correctional institution who is serving a sentence of life imprisonment with parole eligibility after serving twenty years of imprisonment imposed pursuant to section 2929.022 or 2929.03 of the Revised Code and who is not eligible for parole before serving twenty years of imprisonment under that sentence, is entitled, for faithfully observing the rules of the institution, to a diminution of thirty per cent of the time that is required to be served before parole eligibility, as determined under section 2967.13 of the Revised Code. A person confined in a state correctional institution who is serving a life sentence imposed pursuant to section 2929.022 or 2929.03 of the Revised Code and who is not eligible for parole before serving a term of twenty full years of imprisonment or thirty full years of imprisonment under that sentence is not entitled to any diminution of the twenty full years or thirty full years that he is required to serve before parole eligibility. A person confined in a state correctional institution for life for the offense of first degree murder or aggravated murder, which sentence was imposed for an offense committed prior to October 19, 1981, or for the offense of rape or felonious sexual penetration, is not entitled to any diminution, pursuant to this section, of the time that is required to be served before parole eligibility, as determined under section 2967.13 of the Revised Code.

(C) When a person is serving consecutive sentences of imprisonment, at least one of which is a sentence referred to in division (B) of this section, and is eligible for the diminution provided in divisions (A) and (B) of this section, the diminution shall be separately calculated for the sentences included within the provisions of division (A) of this section and for the sentences included within the provisions of division (B) of this section. The diminution separately calculated for each sentence under divisions (A) and (B) of this section shall be aggregated, and the total aggregated diminution shall be subtracted from the base number of years that is required to be served on the consecutive sentences before the prisoner becomes eligible for parole, as determined under divisions (G), (H), (I), and (J) of section 2967.13 of the Revised Code.

(D) A prisoner sentenced to a state correctional institution pursuant to division (F) of section 2929.41 of the Revised Code shall be allowed a deduction equal to one-third of his sentence.

(E) The thirty per cent diminution of a prisoner's sentence that is provided in divisions (A), (B), and (C) of this section and the diminution of a prisoner's sentence that is provided in division (D) of this section shall be prorated on a monthly basis and shall be credited to each prisoner at the expiration of every calendar month. After a prorated diminution has been credited for a given month, it shall not be reduced or forfeited for any reason. The department of rehabilitation and correction shall adopt rules that apply uniformly to all state correctional institutions, that establish criteria for denying the diminution of sentence that a prisoner could be credited under this section, identify the violations of rules of the institutions for which the diminution will be denied, and specify the percentage and number of months of denial for each rule violation. If a prisoner violates the rules of the institution in which he is confined, he may be denied the diminution of his sentence for a specified number of months after the violation, but shall not be required to forfeit any of his accumulated diminution of sentence. The denial of diminution of a sentence shall be recorded for the prisoner at the expiration of each calendar month for which the diminution is denied.

(F) A person who is confined in a state correctional institution shall not have his minimum or definite term diminished pursuant to any statute or rule other than this section and sections 2967.193 or 5145.11 of the Revised Code. The total of any diminution of sentence granted pursuant to division (A), (B), or (C) of this section shall not exceed, for any prisoner, thirty per cent of the minimum or definite sentence, or in the case of a sentence of life imprisonment, thirty per cent of the number of years before parole eligibility, of the sentence imposed upon the prisoner. The cumulative total of any diminution of sentence granted pursuant to this section, any days of credit awarded pursuant to section 2967.193 of the Revised Code, and any diminution of sentence granted under section 5145.11 of the Revised Code shall not exceed, for any prisoner, one-third of the minimum or definite sentence, or in the case of a sentence of life imprisonment, one-third of the number of years before parole eligibility, of the sentence imposed upon the prisoner.

A person confined in a state correctional institution who is serving a period of imprisonment that constitutes a portion of a sentence of shock incarceration, which period of imprisonment is of the type described in division (B)(2)(a) of section 5120.031 of the Revised Code, shall not have his minimum or definite term diminished pursuant to this section during that period of imprisonment. A person who is serving a period of electronically monitored early release under sections 5120.071 to 5120.074 of the Revised Code is not to be considered for purposes of this section as being confined in a state correctional institution and shall not have his minimum or definite term diminished pursuant to this section during that period of electronically monitored early release.

(G)(1) The department of rehabilitation and correction shall maintain statistical data that will enable it to analyze the impact of the diminution of sentence provided to prisoners by this section upon the correctional population of this state and upon prisoners to whom it is provided. The data shall include, but shall not be limited to, all of the following:

(a) The total diminution granted each month to all persons confined in a state correctional institution.

(b) The number of persons each month who are denied the diminution and the total amount of diminution denied each month;

(c) The number of persons who are granted diminution and actually are granted parole prior to the earliest date of parole eligibility they would have had without the diminution;

(d) The number of persons who are granted diminution and actually are released before the expiration of their definite term of imprisonment as it existed without the diminution;

(e) The number of persons described in division (G)(1)(c) or (d) of this section who are returned to a department institution as parole violators, or who are convicted of another offense and are confined in a department institution.

(2) The department annually shall analyze the data it maintains under division (G)(1) of this section and shall prepare a report containing its analysis, which report shall be distributed to each member of the general assembly.

(1994 H 571, eff. 10–6–94; 1992 H 725, eff. 4–16–93; 1990 S 258; 1987 H 261; 1983 S 210; 1982 H 269, § 4, S 199; 1981 S 1; 1972 H 511; 130 v Pt 2, H 28)

2967.191   Credit for confinement awaiting trial and commitment

The adult parole authority shall reduce the minimum and maximum sentence or the definite sentence of a prisoner by the total number of days that the prisoner was confined for any reason arising out of the offense for which he was convicted and sentenced, including confinement in lieu of bail while awaiting trial, confinement for examination to determine his competence to stand trial or sanity, confinement in a community based correctional facility and program or district community based correctional facility and program, and confinement while awaiting transportation to the place where he is to serve his sentence.

(1982 H 269, § 4, eff. 7–1–83; 1982 S 199; 1980 H 1000; 1978 H 565; 1972 H 511; 131 v S 133)

2967.192   Applicable law by time of offense; multiple sentences

(A) Section 2967.19 of the Revised Code, as amended by Amended Substitute Senate Bill No. 199 of the 114th general assembly, shall apply only to persons sentenced to state correctional institutions for offenses committed on or after July 1, 1983, and prior to November 1, 1987. The diminution of a person's minimum or definite term for good behavior or for obeying the rules of the institution in which he is incarcerated shall be calculated pursuant to the statutes and rules that existed immediately prior to July 1, 1983, if the person is or was sentenced, before or after January 5, 1983, to a state correctional institution for an offense committed prior to July 1, 1983, and the person is not serving a term of imprisonment for any offense committed on or after July 1, 1983, and prior to November 1, 1987.

If a person is serving one or more terms of imprisonment for offenses committed before July 1, 1983, and also one or more terms of imprisonment for offenses committed on or after July 1, 1983, and prior to November 1, 1987, the diminution of the person's minimum or definite terms for good behavior or for obeying the rules of the institution in which he is incarcerated shall be calculated as follows:

(1) If the terms of imprisonment are being served concurrently, the diminution of the minimum or definite terms shall be earned concurrently, and the person shall be eligible for parole or be released, whichever is applicable, after the expiration of the longest diminished minimum or definite term.

(2) If the terms of imprisonment are being served consecutively and the minimum and definite terms do not in the aggregate exceed the applicable maximum set forth in division (E) of section 2929.41 of the Revised Code, each minimum and definite term shall be diminished separately with the minimum terms that were imposed for offenses committed prior to July 1, 1983, being diminished first and in the same order that the applicable offenses were committed.

(3) If the terms of imprisonment are being served consecutively and the minimum and definite terms in the aggregate exceed the applicable maximum set forth in division (E) of section 2929.41 of the Revised Code, the diminution shall be applied to the minimum and definite terms and any part of a minimum or definite term that in the aggregate equal the applicable maximum and that were imposed for the offenses that were first in chronological sequence.

(B) The provisions of section 2967.19 of the Revised Code, as amended effective November 1, 1987, shall apply to all persons who are confined in a state correctional institution on or after November 1, 1987, regardless of the date on which the person committed the offense for which he is confined. However, if, on November 1, 1987, the person is serving one or more terms of imprisonment for offenses committed before November 1, 1987, the provisions of section 2967.19 of the Revised Code, as amended effective November 1, 1987, apply only in relation to the portion of the term or terms served on or after November 1, 1987, and the diminution of the person's minimum or definite term for good behavior or for obeying the rules of the institution in which he is incarcerated in relation to the portion of the term or terms served prior to November 1, 1987, shall be governed by division (A) of this section.

(1994 H 571, eff. 10–6–94; 1987 H 261, eff. 11–1–87; 1982 H 269, § 4)

2967.193 Deduction from sentence for participation in rehabilitation programs; procedures

(A) Except as provided in division (D) or (E) of this section, any person confined in a state correctional institution is entitled to earn days of credit as a deduction from his minimum or definite sentence as follows:

(1) Two days shall be awarded to the prisoner and be deducted from his sentence for each full month during which he productively participates in any of the following programs approved by the department of rehabilitation and correction:

(a) Academic or vocational education;

(b) Prison industries;

(c) Alcohol and drug abuse rehabilitation.

(2) Three days shall be awarded to the prisoner and be deducted from his sentence for each full month during which the prisoner remains at minimum security status, as defined by the department of rehabilitation and correction.

(B) Except as provided in division (E) of this section, the director of rehabilitation and correction, at his discretion, may award not more than one hundred twenty days of credit to any person confined in a state correctional institution for meritorious conduct involving the protection of persons or property while incarcerated.

(C) Any days of credit earned by a prisoner under division (A) of this section shall be awarded to the prisoner at the expiration of the calendar month in which they are earned, and, after those days have been awarded, they shall not be reduced or forfeited for any reason. Any days of credit awarded to a prisoner under division (B) of this section shall not be reduced or forfeited for any reason.

(D) No prisoner is entitled to earn the days of credit described in division (A)(1) of this section unless his participation in the program described in division (A)(1)(a), (b), or (c) of this section is a productive participation. The department of rehabilitation and correction shall adopt rules that establish criteria for determining whether a prisoner's participation in any of the programs listed in division (A)(1)(a), (b), or (c) of this section is sufficiently productive for the prisoner to qualify for the days of credit described in division (A)(1) of this section. The rules shall ensure that mere participation in any such program without any benefit to, or positive experience on the part of, the prisoner does not constitute a sufficiently productive participation in the program.

(E)(1) The provisions of this section apply to all persons who are confined in a state correctional institution on or after November 1, 1987, provided that no days of credit may be earned by or awarded to any such person under division (A) or (B) of this section for any program participation, any period of minimum security status, or any meritorious conduct that occurred prior to November 1, 1987.

(2) No person who is serving a term of actual incarceration imposed pursuant to section 2929.71 or 2929.72 of the Revised Code shall be awarded any days of credit under division (A) or (B) of this section for any program participation, any period of minimum security status, or any meritorious conduct that occurred during the term of actual incarceration. No person who is serving a sentence of imprisonment for life with parole eligibility after serving fifteen full years, twenty full years, or thirty full years of imprisonment, as described in division (B), (D), or (E) of section 2967.13 of the Revised Code, shall be awarded any days of credit under division (A) or (B) of this section for any program participation, any period of minimum security status, or any meritorious conduct that occurred before the person becomes eligible for parole. No person who is serving a term of imprisonment for which he becomes eligible for parole after serving a term of ten full years' imprisonment, as described in division (F) of section 2967.13 of the Revised Code, shall be awarded any days of credit under division (A) or (B) of this section for any program participation, any period of minimum security status, or any

meritorious conduct that occurred before the person becomes eligible for parole. No person who is serving a period of imprisonment that constitutes a portion of a sentence of shock incarceration, which period of imprisonment is of the type described in division (B)(2)(a) of section 5120.031 of the Revised Code, shall be awarded any days of credit under division (A) or (B) of this section for any program participation, any period of minimum security status, or any meritorious conduct that occurred during that period of imprisonment. A person who is serving a period of electronically monitored early release under sections 5120.071 to 5120.074 of the Revised Code is not to be considered for purposes of this section as being confined in a state correctional institution and shall not be awarded any days of credit under division (A) or (B) of this section for any program participation, any period of minimum security status, or any meritorious conduct that occurred during that period of electronically monitored early release.

(3) The cumulative total of any days of credit awarded under division (A) or (B) of this section, any diminution of sentence granted pursuant to section 2967.19 of the Revised Code, and any diminution of sentence granted pursuant to section 5145.11 of the Revised Code shall not exceed, for any prisoner, one-third of the minimum or definite sentence, or in the case of a sentence of life imprisonment, one-third of the number of years before parole eligibility, of the sentence imposed upon the prisoner.

(F)(1) The department of rehabilitation and correction shall maintain statistical data that will enable it to analyze the impact of the days of credit provided to prisoners under division (A) or (B) of this section upon the correctional population of this state and upon prisoners to whom the days of credit are provided. The data shall include, but shall not be limited to, all of the following:

(a) The total days of credit granted each month to all persons confined in a state correctional institution;

(b) The number of persons who are granted days of credit and actually are granted parole prior to the earliest date of parole eligibility they would have had without the days of credit;

(c) The number of persons who are granted days of credit and actually are released before the expiration of their definite term of imprisonment as it existed without the days of credit;

(d) The number of persons described in division (F)(1)(b) or (c) of this section who are returned to a department institution as parole violators, or who are convicted of another offense and are confined in a department institution.

(2) The department annually shall analyze the data it maintains under division (F)(1) of this section and shall prepare a report containing its analysis, which report shall be distributed to each member of the general assembly.

(1994 H 571, eff. 10–6–94; 1992 H 725, eff. 4–16–93; 1990 S 258; 1987 H 261)

2967.20 Transfer of prisoners—Repealed

(1994 H 571, eff. 10–6–94; 1972 H 494, eff. 7–1–72 [1]; 130 v Pt 2, H 28)

[1] 1972 H 494, § 3, states that 2967.20 takes effect 7–1–72. The Ohio Constitution provides that "no law passed by the general assembly shall go into effect until ninety days after it shall have been filed by the governor in the office of the secretary of state" (Art II, § 1c)—*except* for emergency laws and laws providing for tax levies or appropriations for current expenses, which take effect immediately (Art II, § 1d). Since H 494 is apparently not an exception, and 7–1–72 is within the ninety-day period, the effective date of 2967.20 is probably 7–12–72.

2967.21 Effect of transfer on term of sentence

Any prisoner sentenced or committed to a state correctional institution may be transferred from that institution to another state correctional institution, but he shall continue to be subject to the same conditions as to term of sentence, diminution of sentence, and parole as if confined in the institution to which he was originally sentenced or committed.

(1994 H 571, eff. 10–6–94; 130 v Pt 2, H 28, eff. 3–18–65)

2967.22 Parolee or probationer appearing to be mentally ill; procedures; effects of escape and of return

Whenever it is brought to the attention of the adult parole authority or county department of probation that a parolee, furloughee, or probationer appears to be a mentally ill person subject to hospitalization by court order, as defined in section 5122.01 of the Revised Code, or a mentally retarded person subject to institutionalization by court order, as defined in section 5123.01 of the Revised Code, the parole or probation officer may, subject to the approval of the chief of the adult parole authority or his designee or chief probation officer, file an affidavit under section 5122.11 or 5123.71 of the Revised Code. A parolee or probationer who is involuntarily detained under Chapter 5122. or 5123. of the Revised Code shall receive credit against the period of parole or probation for the period of involuntary detention.

If a parolee, probationer, or furloughee escapes from an institution or facility within the department of mental health or the department of mental retardation and developmental disabilities, the superintendent of the institution shall immediately notify the chief of the adult parole authority or the chief probation officer. Notwithstanding the provisions of section 5122.26 of the Revised Code, the procedure for the apprehension, detention, and return of the parolee, probationer, or furloughee is the same as that provided for the apprehension, detention, and return of persons who escape from institutions operated by the department of rehabilitation and correction. If a parolee or furloughee is not apprehended and returned to the custody of the department of mental health or the department of mental retardation and developmental disabilities within ninety days after his escape, he shall be discharged from the custody of the department of mental health or the department of mental retardation and developmental disabilities and returned to the custody of the department of rehabilitation and correction. If a probationer is not apprehended and returned to the custody of the department of mental health or the department of mental retardation and developmental disabilities within ninety days after his escape, he shall be discharged from the custody of the department of mental health or the department of mental retardation and developmental disabilities and returned to the custody of the court that sentenced him.

(1990 H 569, eff. 7–1–91; 1980 H 965, S 52; 1978 H 565; 1972 H 494; 130 v Pt 2, H 28)

2967.23 Early release of prisoners to halfway house or community-based correctional facility

(A) The department of rehabilitation and correction may release a prisoner who is serving a definite sentence to a halfway house licensed pursuant to section 2967.14 of the Revised Code or, with the approval of the judicial corrections board of the facility, to a community-based correctional facility and program as provided in section 2929.221 of the Revised Code for the last one hundred twenty days of the definite sentence.

(B) The department of rehabilitation and correction shall adopt rules for granting releases under this section, supervising prisoners on release, and administering the release program. No prisoner shall be released under this section if he has ever been convicted of an offense of violence. A prisoner who violates any rule established by the department under this section may be returned to the state correctional institution from which he was released.

(1994 H 571, eff. 10–6–94; 1992 S 331, eff. 11–13–92)

2967.25 Parole eligibility when serving consecutive sentences

A person serving several indeterminate sentences consecutively becomes eligible for parole upon the expiration of the aggregate of the minimum terms of his several sentences diminished as provided in section 2967.19 of the Revised Code.

(1972 H 511, eff. 1–1–74; 1969 H 1; 132 v H 65; 130 v Pt 2, H 28)

2967.26 Furloughs for employment or education; furlough services fund

(A)(1) The adult parole authority may grant furloughs to trustworthy prisoners, other than those serving a term of actual incarceration or those serving a sentence of imprisonment for life imposed for an offense committed on or after October 19, 1981, who are confined in any state correctional institution for the purpose of employment, vocational training, educational programs, or other programs designated by the director of rehabilitation and correction within this state. The adult parole authority shall not grant a prisoner who is serving a term of actual incarceration or sentence of imprisonment for life imposed for an offense committed on or after October 19, 1981, a furlough under this section. Additionally, the adult parole authority shall not grant a prisoner a furlough under this section if the prisoner has more than six months of imprisonment to serve until parole eligibility, as determined under section 2967.13 of the Revised Code, or in relation to a definite sentence of imprisonment, if the prisoner has more than six months of imprisonment to serve until the expiration of his definite sentence, diminished as provided in section 2967.19 of the Revised Code.

(2) If the victim of an offense for which a prisoner was sentenced to a term of imprisonment has notified the department of rehabilitation and correction of his name and address, the adult parole authority, at least three weeks prior to granting a furlough to the prisoner pursuant to this section, shall notify the victim of the pendency of the furlough. If the victim subsequently submits a statement to the authority regarding the impact of the release of the prisoner on furlough, the authority shall consider the statement in deciding whether to grant the furlough.

(B) The department of rehabilitation and correction shall place conditions on the release of any prisoner who is granted a furlough pursuant to this section. Each such prisoner shall be confined during any period of time that he is not actually working at his approved employment, engaged in a vocational training or other educational program, engaged in another program designated by the director pursuant to division (A) of this section, or engaged in other activities approved by the department.

While a prisoner who is granted a furlough pursuant to this section is confined during the furlough period, the confinement shall be in a suitable facility that has been licensed by the division of parole and community services pursuant to division (C) of section 2967.14 of the Revised Code. The division may enter into agreements with any agency, public or private, or a department or political subdivision of the state, that operates a facility that has been licensed by the division pursuant to division (C) of section 2967.14 of the Revised Code. An agreement shall provide for housing, supervision, and other services that are required for furloughed prisoners who are assigned to the facility. An agreement shall provide for per diem payments to the agency, department, or political subdivision on behalf of each furloughed prisoner who is assigned to a facility that is operated by the agency, department, or political subdivision and that has been licensed by the division. The per diem payments shall be equal to the facility's average daily per capita costs with its facility at full occupancy. The per diem payments shall not exceed the total operating costs of the facility during the term of an agreement. The director of rehabilitation and correction shall adopt rules in accordance with Chapter 119. of the Revised Code for determining includable and excludable costs and income to be used in computing the agency's average daily per capita costs with its facility at full occupancy.

(C) The adult parole authority, subject to approval by the director of rehabilitation and correction, shall adopt rules for granting furloughs, supervising and confining prisoners on furlough, and administering the furlough program. The rules shall reflect the fact that no prisoner is eligible for furlough who is serving a term of actual incarceration or a sentence of imprisonment for life imposed for an offense committed on or after October 19, 1981, and shall provide that no prisoner is eligible for furlough who is serving another type of sentence and who has more than six months of imprisonment to serve until parole eligibility, as determined under section 2967.13 of the Revised Code, or in relation to a definite sentence of imprisonment, who has more than six months of imprisonment to serve until the expiration of his definite sentence, diminished as provided in section 2967.19 of the Revised Code.

(D) The authority may provide for payment by the prisoner on furlough to the division of reasonable expenses incurred by the division in supervising or confining the prisoner on furlough. Inability to pay such expenses shall not be grounds for refusing to grant a furlough to an otherwise eligible prisoner. Amounts received by the division under this division shall be deposited into the furlough services fund, which is hereby created in the state treasury. The fund shall be used solely to pay costs related to the operation of the furlough education and work release program. The director of rehabilitation and correction shall adopt rules in accordance with section 111.15 of the Revised Code for the use of the fund.

(E) A prisoner who violates any rule established by the authority under division (C) of this section may be returned to the state correctional institution in which the prisoner had been confined prior to furlough, but he shall receive credit towards completing his sentence for the time he was on furlough.

(1994 S 186, eff. 10–12–94; 1994 H 571, eff. 10–6–94; 1993 H 152, eff. 7–1–93; 1988 S 94; 1983 S 210; 1982 H 269, § 4, S 199; 1981 H 694, S 1; 1976 H 637; 1971 H 567)

Historical and Statutory Notes

Ed. Note: A special endorsement by the Legislative Service Commission states, "Comparison of these amendments [1994 S 186, eff. 10–12–94 and 1994 H 571, eff. 10–6–94] in pursuance of section 1.52 of the Revised Code discloses that they are not irreconcilable, so that they are required by that section to be harmonized to give effect to each amendment." In recognition of this rule of construction, changes made by 1994 S 186, eff. 10–12–94, and 1994 H 571, eff. 10–6–94, have been incorporated in the above amendment. See *Baldwin's Ohio Legislative Service*, 1994 Laws of Ohio, pages 5–929 and 5–1170, for original versions of these Acts.

2967.27 Furloughs for trustworthy prisoners; rules to be adopted; limitations

(A)(1) The department of rehabilitation and correction may grant furloughs to trustworthy prisoners confined in any state correctional facility for the custody and rehabilitation of persons convicted of crime, except that the department shall not grant a furlough for any purpose other than the purposes described in division (A)(1)(a) or (b) of this section to a prisoner serving a sentence of life imprisonment that was imposed for an offense committed on or after October 19, 1981. The department may authorize furloughs under this section for the purpose of:

(a) Visiting a dying relative;

(b) Attending the funeral of a relative;

(c) Arranging for a suitable parole plan, or an educational or vocational furlough plan;

(d) Arranging for employment;

(e) Arranging for suitable residence;

(f) Visiting with family;

(g) Otherwise aiding in the rehabilitation of the inmate.

(2) If the victim of an offense for which a prisoner was sentenced to a term of imprisonment has notified the department of rehabilitation and correction of his name and address, the department, at least three weeks prior to granting a furlough to the prisoner pursuant to this section, shall notify the victim of the pendency of the furlough. If the victim subsequently submits a statement to the department regarding the impact of the release of the prisoner on furlough, the department shall consider the statement in deciding whether to grant the furlough.

(B) The department of rehabilitation and correction shall adopt rules for granting furloughs under this section, supervising prisoners on furlough, and administering the furlough program. Such rules shall provide that no prisoner shall be eligible for furlough under this section who has served less than six months in a state correctional institution, except in the situation of attending the funeral of a member of the immediate family, or attending a bedside visit with a member of the immediate family who is ill and bedridden.

(C) No person shall be granted a furlough under this section who is likely to pose a threat to the public safety or has a record of more than two felony commitments (including the present charge), not more than one of which may be for a crime of an assaultive nature.

(D) Furloughs may be granted only upon the written approval of the director of the department of rehabilitation and correction or if the director deems it appropriate, by the assistant director of the department of rehabilitation and correction, or the wardens within the department of rehabilitation and correction.

(E) Furloughs granted pursuant to this section shall be for a period no longer than is reasonably necessary to accomplish the purposes of this section, but in no event shall such furlough extend beyond seven days, nor shall the total furlough time granted to any inmate within any calendar year exceed fourteen days except furloughs granted under divisions (A)(1)(c) and (d) of this section.

(F) A prisoner who violates any rule established by the department of rehabilitation and correction under this section may be returned to the state correctional facility from which he was furloughed, but such violation does not constitute cause for denial of credit toward completion of his sentence of the time the prisoner was on furlough.

(1994 S 186, eff. 10–12–94; 1994 H 571, eff. 10–6–94; 1981 S 1, eff. 10–19–81; 1974 H 217)

Historical and Statutory Notes

Ed. Note: A special endorsement by the Legislative Service Commission states, "Comparison of these amendments [1994 S 186, eff. 10–12–94 and 1994 H 571, eff. 10–6–94] in pursuance of section 1.52 of the Revised Code discloses that they are not irreconcilable, so that they are required by that section to be harmonized to give effect to each amendment." In recognition of this rule of construction, changes made by 1994 S 186, eff. 10–12–94, and 1994 H 571, eff. 10–6–94, have been incorporated in the above amendment. See *Baldwin's Ohio Legislative Service*, 1994 Laws of Ohio, pages 5–929 and 5–1171, for original versions of these Acts.

2967.31 Shock parole

Notwithstanding any other provision for determining parole eligibility, a prisoner confined in a state correctional institution may be released on parole at any time after serving six months in the custody of the department of rehabilitation and correction, when all of the following apply:

(A) The offense for which the prisoner was sentenced was an offense other than aggravated murder, murder, an aggravated felony of the first degree, an aggravated felony of the second degree, an aggravated felony of the third degree, or a felony of the first degree.

(B) The prisoner has not previously been convicted of any felony for which, pursuant to sentence, he was confined for thirty days or more in a correctional institution in this state or in a similar institution in any other state or the United States.

(C) The prisoner is not a dangerous offender as defined in section 2929.01 of the Revised Code.

(D) The prisoner does not need further confinement in a correctional institution for his correction or rehabilitation.

(E) The history, character, condition, and attitudes of the prisoner indicate that he is likely to respond affirmatively to early release on parole, and is unlikely to commit another offense.

(F) The prisoner is not serving a term of actual incarceration.

(G) The prisoner is not ineligible for shock parole pursuant to division (C) of section 2903.06 or 2903.07 of the Revised Code.

(1994 H 571, eff. 10–6–94; 1982 H 269, § 4, eff. 7–1–83; 1982 S 432, S 199; 1975 H 1; 1972 H 511)

CHAPTER 2969

RECOVERY OF OFFENDER'S PROFITS; CRIME VICTIMS RECOVERY FUND

RECOVERY OF OFFENDER'S PROFITS

RECOVERY OF OFFENDER'S PROFITS

2969.01 Definitions

As used in sections 2969.01 to 2969.06 of the Revised Code:

(A) "Offender" means a person who pleads guilty to, is convicted of, or is found not guilty by reason of insanity of an offense in this state or a person against whom a complaint or information has been filed or an indictment has been returned in this state.

(B) "Victim" means a person who suffers personal injury, death, or property loss as a result of any of the following, or the beneficiaries of an action for the wrongful death of any person killed as a result of any of the following:

(1) An offense;

(2) The good faith effort of a person to prevent an offense;

(3) The good faith effort of any person to apprehend a person suspected of engaging in an offense.

(C) "Member of the family of an offender" means an individual who is related by consanguinity or affinity to an offender.

(1995 S 91, eff. 11–15–95; 1984 S 172, eff. 9–26–84)

2969.02 Offender's contract to publish material related to his offense; money due to be paid to clerk of court of claims; liability

(A) Except as provided in section 2969.05 of the Revised Code, a person that enters into a contract with an offender, an agent, assignee, conspirator, or accomplice of an offender, a member of the family of an offender, or an agent or assignee of a member of the family of an offender shall pay the money, and the monetary value of the property other than money, due under the contract to the clerk of the court of claims for deposit in the recovery of offender's profits fund, if the terms of the contract provide for any of the following:

(1) The reenactment or description by the offender or by a member of the family of the offender in any of the following of an offense that the offender committed:

(a) A movie, book, magazine, newspaper, article, or other form of literary expression;

(b) A program on television, radio, or another broadcasting medium;

(c) A play, speech, or another form of live entertainment, instruction, or presentation.

(2) The expression or description of the thoughts, feelings, opinions, or emotions of the offender or of a member of the family of the offender regarding or experienced during the

offense in a material, performance, or program described in division (A)(1)(a), (b), or (c) of this section;

(3) The life story or a part of the life story of the offender or of a member of the family of the offender or an interview or a part of an interview with the offender, an agent, assignee, conspirator, or accomplice of the offender, a member of the family of the offender, or an agent or assignee of a member of the family of an offender that is to be used in a material, performance, or program described in division (A)(1)(a), (b), or (c) of this section, if the publication value of the story or interview results in part from the notoriety brought by the commission of an offense.

(B) An offender, an agent, assignee, conspirator, or accomplice of an offender, a member of the family of an offender, or an agent or assignee of a member of the family of an offender who enters into a contract described in division (A) of this section or a person who receives money or property other than money pursuant to a contract of that nature shall pay the money or the monetary value of the property received pursuant to the contract to the clerk of the court of claims for deposit in the recovery of offender's profits fund. If a person receives money or property pursuant to a contract described in division (A) of this section and fails to pay it or its monetary value to the clerk of the court of claims for deposit in the fund as required by this division, the state has a lien upon the money or property and upon property that is purchased or otherwise obtained with the money or property. The attorney general shall enforce the lien in the same manner as a judgment lien may be enforced by a private individual.

(C)(1) A person who fails to pay money or the monetary value of property other than money to the clerk of the court of claims for deposit as required by this section is liable to the state for the money or the monetary value of the property.

(2) If a person who is required by this section to pay money or the monetary value of property other than money to the clerk of the court of claims for deposit in the recovery of offender's profits fund fails to do so, the attorney general shall bring an action to recover the money or the monetary value of the property against the person who has possession, custody, or control of the money or property or against the person who failed to pay the money or the monetary value of the property to the clerk for deposit in the fund as required by this section. The action shall be brought in the appropriate court. If the court determines in an action brought pursuant to this division that money or the monetary value of property is to be paid to the clerk for deposit in the fund, it shall order that the money be paid to the clerk for deposit in the fund and that the property be sold and the money received from the sale be paid to the clerk for deposit in the fund.

(1995 S 91, eff. 11–15–95; 1985 H 201, eff. 7–1–85; 1984 S 172)

2969.03 Any person may bring declaratory judgment action concerning such a contract

Any person may bring an action for a declaratory judgment to determine if section 2969.02 of the Revised Code applies to a particular contract. The action for a declaratory judgment shall be brought in the Franklin county court of common pleas.

(1984 S 172, eff. 9–26–84)

2969.04 Administration of recovery of offender's profits fund; separate accounts; procedures

(A) The clerk of the court of claims shall administer the recovery of offender's profits fund created by section 2969.06 of the Revised Code and shall maintain in the fund in the name of each offender a separate account for money received, or money received from the sale or other disposition of property, pursuant to section 2969.02 or 2969.03 of the Revised Code. The clerk shall distribute the money in each account in accordance with division (C) of this section.

If money is deposited in the fund and maintained in a separate account in the name of an offender and if the offender is found not guilty of all of the charges against the offender in this state, all of the charges against the offender in this state are dismissed, or the offender is found not guilty of some of the charges against the offender in this state and the remaining charges against the offender in this state are dismissed, the clerk shall return all of the money in the separate account plus the interest earned on the money to the persons from whom it was obtained.

(B) Notwithstanding a contrary provision of any section of the Revised Code that deals with the limitation of actions, a victim of an offense committed by an offender in whose name a separate account is maintained in the recovery of offender's profits fund may bring a civil action against the offender or the representatives of the offender, and, if money in the separate account was obtained from a member of the family of the offender or an agent or assignee of a member of the family of the offender, against the family member, agent, or assignee at any time within three years after the establishment of the separate account.

In order to recover from a separate account maintained in the fund in the name of an offender, a victim of that offender shall do all of the following:

(1) Within the three-year period or, if the action was initiated before the separate account was established, within ninety days after the separate account is established, notify the clerk of the court of claims that a civil action has been brought against the offender or the representatives of the offender and, if money in the separate account was obtained from a member of the family of the offender or an agent or assignee of a member of the family of the offender, against the family member, agent, or assignee;

(2) Notify the clerk of the court of claims of the entry of any judgment in the civil action;

(3) Within ninety days after the judgment in the civil action is final or, if the judgment was obtained before the separate account was established, within ninety days after the separate account is established, request the clerk of the court of claims to pay from the separate account the judgment that the victim is awarded in the civil action.

If a civil action is brought against an offender or the representatives of the offender and, if money in the separate account was obtained from a member of the family of the offender or an agent or assignee of a member of the family of the offender, against the family member, agent, or assignee and if the civil action is brought after the expiration of the statute of limitations that would apply to the civil action but for this division, the court shall state in a judgment in favor of the victim that the judgment may be enforced only against the separate account maintained in the name of that offender in the recovery of offender's profits fund.

(C)(1) The clerk of the court of claims shall not make a payment from the separate account maintained in the name of an offender in the recovery of offender's profits fund to a victim of the offender until the expiration of the later of the following periods:

(a) The expiration of three years after the establishment of the separate account, provided that no action of which the clerk was notified under division (B)(1) of this section is pending;

(b) If three years has elapsed since the establishment of the separate account and if one or more actions of which the clerk was notified under division (B)(1) of this section is pending at the expiration of that three-year period, the date of the final disposition of the last of those pending actions.

(2) Upon the expiration of the applicable period of time set forth in division (C)(1) of this section, the clerk of the court of claims shall make payments from the separate account maintained in the name of an offender in the recovery of offender's profits fund to any victim of the offender who has obtained a judgment against the offender or the representatives of the offender and, if money in the separate account was obtained from a member of the family of the offender or an agent or assignee of a member of the family of the offender, against the family member, agent, or assignee for damages resulting from an offense committed by the offender. The payments shall be made as provided in this division.

After an offender in whose name a separate account is maintained in the recovery of offender's profits fund is convicted of or found not guilty by reason of insanity of any offense in this state, the clerk of the court of claims shall determine on the second day of January and the first day of April, July, and October of each year the amount of money in that separate account. After the expiration of the applicable period of time set forth in division (C)(1) of this section, the clerk shall pay from that separate account any judgment for which a victim of that offender has requested payment pursuant to division (B)(3) of this section and has requested payment prior to the date of the most recent quarterly determination described in this division. If, at a time that payments would be made from that separate account, there are insufficient funds in that separate account to pay all of the applicable judgments against the offender or the representatives of the offender and, if money in the separate account was obtained from a member of the family of the offender or an agent or asignee [*sic*] of a member of the family of the offender, against the family member, agent, or assignee, the clerk of the court of claims shall pay the judgments on a pro rata basis.

(1995 S 91, eff. 11–15–95; 1985 H 201, eff. 7–1–85; 1984 S 172)

2969.05   Distribution of moneys

If a separate account has been maintained in the recovery of offender's profits fund and if there is no further requirement to pay money or the monetary value of property into the fund pursuant to section 2969.02 of the Revised Code, unless otherwise ordered by a court of record in which a judgment has been rendered against the offender or the representatives of the offender and, if money in the separate account was obtained from a member of the family of the offender or an agent or assignee of a member of the family of the offender, against the family member, agent, or assignee, the clerk of the court of claims shall pay the money remaining in the separate account to the persons from whom the money was obtained, if all of the following apply:

(A) The applicable period of time that governs the making of payments from the separate account, as set forth in division (C)(1) of section 2969.04 of the Revised Code, has elapsed.

(B) None of the civil actions against the offender or the representatives of the offender and, if money in the separate account was obtained from a member of the family of the offender or an agent or assignee of a member of the family of the offender, against the family member, agent, or assignee of which the clerk of the court of claims has been notified pursuant to division (B)(1) of section 2969.04 of the Revised Code is pending.

(C) All judgments for which payment was requested pursuant to division (B)(3) of section 2969.04 of the Revised Code have been paid.

(1995 S 91, eff. 11–15–95; 1985 H 201, eff. 7–1–85; 1984 S 172)

2969.06   Recovery of offender's profits fund

All moneys collected pursuant to sections 2969.02 and 2969.03 of the Revised Code shall be credited by the treasurer of state to the recovery of offender's profits fund, which is hereby created in the state treasury. Except as provided in division (A) of section 2969.04 of the Revised Code, any interest earned on the money in the fund shall be credited to the fund.

(1985 H 201, eff. 7–1–85; 1984 S 172)

CRIME VICTIMS RECOVERY FUND

2969.11   Definitions

As used in sections 2969.11 to 2969.14 of the Revised Code:

(A) "Crime victims recovery fund" means the fund created by division (D) of section 2929.25 of the Revised Code.

(B) "Victim" means a person who suffers personal injury, death, or property loss as a result of any of the following, or the beneficiaries of an action for the wrongful death of any person killed as a result of any of the following:

(1) An offense committed by an offender in whose name a separate account is maintained in the crime victims recovery fund pursuant to section 2969.12 of the Revised Code;

(2) The good faith effort of a person to prevent an offense committed by an offender in whose name a separate account is maintained in the crime victims recovery fund pursuant to section 2969.12 of the Revised Code;

(3) The good faith effort of a person to apprehend a person suspected of engaging in an offense committed by an offender in whose name a separate account is maintained in the crime victims recovery fund pursuant to section 2969.12 of the Revised Code.

(1995 S 91, eff. 11–15–95)

2969.12   Administration of fund; separate accounts; civil actions; distribution of moneys

(A) The clerk of the court of claims shall administer the crime victims recovery fund and shall maintain in the fund in the name of each offender a separate account for money received, or money received from the sale or other disposition of property, pursuant to section 2929.25 of the Revised Code in connection with that offender.   The clerk shall distribute the money in that separate account in accordance with division (C) of this section.

(B) Notwithstanding a contrary provision of any section of the Revised Code that deals with the limitation of actions, a victim of an offense committed by an offender in whose name a separate account is maintained in the crime victims recovery fund may bring a civil action against the offender or the representatives of the offender at any time within three years after the establishment of the separate account.

In order to recover from a separate account maintained in the fund in the name of an offender, a victim of that offender shall do all of the following:

(1) Within the three-year period or, if the action was initiated before the separate account was established, within ninety days after the separate account is established, notify the clerk of the court of claims that a civil action has been brought against the offender or the representatives of the offender;

(2) Notify the clerk of the court of claims of the entry of any judgment in the civil action;

(3) Within ninety days after the judgment in the civil action is final or, if the judgment was obtained before the separate account was established, within ninety days after the separate account is established, request the clerk of the court of claims to pay from the separate account the judgment that the victim is awarded in the civil action.

If a civil action is brought against an offender or the representatives of the offender after the expiration of the statute of limitations that would apply to the civil action but for this division, the court shall state in a judgment in favor of the victim that the judgment may be enforced only against the separate account maintained in the name of that offender in the crime victims recovery fund.

(C)(1) The clerk of the court of claims shall not make a payment from the separate account maintained in the name of an offender in the crime victims recovery fund to a victim of the offender until the expiration of the later of the following periods:

(a) The expiration of three years after the establishment of the separate account, provided that no action of which the clerk was notified under division (B)(1) of this section is pending;

(b) If three years has elapsed since the establishment of the separate account and if one or more actions of which the clerk was notified under division (B)(1) of this section is pending at the expiration of that three-year period, the date of the final disposition of the last of those pending actions.

(2) Upon the expiration of the applicable period of time set forth in division (C)(1) of this section, the clerk of the court of claims shall make payments from the separate account maintained in the name of the offender in the crime victims recovery fund to the victims of the offender who obtained a judgment against the offender or the representatives of the offender for damages resulting from the offense committed by the offender.   The payments shall be made as provided in this division.

When a separate account is maintained in the name of an offender in the crime victims recovery fund, the clerk of the court of claims shall determine on the second day of January and the first day of April, July, and October of each year the amount of money in that separate account.   After the expiration of the applicable period of time set forth in division (C)(1) of this section, the clerk shall pay from that separate account any judgment for which a victim of that offender has requested payment pursuant to division (B)(3) of this section and has requested payment prior to the date of the most recent quarterly determination described in this division.   If at a time that payments would be made from that separate account there are insufficient funds in that separate account to pay all of the applicable judgments against the offender or the representatives of the offender, the clerk of the court of claims shall pay the judgments on a pro rata basis.

(1995 S 91, eff. 11–15–95)

2969.13 Moneys deposited in crime victims recovery fund

All moneys that are collected pursuant to section 2929.25 of the Revised Code and required to be deposited in the crime victims recovery fund shall be credited by the treasurer of state to the fund. Any interest earned on the money in the fund shall be credited to the fund.

(1995 S 91, eff. 11–15–95)

2969.14 Application of remainder of moneys to cover cost of incarceration

(A) If a separate account has been maintained in the name of an offender in the crime victims recovery fund and if there is no further requirement to pay into the fund money, or the monetary value of property, pursuant to section 2929.25 of the Revised Code, unless otherwise ordered by a court of record in which a judgment has been rendered against the offender or the representatives of the offender, the clerk of the court of claims shall pay the money remaining in the separate account to the state to cover the cost of all imprisonment and incarceration of the offender, if all of the following apply:

(1) The applicable period of time that governs the making of payments from the separate account, as set forth in division (C)(1) of section 2969.12 of the Revised Code, has elapsed.

(2) None of the civil actions against the offender or the representatives of the offender of which the clerk of the court of claims has been notified pursuant to division (B)(1) of section 2969.12 of the Revised Code is pending.

(3) All judgments for which payment was requested pursuant to division (B)(3) of section 2969.12 of the Revised Code have been paid.

(B) If the clerk of the court of claims is required by division (A) of this section to pay the money remaining in the separate account established in the name of an offender to the state to cover the cost of all imprisonment and incarceration of the offender and if, after payment of that cost, any of that money remains in the separate account, or if there was no cost incurred for imprisonment and incarceration of the offender, the clerk of the court of claims shall distribute the amount of the money remaining in that separate account as otherwise provided by law for the distribution of money paid in satisfaction of a fine, as if that amount was a fine paid by the offender.

(1995 S 91, eff. 11–15–95)

END OF VOLUME